#23—

TIDE OF TERROR

TIDE OF TERROR

America, Islamic Extremism, and the War on Terror

Carl Hammer

PALADIN PRESS • BOULDER, COLORADO

Tide of Terror: America, Islamic Extremism, and the War on Terror
by Carl Hammer

Copyright © 2003 by Carl Hammer

ISBN 1-58160-412-2
Printed in the United States of America

Published by Paladin Press, a division of
Paladin Enterprises, Inc.
Gunbarrel Tech Center
7077 Winchester Circle
Boulder, Colorado 80301, USA
+1.303.443.7250

Direct inquiries and/or orders to the above address.

Visit our Web site at: www.paladin-press.com

Table of Contents

Introduction 1

**I. The Rise of Usamah bin Ladin and Modern
Islamic Terrorism** 7

Chapter 1: The Wahhabis of Arabia and the House of Saud .9

Chapter 2: The Muslim Brotherhood of Egypt 15

Chapter 3: Islamic Jihad and the Islamic Society 23

Chapter 4: The Thrill of Modern Salafi Islam 33

Chapter 5: The Ikhwan Revival: Retaliation against
  Saudi Arabia 45

Chapter 6: The Afghan Jihad against the Soviet Union 49

Chapter 7: Usamah bin Ladin and the Arab Afghans in
  the 1990s 61

  Extremists Triumphant 61

  Usamah bin Ladin 63

  Al-Qaida 69

  Usamah bin Ladin Moves to Sudan 79

  Usamah bin Ladin in Afghanistan 86

Chapter 8: The Terrorist Ideology: Why They Hate Us . . .113

II. Background to the Afghan War 123

Chapter 9: The Afghan Factions, September 2001 133

  The Taliban 134

The Arab Afghan Movement and Al-Qaida 148
The Northern Alliance 151
Chapter 10: The Regional Context 165
Saudi Arabia 165
Pakistan 167
Iran 171
Turkmenistan 176
Uzbekistan 178
Tajikistan 181
Kyrgyzstan 184
China 186
The Russian Federation 188
The United States of America 190

III. The War on Terror **201**
Chapter 11: The Intelligence War against Usamah bin Ladin
and Al-Qaida 203
Chapter 12: The Military Campaign in Afghanistan 223
American and British Forces at Sea 225
U.S. Military Present 226
U.S. and British Forces on Bases Within the Region . .233
Chapter 13: The Coalition Deploys 247
The New Bases 250
Chapter 14: Operation Enduring Freedom 261
The War in the Air 262
The Special Forces War 267
The War on the Ground 274
The Information War: The United States
versus Al-Jazeera 283
Chapter 15: After the War: Implications for Afghanistan . .293
Chapter 16: Can the War on Terror Be Won? 307
Usamah bin Ladin and Weapons of Mass Destruction .312
Ways to Successfully Combat Islamic Extremism
and Terrorism 319

IV: Appendices **329**
Appendix 1: Key Events of the Arab Afghan Movement
   and Al-Qaida 331
Appendix 2: Chronology of the War on Terror 341
Appendix 3: Islamic Extremism in Pakistan 383
Appendix 4: Islamic Extremism in Kashmir 399
Appendix 5: Islamic Extremism in Yemen 411
Appendix 6: Islamic Extremism in Sudan 419
Appendix 7: Islamic Extremism in Somalia 425
Appendix 8: Islamic Extremism in Algeria 433
Appendix 9: Islamic Extremism in Tunisia 443
Appendix 10: Hizb ut-Tahrir 445
Appendix 11: The Islamic Movement of Uzbekistan 453
Appendix 12: Islamic Extremism in Chechnya and
   the Caucasus 471
Appendix 13: China and the Uighur East Turkestan
   Movement 481
Appendix 14: Islamic Extremism in Palestine 489
Appendix 15: Islamic Extremism in the Balkans: Bosnia,
   Albania, Kosovo, and Macedonia 495
Appendix 16: Islamic Extremism in the Philippines 505
Appendix 17: Islamic Extremism in Indonesia, Malaysia,
   and Singapore 517
Appendix 18: Sunni Islamic Extremism in the Americas ..525

Note on Transliteration

Arabic, Persian, and other foreign words and place or personal names appear in this book, wherever possible, in the spelling with which English-speaking readers are most familiar. Arabic is spoken in many countries and exists in several dialects. The same Arabic name can accordingly be transliterated into English in different ways. When in doubt, I have attempted, not always successfully, to use the form of the name that is actually used by the person or group itself when writing in English. So I have, for instance, referred to the well-known Arabic news network as Al-Jazeera instead of the more correct Al-Jazirah. On the other hand, I use the somewhat more accurate form Usamah bin Ladin instead of Osama bin Laden because he seldom, if ever, uses English and nobody knows which form he would employ.

Introduction

During the early 1980s, I was one of the many Western intelligence officers, volunteers, and journalists who visited the Afghan *mujahidin* (warriors in the way of God). At that time, I also met several of the Islamic extremists who currently look up to Usamah bin Ladin as their leader and role model. The Soviet Union had intervened in a political conflict in Afghanistan, in effect occupying the country, and was at war with a large number of *mujahidin* groups. The latter, who enjoyed substantial financial, military, and political support from the West, Saudi Arabia, Pakistan, and China, eventually inflicted such losses on the Soviets that Mikhail Gorbachev pulled out the Soviet forces. During the war years, many Americans and Europeans visited the Afghan mujahidin, often for extended periods.

Due to these experiences, in the late 1990s my ministry of defence called upon my services, and my job became to follow the developments within Afghanistan and Islamic extremism. This resulted in a series of briefings written for European government use but eventually also distributed to selected American military personnel.

I have based the present book on these briefings. This book, or rather primer, on Afghanistan and Islamic terrorism, should be regarded as a summary of the briefings. For several reasons, including personal security, I have written little or nothing of my own experiences in Afghanistan. Despite the fall of the Taliban regime, the American-led War on Terror, which began in autumn 2001, shows no signs of being even remotely close to a formal end. This primer is written to give the reader a real understanding of the issues that caused the emergence of Islamic terrorism and thereby the American war in Afghanistan and elsewhere.[1]

The present book is divided into four general sections. First, it describes the rise of 20th-century Islamic extremism. The story begins in Saudi Arabia, the origin and centre of the Wahhabi religiously inspired terrorism that came to the fore during the Soviet war in Afghanistan. (Wahhabism is also known as Salafism; the two terms are interchangeable, since Wahhabism is a form of Salafism and claims to be the only true form of Salafism.) The chief propagandists and supporters of Wahhabi-inspired terrorism, including Usamah bin Ladin, are described in some detail, as are the various organisations they created, including Al-Qaida. Part II describes the political and military situation in Afghanistan and the neighbouring countries at the outset of the 11 September 2001 terrorist attacks on the United States and the subsequent War on Terror. This is followed by a specialised section that describes the military aspects of the War on Terror, with a particular emphasis on the U.S.-led campaign in Afghanistan. However, the War on Terror was not only played out in the hills and deserts of Afghanistan, so the last part of the book details the evolution of Islamic extremism in other key countries and regions, as well as how the West has attempted to combat it. This final section consists of a series of appendices describing the situation in countries as diverse as Algeria, Yemen, and the Philippines, among others. While the internal political situation in some of these countries is extremely complicated and accordingly may produce difficult reading, these appendices are not really necessary for those who are primarily interested in Usamah bin Ladin and the Afghan war.

The book also attempts to analyse to what extent Islamic extremism and terrorism present a global security threat. It analyses the objectives, activities, and strength of the armed Islamic movements by examining their own writings, where such writings exist and are known; the views of their enemies (the states on whose territory the Islamic extremist movements emerged); and, most importantly, the events within the region of the last decade. It also explores ways to deal with the problem, and in the long run possibly eradicate it. However, the book's purpose is not to describe the rise of Islamic fundamentalism as a religious phenomenon. This has been done elsewhere. Nor will I go on at length about the Shia Islamic revolution that brought Ayatollah Ruhollah Khomeini to power in Iran. Islam had already to split into Sunni and Shia sects within a generation of the seventh-century Prophet Muhammad, and the two sects have remained estranged since. Mutual relations have often been hostile. In fact, Usamah bin Ladin and his Sunni extremists hate Shia Iran no less, and usually more, than they hate the United States and the West.

I aim to describe the rise and current situation of Sunni Islamic extremism, the kind espoused by bin Ladin, and how it affects the world as a political and security problem. The emphasis will be on Afghanistan and Central Asia, because this is the region—after Saudi Arabia—where Sunni extremism came closest to realising its objectives of not only recreating early Islamic society but also waging eternal *jihad* (holy war) against the rest of the world.

Sunni extremism and terrorism do not represent an isolated problem but rather are the result of a comprehensive, if somewhat simplistic, ideology that purports to explain Islam's role in the world. According to Sunni extremist thought, the modern state is fundamentally incompatible with true Islam and has to be fought in a jihad. Traditional Islamic law distinguishes between those born as infidels and those born as Muslims who later become infidels. The latter are regarded as apostates and must be exterminated. Wahhabi thought takes this concept one step further: all those who fail to rise against the corrupt, modern state by definition are infidels and, if Muslims, apostates. This makes them enemies, to be killed by all true Muslims. The killing of apostates is not only sanctioned by Islamic law but is in many countries indeed regarded as the sacred duty of each true Muslim under Islamic law. Jihad in this case is not only a collective responsibility of the community, but the individual responsibility of every Muslim.

A paradox in the U.S.-led War on Terror is that the Bush administration, for reasons of expediency, has chosen to treat the two countries that always were bin Ladin's chief supporters, Saudi Arabia and Pakistan, as close allies, while continuing to regard the one Muslim country that always recognised the danger of Wahhabi extremism, Iran, as part of the "axis of evil." Although old habits die hard, especially in politics, this seems to be one of the less prudent policy decisions in what otherwise has been a comparatively successful War on Terror.

This begs the question of evaluating the success, or lack thereof, of the various policy decisions taken during the war. In the early months of the campaign, it was regarded as unpatriotic to criticise the Bush administration or the U.S. military leadership for any errors of judgement or failures in the management of the war. Now, when the Taliban have since long been defeated, an objective analysis can no longer wait—or similar mistakes are likely to occur in subsequent wars. Tactical and in some cases strategic mistakes were made in the war. The speed with which the Taliban government collapsed should not blind the observer to the fact that the Afghan war was fought under extremely difficult conditions on all fronts: military, diplomatic, and political. U.S. forces had never before fought in such a remote location as Afghanistan, nor against an enemy that lacked almost any kind of fixed targets, infrastructure, and command posts. In addition, the United States had never before needed to create such a diverse coalition of foreign countries, political groups, warlords, and mercenaries in order to wage war successfully, nor to massage public opinion in especially the Muslim countries so as not to cause further hostilities. The United States could not have fought and won alone. As will be shown, some coalition partners made contributions without which it was unlikely that the Afghan war could have been concluded successfully. Yet, despite all these difficulties, the United States and the coalition liberated Afghanistan, crushed the Al-Qaida networks there, and drove the surviving terrorists into hiding.

INTRODUCTION

It would be foolish to believe that terrorist attacks as well organised and deadly as those on 11 September 2001 cannot take place again, aimed at the United States or other favoured targets of the Wahhabi extremists such as Russia, Britain, Israel, or even, perhaps surprisingly, the Vatican. While there are several reasons for this eclectic choice of targets, the United States in any case tops the list because of its troops stationed in Saudi Arabia. Wahhabi extremists loathe the non-Muslim military presence on what they regard as hallowed ground of Saudi Arabia, regarding this as no less than a continuation of the medieval Crusades. In fact, bin Ladin has singled out what he describes as "Jews and Crusaders" as his particular enemies and targets. The fact that the United States responded with air attacks after earlier acts of terrorism, and invaded Afghanistan in 2001, is obviously another cause of hatred. The threat from the Islamic extremist movement will last as long as it retains widespread appeal in the Islamic world. It will not disappear with the fall of key leaders such as bin Ladin or the Taliban.

It is imperative, therefore, that the United States and the West thoroughly understand the enemy they are facing. Only then can the threat from Islamic terrorism be defeated.

End Notes

1.   See, for instance, Dilip Hiro, *Islamic Fundamentalism* (London: Paladin, 1988).

PART I

The Rise of Usamah bin Ladin
and Modern Islamic Terrorism

All who are taken with arms are unmercifully put to death. This savage custom has inspired the Wahabys with a ferocious fanaticism that makes them dreadful to their adversaries.

—Jacob Burckhardt, *History of the Wahabys*

CHAPTER 1

The Wahhabis of Arabia and the House of Saud

If one wishes to name a place and a date for the origin of modern Sunni Islamic extremism, then one can do worse than to pick Riyadh in the Arabian Peninsula and a moonlit night following 15 January 1902. The young Arab nobleman Abdul Aziz ibn Abdul Rahman al-Saud (1876–1953), who was to become Saudi Arabia's founding father and is known to history as Ibn Saud, led 40 companions in an audacious raid on Riyadh that has since become both official history and legend. Under cover of darkness, the band scaled the city walls with grappling irons. Having penetrated the city without anybody seeing them, Ibn Saud and his men took up positions in an empty house close to the fortified residence of Ajlan, the governor of Riyadh. There they waited. Dawn came, and as the governor emerged from his quarters, Ibn Saud and his men attacked him. In the brief, desperate, and disordered struggle, the governor died and the Riyadh garrison, shocked and demoralised by the death of its leader, surrendered. Ibn Saud had gained a base, from which he sallied forth in the following decades to conquer much of the Arabian Peninsula. In September 1932, he proclaimed the unified Kingdom of Saudi Arabia: the only modern state named after the family that owns it. Ibn Saud ruled until his death in 1953.[1]

The dawn raid on Riyadh was the outcome of a young man's ambition and daring rather than religiosity, but the secret behind Ibn Saud's continued success was his family's traditional relationship with what were arguably the most conservative and puritan *mullahs* (preachers) of the Arabian Peninsula. These were the Wahhabi sect of Islam, and the sect is still very prominent in Saudi Arabia due to this close relationship. The tie had begun already in 1744, when Muhammad ibn Saud (1710–1765), the founder of the House of Saud, sealed a political and family alliance with Muhammad ibn Abdul Wahhab (1703–1792), the founder of the Wahhabi movement. The two men swore an oath to work together to revive a purer form of Islam under the clerical authority of Wahhab and the temporal authority of the House of Saud. To seal the pact, the son of Muhammad ibn Saud married the daughter of Wahhab.

Politically, the alliance was expedient. Muslims are technically not supposed to go to war against Muslim lands. What distinguished the Wahhabi movement, however, was that it had, from its foundation, proclaimed itself the only true form of Islam. The rulings of the movement's religious leaders (using the *fatwa*—a religious verdict or a formal legal opinion or decision of traditional religious scholars on a matter of Islamic law), which in effect excommunicated all other Muslims by declaring them apostates, made it possible for Saudi rulers to invade and conquer neighbouring territories with impunity, even though the latter were already ruled by Muslims.[2] Having labelled their enemies apostates, the Saudi rulers and their Wahhabi followers demolished the graves of the leading figures of early Islam and killed all inhabitants of the sites of important shrines, especially Shia shrines. Shia Islam filled the Wahhabis with particular hatred and revulsion.[3] When they were on a *jihad*, Wahhabi armies took no prisoners. "All who are taken with arms are unmercifully put to death," wrote the explorer Jacob Burckhardt of the 19th-century armies of the House of Saud.[4]

Yet, the political fortunes of the House of Saud rose and fell several times. By the early 19th century, for instance, Wahhabism and the House of Saud had again fallen on hard times. The fortunes of both were revived by Ibn Saud with his raid on Riyadh, and Wahhabism became the unifying ideology behind the creation of Saudi Arabia.[5] Saudi Arabia is the only modern country that still is named after its ruling family, and it is also the only modern Muslim state to have been created solely by jihad. In his conquests, Ibn Saud from the mid-1910s depended on fanatic Bedouin youths who, whipped into a frenzy to purge the faith of whatever Ibn Saud's Wahhabi missionaries declared un-Islamic, followed Ibn Saud in any desperate venture. These recruits in the jihad against all enemies of the House of Saud became known as *Ikhwan* (brothers). Scorning traditional Arab dress, each dressed in a white robe, cut short above the ankles or indeed near the knees, and a simple white headcloth. They also cut their hair very short, trimmed their moustaches, and let their beards grow freely, believing that these were God's requirements, imposed through the Koran. When Ibn Saud's armies conquered most of the Arabian Peninsula, he used the Ikhwan as shock troops. These forces also conquered the two holiest cities: Mecca, the birthplace of the Prophet Muhammad and the site of the Kaaba, which contains the sacred black stone; and Medina, where Muhammad died and which is the location of the Nabavi Mosque, which contains the Prophet's tomb.[6]

Religious fervour was the strongest component of the extraordinary fighting spirit and motivation of the Ikhwan. They believed that they fought for God against evil, for virtue against sin. They were God's instruments, killing as they pleased, because He willed it. Furthermore, any of the Ikhwan who fell on the field of battle would be transformed into martyrs and thus guaranteed a place in paradise. The death of the martyr, Muslims usually argue, is the happiest, best, easiest, and most virtuous of deaths. In paradise, each receives the undivided attentions of 72 beautiful *houris*, luscious and shapely women dedicated to the martyred man and eager to fulfil his every desire. Even the family of the martyr is ensured a place in paradise, regardless of past conduct. For this reason, death in jihad was not only deemed an acceptable sacrifice, it was welcomed. (Muslims have been known to cry in despair if they were unfortunate enough to survive a battle against infidels.) However, even those who survived the battle could look forward to many privileges. When engaged in jihad, the survivors were entitled to no less than four-fifths of any booty. The Wahhabi mullahs argued that conquered women could be freely raped, and the possessions of infidels and apostates could be appropriated as the holy warrior's just reward. It is thus hardly surprising that Ibn Saud justified every new campaign of conquest through the Wahhabi claims of punishing apostates.[7]

Although the Ikhwan were highly useful in times of war, Ibn Saud soon realised that ruthless religious fanatics were incompatible with nation building and had no place in the creation of a modern country. The Ikhwan hated such modern devices as motor cars, telegraphs, telephones, airplanes, and electric power, convinced that these relied on the work of magic and therefore the devil. (This did not prevent them, however, from blessing the rifle.) They also hated infidels and strongly disapproved of Ibn Saud's connections with foreign oil companies (from 1933 an increasingly important component of the Saudi economy). Besides, they had grown numerous, by the mid–1920s numbering more than 150,000 men settled in 222 colonies.[8] They also refused to abandon the jihad. In particular, the Ikhwan wanted to destroy Iraq's large population of Shia Muslims and seize their possessions and their women. The Ikhwan cared little for recognised international frontiers or, for that matter, the high likelihood of British retaliation, since Britain controlled Iraq. Undeterred by such matters unimportant in the eyes of God, the Ikhwan in 1927 began to raid Iraq. The British Royal Air Force (RAF) responded by bombing the invaders, and Ibn Saud realised that he had to solve the Ikhwan problem. Having incited the Ikhwan to hate every non-Wahhabi as the tool of the devil, he could not persuade them not to attack Shia Muslims and infidel Britons. He had also made them the main component of his armies, so even to try to talk the Ikhwan out of the raiding would be tantamount to risking his own life and throne. Ibn Saud accordingly gave up on the Ikhwan, instead embarking on a plan to enlarge his army with fresh recruits, many of them townsmen who were less fanatic than the Ikhwan. In March 1929, Ibn Saud, with an army of

30,000, confronted 8,000 Ikhwan at Sabilah, 200 miles north of Riyadh. Making good use of his modern, truck-mounted machine guns, Ibn Saud permanently destroyed the Ikhwan bands confronting him. The survivors, finding themselves caught between Ibn Saud and the British forces in Kuwait, surrendered to the British in December 1929. They were extradited to Ibn Saud in several groups, most of which were mercilessly slaughtered by Ibn Saud's new army.[9]

Yet, Saudi Arabia remained a centre of Wahhabism, and Islamic law (*shariah*) still governs civil and criminal law. Wahhabi clerics remain the most influential political force, and the thousands of princes of the House of Saud are wary of saying anything in public that might provoke them. School textbooks continue to insist that Muslims should shun infidels. Some provincial Saudis still refuse to respond to greetings from non-Muslims, as such un-Islamic behaviour is frowned upon by the Wahhabi mullahs and religious police.

During an accidental fire in a girls' school in Mecca on 11 March 2002, 15 girls died because the school doors, as usual, were locked from the outside so as to prevent the girls from straying out. In addition, religious police reportedly refused male firefighters entry into the burning building because there was a possibility of the girls' not being dressed in a way that would shield them from the view of male strangers, and some girls, who had managed to escape, were even pushed back inside the burning building to retrieve the mandatory black cloaks and veils that they were supposed to wear in public. High-ranking clerics regularly preach violence against Jews, infidels, and apostates, the latter a group that still includes most or all non-Wahhabi Muslims. Saudi Arabia is also the land that produced Usamah bin Ladin, many of his followers and financial backers, and 15 out of 19 identified hijackers of the 11 September 2001 terrorist attack on the United States.[10] These attacks did not change Saudi public opinion. In October 2001, a Saudi intelligence survey of educated Saudis, ages 25 to 41, reportedly showed that no less than 95 percent supported Usamah bin Ladin.[11]

End Notes

1   When no other source is given, this section is based on Robert Lacey, *The Kingdom: Arabia & the House of Sa'ud (New York: Harcourt Brace Jovanovich, 1981)*. See also David Holden and Richard Johns, *The House of Saud* (London: Sidgwick & Jackson, 1981).

2   See, for instance, M. J. Gohari, *The Taliban: Ascent to Power* (Oxford: Oxford Logos Society, 1999), 39–41, 54–6.

3   Hiro, *Islamic Fundamentalism*, 41–3.

4   Jacob Burckhardt, *History of the Wahabys* (1831), 57; as quoted in Lacey, *Kingdom,* 145.

5   Hiro, *Islamic Fundamentalism*, 109–16.

6   The modern Ikhwan movement emerged around 1912 but did not make significant contributions to Ibn Saud's wars until a few years later.

7   Hiro, *Islamic Fundamentalism*, 111.

8   Hiro, *Islamic Fundamentalism*, 113.

9   Hiro, *Islamic Fundamentalism*, 115.

10 *USA Today,* 25 April 2002.

11 *Economist,* 2 February 2002, referring to *New York Times.*

CHAPTER 2
The Muslim Brotherhood of Egypt

The Koran is our constitution, the Prophet is our Guide; Death for the glory of God is our greatest ambition.

—The Muslim Brotherhood

As Ibn Saud destroyed his Ikhwan bands in 1929, a similarly named but yet quite different organisation was already being formed in Egypt. This was the Muslim Brotherhood (*Jamaat al-Ikhwan al-Muslimin,* or Society of Muslim Brethren, usually referred to as the Muslim Brotherhood). This movement was founded as a youth organisation in March 1928 by Hassan al-Banna (1904–1949), an elementary school teacher who wished to create a new ruling class whose ideology would be a form of modernised and Westernised Islam. Founded in Ismailiya, capital of the British-held Suez Canal Zone, the movement was at first deeply influenced by Western political thought, though strongly opposed to British rule. The brotherhood from the outset stressed moral and social reform through communication, information, and propaganda.[1]

The brotherhood was gradually politicised in the 1930s but transformed itself into a political entity only in 1939, no doubt inspired by the militant resistance to the 1936 Anglo-Egyptian Treaty as well as the 1936 Arab uprising in Palestine (sometimes called the first *intifada*) against the British mandate and Zionist colonisation. Borrowing the structure of Western, clandestine Marxist organisations, the members were grouped into cells of five, which were called families. The cells, sometimes known to the public but later more often clandestine, were then assembled into higher-level clans, groups, and battalions. The brotherhood declared that "(a) Islam is a comprehensive, self-evolving system; it is the ultimate path of life in all its spheres; (b) Islam emanates from, and is based on, two fundamental sources, the Quran [Koran] and the Prophetic Tradition; and (c) Islam is applicable to all times and places." Banna also declared that the brotherhood stood firmly for Wahhabi Islam. In the view of the brotherhood, Islam was a total ideology that offered to regulate every detail of the political, economic, social, and cultural life of the believer. But the popular slogan of the movement emphasised martyrdom rather than life: "Death for the glory of God is our greatest ambition."[2]

Despite its Wahhabi borrowings, the early ideology of the Muslim Brotherhood was not the mere rejection of any tenets not espoused by Wahhabism, although this was how the movement and its many offshoots developed later. Instead, the early ideology can only be described as Islamism: the perception of Islam more as a political ideology than a mere religion. The Islamism of the 1930s can best be understood when seen in the international context of the time. The desire among some intellectuals was to revolt against modernisation (what today is called globalisation, which is a particular hatred of the modern Islamic movement) and create a new, better society by returning to national roots, exemplified by fascism in Italy and nazism in Germany. The early Islamists—who were not simple fundamentalist *mullahs* but members of the intelligentsia and students at secular universities, and mostly in the sciences— wished to reshape society entirely along Islamic lines, not only through the introduction of Islamic law, but also by reforms in the political, economic, and indeed cultural systems of the Islamic world. Unlike the Wahhabism that had inspired it, Islamism was a modern movement, aimed at reforming the modern world by modern means but based on Islamic society as it was believed to have been in the seventh century, the time of the Prophet. Islamists also tended to play down the rift between Sunni and Shia Islam. Even women were accepted into the political and economic arena, which would have made most Wahhabis turn in their graves.[3] It is conspicuous that many of the Islamists were educated men, with a preponderance of doctors, scientists, and in particular engineers. In Egypt, this even gave rise to a joke in Arabic, as some bright sparks asserted that the Muslim Brotherhood (*al-Ikhwan al-Muslimin*) was really the Engineering Brotherhood (*al-Ikhwan al-Muhandisin*).[4]

The Muslim Brotherhood grew rapidly, developing into a political party with a mass following. In 1940, the movement had 500 branches, each with a mosque and school. The brotherhood schools began by offering religious classes but soon also provided military training to prepare the members for the jihad to first liberate Egypt and then the entire Islamic world. The membership consisted predominantly of students, civil servants, lower-middle-class traders, and peasants.[5] This established a pattern for later Islamic extremist movements: Westernised, educated radicals led the movement, while lower-class, uneducated followers filled the ranks. (Fundamentalist movements within Islam have traditionally drawn the bulk of their members from Muslims who felt discriminated against. In the early centuries of Islam, this meant predominantly non-Arab Muslims. These days, the main constituency of the fundamentalists consists of impoverished recent migrants from rural areas to the cities in the Islamic world or migrants from third-world countries to the West. Fundamentalist leaders are typically found among low- and medium-ranking clerics and middle-class professionals and traders.)[6]

By 1946, the Muslim Brotherhood claimed to have grown into 5,000 branches with half a million active members and another half a million sympathisers. As numerous Muslim Brotherhood volunteers took part in the 1948 Arab-Israeli War, many military officers came to share their beliefs and joined the movement. However, the brotherhood blamed the corrupt Egyptian political establishment for the defeat in the war and began to engage in terrorism, assassinations, and subversive activities. The organisation was banned in December 1948, and Banna was killed by government agents on 12 February 1949 (the ban on the Muslim Brotherhood was lifted in the following year, but only in its capacity as a religious body, not as a political organisation).[7]

The military staged a successful coup in Egypt on 23 July 1952. At first, the military leaders enjoyed the support of the Muslim Brotherhood. In late 1953, however, one of them, Gamal Abdel Nasser (1918–1970, ruled 1952–1970), assumed sole power and introduced new secular revolutionary policies in the form of a doctrine of "Arab socialism," also known as Nasserism. This was not to the liking of the brotherhood, which responded by reviving the secret cells, also known as the Spiritual Order, with orders to carry out assassinations and subversion. In February 1954, the Muslim Brotherhood was again banned due to differences with the government over whether Egypt should be ruled by Islamic or secular law. By then, the brotherhood had also acquired a new leading ideologue: Sayyid Qutb (1906–1966). Militant and full of hatred from the outset, his writings grew increasingly radical over time, especially after he had spent from 1954 to 1964 in a squalid Egyptian prison. Sayyid Qutb fully agreed with the Wahhabis that it was necessary to return to the kind of society he believed had existed during the first years of Islam. He also claimed that there could be no compromise between Islam and the non-Islamic world (in his words *jahiliyyah*, the term used for the pre-Islamic world) and that the non-Islamic world must be thoroughly destroyed so that true Islam could prevail over the entire human race. The means to accomplish this was an ongoing jihad against all apostates, Jews, Christians, and believers of all other religions.[8] In addition, Qutb hated the West out of what can only be described as an acute feeling of Muslim cultural superiority, if not outright xenophobia; in 1946, he wrote, "All these Westerners are the same, . . .how I despise all of them without exception."[9]

On 23 October 1954, a member of the brotherhood attempted to assassinate Nasser. This caused a forceful government reaction. More than 4,000 brotherhood members were imprisoned along with Sayyid Qutb, and several thousand others fled to Syria, Saudi Arabia, Jordan, and Lebanon. This led to increased contacts between the Egyptian brotherhood and the Saudi Wahhabis.The Saudis began financial aid to the Muslim Brotherhood as a way to oppose Nasser's secular policies, and thence became the major financial backer of the organisation. From then on, Wahhabi thought grew dominant in the movement and was adopted by the vast majority of the brotherhood. The emphasis on modern means and political ideology of the early Islamists wilted and then died, discouraged by the failures of the politics of the essentially secular nationalistic post-colonial regimes of the Arab states. In 1964, Nasser granted a general amnesty to imprisoned members of the Muslim Brotherhood. This act of reconciliation failed because extremist thought was spreading within the brotherhood. Besides, within a decade Nasser was engaged in a conflict with the House of Saud, the main benefactor of the brotherhood, for supremacy in North Yemen (following a republican coup there in September 1962). In 1966, the Egyptian government therefore again suppressed the Brotherhood, arresting and executing its top leaders, including Sayyid Qutb, the movement's chief ideologue. Many lower-ranking members were imprisoned.[10]

The government reaction did not silence the brotherhood. Since the earlier period of suppression in the 1950s, the Muslim Brotherhood had turned into an increasingly international organisation. It had already formed branches elsewhere in the Middle East, as early as 1942, when Hassan al-Banna had travelled abroad. When the organisation was first banned in Egypt in 1948, hundreds of members had left the country, followed by thousands more in the aftermath of the failed assassination attempt in 1954. The Muslim Brotherhood accordingly has branches throughout the Middle East, formed either overtly or covertly under different names. In countries such as Jordan and the Persian Gulf states, where political parties were outlawed, the organisation registered as a charity or association such as the *Al-Jamiyyah al-Islah al-Ijtimai* (Society of Social Reform).[11] The brotherhood had developed into (and still remains) the main instrument for propagating international Wahhabism.[12] The brotherhood also began to operate increasingly through affiliated subgroups, many of which were difficult to distinguish from each other or legitimate political and social movements. They were, for this reason, also very difficult for internal security forces to contend with. Modern Islamic extremist groups remain organised according to this pattern, in loose networks that lack hierarchical leaders and fixed structures.

On 28 September 1970, Nasser died unexpectedly of a heart attack. Anwar Sadat (1918–1981, ruled 1970–1981) became president of Egypt. Being a deeply religious man, he reversed the secular policies of his predecessor and released all remaining imprisoned Muslim Brotherhood members. Soon after his May 1971 palace coup against the left-leaning political establishment then in charge, Sadat co-opted the moderate segments of the Islamic movement into the political-religious establishment by the active encouragement of Islamic sentiments to fight atheistic Marxism. He also established about a thousand "Islamic Societies" in universities and factories. As a part of this process, in July 1972 he also abruptly expelled most of the 16,000 Soviet military advisers in Egypt, invited there by Nasser, and from 1974 initiated increasingly close contacts with the United States. Soon Muslim Brotherhood exiles began to return to Egypt from Saudi Arabia and elsewhere.

End Notes

1. Hiro, *Islamic Fundamentalism*, 60–64. See also Richard P. Mitchell, *The Society of Muslim Brothers* (Oxford: Oxford University Press, 1969). The California branch of the Muslim Brotherhood maintains a Web site, www.ummah.net/Ikhwan.

2. Ibid., 61–62, 63–64, 272. See also Charles Wendell, ed., *Five Tracts of Hassan al Banna (1906–49)* (Berkeley: University of California Press, 1978).

3. Olivier Roy, "Has Islamism a Future in Afghanistan?" in William Maley, ed., *Fundamentalism Reborn? Afghanistan and the Taliban* (New York: New York University Press, 1998), 199, 210.

4. Steven Emerson, *American Jihad: The Terrorists Living Among Us* (New York: Free Press, 2002), 172.

5. Hiro, *Islamic Fundamentalism*, 61–62.

6. Ibid., 24–25.

7. Ibid., 63–65.

8. Ibid., 66–67, 141. Sayyid Qutb's most important book was *Maalim fi al-Tariq* (published in English as *Milestones* [Kuwait: New Era Publishers, 1978]; as well as Syed Qutb, *Signposts on the Road* [Bombay: Bilal Books, 1998]). Among his other writings translated into English are *Islam: The Religion of the Future* (Kuwait: New Era

2

Publishers, 1977), and *This Religion of Islam* (Kuwait: New Era Publishers, 1977).

9. Emerson, *American Jihad,* 229.

10. Hiro, *Islamic Fundamentalism*, 66–67, 141.

11. Ibid., 86–87.

12. See, for instance, Abdul Hadi Palazzi, "The Islamists Have It Wrong," *Middle East Quarterly* 8:3 (Summer 2001), 3–11.

Islamic Jihad and the Islamic Society

If, in order to kill infidels, you kill their women and children at the same time, it is of little importance.

—Excerpt from an Islamic Society document
attributed to Muhammad Abdul Salam Faraj (1952–1982)

As the deeply religious Anwar Sadat allowed the Islamic extremists increased freedom, the number of Islamic groups increased rapidly, each with a yet more radical agenda. As the moderate Muslim Brotherhood members were co-opted by Sadat, the radical Brotherhood leaders responded by establishing large numbers of clandestine militant groups to fight the government. These soon resorted to armed resistance and assassinations. The first such group already existed, having emerged in the 1960s as the premier group formed in the spirit of Sayyid Qutb. This was the *Jamaat al-Muslimin* (Society of Muslims), founded by Ali Abduh Ismail, a young Al-Azhar University graduate. In the increasingly free religious-political climate under Sadat, it was followed by a multitude of other groups, with such names as *Mukfirtiya* (Denouncers of the Infidel) and *Jundullah* (Soldiers of God).[1]

Among the members of the Society of Muslims was an imprisoned young member of the Muslim Brotherhood, known as Shukri Ahmad Mustafa (executed 1978), an agricultural engineer by profession. While in prison, he became an ardent supporter of Ali Abduh Ismail, left the Muslim Brotherhood, and joined Ismail's group—though this did not prevent him from forming his own group as soon as he was released from jail: *Jamaat al-Takfir wa'l-*

Hijrah (Society of Denunciation [of unbelievers] and Migration [from the secular world, as when the Prophet fled the enemies of Islam in Mecca by going to Medina]). Mustafa, who even refused to have his writings printed because printing was un-Islamic, had his followers withdraw from what he regarded as a society of infidels and apostates. They refused to visit the mosques, refused to let their children attend state schools, refused military service, and married only among themselves. Many of them went into hiding in mountain caves in Upper Egypt, where they also embarked on weapons training to fight the government. They were discovered by the security forces in September 1973, caught, and imprisoned; but Sadat, still wishing to encourage Islam, had them pardoned and released in April 1974.[2]

While all these groups engaged in violence and bloodshed, they were soon eclipsed by yet another extremist group: the *Munnazamat al-Jihad* (Jihad Organisation; also known as *Al-Jihad al-Islami*, Islamic Jihad). Islamic Jihad originated in a coalition that appeared in the 1970s of three militant groups devoted solely to overthrowing the Egyptian state. One of these was established in 1973 by a medical student named Ayman al-Zawahiri. Born on 9 June 1951 in Maadi, a Cairo suburb, Zawahiri hailed from a prominent Egyptian family of medical doctors on his father's side and diplomats and statesmen on his mother's. Yet, he had been active in militant Islam from an early age. Zawahiri was arrested the first time, for membership in the Muslim Brotherhood, in 1966, when he was only 15 years old. He received a medical degree in 1974 from Cairo University and in 1978 graduated with a master's degree in surgical medicine. Zawahiri picked Sheikh Omar Abdel Rahman (born *c*. 1938) as spiritual leader of Islamic Jihad. The Egyptian sheikh, already blind from diabetes as an infant, had graduated from Al-Azhar in 1971. When Zawahiri chose him, he served as a lecturer at Asyut University, where he was notorious for his militant opinions.[3]

In the meantime, however, Egypt also felt the presence of an ultimately foreign extremist group, the *Hizb ut-Tahrir al-Islami* (Islamic Liberation Party), an international party of ultimately

Palestinian origin, since banned in almost all Muslim countries and therefore mostly active in the West (see Appendix 10). In Egypt, the group was also known as *Shabab Muhammad* (Youth of Muhammad) and was led by Dr. Salih Abdullah Siriyya. In June 1974, Hizb ut-Tahrir members attacked the Technical Military Academy in Cairo to capture weapons with which to overthrow Sadat. They killed 30 soldiers but failed to achieve their objective. The group was soon suppressed. However, the attempted coup made Sadat, unlike Nasser before him, respond with a general amnesty for imprisoned Islamic extremists in 1975. As part of the reconciliation process, he also allowed the Muslim Brotherhood to reorganise and stand for election to parliament, although as independents or members of the ruling party.[4]

By January 1977, the Islamic extremist groups (especially the Society of Denunciation and Migration) rioted and burned nightclubs, cinemas, and bars in Cairo. They also kidnapped and murdered a former government official and newspaper writer. Sadat finally let the security forces deal with the group. Of the estimated 3,000 to 5,000 members throughout the country, the security forces arrested 620. Five leaders, including Shukri Ahmad Mustafa, were sentenced to death and executed. Many members of the groups were university students, and it was soon found that the Islamic extremists had not only managed to gain control of the university campuses and student unions but also most of the thousand Islamic societies earlier established by Sadat. What especially angered the students, and also the rural lower-middle classes, was Sadat's policy to encourage private enterprise and foreign investment in Egypt. In light of Nasser's earlier socialist policies, this was probably necessary for Egypt in the long run, but Sadat's economic policy had increased the cost of living, thereby widening the gap between rich and poor.

But for the Islamic extremists, worse was to come. In March 1979, in a peace treaty brokered by the United States and signed by Egypt and Israel at Camp David, Maryland, Sadat recognised the state of Israel. This act of betrayal against God and Islam infuriated the radicals. How could any true Muslim ever allow Muslim lands to revert to infidel control, they argued. The peace process also deeply angered the moderate Muslim Brotherhood, which thence began to oppose Sadat, accusing him of selling Egypt's independence to the United States, among other sins. By 1981, 100,000 militants demonstrated in Cairo against Sadat and against the Camp David peace accords. They also, for good measure, attacked Egypt's native Coptic Christians in bloody riots.[5]

The three militant groups that formed the Islamic Jihad formally merged in June 1981. Led by a 10-man council (*shura*) under Muhammad Abdul Salam Faraj (1952–1982), a former member of the Muslim Brotherhood, the group grew increasingly militant. Faraj was close to Wahhabi tenets in his insistence that all Muslims who did not rise against the state were apostates and had to be killed, and that the only acceptable form of jihad was armed struggle. He also regarded jihad as a continuous obligation until the entire world was a single Islamic state. Islamic Jihad also formed a military wing, headed by Abbud Abdul Latif Zumur, a military intelligence lieutenant colonel. In a 1980 book, Faraj, an Islamic ideologue and the organisation's chief theoretician, finalised the extremist doctrine: he advocated an Islamic state headed by a *caliph* (spiritual head of Islam) and asserted that such a state could only be created by fighting the current state by jihad. He also emphasised his strong desire to exterminate all Jews and Christians. The latter he regarded as the embodied continuation of the medieval Crusades, implacably hostile to God and the forces of Islam.[6] Not to be outdone, Sheikh Omar Abdel Rahman, primarily based in Saudi Arabia from 1979 to 1982 because of his extremist views, issued a fatwa in 1980 in which he declared "a ruler who does not obey the laws of God" (implicitly referring to Sadat) to be an apostate who must be killed.[7]

Sadat finally realised that he needed to take action against the extremists. On 3 September 1981, he had nearly 2,000 of them imprisoned, purged the military of officers with ties to the Muslim Brotherhood, and ordered all independent mosques, religious societies, and preachers to register with the government. In retaliation, four soldiers belonging to Islamic Jihad assassinated Sadat during a military parade on 6 October 1981. Soon fighting took place between Islamic Jihad extremists and security forces in several towns, but despite the expectations of the extremist leaders, the general population did not rise up against the government as had happened in Iran in 1979.[8]

Sadat's successor, Hosni Mubarak (born 1928), reacted by imprisoning more than 3,000 extremists, chiefly from Islamic Jihad and its predecessor, the Society of Denunciation and Migration. In retaliation, Islamic extremists on 25 April 1982 attempted to assassinate him as well. They failed. Mubarak ordered further arrests, and the security organisations intensified the infiltration of the extremist groups. From 1984, Mubarak also accepted the moderate elements of the by then more staid Muslim Brotherhood as a religious group—but not as a political organisation and only under heavy-handed government control. Yet, the extremist movements grew increasingly powerful and found additional public support. Having tried both socialism and capitalism and failed, it was argued, Egypt needed to return to the Islamic model. A growing number of women began to wear the veil, and, in contrast to earlier times, this became an increasingly common sight in the streets. Men grew beards, the number of religious publications increased rapidly, and the student unions demanded sexual segregation as well as new curricula and textbooks in line with Islamic precepts. The overt signs of a rise in Islamic extremism were obvious. Islamic Jihad and the other groups also continued to actively recruit officers in the military and the security and intelligence services. By 1987, it was estimated that the clandestine extremist groups had a membership of between 70,000 and 100,000.[9]

From this year on, when the Muslim Brotherhood did well in the April elections, Islamic extremism again grew increasingly radical. The groups confronted the government and security forces on various issues, harassed secular Egyptians, closed down discotheques and bars, and attacked Christian churches. After the murder of a policeman in late September 1988, the government responded by arresting 2,000 extremists. Despite severe government repression, which included the frequent use of torture, Islamic extremism remained popular.[10]

However, Islamic Jihad suffered major losses. Faraj was executed and numerous members were arrested following the assassination of Sadat in 1981. Zawahiri was sentenced to three years in jail. Upon his release, he left for Saudi Arabia and then Pakistan, whence he continued to Afghanistan as a jihad volunteer. He also relaunched Islamic Jihad as the *Talai al-Fatah* (Vanguards of Conquest). His group made unsuccessful attempts to assassinate Egypt's interior minister in 1993 and prime minister in 1995. Under Zawahiri's leadership, Islamic Jihad also grew increasingly international. His men successfully bombed the Egyptian Embassy in Islamabad, Pakistan, in 1995, but this attack in most respects marked the end of Islamic Jihad's interest in domestic Egyptian affairs and the full development of the group as an international terrorist organisation.[11]

Sheikh Omar Abdel Rahman, safe from the Egyptian government in Saudi Arabia (and also under CIA protection due to his role in the Afghan jihad against the Soviet forces in Afghanistan), gradually abandoned Islamic Jihad and instead began to devote time to a new coalition of some 40 extremist groups, generically known as the *Jamaat al-Islamiyyah* (Islamic Society). This coalition of extremist groups appears to have grown out of some of Sadat's Islamic societies. The Islamic Society, like most other Egyptian extremist groups, was organised into cells. Each cell was called an *anqud*, Arabic for a bunch of grapes, because each cell was self-contained and if plucked, as from a grapevine, would not affect the others. The leaders of each cell, each usually called an *amir*, would meet in a consultative assembly (*majlis al-shura*). In the mid-1980s, Sheikh Omar reorganised this group and also became its spiritual leader. Although he moved to the United States in 1990, he remained the group's spiritual leader. (Sheikh Omar was arrested in 1995. Since 1997 he has been serving a life sentence for terrorism for his role in the June 1993 attempts to bomb the United Nations headquarters, the Lincoln and Holland Tunnels, the George Washington Bridge, and the Federal Building in New York. Until quite recently, he spent this in a federal medical prison facility in Rochester, Minnesota, relying on staff from the neighbouring Mayo clinic, a first-class medical institution frequently used by Saudi princes and other wealthy Arabs.)[12]

Extremist violence in Egypt continued well into the 1990s, becoming a virtual terrorist campaign during 1996 and 1997, in which several hundred people were murdered, mostly Coptic Christians and foreign tourists. Sheikh Abu Yassir Rifai Ahmad Taha, a disciple of Sheikh Omar safely in exile in London, assumed the leadership of the Islamic Society. The terrorist campaign culminated in the 17 November 1997 Luxor massacre in which Islamic extremists killed 58 foreign tourists (the majority Japanese, Swiss, British, and Spanish) and about 10 Egyptians and wounded about 26 more at an archaeological site. The attack was probably planned by Sheikh Rifai Ahmad Taha and executed by an Islamic Society cell.[13]

The Islamic Society also maintained links with cells abroad. One appears to have been the London-based Islamic organisation Al-Murabitun. The Egyptian Islamic Society also maintained the Al-Murabitun camp in Afghanistan and published the journal *Al-Murabitoun*, the organ of the Islamic Society.[14]

However, government repression was taking its toll among the extremists. In July 1997, well before the Luxor massacre, several imprisoned leaders of the Islamic Society had declared a unilateral cease-fire and asked their supporters to respect it. Yet it took until March 1999 before the active components of the Islamic Society agreed to announce such a cease-fire. The more extreme—and much smaller—Islamic Jihad vowed to continue fighting, particularly against the United States and Israel (but not, apparently, against the Egyptian government). Perhaps lacking a safe infrastructure inside Egypt, it had already, as noted, moved most of its operations abroad, primarily to Afghanistan.[15] Eventually, the extremist leaders still in Egypt asked Zawahiri and Taha to resign from their leading positions in, respectively, Islamic Jihad and Islamic Society because of their continued support for jihad (as well as Al-Qaida, of which both by then were prominent members). Since early 2000, the two men do appear to have either resigned or been dismissed.[16] Control of the Egyptian-based Islamic Jihad was then apparently assumed by one Ahmad Hussain Agiza, while Mustafa Hamzah seems to have taken charge of Islamic Society.[17] On 7 April 2000, another prominent Islamic Jihad leader, Muhammad Rabie al-Zawahiri, brother of Ayman al-Zawahiri and known as the "engineer," was arrested at the Dubai airport and extradited to Egypt.[18] Before his arrest, he was known to have been running Islamic extremist networks in the Balkans.[19]

In August 1992, Ayman al-Zawahiri reportedly signed a cooperation agreement with the Iranian-supported Hezbollah. However, conflicts soon broke out because the Iranians wished to assume control over Zawahiri's group and the Sunni extremists refused to acknowledge Shia leadership.[20] Contacts since then have been limited. In addition, Sunni terrorist attacks on Iranian targets such as at the shrine of Reza (one of the holiest Shia sites) in Mashhad on 20 June 1994, in which at least 26 pilgrims died,[21] would probably preclude any close relationship, even if the two parties had been in favour of cooperation.

The Egyptian government has spent considerable resources and demonstrated ferocity in attempts to crush the Islamic extremist movement. Since 1991, more than 100,000 extremists have been detained without trial in Egypt, and by the beginning of June 1999, it seemed as if the government forces had turned the tide and were winning the battle against extremism. However, Islamic extremism has not been eradicated in Egypt, and it does not seem that the extremists will ever fully give up their struggle. Egypt has the largest population of the Arab states and remains the world's leading centre of Sunni Islamic learning. Al-Azhar University is the oldest and most prestigious of all Islamic institutions of higher education. The mainstream (radical but at least, for the time being, nonviolent) Islamic opposition in the form of the Muslim Brotherhood has capitalised on the disorder by pressing Mubarak to accept ever more aspects of Islamic law in exchange for its allegiance against the more militant extremists. Should Egypt fall prey to Islamic extremism, even by democratic vote as almost happened in Algeria in 1992, the takeover would have far-reaching consequences.[22] Already there have been several cases in which Islamic extremist thought has been found to have penetrated the highest levels of the Egyptian judiciary, administration, universities, and trade unions and thereby affected the rulings and decisions of these bodies. Other overt signs are the prevalence of bearded men and veiled women on the streets of Cairo.[23] Besides, new extremist groups are constantly emerging. In September 2001, Egyptian police arrested many members of what appeared to be a new group, *Al-Waad* (The Promise), which was allegedly linked to Al-Qaida, although its main activity appears to have been collecting money for the Palestinian intifada. Eighty-three of them were eventually charged with seeking to overthrow President Mubarak.[24]

End Notes

1. Hiro, *Islamic Fundamentalism*, 3, 70–72; Avraham Sela, ed., *Political Encyclopedia of the Middle East* (New York: Continuum, 1999), 234, 375–376.

2. Hiro, *Islamic Fundamentalism*, 72–78.

3. Ibid.,78–80; Simon Reeve, *The New Jackals: Ramzi Yousef, Osama bin Laden and the Future of Terrorism* (Boston: Northeastern University Press, 1999), 166–167; Peter L. Bergen, *Holy War, Inc.: Inside the Secret World of Osama bin Laden* (New York: Free Press, 2001), 52–53, 200–201; Jacquard, *Osama Bin Laden,* 102, 279 note 11; John K. Cooley, *Unholy Wars: Afghanistan, America and International Terrorism* (London: Pluto Press, 1999), 40–44; Sela, *Political Encyclopedia,* 377; Ed Blanche, "Ayman al-Zawahiri: Attention Turns to the Other Prime Suspect," *Jane's Intelligence Review* 13: 11 (November 2001), 18–19.

4. Hiro, *Islamic Fundamentalism*, 3, 70–72; Sela, *Political Encyclopedia,* 234, 375–376.

5. Hiro, *Islamic Fundamentalism*, 72–78. See also Gilles Kepel, *Muslim Extremism in Egypt: The Prophet and Pharaoh* (Berkeley: University of California Press, 1984); Walid M. Abdel Nasir, *The Islamic Movement in Egypt: Perceptions of International Relations, 1967–1981* (London: Kegan Paul International, 1994).

6. Hiro, *Islamic Fundamentalism*, 78–80; Sela, *Political Encyclopedia,* 376–377.

7. Hiro, *Islamic Fundamentalism*, 78–80; Cooley, *Unholy Wars,* 40–44; Sela, *Political Encyclopedia,* 377.

8. Hiro, *Islamic Fundamentalism*, 78–79.

9. Ibid.,79–86, 101–102, 282.

10. Ibid., 285–286.

11. Reeve, *New Jackals,* 166–167; Bergen, *Holy War,* 200–201; Jacquard, *Osama Bin Laden,* 102, 176, 279 note 11.

12. Hiro, *Islamic Fundamentalism,* 78–80, 286–286; Cooley, *Unholy Wars,* 40–44; Sela, *Political Encyclopedia,* 377.

13. Bergen, *Holy War,* 203; Jacquard, *Osama Bin Laden,* 107; Fawaz A. Gerges, "The End of the Islamist Insurgency in Egypt? Costs and Prospects," *Middle East Journal* 54: 4 (Autumn 2000), 592–612, on 594; Cooley, *Unholy Wars,* 183–185.

14. Jacquard, *Osama Bin Laden,* 107. The group maintains a web site, *www.eldarco.com/murabit*

15. Gerges, "End of the Islamist Insurgency in Egypt?," 594–595; *Economist,* 27 October 2001.

16. Bergen, *Holy War,* 203; Jacquard, *Osama Bin Laden,* 107.

17. See, for instance, Department of State, *Patterns of Global Terrorism 1999* (Washington, D.C.: Department of State, 2000); Kenneth Katzman, *Terrorism: Near Eastern Groups and State Sponsors, 2001* (Washington, D.C.: Congressional Research Service, Library of Congress, 10 September 2001).

18. Jacquard, *Osama Bin Laden,* 108; Yonah Alexander and Michael Swetnam, *Usama bin Laden's al-Qaida: Profile of a Terrorist Network* (Ardsley, N.Y.: Transnational Publishers, 2001), 28.

19. Yossef Bodansky, *Bin Laden: The Man Who Declared War on America* (Roseville, Calif.: Prima Publishing, 2001), 298. Although offering numerous interesting details, Bodansky's work is marred by his overall assumption that a highly structured, Islamic terrorist international led by Iran is in firm charge of Al-Qaida and virtually all other Muslim terrorists. This view does not correspond to the available evidence, is simply not credible, and may have been coloured by Bodansky's professional roles as director of the Congressional Task Force on Terrorism and Unconventional Warfare and former consultant to the Departments of Defense and State. See, for instance, Mark N. Katz, "Bin Laden Biography Raises Doubts," *Eurasia Culture,* 27 October 2000 (www.eurasianet.org).

20. Jacquard, *Osama Bin Laden,* 109.

21. See, for instance, Reeve, *New Jackals,* 65–67.

22. Reeve, *New Jackals,* 229. For U.S. worries about, and policy toward, Egypt and its extremists, see also Gerges, "End of the Islamist Insurgency in Egypt?" 605–609.

23. Cooley, *Unholy Wars,* 191–2; Gerges, "End of the Islamist Insurgency in Egypt?" 603–604.

24. *Washington Post,* 28 October 2001; *Economist,* 2 February 2002.

CHAPTER 4
The Thrill of Modern Salafi Islam

All these Westerners are the same: a rotten conscience, a false civilization.
How I hate these Westerners, how I despise all of them without exception.
—Sayyid Qutb, 1946

Clearly, Islamic extremism held a strong fascination for the Muslim masses of Egypt. It was not a question of a lack of education, for a Western-style education clearly did not prevent ever-greater numbers of young men and women from joining the struggle against the secular regime. The very real threat of imprisonment, torture, and death at the hands of the security forces did little to discourage them. But these young men and women were not drawn only from the ranks of the poor; often they were members of the comparatively prosperous middle classes, sometimes even of the elite. What distinguished the young Egyptian Islamic extremists, regardless of background, was that they were followers of Salafi Islam, the variant of the Saudi extremist faith known as Wahhabism propagated by Hassan al-Banna and the Muslim Brotherhood. What is it that makes Salafi Islam such a potent source for extremism? What makes Salafi Islam different from other types of Islam? Is Salafi Islam becoming the new mainstream of Islam? Is Islam set for an inevitable confrontation with the Western world, in what some claim to be a clash of civilisations? What is, ultimately, the thrill offered by contemporary Islamic extremism?

Islam is not an immutable and unchanging system of norms and beliefs. To say that Islam is a peaceful, tolerant religion, the mere name of which is abused by those misguided political extremists and terrorists who kill in its name, is as wrong as to claim that Islam is a violent creed by historic necessity involved in a life-or-death struggle with Western civilisation. Islam is a dynamic system of norms, rules, ideas, and opinions, each formulated in its time and place. There is any number of clashing opinions about almost any aspect of Islam. Unlike, for instance, the Catholic Church, in which the pope has the final word on questions of dogma, there is in Islam no generally accepted procedure to approve a norm or a system of norms as the genuine one. Islam is more akin to the popular concept of the British legal system, a vast repository of rules of all past epochs, most of them dormant and fallen out of use as they became incompatible with later events but none totally forgotten or permanently jettisoned.[1]

The interpretation of Islam, which until the age of global telecommunications invariably was different in each locality, has always been the result of a process of selective revival. Current ideas have been recombined with dormant ones to produce an interpretation of Islam that fulfilled the purpose for which it was needed in each time and place. This was typically not a spontaneous development. It may sound cynical, but Islam was almost always interpreted to conform to the needs of the ruling class or group. The interpretation of Islam was an institutional process, in which the Islamic scholars (*ulama*) involved needed support and sponsorship (as did the dissemination of their rulings). Man cannot live on words alone. Somebody has to provide the necessities of daily life, and Muslim clerics often had large families. This made the support—and acquiescence—of the leading social groups or ruling strata a necessary requirement to any interpretation or reinterpretation of Islamic thought. The whole process of interpretation and reinterpretation of Islam was, and is, determined by political conditions.[2] The *ulama* are dependent on the state for their upkeep, often enjoying salaries like other civil servants, as in most Sunni countries even today, including Saudi Arabia.[3]

Salafism and Wahhabism

Salafi Islam (*Salafiyyah*) is one variant of selective revival and reinterpretation of Islam. The faith is named after *as-salaf as-salih*, "the righteous predecessors" or "righteous roots" of early Islam. This interpretation of Islam emerged by the late 20th century as the dominant form of Sunni Islamic radicalism. The first 20th-century proponents of Salafi Islam regarded the various secular left-wing political associations in the Arab world as a threat to Islam. The guiding idea of Salafi Islam accordingly became to purify the Arab world by recreating what its proponents, *salafiyyin* (followers of predecessors), regarded as the perfect Islamic society, a goal to be achieved by turning society back to an essentially imagined model of seventh-century Arabia, the time of the Prophet.[4]

Such views were not new. They had formed the foundation of the 18th-century Wahhabi movement (*Wahhabbiyyah*) in the Arabian Peninsula, a movement that can well be described as Salafi, as well as several even earlier Islamic movements. However, the 20th-century Salafi movement soon took the ideology one step further: this time, the righteous early Islamic society was to be recreated not only in the Arab world but on a global scale.[5] This can only be achieved by jihad, against less-than-pious Muslim rulers as well as non-Muslims. A modern state was regarded as fundamentally incompatible with true Islam. The proponents of Salafism made one key ideological innovation: the flexible definition of the concept of enemy in a jihad. Traditional Wahhabis hated infidels, Shia Muslims, and many others, but they had occasionally respected noncombatants and at times offered captives the opportunity to embrace Wahhabism and thus avoid being killed. But this was no longer the case. Salafism proposed a new and much longer list of enemies, all of whom had to be destroyed. At the top of the list was obviously the leader of the corrupt, modern state, whether nominally Muslim or not. He was followed by all members of the state machinery who served him—soldiers, policemen, administrators, and the like. Because these individuals had left the path of true Islam by serving a corrupt, modern state, each must be declared an infidel (*kafir*). Traditional Islamic law distinguishes between those born as infidels and those born as Muslims who later become infidels. The latter are regarded as apostates (*murtadd*) and must be exterminated. Salafi thought took this concept one step further and came to the conclusion that all those who failed to rise against the corrupt, modern state by definition must be infidels and, if Muslims, apostates. The logical conclusion was that the entire Muslim population must be exterminated, except those who followed the Salafi ideology and accordingly had to carry out the wishes of God. According to Salafi thought, the killing of apostates is not only sanctioned by Islamic law, it is regarded as the sacred duty of each true Muslim. Jihad in this case is not only a collective responsibility of the community but an individual responsibility of every Muslim.[6]

Unlike most earlier interpretations of Islam, Salafi Islam was obviously not chosen to accommodate the ruling groups of the state. The ideology, in the form of Wahhabism at first encouraged by the early rulers of the House of Saud as a way of justifying their wars of conquest, had turned itself into a potent force from which the Saudi princes could not, indeed dared not, dismount. Ibn Saud had managed to crush his Ikhwan bands through superior fire power, but Salafi Islam had somehow managed to survive, and even grow stronger. By the late 20th century, the Saudi rulers were held hostage by a monster of their own creation. Unlike their ancestor Ibn Saud, who killed off his Ikhwan, they did not seem to know how to eliminate the beast, or indeed if they wanted to—nor have they made the attempt since.

Some intellectuals, both Muslims and non-Muslims, see the objective of Sunni Islamic extremism in a more positive light, not as the reproduction of the past but as the reconstruction of society through a process of Islamic reform in which the principles of Islam are applied to contemporary needs. There is indeed a fundamental desire for social justice in most Islamic extremist groups. Western models of every variety are regarded as having been tried and failed. When the colonial powers withdrew from the Islamic world, they were replaced by nationalist dictators such as Gamal Abdel Nasser in Egypt and Achmad Sukarno (1901–1970) in Indonesia. As nationalism and socialism failed, Islamic reformers moved into the ideological void, relying on the urban poor and the devout middle class—including those over-educated and under-employed. In the Islamic world, a Western type of democracy far too often degenerated into destructive rivalry among elites, all more or less corrupt (a typical example is Pakistan). In Nasser's Egypt, Western-style socialism brought superficial reforms but failed to raise the standard of living of the poor and did not bring about the promised revival and unification of the Arab world. Western-style military dictatorship, too, brought its share of suffering, such as in Saddam Hussein's Iraq. Most important, each type of regime was perceived as dividing society into the modernised, Westernised secular elite and the majority of the population, which is seen by the extremists as poor, exploited, and in essence more Islamic.[7] Historical developments are regarded as evidence for the fact that injustice rules the world. Many Muslims, being convinced of their cultural superiority over the West and being proud of Islam as the only true religion, cannot fathom why the West is currently wealthier, more advanced, and militarily more powerful than the Islamic world. Suffering from what can only be described as an inferiority complex, these Muslims feel bitter toward the West, which they feel is perpetually colonialist and imperialistic, always eager to impose its godless materialistic values on the traditional, and in their view higher, cultural and religious values of the Islamic world.[8] Since none of them is prepared to concede the inferiority of Islam to any other social system, the West's superiority can only be explained by the inevitable conclusion that Muslims had deviated from the true path.[9] In short, a very real desire for social justice and Islamic reform is coupled with a xenophobic, virtually racist feeling of superiority based on a historical past. Sunni Islamic extremism in the Islamic world accordingly shows clear similarities with 20th-century nazism in the Western world. In both cases, charismatic leaders gain power by exploiting feelings of resentment among those who suffer from economic exploitation, poverty, and feelings of having been let down by history and taken advantage of by the outside world.

The Islamic extremists find a ready audience among the young, urban poor. In Algeria, for instance, the majority of young men remain unable to find regular employment and spend most days on street corners or in coffee houses, daily growing more embittered. For them, there are only four options: continued unemployment and inability to marry due to a lack of income; involvement in criminal activities with the risk of imprisonment; emigration to France for the chance to become a menial labourer; or enrollment in an Islamic extremist organisation that offers a sense of purpose in life.[10] There is, however, a sharp distinction between those Islamic extremists who engage in irregular warfare in third-world countries such as Afghanistan, who are usually uneducated, unemployed, underprivileged, and embittered, and those who engage in international terrorism against the West. The typical social profile of the latter is young (early 20s); of rural or small-town background, with high achievement motivation; upwardly mobile, with science or engineering education; and from a normally cohesive family background. Those who took part in the 11 September 2001 attacks are all believed to have received higher education and can be said to have had good careers waiting for them. They were, in fact, model middle-class young men, very normal and very common.[11] In countries such as

Egypt and Saudi Arabia, many young extremists are indeed university educated.[12]

Islam is an uncompromising faith. A Muslim feels solidarity with other Muslims, even if they are far away. A Muslim does not readily accept the surrender of Muslim lands to the forces of other faiths, or worse, atheism. Yet, while Muslims should not be depicted as stereotypical immature and militant fanatics, an objective analysis of the root causes of terrorism and extremism should not be pushed aside by a surfeit of cultural sensitivity. Western, as well as Muslim, political leaders, in their need to massage public opinion in the Islamic countries, invariably go out of their way to emphasise that they are at war with terrorism, not with Islam. Yet, their enemy is Islamic terrorism, not any other variety. Islam as a religion, through its scholars and believers, needs to confront the three questions of why Islam allows extremists to interpret the faith in militant and destructive terms; why Islam has endorsed the creation of so many extremist organisations; and why Islam apparently includes no ideological defences against the spread of political extremism and the advocacy of violence.[13]

Western scholars of Islam tend to play down the extremist features of the religion.[14] They have thus largely failed to predict or explain the phenomenon of Sunni Islamic extremism. No doubt this is a legacy of the general respect for all religious creeds that is prevalent, especially in the United States, as well as a scholarly wish to treat one's subject in a way that will not anger or alienate its believers. While this approach is no doubt beyond reproach in the current academic and political climate, it does appear to have clouded the issue of gaining an objective view on the subject of Islamic extremism. For this reason, it is usually worthwhile instead to consult the Russian scholars of Islam. Partly because of their legacy of actually having to deal with Muslims in their own country—and not at a safe distance as had usually been the case in the West—and partly because of the atheistic legacy of the Soviet Union, they seem generally to have gained a clearer understanding of the militant aspects of Islam. For this reason, this writer has chosen to follow the Russian rather than Western authorities on controversial questions that might appear insensitive to Islam, yet are of the highest importance in evaluating the beliefs of Islamic extremism.

It is sometimes asserted that the higher a religious leader's level of knowledge, the more liberal and tolerant he will be. Not so. For the Muslim with strong Salafi beliefs, a good knowledge of religious norms and rules instead makes him determined to use any means to prevent the norms and rules from being violated.[15] It is also often held that tolerance depends on mutual understanding. However, for someone who is not a proponent of Salafi ideology to remain tolerant after having understood its tenets may be as difficult as for a Salafi believer to be tolerant of an apostate. It is then far easier to understand—and tolerate—the reason the state structures of such countries as Iran and Uzbekistan fight to destroy what they consider the Wahhabi threat. Muslims, after all, including the leaders of Iran and Uzbekistan, are men who "do not believe in turning the other cheek. They are commanded to challenge what they see as injustice or what is tyrannical. . . .They cannot be passive."[16] An authoritarian state may in time develop liberal tendencies. For the Salafi ideology to do so seems improbable.

The Difficulty in Defining Religious Beliefs

In Russia and Central Asia, the term Wahhabism has since the late 1980s often been misused as a synonym for any kind of Islamic fundamentalism, or at times, the doctrine of any believing Muslim opposed to the ruling government. Rhetoric about Islam, and in particular what was referred to as the Wahhabi threat, has been used to justify the suppression of groups that certainly formed part of the political opposition but by no means could be described as proponents of Wahhabism. Some Western academics accordingly condemn the use of the term Wahhabism as incompatible with serious scholarship, claiming that a significant Wahhabi movement does not exist in Central Asia.[17] Both views are simplistic.

The fact that accusations of Wahhabism have been used to justify political repression has already been proven, so there is no need to elaborate further on this subject here. However, Salafism/Wahhabism comes in degrees. Few who demonstrate Salafi/Wahhabi tendencies would describe themselves as followers of Wahhabism; they regard themselves as Muslims and nothing else. Some would consider it sinful to use the name because it would place the movement's founder, Muhammad ibn Abdul Wahhab, next to God by naming the religion after him. Moreover, the groups in Central Asia who display Salafi thought follow leaders such as Usamah bin Ladin, wanted by the United States for his part in several terrorist attacks, and Sheikh Omar Abdel Rahman, currently in a U.S. prison for his role in terrorism in New York. These men themselves reinterpreted the creed of original Wahhabism according to their own needs. For this reason, some academics prefer to use the term neo-Wahhabism.[18]

But the main reason the arguments for or against a Wahhabi presence are simplistic is that the average member of the so-called Wahhabi extremist movement in Central Asia—a rank-and-file member of the Afghan Taliban or a young man attracted by the views of Usamah bin Ladin—is no religious scholar. He does not, indeed cannot due to his limited education, distinguish between the different schools of Islam. The religious roots of the Taliban, for instance, lie in the Hanafi tradition (*Hanafiyyah*), originated by the theologian Imam Abu Hanifa (699–767) and one of the four schools of orthodox Islamic law, or, to be precise, the Deobandi school, named after the Deoband *madrasah* (religious boarding school) Dar ul-Ulum Deoband (House of Learning of Deoband), 60 miles north of Delhi, India.

Since its establishment in 1867 the Deoband school has been the leading Islamic centre in the Indian subcontinent, and thus the leading Hanafi centre. Deoband is the second oldest Islamic university, after Al-Azhar in Cairo. The Hanafi and Wahhabi movements ostensibly follow different traditions. However, Deobandi scholars and followers often demonstrate Wahhabi tendencies, as this theological centre was strongly influenced by Wahhabis at least since 1925 (when the first Indian Muslims went on a pilgrimage to Mecca after its occupation by Saudi Wahhabi forces, bringing home "glowing reports" of the new Wahhabi regime.)[19] Deoband's Islamic scholars quickly established local branches of the seminary in what today is Pakistan. Many of today's Afghan religious leaders have studied there.[20] Other religious scholars, who at least eventually referred to themselves as Wahhabis (including Sayyid Shari Muhammad, a native of Medina), established a presence in Tashkent, in the present Uzbekistan, and the Ferghana Valley of Central Asia in 1912 and have remained there since. They too appear to have come primarily from India.[21] Few followers of either tradition have gone to the lengths of scholarship required to ponder whether they were, or were not, Wahhabis.

Although one could argue that followers of the Hanafi school are not genuine Wahhabis even though many of them are strongly influenced by Wahhabism, and that, strictly speaking, the Taliban were Hanafi rather than Wahhabi, for all practical purposes they acted as Wahhabis. Schools of Islamic thought change and adapt according to the demands of their times, as well as popular sentiments among their leaders. They also frequently borrow ideas and norms from each other. It is accordingly just as easy to underrate as overrate the

Wahhabi presence in any given part of Central Asia. It should also be noted that in countries such as Uzbekistan, where any form of Islamic opposition is routinely labelled Wahhabism, this very persecution has given the Wahhabis a popular mystique that in fact encourages local Muslims to regard them as the persecuted Muslim faithful.[22]

For all practical purposes, perhaps the definition of Islamic extremism proposed by the Council of the Muftis (Islamic religious leaders) of Russia on 30 June 2000 is the best one. On that occasion the council singled out as extremist those movements that (1) rejected the basic Islamic traditions, (2) claimed the right to brand as "non-Muslims" traditional believers who happened to disagree with their interpretation of Islamic law, and (3) claimed the right to kill "infidels," including traditional Muslims who had failed to side with them.[23] This will be the definition of Islamic extremism adopted here, because this definition includes all varieties of Sunni extremism, whether referred to as Salafi or Wahhabi.

End Notes

1. Ignatenko, Alexander, "Islamic Radicalism: A Cold War By-Product," *Central Asia and the Caucasus* 1, 2001, 101–112.

2. Ibid., 101–112; Alexander Ignatenko, "Endogeneous Radicalism in Islam," *Central Asia and the Caucasus* 2, 2000, 118–130.

3. Hiro, *Islamic Fundamentalism*, 119.

4. Ignatenko, "Islamic Radicalism," 101–112; Ignatenko, "Endogeneous Radicalism," 121.

5. See, for instance, Ahmed Rashid, *Taliban: Islam, Oil and the New Great Game in Central Asia* (London: I. B. Tauris, 2000), 43.

6. Ignatenko, "Islamic Radicalism," 101–112.

7. See, for instance, Georgii Mirskiy, "Islamic Fundamentalism and International Terrorism," *Central Asia and the Caucasus* 6 (12), 2001, 28–37, 29; John L. Esposito, *The Islamic Threat: Myth or Reality?* (Oxford: Oxford University Press, 1992), 165; Kepel, *Muslim Extremism in Egypt;* Gilles Kepel, *Jihad: The Trail of Political Islam*

(Cambridge: Harvard University Press, 2000).

8. See, for instance, Mirskiy, "Islamic Fundamentalism," 30.
9. Hiro, *Islamic Fundamentalism*, 46.
10. See, for instance, Mirskiy, "Islamic Fundamentalism," 30.
11. Ibid., 34; Esposito, *Islamic Threat,* 138.
12. Reeve, *New Jackals,* 4.
13. See Mirskiy, "Islamic Fundamentalism," 37.
14. See Martin Kramer (editor of the *Middle East Quarterly*), *Ivory Towers on Sand: The Failure of Middle Eastern Studies in America* (Washington, D.C.: Washington Institute for Near East Policy).
15. Bakhtiyar Babadzhanov, "The Fergana Valley: Source or Victim of Islamic Fundamentalism?" *Political Islam and Conflicts in Russia and Central Asia* (Stockholm: Swedish Institute of International Affairs, 1999), 112–123.
16. Akbar S. Ahmed, *Living Islam: From Samarkand to Stornoway* (London: Penguin, 1995), 239.
17. See, for instance, Muriel Atkin, "The Rhetoric of Islamophobia," *Central Asia and the Caucasus* 1, 2000, 123ff; Ahmed Rashid, *Jihad: The Rise of Militant Islam in Central Asia* (New Haven and London: Yale University Press/World Policy Institute, 2002), 46.
18. Ignatenko, "Islamic Radicalism," 101–112.
19. Lacey, *Kingdom,* 195.
20. See, for instance, Mehrdad Haghayeghi, *Islam and Politics in Central Asia* (New York: St. Martin's Press, 1995), 163–164; Maley, *Fundamentalism Reborn?* 14–16, 75; Gohari, *Taliban,* 31–32. Some scholars play down the Wahhabi tendencies of Deoband while acknowledging its orthodoxy and rejection of innovation. Olivier Roy, *Islam and Resistance in Afghanistan,* 2d ed. (Cambridge: Cambridge University Press, 1990), 57–58. See also Barbara D. Metcalf, *Islamic Revival in British India: Deoband, 1860–1900* (Princeton, N.J.: Princeton University Press, 1982).
21. Ahmed Rashid, *The Resurgence of Central Asia: Islam or Nationalism?* (London: Zed Books, 1994), 44; Rashid, *Taliban,* 85; Rashid, *Jihad,* 45; Babadzhanov, "Fergana Valley," 112–123; Ashirbek Muminov, "Traditional and Modern Religious-Theological Schools in Central Asia," *Political Islam and Conflicts in Russia and Central Asia* (Stockholm: Swedish Institute of International Affairs, 1999), 101–111.
22. Rashid, *Jihad,* 46.
23. Ignatenko, "Islamic Radicalism," 101–112.

CHAPTER 5

The Ikhwan Revival:
Retaliation against Saudi Arabia

Jihad and the rifle alone: no negotiations, no conferences, and no dialogues.
—Abdullah Azzam (1941–1989)

The House of Saud had risen to power through the violent fanaticism of the early Wahhabis, and Saudi Arabia indeed was created on a foundation of Wahhabism. The Wahhabi argument was and is that all those who fail to rise against the corrupt, modern state by definition are infidels and, if Muslims, apostates who have to be killed. This argument has troubled the relationship between the House of Saud and the Wahhabis on whom the Saudi rulers rely.

There have been literally thousands of wealthy and fun-loving princes and princesses of the House of Saud. Educated in the West, they preferred gambling in Monaco, dressing in the fashions of Paris, and dancing the night away in London and New York to doing nothing much in their often bleak native country. The average Wahhabi, on the other hand, while not necessarily poor, has regarded even the use of radio and television as sins sufficient to damn any believer for eternity.

In September 1965, a young prince named Khalid ibn Musaid led his followers in an attack on the Riyadh television station. In the ensuing fight, he and his men were killed by security forces. It turned out that the prince, a young man who after a period of debauchery in the West had undergone a religious crisis, was the self-proclaimed leader of the revived Ikhwan movement. He and his followers had adopted Ikhwan dress: garments cut short above the ankles, hair cut short, moustaches clipped, and beards grown long. That Islamic forces would turn against the House of Saud came as a surprise for the Saudi rulers. There had always been secular and tribal enemies of the House of Saud in the kingdom, but these had largely been bought off, at least into the late 1970s. Nobody had expected that the remaining opposition would manifest itself in Islamic terms.[1]

In the aftermath of the Camp David agreement of 1979, the House of Saud, realising that it could no longer trust its own people, reacted by making an agreement with Pakistan. In exchange for a generous financial aid package, the Saudi rulers first received the assistance of two battalions of Pakistani army commandos, and then no fewer than three brigades. The Pakistanis, wearing Saudi uniforms, acted as a special royal guard. Being mercenaries without roots in Saudi society, it was argued, the Pakistani soldiers would be far more reliable than any native troops.[2] At first, the plan worked well: the Pakistanis were not only more dependable but also considerably more professional than the Saudi forces. But by entering into this agreement, which essentially made the two states symbionts of each other, the countries could not avoid religious repercussions. Pakistan, increasingly desperate for the financial aid from the Saudi government, had to accept the increasing numbers of Wahhabi proselytisers and preachers who always came as part of the package with Saudi aid. These men began to acquire influence in Pakistan, gradually turning the country into another state based on Islamic extremism and never-ending jihad. By encouraging Wahhabism in Pakistan, the Saudis inadvertently paved the ground for the possibility that even the house Pakistani troops one day would take up the call of the Ikhwan and rise against the House of Saud.

The extremist activities of the revived Ikhwan movement culminated early in the morning of 20 November 1979, when some 200 to 400 armed Ikhwan extremists (and dozens of women and children supporters) infiltrated and occupied Islam's holiest shrine, the Grand Mosque in Mecca. They were led by Juhaiman ibn

Muhammad ibn Saif al-Utaiba and his brother-in-law Muhammad ibn Abdullah al-Qahtani. Juhaiman, whose grandfather had been one of the Ikhwan who died at Sabilah in 1929, had studied at the Islamic University of Medina, which was established by the Egyptian Muslim Brotherhood. Later he had taken up preaching. His own development of the Wahhabi doctrine was the concept of the *mahdi* (guide), or the one guided by God, a messiah to restore the faith to its original purity, free it from all modern innovation and compromise, and bring a golden age under divine sanction. Juhaiman had expected to find Saudi King Khalid present in the mosque at this particular time. By killing the king in the holiest of shrines, he no doubt expected all true Muslims to rise in support of him and his brother-in-law, on behalf of whom Juhaiman claimed mahdiship, and to overthrow the government.

All this came to nothing. The king was not there, and the occupation turned into a bloody siege. While there was considerable popular support for the extremists, and many—perhaps as many as 3,000—of the Muslims who happened to be in the mosque at the time joined Juhaiman, the general population of Mecca did not rise. The government had to deploy 10,000 Saudi troops, thousands of Pakistani troops, and—even more shockingly to pious Muslims—a contingent of French advisers, antiterrorist fighters from the *Groupe d'Intervention de la Gendarmerie Nationale* (who instantly converted to Islam before they entered the holy site). The battle lasted for more than two weeks, ending only on 5 December. Among the extremists, at least 117 were killed during the siege, while 63 survivors were subsequently beheaded. As many as 127 soldiers were killed and 461 wounded in the struggle. At least a dozen innocent worshippers were also killed in the crossfire, many of them murdered by the extremists. About 7,000 suspected sympathisers of the Ikhwan were arrested. Among the extremists were not only Saudi citizens. There were Egyptians (members of the Muslim Brotherhood), Sudanese (from a group called the Ansars [Helpers], so named after the first supporters of the Prophet Muhammad), Kuwaitis (members of *Al-Jamiyyah al-Islah al-Ijtimai* [Society of Social Reform], a subsidiary of the Muslim Brotherhood), and Yemenis.[3]

Since the Mecca incident, Islamic extremism increased in Saudi Arabia. The number of members of the militant *Jamaat al-Dawa* (Society of the Call—with *dawa* having the meaning of proselytising) grew rapidly, especially among university-level students of science and technology. These refused enrollment at Western universities, let their beards grow, cut their hair very short, and dressed in a short white robe reaching only to the knees instead of the ankle-long conventional white robe, and wore caps or head-cloths. The Society of the Call, which has functioned openly, is a proven a recruiting base for more violent organisations.[4] It is believed that as many as 25,000 Saudi extremists went to fight the jihad abroad, chiefly in Afghanistan and Bosnia.[5]

There currently seems to be little long-term hope for the House of Saud: the royal family no longer controls the country as it used to.[6] Attempting to base one's power on those holding extremist views while half-heartedly suppressing those very same views is unlikely to work forever. Numerous individuals in Saudi Arabia, including members of the vast royal family, are known to sponsor Islamic extremism, directly and indirectly. The extremist groups have sources of income throughout the Islamic world, but their chief financial support has come from wealthy and influential members of the Saudi elite. If the current leadership of Saudi Arabia were to condemn extremist views that are rife among its own members and in the general population, this could lead to the fall of the House of Saud. If not, Saudi Arabia will remain a source of funds as well as recruits for the jihad against the West.

End Notes

1. Hiro, *Islamic Fundamentalism*, 125–126.
2. Lacey, *Kingdom*, 455; Hiro, *Islamic Fundamentalism*, 133–134.
3. Lacey, *Kingdom*, 478–487; Hiro, *Islamic Fundamentalism*, 125–126, 128–133; Jacquard, *Osama Bin Laden*, 13.
4. Hiro, *Islamic Fundamentalism*, 134–135.
5. *Economist*, 29 September 2001.
6. Reeve, *New Jackals*, 229–230.

CHAPTER 6
The Afghan Jihad
against the Soviet Union

In some ways, the Saudi rulers must have regarded the Soviet intervention in Afghanistan on 26 December 1979, only about a month after the Mecca occupation, as a godsend.[1] When the United States, Britain, and France began to organise the jihad in Afghanistan, the House of Saud eagerly took the opportunity to send off its most radical extremists to distant Afghanistan, where they could fight the Soviets to their hearts' content and at the same time cease being an immediate threat to their rulers. Or so, at least, it was believed at the time.

Paradoxically, the Soviet intervention in Afghanistan was to some extent engineered in Washington, D.C. As early as 3 July 1979, President Jimmy Carter had decided to provide clandestine aid to the Islamist opponents of the then pro-Soviet Afghan government. There is little doubt that President Carter was aware that the likely Soviet response would be a full-scale intervention and that the Carter administration saw this as a means to bog the Soviet Union down into a bloody war in which the United States would not be directly involved. Carter's national security advisor, Zbigniew Brzezinski, on the very same day wrote a note to the president in which he explained that, in his view, the aid would bring a military intervention by the Soviets. According to his own statement several years later, Brzezinski's intention was to draw the Soviets into their own Vietnam War.[2]

Brzezinski's calculation may have been cynical, but it was based on solid facts. Afghanistan was then a Soviet client state, and it seemed about to fall into anarchy. The Soviets also, quite correctly, realised that their client government was under threat not only from the domestic opposition but from hostile foreign forces as well, in particular Pakistan. Probably correctly, the Soviet government believed that Afghanistan was in the process of switching its allegiance to the West. When the Soviet leaders also received alarming reports describing how the U.S., British, German, and other foreign intelligence services were establishing a presence in Afghanistan, they responded by ordering a preemptive military intervention. On 26 December 1979, the first regular Soviet military units crossed the border into Afghanistan.[3]

Soon after, apparently already in early 1980, the West began to encourage its Muslim allies to send volunteer fighters to Afghanistan, to rouse the Afghans and to fight the Soviets in a jihad. Exactly when this decision was made remains unclear. The policy may have been formulated already at the time that President Carter decided to provide aid to the Islamists, or perhaps it was the effect of the Soviet intervention half a year later. Be that as it may, many Muslims needed no further encouragement: in their view, an atheist superpower had invaded a pious Muslim country. Following the Soviet intervention, those extremists who had the means immediately made their way to Pakistan and the Afghan border. In time the survivors became known as the Arab "Afghan veterans," or merely "Afghans"—extremists so named because they fought against the Soviet occupation forces (whose soldiers also, coincidentally, are known in Russian as *afgantsy,* "Afghans").[4]

Among the Arab Afghans were two men who would become key leaders of the Islamic extremist movement: Abdullah Yussuf Azzam (1941–1989), a Palestinian, and Usamah bin Ladin (1957–), a young, wealthy Saudi. Together they turned the Islamic extremist movement into a global endeavour and created what appears to be a lasting international support structure for worldwide jihad activities. During the anti-Soviet jihad, the older of the two, Abdullah Azzam, was by far the more influential. Azzam was born in a village near Jenin in Palestine in 1941. Like so many other Palestinian refugees, his family fled to Jordan after the Israeli occupation of Palestine. Having graduated with a degree in Islamic law from Damascus University in 1966, Azzam volunteered to fight against Israel, which he hated vehemently, in the 1967 war. After the war, Azzam went on to study Islamic law at Al-Azhar University in Cairo, receiving a doctorate in 1973. (It was a heady time at Al-Azhar. Among other students there at roughly the same time was Sheikh Omar Abdel Rahman.) Azzam subsequently lectured in Islamic law at the University of Jordan in Amman. Dismissed because of his extremist views, Azzam moved on to Saudi Arabia, where extremism was more appreciated. He continued teaching at King Abdul Aziz University in Jeddah. In 1980, he met the first Afghan mujahidin leaders, after which he moved to Pakistan with a small band of followers. There he became a lecturer at the International Islamic University in the capital, Islamabad. However, he soon settled in Peshawar, close to the Afghan border and a centre for jihad activities. There, with the assistance of Usamah bin Ladin, Azzam founded the Bait ul-Ansar (House of the Helpers), a guest house for jihadists, in 1984.[5]

Together Azzam and Usamah bin Ladin, with the full backing of Saudi Arabia, established the Islamic Salvation Foundation. This organisation would pay to fly willing but poor Islamic fighters recruited by Azzam throughout the world to Pakistan and compensate their families whenever needed, especially if they were killed—martyred—in the jihad. In addition, Usamah bin Ladin played a small part in helping Azzam establish *Maktab al-Khidamat al-Mujahidin al-Arabi* (Office of Services of the Arab Mujahidin), which would train the volunteers and supply them with the necessary weapons. These two organisations (the Islamic Salvation Foundation and the Office of Services) became the heart of what eventually was to be the modern worldwide jihad organisation: Islamic charities to pay the fighters and their families while maintaining a legitimate front and special clandestine organisations to arm and train the fighters and send them into combat.

As the war continued and U.S. and Saudi funding increased, the Office of Services established the *Al-Kifah* (The Struggle, also known as Al-Kifah Refugee Center in the United States) recruitment centres. Their purpose was to raise money and fighters for the anti-Soviet jihad throughout the world, especially in Muslim countries and wherever there were large Muslim immigrant populations. Azzam opened branches in many Western countries, including the United States, Britain, France, Germany, Sweden, and Norway, as well as throughout the Middle East. The organisation also established military training camps in Afghanistan and Pakistan.

The Office of Services/Al-Kifah Refugee Center in the United States

In the United States, the main office of the Office of Services/Al-Kifah Refugee Center was located in Brooklyn.[6] In Brooklyn and an office in Tucson, Arizona, the organisation also published an Arabic-language monthly magazine, *Al-Jihad*. Tucson had an Islamic Center as well as an Islamic Association for Palestine (IAP), the latter eventually growing into an information centre for the Palestinian organisation Hamas.

Important regional Office of Services/Al-Kifah Centers were established in the following cities:

Arlington, Virginia
Atlanta, Georgia
Boston, Massachusetts
Boulder, Colorado
Chicago, Illinois
Clearwater, Florida
Columbia, Missouri
Dearborn, Michigan
Jersey City, New Jersey

Las Cruces, New Mexico
Lincoln, Nebraska
Los Angeles, California
Madison, Wisconsin
Nashville, Tennessee
New Haven, Connecticut
Philadelphia, Pennsylvania
Phoenix, Arizona
Pittsburgh, Pennsylvania
Portland, Oregon
Sacramento, California
Tucson, Arizona
Washington, D.C.

Al-Kifah ceased most operations in 1994.[7] The Office of Services was closed by the Pakistani government following the 1995 attack on the Egyptian Embassy in Islamabad.[8]

For Azzam, the Afghan jihad was only the beginning. He demanded that no Muslim rest until all lands that once had been under Muslim rule would be returned to Islam, including places as diverse as Spain, Burma, and the Philippines.[9] Azzam was also one of the founders of the Palestinian Hamas movement in the Gaza Strip and the West Bank. Azzam travelled widely to recruit men and raise funds for the jihad. From 1985 to 1989, he toured the United States recruiting Muslims for jihad, certainly for Afghanistan but possibly also for the December 1987 Palestinian uprising, the intifada, against Israel in the occupied territories.[10]

On 24 November 1989, Azzam was murdered in a car-bomb attack in Peshawar, Pakistan, that also killed two of his four sons. Suspects included almost all of Azzam's friends and enemies, including at least five intelligence services: the Israeli Mossad, the Soviet KGB, and the Afghan Khad (all three regarded as Azzam's enemies), as well as the CIA and the Pakistani Inter-services

Intelligence Agency (ISI), which where both regarded as his friends, but for whom Azzam had become an embarrassment due to his worldwide jihad aspirations.[11]

In the 1980s, the least problem for jihad organisers such as Azzam was funding. Money for the jihad in Afghanistan was generous and handed out with no questions asked. Beginning with $30 million allocated by the United States in 1980, the volume of funding grew steadily during the decade. Saudi Arabia matched the U.S. aid approximately dollar for dollar. By 1986, combined U.S. and Saudi military aid reached about $1 billion a year. Not every resistance group in Afghanistan received support, however. Since the funds were channelled through the ISI, and the United States chose to trust the judgement of the Pakistanis, the bulk went to groups favoured by Pakistan (invariably the religiously more extreme because the ISI feared Afghan nationalism), Saudi Arabia, and individual Arab donors. Most accordingly went to Pakistan's favourite Islamist, Gulbuddin Hekmatyar, and various Saudi-inspired Wahhabi groups. Funding remained plentiful throughout the war. The U.S. military aid program was, for undeclared reasons, not terminated until in 1992—despite the fact that the Soviet Union had pulled out of Afghanistan in 1989 and then dissolved in late 1991.[12]

The United States also made important contributions to the educational activities of the jihad proponents. Special textbooks written in Dari and Pashto were in the early 1980s designed by the Center for Afghanistan Studies at the University of Nebraska–Omaha under a USAID grant. Aiming to promote jihad and militancy, they taught students basic arithmetic "by counting dead Russians and Kalashnikov rifles." More than 13 million were distributed in Afghan refugee camps and Pakistani religious boarding schools. The textbooks were so effective that in the 1990s even the Taliban endorsed them.[13]

This does not mean, however, that U.S. personnel took an active part in the anti-Soviet war. Although British and French intelligence personnel entered Afghanistan, few of their U.S. colleagues did. Instead, the CIA arranged for funds and weapons to be sent to the Pakistani ISI, which undertook the training of fighters and delivery of supplies to those fighting the Soviets in Afghanistan, or at least to those groups that remained firmly under the control of the ISI. U.S. officers were generally ordered to stay out of Afghanistan during the war for fear of being captured by the Soviets, thus offering them evidence of an anti-Soviet operation to present to the world. The name of the game, at least until the United States began to supply Stinger surface-to-air missiles in 1986, was plausible deniability. Until then, the CIA had even used its U.S. and Saudi funds to buy weapons from China and Egypt so that no support could be traced back to the United States.[14]

Fighters for the Afghan jihad were actively recruited throughout the Muslim world. The CIA was not directly involved in the recruitment process, except so far as the agency at times facilitated the travels of important Muslim leaders.[15] Partly for practical reasons—and partly for reasons of deniability—the CIA instead worked through its Saudi allies. The Saudis, in their turn, worked through a vast number of Islamic organisations and charities. Indeed, many Muslims paid for their own participation in the jihad, regarding the jihad as a spiritual experience and expecting a reward only in paradise. As a consequence, most jihad recruits came from Egypt, Saudi Arabia, Yemen, and Algeria. Saudi Arabia's national airline even gave a 75-percent discount to those who flew to Pakistan for the purpose of holy war.[16]

Of several important fronts for jihad support, one was the organisation already in existence and generally known as the *Tabligh* (Revelation; also known as *Jamaat-e Tabligh, Jamaat al-Tabligh,* and *Tablighi Jamaat*). The Tabligh grew from a group of a few dozen Muslims preaching and doing missionary work in 1926 in the region of Mewat, near Delhi, India. The founder was Maulana Muhammad Ilyas (1885–1994). This movement, formally established in 1927, had by 1988 grown into a loosely organised but well-funded global mass movement that attracted more than 1 million Muslims from 90 countries for its annual conference in Raiwind, near Lahore, Pakistan. By the late 1990s, the annual Raiwind meeting was the second largest congregation of Muslims after the annual pilgrimage to Mecca. The Tabligh also maintains a

European headquarters in Britain (in Dewsbury, a suburb of Leeds) as well a major office in Paris.

By the mid-1980s, the Tabligh was devoting considerable attention to the recruiting of young men for the Afghan jihad in North Africa. The organisation is known to have been active in Tunisia (see Appendix 9) but almost certainly was also active in the other North African states and doubtless throughout the world. Most fighters were recruited on university campuses and at colleges, where Islamic extremism by then was spreading rapidly. Others were recruited in the prisons, where members of the illegal Islamic extremist parties could be found. Many were offered free trips to Pakistan for religious studies. After a six-week period of religious education, the students would be approached and offered the opportunity for military training.[17] In 1988, the Tabligh held a convention in Chicago, attracting more than 6,000 Muslims from around the world.[18] In 1990, a similarly huge convention was held in Dallas.[19]

The Tabligh, as well as many other Islamic charities and missionary organisations, remains active in the recruitment of fighters for the jihad and the delivery of supplies to jihad groups throughout the world. It may, for instance, have been involved in the war in Chechnya: it has two religious establishments near Baku, the capital of Azerbaijan.[20] The Tabligh was also the organisation that, through its system of mosques in Western countries, originally recruited American Taliban John Walker Lindh and British "shoe bomber" Richard Reid.[21] (One of its earlier successes was the conversion to Islam of the British rock musician Cat Stevens, now known as Yusuf Islam.)[22]

The jihad support organisation then firmly established itself in the United States. The First Conference of Jihad in the United States was held at the Al-Farook Mosque on Atlantic Avenue in Brooklyn in 1988.[23] The American jihad movement had by then already grown into a powerful and increasingly wealthy organisation, which became clear after the 1989 death of Abdullah Azzam as a power struggle immediately broke out for control of the American end of his organisation. Azzam had appointed Mustapha

Shalabi, an Egyptian, but the latter was soon challenged by Sheikh Omar Abdel Rahman, another Egyptian, who came to settle in Brooklyn. (Sheikh Omar in some ways had competed with Azzam in Islamic extremism; he had also founded a guest house in Peshawar, a city he visited at least twice under the protection of Gulbuddin Hekmatyar.)[24]

At the core of the dispute was disagreement on how to use the hundreds of thousands of dollars and thousands of fighters that were the prime assets of the American side of the organisation. Shalabi wished to continue the war against the secular government in Afghanistan, even though the Soviets had pulled out, while Sheikh Omar Abdel Rahman wanted to move the jihad to Egypt and take the struggle to the international arena. On 26 February 1991, the dispute was solved by Shalabi's murder at the hands of unknown assailants, allegedly followers of Sheikh Omar.[25] The CIA had facilitated the entry of Sheikh Omar, the Egyptian terrorists' spiritual leader, into the United States. Despite being a known terrorist suspect, he had been granted visas in 1987 and 1990—in at least one case issued by an undercover CIA officer in the consular section of the U.S. Embassy.[26] Sheikh Omar also obtained a green card, no doubt because he worked closely (according to some sources) until at least 1992 with the CIA to facilitate the support to the mujahidin in Afghanistan.[27] This close cooperation with Sheikh Omar must rank as one of the CIA's most spectacular errors of judgement. The sheikh's plan in 1993 to bomb various targets in New York soon proved that he would not hesitate to bring the jihad to the United States as well as to Afghanistan.[28] Sheikh Omar's two sons, Muhammad and Assadallah (Abu Asim), were last seen in September 2000 in Afghanistan, where they vowed to continue the jihad.[29] On 21 September 2000, the Jihad Media Centre in Afghanistan produced a video featuring the leaders of four Muslim groups, including the Egyptian Islamic Jihad and Islamic Society as well as Al-Qaida, in which the leaders reaffirmed their determination to fight for the release of Sheikh Omar.[30]

When the Soviet Union pulled out of Afghanistan in 1989 and disintegrated in late 1991, the West celebrated. Through the use of the massive Western and Saudi financial resources and eager Muslim manpower, it was believed, the West had triumphed over the "evil empire" and could relax, confident that a new and better world would emerge by itself. Unfortunately, the worldwide jihad movement did not disintegrate but turned on the West. That the support of the Arab Afghans had been a mistake was, in hindsight, acknowledged by U.S. officials. "We did spawn a monster in Afghanistan," admitted Richard Murphy, the assistant secretary of state for Near East and South Asian Relations during the Reagan administration and former U.S. ambassador to Syria and Saudi Arabia. Charles G. Cogan, the CIA's operations chief in the Near East and South Asia between 1979 and 1984, was even more forthright: "The hypothesis that the mujahidin would come to the United States and commit terrorist actions did not enter into our universe of thinking at the time. We were totally preoccupied with the war against the Soviets in Afghanistan."[31]

Yet signs had been obvious for a long time. As early as September 1989, the head of the CIA Afghan Task Force had been dismissed due to charges in Congress of CIA incompetence and acquiescence in ISI politics, as well as the agency's complete reliance on its Pakistani counterpart. The main charge was that the ISI continued to favour its own chosen leaders, invariably ethnic Pashtuns such as Hekmatyar, who were almost always Islamists or extremists, while independent but far more important leaders such as Ahmad Shah Masud received little of the U.S. largesse distributed through the ISI. In addition, Arab aid continued to be directed to favoured leaders, primarily Hekmatyar and an Al-Azhar graduate named Abdul Rasul Sayyaf. Despite the allegations by Congress, the CIA, which maintained close links with Pakistani and Saudi intelligence, continued to rely on the ISI.

Both the ISI and CIA had made a huge investment in Hekmatyar and wished to see him as the key guarantor of Pakistani interests in Afghanistan, and no doubt Soviet Central Asia as well. Neither agency wanted to admit that 10 years of intensive funding had been a mistake.[32] And despite the knowledge that Saudi Arabia had at least matched the U.S. volume of funding, no Western official could foresee that the jihad would continue after the U.S. support was cut off. After all, Saudi Arabia was the friend of the United States, or so everybody believed.

End Notes

1. For more information on the Soviet war in Afghanistan, see Russian General Staff, *The Soviet-Afghan War: How a Superpower Fought and Lost* (Lawrence: University Press of Kansas, 2002); Mark Urban, *War in Afghanistan*, 2d ed. (New York: Macmillan, 1990); David C. Isby, *War in a Distant Country: Afghanistan—Invasion and Resistance* (London: Arms and Armor Press, 1989); Mohammad Yousaf and Mark Adkin, *Afghanistan: The Bear Trap—The Defeat of a Superpower* (Havertown, Penna.: Casemate, 1992, 2001). Details on Afghan tactics are found in Ali Ahmad Jalali and Lester W. Grau, *Afghan Guerrilla Warfare* (St. Paul: MBI, 2001; first published in 1995 as *The Other Side of the Mountain*).

2. Cooley, *Unholy Wars*, 13, 19; Bergen, *Holy War*, 67–68. See also Yousaf and Adkin, *Afghanistan*, 25–26.

3. See, for instance, Svetlana Savranskaya, ed., *The Soviet Experience in Afghanistan: Russian Documents and Memoirs*, 9 October 2001 (*www.gwu.edu/~nsarchiv*); Mark Galeotti, *Afghanistan: The Soviet Union's Last War* (London: Frank Cass, 1995), 10–13; Orozbek Moldaliev, "Islamism and International Terrorism: A Threat of Islam or a Threat to Islam?" *Central Asia and the Caucasus* 3 (15), 2002, 91.

4. Cooley, *Unholy Wars;* James Bruce, "Arab Veterans of the Afghan War," *Jane's Intelligence Review* 7:4 (April 1995), 175–179.

5. Bergen, *Holy War*, 52–53.

6. When no other source is given, this section is based on Emerson, *American Jihad*, 128–133, 180. The Brooklyn office was first located at the Al-Farooq Mosque, then on 566 Atlantic Avenue. Alexander and Swetnam, *Usama bin Laden's al-Qaida*, 37.

7. Emerson, *American Jihad*, 132–133.

8. Jacquard, *Osama Bin Laden*, 59.

9. Bergen, *Holy War*, 52–53.

10. Cooley, *Unholy Wars*, 86–87, 202, 223; Reeve, *New Jackals*, 169; Bergen, *Holy War*, 52–53.

11. Cooley, *Unholy Wars*, 86–87, 202, 223; Reeve, *New Jackals*, 169. Some also suspected the Egyptian extremists and indeed Usamah bin Ladin. Ed Blanche, "The Egyptians around Bin Laden," *Jane's Intelligence Review* 13:12 (December 2001), 19–21.

12. Barnett R. Rubin, *The Fragmentation of Afghanistan: State Formation and Collapse in*

the International System (New Haven: Yale University Press, 1995), 179–183.

13. International Crisis Group (ICG), *Pakistan: Madrasas, Extremism and the Military* (Islamabad/Brussels, ICG Asia Report 36, 29 July 2002), 13–14. The United States in March 2002 reintroduced edited versions of the same books into Afghan schools.

14. Yousaf and Adkin, *Afghanistan*, 81; Bergen, *Holy War*, 68.

15. Among them Sheikh Omar Abdel Rahman. Bergen, *Holy War*, 66–67; Jacquard, *Osama Bin Laden*, 7.

16. See, for instance, Bergen, *Holy War*, 55, 66–67, 90.

17. Cooley, *Unholy Wars*, 82–85; Jacquard, *Osama Bin Laden*, 61.

18. Cooley, *Unholy Wars*, 82, referring to Mumtaz Ahmed, "Islamic Fundamentalism in South Asia," in Martin E. Marty and Scott Appleby, eds., *Fundamentalisms Observed* (Chicago: University of Chicago Press, 1994), 510.

19. Reeve, *New Jackals*, 224.

20. Jacquard, *Osama Bin Laden*, 49.

21. Stephen Schwartz, "Recruiters for Jihad," *Weekly Standard* (New York), 28 January 2002.

22. *Economist*, 3 November 2001. See also the web site, *www.yusufislam.org.uk*

23. Emerson, *American Jihad*, 129–130.

24. Bergen, *Holy War*, 53–54.

25. Emerson, *American Jihad*, 134–135.

26. Bergen, *Holy War*, 66–67.

27. Jacquard, *Osama Bin Laden*, 7.

28. See, for instance, Laurie Mylroie, *The War Against America: Saddam Hussein and the World Trade Center Attacks—A Study of Revenge*, 2d ed. (New York: ReganBooks, 2001), 4, 182–192; Emerson, *American Jihad*, 29.

29. Jacquard, *Osama Bin Laden*, 102–103; Blanche, "Egyptians around Bin Laden," 19–21.

30. Jane's World Insurgency and Terrorism 13, Jane's Information Group, 4 October 2001.

31. Reeve, *New Jackals*, 3.

32. Rubin, *Fragmentation of Afghanistan*, 251, 252.

CHAPTER 7

Usamah bin Ladin and the Arab Afghans in the 1990s

If anything, I think that our children will be stricter Muslims than we are.
—Prince Turki ibn Faisal, director of the Saudi intelligence service,
on the rise of Wahhabism (November 1980)

EXTREMISTS TRIUMPHANT

When Soviet leader Mikhail Gorbachev pulled out of the Afghan war (the withdrawal began on 15 May 1988 and ended on 15 February 1989) and the Soviet Union was subsequently dissolved in December 1991, the Arab Afghans triumphantly, but wrongly, drew the conclusion that they had singlehandedly destroyed a superpower. Not so. The Soviet Union fell because of economic problems, corruption, and a general systems failure that undermined the loyalty to the one-party state.

The war in Afghanistan accounted for only about 1 or 2 percent of the total annual Soviet defence budget, and its total cost over 10 years amounted to no more than about a single year's subsidy for the production of basic foodstuffs in the Soviet Union. Neither were the human losses due to the war that great. The Soviet Union never deployed more than about 120,000 troops at any time in a country as large as Texas and twice the size of Vietnam: this equalled only some 3.6 percent of the entire military establishment of that decade. Of the troops that were deployed to Afghanistan, perhaps only 40 percent took part in combat, and fewer than 26,000 soldiers, at the very most, died in Afghanistan during an entire decade of war (14,453 according to official figures, probably somewhat underestimated). At the same time, between 35,000 and 76,000 Soviet servicemen died at home in circumstances ranging from accidents to suicide to bullying. Some 65,000 Soviet citizens died in car accidents each year, compared with the typically less than 3,000 a year who fell in battle during the Afghan war. While some Soviet soldiers did succumb to drug addiction while in Afghanistan, this was only a small minority of the total and has been shown to have had a smaller impact on Soviet society than was widely rumoured in the West at the time.[1]

The Arab Afghans also conveniently forgot that although the major share of the monetary costs of the jihad had been paid by Saudi Arabia, almost as much cash and, more important, all advanced weapons had been provided by the West. As a result, many Islamic extremist leaders thought that it would not be beyond their power to destroy the West as well, or at least to push all Western forces out of the Islamic world. These views became particularly pronounced at the time of the 1991 Gulf War. Many Muslims could not understand why Saudi Arabia and the other Arab rulers of the coalition had accepted Western help in repelling the forces of Iraqi leader Saddam Hussein. In their excitement, it seemed crystal-clear to the extremist leaders that the Arab Afghans, the instruments of God, easily could have routed the secular Iraqis all by themselves, without any foreign assistance. In addition, the continued presence of U.S. forces in what these leaders regarded as the holy territory of the Arabian Peninsula seemed to them to be that of an occupying army of crusaders bent on destroying Islam.

Two other important events inspired and excited the Arab Afghans. First, the civil turmoil in Algeria in 1992 developed into a genuine civil war between Islamic extremists and the far more secular Algerian government and military. Second, in 1994 Pakistan formed the Taliban movement in Afghanistan as a counterweight to the old generation of anti-Soviet mujahidin and launched it in a bid for power. Many Arab Afghans took part in both these events.

Soon to become chief among the new leaders of the Islamic extremists was Usamah bin Ladin. Although he, like many other likeminded leaders, soon turned against the House of Saud, the type of Islam he and his fellow extremists espoused remained closely connected to Wahhabism. While the extremist groups found sources of income throughout the Islamic world, their primary financial support came from wealthy and influential members of the Saudi elite. This included members of the vast royal family, who have been known to directly and indirectly sponsor Islamic extremism—despite the fact that Usamah bin Ladin and his followers were soon to confront them.

USAMAH BIN LADIN

Usamah bin Ladin was born in Riyadh, Saudi Arabia, on 10 March 1957, the 17th of the 20 sons of Muhammad bin Oud bin Ladin (who also fathered 32 daughters), one of the wealthiest businessmen of the Arabian Peninsula.[2] Usamah means "young lion" in Arabic. Usamah bin Ladin's mother was the 11th and last wife of the elder bin Ladin and hailed from Syria.

Muhammad bin Oud bin Ladin was an engineer and builder originally from Al-Ribat in the southern Yemeni province of Hadhramaut. A few years before Ibn Saud proclaimed the kingdom of Saudi Arabia in 1932, he moved to the key Red Sea port of Jeddah, as had many other Yemenis at the time. In 1931 he established a construction business. He eventually won the contract to build a new royal palace in Jeddah, thus gaining access to the House of Saud. This led to a string of other lucrative contracts that made Muhammad bin Oud bin Ladin increasingly wealthy. It also enabled him to develop close relations with the Saudi rulers. By the early 1960s, he was a close advisor to the king and on one occasion even stepped in to pay the wages of the entire Saudi civil service for four months. As a reward, he was appointed minister of public works. More important, of course, was that all subsequent contracts for public works were entrusted to him and his successors. By the mid-1990s, his firm, the Saudi Binladin Group, had an estimated turnover of $36 billion and was engaged in the rebuilding of Kuwait City as well as Beirut. There are no indications that it ever engaged in the support of terrorism (in the years around 1980, Usamah bin Ladin's oldest brother, the late Salem bin Ladin, was even connected through his American business representative with George W. Bush, then a junior oilman).[3]

Usamah bin Ladin received a traditional education and finished his secondary schooling in Jeddah in 1973. Although young Usamah grew up a devout Wahhabi, in the same way as many other wealthy young Saudis he made frequent pleasure trips abroad. Photos from the time, apparently depicting young Usamah, show what appears to be any Western European teenager, dressed in flared jeans and other clothes typical of the time and place. Some claim that young Usamah in particular travelled to the fleshpots of Beirut, where he could indulge in a less puritanical lifestyle. The truth in this is hard to ascertain; Usamah bin Ladin was still quite young. He is unlikely to have been as depraved as some Western newspapers after the 11 September 2001 attacks made him out to have been. However, like many other young Saudis, he eventually appears to have gone through a religious crisis, suddenly turning his back on pleasure trips and instead devoting himself to Wahhabism.[4] Exactly why and when young Usamah transformed from a Westernised teenager into a Wahhabi zealot remains unknown to outside observers. His close relatives probably know, but they do not talk.

At about this time, at age 17, Usamah bin Ladin also married his first wife, a Syrian relative, in a marriage arranged by his family. He began to study economics, public administration, and some civil engineering at King Abdul Aziz University in Jeddah.

Jeddah is Saudi Arabia's main port on the Red Sea, thus being more exposed to Western and Egyptian influences than most of the kingdom. So many of the lecturers at the university, as well as in the city's mosques, were Egyptians. Jeddah accordingly was a hotbed of Islamic extremism and a centre for the Muslim Brotherhood. Usamah bin Ladin came under the influence of Abdullah Azzam (then a lecturer there) and Muhammad Qutb, the brother of executed Egyptian extremist and writer Sayyid Qutb. They argued that extremism in the form of Wahhabism was the solution to all ills. And the Arab world then had its share of social ills. On 25 March 1975, for example, Saudi King Faisal was killed by a deranged nephew, and the Wahhabi clerics blamed the young man's illness on the time he had spent in the United States and the insidious influence of Western culture. So who were Usamah and his friends to disagree? Then the Lebanese civil war broke out in April 1975. Young Usamah, like many other Saudis, saw this as God's punishment for the depravity of Beirut. He grew increasingly radical in his beliefs and wholeheartedly adopted the views of the Muslim Brotherhood.

After his father died in 1968,[5] young Usamah had received a considerable inheritance. A source reportedly close to the family claimed that Usamah's share of the estate was $35 million. However, American officials in 1991 estimated Usamah bin Ladin's total worth at $250 million. Yet others reported an inheritance in excess of £300 million (about $750 million at the time). Thus there were no financial worries in his life: if he wished, he could indulge in a life of leisure. As he grew older, though, Usamah bin Ladin was known to enjoy horseback riding as well as reading in the fields of Islamic thought and current affairs.[6] He also acquired a sympathetic contact in Prince Turki ibn Faisal ibn Abdul Aziz (born in 1945), the director of the Saudi intelligence service, the two men apparently becoming friends in 1978. Prince Turki, despite graduating from an American university and pursuing postgraduate studies in Islamic law at London University, had remained a devout Wahhabi. He also had a genuine reputation for honesty and lack of corruption, despite being a Saudi prince, and Usamah bin Ladin appears to have admired these qualities. As for Prince Turki, he soon realised that Usamah bin Ladin, then in his early 20s, was the ideal candidate to act as a Saudi representative abroad.

The cause both men needed became apparent with Soviet interference in Afghanistan in December 1979. Usamah bin Ladin, furious over the Soviet intervention in a Muslim country, seems to have been eager to go there to fight. However, Prince Turki was taking part in the arrangements being made by the United States and some major Western powers to supply the Islamist insurgents in Afghanistan. Since Saudi Arabia had offered to match the Western contributions dollar for dollar, or more, Turki persuaded young bin Ladin instead to organise the clandestine network to supply the jihad in Afghanistan with cash, weapons, and willing volunteers from throughout the Islamic world. Bin Ladin flew to Peshawar, Pakistan, where he soon teamed up with Abdullah Azzam (the two men may have met earlier when Azzam taught at King Abdul Aziz University). Together Azzam and Usamah bin Ladin, as noted earlier, established the Islamic Salvation Foundation and the *Maktab al-Khidamat al-Mujahidin* (Office of Services of the Mujahidin). Usamah bin Ladin's first modest contribution was the Bait al-Ansar (House of the Helpers) in Peshawar for Muslims on their way to the Afghan jihad. He also arranged much needed construction work in the liberated areas through his contacts with the family firm, by then known as Bin Laden Brothers for Contracting and Industry.

While Usamah bin Ladin spent the Afghan war as an organiser of rear services rather than a fighter, he did take part in battle at least once. Laudatory accounts tell about his and Abdullah Azzam's heroism when, in early 1986, they were part of a small force of between 50 and 100 fighters defending a tactically unimportant village named Jaji, apparently holding out for more than a month against massive Soviet attacks. While it seems clear that Usamah bin Ladin was at Jaji, his actual battlefield role remains unknown to those who were not there. He also seems to have taken part in a leading position in the battle of Shaban in 1987. Yet, while Usamah bin Ladin won considerable popularity among the foreign jihad volunteers, many of the native Afghan fighters cared little for him, in the same way they thought little of most foreign volunteers.

This was hardly surprising; not only was foreign aid exclusively directed to the most vehemently Islamic groups, but the quality of many foreign fighters left much to be desired. Many of those who survived the war returned to Pakistan with crippling wounds, which were not always caused by fighting. (I personally met an Egyptian volunteer who confided that he had lost several toes to frostbite from playing soccer barefoot in the snow, not exactly the sort of behaviour meant to inspire the Afghans, who fought as much, if not more, for their homes and families as for the glory of Islam.)

In Afghanistan, bin Ladin made friends with several Islamic extremists who were to acquire lasting renown within the movement. And in this, as with bin Ladin's combat experience, it is often hard to distinguish between facts and myths. For instance, it is often claimed that bin Ladin at some time in the early 1980s contributed money to the then virtually unknown Binnori mosque in the Newtown area of Karachi. He also reportedly bought a house there for the prayer leader of the mosque, Mullah Muhammad Omar, who in 1994 became the leader of the Afghan Taliban. Yet it remains unknown to outside observers whether Mullah Omar ever visited Karachi.

However, Usamah bin Ladin undisputedly met the Egyptian extremist Ayman al-Zawahiri, a leader of the Egyptian Islamic Jihad. The two probably first met in 1985 after Zawahiri had gone to Afghanistan in the mid-1980s as a jihad volunteer. Zawahiri, six years older than bin Ladin, had already spent three years in prison in Egypt, an experience that must have given him the bitter, steely edge that bin Ladin, despite everything, never acquired. Zawahiri has since become the key ideologue and planner in Al-Qaida and may even be the true leader of the organisation. He certainly was a major influence on the later development of Usamah bin Ladin and his views on how to conduct the struggle.[7]

Through the influence of Al-Zawahiri, bin Ladin also acquired the help of two other Egyptians from Islamic Jihad who were to make names for themselves in the jihad organisation: Abu Ubaidah al-Banshiri and Muhammad Atef Mustafa. Abu Ubaidah al-Banshiri (also known as Ali Al-Rashidi) was a former Egyptian police officer who had been a clandestine member of Islamic Jihad since the 1970s. He was arrested in 1981 and, after being released, went to Afghanistan in 1986. He reportedly fought alongside Usamah bin Ladin at Jaji, which led to his subsequent appointment as bin Ladin's military commander when the latter later set up his own organisation. Abu Ubaidah was also reported to have been involved in jihad activities in other areas, including Eritrea, Kashmir, Tajikistan, Chechnya, Bosnia, and Libya, claims which do not all seem credible. He drowned in a mysterious ferry accident on Lake Victoria, in Tanzania, in the spring of 1996.[8]

Muhammad Atef Mustafa (also known as Abu Hafs, Sheikh Taysir Abdullah, Abu Afez al-Masri al-Khabir, and Subhi Abdul Aziz Abu Sittah) was an Egyptian army or police officer during the 1970s. He arrived in Peshawar in 1983, where he worked closely with Azzam.[9] One of his daughters married Usamah bin Ladin's son Muhammad in early 2001.[10] Muhammad Atef, who was accused of organising the 11 September 2001 attacks on the United States,[11] reportedly died in November 2001 in an air raid on Kabul.[12]

After the Soviet forces withdrew from Afghanistan, bin Ladin returned to Saudi Arabia. By then, however, he was full of enthusiasm for the jihad. When the United States and the other Western members of the anti-Soviet coalition cut back on their support to the Islamic extremists in 1989 (and then abandoned them completely in 1992), he regarded this as a betrayal. When the various Afghan groups soon after began to compromise with the formerly Soviet-supported Afghan government, and when the Afghan groups subsequently took up arms against each other, he saw this too as the work of traitors. Even worse, the wide gap between the wealthy Saudi princes and the general population of Saudi Arabia remained as wide as ever, and the Saudi upper classes spent as much time on leisure tours to the West as before. Saudi women appeared outside their homes without male guardians, flaunting Western dress. Alcohol was available to those who wanted it. Infidel Westerners lived and worked openly in the country of the Prophet. All this filled bin Ladin with revulsion. In his view the entire country was suffering from moral degradation caused by Western influences. (As a further insult, the United States continued to support Israel against the Palestinians. Bin Ladin realised that part of the vast profits U.S. companies made in the Middle East went to the U.S. government in taxes that were then used to subsidise Israel. Muslims were thus unknowingly supporting the hated Jews.) The final insult to Usamah bin Ladin's values came with the Gulf War of 1991, the response by the United States and allies to Iraqi President Saddam Hussein's invasion of Kuwait in August of 1990. Western troops, with the full support of the House of Saud, entered Saudi Arabia in strength, ostensibly to protect the kingdom against Iraqi aggression but ultimately to launch a war against Iraq to liberate Kuwait. From bin Ladin's perspective, the holy country of the Prophet was suddenly being invaded by Western crusader hordes— and their purpose was to bring down the Iraqi ruler Saddam Hussein, who, despite his secular regime, was the leader of a Muslim nation. That the House of Saud directly supported and facilitated the invasion by crusaders only further inflamed the situation and bin Ladin's hatred. In this he was not alone. The admission of Western forces into the Arabian Peninsula was, as noted earlier, the final straw for the other Arab Afghans as well.

AL-QAIDA

Usamah bin Ladin was prepared for the new struggle. As early as 1988 or 1989, with the help of Muhammad Atef, he had reorganised the Office of Services into Al-Qaida (The Base) to combat the manifold Western influences on the Islamic world.[13] The name of the new organisation has been explained as deriving from the fact that when bin Ladin could not give answers to Muslim families who inquired about their relatives missing in Afghanistan, he decided in 1988 to arrange for proper documentation of each volunteer sent to the jihad. He reportedly kept records of all his visitors thereafter, with their dates of arrival and final departure, and these became known as the records of "the base." The whole complex then took on the same name.[14] Be that as it may, the purpose of Al-Qaida was to support the global jihad by raising money and fighters, as its predecessor had done during the Afghan war.[15]

Al-Qaida was led by a council (*majlis al-shura*), which included bin Ladin and Zawahiri and discussed the projects undertaken by the group. In addition, Al-Qaida had a military committee, among the members of which were Muhammad Atef and Abu Ubaidah al-Banshiri (until his drowning in 1996). The general policies of Al-

Qaida were formulated by Usamah bin Ladin and the council, which together made all executive decisions. According to some testimony, there were three committees subordinate to the council: military, religious, and financial. There was also a media committee, led by one Abu Musab, known as "Reuters," and a travel committee responsible for travel arrangements and the acquisition of passports and other identity papers. In addition, there was a security detail, reportedly led by Muhammad Musa.[16] A number of businesses were established to act as fronts for money transfers as well.[17]

Bin Ladin also closed down the various remaining overt support offices in the West after making sure that valuable assets and personnel had been transferred into the more secretive Al-Qaida. Al-Kifah ceased most operations in 1994.[18] The Peshawar-based Office of Services was conveniently closed by the Pakistani government following the 1995 attack on the Egyptian Embassy.[19]

One of Al-Qaida's first tasks was to safeguard the security of its camps in Pakistan. Bin Ladin made substantial payments to Sami ul-Haq, a senior politician and Muslim cleric, who spent them on the election campaign of Nawaz Sharif, who ran for Pakistani prime minister in October 1990. Sharif won the election, and it appears that bin Ladin supported him and his Islamic Democratic Alliance for several years.[20]

Al-Qaida recruited its members among the informally connected groups of Arab Afghans. The early members were those who had been with bin Ladin since the Afghan war. Unlike traditional Middle Eastern terrorist organisations, the Arab Afghans typically formed part of a complex network of relatively autonomous, loosely organised groups rather than hierarchical organisations. These were joined by their common ideology of Salafi Islamic principles translated into politics rather than a shared organisational structure. For this reason, very little was known about these groups outside their immediate circles until recently. Important evidence in the form of computers and documents was captured in Afghanistan at the time of the fall of the Taliban. However, the vast amount of abandoned documents and other evidence seems to have overwhelmed the few available Western intelligence personnel present, and much of it was dispersed among locals and journalists before it could be secured and analysed.[21] Because of the lack of formal hierarchy, the extremist groups were also difficult to influence through their leaders, even if such leaders were known. The groups were, as far as is known, generally financed by private sources rather than by state sponsors. Most groups of this kind appeared to be funded partly by donations from like-minded religious groups in various countries and partly from involvement in narcotics trafficking. The chief objective of the Arab Afghan movement was global opposition to perceived threats to its interpretation of Islam. Most or all of these extremists were to some extent influenced by Salafi Islam, and in particular the Wahhabis of Saudi Arabia. (This was due, at least in part, to the financial contributions from Saudi Arabia and the close relationship between the Saudi rulers and the Wahhabi religious leaders.)[22] Of the thousands of men who eventually received training in the Al-Qaida camps in Afghanistan, only a small percent formally became Al-Qaida members. Those who did had to swear the *bayah,* a traditional oath of allegiance in Arabic to the organisation and its leader.[23]

A characteristic of the Arab Afghan movement that Al-Qaida subsequently made its trademark was the ability to quickly relocate members and operations from one geographic area to another in response to changing circumstances and needs. Many of the fighting members of the movement appeared to constantly move from one war zone to another or one Islamic group to another, turning up in places as diverse as Algeria, Egypt, Chechnya, and Tajikistan. The relocations also appeared to serve as a security measure. Moving members responsible for an act of terrorism after it took place often enabled them to avoid arrest or extradition, and this ability to move and act swiftly was one major factor in the movement's success.[24] The Arab Afghan movement can be said to operate on a truly global scale, recruiting, training, profiting, and striking wherever opportunities present themselves or the defences of the movement's enemies are down.

Another characteristic of the movement was that the its average members, the foot soldiers, typically knew little or nothing of the

wider plan of whatever operation they were conducting. Members
involved in terror activities were organised into cells, usually of
three people, with each cell designated a certain task. Four cells
were usually employed. The first consisted of the planners. A surveillance cell would collect information on possible targets and send
it to the planners, who decided which target to attack. A logistical
cell would then provide weapons and explosives. A fourth cell was
to carry out the attack. Even when the system was not fully used,
those who executed the attack would be separate from those who
planned and prepared the mission.[25] The planners, who had full
knowledge of at least their particular operation, usually moved out
of the country of operations immediately after, or even before, the
attack took place. Examples include Ramzi Yousef, who fled the
United States after the February 1993 World Trade Center bombing;
a mysterious and never identified Egyptian explosives expert known
as Abdul Rahman, who prepared the Nairobi bomb in 1998; an
equally unidentified Hussain who facilitated the Dar-es-Salaam
bomb in the same year; Muhammad Omar al-Harazi (also known as
Abdul Rahman Hussain Muhammad al-Saafani), who led the attack
on the USS *Cole* but left Yemen for Afghanistan after the attack;
and perhaps Mustafa Muhammad Ahmad al-Hawsawi (also known
as Sheikh Saeed), believed to be one of bin Ladin's most trusted
financial officers, who was in constant contact with the lead hijack-
er Muhammad Atta in the days leading up to the 11 September 2001
terrorist attacks. Ahmad al-Hawsawi left his base in the United Arab
Emirates and flew to Pakistan on 11 September 2001, where he
promptly went into hiding. More important, some comments by
Usamah bin Ladin in a mid-November 2001 videotape, presented as
evidence by the U.S. government, indicated that the Saudi members
of the 11 September conspiracy were not told the details of the mission until just before they boarded the airliners they were going to
hijack and crash into the targets.[26]

Although Al-Qaida to some extent functioned as the centre of
what was quickly evolving into a vast, loose international network
of Islamic extremist groups, Al-Qaida always retained the nature of
a general support organisation rather than an operations centre, in

the same way that bin Ladin had provided logistical support to the Afghan jihad.

Usamah bin Ladin was believed (not necessarily correctly) to support, finance, and coordinate much of what went on within the Arab Afghan movement. The members of Al-Qaida sometimes conducted missions on their own, but more often they acted in conjunction with other groups or elements of the movement. In bin Ladin's declaration of holy war against the United States and the West in 1996, he specified that this war would be fought by irregular, light, highly mobile forces using guerrilla tactics.[27] This has proven a good description of the Arab Afghan movement (see Appendix 1). However, even though Usamah bin Ladin is believed to finance many Arab Afghan terrorist activities and direct some operations, he never claimed to be in direct command of all operatives in the movement and is unlikely to have played such a role. Usamah bin Ladin did not function as a traditional leader in control of these various activities.[28] He often appeared to be the inspiration rather than organiser or financier of extremist activities. Even after he founded the World Islamic Front for Jihad against the Jews and the Crusaders in February 1998, and together with some other extremist leaders issued a fatwa declaring it legitimate to kill any American, civilian or military, the groups participating in the front remained independent.

While the ordinary members of the Islamic extremist groups typically were recruited among the underprivileged, impoverished, and embittered masses who usually constitute the recruits for extremist and terrorist movements, the leaders belonged to the affluent, privileged, educated, and Westernised elite of their society. However, by exchanging the easy life into which they were born for the path of Islam, these men turned themselves into populist leaders of the first magnitude, expecting and receiving the adoration of the vast majority of the masses. None had sacrificed a more luxurious life than Usamah bin Ladin, and he accordingly became most admired of all.

Few if any of the movement's rank-and-file members in Afghanistan had any but the most basic education, and whatever education they may have received was in most cases exclusively religious. The main recruiting ground was until 2001 among poor, uneducated young men, often orphans or refugees, who had literally nothing to lose. These men viewed membership in a well-funded international extremist Islamic organisation with pretensions of equality and brotherhood, as well as good political connections in certain Arab countries, as a sound career move. However, the movement also had a core of extremists with higher education, typically attracted to it by feelings of resentment because of high unemployment in their native countries, among them Algeria and, in recent years, Uzbekistan[29] (just two among the Middle Eastern and Central Asian countries whose governments face severe danger from extremist activities.) Such men usually entered Afghanistan from Pakistan.[30]

The background of the typical Islamic extremist changed over the years, showing a clear trend away from the intelligentsia that had led the early Islamist movement. In the 1970s about 80 percent of the Egyptian Islamic extremists arrested were college or university graduates.[31] By the early 1980s, an estimated 40 percent of the members were college or university students and six percent were professionals.[32] By the mid-1990s, the figure had dropped to a mere 20 percent. Furthermore, it had become clear that many recruits could be found in the lower ranks of various nations' armies and paramilitary forces.[33] The majority of the foreign volunteers with the Taliban captured by the Northern Alliance were uneducated and gave no impression of being able to operate efficiently as international terrorists. This supports the suggestion that Usamah bin Ladin eventually chose the U.S. Embassies in Tanzania and Kenya for the 1998 bombings simply because they were easy targets. Security was weak, and the men who were sent to do the job could not operate effectively in more organised and advanced countries. The attacks were successful, but they were sloppily executed and several perpetrators botched their flight from the countries. In Aden, Yemen, would-be suicide bombers in January 2000 overloaded a small boat with explosives, thereby sinking it and blowing their chance of attacking the USS *The Sullivans*. Such an attack, however, succeeded in crippling the USS *Cole* in October of the same year. That most Arab Afghans lacked education was also the assessment of the Afghan Northern Alliance commander Ahmad Shah Masud's intelligence service. According to his analysis, of the 700 or so Arab Afghans in Afghanistan, very few were capable of anonymously and securely travelling abroad.[34]

Yet there were technically capable men within Al-Qaida. This is perhaps most clearly shown in the multivolume book that in various forms is known as the *Encyclopedia of the Afghan Jihad* (*Mawsuat al-Jihad al-Afghani*). This CD-ROM textbook in terrorism has seen widespread distribution among Arabic-speaking Islamic extremists.

The *Encyclopedia of the Afghan Jihad* (*Mawsuat al-Jihad al-Afghani*)

Of the apparently numerous editions of the encyclopedia, several versions as well as condensations have turned up in the United States, Britain, France, Italy, Belgium, Croatia, Pakistan, the Philippines, Jordan, Egypt, and Canada. What appears to have been a complete copy of the encyclopedia, 8,000 pages in all, is reputed to have been discovered in the possession of Islamic extremists in Belgium in 1995, according to some reports, on a diskette (although an ordinary diskette would not have held that amount of information). Copies were subsequently distributed to Israeli and French intelligence organisations. By 1999, the CIA had received a copy of an abridged version of approximately 1,000 pages found by Jordanian intelligence.[35]

The full encyclopedia consists of 11 volumes. One volume details weapons, from handguns to antiaircraft guns, as well as the weak points of tanks of assorted models and how these can be attacked with various weapons. Another volume details explosives, mines, and grenades, as well as the uses of TNT and Semtex and information on how to blow up bridges and other structures. Other sections of the encyclopedia describe battlefield first aid, topography, strategy, manufacture of improvised weapons, and special tactics such as street fighting.[36]

The first volume, on explosives, is a 200-page manual with diagrams and illustrations on how to make booby traps in the form of exploding chairs, sofas, beds, radios, irons, teapots, books, cigarette packs, lighters, whiskey bottles, stethoscopes, hairbrushes, whistles, pipe bombs, letter bombs and more powerful bombs for cars, trucks, and houses. The volume also includes instructions on fuses and timers, as well as instructions on how to make explosives with the name of ingredients in both Arabic and English. One edition of this work, found in the hands of Arab Afghans, was dedicated to Abdullah Azzam, the founder of the Office of Services, as well as to Usamah bin Ladin.[37] What appears to have been volume five of the encyclopedia details weapons in nearly 1,000 pages, with diagrams and detailed instructions on how to use Western and Soviet weapons, including the Stinger shoulder-fired, portable surface-to-air missile delivered by the CIA starting in 1986.[38]

Although the encyclopedia clearly has been updated and improved since the Soviet Union pulled out of Afghanistan, major parts of it appear to be direct translations of U.S. military field manuals used at the time of the war. Even the illustrations are reproduced. So are, for instance, two pages describing booby-trap designs found and made public in 2001 by a former CIA analyst based on pages 72 to 74 of the U.S. Army Field Manual FM 5-31, *Booby Traps*.[4] Two of the four pages of a 6,000-page text on CD-ROM reportedly acquired and published by *Time* magazine were also based on FM 5-31.[40] A page on how to blow up bridges, illustrated by a

French writer, is at least in part based on FM 5-25, *Explosives and Demolitions*.[41] However, according to some analysts, the authors of the encyclopedia did not only copy field manuals but also often simplified the material available, thus ensuring that even the relatively uneducated could use it. This made some of the processes described risky also to the user.[42] One of the no doubt many who have done their share of the work was probably Ramzi Yousef, who planned and executed the World Trade Center bombing in 1993. In 1992, he is known to have taught the use of explosives and bomb-making at a camp roughly 30 miles east of Peshawar, called the University of Dawa (*dawa*, "call" or proselytising) and Jihad.[43]

The digital version of the encyclopedia appears to be the work of Khalil al-Deek, a Palestinian with dual Jordanian-U.S. citizenship. Deek, a computer technician, lived in California where he worked in Web site design. Later he went to Pakistan, ostensibly to prepare a CD-ROM with Islamic texts. However, Deek, being implicated with 13 others in the preparation of an attack planned to coincide with the millennium, was expelled from Pakistan and arrested in Jordan on 16 December 1999. When Pakistani police subsequently searched his home, they found evidence that implicated Deek in the digital preparation of the encyclopedia.[44]

Since then, yet another CD-ROM has been found. This, with 5,800 pages on the deployment of bacteriological and chemical weapons, turned up in the investigations following the 11 September 2001 attacks. It was apparently only released to key Al-Qaida members.[45] No further details on its contents have been made public.

The overall number of Arab Afghans is hard to estimate. A reasonable estimate in the mid-1990s was a total in excess of 14,000, including some 5,000 Saudis, 3,000 Yemenis, 2,000 Egyptians,

2,800 Algerians, 400 Tunisians, 370 Iraqis, 200 Libyans, and scores of Jordanians.[46] The Pakistani government in the early 1990s asked Arab militants in the country to register with the government (a request many obviously did not heed); those in the North-West Frontier Province who did included 1,142 Egyptians, 981 Saudis, 946 Yemenis, 792 Algerians, 771 Jordanians, 326 Iraqis, 292 Syrians, 234 Sudanese, 199 Libyans, 117 Tunisians, and 102 Moroccans.[47] Although the real numbers no doubt were higher, at least the proportions are likely to be correct. In the late 1990s, a former senior CIA official estimated that the number of Arab Afghans was closer to 17,000.[48] Jihad veterans subsequently took the war home to more than 25 countries, including Algeria, Azerbaijan, Bangladesh, Bosnia, Britain, Burma, Chechnya, China, Egypt, France, India, Morocco, Pakistan, the Philippines, Saudi Arabia, Sudan, Tajikistan, Tunisia, the United States, Uzbekistan, and Yemen.[49]

Only a few Arab Afghans were actually members of Al-Qaida. The total worldwide membership of Al-Qaida was usually estimated to be between 3,000 and 5,000. Most observers estimated Al-Qaida's membership as 4,000 Arab Afghans.[50] In an interview in November 2001, an anonymous Al-Qaida leader claimed a total membership of 6,000, ruled by a worldwide, 156-strong central committee of which 24 were in Pakistan. He also claimed that bin Ladin, despite his value to the organisation, was not its leader. Al-Qaida, he said, was really led by two Egyptians.[51] Others have put the total membership lower, at from 1,500 to 3,000 people.[52] In early November 1998, Egyptian intelligence reportedly estimated the number of Arab Afghans with bin Ladin in Afghanistan at 2,830. Among them were 594 Egyptians, 410 Jordanians, 291 Yemenis, 255 Iraqis, 177 Algerians, 162 Syrians, 111 Sudanese, 63 Tunisians, 53 Moroccans, and 32 Palestinians, in addition to scores of extremists from various other states, mainly in the Persian Gulf.[53]

The statement that Al-Qaida was led by two Egyptians (if so, no doubt Zawahiri and probably Muhammad Atef) is not as far-fetched as it may sound. After all, U.S. officials claim that Al-Qaida merged with the Egyptian Islamic Jihad in 1998. However,

Islamic Jihad was by far the larger group, and currently all key members of the joint group—with the single exception of bin Ladin himself, who provides the public face of the organisation—are Egyptians. In addition, as far as can be ascertained, the combined group follows ideology and tactics based on the Egyptian model. It can thus be argued that Islamic Jihad assumed control over Al-Qaida rather than vice versa. This would hardly be surprising because Egypt, due to Al-Azhar University and the legacy of Sayyid Qutb, is the fount of all Islamic extremist ideology more sophisticated than the village mullah type espoused by the arch conservative Saudi Wahhabis and the Afghan Taliban.[54]

USAMAH BIN LADIN MOVES TO SUDAN

Islam is light, democracy is darkness.
    —Declaration by the Algerian extremist movement

After 1989, when Usamah bin Ladin returned from Afghanistan, the Saudi government denied him the ability to travel abroad to discourage further extremist activities. According to some, this was in response to a request from Pakistan. Due to his repeated criticism of the ruling House of Saud, however, bin Ladin was either expelled from or quietly permitted to leave Saudi Arabia in April 1991. He promptly flew to first Peshawar and then, in mid-1992, to Sudan (reportedly in his private executive jet).[55] Welcomed by Hassan al-Turabi, the Islamic extremist who was the true power behind the Sudanese government at that time (see Appendix 6), bin Ladin settled in the Riyadh section of Sudan's capital, Khartoum. Usamah bin Ladin also brought an entourage of aides and bodyguards, which eventually grew into a force of approximately 500 Arab Afghans. These were men of fundamentally three different types: those without a purpose who needed a leader—any leader—to tell them what to do, religious fanatics who had only minimal clerical knowledge, and ruffians who were itching for a fight—any fight—against whomever they believed were enemies of Islam. Most were Egyptians, Algerians, Palestinians, and Tunisians, but there were also Saudis, Syrians, Iraqis, and Moroccans. Among them was Ayman al-Zawahiri, who joined bin Ladin in Sudan in 1992 and 1993. In Sudan, quite a few Sudanese joined the movement as well, as did Somalis, Ethiopians, Eritreans, Bosnians, and a handful of African-Americans.

Sudan was deeply divided by a civil war between Islamic and non-Islamic forces, and the Islamic government, based on the National Islamic Front (NIF), needed all the help it could get. Bin Ladin helped the NIF build an impressive complex of training camps for Islamic extremists. Some camps were located in the Al-Khalafiyya area, roughly 25 miles north of Khartoum (from 1994 reportedly used by two rival Algerian groups: the Islamic Salvation Army and the Armed Islamic Group [Groupe Islamique Armé, or GIA]); at Akhil al-Awliya, on the banks of the Blue Nile south of Khartoum (used by Palestinians, Syrians, and Jordanians); Al-Mrihat, north of Umm Durman (used by Egyptian members of the Muslim Brotherhood, Islamic Society, and Zawahiri's faction of the Islamic Jihad, the Vanguard of Conquest); and Mukhayyamat al-Mazari, northwest of Khartoum (used by extremists of all nationalities, including Libyans, Tunisians, Palestinians, Syrians, Saudis, Lebanese, Algerians, and even Americans).[56]

Usamah bin Ladin also set up a number of corporations to assist the Sudanese with numerous badly needed infrastructure developments, as well as to ensure a flow of funding for his political activities.[57] He formed the company Al-Hijrah Construction and Development, jointly owned with the Sudanese government. The firm built a new airport at Port Sudan and a vitally needed road between Khartoum and Port Sudan that formed part of a new network of north-to-south roads. He also invested more than $50 million in the Al-Shamal Islamic Bank in Khartoum, a joint venture with senior members of Turabi's NIF. Along with other NIF members, bin Ladin was one of the founders of the holding company Wadi al-Aqiq, which soon assumed control over Sudan's important exports of corn, sunflower, and sesame seed products. Some claim that bin Ladin also invested in the agricultural company Al-Themar al-Mubaraka, the trucking firm Al-Qudarat Transport

Company, a fleet of fishing boats, and Khartoum Happ Tannery, a factory that processed goat skins. Most interesting, he invested in Gum Arabic Company Limited, a Khartoum-based corporation heavily involved in Sudan's lucrative exports of gum arabic, a commodity of which Sudan controls around 80 percent of the world's supply. (Gum arabic, from the sap of the Sudanese acacia tree, is used for a number of key products in the Western world, including canned drinks, sweets, and medical pills, and was the key Sudanese export to the West.)[58]

The Crucial Year of 1994

The year 1994 was a watershed for Usamah bin Ladin personally, as well as for the development of Al-Qaida and the Sunni Islamic extremist movement.

First, following the deaths of 18 U.S. servicemen in skirmishes with Somali warlords in late 1993, all remaining U.S. forces pulled out of Somalia by March 1994 (see Appendix 7). The Islamic extremists saw the development as a glorious victory for Islam that proved the United States was even easier to defeat than the Soviet Union.

On 7 April 1994, the Saudi government retaliated for Usamah bin Ladin's repeated criticisms and his refusal to return home to an unspecified punishment by revoking his Saudi citizenship (he travelled thereafter on a Sudanese diplomatic passport).[59] Furthermore, all his financial assets in the kingdom were seized—a considerable fortune that he rightly regarded as his birthright.[60] Bin Ladin retaliated in turn on 11 July 1994 by forming an exile opposition group to the Saudi regime, the Advice and Reformation Committee (ARC, also occasionally known as the Office of Council and Reforms) in London. Usamah bin Ladin appointed Khalid bin Abdhuram al-Fawwaz, a former Saudi civil engineer who had fought in Afghanistan, as director of the new organisation. Local branches of the ARC were also established in Kansas City, Missouri, and Denver, Colorado. (In 1998, the United States moved against the ARC, treating it as an extension of Al-Qaida. The government designated Fawwaz a foreign terrorist, closed down the ARC offices, and blocked the organisation's possessions and funds.

Fawwaz was arrested in Britain in October of the same year.)[61]

Then, also in April 1994, civil war between northern Islamic extremist and southern secular forces broke out in recently unified Yemen, bin Ladin's ancestral land (see Appendix 5). Although the secessionist south was comparatively secular, and many battle-hardened Arab Afghans in the ensuing war fought on the northern, more Islamic-oriented side, the secessionists, to bin Ladin's horror, received some support from Saudi Arabia. No doubt seeing the Saudi support as a further betrayal of the Wahhabi ideals, he responded by moving weapons and money into Yemen to assist the northern side. By July 1994, the northern army and the Arab Afghans had defeated the southern forces.[62]

Islamic extremism was also on the rise in Algeria. On 13 May 1994, the most violent Islamic extremists in Algeria, most of them Arab Afghans, merged into the GIA (in Arabic *Jamaat al-Islamiyyah al-Musallahah*). The GIA quickly acquired the reputation of being the most brutal of the many violent Algerian Islamic extremist groups (see Appendix 8).

In April 1994, Usamah bin Ladin also visited Albania, an underdeveloped, corrupt, largely (nominal) Muslim state in the Balkans. Amazingly, Usamah bin Ladin arrived there as a member of an official Saudi Arabian delegation and was introduced as a friend of the Saudi government who would finance the construction of apartment buildings and a health-care centre. He negotiated an agreement with Bashkim Gazidede, an Islamic intellectual who then was the head of the Albanian intelligence service. Probably in exchange for payments, Gazidede later arranged entry into Albania for several Islamic extremists, including four men believed to be responsible for the 1993 assassination of Rifat el-Mahgoub, the speaker of the Egyptian Parliament. He also enabled numerous Islamic charities to establish offices in Albania; these could then be used as a source of funds as well as cover for terrorism. Bin Ladin forged bonds with members of the very top of Albanian society. Even the then president of Albania, Sali Berisha, had close links with groups that later proved to be fronts for Islamic extremists. Al-Qaida soon became heavily involved in the

Balkan wars of the times, as Arab Afghan volunteers rushed to join the Muslim Bosnians and Kosovo Albanians in their wars with Serbs, Croats, Macedonians, and others. Due to its proximity to the Balkans and Albania, Italy became a key stopover point and accordingly a centre for Al-Qaida activities. Fighters on their way to and from the Balkans could easily cross the Adriatic Sea illegally by boat; safehouses were available in Rome, Bologna, and Milan (see Appendix 15).

Unfortunately for bin Ladin and his followers, other news followed that was not so good. In October 1994, Jordan signed a formal peace treaty with Israel, thereby aligning itself with the other more or less secular Arab regimes that bin Ladin saw as traitors to Islam.

A small consolation was that in October 1994 the Palestinian movement Hamas embarked on the ongoing campaign of suicide bombings against the hated Jews (see Appendix 14). Palestine was never a major interest of Usamah bin Ladin's, but he maintained occasional contacts with Hamas, at least since 1994, when he first appears to have offered financial assistance to the Palestinian Islamic movement (although his support is unlikely to have been very substantial, since he had lost much of his personal fortune).[63]

Better news followed the next month. In November 1994, the Taliban emerged in Afghanistan, with Pakistani support.[64] In the eyes of Usamah bin Ladin, the Taliban opened up an entire new front in the global jihad. It also served to safeguard the Al-Qaida bases in Afghanistan, until then increasingly at risk from Afghan warlords who did not particularly like foreign fighters' meddling in Afghan internal affairs.

Then, on 11 December 1994, Russian regular military units marched into Chechnya, a Muslim Russian republic in the Caucasus that earlier had declared independence. This resulted in a bloody war between Chechen and Russian forces (see Appendix 12). For bin Ladin, the Russian move was probably seen in the same light as the Soviet intervention in Afghanistan 15 years earlier: Islam was under threat from the superpowers, and the global jihad had to continue. Usamah bin Ladin, still a quartermaster rather than ideologue, probably reached this conclusion together with Ayman al-Zawahiri, who joined him in Sudan the previous year.

Although bin Ladin's personal involvement in the events of 1994 was fairly limited, he suddenly became noticed by a few specialists within the intelligence services.

The CIA, still obsessed with Iran, identified Usamah bin Ladin as a threat only in the aftermath of the investigation into Ramzi Yousef's February 1993 bombing of the World Trade Center. The investigation revealed that many of the conspirators had fought in Afghanistan with U.S. support. This, which became known as the "blowback" problem from Afghanistan, caused James Woolsey, then the head of the CIA, to fly to Cairo discuss the problem with the Egyptian Intelligence agency (*Mukhabarat al-Amah*). The Egyptians promptly notified their U.S. allies that bin Ladin was on top of their list of suspected extremists. Then telephone numbers connected to Usamah bin Ladin were found among the many calls made by Ramzi Yousef and his associates from New York. No longer doubting that the United States had an Arab Afghan problem, the CIA from the summer of 1993 began to monitor bin Ladin and his activities. However, it took almost three years and an additional seven dead Americans in terrorist attacks in Karachi, Pakistan, and Riyadh (as well as dozens of murdered Iranians, Egyptians, Ethiopians, and Indians) to convince the CIA to direct sufficient resources against the new threat. Following the November 1995 terrorist attack on a joint Saudi-U.S. facility in Riyadh, the CIA's Counterterrorist Center formed a special Usamah bin Ladin task force in January 1996. After a long investigation, the conclusion was that funds were still reaching bin Ladin from supporters among businessmen and senior politicians in Saudi Arabia, Kuwait, and Qatar.[65]

Russia responded more quickly and decisively. Although Russia, like the United States, initially was concerned about the possible spread of Islamic fundamentalism from Iran, in 1994 the Russian Foreign Intelligence Service, headed by Yevgeni Primakov, stressed the distinction between "Islamic fundamentalism" and "Islamic extremism" and pointed out that only the latter was a threat to

Russia. Primakov, himself a Middle East expert, realised that Iran no longer posed a threat but that Sunni extremism as espoused by Al-Qaida did. Henceforth, Russian intelligence devoted substantial resources to tracking the Wahhabi extremists, especially when they were active in what Russia regarded as its zone of interest: the Caucasus and Central Asia. The threat reevaluation also enabled Russian intelligence to begin an increasingly fruitful cooperation with Iranian intelligence, itself the target of Sunni Islamic extremism but better informed about it than the Western services.[66]

There may be another, more sinister reason the CIA did not respond more decisively. In collaboration with Pakistan, it supported the creation of Sunni sectarian extremism and power in South Asia as a way to counter the influence of Ayatollah Khomeini's Iranian, and therefore Shia, Islamic revolution.[67] Nowhere was this better shown than in Afghanistan, where early on the CIA and other U.S. government entities in most cases welcomed the creation and victories of the ethnic Pashtun and religiously Sunni Taliban at the expense of the Tajiks, who speak a Persian language and are therefore suspect, and the Northern Alliance, which is in part Shia. After all, there seemed no better way to oppose Shia Iran than to support Sunni extremists, who hated Shia Iran vehemently and never would cooperate with the Iranians.[68]

The preoccupation with Iran has consistently bedevilled the attempts of U.S. policy makers to formulate policy with regard to Afghanistan. What appears to be an instinctive rather than reasoned belief that the Persian-speaking Tajiks and Hazara must be the bad guys, while the Pashtuns, who opposed them, must be good, also remains prevalent among many American academics.[69] This mindset has not changed with the War on Terror. In fact, since President Bush's 29 January 2002 declaration that an "axis of evil" consisting of the three disparate countries of Iran, Iraq, and North Korea threatened world peace and that Iran has actively aided the Al-Qaida network, and in particular has assisted many Al-Qaida members to escape to Iran and receive protection,[70] his administration's unspoken desire to make Iran guilty for acts of Sunni terrorism appears to have intensified.

USAMAH BIN LADIN IN AFGHANISTAN

It is our duty to lead people to the light.
—Usamah bin Ladin to ABC reporter John Miller, May
1998

While Usamah bin Ladin was in Sudan, two attempts were
made on his life. First, in late 1995, four Yemenis, believed to be
mercenaries recruited by elements within the House of Saud,
attacked his residence in Khartoum. All the assailants were killed,
together with two of bin Ladin's guards. Second, a lone assailant,
probably a bodyguard, made an unsuccessful attempt to kill
Usamah bin Ladin in the spring of 1996. Since the second attack
followed closely upon an offer from the Saudi government to
restore Usamah bin Ladin's citizenship and return his confiscated
funds in exchange for a public expression of allegiance to the king
(an offer that was refused), it is believed that this too was a Saudi
attempt to get rid of the highly visible dissident.[71]
Pressure also mounted on the Sudanese government to evict the
Arab Afghans. The United States and Saudi Arabia wanted bin Ladin
expelled, while Egypt demanded the extradition of several Egyptian
extremists who had attempted to assassinate President Mubarak in
Ethiopia in June 1995. Finally, in April 1996, the Sudanese government asked bin Ladin to leave the country, reportedly by leaking
rumours through Isam al-Turabi, the youngest son of Hassan al-
Turabi, to bin Ladin about the planned extradition to Saudi Arabia.[72]
On 15 May 1996, Sudan formally asked Usamah bin Ladin to
leave.[73] On 18 May 1996, Usamah bin Ladin flew to Afghanistan
with his wives, children, and around 150 supporters in a chartered
aircraft, landing at Jalalabad.[74]Other supporters followed later. Yet
more militants coming from Pakistan joined the movement, including some who were encouraged to do so by the Pakistani internal
security agency, the Intelligence Bureau (IB). In addition, the IB provided safehouses in Karachi for Al-Qaida members.
However, Usamah bin Ladin reportedly lost up to $150 or even
$170 million on his investments in Sudan and in deals where the

Sudanese government failed to pay its debts in breach of written contracts. He also lost the proceeds of the various monopolies over Sudanese agricultural products and other benefits that the NIF had guaranteed his companies in return for their investments.[75] In fact, having already lost his fortune in Saudi Arabia in early 1994, Usamah bin Ladin by this time likely had little more than a few million dollars in cash or disposable assets. However, this no longer mattered much. His organisation abroad was largely self-supporting: as his followers worked for God, not for financial gain, and Al-Qaida usually paid no more than initial start-up costs whenever new cells were established. Besides, money still flowed in through the many Islamic charities and wealthy supporters who themselves did not wish to join the jihad but were more than happy to relieve their collective bad conscience by paying large amounts to those who did. Al-Qaida was also soon involved in the lucrative Afghan drug trade.

In Afghanistan, Usamah bin Ladin quickly forged a close alliance with the Taliban rulers. He bought a new house in Kandahar's Shahar-e Nau (New Town) area for Taliban leader Mullah Muhammad Omar. He also funded various badly needed infrastructure projects in Kandahar (as he had previously done in Sudan), as well as a new mosque in 1998.

According to some reports, Mullah Omar and bin Ladin grew so close that bin Ladin married off his oldest daughter to the mullah. Other reports claim that Usamah bin Ladin himself married one of Omar's daughters. The latter is unlikely, however, and has been denied by Taliban officials. He may have married another Pashtun woman around 1998, as some claim.[76] If so, the marriage appears not to have lasted long. Bin Ladin married his fourth and last wife, a Yemani, in Kandahar in 2000.[77] Yet, when Mullah Omar married bin Ladin's daughter, bin Ladin became related by blood to the Pashtun leader—no doubt a major reason why the mullah so fiercely refused to extradite Usamah bin Ladin. In 2001, Usamah bin Ladin was appointed the Taliban's defence minister.[78]

On 23 August 1996, Usamah bin Ladin issued his first fatwa, a declaration "to His Muslim Brothers in the Whole World and

Especially in the Arabian Peninsula: Declaration of Jihad Against
the Americans Occupying the Land of the Two Holy Mosques;
Expel the Heretics from the Arabian Peninsula." This has since
been regarded as his formal declaration of war against the United
States. In it, he also outlined the means he wished to implement to
defeat the superpower: "fast-moving light forces that work under
complete secrecy. In other words, to initiate a guerrilla warfare,
where the sons of the nation, and not the military forces, take part
in it."[79]

Usamah bin Ladin also moved his headquarters into a fortified
cave. This, one of several that had been tunnelled into the side of a
mountain to protect it against air attacks during the Soviet war in
Afghanistan, was located at Milawa near the city of Jalalabad in
eastern Afghanistan. The approach road, in a narrow ravine, was
guarded by several hundred men armed with machine guns, heavy
weapons, and even tanks. Yet, the cave was minimally outfitted.
Usamah bin Ladin was known only to have two laptop computers,
one or more satellite telephones, several low beds with thin mat-
tresses, and a library of Islamic books. The cave was his headquarters, but in fact he rarely stayed there. For security reasons, he seldom spent two nights in the same place. Instead, he shuttled around
Afghanistan in a convoy of up to 20 vehicles, protected by his most
devoted followers, armed with small arms, grenade launchers, and
according to some, even Stinger surface-to-air missiles to protect
against air attack.

Meanwhile, his followers for the most part lived in camps, as
did many Taliban soldiers. The Taliban and Arab Afghan camps,
seen from a distance while in use, consisted of numerous tents with
immense green canvasses staked on poles undulating in long
waves. At prayer times, the camp inhabitants all prostrated themselves together for prayer.[80]

In February 1998, bin Ladin chaired a meeting in Afghanistan
with several other Islamic extremist leaders, including Ayman al-
Zawahiri, head of Egyptian Islamic Jihad; Abu Yassir Rifai Ahmad
Taha, head of Egypt's Islamic Society; Fazlur Rehman Khalil, the
leader of the Pakistani extremist movement *Harakat ul-Ansar*;

Sheikh Abdul Salam Muhammad, a leader of the *Harakat ul-Jihad Islami* (Islamic Jihad Movement) in Bangladesh;[81] and Sheikh Mir Hamzah, secretary of the Society of Pakistani Religious Scholars (*Jamiat-e Ulama-ye Pakistan*). The result of the conference was the establishment of the World Islamic Front for Jihad against the Jews and Crusaders on 23 February 1998. In a concluding fatwa, signed by Usamah bin Ladin, Ayman al-Zawahiri, Abu Yassir Rifai Ahmad Taha, Fazlur Rehman Khalil, and Sheikh Mir Hamzah, bin Ladin and his associates authorised attacks on Americans, military and civilian, throughout the world. The fatwa states: "We—with God's help—call on every Muslim who believes in God and wishes to be rewarded to comply with God's order to kill the Americans and plunder their money wherever and whenever they find it." The fatwa also indicated that "to kill the Americans and their allies— civilians and military—is an individual duty for every Muslim who can do it in any country in which it is possible to do it."[82]

The establishment of the World Islamic Front for Jihad against the Jews and Crusaders brought widespread attention to the Islamic extremist cause but remained mainly a propaganda venture. The front never engaged in operations as a unified organisation. Any activities beyond the issue of the 1998 fatwa were left to the very active networks of Islamic extremist cells that made up the membership—or supporters—of the front.

Usamah bin Ladin's fame increased as the U.S. attempts to catch or kill him failed: he finally reached almost legendary status in the Islamic world. Many Muslims who had never met him, whose only contact was through a radio broadcast or Internet site, declared themselves ready to die for him and his interpretation of Islam. The secret of bin Ladin's power was his renown and the understated but firm resolve he invariably displayed in public: he was reserved, never seeming to order a fighter to die in a suicide attack, yet there was always somebody, somewhere, who was willing to obey what was believed to be bin Ladin's implicit request or, at the very least, intention. Often these men cared for nothing more than fulfilling bin Ladin's wishes, spoken or not. And to carry out the presumed intentions of Usamah bin Ladin was easy: it took no more than some explosives or a gun and the willingness to sacrifice oneself, or to accomplish the mission and return to the anonymity whence one had come. Compared to the media-led Western politicians, exemplified by President Bill Clinton, and the Middle Eastern leaders who were widely held to be their puppets, bin Ladin displayed moral integrity and a sense of purpose. In many ways he was a myth, not a man.

In an e-mail poll of its international viewers conducted by the Al-Jazeera satellite television network on 10 July 2001, it was found that 82.3 percent of the respondents regarded Usamah bin Ladin as a respected *mujahid* (holy warrior), whereas only 8.8 percent saw him as a terrorist. The remaining respondents were noncommittal. The television station pointed out, however, that its viewers were not a representative sample of the Muslim masses but the elite, and that if less sophisticated Arabs had been asked, those in favour of him would have been even higher.[83] After the 11 September 2001 terrorist attacks, a common reaction in the Muslim Middle East, including Saudi Arabia was, in its more moderate form, that the United States was trying to frame Usamah bin Ladin for an act committed by others, or, more radically, that the United States itself had arranged the attack to frame Muslims.[84] In Pakistan, a poll released in mid-October 2001, after the U.S.-led air raids on Afghanistan had begun, found that 82 percent of urban Pakistanis regarded Usamah bin Ladin as a freedom fighter.[85] Among rural Pakistanis he was no doubt even more popular.

By early 1998, the Al-Qaida core group appeared to have merged with Egyptian Islamic Jihad. Usamah bin Ladin was also clearly cooperating closely with, at the least, Rifai Ahmad Taha's wing of the Egyptian Islamic Society.[86]Al-Qaida had also become an umbrella organisation that harboured a network of like-minded organisations throughout the world, all of which looked up to bin Ladin as an inspiration. Some of the affiliated organisations worked so closely with Al-Qaida that it was difficult to distinguish among them. Among them were Egyptian Islamic Jihad and the Islamic Movement of Uzbekistan (IMU; see Appendix 11). Others, however, were completely independent groups that merely cooperated with

Al-Qaida, including several Pakistani and Algerian organisations, ethnic Uighur groups from Chinese Xinjiang, and radical Palestinian, Yemeni, and other Middle East groups. Al-Qaida also maintained links with various Islamic extremist groups in Russia, in particular in the Caucasian republics of Chechnya and Dagestan. Al-Qaida is believed to have operated either directly or through affiliates in some 40 countries. Some organisations, such as the Moro Islamic Liberation Front in the Philippines and groups in Indonesia, Malaysia, and Singapore, received money and support from Al-Qaida but were largely independent (see Appendix 16 and 17).

The 11 September 2001 Attacks

On 11 September 2001, in a well-coordinated operation in the United States, terrorists hijacked four passenger airliners and successfully crashed three into the World Trade Center in New York (two airliners, one aimed at each tower) and the Pentagon in Washington, D.C. (one airliner). The fourth airliner, probably aimed at the White House, crashed in Pennsylvania as passengers, learning about the previous attacks, attempted to regain control over it. Altogether, more than 3,000 men, women, and children died. The burning aircraft fuel generated such heat that the steel girders that supported the World Trade Center buildings melted, causing the two towers to collapse.[87] Within hours, suspicions fell on Usamah bin Ladin, although at first he was not the only suspect.[88]

It is unlikely that the U.S. government, with the means then at its disposal and based on evidence from the few clandestine operations in operation against Al-Qaida, could have predicted the 11 September attacks or prevented them. This, however, does not mean that either the means or the tactics employed by the terrorists came as any particular surprise to those who were familiar with Islamic extremism and terrorism. That Islamic extremists dreamed of, and planned, the use of aircraft as bombs had been shown on a number of occasions, sometimes years earlier. On 24 December 1994, four Algerian terrorists, members of the Phalange of the Signers in Blood, a subsidiary of the GIA, hijacked an Air France passenger airliner from Algiers. They demanded that it be flown to Marseille, where it was to be refueled for a flight to Paris. The terrorists also demanded that the aircraft, an Airbus A300, be loaded with 27 tons of fuel, almost three times what was needed for the flight. However, French antiterrorist personnel of the Groupe d'Intervention de la Gendarmerie Nationale, under Commander Denis Favier, successfully stormed the airplane on the ground. In the subsequent investigation, it was determined that the terrorists had intended either to explode the aircraft over Paris or crash it into the Eiffel Tower.[89] There is little doubt that the extra fuel was expected to make the aircraft into a more potent bomb. In addition, Ramzi Yousef, who had been involved in the bombing of the World Trade Center already in 1993, had plans he had developed by January 1995 in the Philippines (which Philippine intelligence later passed on to the United States) with his follower Abdul Hakim Murad, a trained pilot. The plans included hijacking an airliner and crashing it into the CIA headquarters in Langley, Virginia. He had developed another plan, never carried out, that included multiple simultaneous airline hijackings.[90]

Even if these warnings had been forgotten, there were more recent causes of suspicion. In July 2001, Kenneth Williams, an FBI agent in Phoenix, Arizona, noticed that many Muslims were signing up to attend local flight-training schools. The agent's supervisor, Bill Kurtz, wrote a lengthy report to FBI headquarters, voicing suspicions that the men might be connected to Usamah bin Ladin. The report was ignored.[91] On 17 August 2001, Zacarias Moussaoui, a French citizen of Algerian descent, was arrested in Minnesota for carrying a false passport. He had already failed to qualify as a light-aircraft pilot, but was known to have offered a flight school large amounts of cash for the opportunity to practice in a jumbo-jet flight simulator. He somewhat foolishly pointed out that he was only interested in learning to steer the jumbo jet, not to land it. Again local FBI officials were eager to investigate the case further, by searching his personal computer for additional information, but this request was denied on legal grounds.[92] In a separate development, the arrest in the United Arab Emirates in July 2001 of a French Algerian, Djamel Begal, reportedly uncovered a plot to crash a helicopter into the U.S. Embassy in Paris.[93]

Although the FBI was severely criticised for its failure to prevent the subsequent 11 September attacks, it is doubtful exactly how much the bureau could have done based on the Phoenix report alone or whatever information might have been found in the computer belonging to Zacarias Moussaoui. In addition, legislation and constitutional protections were designed to protect U.S. citizens and legal residents (which the hijackers were) from the monitoring for intelligence purposes of their telephone and e-mail communications.

In all fairness, it seems unlikely that even a quick and vigorous investigation of either of these cases, although desirable, would have saved the United States from the subsequent attacks. The flaw in the work of the FBI appears, rather, to have been a systemic failure: the FBI was simply not organised and led to conduct active counterterrorism operations. There were too few agents with appropriate language skills or knowledge of the enemy. In addition, the FBI appears to have encouraged a culture of political correctness and sloppy investigations—which was clearly shown in the agency's failure to coordinate its activities with those of other government agencies (several men on the FBI watch list had been admitted to and were living openly in the United States). In at least one case, a terrorism suspect was even listed in the San Diego telephone directory. Yet the FBI failed to find any of them until it was too late.[94]

By the time of the 11 September attacks, there was a considerable lack of knowledge about and insights into the Arab Afghan movement within the U.S. government. This made it all too easy to prematurely dismiss the movement as being of no consequence (the typical government official's or academic's approach), or to go overboard and, in a media frenzy, portray an individual leader of the Arab Afghan movement, such as Usamah bin Ladin, as a terrorist mastermind bent on world domination (the typical media or spin doctor's approach).

This writer has no reasons to believe that Usamah bin Ladin was innocent of any involvement in the 11 September attacks. For him to participate in the operation would be fully in line with his stated aspirations and desires as well as his known capability. Yet, despite the hearsay from U.S. intelligence sources and various official claims, there appears to be no conclusive evidence that bin Ladin's organisation in Afghanistan was directly involved in terrorist activities (although the organisation's members were certainly involved in irregular warfare on the side of the Taliban movement). The much publicised videotape of mid-November 2001, in which bin Ladin apparently claims involvement in the 11 September attacks, was obviously recorded after the United States had already attacked Afghanistan and there was no turning back.[95] While there is little reason to dispute bin Ladin's videotaped statement, the video recording merely shows that he took credit for it when it was obvious that (1) many Muslims celebrated the attack, and (2) the United States would go after him regardless of whether any involvement could be proven.

On 12 September 2001, CIA Director George Tenet briefed President George W. Bush on the available intelligence that linked the attacks to Usamah bin Ladin and Al-Qaida. All evidence presented was of an intelligence rather than legal nature, which means that it depended on hearsay, unconfirmed reports from unknown or barely known sources, and the interpretations by intelligence analysts of hard-to-evaluate information such as monitored telephone conversations. Though not necessarily wrong, it was not the kind of evidence that could be used in a court of law—or to convince the international community. One report out of Kandahar, probably from the CIA's source within the Taliban (who, as will be shown, had a history of producing reports that could not be confirmed by other means), indicated that the attacks were "the results of two years' planning." Another report (the source of which was never disclosed) suggested that the attacks were "the beginning of the wrath"—a conclusion that could be found in any Arab newspaper. Several reports specifically identified Capitol Hill and the White House as targets on 11 September. One claimed that a bin Ladin associate—in error, as it turned out—"gave thanks for the explosion in the Congress building." Another, allegedly a key leader, named Wafa, in what the CIA described as the Al-Qaida financial support organisation (perhaps a reference to the Al-Wafa Humanitarian Organisation, a group based in Kandahar that built roads and infrastructure in Afghanistan), initially claimed that "the White House has been destroyed," which obviously was another misunderstanding. Unfortunately, these two reports proved nothing. News reports showed that numerous Muslim leaders gave thanks for the attacks—after watching them on television.[96]

Perhaps more credible was another report indicating that Al-Qaida members in Afghanistan at 9:53 AM on 11 September, shortly after the Pentagon was hit, said (due to the given exact time, obviously in a telephone conversation monitored by the U.S. National Security Agency) that the attackers were following through with "the doctor's program." This might have been a reference to Ayman al-Zawahiri, who because of his background as an Egyptian physician was often referred to as "the doctor." Unfortunately, other prominent Arab Afghans were known by the same title, including Khattab, a Jordanian-Chechen commander busy fighting Russia at the time, as well as many religious sheikhs who were certainly extremists but not necessarily Al-Qaida members. One report, regarded as a central piece of evidence but one whose source was never disclosed, involved Al-Qaida member Abu Zubaydah, whom the CIA had earlier identified as the chief field commander of the October 2000 attack on the USS *Cole* in the Yemeni port of Aden. According to "a reliable report" received after the terrorist attacks, Abu Zubaydah at some unspecified point had referred to "zero hour" in conversation with people whose identity was never disclosed. As a final point, and of this at least there was little doubt, the CIA and the FBI had evidence of connections between at least three of the 19 hijackers and the Al-Qaida camps in Afghanistan. In Tenet's view—and this was the conclusion he presented to President Bush—the evidence of Usamah bin Ladin's guilt was conclusive.[97]

On earlier occasions, to protect its sources, the CIA might have asked to withhold evidence from use in court or to convince the international community. A source within the Taliban, for instance, could no doubt be killed if exposed by the disclosure of such information, and the CIA would lose a valuable and hard-to-replace intelligence asset. In addition, the exposure and loss would discourage other potential sources from offering their services to the agency. On this occasion, however, the situation was different: Bush wanted results, even if sources had to go. If there was a question between protecting a source and protecting the American people, he told Attorney General John D. Ashcroft on 12 September 2001, "we burn the source and we protect the American people."[98]

If Usamah bin Ladin was not directly responsible (and he surely may have been), then what did he do? Bin Ladin and Al-Qaida, for a number of years, unquestionably served as inspiration and possibly sponsors of terrorism taking place outside Afghanistan. One could argue that this made Al-Qaida a dangerous force against global security but hardly a terrorist group. His presence in Afghanistan can be seen to have promoted terrorism, but that in itself did not make Afghanistan or the Taliban leadership a promoter of international terrorism. A parallel case was in London, where similar Islamic extremist leaders lived and agitated at the same time that bin Ladin did likewise in Afghanistan.

It is not unusual for past and present leaders of movements fighting for whatever cause, secular or clerical, to act as a higher legal or moral authority while based in another country. Revolutionaries such as Vladimir Lenin, Ho Chi Minh, and many of the leaders of the African National Congress of South Africa used European capitals as sanctuaries and bases from which to plot the overthrow of their respective governments. Until the War on Terror got under way, London remained the base for, among others, the Kurdistan Information Centre, associated with the Kurdish Workers' Party, fighting in Turkey, and the Tamil Eelam group, the political wing of the Tamil insurgents in Sri Lanka. Both groups have been accused of terrorist activities by the U.S. State Department.[99] Modern telecommunications and the Internet ensure that such leaders can keep in touch with their followers. Among current Islamic leaders, Sheikh Abu Qatada (real name Omar Mahmoud Uthman Abu Omar), a Jordanian Palestinian who served as the spiritual leader for the GIA, and Sheikh Abu Hamza al-Masri, an Egyptian propagandist for the Algerian GIA and former Afghan veteran who was the spiritual leader of the Yemeni Islamic Jihad movement and preached jihadist beliefs at the Finsbury Park mosque in London, both lived in London. (Abu Hamza is currently a British citizen; Abu Qatada, who began preaching in Pakistan in 1989 and received asylum in Britain in 1993, went into hiding after Britain in late 2001 passed emergency anti-terrorist legislation.)[100] Numerous other, less well-known Islamic extremists were also based in Britain.[101] One such was Yassir Tawfiq al-Sirri, an Egyptian who ran the Islamic Observation Centre that was devoted to Islamic propaganda. Al-Sirri, who was accused by Egypt of attempting to assassinate the Egyptian prime minister in 1993, had fled to Britain in 1994; alleged to have aided the men who assassinated the Afghan anti-Taliban commander Masud in September 2001, he was detained on 24 October 2001.[102] More than 60 Islamist newsletters, the majority produced by Egyptian and Algerian extremists, were published in London.[103] Yet nobody could accuse the British government of sponsoring terrorism, even though it offered asylum to alleged terrorist leaders and supporters. Before 11 September 2001, one could accordingly sympathise with the Taliban leaders who failed to see why they should be targeted with sanctions and cruise missiles only because they did not wish to surrender bin Ladin to a quite possibly biased trial in the United States that would no doubt result in very harsh punishment. In November 1998, the United States offered a $5 million reward for Usamah bin Ladin's capture, and in November 2001 this reward was increased to $25 million.[104]

The reason the Taliban refused to hand over bin Ladin was not pure intransigence. First, the United States rather carelessly never bothered to present the Taliban leadership with evidence against him. This enabled to Taliban to put bin Ladin on a trial of their own in September 2000, during which he swore on the Koran that he had nothing to do with the terrorist bombings and that he was not responsible for what others do who claim to know him or claim to act in his name. This trial may well have been biased and flawed according to most standards, yet the U.S. government conceded by not presenting its case. (Some have explained the U.S. inaction as a means of avoiding a claim of double jeopardy by the defence in case Usamah bin Ladin were ever brought to justice in the United States.[105] This is probably a dubious claim because the government no doubt could get around such details.) Second, it should be noted that the U.S. case against bin Ladin, such as it was, appears to have been primarily based on testimony received from already convicted terrorists during the plea bargain process. This concept, while often relied on in U.S. courts, is not universally accepted and, more important, does not form part of Islamic law. Many people outside the United States (including this writer), and not only Muslims, would agree with Rahmatullah Hashimi, Mullah Omar's ambassador: "Plea bargains pervert the very essence of justice."[106]

Another reason for the United States' failure to deal with bin Ladin was the distinct lack of knowledge, both in its legal system and among many intelligence chiefs, of the Islamic world and Islamic extremism. When Ramzi Yousef was sentenced on 5 September 1996, the judge tried to make a moral point of the fact that the airliners Yousef and his fellow conspirators were convicted of plotting to bomb "could have been filled with Muslims, indeed, they could have been filled with imams or mullahs or even the Ayatollah."[107] By making this undoubtedly correct statement, the judge inadvertently betrayed his lack of understanding of not only the differences between Sunni and Shia Islam, but also of the sad fact that nobody would have been happier than the terrorists if they had been able to kill the Shia ayatollah, whom they hated no less than the president of the United States.

In fact, the policymakers of the United States have generally been unable (or unwilling) to distinguish between Sunni Islamic extremism and the Shia Islamic revolution of Ayatollah Khomeini's Iran. So, for instance, CIA Director James Woolsey testified before the Senate Intelligence Committee on 25 January 1994 that the 1993 World Trade Center bombing was the work of a combination of local Sunni and Shia, obviously a cheap trick to connect the perpetrators to Iran. No Shia Muslims were ever indicted for the bombing.[108] Likewise, the U.S. ambassador to Israel, Edward Walker, astonishingly blamed Iran for the 17 November 1997 Luxor massacre, even though there was ample evidence that domestic Sunni extremists had committed the attack.[109] On 21 June 2001, a federal grand jury in Alexandria, Virginia, caused a diplomatic row by indicting several Saudis (and a Lebanese) who were suspected as members of what the court claimed to be an Iranian-supervised organisation called "Saudi Hizbullah" for the 1996 Khobar Towers bombing.[110]

If we assume that Usamah bin Ladin was actively involved in the 11 September attacks, and this after all seems most probable, what could he conceivably expect to gain from such a massive strike? He was not a stupid man; he knew that the United States would not collapse from a terrorist strike, however powerful. He also must have expected that the United States, finally roused from its complacency, was almost certain to retaliate against him personally and his organisation.

Although bin Ladin's thoughts are known only to himself, it seems fair to assume that he wished to provoke the United States into retaliating not only against him personally but the entire Islamic world. If he could push the United States into an exaggerated military response against Muslim targets, he could thereby increase Muslim indignation and fan even greater hatred against America and the West. With some luck, he might have argued, the United States would even retaliate by launching nuclear missiles on innocent Muslims (an argument not as cynical as it might appear, since the dead Muslims, even if counted in millions, would then go to paradise as martyrs), thus causing a popular uprising against the West throughout the Islamic world. By assuming the worst possible outcome, Usamah bin Ladin probably hoped that the attacks would be the spark that would ignite an apocalyptic, global showdown between Western and Muslim forces. Such a scenario could only end in God's final, triumphant victory over the forces of evil, with bin Ladin himself as the chief instrument of God, the *mahdi*, a God-inspired leader who appeared to command the Muslims at the time of the final battle between good and evil.[111] As a secondary objective, if no violent retaliation was forthcoming, Usamah bin Ladin paradoxically might have wished the United States to reinforce its support to various despotic regimes in Muslim countries, for instance Saudi Arabia, Pakistan, and Uzbekistan, for this too would create domestic hatred and resentment against the United States and the West. Although far short of the apocalyptic catastrophe he yearned for, this last would at least fulfill one of his apparent goals: the destabilisation of Pakistan and Saudi Arabia, the respective holders of nuclear weapons and holy sites. Such a goal was also indicated by his speech on the videotape released soon after the air raids on Afghanistan began, which appears to have been intended to incite violence by Muslims against their rulers in these countries and elsewhere.

Fortunately, President Bush did not immediately oblige bin Ladin by initiating a global, apocalyptic war. However, bin Ladin did achieve his presumed secondary objective. As will be shown, several despotic regimes in the Middle East and Asia (e.g., Pakistan, Uzbekistan, China) have since, with the full support of the West, launched their own wars on terrorism. Unfortunately, they do not only target terrorism but all forms of domestic dissent—and the West no longer has the moral authority to tell them to clean up their act. As Amnesty International pointed out in its annual report in 2002, "It was not autocratic regimes but established democracies that took the lead in introducing draconian laws to restrict civil liberties in the name of public security. In the United Kingdom (UK), the government passed "emergency" legislation that provided for detention of foreign nationals without charge or trial, thereby creating a shadow criminal justice system without the essential safeguards of the formal system. Legislation was passed in the United States allowing for indefinite detention on national security grounds of non-U.S. nationals facing deportation."[112] It will henceforth be difficult to persuade authoritarian regimes to change their ways, since they can always justify their means by claiming that they merely copied the antiterrorism legislation in the West.

The Attempts to Assassinate Pope John Paul II

Usamah bin Ladin is a suspect in two plots to assassinate Pope John Paul II. Ramzi Yousef planned the first attempted assassination during the papal visit to Manila in mid-January 1995. Yousef considered various inventive methods, including an air raid on the pope's motorcade, which would involve manually dropping bombs from a small airplane. In the end, he probably settled for a traditional terrorist bomb, possibly to be used by a suicide bomber. However, something went wrong about a week before the pope's visit, when Yousef was preparing the chemicals for the bomb in his kitchen. Smoke began to billow out of the room, and Yousef and a co-conspirator had to flee the place as police and firemen arrived, abandoning all their preparations, materials, bomb-making reference books, and even a laptop full of incriminating documents in the process.[113]

A second attempt to kill the pope, for which Usamah bin Ladin is also reputed to be responsible, took place on 11–12 April 1997 in Bosnia. No less than 23 antitank mines, set for triggering by remote control, were placed under a bridge across a deep ravine on the route the pope was to travel to Sarajevo. The pope's visit to Muslim Bosnia angered many local Muslims, who regarded the visit as an attack on Islam. At least one local Muslim was arrested for tearing down posters announcing the pope's planned visit.[114]

Al-Qaida's Financial Support Organisation

The Al-Qaida network is believed to have benefited financially from various commercial enterprises in the Middle East and North Africa, particularly in Yemen and Somalia, as well as some enterprises in the West. The United States has singled out the Barakaat group of companies and the Al-Taqwa group, alleged as major sources of income. Al-Taqwa finance company is headquartered in the Italian enclave of Campione, a corporate tax haven near Lugano, Switzerland. While Al-Taqwa has clear connections to the Egyptian Muslim Brotherhood, it remains by no means certain, despite the U.S. suspicions, that the firm was involved in terrorism. On 7 November 2001, the U.S. Treasury shut down the Al-Barakaat Group in the United States and urged its coalition partners to do likewise. U.S. Secretary of the Treasury Paul H. O'Neill said that Al-Barakaat Group was "a principal source of funding, intelligence, and money transfers for Osama bin Laden." The company, however, maintains that it has done nothing wrong. Nonetheless, the United Arab Emirates, the headquarters of Al-Barakaat Group, followed the U.S. request by blocking the accounts of the group. Another suspect was Mamoun Darkazanli (also known as Abu Ilyaf), the owner of the Darkazanli Import-Export Company in Hamburg, Germany, founded in 1993 and involved in wholesale merchandising of such appliances as television sets and electric equipment. (Darkazanli was believed to be a close associate of Usamah bin Ladin, and his company also found its assets frozen.) The commercial enterprises in the Al-Qaida network also allegedly included two investment companies: Ladin International and Taba Investment Company.[115]

Much of the Al-Qaida funding, perhaps most, has come from Islamic charities. For obvious reasons, most of them are located in the Islamic world, but there are also many offices in the West. Not all were formed to promote terrorism. Islamic charities do provide health services, schools, and often a means of living for the unemployed. In other words, they are doing what the state cannot, or will not, do in so many third-world countries. Yet it is the nature of Islamic charities to assist in jihad activities: this is regarded as a sure way to promote Islam and do God's work. So, for instance, the Qatar Charitable Society (also known as the Charity Fund of Qatar), in addition to its normal charitable activities, was also used by Al-Qaida as a source of funding and transferring funds. The charity was banned in Russian Dagestan in conjunction with the outbreak of the second Chechen war in 1999 for its use in support of the separatist government in Chechnya.[116] Another example is the International Islamic Relief Organisation, reportedly another backer of Al-Qaida, which Britain in late September 2001 removed from the list of registered charities.[117] Mercy International Relief Agency supported Al-Qaida as well.[118] The Global Relief Foundation, a Chicago-based charity, is suspected of having been an Al-Qaida front. Another Chicago-based Muslim charity, the Benevolence International Foundation (BIF, also known as the Benevolentia International Foundation, occasionally referred to as Bosnian Ideal Future) was accused of aiding Al-Qaida in late April 2002. This organisation was headed by Enaam Arnaout, a Syrian-born U.S. citizen who has been a close friend of Usamah bin Ladin at least since 1989. The BIF was deeply involved in Bosnia, and evidence found at eight BIF offices there on 19 March 2002 indicated the charity's involvement with Al-Qaida.[119]

There are several charities that also supported the Taliban. The Al-Wafa Humanitarian Organisation, a group based in Kandahar that built roads and infrastructure in Afghanistan, eventually found its assets frozen. Assets belonging to the Al-Rashid Trust, run by Mullah Khail al-Rashid, were frozen because the charity was accused of smuggling weapons and supplies to the Taliban and IMU, disguised as humanitarian aid.[120] The London-based group *Harakat al-Muhajiroun* (Movement of Those Who Made Hijrah—that is, migration from the secular world), with offices in 21 countries, also raised funds and recruited foreign Muslims for the Taliban, especially in Britain. This group, Harakat al-Muhajiroun, headed by Omar Bakri Muhammad, a Syrian, claimed, among other statements, that a *shariah* court in Britain had issued a fatwa calling for the murder of Pakistani President Pervez Musharraf.[121]

One global Islamic charity on the early list of financial entities to be sanctioned by the United States was the Rabita Trust for the Rehabilitation of Stranded Pakistanis. However, it was removed from the list of sanctioned entities when it was found that President Musharraf, a key U.S. ally, was a member of Rabita's board of directors. After Musharraf was given time to remove himself from the board, Rabita was eventually sanctioned on 12 October 2001.[122]

Usamah bin Ladin's Financial Assets

The question of Usamah bin Ladin's financial resources is complex. Although he is invariably said to be very wealthy, his funds in Saudi Arabia were confiscated in February 1994 when his Saudi citizenship was revoked.[123] Nobody outside Al-Qaida today appears to know with what money he allegedly funded the terrorist activities of the Arab Afghan movement. If bin Ladin truly was financing the movement, his main source of income could hardly be anything but the proceeds of the lucrative smuggling of narcotics out of Central Asia.[124] If so, this might make him a key figure in organised crime rather than an Afghanistan-based terrorist. This also means that Al-Qaida's source of funding may remain available to the various leaders of the movement after bin Ladin himself has left the scene.

Usamah bin Ladin lost most of his personal funds when Saudi Arabia confiscated his assets in 1994 and Sudan forced him to leave in 1996. Arab confidants of bin Ladin afterward claimed that he was short of money: all investments in Sudan were lost as he left the country, salaries were cut, and no money remained even for minor expenses. For a while, Al-Qaida had to survive on donations from wealthy Arab businessmen, including Saudi banker Khalid bin Mahfouz, who was put under house arrest in Saudi Arabia for allegedly transferring funds to Islamic charities that were Al-Qaida fronts, or an exiled Saudi businessman in Ethiopia, Sheikh Muhammad Hussain Al-Almadi.[125]

One of the most striking aspects of the 11 September 2001 attacks is that they were carried out with a minimum of cash. First, the terrorists lived in cheap motels, did their own cooking and laundry, and drove 10-year-old cars. Their personal expenses seem to have been limited to very occasional visits to strip clubs. Second, the weapons used to hijack four aircraft were ridiculously cheap: box cutters and knives. The only major cost of the entire operation was in the flying lessons and the mandatory airline tickets on the hijacked flights as well as travel into and (in some cases) out of the country. The total cost for the operation, which is believed to have involved 19 hijackers and perhaps another dozen support staff, is estimated not to have exceeded $2 million.[126] What money that was needed appears to have been wired to Muhammad Atta, the apparent leader of the attack, from Mustafa Muhammad Ahmad al-Hawsawi (Sheikh Saeed), who is believed to be one of bin Ladin's most trusted financial officers. Intriguingly, the hijackers returned the leftover money to Hawsawi on the eve of the attack.[127]

Besides, Usamah bin Ladin seldom seems to have sent regular payments to his agents. It appears that it was far more common for the men he dispatched to receive only a lump sum and then be expected to finance themselves. For instance, Ahmed Ressam, arrested in December 1999 in Port Angeles, Washington, for plotting to attack targets in the United States, claimed that he had been given $12,000 to set himself up and was then told to finance any other expenses by credit-card fraud.[128]

End Notes

1. Galeotti, *Afghanistan,* 30, 38, 53, 97, 224; Russian General Staff, *Soviet-Afghan War,* xix. For the Russian casualty figures, see Russian General Staff, *Soviet-Afghan War,* xix, 43–44, 332, note 8.

2. Numerous biographies of Usamah bin Ladin are available. When no other source is given, this section is based on Reeve, *New Jackals,* 156–221; Rohan Gunaratna, "Blowback," *Jane's Intelligence Review* 13:8 (August 2001), 42–45. Fundamentally the same information is given in Bergen, *Holy War,* 41–59. Ultimately, much of the pub-

lished information derives from a document given to an American reporter by an anonymous source reportedly close to Usamah bin Ladin (*www.pbs.org/frontline/*). The source may possibly be Dr. Saad al-Faqih, a prominent Saudi dissident living in exile in London, who has in interviews with PBS has presented essentially the same information. Dr. al-Faqih heads the London-based Movement for Islamic Reform in Arabia (MIRA). See, for instance, MIRA's web site, *www.miraserve.com* There is no suggestion that he is connected with terrorism.

3.   See, for instance, Bergen, *Holy War,* 45–46.

4.   For similar experiences among other wealthy young Saudis, see Lacey, *Kingdom,* 370.

5.   *Observer* (London), 28 October 2001.

6.   Bergen, *Holy War,* 80.

7.   Reeve, *New Jackals,* 166–167; Bergen, *Holy War,* 200–201; Jacquard, *Osama Bin Laden,* 102, 279, note 11.

8.   Bodansky, *Bin Laden,* 83–84; Bergen, *Holy War,* 57.

9.   Jacquard, *Osama Bin Laden,* 102; Blanche, "Egyptians around Bin Laden," 19–21.

10. Bergen, *Holy War,* 204; Blanche, "Egyptians around Bin Laden," 19–21; Blanche, "Ayman al-Zawahiri," 18.

11. Bergen, *Holy War,* 82; *Washington Times,* 22–28 October 2001 (National Weekly Edition).

12. *Washington Post,* 17 November 2001.

13. Peter Bergen, "The Bin Laden Trial: What Did We Learn?" *Studies in Conflict & Terrorism* 24:6 (2001), 429–434; Bergen, *Holy War,* 59; *Economist,* 22 September 2001.

14. The explanation derives from a document given to an American journalist by an anonymous source reportedly close to Usamah bin Ladin (www.*pbs.org/frontline/*).

15. Reeve, *New Jackals,* 170ff.

16. Gunaratna, "Blowback," *Jane's Intelligence Review* 13:8 (August 2001), 43; Phil Hirschkorn, "Convictions Mark First Step in Breaking up Al-Qaeda Network," *Jane's Intelligence Review* 13:8 (August 2001), 46; Bergen, *Holy War,* 30; Jacquard, *Osama Bin Laden,* 283–284, note 4; Jane's Sentinel Security Assessment: Afghanistan, Jane's Information Group, 31 May 2002.

17. *Economist,* 22 September 2001.

18. Emerson, *American Jihad,* 132–133.

19. Jacquard, *Osama Bin Laden,* 59.

20. Reeve, *New Jackals,* 171.

21.   See, for instance, *Economist,* 24 November 2001; Anthony Davis, "The Afghan Files: Al-Qaeda Documents from Kabul," *Jane's Intelligence Review* 14:2 (February 2002), 14–19.

22. Michele Zanini, "Middle Eastern Terrorism and Netwar," *Studies in Conflict & Terrorism* 22:3 (1999): 250.

23. *Washington Post,* 19 December 2001; Bergen, *Holy War,* 28.

24. Zanini, "Middle Eastern Terrorism," 250.

25. Stefan Leader and Aaron Danis, "Tactical Insights from the Trial," *Jane's Intelligence Review* 13:8 (August 2001), 48.

26. Ramzi Yousef: Reeve, *New Jackals,* 26; Abdel Rahman: Bergen, *Holy War,* 108, 112; Hussain: Bergen, *Holy War,* 111, 112; Harazi: Bergen, *Holy War,* 186; Hawsawi: *Newsweek,* 19 November 2001. Video tape: Transcript and annotations of the video tape independently prepared by George Michael, translator, Diplomatic Language Services, and Dr. Kassem M. Wahba, Arabic language program coordinator, School of Advanced International Studies, Johns Hopkins University, 13 December 2001.

27. Translation per the 12 October 1996 statement by the London-based Saudi dissident organisation, the Committee for the Defense of Legitimate Rights,posted at www.*msanews.mynet.net*

28. For an explanation of the movement and the ideology behind it, see Bernard Lewis, "License to Kill: Usama bin Ladin's Declaration of Jihad," *Foreign Affairs,* November/December 1998, 14–19. For the text see also Gohari, *Taliban,* 146–149. See also Zanini, "Middle Eastern Terrorism," 250; Cooley, *Unholy Wars,* 224.

29. See, for instance, Center for Preventive Action (Nancy Lubin and Barnett R. Rubin), *Calming the Ferghana Valley: Development and Dialogue in the Heart of Central Asia* (New York: Century Foundation Press, 1999), 65–68.

30. Ibid., 65–68.

31. Cooley, *Unholy Wars,* 187.

32. Hiro, *Islamic Fundamentalism,* 101–102.

33. Cooley, *Unholy Wars,* 187.

34. See, for instance, Reuel Marc Gerecht, "The Terrorists' Encyclopedia," *Middle East Quarterly* 8:3 (Summer 2001), 77–78; Leader and Danis, "Tactical Insights from the Trial," 48.

35. See Gerecht, "Terrorists' Encyclopedia," 81–82.

36. Jacquard, *Osama Bin Laden,* 155.

37. See Gerecht, "Terrorists' Encyclopedia," 78–79; Bergen, *Holy War,* 84.

38. Gerecht, "Terrorists' Encyclopedia," 81.

39. Ibid., 71–85, illustrated on 80; Department of the Army, *Field Manual FM 5–31: Boobytraps* (Washington, D.C.: Department of the Army, September 1965), 72–74.

40. *Time,* 26 November 2001, 50–54; *FM 5–31: Boobytraps,* 76–77, 107.

41. Jacquard, *Osama Bin Laden*, 256; Department of the Army, *Field Manual FM 5–25, Explosives and Demolitions* (Washington, D.C.: Department of the Army, 1967), 129, 136. The discrepancies may be due to the fact that this writer worked with an early edition of the field manual, while the extremists may have had access to one of the later editions.

42. See Gerecht, "Terrorists' Encyclopedia," 81.

43. Reeve, *New Jackals*, 137–138.

44. Jacquard, *Osama Bin Laden*, 154.

45. Ibid., 146.

46. Bruce, "Arab Veterans," 175.

47. Bergen, *Holy War*, 90.

48. Reeve, *New Jackals*, 3.

49. Ibid., 3.

50. Bergen, *Holy War*, 5; *Economist*, 24 November 2001.

51. Kazuharu Ogi in *Shukan Asahi* (Japan), 9 November 2001.

52. See, for instance, *Novye Izvestiya* (Russia), 31 October 2001.

53. Bodansky, *Bin Laden*, 318–320. The numbers of course add up to only 2,148.

54. Bergen, *Holy War*, 199; Blanche, "Egyptians around Bin Laden," 19–21.

55. See, for instance, transcript of the interview with Usamah bin Ladin entitled "Usamah bin Ladin, the Destruction of the Base," conducted by Jamal Ismail in an unspecified location in Afghanistan and presented by Salah Najm (Al-Jazeera, 10 June 1999). When no other source is given, this section is based on Reeve, *New Jackals*, 156–221; Gunaratna, "Blowback," 42–45; and Bergen, *Holy War*, 41–59.

56. Emerson, *American Jihad*, 145–146.

57. In addition to Reeve, *New Jackals*, see Bergen, *Holy War*, 80.

58. Emerson, *American Jihad*, 137; Jacquard, *Osama Bin Laden*, 28; Gunaratna, "Blowback," 44; Trifin J. Roule, Jeremy Kinsell, and Brian Joyce, "Investigators Seek to Break Up Al-Qaeda's Financial Structure," *Jane's Intelligence Review* 13:11 (November 2001), 9.

59. Bodansky, *Bin Laden*, 91, 102.

60. See Cooley, *Unholy Wars*, 120, 123; Gohari, *Taliban*, 144; *Intelligence Newsletter* 300 (Paris: Indigo Publications, 28 November 1996), 7. The Saudi government probably revoked bin Ladin's citizenship and confiscated his assets because had become increasingly critical of the House of Saud. However, some claim, perhaps less convincingly, that the Egyptian security services in a joint Egyptian-Saudi investigation had discovered that bin Ladin had given money to a group of Egyptian extremists to buy printing presses and weapons, and that Egypt accordingly put tremendous pressure on the

Saudis to move against him. Reeve, *New Jackals*, 182. The anonymous document obtained by PBS suggests that his assets may have been frozen earlier, perhaps as early as in 1992 (www.pbs.org/frontline/).

61. Jacquard, *Osama Bin Laden*, 220, who publishes the incorporation document signed by bin Ladin. See also Reeve, *New Jackals*, 180; Bergen, *Holy War*, 88–89, 205–206; Emerson, *American Jihad*, 180.

62. *Economist*, 16 February 2002; Cooley, *Unholy Wars*, 122, 124; Bergen, *Holy War*, 174.

63. Jacquard, *Osama Bin Laden*, 64, 282, note 8.

64. See Ralph H. Magnus and Eden Naby, *Afghanistan: Mullah, Marx, and Mujahid* (Boulder, Colo.: Westview Press, 1998), 239–240.

65. Reeve, *New Jackals*, 184–185; *Washington Post*, 3 October 2001.

66. Lena Jonson, *Russia and Central Asia: A New Web of Relations* (London: Royal Institute of International Affairs, 1998), 30; Yevgenyi Primakov, "Rossiya ne protivodeistvuet islamu: My ne stavim znak ravenstva mezhdu islamskim fundamentalizmom i islamskim ekstremizmom," *Nezavisimaya Gazeta*, 18 September 1996. See also Rashid, *Taliban*, 177.

67. See, for instance, Cooley, *Unholy Wars*, 222; ICG, *Pakistan: Madrasas*, 13.

68. The Clinton administration, too, was initially eager to support the Taliban. Maley, *Fundamentalism Reborn?* 45–46, 49, 91, 96–97, 99, 134.

69. See the emotional arguments raised in S. Frederick Starr, "Restrain Northern Alliance," syndicated in *Japan Times*, 27 October 2001; S. Frederick Starr, "A Federated Afghanistan?" *Central Asia – Caucasus Analyst Biweekly Briefing*, 7 November 2001 (www.cacianalyst.org).

70. See, for instance, *Economist*, 2 February 2002, 23 February 2002; Ariel Cohen, "The Bush Administration Casts a Wary Eye on Iran," *Eurasia Insight*, 16 March 2002 (www.eurasianet.org).

71. When no other source is given, this section is based on Reeve, *New Jackals*, 156–221; Gunaratna, "Blowback," 42–45; Bergen, *Holy War*, 41–59.

72. Jacquard, *Osama Bin Laden*, 35.

73. *Washington Post*, 3 October 2001.

74. Some claim that bin Ladin's aircraft departed Khartoum Airport only to immediately land in Wadi Saydna Airport, a few miles away. There he spent the following weeks, assisted by Sudanese intelligence, in organising the transfer of men and assets until all was concluded. If so, he departed for Jalalabad only later in May. Bodansky, *Bin Laden*, 186.

75. Al-Jazeera (in Arabic), 10 July 2001; Bergen, *Holy Wars*, 102–103.

76. Bodansky, *Bin Laden,* 307.

77. Bergen, *Holy War,* 248, note 42. By 1991 bin Ladin had three wives, one Syrian and two Saudis (some claim that he also had a wife from the Philippines; Jacquard, *Osama Bin Laden,* 21). Three of his wives obtained high academic degrees. Of the four putative wives three remained with him during his travels. *Al-Watan al-Arabi* (France), 18 January 2002. Bin Ladin also had 15 children, including his three eldest sons, Muhammad, Omar, and Saad. Reeve, *New Jackals,* 172. A fourth son, Abdullah or Abdul Rahman, was apparently with bin Ladin in Afghanistan. *Newsweek* (Asia edition), 19 August 2002; *Intelligence Newsletter* 294 (5 September 1996), 6.

78. Jane's World Insurgency and Terrorism 13, 27 November 2001.

79. Emerson, *American Jihad,* 147–148. Translation per the 12 October 1996 statement by the London-based Saudi dissident organisation, CDLR (posted at *www.msanews.mynet.net*).

80. See, for instance, Gerecht, "Terrorists' Encyclopedia," 71–85.

81. The two important Bangladeshi extremist organisations, Harakat ul-Jihad Islami and Harakat ul-Mujahidin, were, for instance, suspected of the attempted assassination of the celebrated Bangladeshi poet Samsur Rahman on 18 January 1999. Police afterward arrested one Pakistani and one South African, who told investigators that they had received financial support from Usamah bin Ladin for training and recruiting fighters in Bangladesh. *Patterns of Global Terrorism 1999.*

82. See Cooley, *Unholy Wars,* 224–225; Reeve, *New Jackals,* 270. For the full text of the *fatwa,* see Reeve, *New Jackals,* 268–270; FAS Intelligence Resource Program (www.fas.org).

83. Al-Jazeera (in Arabic), 10 July 2001.

84. *Economist,* 29 September 2001.

85. Richard Behar, "Kidnapped Nation," *Fortune,* 29 April 2002, 86.

86. *Economist,* 22 September 2001.

87. See *Economist,* 15 September 2001. For a final confirmation that the White House was the final target, see *Washington Post,* 23 May 2002.

88. *Washington Post,* 12 September 2001.

89. See Department of State, *Patterns of Global Terrorism 1994* (Washington, D.C.: Department of State, April 1995); Rohan Gunaratna, "Terror from the Sky," *Jane's Intelligence Review* 13:10 (October 2001), 7.

90. Reeve, *New Jackals,* 87; Bergen, *Holy War,* 138.

91. See *Washington Post,* 22 May 2002; *Newsweek,* 27 May 2002.

92. See *Economist,* 22 September 2001, *Washington Post,* 12 December 2001, 31 January 2002.

93. Alexander and Swetnam, *Usama bin Laden's al-Qaida,* 52, referring to *Times of London,* 27 September 2001.

94. *Newsweek,* 27 May 2002.

95. Transcript and annotations of the video tape independently prepared by George Michael, translator, Diplomatic Language Services; and Dr. Kassem M. Wahba, Arabic language program coordinator, School of Advanced International Studies, Johns Hopkins University, 13 December 2001.

96. See, for instance, Al-Jazeera (in Arabic), 13 September 2001.

97. *Washington Post,* 28 January 2002 (a report on the decision-making process inside the Bush administration's war cabinet in mid-September 2001). For more information on Abu Zubaydah, see, for instance, Blanche, "Egyptians around Bin Laden," 21.

98. *Washington Post,* 28 January 2002. The account does not specify whether the president had already given the instruction to Ashcroft on 11 September or, which seems most likely, on 12 September.

99. *Economist,* 25 November 2000, 56–58. See also U. S. Department of State web site, *www.usinfo.state.gov*

100. *Economist,* 12 January 2002.

101. Michael Whine, "Cyberspace: A New Medium for Communication, Command, and Control by Extremists," *Studies in Conflict & Terrorism* 22:3 (1999), 240; *Economist,* 25 November 2000, 56. On Abu Qatada, see also *Washington Post,* 28 October 2001.

102. *Newsweek,* 5 November 2001; Ed Blanche, "Egypt Takes Chance to Bring Home Militants," *Jane's Intelligence Review* 13:12 (December 2001), 2.

103. Jacquard, *Osama Bin Laden,* 281, note 4.

104. Rashid, *Taliban,* 135; US Department of State web site, *www.secretary.state.gov*

105. Bodansky, *Bin Laden,* 304.

106. UPI, 14 June 2001.

107. Reeve, *New Jackals,* 239.

108. Mylroie, *War Against America,* 282, note 7.

109. Cooley, *Unholy Wars,* 184.

110. Ed Blanche, "US Indictments Strain Saudi Links," *Jane's Intelligence Review,* August 2001, 4. For some of the issues involved, see Ed Blanche, "Security and Stability in the Middle East: The Al-Khobar Factor," *Jane's Intelligence Review* 13:6 (June 2001), 32–35.

111. Timothy R. Furnish, "Bin Ladin: The Man Who Would Be Mahdi," *Middle East Quarterly* (Spring 2002), 53–59.

112. Amnesty International (http://web.amnesty.org).

113. Reeve, *New Jackals,* 78, 86–89.

114. See Cable News Network (CNN), 12 April 1997; Catholic World News, 15 April 1997 (*www.cwnews.com*).

115. Presidential Executive Order 13224, 23 September 2001. The ever-growing list of blocked companies and individuals (which since has come to include a highly eclectic group of people and groups, not all suspected of association with Al-Qaida) is available from the Office of Foreign Assets Control, U.S. Department of the Treasury. See also *Washington Post,* 21 September 2001; *New York Times,* 25 September 2001; Emerson, *American Jihad,* 137; Jacquard, *Osama Bin Laden,* 28, 134; Roule, Kinsell, and Joyce, "Investigators Seek to Break Up Al-Qaeda's Financial Structure," 8–11; Laurence Caramel, "La communauté internationale déclare la guerre financière au terrorisme," *Bilan du Monde 2002* (Paris: *Le Monde,* 2001), 13; Gunaratna, "Blowback," 44.

116. Emerson, *American Jihad,* 152. See also Valentina Kurganskaia, "New Spiritual Trends in Kazakhstan," *Central Asia and the Caucasus* 3 (15), 2002, 106.

117. *Economist,* 22 September 2001; Roule, Kinsell, and Joyce, "Investigators Seek to Break Up Al-Qaeda's Financial Structure," 9.

118. Alexander and Swetnam, *Usama bin Laden's al-Qaida,* 29.

119. *Washington Post,* 1 May 2002; *USA Today,* 1 May 2002.

120. *New York Times,* 25 September 2001.

121. *Time,* 3 June 2002; *Economist,* 22 September 2001; Jane's World Insurgency and Terrorism 13, 27 November 2001.

122. Roule, Kinsell, and Joyce, "Investigators Seek to Break up Al-Qaeda's Financial Structure," 11; Executive Order 13224, supplementary list of 12 October 2001.

123. Cooley, *Unholy Wars,* 120, 123; Gohari, *Taliban,* 144; *Intelligence Newsletter* 300 (28 November 1996), 7.

124. See, for instance, "Central Asia's Narcotics Industry: The New 'Golden Triangle,'" *IISS Strategic Comments* 3:5 (June 1997).

125. Al-Jazeera (in Arabic), 10 July 2001; Bergen, *Holy Wars,* 102–103; Bergen, "Bin Laden Trial," 429–434; Gunaratna, "Blowback," 44.

126. *Economist,* 29 September 2001.

127. See, for instance, *Economist,* 6 October 2001.

128. *Economist,* 22 September 2001.

CHAPTER 8
The Terrorist Ideology: Why They Hate Us

Democracy is a great sin for God and an oppression for the people.
—From a communiqué of the Islamic Society (Morocco),
signed by the movement's emir, Abu Abdullah al-Sharif

Usamah bin Ladin's 1998 fatwa clearly spelled out his grievances.[1] These, incidentally, were what bothered not only him but most Sunni Islamic extremists. In Usamah bin Ladin's vocabulary the grievances were these:

U.S. occupation of Saudi Arabia, the holy land of Islam
U.S. aggression against the Iraqi people
Israeli occupation of Palestine

Even though bin Ladin's complaints were presented in the terms of political goals, his demands were firmly based on Islamic beliefs. Most important, in his opinion, was that true Muslims regain control over Islam's holy sites. After the holy cities of Mecca and Medina, which in his view were occupied with U.S. support by the apostate House of Saud, Jerusalem is the third most holy city to Islam. Arabs call the city Al-Quds, or even Al-Quds al-Sharif ("Noble and Holy City"). More specifically, Jerusalem's walled-off Old City is the site of two Muslim shrines located on the Temple Mount (known to Muslims as *al-Haram al-Sharif,* "the Noble and Inviolable Sanctuary"). These are the Al-Aqsa Mosque (al-Masjid al-Aqsa, "The Farthest Mosque") and the Dome of the Rock

(Qubbat al-Sakhra). Muslim tradition has it that the Prophet ascended to the seven heavens from this place.[2]

However, the order in which Usamah bin Ladin listed his grievances was significant. Islamic extremists, and indeed many if not most Muslims throughout the world, regard the Israeli occupation of Jerusalem (and, to a far lesser extent, other Palestinian territories) as a tragedy and an insult to Islam. In addition, most also believe that Israel is firmly controlled by the United States, which, in turn, is ruled by Zionists, according to what appears to be the belief of a majority of Arabs. These circumstances make the United States the paramount enemy of the Islamic world. Usamah bin Ladin, however, did not regard the Jerusalem issue as a priority. For him, the most important crime of the United States was its occupation of Saudi Arabia. Second was the war against Iraq, while support of Israel came last.[3]

Muslims are also outraged by the presence of Western troops in Saudi Arabia. Bin Ladin founded the World Islamic Front for Jihad against the Jews and the Crusaders to fight the U.S. "occupation" of Saudi Arabia, the holy land of Islam. He has accused the Saudi government of betraying Islam by allowing the United States to base thousands of troops in the kingdom.

After the holy sites, bin Ladin's other main complaint was the U.S. aggression against Muslims throughout the world, most important in Iraq. Like many Muslims, bin Ladin argued that an attack on one Muslim is an attack on them all, so Muslims resent the military attacks and economic sanctions against Iraq. The estimate that nearly a million Iraqi children, according to World Health Organisation and UN Children's Fund (UNICEF) reports, are malnourished and that thousands have died because of UN sanctions imposed at the time of the Gulf War, continues to enrage Muslims.[4]

The plight of the Palestinians under Israeli occupation has also aroused hostility throughout the Muslim world.[5] However, it was not only the fate of the Palestinians that concerned bin Ladin. He was probably more interested in recovering the holy places in Jerusalem. Also, from the Muslim point of view, there is no doubt that Israel has been treating the Palestinians badly and that the international community has sided with Israel in the Palestinian misfortune. The 1947 Arab-Israeli war, which marked the emergence of the independent state of Israel, produced between 600,000 to 800,000 Palestinian refugees who fled or were evicted from Jewish-held areas. The vast majority remained unable to return home or get any compensation for their loss. The Israeli occupation of the Gaza Strip and the West Bank in the Six Day War of 1967 further exacerbated the plight of the Palestinians: despite UN Resolution 242, which calls for withdrawal from occupied territories, Israel has not done so. Instead, it has built permanent Israeli settlements and infrastructure there, obviously in preparation for a permanent annexation. Moreover, Israel's victory in the Six-Day War led to the formation of a powerful Israeli lobby in the United States, headed by the American-Israeli Public Affairs Committee (AIPAC). Since then, the American Jewish community, and not only Jewish conservatives, has remained united in its support for Israel and U.S. support for Israel. In 1984, Israel also became a useful American ally and client state in the Cold War. In the end the issue has been transformed from a matter of geopolitics into a question of faith. This is most clearly shown by the support to Israel from the increasingly powerful American evangelical Christian right, since its followers regard Israel as a land promised to the Jews by God.[6]

There are other reasons for radical Muslims to hate the West, which have nothing to do with Usamah bin Ladin's fatwa. First—perhaps a more objective cause of anger, in Western eyes—is the dismal record with regard to human rights and economic development of many of those Middle Eastern governments the United States supported during the Cold War. Because of this support, dictatorship and prevention of economic reform also appear to be chief characteristics of U.S. policy in the region.[7] While many Muslims have been attracted by Western principles of democracy and personal freedom, these two concepts have to some extent been integrated into the popular versions of Islam. Unfortunately, other, less attractive, characteristics of Western culture came to symbolise the decadence of the West: crime, homosexuality, adultery, divorce, and materialism. Because the United States was the leading country in the West, it had to take the blame for what most Muslims seem to regard as the ills of Western culture.[8]

The Islamic extremists feel that the Koran, God's own, irrefutable words, justifies the use of terrorist tactics against infidels and apostates:[9]

> And We shall cast terror into the hearts of those who disbelieved . . . Their abode is the Fire; and evil is the habitation of the wrongdoers.[10]
>
> When thy Lord revealed to the angels, saying, . . . "I will cast terror into the hearts of those who disbelieve. Smite them above their necks, and smite off all fingertips. That is because they have opposed God and His Messenger."[11]
>
> Against them make ready your strength to the utmost of your power including steeds of war, to strike terror [into the hearts of] the enemies of God and your enemies. . . .[12]
>
> And God turned back the disbelievers in their rage. . . . And He brought those of the People of the Book [*that is, Christians, Jews*] who had aided them down from their fortresses, and cast terror into their hearts. Some you slew, and some you took captive. And He made you inherit their land and their houses and their wealth. . . .[13]

Incidentally, the Koran can also be used to justify robbery and murder to raise funds for Islamic activities, as long as the crimes are directed at infidels.[14] Many Muslim criminals have taken advantage of this convenient scriptural permission.[15]

Many Islamic extremists also show, in public, a very harsh toward sexual activities, especially sexual attitudes as they perceive them to be in the West. So did, for instance, Usamah bin Ladin and other Arab Afghan returnees to Saudi Arabia loath the fact that some Saudi women had begun to wear Western dress and even moved about without male guardians. They assumed that these women had adopted not only Western dress but also Western sexual mores. Yet, what the Arab Afghans expressed in public was of course not necessarily what they thought in private. Although seldom remarked upon by Western academics, it is hard to spend more than a few minutes with most young Islamic extremists—unless they are in the presence of their elders—before they raise the subject. These young men often seem overwhelmed by what they imagine to be the uninhibited sexual activities in all infidel countries, and they can literally spend hours discussing the brothels they would visit in the non-Islamic world (for instance, the United States or the Philippines)—if they ever got the money to travel there. Even if the subject is raised as a moral lesson, to accentuate the righteousness of their own beliefs, the discussion quickly turns to uninformed gossip: "Women should not dance or go to bars because it cheapens them, and then they are treated like animals or used by men as prostitutes, and then people come to watch them copulating (in) live sex shows," the 29-year-old Taliban leader Mullah Shah Mahmood told reporter Martin Regg Cohn in an interview. It did not take long, however, before the Mullah's disciples in this unexpected meeting with a Westerner turned to questions such as whether an uncircumcised man could achieve orgasm. Predictably, the interviewer later learned that Taliban leaders as well had secret television and video sets.[16]

The West has gone out of its way to assert that it is at war with terrorism, not Islam. Many Muslim leaders and Islamic teachers have likewise asserted that Islamic extremism is not a legitimate form of Islamic expression, even before the 11 September attacks. Traditional Islam accepts four legal schools of Islam as legitimate and authoritative, but the extremists often see the existence of these schools as an obstacle to their concept of Islamic unity. Traditional Islam follows various rules on how to appoint scholars as authorised interpreters of Islamic law, and makes the authority of such scholars dependent on the possession of written documents of appointment signed by their predecessors. Islamic extremists frequently install those with little or no theological or legal education in positions of Islamic authority, and in any case usually recognise the only authority of the leaders of their group. Yet more striking is perhaps that although Sunni Islam traditionally lacks any centralised leadership similar to that of a pope or patriarch, Sunni extremists typically regard their own leaders as *the* Islamic leadership. Sunni extremism is, in fact, an Islamic type of totalitarianism, in many respects drawing more on Western than Islamic organisation models.[17] Even so, it remains a paradox that the very fact that Sunni Islam lacks a centralised leadership makes it susceptible to the claims of extremist leaders as self-proclaimed religious authorities.

When the 18th-century extremist Muhammad ibn Abdul Wahhab began preaching his narrow ideology, rejecting traditional scholars, scholarship, and practices, the mufti of Medina declared Wahhabi belief a heresy and formally excommunicated him by issuing a fatwa, which said, "This man is leading the ignoramuses of the present age to a heretical path, He is trying to extinguish Allah's light." Wahhab, like many other fiery populist leaders throughout the ages, found it easy to get new converts, ruling that whoever did not agree with him was an apostate, and thus someone whose blood should be shed, whose women could be raped, and whose wealth could be confiscated. These views are still perpetuated in mosques throughout the Islamic world and in the West, as well as on the Internet, although usually not in the English-language versions of the Web sites of the various Islamic groups— only in languages such as Arabic and Malay.[18]

As noted already, most Islamic extremist leaders belonged to the privileged upper classes even though one significant root cause of Islamic extremism was the widespread poverty, unemployment, and lack of opportunity in the Muslim world. These conditions were what drove so many of the present rank-and-file members of the extremist movement into the hands of fanatic mullahs— although extremism may not necessarily have been their first career choice, had there been any other. A further understanding of the process may be found in the *madrasahs*, which are essentially schools for the poor. Most *madrasahs* offer destitute young men food and shelter regardless of their Islamic qualifications or lack thereof. Once there, many of the young men who at first had little interest in religion could be turned into fanatics after being taught a simplistic but attractive ideology that glorified martyrs—that is, young men who were empowered by God to take up arms and seize the leading role in society.

The economic and social failure of the Muslim world, as well as the plight of Muslims in Palestine, Chechnya, Kashmir, and other places, has generated a strong persecution complex. Usamah bin Ladin, seemingly a lone man hunted by the vast resources of the Western world, has come to embody this complex. The demonisation of bin Ladin by the Western media and leading figures in the world only reinforces this feeling. When George W. Bush, the leader of the world's only superpower, declared the War on Terror, he in effect declared war on a single man. Bush thereby put bin Ladin on a pedestal and in the dignified position of Islam's leading protector and defender, a saint commanding the forces of God against the arrogant and infidel imperialists of the West. This image will not easily be removed, and if bin Ladin dies in the struggle, or is shown to have died, he will long be remembered as a martyr of the faith and the victim of the evil West. Usamah bin Ladin is currently the hero of the Muslim world, and his face remains visible not only in all news media but on posters, sweet wrappers, and any number of commercial goods throughout the Islamic world. His name and face also obviously command attention in the West. In the United States he is even marketed as an action figure. In the marketers' thinking, Usamah bin Ladin equals instant brand-name recognition.

In the final analysis, Islam as a religion has proven unable and unwilling to keep up with the times. Unlike Christianity, which developed the concept of separation of church and state, Islam refused to consider such a division. Islam thereby proved incapable of formulating a modern conception of state and government. This would have made Islam able to cope with a non-Islamic world that in time grew not only far more powerful in military strength through organisational means, but also in science. Unlike the West, Islam failed to distinguish philosophy from theology, which ability in the long run enabled the Western world to embrace scientific findings regardless of whether these were in apparent conflict with theological doctrine. No such development was possible in Islam because, unlike Christianity, it continued to insist on complete submission to the Koran, which is regarded as the genuine, complete, and infallible word of God. Moreover, unlike most Christian states, Islam typically could not accept harmonious relations with those it could not conquer. According to the Koran, a Muslim could in theory only serve a Muslim leader, not an infidel one. By extension, an Islamic state could not accept any decision or even a border demarcated by a non-Islamic state. This belief also ruled out the adoption of non-Muslim innovations in science and administration, although this was perhaps so more in theory than actual practice.

As long as Islam could expand its territory by waging war on non-Muslims, the religion flourished and its leaders, somewhat contradictorily but fully supported by the clerics, made full use of scientific as well as cultural innovations. However, when expansion was no longer possible, religious leaders found it far preferable to contemplate the purity of the faith rather than accept that the world had changed. They could not do otherwise; the very foundation of Islam is that all truth was revealed by God, once and for all, to the Prophet. With the evident decline of many Islamic nations, this world view invariably led to a search for scapegoats. Either the infidels were to blame for the decline of Islam, or else the Muslim general population had strayed from the early purity of the faith and had to be forced back into the fold. Islamic governments, never clearly separated from the local religious leadership, supported conservative mullahs who encouraged the population not to the blame the government, which, after all, did represent God's infallible word. Instead, the governments also said that others were to blame: apostates at home or evil infidels abroad.[19]

It seems wishful thinking to hope that mainstream Islam, let alone Salafi or Wahhabi Islam, will reform itself and recover an influential position among world religions. For every Muslim reformist, there seems to be vast numbers of ignorant mullahs who refuse to even consider improvements of any kind. If so, Islam is doomed to remain the mass movement of poor, uneducated people in third-world countries who, even when they migrate to the West, which seems to be the outspoken hope of many, will remain consumed by their own self-pity rather than actively seeking to create a better life. Few will question their own faith, but many will be quick to blame any Western government that does not provide each one with welfare and benefits in the form of a full table, whether at home or abroad.

End Notes

1. For the full text of the fatwa, see Reeve, *New Jackals,* 268–70; or FAS Intelligence Resource Program (www.fas.org).

2. See, for instance, Mirskiy, "Islamic Fundamentalism," 30–31.

3. See, for instance, Mirskiy, "Islamic Fundamentalism," 30–31.

4. See, for instance, the Unicef statement of 27 November 1997 (www.unicef.org); BBC, 1 October 2002. See also *Observer* (London)/*Japan Times* (Tokyo), 27 October 2001, for yet higher casualty rates.

5. *Economist,* 29 September 2001.

6. See, for instance, *Economist,* 6 October 2001, 6 April 2002; *Time,* 6 May 2002. For some details on US-Israeli defense and intelligence cooperation, see Samuel W. Lewis, "The United States and Israel: Evolution of an Unwritten Alliance," *Middle East Journal* 53: 3 (Summer 1999), 364–78, on 373–5.

7. *Economist,* 29 September 2001.

8. *Economist,* 29 September 2001.

9. The translations are based on those by Maulvi Sher Ali, Yusufali, and J. M. Rodwell (www.concordance.com; http://promo.net/pg).

10. Koran 3.152.

11. Koran 8.13–14.

12. Koran 8.60.

13. Koran 33.26–8.

14. See, for instance, Koran 9: "Make war upon such of those to whom the Scriptures have been given as believe not in God, or in the last day, and who forbid not that which God and His Apostle have forbidden, and who profess not the profession of the truth, until they pay tribute out of hand, and they be humbled."

15. For instance in Indonesia. International Crisis Group (ICG), *Al-Qaeda in Southeast Asia: The Case of the "Ngruki Network" in Indonesia* (Jakarta/Brussels: ICG Indonesia Briefing, 8 August 2002), 8, 13, 14.

16. *Toronto Star,* 29 April 2001 (www.thestar.com). The present writer has had the dubious honor of spending many hours in the company of Islamic extremists, and he is fed up with discussions that would make Dr Ruth blush.

17. See, for instance, Palazzi, "Islamists Have It Wrong,"3–11.

18. See, for instance, Palazzi, "Islamists Have It Wrong," 3–11 (for the mufti's words, on 7). Among prominent Islamic web sites in spring 2002 were www.azzam.com and www.almaqdese.com, both registered in London; www.jehad.net, registered in Sweden; www.aljihad-online.has.it, registered in Italy; www.attawhid.com, registered in Warsaw, Poland; www.alneda.com, registered in Singapore and activated from Malaysia; www.aloswa.org, registered in Malaysia; and www.sahwah.net and www.erhap.com, both registered in Mecca, Saudi Arabia. Some have since been closed down while the United States has limited access to the others through its servers.

19. Some of these points are further explored in Bernard Lewis, *What Went Wrong? Western Impact and Middle Eastern Response* (Oxford: Oxford University Press, 2001).

PART II
Background to the Afghan War

The extremists are more savage than the Communists because they kill and loot under the cloak of Islam. If they take power the bloodbath will continue for another ten years.

—A spokesman for the traditional Afghan leader
Pir Sayyid Ahmad Gailani, 1989

Central Asia was historically the heartland of Eurasia. Its location at the intersection of the overland communications routes known as the Silk Road, linking China and the Far East with the Mediterranean and India and then Russia and Europe, made the region a hub of commerce from early times. The same tribesmen who then ran the caravans today drive the lorries that move goods across the often hostile borders of the region. The region played an important role in the development and dissemination of science and culture. However, while Central Asia remains an important transportation nexus, especially with regard to future exploitation of the region's oil and natural gas resources, the chief importance of the region may today be that of a powder keg. Central Asia has developed into a global security threat, and this would be greatly increased if Pakistan with its nuclear weapons program were to follow Afghanistan and parts of Tajikistan on their descent into warlordism.[1]

Central Asia was long a contested territory in a great geopolitical game among great powers. The traditional Great Game was played out in the 19th century between Britain and Russia for the territories between the British South Asian and the Russian Siberian and Central Asian possessions.[2] These territories eventually came to serve both powers, but at that time they benefited

Britain in particular, constituting a buffer area. In a geopolitical contest, buffer territories or states are of great use against an external political-military threat because of their ability to contribute not only their own interposed forces but also their capacity to absorb whatever the threat may offer. Any buffer state provides geographic depth, which allows time to move additional forces to a theatre of war. It also discourages aggression because the power against which the buffer is intended must calculate the cost of absorbing the buffer state and at the same time risk war with the rival power.

Afghanistan retained its role of buffer state with the rise of the Soviet Union and the onset of the Cold War. As Britain pulled out of the game, Afghanistan became the prize in a geopolitical contest between the United States and the Soviet Union. The latters' rivalry culminated in the Afghan civil war that led to Soviet intervention and the massive Western and Arab support of the mujahidin who fought against the Soviet-supported regime.[3] The Soviet Union lost the Cold War, and Afghanistan fell back into civil war and anarchy. In recent years there has been talk about the new Great Game—a term that understandably has excited public attention—over the oil and gas resources in the Caspian region and Central Asia, and the issue of optimal pipeline routes from an economic and geopolitical point of view.[4]

The current geopolitical contest for domination of Afghanistan has been bloodier than the traditional Great Game and financially more devastating than the new Great Game. More people, certainly more than 1.5 million,[5] have been killed in Afghanistan since civil war broke out in 1979 than in all the battles between the British and Russians and their proxies more than a century ago. The huge investments of the New Great Game for oil and gas were at least made with the purpose of eventually turning a profit, even if the economic costs for neighbouring countries because of military expenditures, refugee problems, social disruption, and such criminal activities as narcotics trafficking caused by the long war in Afghanistan are almost certainly far greater.

With the exception of Afghanistan, Central Asia is no longer territory to be fought over. Few borders are seriously contested, unlike the situation in the Middle East and the Indian subcontinent. Despite regional problems involving the exploitation of water resources, inter-ethnic distrust, economic reform, and the development of democracy, the risk of open warfare erupting between the states of the region is small.

However, a geopolitical and ideological game is still being played over Afghanistan, the most volatile spot in the region. The civil war in Afghanistan has served as a catalyst in creating new boundaries and dividing neighbouring states according to how they respond to the resultant political, religious, social, and military turmoil. The rise to power of extremist Islamic groups in Afghanistan was in recent years the major security threat to the region, inspiring a similar development in some parts of Tajikistan and nuclear weapons-armed Pakistan. The extremist groups suffered a severe setback when a coalition led by the United States destroyed the Afghan Taliban government in late 2001. Yet extremist Islamic thought remains widespread in Afghanistan, and the country remains dangerously unstable despite a new Afghan government set up by the victors.

The Afghan state as we recognise it today was first formed around Kandahar in 1747 by Ahmad Shah Durrani (reigned 1747–1773), an ethnic Pashtun. The people incorporated into his political entity were united by neither language nor religion, being both Turkic- and Persian-language speakers, as well as both Sunni or Shia Muslims. The latter group included the Hazara, descendants of Mongol invaders. The population was pastoral rather than nomadic, yet the early Afghan rulers frequently raided the neighbouring countries in the tradition of the earlier nomadic Mongol and Turkic conquest dynasties. However, this period of expansion soon ended, and in 1772 the early Afghan state shifted its capital from pastoral, clerical Kandahar to mercantile, secular Kabul. One reason for the shift was that it allowed the secular rulers to escape clerical domination. The Afghan monarchy, although frequently torn by succession disputes and threatened at times by British annexation, managed to survive until 1973, when it fell in a coup d'etat.[6]

The ethnic term Afghan originally referred exclusively to the Afghan or Pashtun people. Since the late 19th-century nation-building project of Amir Abdul Rahman Khan (reigned 1880–1901), the term has come to encompass all those peoples who live within the borders inherited, conquered, or pacified by this monarch. The nation-building project, in the form of "pashtunisation"—an emphasis on the Pashtun origins of the state and Pashtun language (Pashto) and culture—has since remained the goal of all succeeding governments. Within Afghanistan, research on the non-Pashtun origins of the state or the languages and cultures of the minorities was severely discouraged. As foreign observers and scholars during that period spent most of their time in contact with Pashtun government entities, this is also the view that eventually came to dominate foreign research on Afghanistan. This led to such things as introduction and codification of customs, for example, the Pashtunwali code of conduct of the Pashtuns in a form that had little or nothing to do with genuine historical traditions but everything to do with nation-building in the modern sense. The territory currently recognised as Afghanistan was, until about 150 years ago, known as Khorasan. Even when the territory won independence after the fall of the Persian Safavid Empire in 1736, the new state was still referred to internationally as Khorasan until 1801—and far longer in the country itself, at least until the 1890s.[7]

Geographically, the massive Hindu Kush mountain range (which in the northeast corner rises into the Pamir Mountains, colorfully known as the "Roof of the World") divides modern Afghanistan into the north and south. The north is mainly populated by Persian- and Turkic-speaking groups (although some Pashtun groups were relocated there in the late 19th century to ensure royal control of the area), while the south is mostly inhabited by Pashtuns and some Persian-speaking groups. The Hindu Kush itself is inhabited by Tajiks and, particularly in the central regions of the country, Hazara. Both of these ethnic groups are Persian speakers. Tajik was originally a term mainly used by outsiders for mostly Sunni Persian speakers who do not belong to a tribal society; however, since the civil war began there is an increasing tendency for nontribal Persian-speakers to identify themselves as Tajiks.[8] Both Tajiks and Hazara also constitute significant population segments of most large cities, including Kabul, which indeed is located in the southern foothills of the Hindu Kush. Along the border to the east with Pakistan are several smaller mountain ranges, including the Suleman Range, which is traversed by the well-known Khyber Pass. Pashtuns live on both sides of this range. Western and southern Afghanistan are on the eastern end of the flat and arid Iranian Plateau. Northern Afghanistan, on the other hand, forms a southern extension of the Central Asian steppe. Most good farm land is limited to the fertile valleys in the foothills of the Hindu Kush.[9]

The modern state of Afghanistan, as created after 1880 by Amir Abdul Rahman Khan with weapons and subsidies from Britain, was always a rentier state, that is, a state dependent on foreign aid from a sponsor (or group of sponsors) that wished to use the state for its own strategic reasons. When Britain resigned its role in Afghanistan after World War II, the sponsorship was taken up by a not very enthusiastic United States and the considerably more eager Soviet Union. During the period 1979–1989, the two superpowers fought a war by proxy in Afghanistan, with the Soviet Union supporting the central government and the United States supporting various Islamic groups opposed to the secular Afghan government. However, with the dissolution of the Soviet Union in December 1991, the bipolar strategic conflict ended. So did most of the foreign aid. The aid that remained came exclusively from Arab sources. Through this, the subsequent Taliban government could be regarded as a rentier government as well.[10]

Due to the long civil war that commenced in early 1979, exacerbated by the Soviet intervention in the period 1979–1989 and not yet fully resolved, Afghanistan remains what can best be described as a failed state.[11] The country is no longer characterised by any real sovereignty but by de facto, if fluid, internal borders between mutually antagonistic groups. The internal borders were for some time considered as approximating ethnic borders, although these were always hard to define due to historical population movements. Since most ethnic groups in Afghanistan also maintained contacts with ethnic cousins beyond national borders, the civil war caused even national territorial ambiguity. It became increasingly hard to pinpoint where Afghan state power, such as it was, began and ended. The Pashtuns, for instance, since 1979 have received support from Pakistan, homeland of the other main population of Pashtuns, while the Tajiks in due time began to receive assistance from neighbouring Tajikistan.[12] In addition, the civil war included successful uprisings among two minorities, the Hazara and Nuristanis, who thereby regained the autonomy they had lost to Amir Abdul Rahman Khan in 1893 and 1896, respectively. (Hazarajat and Nuristan, the latter known as Kafiristan—"Country of Infidels"—before its conquest and forced conversion to Islam, were the last two regions conquered and incorporated into the state of Afghanistan).[13] During the war, the government of the Soviet-supported People's Democratic Party of Afghanistan (PDPA) increasingly came to rely on tribal-based militias known as *operatifi*. These were for all intents and purposes identical to the irregular forces on which earlier Afghan governments had relied. The militias were exempted from any government programs they did not choose to join and were primarily supposed to keep their own areas free of enemy fighters and to keep the major roads open. The most important of the *operatifi* became the Jowzjani Uzbek militia, led by Abdul Rashid Dostum.[14] As the *operatifi* system increased in importance, even the identity of Afghan state power became unclear as warlords and political groups battled for power.

Salafi Islamic thought came to Central Asia during the 1979--1989 war in Afghanistan. It came with Arab volunteers for the *jihad* against the Soviet intervention force, and therefore in the form of Wahhabism.[15] In 1988, the first purely Wahhabi group rose to prominence in eastern Afghanistan. This was the *Jamaat al-Dawa ila al-Quran wa Ahl al-Hadith* (Society for the Call to the Koran and People of the Prophetic Tradition), led by a former *Hezb-e Islami* (Islamic Party) commander and largely supported by Arab sympathisers. Among the Afghans it became known as the Wahhabi group.[16]

In 1994, Pakistan switched its support to (indeed, in all essentials created) another Wahhabi group known as the Taliban movement. This movement of Islamic extremists (*taliban* is the plural form of *talib,* "religious student" in a traditional Islamic *madrasah*), dominated by Pashtuns with massive Pakistani support, came to control most parts of the country within a few years.[17] Despite some claims that the movement had already passed its zenith of power,[18] the Taliban remained in control of the major cities and their surrounding lands. The 11 September 2001 terrorist attacks on the United States again changed the situation. The Taliban were pushed out of power in a major offensive in late 2001 by the predominantly non-Pashtun Northern Alliance, this time considerably well armed and equipped by Iran and Russia, and with air support from the United States and several coalition countries.[19] Following discussions outside Bonn, Germany, under the aegis of the United Nations, an interim Afghan government was formed on 4 December 2001, to assume power on 22 December. Most key Afghan leaders or their representatives, as well as their foreign sponsors (primarily the United States, Russia, Pakistan, and Iran) participated. The United States and Pakistan nominated a Pashtun, Hamid Karzai, as leader of the interim government, while accepting the realities on the ground by awarding all key ministries (defence, internal affairs, and foreign affairs) to leaders from the Northern Alliance.[20]

Since the assumption of power by Karzai's interim government, some foreign aid from the West is again available. This leaves Afghanistan essentially where it started 100 years ago: a rentier state unable, and to some extent unwilling, to depend on its own resources. In striking similarity to the various Afghan governments before the civil war (most recently, the Soviet-supported PDPA government), the Afghan government at the time of this writing presides over a state whose finances seem to be ever more dependent on external support. In addition, the activities of the government seem increasingly concentrated on maintaining its own security.

Since all the kings of the 1747–1973 monarchy, except one, were ethnic Pashtuns, it is often argued that the Afghan national identity is based on Pashtun domination over other such ethnic

groups as the Tajiks, Hazara, Uzbeks, and several others.[21]
President Bush appeared to reach the same conclusion, a view
shared by the fallen Taliban government's main sponsor, Pakistan.
However, after more than two decades of civil war and a Soviet
intervention that pitched both Afghan government forces and
Soviet troops against mujahidin forces, very little appears to remain
of Afghan national identity. Indeed, ethnic divisions became more
divisive with the disappearance of the threat from the Soviet Union.
First, the Soviet-inspired nationality policy of the PDPA government reinforced ethnic identities. Second, assertiveness increased
among the minorities due to their military successes against the
Soviets and their ability to survive in a war seen increasingly to be
against the Pashtun majority. This newly acquired political aware-
ness has made the traditional Pashtun political domination in
national politics unsustainable, especially as the new political and
military organisation of many minorities facilitates protests.[22] The
collapse of the Afghan state accordingly devalued the national
identity and instead reinforced ethnic identities. The defeat of the
Taliban movement and its replacement by an interim government
has done little to change this situation.

A large portion of the surviving Afghan population is no longer
able to support itself, having been totally dependent on foreign aid
for years.[23] As long as such aid is provided, the Afghan warlords
(whether Taliban, leaders in the new government, or commanders
who retain military forces but were not offered government positions) are relieved of the responsibility of providing for their supporters and their dependents. So they are free, if they so wish, to
spend all revenues on their wars. Without foreign aid, there would
be far less opportunity for internecine strife, since armed groups
need cash to acquire weapons, ammunition, and fuel, and local
resources in most cases would be insufficient to arm any substantial force.

The Pashtuns are the largest ethnic group in Afghanistan (about
40 percent of the population, which may have reached 26 million),
followed by Tajiks (25 percent), and Hazara and Uzbeks (together
roughly 25 percent).[24] However, although most of Afghanistan's

population is concentrated in the largely Pashtun south, 60 percent of the country's agricultural resources and 80 percent of its industrial, mineral, and gas wealth are in the chiefly Uzbek and Tajik north. This is a further incentive for the Pashtuns to recover their leading position, while the non-Pashtuns will try to keep their natural resources beyond Pashtun control.[25]

End Notes

1. When no other source is given, this chapter is based on Michael Fredholm, *Afghanistan and Central Asian Security* (Stockholm: Stockholm University, Asian Cultures and Modernity Research Report 1, March 2002).

2. See H. W. C. Davis, *The Great Game in Asia (1800–1844)* (London: Oxford University Press for the British Academy, The Raleigh Lecture on History, 10 November 1926); Peter Hopkirk, *The Great Game: The Struggle for Empire in Central Asia* (New York: Kodansha International, 1992); Karl E. Meyer and Shareen Blair Brysac, *Tournament of Shadows: The Great Game and the Race for Empire in Central Asia* (Washington, D.C.: Counterpoint, 1999).

3. See, for instance, Isby, War in a Distant Country; Rubin, Fragmentation of Afghanistan; Magnus and Naby, Afghanistan.

4. See Ariel Cohen, "The New Great Game: Oil Politics in the Caucasus and Central Asia," Heritage Foundation *Backgrounder* No. 1065 (25 January 1996); Ahmed Rashid, "The New Great Game: The Battle for Central Asia's Oil," *Far Eastern Economic Review,* 10 April 1997. See also Rashid, *Taliban.*

5. Rashid, *Taliban,* vii.

6. Magnus and Naby, *Afghanistan,* 24–47; S. A. M. Adshead, *Central Asia in World History* (New York: St. Martin's Press, 1993), 197–198.

7. Sayed Askar Mousavi, *The Hazaras of Afghanistan: An Historical, Cultural, Economic and Political Study* (Richmond, Surrey: Curzon Press, 1998), xv, 2–9; M. Nazif Shahrani, "The Future of the State and the Structure of Community Governance in Afghanistan," Maley, *Fundamentalism Reborn?,* 214.

8. Bernt Glatzer, "Is Afghanistan on the Brink of Ethnic and Tribal Disintegration?" in Maley, *Fundamentalism Reborn?,* 170. For the current fast changes in ethnic self-identification, see also Olivier Roy, "Has Islamism a Future in Afghanistan?" in Maley, *Fundamentalism Reborn?,* 206.

9. See, for instance, Rashid, *Taliban,* 7–8.

10. Rubin, *Fragmentation of Afghanistan*, passim, in particular 265–269; Shahrani, "Future of the State," 225.

11. See, for instance, Rubin, *Fragmentation of Afghanistan*, passim, in particular 265–280; Rashid, *Taliban*, 83, 207–208. See also Antonio Giustozzi, *War, Politics, and Society in Afghanistan: 1978–1992* (Washington, DC: Georgetown University Press, 2000).

12. Rashid, *Taliban*, 53–54, 61, 78, 146; Gohari, *Taliban*, 122–123.

13. Rubin, *Fragmentation of Afghanistan*, 180, 186.

14. Ibid., 144, 148, 158, 159.

15. See, for instance, Gohari, *Taliban*, 39–41, 54–56.

16. Rubin, *Fragmentation of Afghanistan*, 89, 314 , note 26. The Arabic term *hadith*, here translated as "prophetic tradition," indicates the collection of authenticated precepts attributed to the Prophet Muhammad, which constitutes an important source of Islamic law.

17. Maley, *Fundamentalism Reborn?* 43–89; Rashid, *Taliban*, 44–45, 72, 183–184; Gohari, *Taliban*, 32. See also Michael Griffin, *Reaping the Whirlwind: The Taliban Movement in Afghanistan* (London: Pluto Press, 2001).

18. Peter Tomsen, "A Chance for Peace in Afghanistan: The Taliban's Days Are Numbered," *Foreign Affairs* 79:1 (January/February 2000), 179–182.

19. See *Economist,* 17 November 2001.

20. *Washington Post,* 5 December 2001; *Economist,* 8 December 2001.

21. Magnus and Naby, *Afghanistan,* 161–165.

22. Kristian Berg Harpviken, "War and Change in Afghanistan: Reflections on Research Priorities" in Mirja Juntunen and Birgit N. Schlyter, eds., *Return to the Silk Routes: Current Scandinavian Research on Central Asia* (London: Kegan Paul International, 1999), 170.

23. See, for instance, Peter Marsden, *The Taliban: War, Religion and the New Order in Afghanistan* (London: Zed Books, 1998), 108.

24. Central Intelligence Agency, *The World Factbook 2001* (www.cia.gov).

25. Rubin, *Fragmentation of Afghanistan*, 237–238; Rashid, *Taliban*, 55.

CHAPTER 9
The Afghan Factions, September 2001

By September 2001, the military situation in Afghanistan was comparatively stable. With Pakistani support, the Taliban had occupied large parts of the Afghanistan, although not the 95 percent of its territory that a patently untrue Taliban claim had quickly convinced the international media to accept without question.[1] The Northern Alliance, due to its foreign sponsors, remained in the north and in various inaccessible locations throughout the country. The Taliban held the major cities, but the country remained vulnerable to Northern Alliance strikes and in many regions had not even seen any Taliban presence.

The various parties in the Afghan civil war could best be summarised as two main forces: the Pashtuns (until late 2001 represented by the Taliban) and their chief opponent, the Northern Alliance (also known as the United Front), primarily made up of ethnic Tajik, Hazara, and Uzbek forces under such leaders as the late Ahmad Shah Masud and Abdul Rashid Dostum. A third force, although allied and ideologically sympathetic to the Taliban, was until late 2001 made up of the loose network of Arab Afghan Islamic extremists under Usamah bin Ladin.

THE TALIBAN

The Taliban, September 2001
Objective: Assumption of full power and the promotion of traditional Pashtun domination over the Afghan state.
Allies: The Arab Afghan movement.
Sponsor: Pakistan.
Proxies: None.
Population: Pashtuns are estimated to comprise around 40 percent of the total population of Afghanistan (which may be as high as 26.8 million).[2]
Armed forces: At most perhaps 45,000, including an estimated 9,000 to 10,000 part-time Pakistani volunteers who served for short periods before being replaced by other Pakistanis and at least 500 to 600, perhaps as many as 1,000 to 1,500, Arabs).[3]

The Taliban was a military force created in 1994, in all essentials by and for Pakistani interests, although few, if any, Taliban leaders were much concerned about following Pakistani orders.[4] The movement's leaders seemed to regard themselves as the world's only true Islamic government, on the lines of the righteous caliphate of the early years of Islam.[5] The Taliban government accordingly styled itself the Islamic Emirate of Afghanistan.[6]

The Taliban were also reinforced by large numbers of Pakistanis, including religious volunteers and regular Pakistani military units. Indeed, the very first Taliban incursion into Afghanistan in 1994 was reportedly supported by Pakistani army artillery and motor transportation from the Pakistani side of the border.[7] The volunteers, first reported by the Pakistani press in mid-June 1997,[8] were initially mostly Pashtuns of Afghan or Pakistani origin, but from 1999 on, Pakistani Punjabis arrived in increasing numbers and eventually formed the majority of the Pakistani volunteers.[9]

The Pakistani military played a considerable role in the military success of the Taliban. Senior intelligence and army officers were involved in strategic planning. Regular army units served in combat roles or were detached from their units for the provision of such special skills as tank driver and aircraft pilot and in technical and rear support, maintenance, and administrative functions. Pakistani aircraft assisted with troop rotations for Taliban forces during combat operations at least in late 2000. Pakistani military officers from the ISI, as well as commandos from Pakistan's Special Services Group (a regiment of about 2,800 men based at Cherat, near Peshawar), also appeared to take considerable responsibility for the planning and execution of major operations. This was shown by the Taliban's impressive use of mobility, speed, and logistics, as well as efficient contemporary command, control, communications, and intelligence. This level of efficiency had never been seen among Afghan troops and was certainly not to be expected from a comparatively new military formation, even considering that the Taliban had also recruited numerous officers and men of the pre-1992 Afghan army, many from the hard-line, Pashtun nationalist Khalq ("Masses") wing of the Communist Party.[10]

Afghanistan being full of weapons, the Taliban did not really have a supply problem with regard to small arms. Fuel, heavy weapons, and ammunition were another matter. The Taliban depended on Pakistan for delivery of ammunition, particularly for tanks and artillery; some small arms; pickup trucks; and petroleum (both motor and aviation fuel), oil, and lubricants. They also received financial payments. A significant share of the Taliban procurement of arms, munitions, and spare parts was handled by Pakistani private companies, often run by retired military officers. The companies bought considerable quantities from Chinese manufacturers through dealers in Hong Kong and Dubai. The supplies were usually shipped in sealed containers to the Pakistani port of Karachi, whence they were trucked to Afghanistan without normal customs inspection, since this was not required by the two countries' trade agreement, the Afghan Transit Trade Agreement (ATTA).[11] Some were probably paid for through financial assistance to the Taliban from private or state supporters in the Arabian Peninsula through the use of such Islamic charities as the

Al-Rashid Trust (since accused of smuggling weapons and supplies disguised as humanitarian aid to the Taliban).[12] The Taliban were funded partly from contributions from abroad, typically from supporters in the Arab Afghan movement, and partly from taxes, in particular deriving from narcotics production in Afghanistan.[13]

Many Pakistanis, too, profited from business connections with the Taliban. Taliban leaders soon developed relations with a number of Pakistani businessmen close to Asif Ali Zardari, the husband of Pakistani Prime Minister Benazir Bhutto, who in turn were given highly lucrative permits for fuel deliveries from Pakistan to the Taliban. Pakistan also assisted in the development of necessary infrastructure in Taliban-controlled Afghanistan. (For instance, Pakistan Telecom set up a microwave telephone network in Kandahar that became part of the Pakistani telephone grid. Kandahar received the same prefix (081) as that for Quetta, so a call to Kandahar from Pakistan was a local call.[14]

In the early years of the movement, the Taliban also received considerable material and financial support from Saudi Arabia. By then, every major Taliban offensive seemed to be preceded by a visit from Prince Turki ibn Faisal al-Saud, head of the Saudi General Intelligence Agency (*Istakhbarah al-Amah,* or simply *Istakhbarat)*, and his staff. Prince Turki had also played a major role in organising the mujahidin front against the Soviets during that war. However, in the opinion of some analysts, Saudi intelligence depended too much on the Pakistani ISI for information on what was happening in Afghanistan. In September 1998, the uncompromising Taliban leader Mullah Omar insulted Prince Turki and the Saudi royal family. Saudi Arabia then ceased supporting the Taliban, although the diplomatic recognition pushed through by Pakistan in 1997 was not withdrawn. Significantly enough, from October 1998 the Taliban, who previously had generally been able to seize the initiative in any military offensive, began to lose ground to a Northern Alliance offensive that managed to maintain its momentum until the summer of 1999.[15]

Mullah Omar Insults Prince Turki

Several stories purport to explain exactly how and why the Taliban broke with Saudi Arabia in September 1998. According to one, while Prince Turki was lecturing Mullah Omar about his lack of gratitude to his Saudi benefactors, Mullah Omar reportedly responded by grabbing a water jug, then emptying it over himself. Then he said: "I nearly lost my temper. Now I am calm. I will ask you a question and then you can leave. How long has the royalty of Saudi Arabia been the hired help of the Americans?"[16] Another tale says that Turki met with Mullah Omar together with Salman al-Umari, the Saudi chargé d'affaires for Kabul, normally based in Pakistan. Turki, frustrated by Mullah Omar's lack of understanding of international affairs, curtly told Mullah Omar that the Taliban were wasting his time. Salman al-Umari then accused the Taliban of being ungrateful for the Saudi support and threatened them with dire consequences unless they surrendered Usamah bin Ladin to the United States. Mullah Omar responded by demanding that Salman al-Umari immediately leave the country, in effect expelling the Saudi diplomat.[17]

As for the United States, the Clinton administration at first rushed to support the Taliban. Hours after the Taliban advanced into Kabul in September 1996, a state department spokesman concluded that the United States could see "nothing objectionable" in the harsh Taliban version of Islamic law already imposed in the areas under their control. Two months later, then assistant secretary of state for South Asian affairs, Robin L. Raphel, insisted that the Taliban had to be "acknowledged" as an "indigenous" movement—despite the widespread knowledge among Pakistan-based Western diplomats that the ISI had been instrumental in forming and supporting the movement.[4] As late as in 1997, the United States signalled that it would accept any Taliban-appointed diplomat to

Afghanistan's mission in Washington.[19] U.S. policy then saw the
Taliban occupation of Afghanistan as a means primarily to (1) create a buffer state in Afghanistan to prevent Russian access to the
former Soviet oil and gas resources in Central Asia and to isolate
Iran, (2) restore order and evict Usamah bin Ladin and other foreign terrorists, and (3) allow the American oil company Unocal, its
Saudi associate Delta Oil, and apparently loyal U.S. ally Pakistan
overland access to what was believed to be the rich financial
opportunities of the former Soviet Central Asian republics. There
was also some hope that the Taliban would bring an end to the
opium trade out of Afghanistan, and—most unrealistically of all—
pave the way for the return of the former king, Zahir Shah.

There is no real evidence that the United States actually supported the Taliban with weapons or funding; however, officials in
the CIA, and probably elsewhere, were almost certainly informed
about Pakistan's support of the Taliban and chose to regard this as
beneficial to the interests of the United States. As for Unocal, the
firm often developed its policy in cooperation with the U.S.
Embassy in Islamabad, which also frequently hosted functions and
meetings on behalf of the oil company.[20] By 1996, senior officers
from both the State Department and the CIA were dispatched regularly to meet with Taliban leaders both inside and outside
Afghanistan.[21] The United States can be said to have offered political support to the Taliban at this time, albeit in a vague and ill-considered manner, but this was more due to U.S. support of Pakistan
than any properly defined policy toward Afghanistan.

The Taliban movement was hostile to what it regarded as the
"wicked and corrupt" religious beliefs of Shia Iran in the same way
that it was opposed to Shia beliefs among Afghanistan's
minorities.[22] The movement was also known to provide bases for
members of various small Iranian Sunni opposition groups (such as
the *Ahl-e Sunnah W'al Jamaat*, or People of the Beaten Path and
Society) at Herat.[23] However, for all their indignant rhetoric, the
Taliban leaders no doubt realised that their military strength was
insufficient to confront Iranian military forces directly.

The Taliban military chain of command was vague and ill

defined. The top decision-making body was the Supreme Shura in Kandahar, headed by Mullah Omar and made up of 10 members dominated by his original friends and cofounders of the movement. There were also other, lower shuras that reported to the Kandahar shura: those in Kabul and the military. The Kabul shura was fundamentally a cabinet of acting ministers in the capital. It dealt mostly with day-to-day problems and local military and political activities; all important decisions were made in Kandahar. The military shura, another loose body of senior Taliban officials, was technically in charge of military affairs. However, Mullah Omar remained head of the Taliban armed forces, and the military shura accordingly seemed to limit itself to planning strategy and in some cases the implementation of tactical decisions. It had no strategic decision-making powers, and all decisions on military strategy, appointments of key commanders, and allocation of funds were made by Mullah Omar. Under Mullah Omar, there was a chief of the general staff and chiefs of staff for the army and air force, respectively.[24] Military operations were supposed to be directed by the minister of defence, Mullah Obaidullah, or the military chief of staff, Mullah Muhammad Hassan. At task force level, the chief of army staff, Mullah Rahmatullah Akhund, was supposedly in command of ground operations, while the air force chief of staff, General Muhammad Gailani, was responsible for air operations. However, it seems that ground operations remained in the hands of various local task force commanders, several of whom were also members of the Taliban government. Two key commanders in 1998 were, for instance, Mullah Khairullah Khairkhwa, minister of internal affairs, and Mullah Amir Khan Mutaqi, former minister for information and culture. Key local commanders such as these were probably directly subordinated to Mullah Omar.[25]

The Taliban ran an intelligence service, the *Istakhbarat* (named after, and no doubt at first assisted by, the Saudi intelligence service). From 1998 on it was headed by Taliban Minister of Security Qari Ahmadullah, a former Taliban interior minister.[26] He was killed in a bombing raid in eastern Afghanistan in late December 2001.[27]

For all its harsh policies, the Taliban movement never

engaged in terrorist activities against neighbouring states, although the movement at times during its offensives indulged in what can only be called terrorist activities aimed at its Afghan enemies. Among these were the torture, castration, and killing of former President Sayyid Muhammad Najibullah in 1996, followed by the public display of his corpse, and the massacres of an estimated 6,000 to 8,000 civilians in Mazar-e-Sharif, Maimana, and Shiberghan in 1998. Although these acts of terrorism were ordered by the Taliban leadership, this does not exonerate individual Taliban soldiers from the acts they committed.[28] However, neither the Taliban nor any other indigenous Afghan organisation was known to participate in international terrorism.[29] Instead of terrorism, Afghans typically practised irregular warfare, preferably against each other. All the same, the collapse of the Afghan state and the Taliban policy of protecting foreign Islamic extremist groups posed a serious threat to regional stability. These foreign extremists included Usamah bin Ladin and the Arab Afghans, the Islamic Movement of Uzbekistan (IMU; see Appendix 11), the Chechen Wahhabis (see Appendix 12); and elements of the Uighur East Turkestan movement (see Appendix 13). The Taliban also recognised the separatist government in the Russian republic of Chechnya in January 2000, an act that caused the lasting enmity of Russia.[30]

The Taliban forces varied widely in training and experience. Some had considerable military experience, and many men had received military training in Pakistan, around Kabul, or in other quiet areas of Afghanistan. Others, however, especially some of the recent recruits from Pakistan, had received virtually no training and were frequently trucked straight to the front to take part in combat operations.[31] Most Taliban soldiers received regular salaries. Among those who did were the professional soldiers from the former Soviet armed forces, serving as gunners, tank crew, mechanics, and aircraft pilots. Although the majority of the professionals were Pashtuns, they were seldom as religiously motivated as other Taliban soldiers, in particular the volunteers from Pakistan.[32]

The Taliban Army

The Taliban military remained organised into temporary task forces under various local commanders in most cases. A few attempts had been made to reorganise the Taliban into a modern kind of army; however, the only known results of these attempts were the creation, on paper at least, of an army corps based in Kabul (commanded by Mullah Muhammad Fazl) and an independent armoured brigade, known as Armoured Force No. 4, under Mullah Muhammad Zahir. In addition, there were at least four largely independent commands known as army divisions, headed by members of the military shura.[33]

The most important Taliban army bases were in Kabul, Herat, and Kondoz. Smaller Taliban garrisons existed in other cities that formerly had been Afghan Army corps headquarters, specifically Kandahar and Jalalabad. There were also Taliban bases in several occupied northern cities, among them Mazar-e-Sharif, Shiberghan, and Maimana.[34]

Taliban soldiers were generally dressed in their usual civilian clothes, although there was a movement to adopt the Afghan or Pakistani version of Wahhabi dress as military uniform: a white shalwar kameez (long shirt and baggy trousers, the Pakistani national dress), a white or black turban, a clipped moustache, and an untrimmed beard. This trend was particularly conspicuous among the Pakistani volunteers to the Taliban. Taliban units also flew black and white flags.[35]

The Taliban used fast-moving fleets of small Japanese pickup trucks, each carrying about eight men. The trucks, usually double-cab Toyotas or Datsuns, were mounted with machine guns, automatic cannons, or multiple rocket launchers (MRLs), apparently inspired by a practice that grew out of the Somalian clan wars in the years before the Taliban rose to power (see Appendix 7).

Large numbers of new pickup trucks reached the Taliban from across the Pakistani border in 1995.[36] The earliest may have been flown into Kandahar in January and February 1995, when Pakistani extremist leader Fazlur Rahman organised the initial bustard-hunting trips for Gulf Arab princes and in the process established the first direct contacts between the Taliban and their Arab sponsors. Dozens of luxury jeeps were flown in on huge transport planes to be used while hunting, and many of these remained as gifts from the Arabs for their Taliban hosts.[37] The pickup trucks were soon equipped with truck-mounted ZU-2 antiaircraft cannon and BM-21 MRLs. Used for fast transportation and fire support by the Taliban company-sized units of 100 or 200 men in what can only be described as blitzkrieg tactics, the outfitted trucks proved a highly effective weapon, one hitherto almost unknown in Afghanistan.[38]

Personal and Support Weapon Inventory[39]
7.62mm AKMS assault rifles
7.62mm Type 56/56-1 assault rifles
7.62mm RPD/RPK machine guns
7.62mm PK general-purpose machine guns
RPG-7/Type 63 rocket launchers
12.7mm DShK-38 heavy machine guns
23mm ZU-23-2 (usually truck-mounted) automatic cannons
23mm ZSU-23-2 (usually truck-mounted) automatic cannons
30mm AGS-17 automatic grenade launchers
122mm BM-21 MRLs
75mm Type 76 recoilless rifles
82mm Type 65 recoilless rifles

As early as in January 1995, Afghan former Khalq communist military officers fulfilled the technical functions needed by the Taliban to operate armoured units.[40] The Taliban were estimated to field some 650 main battle tanks and armoured fighting vehicles (AFVs) of various types, an estimated 250 of which had been captured from the Northern Alliance during the summer and autumn offensives of 1998. Not all were expected to be serviceable, although the Taliban did have functional repair shops in the Kabul area. Most armoured elements were attached as needed to infantry task forces, apparently without a fixed structure. Some of these elements, as well as several others, were reportedly organised into an armoured brigade (or brigade equivalent) based in Kabul and tentatively identified as the Armoured Force No. 4. This unit never operated as an independent unit and indeed appears to have been a mere paper unit. The Taliban had, however, on at least one occasion, used armoured elements in an independent role, as distinct from the more common mobile artillery or fire-support. In July 1998, they used an armoured column of T-54/55 and T-62 tanks in a breakthrough on one flank of a twin-pronged advance on Maimana in northwestern Afghanistan.[41]

Armoured Vehicle Inventory[42]
T-62 tanks
T-54/55 tanks
BMP-1/2 AFVs
BTR-60PB AFVs
BTR-70 AFVs
BRDM-2 AFVs

Artillery was the most effective of the Taliban specialised arms. As early as in January 1995, former Khalqi communist military officers had enlisted as Taliban artillery officers.[43] The artillery consisted of several hundred artillery pieces, as well as truck-mounted MRLs. Artillery batteries were attached to infantry task forces as required.[44]

Artillery Inventory[45]
76mm GP M1966 mountain guns
152mm M-1 (towed) howitzers
152mm D-1 (towed) howitzers
122mm D-30 (towed) guns
100mm M1944 (towed) antitank guns
100mm M1955 (towed) antitank guns
220mm 9P140 Uragan MRLs
140mm BM-14-16 MRLs

Artillery Inventory cont.

122mm BM-21 MRLs
107mm Type 63 MRLs
120mm mortars
82mm mortars

Air defence weapon systems were typically deployed wherever infantry groups were operating or, alternatively, based on mountain heights.[46] It was estimated that the Taliban had about 300 to 500 air defence weapons, most of them cannons.[47] The Taliban also used several types of old Soviet surface-to-air missiles (SAMs); exactly which types and how many was unknown to Western observers. Since all identified or suspected SAM sites were soon destroyed in the U.S.-led air raids, it is impossible to estimate the true numbers and state of the Taliban air defence establishment. Some reports, for instance, suggested that the Taliban used SA-2, SA-3, SA-7, and SA-14 missiles.[48] Later it was alleged that the Taliban only had three rather obsolete SA-3 missile sites.[49] However, they also probably had small numbers of U.S.-made FIM-92A SAMs.[50]

Air Defence Inventory[51]

100mm KS-19 antiaircraft guns
85mm KS-12 antiaircraft guns with Fire Can radar
57mm S-60 antiaircraft guns
23mm ZSU-23-4 self-propelled antiaircraft guns
23mm (twin) ZU-23-2 automatic cannons
14.5mm ZPU-1/2/4 heavy machine guns
12.7mm DShK-38 heavy machine guns
SA-3 Goa SAM missile batteries
SA-7 Grail manportable SAMs
SA-13 Gopher SAM batteries
FIM-92A Stinger manportable SAMs

Although the Taliban captured a few Soviet-made SS-1B Scud surface-to-surface missiles in 1998, none were believed to be operational in late 2001. The Taliban also had access to some Frog-7 (Lunar) missiles,[52] although their number remains unknown to Western observers. Whatever the Taliban had in the form of surface-to-surface missiles, whether operational or not, were destroyed in the U.S.-led air raids.

The Taliban Air Force

The strength and state of the Taliban air force in late 2001 was also largely unknown to Western observers. Since whatever they had—whether permanently grounded or operational—was soon destroyed in the U.S.-led air raids, no reliable estimate could ever be made.

By mid-2000, the Taliban were estimated to have about fifteen operational combat aircraft: about ten Su-22 Fitter ground attack aircraft and about five MiG-21 Fishbed fighters.[53] However, U.S. and European analysts had widely divergent opinions on the number of operational Taliban aircraft. The Europeans generally suggested lower numbers than their U.S. counterparts. Some Pentagon sources claimed that the Taliban had a far more impressive air capability, at times bordering on the ridiculous (i.e., some thirty MiG-23 Flogger fighter-bombers and as many as eighty MiG-21 fighters).[54] A more serious U.S. analysis assumed a total of about thirty operational Su-22 ground attack aircraft and MiG-21 fighters, and even this estimate was later revised to no more than twenty operational combat aircraft.[55] It appears that the lower estimates were more correct. An Asian analyst in early October 2001 claimed that the Taliban indeed had no more than six operational MiG-19 (by which the source perhaps meant Su-22) and MiG-21 fighters.[56]

The Taliban air force also included a small but significant helicopter contingent consisting of about six Mi-8/17 Hip utility helicopters and about five Mi-35 Hind attack helicopters. For transportation duties, the Taliban also had a fleet of various transports, primarily Soviet-made Antonovs.[57]

Most of the few remaining pilots were veterans of the former communist government. The lack of organisation and trained pilots in the Taliban air force prevented the mounting of serious attacks on opposition airbases. Yet, the Taliban did possess air superiority as long as they only faced the Northern Alliance. The Pakistani air force also reportedly supported the Taliban forces, at least in 1998 and 1999, and possibly later as well. There was some evidence that Pakistani personnel were involved in maintenance and airport logistics. The Taliban air force usually supported ground operations only with high-altitude bombing, and typically by only one or two aircraft per sortie. Although the Taliban allegedly used attack helicopters in a ground attack role in northern Takhar Province on 21 August 1999 and perhaps later, helicopters were mainly used for transportation and evacuation of supplies and occasionally troops. However, for transport purposes, including the airlifting of troops and the supply of occupied territory in the north, the various Antonov transports were far more important. The Taliban also controlled the Ariana commercial airline. When the UN Security Council Resolution 1267, implemented in November 1999, imposed economic sanctions on the Taliban and forbade Ariana from conducting international flights, the Taliban simply incorporated the Ariana fleet into its air force.[58]

Taliban Air Force Inventory[59]

Type	Number
Role	
Sukhoi Su-22 Fitter	10
Ground Attack	
MiG-21 Fishbed	5
Fighter	
Mil Mi-35 Hind	5
Attack Helicopter	
Mil Mi-8/17 Hip	6
Utility Helicopter	
Aero L-39C Albatros	5
Trainer	
Antonov An-12 Cub	6
Transport	
Antonov An-26 Curl	25

Taliban Air Force Inventory cont.

Transport	
Antonov An-24 Coke/An-32 Cline	12
Transport	
Ilyushin Il-18 Coot	1
Transport	
Yakovlev Yak- 40 Codling	1
Transport	
Boeing 727A/B	2
Transport (Ariana)	
Tupolev Tu-154 Careless	1
Transport (Ariana)	
Antonov An-24 Coke	5
Transport (Ariana)	
De Havilland DHC-6 Twin Otter	1
Transport (Ariana)	

Total   85 (estimated)

Taliban air force bases:[60]
Kabul Khwaja Rawash International Airport
Kandahar
Shiberghan
Shindand
Jalalabad

The Taliban Religious Police

The Taliban maintained a religious police, consisting of several hundred men, along the lines of the Saudi religious police. In Saudi Arabia, the religious police (*mutawiyyin*) form the executive arm of the Committees for Promotion of Virtue and Prevention of Vice. The Taliban counterpart was the executive arm of a fundamentally identical organisation, the Ministry for the Promotion of Virtue and Prevention of Vice (*Amr bi'l-Maruf wa Nahi an al-Munkar*, known in the Persian language Dari as *Amr Bil Maruf wa Nai Az Munkar*).

The duty of the religious police, armed with batons as well as military weapons, was to harass members of the public who failed to stop working or shopping at prayer time, compel shops to close at prayer times, destroy objects deemed un-Islamic, and enforce the religious and social edicts, particularly dress codes. The religious police did not serve in combat roles or as military police.[61]

THE ARAB AFGHAN MOVEMENT AND AL-QAIDA

The Arab Afghan Movement and Al-Qaida, September 2001

Objective: Opposition on a global scale to perceived threats to the movement's interpretation of Islam, which among its rank and file expressed itself as a wish to fight apostates and infidels as a way of life.

Means: Guerrilla warfare and terrorism, financed by narcotics trafficking and donations from supporters.

Allies: The Taliban movement.

Sponsors: Like-minded religious groups in various countries.

Proxies: United Tajik Opposition (UTO) warlords such as Mirzo Zioev and his erstwhile subordinate, Juma-boi Namangani Khojiev, an ethnic Uzbek and a leader of the IMU.

Armed forces: At most an estimated 2,000 armed followers in Afghanistan and another 2,000 (some claim 5,000) in Tajikistan (probably far fewer on both accounts), and many of the Pakistani volunteers in the Taliban.

The actual fighting strength of the Arab Afghan movement

was always very difficult to estimate, especially after the U.S.-led War on Terror drove the movement underground. In Central Asia, the strength of the movement was, at the very most, an estimated 2,000 armed followers in Afghanistan (based around Kabul and Jalalabad)[62] and another 2,000 (5,000 claimed) in Tajikistan.[63] Others, however, suggest far lower numbers (1,200 in Afghanistan and 600 in Tajikistan, respectively).[64] The number of fighters was probably far less in both counts, since the stated numbers, even if correct, probably included dependents. In actual combat the number of fighters was at times augmented by Pakistani recruits in the Taliban. The ethnic composition of the movement was also hard to determine. The number of Arabs seems to have been no more than from 500 to 1,500, again tending to the lower rather than higher figure. In addition to Arabs from countries such as Egypt, Yemen, Algeria, Tunisia, Morocco, and Syria, this figure included Muslims from Sudan, Pakistan, Bangladesh, the former Soviet Central Asian republics, Chinese Xinjiang, and Chechnya. There were also some Muslims from Indonesia, the Philippines, and Burma.[65] It should be noted, however, that some of the Pakistanis who made up the more recent recruits to the Taliban could be expected to join the Arab Afghans in any military venture.[66] Of 113 foreign prisoners captured by the Northern Alliance, all but four were Pakistanis, of which less than a third were ethnic Pashtuns. The others came from Yemen, Britain, and China. There were no Arabs: they often committed suicide rather than allowing themselves to be captured, according to Northern Alliance commanders (a common method was, apparently, to put their heads together and set off hand grenades). Furthermore, only somewhat less than half professed to have been religious students. The rest claimed various occupational backgrounds including, for slightly less than a tenth, the professional fields. The average age was in the mid-20s. Some asserted that they had fought in Kashmir and Tajikistan before they went to Afghanistan. Few had more than a rudimentary primary education, and the overwhelming majority did not understand Arabic, thus depending on their teachers to interpret the Koran. Several had been told by their mullahs in

Pakistan and Kabul that the Tajiks of the Northern Alliance, against whom they were sent to fight, were not really Muslims. Some claimed they had been told that Russians still occupied northern Afghanistan. None of these prisoners had apparently fought in the war against the Soviet Union, which is unsurprising due to their generally young age.[67]

The majority of the fighters in the Central Asian region, except for the Afghan-based Taliban (who were not part of the Arab Afghan movement, although they supported it), apparently belonged to the IMU. The movement included many Arabs; an estimated 500 to 600 formed part of Usamah bin Ladin's 055 Brigade, which was deployed as part of the Taliban forces in Afghanistan.[68] One analysis suggests that of 1,200 IMU fighters, about 600 to 700 were Uzbeks from the Ferghana Valley and about 500 were Tajiks who earlier had formed part of the UTO during the civil war in Tajikistan but never accepted the peace process. The rest included several dozen Arabs sent by Usamah bin Ladin, several dozens of Pakistanis, and a handful of Chechens.[69]

By early 2002, most of the surviving Arab Afghans had probably fled Afghanistan. Those who wished to continue the struggle may well have gone to Kashmir,[70] while many no doubt went into hiding in Pakistan or the Middle East, perhaps aided by disaffected elements in the ISI, a long-time sponsor of the Arab Afghan movement.

The Arab Afghans were far too nebulous in ethnic and organisational composition to have a formal order of battle. They were typically deployed where needed. Because of their fanaticism and the fact that they had little hope of mercy if captured, the Arab Afghans by late 2001 and early 2002 had a reputation for high morale and were expected to fight to the death when cornered.

The only true units of the Arab Afghans that apparently held some form of organisational continuity was Usamah bin Ladin's personal bodyguard, which appears to have been small but well-armed, and the 055 Brigade, which fought as part of the Taliban army.

THE NORTHERN ALLIANCE

The Northern Alliance, September 2001
Objective: Resistance to the Pashtun-dominated Taliban movement and, eventually, introduction of a non-Pashtun-dominated government.

Allies: None.

Sponsors: Iran, Russia, and to some extent Tajikistan, Uzbekistan, and India.

Proxies: None.

Population: Tajiks are estimated to comprise about 25 percent of the total population of Afghanistan (which may be as high as 26.8 million) while Hazara and Uzbeks together may form roughly another 25 percent.[71]
Armed forces: Estimated 12,000 to 15,000, mainly Tajiks from *Jamiat-e Islami;* 5,000 mostly Shia Hazara belonging to *Hezb-e Wahdat;* and 2,000 Uzbeks under Dostum.[72]

The Northern Alliance, also known as the United Front (short for the United Islamic and National Front for the Salvation of Afghanistan), was set up on 13 June 1997. Although formally led by the then president of Afghanistan Burhanuddin Rabbani, the alliance was under the military control of its then defence minister, the late Ahmad Shah Masud.[73] The alliance was the successor to the Supreme Council for the Defence of the Motherland, set up on 10 October 1996.[74] Since 1998, the alliance effectively consisted of Rabbani's *Jamiat-e Islami Afghanistan* (Islamic Society of Afghanistan). The other two main factions of the Northern alliance, Abdul Rashid Dostum's *Jombesh-e Milli Islami* (National Islamic Movement) and the Shia umbrella organisation *Hezb-e Wahdat-e Islami-ye Afghanistan* (Islamic Unity Party of Afghanistan), created in June 1990 by the Iran-based Shia groups, suffered significant losses and were temporarily shattered by the Taliban advances in the summer and autumn of 1998. The far smaller Shia faction, the *Harakat-e Islami-ye Afghanistan* (Islamic Movement of Afghanistan), was by then based in Quetta, Pakistan. The Hezb-e Wahdat eventually regrouped to conduct guerrilla operations in and near the central provinces of Bamian and Samangan, as did the Harakat-e Islami. Jombesh-e Milli leader Abdul Rashid Dostum returned to the region in December 1999, and Dostum met Masud on 19 March 2000 to discuss renewed cooperation; however, for a long while it remained unknown to outsiders exactly how much Dostum subsequently reorganised his forces.[75]

The Northern Alliance received military support from Iran, Russia, and to some extent Tajikistan (which also provided a supply route for the military support from Iran and Russia, including, apparently, the use of the Kulob air base and a helicopter base close to Tajikistan's capital Dushanbe). Iranian and Russian military supplies, including ammunition and T54/55 tanks and truck-mounted 122mm MRLs, arrived in significant amounts by late 2000 and in the first half of 2001. By then, Masud had also purchased a further five secondhand Mi-17 Hip H medium-lift helicopters, in addition to the two he already had.[76] From September 2001 on, Russia increased aid to the Northern Alliance at least fourfold.[77] Yet during the autumn 2001 war, if not before, Iran was clearly the major contributor of munitions. These consisted chiefly of fuel, antipersonnel mines, machine guns, small-arms and artillery ammunition, and some AFVs. Some support also apparently derived from India in the form of aircraft parts, ground radar, and financial assistance, if nothing else. Uzbekistan, too, provided supplies and sanctuary, at least to Dostum's Uzbeks. Dostum is also known to have received financial support from Turkey. Rumours of military support from Israel have never been verified.[78] There is some evidence that Russian military advisors were assisting the Tajik forces before the second half of 2001.[79] Whether such men were on active service or mercenaries contracted by Masud remains unknown to most outside observers. Iran also provided military training to the Northern

Alliance through small teams of approximately five to eight military instructors who would arrive periodically from Iran to conduct courses at a camp for junior officers near Farkhar in Takhar Province in northern Afghanistan. An estimated 80 to 150 men received instruction at any given time.[80] There is no evidence to suggest that any foreign support ceased following the fall of the Taliban government. Instead, Russia and probably Iran stepped up military supplies, including T-55 tanks, SAMs, artillery, mortars, rifles, and ammunition.[81]

The Tajik forces were led by a general staff under first Masud, then Muhammad Fahim Khan, consisting of a small group of senior commanders. At the tactical level, operations were led by individual front commanders, who usually enjoyed considerable autonomy. Of these, the most senior was believed to be Gen. Bismillah Khan, formerly commander of the forces in the Shomali-Kabul theatre.[82]

The Tajik forces of the Northern Alliance commanded by the late Masud were without doubt the most experienced soldiers in Afghanistan, with men and commanders who had been at war continually for two decades. Morale was high, as many younger and less experienced recruits followed in the footsteps of their fathers and uncles. Most of these Tajiks were from the Panjshir Valley as well as adjacent valleys of the Hindu Kush, and from the Shomali region north of Kabul. Local troops under slightly less reliable local leaders, who also acknowledged Masud as their commander, came from Badakhshan Province. The commanders from the Uzbek, Hazara, and other ethnic groups in northern Afghanistan were typically more autonomous.[83]

The forces of the Northern Alliance were experienced, but they were generally better in small-unit tactics than in company- and battalion-level operations. Training took place in the Northern Alliance core territories, primarily the Panjshir Valley and southern Badakhshan. The Northern Alliance also suffered from shortcomings in command and control capability.[84] As noted, there is some evidence that Russian military advisors were assisting the Tajik forces before the second half of 2001.[85]

President Rabbani was excluded from the new interim government formed on 4 December 2001, and all key ministries went to
leaders from the Northern Alliance. Muhammad Fahim Khan was
confirmed as minister of defence, Yunus Qanuni as interior minister, and Abdullah Abdullah as foreign minister.[86] Although the
Northern Alliance *per se* no longer plays an active role in Afghan
politics since the fall of the Taliban government, the term remains
useful because it still defines those Afghan forces primarily made
up of minorities opposed to Pashtun domination.

The Northern Alliance Army
The Northern Alliance forces remained loosely organised; the con-
tinual war precluded any more formal organisation. The basic formation
was a unit of company or half-company strength, generally referred to as
a *kandak* (battalion) and formed locally from regions such as Panjshir,
Andarab, and Farkhar. Some were formally attached to a brigade, for
instance the Guards Brigade battalions headquartered in Panjshir, while
others were independent units. In any case, most operated detached from
their higher formations as determined by the situation. Armor and
artillery support were attached to units or task forces as required.[87]
The organisation can be summarised as follows:

Guards Brigade, Panjshir Valley
Independent brigade, Andarab
Independent brigade, South Badakhshan
Provincial division, Takhar
Provincial division, Badakhshan
Independent guerrilla groups (some still operating under
    their earlier divisional designations)

Note: The provincial divisions based in Takhar and
Badakhshan, respectively, were umbrella formations consisting of
local former mujahidin forces under local commanders who exer-
cised considerable autonomy.[88]

The Northern Alliance operated out of bases primarily in the

Panjshir Valley (Dalansang, Anawa, and Dasht-e-Parakh) and the Andarab Valley (Banu and Deh Sala). Other bases included Khowst-e Fering and Bahrak, southern Badakhshan. Formerly, the Northern Alliance also retained bases in Taloqan and on the Shomali Plain (Charikar and Bagram). Northern Alliance units were, however, active in many other locations, including in ostensibly Taliban-controlled provinces. For instance, Wahdat ground forces also remained in Bamian and Samangan provinces. They were mainly equipped with small arms and infantry support weapons, as well as a limited number of armour, artillery, and transport vehicles (KamAZ heavy-duty trucks and light pickup trucks) recaptured from the Taliban. Northern Alliance guerrillas also operated in the northwestern provinces of Faryab and Sar-e-Pol.[89]

Regular Northern Alliance units, in particular the Tajiks, wore camouflage uniforms of Russian manufacture. Most other troops used their daily dress, as they had done in the Soviet Afghan war.

Most of the personal weapons and support weapons of the Northern Alliance were of Soviet/Russian or Chinese make, so much remained from the Soviet Afghan war.

Personal and Support Weapon Inventory[90]
7.62mm AKM/S assault rifles
7.62mm Type 56/56-2 assault rifles
5.45mm AK-74 assault rifles
7.62mm SVD snipers rifles
7.62mm RPK/RPD machine guns
7.62mm PK general-purpose machine guns
12.7mm DShK heavy machine guns
75mm Type 76 recoilless rifles
82mm Type 65 recoilless rifles
14.5mm ZPU-1/2 heavy machine guns
23mm ZU-23-2 (truck-mounted antiaircraft guns, used as antipersonnel weapons)
30mm AGS-17 automatic grenade launchers
RPG-7 rocket launchers
Type 69 rocket launchers

The Northern Alliance was estimated to field no more than about 60 to 70 main battle tanks and AFVs. Both Dostum and the Hizb-e Wahdat lost all their armour in the Taliban offensives in the summer and autumn of 1998.[91]

Armoured Vehicle Inventory[92]

T-62 tanks
T-54/55 tanks
BMP-1/2 AFVs
BTR-60PB/Pu AFVs
BTR-70 AFVs
BRDM-2 AFVs

While most artillery of larger calibres, such as the 152mm D-1 howitzers, remained in the Panjshir Valley, others, particularly the MRLS and 122mm D-30 guns, were extensively used on all fronts. Both Dostum and the Hizb-e Wahdat lost all their artillery in the Taliban offensives in the summer and autumn of 1998.[93]

Artillery Inventory[94]

152mm D-1 (towed) howitzers
122mm M30/D-30 (towed) howitzers
100mm M1944 (towed) antitank guns
100mm M1955 (towed) antitank guns
76mm M1966 mountain guns
107mm Type-63-1 MRLs
122mm BM-21/BM-21V Grad MRLs
140mm BM-14-16 MRLs
220mm 9P140 Uragan MRLs
120mm mortars
82mm mortars

Air defence weapon systems were typically deployed wherever infantry groups were operating, or alternatively based on mountain heights. Small numbers of Stinger SAMs were also in the theatre after the Soviet Afghan war.[95]

Air Defence Inventory[96]
23mm ZSU-23-4 self-propelled antiaircraft gun (one only)
23mm ZU-23-2 (truck-mounted) automatic cannons
14.5mm ZP-1/2 heavy machine guns
12.7mm DShK-38 heavy machine guns
SA-7 Grail manportable SAMs
SA-13 Gopher SAM batteries
FIM-92A Stinger SAMs (small numbers)

The Northern Alliance also retained a small number of old Soviet surface-to-surface missiles.

Surface-to-Surface Missile Inventory[97]
Frog-7 (Lunar) surface-to-surface missiles, with ZIL-135 transporters (the number of remaining missiles was estimated at fewer than 10)
SS-1B Scud-B (estimated 25 to 30 missiles with two to four MAZ-543 TEL vehicles, based in Panjshir but of uncertain operational readiness)

The air assets of the Northern Alliance remained vital as a means to supply and thereby sustain military operations. The number and identity of the aircraft of the Northern Alliance were usually difficult to determine because several of their transports and helicopters appeared to be only occasionally made available, or perhaps on loan from, Russia, Iran, and, according to some reports, India.[98] From early 1997 on, most Northern Alliance aircraft were based at Kulob Air Base, Tajikistan, the base also used by the Russian combat aircraft that were from time to time made available to the alliance. By early 1999, air assets at Kulob were reportedly increased. The Northern Alliance was also offered 20 (ex-Iraqi) MiG-21 fighters by Iran in late 1997, although there is no evidence that these were actually delivered. The Hizb-e Wahdat was known to have had a single An-32 transport and a single Fokker F-27, both of which were believed to be in Iran.[99]

The aircraft provided by Russia were flown by Russian pilots. Whether these were Russian servicemen, mercenaries, or both remains unknown to most outsiders. A Russian aircrew was captured early on when delivering arms to Afghanistan and subsequently released against payment of ransom. Kulob-based Russian aircraft were also known to have taken part in air raids against the Taliban early in the war;[100] so had Uzbekistani Air Force ground-attack aircraft (Sukhoi Su-24 Fencers). The latter reportedly attacked Taliban positions near the border town of Heiratan on 6 June 2000.[101]

Northern Alliance Aircraft Inventory[102]

Type Number		Role
Mil Mi-35 Hind	2	Attack Helicopter
Mil Mi-8 Hip	1	Utility Helicopter
Mil Mi-17 Hip H	8	Utility Helicopter
Antonov An-12 Cub	1	Transport
Antonov An-32 Cline	6	Transport (one believed grounded in Iran)
Fokker F-27 Friendship	1	Transport (believed grounded in Iran)
Total	17	possibly operational, at least two grounded (estimated)

In addition, the following aircraft were reportedly on loan from, or at least occasionally made available by, Russia:

*Sukhoi Su-22 Fitter	12	Ground Attack
*MiG-21 Fishbed	18	Fighter
*Mil Mi-24 Hind	4	Attack Helicopter
*Antonov An-24 Coke	3	Transport (possibly on loan)

Northern Alliance Aircraft Inventory cont.
Northern Alliance air bases:
Kulob Air Base, Tajikistan. Formerly the Northern Alliance used air bases at Bagram, Feyzabad (Badakhshan Province, only an airstrip), and Khwaja Ghar (Takhar Province) and an airstrip outside Taloqan. Some observers reported that Masud also was constructing an airstrip at Koran-e-Monjan in southern Badakhshan Province.[103]

End Notes

1. See, for instance, Julie Sirrs, "The Taliban's International Ambitions," *Middle East Quarterly* 8:3 (Summer 2001), 68.

2. Magnus and Naby, *Afghanistan,* 10, 93; CIA, *World Factbook 2001.*

3. Jane's Sentinel: Afghanistan, 30 August 2000; Ahmed Rashid, "The Taliban: Exporting Extremism," *Foreign Affairs,* November/December 1999, 22–35; Anthony Davis, "Struggle for Recognition," *Jane's Defence Weekly,* 4 October 2000, 21; Rashid, *Taliban,* 100.

4. Rashid, *Taliban,* 26–30, 125; Maley, *Fundamentalism Reborn?,* 71, 82.

5. Gohari, *Taliban,* 118.

6. Taliban web sites, *www.taleban.com; www.afghan-ie.com*

7. Maley, *Fundamentalism Reborn?* 45–46, 49, 50.

8. Ibid., 12, note 25.

9. Jane's Sentinel: Afghanistan, 30 August 2000; Ahmed Rashid, "Taliban: Exporting Extremism," 22–35; Rashid, *Taliban,* 100; Davis, "Struggle for Recognition," 21; Anthony Davis, "Foreign Fighters Step Up Activity in Afghan Civil War," *Jane's Intelligence Review* 13:8 (August 2001), 14–17.

10. Anthony Davis, "How the Taliban Became a Military Force," in Maley, *Fundamentalism Reborn,* 39, 43–71, in particular 68–71. Jane's Sentinel: Afghanistan, 30 August 2000; Davis, "Struggle for Recognition," 21; Davis, "Foreign Fighters," 14–17; Rashid, *Taliban,* 49; Rashid, *Jihad,* 174; Human Rights Watch (HRW), *Fueling Afghanistan's War* (HRW: Press Backgrounder, 2001).

11. Support from Pakistan: HRW, *Fueling Afghanistan's War;* Jane's Sentinel: Afghanistan, 17 October 2000; 30 August 2000; Jane's Sentinel: Afghanistan, 28 May 1999; Rashid,

Taliban, 44–45, 72, 183–184; Ahmed Rashid, "Heart of Darkness," *Far Eastern Economic Review,* 5 August 1999, 8–12; Magnus and Naby, *Afghanistan,* 190; Maley, *Fundamentalism Reborn?,* 69.

12. *New York Times,* 25 September 2001.

13. Rashid, *Taliban,* 35, 120, 123–124; Rashid, "Heart of Darkness," 8–12.

14. Ahmed Rashid, "Pakistan and the Taliban," Maley, *Fundamentalism Reborn?,* 72–89, on 84–85.

15. Rashid, *Taliban,* 48, 72, 131, 138–139, 201–202, 227–233, 264, note 16.

16. *Observer* (London), 28 October 2001.

17. Bodansky, *Bin Laden,* 302.

18. Maley, *Fundamentalism Reborn?,* 45–46, 49, 91.

19. Anwar-ul-Haq Ahady, "Saudi Arabia, Iran and the Conflict in Afghanistan," Maley, *Fundamentalism Reborn?,* 134; based on *Washington Post,* 29 May 1997, 29.

20. Maley, *Fundamentalism Reborn?,* 96–97, 99.

21. Ibid., 40.

22. Gohari, *Taliban,* 109–110, 134–135.

23. Rashid, "Heart of Darkness," 8–12; Rashid, "Taliban: Exporting Extremism," 22–35; Rashid, *Taliban,* 203. The term *sunnah,* here translated as "beaten path," signifies the worldwide community of Muslims.

24. Rashid, *Taliban,* 95–104, 220–221.

25. Jane's Sentinel: Afghanistan, 30 August 2000.

26. Jason Burke, "Lies, payoffs, traps are allies' weapons," *Observer* (London), as included in *The Japan Times,* 10 November 2001.

27. *Washington Post,* 3 January 2002. A certain Obeidullah held a press conference in Pakistan in early May 2002, claiming to have been Qari Ahmadullah's deputy. If so, it appears that this deputy, Obeidullah, upon his superior's death assumed command of Taliban intelligence, or what remained of it, unless he was instead that Mullah Haji Obaidullah Akhund who was Taliban minister of defence in 1999 and was responsible for military liaison between the Taliban and ISI—which could explain his relaxed presence in Pakistan. *USA Today,* 6 May 2002, based on Associated Press.

28. Rashid, *Taliban,* 49–50, 73–74.

29. Afghanistan was not on the U.S. list of states sponsoring terrorism, since the United States did not recognise the Taliban government.

30. Jane's Sentinel: Afghanistan, 1 June 2000.

31. Ibid, 30 August 2000.

32. Rashid, *Taliban,* 100.

33. Ibid., 99–101, 221; Jane's Sentinel: Afghanistan, 30 August 2000.
34. Jane's Sentinel: Afghanistan, 30 August 2000.
35. See, for instance, Bergen, *Holy War,* 13.
36. Maley, *Fundamentalism Reborn?,* 60.
37. Rashid, "Pakistan and the Taliban," 76.
38. Maley, *Fundamentalism Reborn?,* 60, 62.
39. Based chiefly but not exclusively on Jane's Sentinel: Afghanistan, 30 August 2000.
40. Maley, *Fundamentalism Reborn?,* 54.
41. Jane's Sentinel: Afghanistan, 30 August 2000.
42. Based chiefly on Jane's Sentinel: Afghanistan, 30 August 2000. Exact numbers are unknown to outside observers and may not even have been known to the Taliban leadership, since local leaders jealously guarded their key assets.
43. Maley, *Fundamentalism Reborn?,* 54.
44. Jane's Sentinel: Afghanistan, 30 August 2000.
45. Based chiefly but not exclusively on Jane's Sentinel: Afghanistan, 30 August 2000. Again, exact numbers are unknown to outside observers and may not even have been known to the Taliban leadership.
46. Jane's Sentinel: Afghanistan, 30 August 2000.
47. *Washington Post,* 10 October 2001.
48. *Washington Times,* 8–14 October 2001 (National Weekly Edition).
49. *Washington Post,* 10 October 2001.
50. See, for instance, Bergen, *Holy War,* 74.
51. Based chiefly but not exclusively on Jane's Sentinel: Afghanistan, 30 August 2000, 19 March 2002. Again exact numbers are unknown.
52. *Washington Times,* 8–14 October 2001 (National Weekly Edition).
53. Jane's Sentinel: Afghanistan, 30 August 2000.
54. *Washington Times,* 8–14 October 2001 (National Weekly Edition).
55. *Washington Post,* 10 October 2001.
56. *Far Eastern Economic Review* (Hong Kong), 7 October 1999.
57. Jane's Sentinel: Afghanistan, 30 August 2000.
58. Ibid.
59. Based primarily on Jane's Sentinel: Afghanistan, 30 August 2000.
60. Jane's Sentinel: Afghanistan, 30 August 2000.
61. Ibid., 2 May 2000; Reeve, *New Jackals,* 230.
62. Rashid, "Heart of Darkness," 8–12.
63. See, for instance, Jane's Sentinel: Kyrgyzstan, 31 October 2000.

64. Ahmed Rashid, "Epicentre of Terror," *Far Eastern Economic Review,* 11 May 2000, 16–18.

65. See Davis, "Foreign Fighters."

66. Fredholm, *Afghanistan and Central Asian Security.*

67. See Sirrs, "Taliban's International Ambitions," 61–71; and Gerecht, "Terrorists' Encyclopedia," 71–85.

68. Jane's Sentinel: Afghanistan, 30 August 2000.

69. Ahmed Rashid, "From Deobandism to Batken: Adventures of an Islamic Heritage," CACI Forum Transcription, 13 April 2000.

70. *Jane's Intelligence Digest,* 31 May 2002.

71. Magnus and Naby, *Afghanistan,* 10, 93; CIA, *World Factbook 2001.*

72. Jane's Sentinel: Afghanistan, 30 August 2000; 2 May 2000; Rashid, *Taliban,* 100.

73. Rashid, *Taliban,* 61.

74. Ibid., 52–53.

75. Jane's Sentinel: Afghanistan, 30 August 2000; 17 October 2000; Magnus and Naby, *Afghanistan,* 149–157, 229. See also Viktor Korgun, "Afghan Factor in Regional Geopolitics," *Central Asia and the Caucasus* 5, 2000, 138–146. The Hezb-e Wahdat could be e-mailed at www.*Wahdat_news@yahoo.com* and occasionally displayed press releases on the web site *www.hazaraonline.f2s.com* Other Hazara web sites included *www.hazara.net* and *www.hazara.com* The Jamiat-e Islami maintained the web sites *www.jamiat.com* and *www.afghangovernment.org*

76. Anthony Davis, "Afghanistan: Prospects for War and Peace in a Shattered Land," *Jane's Intelligence Review* 13:8 (August 2001), 31.

77. *Washington Post,* 3 October 2001, referring to an interview with Ali Ahmad, consul at the Northern Alliance's embassy in Tashkent.

78. Support from Iran: HRW, *Fueling Afghanistan's War;* Jane's Sentinel: Afghanistan, 17 October 2000; 28 May 1999; Korgun, "Afghan Factor," 138–146; Rashid, *Taliban,* 44–45, 53, 70, 72, 76, 200, 203; Gohari, *Taliban,* 154; Magnus and Naby, *Afghanistan,* 190; Rashid, *Jihad,* 221. Support from Russia: HRW, *Fueling Afghanistan's War;* Jane's Sentinel: Afghanistan, 17 October 2000; 28 May 1999; Korgun, "Afghan Factor," 138–146; Rashid, *Taliban,* 44, 53–54, 61, 72, 76, 78; Magnus and Naby, *Afghanistan,* 69. Support from Tajikistan: HRW, *Fueling Afghanistan's War;* Jane's Sentinel: Afghanistan, 17 October 2000; Korgun, "Afghan Factor," 138–146; Rashid, *Taliban,* 53–54, 61, 78, 146. Support from Uzbekistan: HRW, *Fueling Afghanistan's War;* Jane's Sentinel: Afghanistan, 17 October 2000; Rashid, *Taliban,* 53–54, 72; Magnus and Naby, *Afghanistan,* 69, 166, 189. Support from India: Jane's Sentinel: Afghanistan, 17 October 2000; Rashid, *Taliban,* 45. Support from Turkey: Rashid, *Taliban,* 154.

Support from Israel: Jane's Sentinel: Afghanistan, 17 October 2000; Rashid, "Epicentre of Terror," 16–18.

79. Jane's World Insurgency and Terrorism 13, 27 November 2001.
80. HRW, *Fueling Afghanistan's War.*
81. *Economist,* 20 October 2001, 17 November 2001.
82. Jane's Sentinel: Afghanistan, 30 August 2000.
83. Ibid.
84. Ibid.
85. Jane's World Insurgency and Terrorism 13, 27 November 2001.
86. *Economist,* 8 December 2001.
87. Jane's Sentinel: Afghanistan, 30 August 2000.
88. Ibid.
89. Ibid.
90. Based primarily on Jane's Sentinel: Afghanistan, 30 August 2000.
91. Jane's Sentinel: Afghanistan, 30 August 2000.
92. Based primarily on Jane's Sentinel: Afghanistan, 30 August 2000. Exact numbers are unknown to most outside observers. Local leaders jealously guarded their key assets.
93. Jane's Sentinel: Afghanistan, 30 August 2000.
94. Based primarily on Jane's Sentinel: Afghanistan, 30 August 2000. Again exact numbers are unknown to most outside observers.
95. Jane's Sentinel: Afghanistan, 30 August 2000.
96. Based primarily on Jane's Sentinel: Afghanistan, 30 August 2000, 19 March 2002. As before, exact numbers are unknown to most outsiders.
97. Based primarily on Jane's Sentinel: Afghanistan, 30 August 2000.
98. Jane's Sentinel: Afghanistan, 17 October 2000; Rashid, *Taliban,* 45.
99. Jane's Sentinel: Afghanistan, 30 August 2000.
100. Ibid.
101. *Jane's Defence Weekly,* 28 June 2000, 14, referring to a report in the Kyrgyz press about a downed aircraft.
102. Based primarily on Jane's Sentinel: Afghanistan, 30 August 2000.
103. Jane's Sentinel: Afghanistan, 30 August 2000.

.

CHAPTER 10
The Regional Context

To thoroughly understand why countries such as Pakistan encouraged Islamic extremism in Afghanistan while others fought it, one must investigate the regional geopolitical context. This is also necessary to evaluate the military capability of the coalition and non-coalition countries in the late 2001 War on Terror in Afghanistan. Because geopolitics is a complex subject, the following summaries are provided to introduce the reader to the issues that have long concerned diplomats and foreign policy specialists.[1]

SAUDI ARABIA

Objective: Preservation of royal rule and, if possible, religious purity of the Wahhabi type.
Means: Religious proselytising and foreign aid.
Allies: To some extent Egypt and Pakistan.
Sponsor: The United States.
Proxies: None at present.
Population: 20.3 million, including more than 5 million non-nationals (2000).[2]
Armed forces: 126,500 troops, 75,000 national (or royal) guardsmen, 15,000 men in the Frontier Force and

Coast Guard, and perhaps 25,000 part-time tribal
National Guard levies. Foreign troops include substantial
air and ground assets, including at least 920 U.S., 280
British, 170 French, and 5,000 Gulf Arab troops.[3]

Since World War II, Saudi foreign policy has had two major
goals in addition to the obvious objectives of ensuring national
security and general domestic stability: the promotion of Wahhabi
Islam and the security of the House of Saud. When the Soviet Union
intervened in Afghanistan in 1979, the Saudi rulers believed that the
Soviets also intended to take control of the oil in the Persian Gulf.
The Saudis also believed that the rise of communism in
Afghanistan, a Muslim country, would in the long run threaten the
stability, and hence the security, of the monarchies of the gulf. This,
together with the perceived need to promote Wahhabism, obligated
the Saudis to oppose the Soviet presence in Afghanistan. In addition, the Saudi rulers feared the emergence of Ayatollah Khomeini's
Iran as a possibly more legitimate Islamic regime, which might be
able to wrest leadership of the Islamic world from Saudi hands.
Although Saudi Arabia itself does not have very strong economic
interests in Central Asian oil and gas, it accordingly wished to support its two allies, Pakistan and the United States, in taking control
of these resources—thus denying them to Iran.[4]

The Saudi kingdom is currently in severe trouble. A decade
ago, Saudi nationals had hardly any unemployment; the official
unemployment rate is currently 18 percent and rising. By 2001,
half of the roughly 15 million nationals are under the age of 18 and
face severe unemployment. In the early 1980s, Saudi Arabia's per
capita annual income was on a par with that of the United States,
$28,000; by 2001, it had fallen below $7,000. These economic
problems have intensified the resentment among especially the
young at the dissolute ways of the 30,000 members of the vast
Saudi royal family, the House of Saud.[5] It is estimated that between
5,000 and 10,000 Saudi extremists have received training in camps
in Afghanistan. After all, 15 of the hijackers on 11 September 2001
were Saudis. Although uncensored news from Saudi Arabia is

scarce, reports indicate that hundreds of Saudi veterans of the jihads in Afghanistan, Bosnia, and Chechnya were detained in the first month after the 11 September 2001 attacks.[6]

In addition, following these terrorist attacks, public Saudi opinion against the U.S. and British presence in the country hardened. By October 2001, a Saudi intelligence survey of educated Saudis, ages 25 to 41, reportedly showed that no less than 95 percent supported Usamah bin Ladin.[7] Soon popular Wahhabi prayer leaders in Riyadh, Jeddah, and Burayda resigned their official posts in protest against the continued U.S. military presence. Public demonstrations in the form of religiously sanctioned occasions, such as the funeral of a Wahhabi cleric, turned into mass meetings. When the telephone numbers of the Saudi families of the Al-Qaida suspects held in U.S. jails were posted on a popular Web site, thousands of people called to comfort them and to announce their support. In January 2002, discussions within the House of Saud indicated that Saudi Arabia wanted the U.S. and British troops based in the country to leave for good.[8]

PAKISTAN

Objective: The creation of a friendly, Pashtun-dominated government in Afghanistan as strategic depth against India, as well as the prevention of Pashtun separatism in Pakistan.
Means: Support of first the predominantly Pashtun Taliban movement, then Pashtun leader Hamid Karzai.
Allies: None.
Sponsor: China (although unlikely to have supported Pakistan's former policy of sponsoring the Taliban), the United States.
Proxies: Formerly the Taliban, now probably Hamid Karzai; possibly also the ethnic Pashtun Afghan warlord Gulbuddin Hekmatyar.
Population: 148.2 million (1998).[9]
Armed forces: 615,100, as well as about 250,000 in paramilitary units, with large forces tied up along the

eastern border. Nuclear weapons. Since September 2001, at most a few thousand U.S. troops in minor air bases in or near Baluchistan.[10]

Until late 2001, due to Pakistan's success in creating and sustaining proxy extremist movements on two fronts, Afghanistan and Indian Kashmir, it was branded a nuclear-armed rogue state but was also looking increasingly like a failing state. Despite a deliberate attempt (following U.S. pressure since 11 September 2001) to move away from this path, Pakistan still suffers from political and social turmoil, Islamic extremism, sectarian violence, and a growing drug problem.[11] Considering the large numbers of the Taliban's co-religionists in Pakistan and the fact that many religious and political groups there share the Taliban worldview, the very example of sustained Taliban rule puts the legitimacy of Pakistan's secular government at risk. It should be remembered that the first fatwa about the jihad in Afghanistan was issued in Pakistan.[12] Moreover, Pakistan's policy toward the Taliban appears to have been very much under the control of ethnic Pashtun officers in the armed forces and the intelligence organs, in particular ISI. Thousands of these men fought for their Afghan Pashtun cousins in Afghanistan (together with volunteers from Pakistani Islamic parties)[13] and appear to identify increasingly with Islamic extremist movements similar to the Taliban in Pakistan (e.g., *Jamaat-e Islami*) rather than with the artificial state construct of Pakistan.

Paradoxically, Pakistan's very determination and success in supporting extremist groups have allowed these to impose their will on key Pakistani institutions and large segments of Pakistan's population. The fact that Pakistan's political leadership tends to be weak and corrupt only serves to reinforce extremist feelings. In Pakistan, Islamic extremists already have all the ingredients for success, including the convenience of language, a considerable population of Pashtuns inspired by their cousins in Afghanistan, an Islamic environment, numerous sympathisers, and well-established financial and educational institutions. Since 1998, neo-Taliban groups have banned TV and videos and imposed other superficial trappings of

Taliban rule in several locations throughout the Pashtun belt of Pakistan.[14] Until the Pakistani policy shift following the U.S. decision to intervene in Afghanistan, for these reasons it seemed probable that Pakistan, too, would collapse. At present, it seems that Pakistan has survived this danger. However, a key issue for Pakistan's neighbours is the possibility of a religious fanatic's gaining control of its nuclear weapons program in the foreseeable future.

Although Pakistan's strategic planners originally saw a need to ensure the continued rule of a friendly, Pashtun-dominated government in Kabul, it can be argued that this policy, as yet not abandoned, today forms a greater threat to Pakistan than to its major opponent, India. The policy is generally regarded as having originated from two perceived strategic needs: (1) to allow Pakistan the use of Afghanistan's territory for strategic depth in a conventional war against India; and (2) to ensure friendly Pashtun hegemony in Afghanistan so that the ethnic Pashtuns on either side of the Pakistan-Afghanistan border would drop any plans to unite in a single Pashtun nation, thus compromising Pakistani territorial integrity.[15] While the first strategic need may have been valid during the early decades of Pakistan-India enmity, current developments in air and missile power make this assumption less tenable. As for the second need, it should be remembered that the Afghan government supported a movement among Pashtun tribesmen to establish an independent state, Pashtunistan, in the years immediately following Pakistan's independence in 1947, leading to sporadic clashes between tribesmen and Pakistani troops.[16] Despite this, the Pashtuns today are in a better position to compromise Pakistani territorial integrity than they were in the past. Pakistan has certainly helped to arm them to the teeth.

As a further objective, Pakistan—or at least powerful commercial interests in the country—needs to ensure safe passage for direct trade and transit routes to Central Asia.[17]

Before the Taliban movement emerged in 1994, Pakistan supported a number of other Pashtun leaders, first and foremost Gulbuddin Hekmatyar. In fact, the Taliban's initial victories, whether by chance or according to plan, would have been more difficult to achieve had not Hekmatyar's frequent military conflicts with Rabbani's Kabul government (of which Hekmatyar himself from time to time was a member) seriously weakened the governing coalition and its forces.[18] Hekmatyar lost his last military base in August 1998 and went to live in exile in Iran until 26 February 2002, when he was forced to leave due to his outspoken support for the Taliban.[19] He probably ended up in Afghanistan, although much fancy guesswork appeared in the media.[20] There still remains the possibility that Hekmatyar and commanders remaining loyal to him of the once ethnically powerful Pashtun Hezb-e Islami may again be employed as Pakistan's proxy if Pakistan finds the current Afghan leaders too independent or if Afghanistan breaks up.

In the international arena, Pakistan has at least since September 1954 relied on U.S. support. Pakistan's alignment with the West was reinforced in 1955, when Soviet leaders Nikita Khrushchev and Nikolai Bulganin stopped at Srinagar in Indian Kashmir, thus marking a new level of cooperation in Indo-Soviet relations. However, Pakistan since about 1960 also grew to depend on Chinese support (against India in particular). While the United States tolerated Pakistan's ties to China, two issues gradually eroded the U.S.-Pakistani relationship. First, the Pakistani nuclear weapons program continued despite opposition from the United States, which in October 1990 for this reason cut off American military aid. Then in 1998, Pakistan responded to Indian nuclear weapons tests by conducting its own nuclear weapons tests.[21] Second, Pakistan failed to persuade the Taliban to hand over Usamah bin Ladin to the United States. China, too, was antagonised, although by Pakistan's inability to persuade the Taliban to cease the support extended to Uighur separatists in the western Chinese province of Xinjiang. Pakistan was indeed not even successful in preventing its own Islamic extremists from assisting separatists in Xinjiang.[22] By 11 September 2001, Pakistan became increasingly isolated and thus vulnerable to ethnic fragmentation and a takeover by Islamic extremists.

Since then, General Pervez Musharraf, Pakistan's leader after the military coup of 12 October 1999, has dramatically reversed the policy of supporting Islamic extremists. Although at first hesitant due to the strong position of the extremists within the country, Musharraf nonetheless declared his and Pakistan's support for the United States against the Taliban and Al-Qaida. He also had little choice but to persuade the army to oppose the Taliban because otherwise, the Pakistanis reasoned, the United States would support India in a war against Pakistan.[23]

On 22 November 2001, when it was clear that the Taliban were losing the war, Pakistan ordered the Taliban embassy in Islamabad closed.[24] Pakistan has since closely aligned itself with the United States. Pakistan's main advantage in the War on Terror is that only a relatively minor part of its population seems to favour Islamic extremism. The Islamic parties have never done well in elections, even though their followers were a force to be reckoned with in the streets.[25] Yet, as many as 80,000 to 100,000 Pakistanis trained and fought in Taliban units between 1994 and 1999, not counting regular Pakistani troops reported to have served with the Taliban. Moreover, Pakistan has an estimated 5,000 to 6,000 religious seminaries that espouse extremist beliefs and continually teach and inspire the spiritual obligation to engage in *jihad* against the enemies of Islam. They are not likely to meekly abide the government's reaction against them.[26] For Musharraf, the struggle against Islamic extremism can be said to have barely begun.

IRAN

Objective: (1) Prevention of Sunni domination in any future Afghan government; and (2) continued influence in Dari-speaking parts of Afghanistan as well as some level of influence in Persian Tajik-speaking Tajikistan.
Means: Support to Shia forces in Afghanistan.
Allies: Russia, to some extent Tajikistan, and (against Pakistan) possibly India.
Sponsor: None.
Proxies: Shia Afghans, including some elements of the Northern Alliance.

Population: 66.8 million (1999).[27]
Armed forces: 538,000 including Islamic Revolutionary
Guards (*Pasdaran-e Enghelab-e Islami*), with large
forces guarding against external threats along the southern and western borders.[28]

Iran's foreign and security policy objectives in Central Asia
might appear highly ambiguous to the casual observer but are in
fact very straightforward. This does not, however, provide for simplistic explanations, since different state actors—primarily the
reformist, essentially secular movement around President
Muhammad Khatami and the revolutionary-conservative clerical
party of supreme leader Ayatollah Seyyed Ali Khamenei—have different agendas. The former could be said to represent the interests
of the state, while the latter represents the ideology of the Islamic
revolution. Iran as a whole accordingly suffers from a fundamental
dilemma of its foreign relations. This is clearly visible in the divergent policies toward the non-neighbouring countries of the Middle
East and Africa, where Iran has felt compelled to support Islamic
radicalism, and Iran's actual neighbours, of far greater importance
because of immediate security concerns. Policy toward the latter
appears to be invariably guided by national interests, especially
considerations of national security, should a conflict between the
interests of the state and those of the Islamic revolution occur.
Overall policy seems in most cases to have been pragmatic since
1985, when Iran and Saudi Arabia mended fences and Iranian leaders, including Ayatollah Khomeini, declared that Iran desired
peaceful coexistence with its neighbours and regarded the export of
the Iranian revolution as an informational rather than military venture. Since the 1991 disintegration of the Soviet Union, Iran has
invariably acted according to its national interests with regard to its
neighbours and been careful to maintain good relations with the
nearby states, above all with Russia.[29]

Russia appears, in fact, increasingly as a strong regional ally of
Iran. This has been obvious in the growing trade between the two
countries since the early 1990s[30] and in the agreements to expand

military cooperation in December 2000 and March 2001.[31] Russia is also Iran's main foreign supplier of conventional weapons.[32] Although Russia was initially concerned about the possible spread of Islamic fundamentalism from Iran, in 1994 the Russian Foreign Intelligence Service, headed by Yevgenyi Primakov, stressed the distinction between "Islamic fundamentalism" and "Islamic extremism" and pointed out that only the latter was a threat to Russia. This paved the way for a more sophisticated policy toward Iran, especially after January 1996, when Primakov became foreign minister.[33]

Until the fall of the Taliban government, Iran's strategy with regard to Afghanistan was apparently to support opposition to the Pakistan-sponsored Pashtun forces to such an extent that a final Taliban military victory would be impossible. This policy was probably expected to force a diplomatic settlement without the need for a direct military confrontation between Iranian and Afghan or Pakistani military forces.[34] In this policy Iran also seemed to enjoy the support of Tajikistan, India, and Russia.[35] No doubt Iran retains the option of supporting at least the Afghan Shia forces close to the Iranian-Afghan border. There have been reports of Iranian contacts with these groups,[36] and such support can be expected to last as long as Pakistan and the United States continue to operate Pashtun forces as proxies in Afghanistan.

That Iran's foreign policy objectives in Central Asia do not appear to include any Islamic revolution does not, of course, rule out clandestine contacts with radical Islamic movements in the region. Little is known about any such contacts,[37] and Iran appears to have very limited, if any, influence over Islamic groups in Central Asia outside some Shia groups in Afghanistan. One reason is surely the difference in faith, since the most active extremist Islamic groups there are Sunni rather than Shia, and in any case until late 2001 they were already supported by Pakistan and like-minded groups in Saudi Arabia.[38] However, Iran appears to put its relations with Russia first, the governments of the Central Asian states second, and the Islamic movements only third and last. This indicates that Iran is not attempting to gain influence among extremist groups to destabilise the region but rather to collect intelligence to keep itself (and perhaps its regional allies) informed about what goes on among radical Muslims. To show sympathy for and augment one's influence among radical movements is not the same as spreading one's ideology.

Although it seems clear that Iran is eager to achieve some level of influence in Tajikistan and the Persian Dari-speaking parts of Afghanistan, this appears primarily to be a cultural rather than religious objective. An interesting example of Iranian pragmatism rather than revolutionary zeal is its educational and media activities in Central Asia. These include regular Persian-language radio and television broadcasts since 1992 for Tajikistan as well as broadcasts in Uzbek to Uzbekistan. However, the television programming aimed at Tajikistan consists of soap operas rather than the religious broadcasting that dominates Iran's domestic television.[39]

Iran's pragmatic foreign policy continued unchanged after the 11 September 2001 attacks that drove the United States to war in Afghanistan. First, Iran publicly pledged to assist in the conduction of search-and-rescue missions for downed U.S. airmen on Iranian territory during the war in Afghanistan and allowed the United States to unload 165,000 tons of American wheat meant for Afghanistan at Iranian ports.[40] Second, and of more long-term importance, reports indicate that direct talks between Iranian and U.S. representatives played a crucial role in promoting the United Nations-sponsored Bonn agreement that led to the creation of the interim Afghan government on 4 December 2001. Iran, for instance, persuaded Burhanuddin Rabbani to step down so that the United States could nominate a Pashtun, Hamid Karzai, as leader of the interim government, and Iran accepted the proposition of a broad-based government that includes Pashtun leaders in addition to those of the Northern Alliance. Iran also persuaded the Northern Alliance commander, Ismail Khan, not to boycott Karzai's inauguration as leader of the interim government.[41]

The United States has persistently alleged—especially since President Bush's 29 January 2002 declaration that an "axis of evil" consisting of the three disparate countries of Iran, Iraq, and North

Korea threatened world peace—that Iran has actively aided the Al-Qaida network, particularly by assisting large numbers of Al-Qaida members to escape into Iran, where they are said to be protected by the government.[42] These allegations disregard the fact that bin Ladin's followers generally hate Shia Iran no less than the United States and have a history of terrorist attacks against Iranian targets.[43] Although some surviving Al-Qaida members, and in particular their dependents, did escape across the Iranian-Afghan border, probably by using the services of local smugglers, Iranian security forces appear to have quietly rounded them up and had them extradited to their native countries, including at least Saudi Arabia, Jordan, and Egypt.[44] For this reason, U.S. allegations of Iran's aiding and abetting terrorism by helping terrorists to escape are in most cases unfounded, and all the more rhetorical, since the United States itself has hinted at the extraditing of its Al-Qaida prisoners as soon as they have been satisfactorily interrogated.[45]

The same can be said about the recurring U.S. reports that Iran is sending agents into Afghanistan to destabilise the current situation, undermine the interim government, and "lure locals away from Karzai's ruling coalition."[46] While Iran no doubt strives to keep itself informed about events in neighbouring Afghanistan, especially among its co-religionists, this is neither more nor less surprising than the fact that the United States and neighbours of Afghanistan are doing likewise. Besides, judging from Iran's long-standing support of the Northern Alliance, that country can be expected to maintain especially good relations with the key ministers in the Afghan government, who all come from the Northern Alliance. It is accordingly hard to see what Iran could possibly stand to gain by undermining that government. Besides, Afghan leader Hamid Karzai visited Iran on 24 February 2002 and, during a meeting with Ayatollah Khamenei, won public endorsement for the interim government.[47] However, the U.S. policy of singling out Iran as the culprit has led to many rumours, particularly among the Pashtuns, as well as speculation that the United States will team up with a 20,000-strong ex-Taliban Pashtun tribal army "keen to put a stop to Iran's interference in the country."[48] Because such rumours only serve to further destabilise the region, particularly Afghanistan, it is hard to see the American allegations as anything but an ill-chosen way to pressure Iran, presumably in the hope that it will abandon its influence in Afghanistan without a struggle. After all, a Pashtun army, even if beefed up with a few U.S. ground units and air support, would be unlikely to have any significant impact on Iran's numerically far superior military forces. A full-scale U.S. military attack on Iran, except by proxy, can almost certainly be ruled out.

Despite what can only be a propaganda war against Iran, and a certain amount of anger engendered in Iran against President Bush because of his "axis of evil" statement, the U.S. War on Terror has not caused any apparent change in Iranian policy. It remains pragmatic, which is fortunate for the prospects of the region. It should be noted that so far, the United Nations, the European Union, and the Karzai government have chosen not to join the United States in its criticism of Iran.

A prominent problem in the world's understanding of Iranian policies appears to be the exaggerated influence of traditional Middle East experts in the analysis of the meaning and impact of Iranian foreign and security policy. The sudden independence of the former Soviet Central Asian republics changed the ethnic character of the Middle East. The addition of more than 50 million people, most of them Muslims but almost none of Arab descent, has irrevocably changed the region.[49] As the region's political focus (if not yet the attention of the world's media) shifts eastward, events in a narrow strip of Middle Eastern land facing the Mediterranean no longer decide every political issue in the Islamic world. Iran has realised this, but quite a few analysts and policy experts in the West still have to catch up.

TURKMENISTAN

Objective: The construction of pipelines through Afghanistan, paid for by a third party and with protection provided by any Afghan government, as a way to revive Turkmenistan's economy.

Means: Tacit support of Pakistan (and by extension, Pakistan's Afghan allies) and attempts to procure foreign investment.

Allies: None.

Sponsor: None.

Proxies: None.

Population: 4.4 million (1999).[50]

Armed forces: 17,000 as well as 12,000 border guards.[51]

Turkmenistan's chief foreign policy concerns appear to be (1) how to remain neutral while surrounded not only by much larger and militarily more powerful neighbours (e.g., Iran, Uzbekistan), but also very turbulent neighbours (primarily Afghanistan); and (2) to revive Turkmenistan's stagnant economy by exporting its oil and natural gas.[52] Although the first objective may be achieved by adhering to a policy of neutrality (Turkmenistan declared itself a "neutral" country in 1993), the second may be impossible without risking involvement in Afghanistan. Turkmenistan is surrounded by countries with oil and natural gas resources of their own, among them Iran, Russia, Kazakhstan, and Uzbekistan. These neighbours thus have little interest in supporting Turkmenistan's exports as long as they can sustain the export of their own resources.[53]

This predicament leaves Turkmen President Saparmurat Niyazov, the state's increasingly autocratic ruler, only one choice: to promote an export pipeline corridor through Afghanistan to Pakistan, from which oil and gas can be shipped on to South Asia and the Far East.

The idea of building a trans-Afghan pipeline from Central Asia to the Indian Ocean was apparently born in Pakistan. In December 1991, a Pakistani delegation visiting Ashgabat, Turkmenistan's capital, expressed its interest in building a gas pipeline across Iran and Afghanistan to Pakistan.[54] In 1992, Turkmenistan and Pakistan agreed jointly to develop their energy sources and build a gas pipeline and a highway across Afghanistan to connect the two countries.[55] The Argentinian oil company Bridas finalised plans for such a venture in 1994. In 1995, the American oil company Unocal and its partner, the Saudi-owned Delta Oil company, also announced plans for a pipeline in response to what they regarded as a threat from Bridas to corner the market.[56] Afghan Taliban troops were expected to secure the highways and routes for oil and gas pipelines. An important objective of the plan was that the energy routes would exit through Pakistan, the U.S. ally, rather than through Iran. For this reason, Turkmenistan has continuously maintained friendly relations with Pakistan as well as Pakistan's Afghan allies.[57] The latter include Afghan leader Hamid Karzai, who during his first state visit to Islamabad on 8 February 2002 declared that the construction of a pipeline carrying natural gas from Turkmenistan across his country to Pakistan was "very essential."[58] It is fair to conclude that U.S. and Pakistani interest in Turkmenistan's natural gas has survived the War on Terror and that Turkmenistan's policy may yet pay off. However, Turkmenistan is being used more and more as a trans-shipment point for illegal drugs from Afghanistan.[59] This means that Turkmenistan is directly affected by further regional instability.

UZBEKISTAN

Objective: Continued existence as a secular state, nation building, and the assumption of a prominent regional role.
Means: Military action; encouragement of ethnic Uzbek warlords in Afghanistan and (at least until 1998) Tajikistan.
Allies: Currently cooperating with the United States; good although hardly cordial relations with Russia, China, Turkey, Kazakhstan, Kyrgyzstan, and (while under U.S. influence) Tajikistan.
Sponsor: To some extent the United States, at least for the duration of its involvement in Afghanistan.

Proxies: Ethnic Uzbek warlords such as Abdul Rashid Dostum.
Population: 23.9 million (1999).[60]
Armed forces: 55,000, in addition to 19,000 to 21,000 internal security troops and border guards; perhaps 3,000 Russian troops primarily concerned with air defence; possibly still around 1,000 U.S. troops stationed at Qarshi/Khanabad Air Base in support of U.S. operations in Afghanistan.[61]

Uzbekistan is a comparatively populous and militarily strong state in the region. Under its autocratic president, Islam Karimov, it seems determined not only to ride out the storms of various forms of potential trouble but to carve out a leading role in the region.[62] Although Russia has offered unconditional support in terms of security and counterterrorism,[63] President Karimov, earlier than other former Soviet Central Asian leaders, showed determination to reduce his dependence on Russia and has avoided returning his country to the ranks of Russian clients. Instead, Uzbekistan has embarked upon an ambitious project of nation building, attempting to create a national identity by promoting the Uzbek language and culture.[64] Uzbekistan is also distancing itself from Russia militarily by, for instance, replacing obsolete military equipment with imports from the West rather than Russia. It has also achieved self-sufficiency in energy, another important means of reducing Russia's influence. In the process, Uzbekistan's government has become increasingly authoritarian, suppressing all potential sources of opposition to the president's rule.[65]

Uzbekistan appears adamant in charting its own course, outside the pale of Moscow. Karimov is a pragmatic ruler who is unlikely to bow either to Russian or Western demands as long as he can find a third way. An example was the clouded relationship with the West because of Karimov's suppression of all opposition during the early years of Uzbekistan's independence. From 1995 on, Karimov began to improve his relations with the United States by seeking good relations with NATO, avoiding links with Iran, and declaring some support for Israel in the United Nations. Karimov's policy paid off, and the United States for a while began to see Uzbekistan as a strategic partner.[66] As U.S. interest in the region from 1998 seemed to wane after 1988, Uzbekistan found itself increasingly on its own. Therefore, in June 2001, Uzbekistan joined the Shanghai Cooperation Organization (SCO), apparently in search of allies to help it deal with the domestic armed opposition group the IMU. Yet, when the SCO on 10 and 11 October 2001 held an emergency meeting in Kyrgyzstan's capital, Bishkek, to discuss the American-led air strikes on Afghanistan, Uzbekistan declined to participate.[67]

Uzbekistan had concluded an agreement with the United States that thereby gave official permission for the deployment of U.S. military forces in the country (a deployment that had already taken place) and the use of an Uzbekistani air base on 6 October 2001.[68] It seems fair to assume that Uzbekistan thereafter regarded itself as a U.S. ally and no longer felt the need to belong to the SCO. Uzbekistan's government has subsequently claimed that the agreement contained secret terms, including a long-term specific U.S. commitment to Uzbekistan.[69] An additional strategic partnership agreement was indeed signed in March 2002, stating that the United States will regard any threats to Uzbekistan as serious and presumably provide some assistance should such a situation arise.[70] Another important consideration for Uzbekistan was no doubt that in return for the use of the base, the United States promised substantial aid payments. The first was in the region of $100 million, and then, following a 2002 proposal by the Bush administration to increase U.S. aid, $160 million.[71]

This pragmatism, as well as the highly personalised nature of Uzbekistan's foreign policy, makes it hard to predict Uzbekistan's responses to different initiatives or threats. Moreover, since the United States and Uzbekistan began to cooperate in the War on Terror, Uzbekistan's government has been able to use this cooperation as an excuse for curbing its remaining domestic opposition, whether of secular or clerical origin. Karimov, probably correctly, perceived that the West would play down its earlier emphasis on human rights issues as long as the war against extremists and terrorists lasted.[72]

Karimov's personal power appears well entrenched. A former
first secretary of the ruling Communist Party of Uzbekistan (CPU),
Karimov banned the CPU in 1991, establishing in its place the
People's Democratic Party of Uzbekistan (PDPU), with essentially
the same structure and membership. He also retained the Soviet
economic system, resisting privatisation and reform. Food riots in
1992 in the former capital, Tashkent, were put down by military
force. Karimov then had his first five-year term extended from
1995 to 2000 in a national referendum. He won a second term in a
January 2000 election widely regarded as rigged. Elections had
been scheduled for January 2005, but in a referendum on 27
January 2002, again criticised by human-rights groups as being
rigged, Karimov gained an extension of the presidential term from
five to seven years.[73] Barring a successful assassination or sudden
illness, Karimov seems unlikely to relinquish power soon. He also
seems unlikely to change the fundamentally Soviet-style political
and economic system that he has retained. In April 2001, the
International Monetary Fund (IMF) gave up on Uzbekistan and
closed its office in Tashkent due to Karimov's lack of economic
reforms.[74] However, within days after the conclusion of the 6
October 2001 agreement between Uzbekistan and the United
States, the World Bank announced that it would send a high-level
delegation to Tashkent to provide new loans, debt relief, and further
benefits from international financial institutions to ensure economic stability.[75]

TAJIKISTAN

Objective: For the presidential faction—national survival and, perhaps, nation and state building. For the
United Tajik Opposition (UTO) faction—fundamentally
the same, though some former UTO leaders appear to be
far more interested in narcotics trafficking and maintain
links with Islamic extremist groups such as the IMU.
Means: Attempts to procure foreign support together
with carefully selected patronage in the country.

Allies: Russia, Iran, and (at least at present) the
United States.
Sponsor: Russia.
Proxies: For the presidential faction—elements in
Afghanistan's Northern Alliance (including, until his
death in 2001, its military commander Ahmad Shah
Masud); for UTO warlord Zioev's faction—the IMU.
Population: 6.1 million (1999).[76]
Armed forces: 7,000, in addition to about 2,500 former
UTO fighters more or less integrated into the armed
forces; perhaps as many as 25,000 paramilitary soldiers
of local, very dubious allegiance; 14,500 Russian border
guards, the rank-and-file, often locally recruited Tajiks;
about 8,500 Russian regular troops (the 201st Gatchina
Motor Rifle Division, which is due to be demoted in status to a garrison unit after 1 January 2002); an undisclosed number (fewer than 1,000) of troops from the
United States and coalition countries.[77]

In 1991, the Communist Party leaders in Tajikistan's capital,
Dushanbe, suddenly found themselves the rulers of an independent
country, even though it is questionable whether there was yet a
state in the territory nominally under their control. Due to the
1992–1997 Tajikistani civil war, the government never achieved
complete control over Tajikistan's territory, large parts of which
remain under the personal control of various local warlords. Most
of these have a background as local leaders in the UTO, the opposition umbrella organisation dominated by Islamic groups that, since
the Peace Accord in June 1997, has transformed itself into part of
the coalition government of Tajikistan. The other part of the coalition, under President Emomali Rahmonov, represents the old Soviet
power structure, the *nomenklatura*.[78] Yet Rahmonov has since 2000
enhanced his position, consolidated presidential power, and succeeded in increasing his control over important areas of the country
by carefully selected patronage.[79]

Among former UTO field commanders who retain sizeable

personal forces is Minister for Emergency Situations and Civil Defence Mirzo Zioev. Widely suspected of narcotics trafficking and ties to extremist groups such as the IMU, Zioev was involved in the latter's armed incursion into neighbouring Kyrgyzstan in 1999.[80] The fact that a leading government member was able to use what ostensibly were government troops (in Zioev's case, 400 men recruited by him personally among the 800 fighters of his UTO command)[81] for armed aggression against a neighbouring country does not bode well for Tajikistan's future. Although this state has never failed as completely as Afghanistan, prospects for building a national identity remain poor.

Continued control over large territories in Tajikistan by local warlords, most of them sympathetic to Islamic extremism and quite capable of engaging in irregular warfare and terrorism due to their experience during the civil war, make certain areas of Tajikistan (in particular the Garm, Jirgatal, and Tavildara districts) prime targets for such extremism. The country's proximity to Afghanistan ensures close contacts between like-minded groups in the two countries. So does the fact that even high-ranking members of government such as Zioev have a major power base among what can only be described as Islamic extremists. A further complication is the close ties between the warlords, government, and crime syndicates involved in narcotics trafficking. Tajikistan is a prime example of a state in which warlordism, extremism, terrorism, and drug trafficking go hand in hand, a phenomenon commonly known as narco-terrorism.[82] While some of the local leaders may be content to devote themselves to their own territories while raising cash through narcotics trafficking, Tajikistan also appears to the be home base for groups of Islamic extremists with interests beyond the borders of the state.[83]

Tajikistan's government is dependent on Russia. There is also a considerable Iranian influence, but since Russia and Iran share the same foreign policy objectives in Tajikistan, the two states complement each other rather than compete for Tajikistani favour. Due to the earlier civil war, however, Tajikistan's government appears to have little choice but to follow Russia's dictates.[84]

Russian and Iranian influence at least ensured that the presidential faction offered support to Afghanistan's Northern Alliance and opposed the Taliban.[85]

The U.S. War on Terror has brought some changes to Tajikistan, although, so far, it remains uncertain whether the U.S. presence will have a lasting impact on the frail state. The Americans arrived early, probably due to their (and especially Britain's) long relationship with leaders of the Afghan Northern Alliance who operated an embassy in Dushanbe, rather than through Tajikistan's government channels.[86] But Tajikistan would not have approved a U.S. presence had Russian President Vladimir Putin not requested it.[87]

Tajikistan's government appears to have taken advantage of its cooperation with the United States to suppress the domestic opposition, whether secular or clerical. As in Uzbekistan, the government has, probably correctly, perceived that the West will play down its earlier emphasis on human rights issues as long as the war lasts.[88]

KYRGYZSTAN

Objective: Continued existence as a secular state and nation building.
Means: Foreign aid.
Allies: Currently cooperating with the United States; good relations with Russia, China, Turkey, Kazakhstan, and (while under U.S. influence) Uzbekistan and Tajikistan.
Sponsor: The United States, at least as long as it maintains a base in Kyrgyzstan.
Proxies: None.
Population: 4.8 million (2000).[89]
Armed forces: 10,900 troops, 800 national guardsmen, and approximately 5,000 border guards, as well as some recently formed self-defence militia units. Foreign troops include a Russian SAM regiment and transportation battalion and headquarters (of more than 100 mili-

tary advisers) in Osh; U.S. special forces advisers in Osh; and 3,000 U.S. personnel at the air base used by NATO at Manas Airport.[90]

Terrorism in Central Asia is also a threat to Kyrgyzstan. It is clear that Kyrgyzstan does not possess the armed strength to repel armed extremist incursions without outside help, nor is the country likely to be able to do so in the near future despite some attempts at military reform and recruitment.[91] Moreover, Islamic extremism and terrorism seem to inhibit the admittedly weak signs of emerging democracy in the region. Terrorism has already (in combination with Russia's financial crisis and, one suspects, President Askar Akaev's growing frustration with the confusions of democracy) turned the government of Kyrgyzstan from what was referred to as the most democratic in the region to one that can only be designated as autocratic. Akaev, at first attempting to rebuild the country by introducing economic reforms, depended heavily on aid from the West and Japan. However, Kyrgyzstan remained weak, and large-scale foreign investments in desperately needed infrastructure projects were not forthcoming. Unemployment rose and living standards fell. This, predictably, gave rise to a growing political opposition. Akaev responded by becoming increasingly authoritarian. His original reputation as a democratically elected president grew increasingly tarnished, corruption scandals engulfed his government, and Akaev's credibility sank fast.[92]

What democracy could not solve in Kyrgyzstan, the threat from the IMU did. Since the IMU raids into Kyrgyzstan began in 1999, Kyrgyzstan has received military aid from the United States, Russia, and China. The extremist threat also enabled Akaev to arrest political opponents, curb the media, and rig elections so that he could stay in office. Most opposition parties were banned before the February 2000 parliamentary elections. Although these measures provided a semblance of control, they also, paradoxically, ensured that the IMU found plenty of new supporters, especially in the impoverished south. Islam was historically never a strong force among the originally nomadic Kyrgyz, yet the depressed living conditions in contemporary Kyrgyzstan encourage the influence of Islamic extremism among the population, hoping to find in religion solutions to widespread social injustices that the state has been unable to redress.[93]

In December 2001, the United States concluded an agreement with Kyrgyzstan, receiving very favourable conditions for a military base at Manas Airport, close to the capital of Bishkek.[94]

CHINA

Objective: Eradication or at least containment of separatism inside China, access to energy sources and transportation routes, retention of influence over Pakistan.
Means: Increased security in the Xinjiang Uighur Autonomous Region and political pressure on foreign states on the territory in which Xinjiang separatists are active.
Allies: None.
Sponsor: None.
Proxies: Pakistan; possibly groups in Afghanistan.
Population: 16.9 million in sparsely populated Xinjiang; total population 1.3 billion.[95]
Armed forces: 288,400 (in Lanzhou Military Region of which Xinjiang forms one of five military districts) out of a total of 2,480,000, as well as some 12 million paramilitary personnel. Nuclear weapons.[96]

China is unlikely to regard its relationship with Afghanistan and the Central Asian states as of primary importance. A far greater Chinese concern is its relative position in the post-Cold War strategic environment and in particular its relation to the only remaining superpower, the United States. This obviously means that China sees the buildup of new U.S. military bases in the region as a cause for some alarm. However, Central Asia holds a place in China's view of global strategy for other reasons: (1) the region's oil and natural gas resources, which are likely to become vital for China's growing energy needs; (2) the region's potential as a market for Chinese goods, as this would enhance the economic development of China's inland regions; and (3) its likely support for Turkestani separatism, Islamic or otherwise, in China's westernmost province, Xinjiang.[97]

At least since at least 1997, China has repeatedly emphasised that it has no choice but to augment domestic energy sources through imports from abroad, particularly from Central Asia and Russia. Another Chinese interest in Central Asia, although perhaps not of immediate concern, is the creation of a regional rail network that, unlike the sea routes, would be beyond the control of the United States. Such a land transportation route, if fully functional, could in the event of a future conflict with the United States be used to move vital natural resources, consumer goods, and war materiel in and out of China. It is accordingly unlikely that China would support any move to increase the influence of the United States in the region or the coming to power of a pro-U.S. government in any country bordering China. Chinese leaders also most likely prefer to retain influence over Pakistan due to the continuing strategic objective of containing India and, in case of war, the hope of forcing it into a two-front war, a strategy that also includes Tibet and Burma.[98]

However, the strategic importance of Pakistan weighs lightly compared with the possibility of growing ethnic unrest in Xinjiang. The Taliban leaders were known to support Islamic extremist movements among the local Uighurs and other Turkic peoples,[99] as did members of the Arab Afghan movement. China in 1997 reportedly erected a fence along its 750-kilometre (470-mile) border with Pakistan to deny Islamic extremists in Pakistan easy access to militant Xinjiang Uighurs.[100]

As a final note, one may speculate on whether China maintains its own clandestine contacts and proxies in Afghanistan and, if so, how strong its influence is in the region.[101] China supported various Afghan factions during the war against the Soviet Union in much the same way as the West did, but little if any information on the Chinese involvement leaked to the public until years after the war ended.[102] The first Chinese delegation went to Kabul to meet

the Taliban on 31 January 1999.[103] One reason for the visit appears
to have been to acquire the right to study and remove two or three
unexploded U.S. Tomahawk cruise missiles launched against Al-
Qaida camps on 20 August 1998.[104] It is in China's interest to keep
itself informed about, if not be a participant in, future developments in Afghanistan.

THE RUSSIAN FEDERATION

Objective: Eradication or at least containment of separatism inside Russia, retention of influence over
Central Asia.
Means: Military bases in Tajikistan and political pressure on foreign states in whose territory separatists orig-
inating in the Russian Federation are active; the ability
to supply selected Afghan commanders with arms and
financial assistance should Russia wish to reassert its
regional influence.
Allies: To some extent Iran and India.
Sponsor: None.
Proxies: The presidential faction within Tajikistan's government; key leaders within Afghanistan's Northern
Alliance (at least until the fall of the Taliban in late
2001; no doubt some Russian influence remains).
Population: 147.2 million.[105]
Armed forces: About 8,500 regular troops and 14,500
border guards (in Tajikistan), out of a total of 860,000.
Nuclear weapons.[106]

Like China, Russia has problems of higher priority and more
pressing engagements elsewhere. For Russia, the primary priority is,
and will no doubt remain in the foreseeable future, its relations with
the United States and Europe. However, the existence of Russian
military bases in Tajikistan, as well as the ongoing war against separatists as well as Islamic extremists in Chechnya, means that Russia
cannot stay quite as aloof as China. The unstable situation in

Afghanistan and the rise of Islamic extremism since the emergence of the Taliban in 1994 has prompted some former Soviet Central Asian states to seek renewed relationships with Russia once they realised the continuing importance of Russia as a regional guarantor of stability.[107] This development, particularly since Vladimir Putin rose to power in 1999, again increased Russia's influence in the region, apparently without its actively seeking it. The last point cannot be overemphasised. Russia, after the demise of the Soviet Union, has far greater problems, and other priorities, than any contemplation of whether it would be worthwhile to return to Central Asia, a region that by the end of the Soviet era was regarded as an economic burden rather than an asset.[108]

By late 2001 the United States in its war against the Taliban had established military bases in several countries close to Afghanistan, and U.S. aid in unprecedented amounts had begun to pour into the region.[109] Despite the outcry of some domestic hawks, Russia did not object to the establishment of new U.S. military bases, did not choose to send troops to fight the Taliban, did not join peace-keeping efforts after the fall of the Taliban, and apparently played no significant role in the United Nations-sponsored Bonn agreement of 4 December 2001. While these decisions caused some domestic criticism,[110] they only confirmed the continuity of Russia's policy of regarding relations with the United States and Europe as its first priority. However, Russia was not without influence in Afghanistan. Russia may perhaps have preferred to see Burhanuddin Rabbani as head of the interim government, but the most powerful ministries of this Afghan government were, after all, controlled by members of the Russian-supported Northern Alliance. While the United States, through sheer military and political power, prevailed in picking Hamid Karzai, a Pashtun, as head of the new government, Russia had long financed and armed the Northern Alliance and could be expected to retain a certain level of influence with its Tajik and Uzbek leaders. Besides, Karzai might well have been acceptable to Russia and Northern Alliance alike, for the very reason that his personal power base among the Pashtuns was comparatively weak.[111] Russia and Iran also supported the Northern Alliance—against the wishes of the United States—in its rapid advance that led to the fall of the Taliban.[112]

Afghanistan remains a concern for Russia because of its potential to cause instability in the region, but the country forms no direct threat to Russian territory. Russian policy toward Afghanistan will no doubt remain pragmatic, as exemplified by Russia's providing support to Masud and his followers, those very Afghan warlords who had fought Russia in the 1979–1989 Afghan war.[113] For this reason, Russia can be expected to continue supporting at least some commanders within the Northern Alliance as long as this seems necessary to contain any Islamic extremism coming out of Afghanistan. If Russia in the future sees the need to meddle in Afghan politics, it can certainly do so by supplying military and financial aid to favoured, probably Tajik or Uzbek, commanders. These means were also available to Russia before U.S. intervention. In other words, despite appearances, Russia has not yet surrendered its regional influence.

In the near future, Russia remains unlikely to get directly involved in substantial military operations in Central Asia. It is far more likely to assist the Central Asian rulers, and probably favoured Afghan commanders, with military support, intelligence, advisors, and international diplomacy. As long as Russian forces remain in Tajikistan, Russia will remain a key player in the region.

THE UNITED STATES OF AMERICA

Objective: Until 11 September 2001, no geopolitical objective except the extradition of Usamah bin Ladin; since then, the removal of the Taliban government and the destruction of Al-Qaida. In the long term, possibly geopolitical gains in connection with Caspian region oil and gas resources.
Means: Financial aid, international recognition, air strikes, and, as a final resort, direct military action.
Allies: NATO, the European Union, Pakistan (since 22

November 2001, when Pakistan ordered the Taliban
Islamabad embassy closed), to some extent Uzbekistan,
Tajikistan, and especially Kyrgyzstan.
Sponsor: None needed.
Proxies: Apparently Hamid Karzai.
Population: 274.6 million (2000).[114]
Armed forces: Until September 2001, none in the
region, although some ability to strike a limited number
of targets from the air. However, several thousand troops
from the United States and coalition countries were
deployed to bases in Pakistan, Tajikistan, Uzbekistan,
Kyrgyzstan, and Afghanistan following the 11 September
terrorist attacks. Substantial additional forces, were
deployed to bases in the Middle East by March 2003 due
to the Iraqi War, putting the total number of troops at
approximately 1.4 million. Nuclear weapons.[115]

In the short term, the United States until recently saw only limited, if any, geopolitical objectives in Central Asia (despite some
claims to the contrary)[116] but remained concerned about a number
of potential developments, such as civil war, the breakup of states,
nuclear proliferation, and anti-Western forms of political Islam.
The United States was (and is) also interested in the oil resources
of some countries in the wider vicinity of Central Asia, notably
Kazakhstan and Azerbaijan, and the means to move the oil from
the region along routes that are safe and do not offer strategic or
trade benefits to any rivals.

After the demise of the Soviet Union in 1991, the United States
did express an interest in the region that culminated in 1997.
Rhetorical public statements, for instance by Deputy Secretary of
State Strobe Talbott in 1997, claimed that the whole of the
Caucasus and Central Asia was of strategic interest to the United
States. U.S. soldiers in September the same year participated in a
highly publicised military exercise with the newly created joint
Kazakhstan-Kyrgyzstan-Uzbekistan peace-keeping battalion within
the framework of the Partnership for Peace program.[117] However,

U.S. interest had by the following year shifted to Usamah bin Ladin, an issue that since 1998 has almost totally overshadowed U.S. relations with the region.

The United States naturally wishes to play a role in the economic growth of Central Asia. But its chief interests and highest priorities are—and likely will remain so, despite some signs to the contrary—China (especially as a Pacific power) and Russia.[118] As long as Russia stays relatively stable and democratic and, above all, friendly, the small countries surrounding Afghanistan are of comparatively minor importance to the United States. One should also note that the United States and Russia share a concern about Islamic extremism. The United States is likely to tacitly support, or at least not oppose, steps taken by Russia to reduce the threat from such groups in Central Asia as well as on its own territory, even if this increases Russian influence in the region. Likewise, Russia has shown that it is not opposed to the deployment of U.S. troops to Central Asia, as long as their purpose is to fight Islamic extremism.

In light of these concerns, it is curious to see how easily purely domestic politics create absurd twists in U.S. foreign policy. In regard to Afghanistan there was the single issue of forcing the extradition of Usamah bin Ladin. From 1998 to 2000, it seemed that the one U.S. policy for Afghanistan was the extradition or extermination of a single individual of foreign origin who currently happened to be living there. Compared to this one objective, everything else—including energy resources, conflict resolution, support of democracy, human rights questions, and indeed the presence of other Islamic extremists than Usamah bin Ladin—appear to have paled in importance.[119] The United States only seemed able to move on in 2000, probably due to more pressing events at home, such as the presidential election. A new policy toward Afghanistan and Central Asia was developed only after the 11 September 2001 terrorist attacks on the United States.

U.S. long-term plans for Central Asia remain unknown outside the inner circle of the Bush administration and may not yet have been finalised. Yet, it is possible that the buildup of a strong U.S. military presence in Kyrgyzstan, at a time when the American operations against the Taliban are already concluded, is intended to serve as the means of acquiring lasting strategic leverage in the region. If so, the U.S. military presence may achieve two political goals: (1) diminishing Russia's ability to influence the region through its support of individuals, often local political leaders, and (2) establishing a new major post for surveillance of China's activities in the region. According to the agreement between the United States and Kyrgyzstan signed in December 2001, the former received very favourable conditions. In stationing its military forces in Kyrgyzstan, the United States gets not only extensive use of the country's only international airport and a 37-acre military base but also the provision that U.S. military personnel are immune to prosecution by the Kyrgyzstani government and are free to enter and leave the country without hindrance, as well as to wear uniforms and carry arms.[120] These are fundamentally the same terms that the United States acquired in Japan and South Korea after the World War II, two countries where the United States has established a lasting military presence.[121]

In the long term, there is also the possibility that groups within the United States, government or commercial, desire geopolitical gains in connection with Caspian oil and gas resources, and in particular the opportunity to build pipelines across Central Asia.[122]

End Notes

1. This section is based on Fredholm, *Afghanistan and Central Asian Security.*

2. Jane's Sentinel: Saudi Arabia, 29 April 2002; CIA, *World Factbook 2001.*

3. Ibid., 3 July 2002, 28 May 2002.

4. Ahady, "Saudi Arabia, Iran and the Conflict in Afghanistan," 117–119, 129.

5. Dilip Hiro, "Days of Darkness Loom for Saudi Arabia," *Observer* (London)/*Japan Times* (Tokyo), 27 October 2001.

6. *Economist,* 13 October 2001, 26 January 2002.

7. Ibid., 2 February 2002, referring to *New York Times.*

8. Ibid., 26 January 2002.

9. Jane's Sentinel: Pakistan, 14 November 2000.

10. Ibid., 20 September 2001.

11. Rashid, *Taliban*, 210.

12. Gohari, *Taliban*, xi, 123–124.

13. Ibid., *Taliban*, 122–123.

14. Ibid., *Taliban*, 127; Rashid, *Taliban*, 93, 187, 194–195.

15. Rashid, "Taliban: Exporting Extremism," 22–35; Rashid, *Taliban*, 186–187.

16. Gohari, *Taliban*, 126.

17. Magnus and Naby, *Afghanistan*, 190; Rashid, *Taliban*, 189–191.

18. Ibid., 180; Gohari, *Taliban*, 19–20.

19. Jane's Sentinel: Afghanistan, 17 October 2000; IRNA, 26 February 2002. His political party, Hezb-e Islami Afghanistan (Islamic Party of Afghanistan) maintained a web site at *www.hezb-e-islami.org*

20. *Washington Times,* 11–17 March 2002 (National Weekly Edition).

21. Victoria Schofield, *Kashmir in the Crossfire* (London: I. B. Tauris & Co, 1996), 178–179, 193, 195, 249; CIA, *World Factbook 2001.*

22. See, for instance, Mark Burles, *Chinese Policy Toward Russia and the Central Asian Republics* (Santa Monica, Calif.: RAND, 1999), 18, based on "Unwelcome Traffic," *Far Eastern Economic Review* (7 December 1995), 40.

23. Ishtiaq Ahmed, presentation on "Pakistan in Crisis," Centre for Pacific Asia Studies (CPAS), Stockholm University, 6 February 2002.

24. Reuters, 22 November 2001. See also RIA Novosti, 8 November 2001; *Dawn* (Pakistan; *www.Dawn.com*), 20 November 2001.

25. *Economist,* 29 September 2001. See also International Crisis Group (ICG), *Pakistan: The Dangers of Conventional Wisdom* (Islamabad/Brussels: International Crisis Group, 12 March 2002), 5–6.

26. Michael Fredholm, "Osama bin Laden and Salafi Islam: More Than a Mere Terrorist Threat," *Central Asia – Caucasus Analyst Biweekly Briefing* 24 October 2001 (*www.cacianalyst.org*).

27. Jane's Sentinel: Iran, 21 November 2001.

28. Ibid., 22 January 2001.

29. See Hiro, *Islamic Fundamentalism*, 215; Edmund Herzig, *Iran and the Former Soviet South* (London: Royal Institute of International Affairs, 1995), 19; David Menashri, "Iran and Central Asia: Radical Regime, Pragmatic Politics," David Menashri, ed., *Central Asia Meets the Middle East* (London: Frank Cass, 1998), 73–97; Ahady, "Saudi Arabia, Iran and the Conflict in Afghanistan," 122.

30. See, for instance, Herzig, *Iran and the Former Soviet South,* 33–34.

31. Ed Blanche, "Iranian, Russian Links Ring US Alarm Bells," *Jane's Defence Weekly,* 24

January 2001, 21; Igor Korotchenko and Ed Blanche, "Iran Goes Shopping," *Jane's Defence Weekly*, 21 March 2001, 18–19.

32. *Jane's Sentinel: Iran*, 17 October 2000.

33. Jonson, *Russia and Central Asia*, 30; Primakov, "Rossiya ne protivodeystvuet islamu." See also, for instance, Rashid, *Taliban*, 177.

34. *Jane's Sentinel: Afghanistan*, 17 October 2000.

35. *Jane's Sentinel: Iran*, 17 October 2000; Rashid, *Taliban*, 44–45.

36. Yasin Bidar, "US Set for Long Stay in Central Asia," *IWPR's Reporting Central Asia* 102 (1 February 2002; *www.iwpr.net*).

37. Menashri, "Iran and Central Asia," 93.

38. Farhad Kazemi and Zohreh Ajdari, "Ethnicity, Identity and Politics: Central Asia and Azerbaijan between Iran and Turkey," in Menashri, *Central Asia Meets the Middle East*, 66.

39. Ibid., 61; Menashri, "Iran and Central Asia," 87; *Jane's Sentinel: Iran*, 17 October 2000.

40. *Washington Post*, 18 October 2001, 29 October 2001.

41. Ibid., 19 January 2002; *Economist*, 9 February 2002; and for more details, Camelia Entekhabi-Fard, "Afghan Leader's Visit to Iran Hands Political Victory to Reformists in Tehran," *Eurasia Insight*, 27 February 2002 (*www.eurasianet.org*).

42. See, for instance, *Economist*, 2 February 2002, 23 February 2002; Ariel Cohen, "The Bush Administration Casts a Wary Eye on Iran," *Eurasia Insight*, 16 March 2002 (*www.eurasianet.org*).

43. See, for instance, Reeve, *New Jackals*, 65–67.

44. *Economist*, 23 February 2002. For further details, see, for instance, *Christian Science Monitor*, 13 August 2002.

45. Ibid., 26 January 2001.

46. Bidar, "US Set for Long Stay"; Artie McConnell, "Iranian Conservatives Seek to Influence Developments in Afghanistan," *Eurasia Insight*, 26 February 2002 (*www.eurasianet.org*); Cohen, "Bush Administration Casts a Wary Eye on Iran."

47. Entekhabi-Fard, "Afghan Leader's Visit to Iran."

48. Bidar, "US Set for Long Stay."

49. Menashri, "Iran and Central Asia," 78; Paul Goble, "The 50 Million Muslim Misunderstanding: The West and Central Asia Today," Anoushiravan Ehteshami, ed., *From the Gulf to Central Asia: Players in the New Great Game* (Exeter: University of Exeter Press, 1994).

50. *Jane's Sentinel, Turkmenistan*, 30 May 2002.

51. Ibid., 28 August 2001; 28 September 2001.

52. Jonson, *Russia and Central Asia,* 9–10. See also Murad Esenov, "Turkmenistan's Foreign Policy and Its Impact on the Regional Security System," *Central Asia and the Caucasus* 1, 2001, 50–57.

53. Michael Ochs, "Turkmenistan: Pipeline Dream II," *Caspian Crossroads Magazine* 1 (Winter 1995), Internet edition; *Economist,* 8 January 2000; Jonson, *Russia and Central Asia,* 63–64, 72.

54. Rashid, *Resurgence of Central Asia,* 203.

55. Esenov, "Turkmenistan's Foreign Policy," 51–52. See also Cooley, *Unholy Wars,* 146.

56. Rashid, *Taliban,* 151, 160–161, 168, 171, 201.

57. Ibid., 152; Marsden, *Taliban,* 131, 136.

58. Radio Free Europe/Radio Liberty (RFE/RL) *Central Asia Report* 2: 6 (14 February 2002), Internet edition.

59. Jane's Sentinel, Turkmenistan, 26 September 2000.

60. Jane's Sentinel: Uzbekistan, 30 May 2002.

61. Ibid., 28 August 2001; 28 September 2001. Active forces only, see also International Crisis Group (ICG), *Central Asia: Fault Lines in the New Security Map* (Osh/Brussels: International Crisis Group, Asia Report 20, 4 July 2001), 10. For U.S. forces, see Bidar, "US Set for Long Stay."

62. See ICG, *Central Asia: Fault Lines.*

63. Jane's Sentinel: Uzbekistan, 31 October 2000.

64. Birgit N. Schlyter, *Language Policy in Independent Uzbekistan* (Stockholm: Forum for Central Asian Studies, Stockholm University, 1997).

65. Jonson, *Russia and Central Asia,* 9, 34–35, 62; Neil J. Melvin, *Uzbekistan: Transition to Authoritarianism on the Silk Road* (Amsterdam: Harwood, 2000), 29–30, 43, 45–47, 91, 100–103.

66. Melvin, *Uzbekistan,* 108–109.

67. Sultan Jumagulov, "Uzbekistan 'Rebuffs' Shanghai Pact," *IWPR's Reporting Central Asia* (19 October 2001; www.iwpr.net).

68. *Washington Post,* 6 October 2001.

69. Rashid, *Jihad,* 184.

70. See, for instance, *Washington Post,* 1 July 2002.

71. *Economist,* 19 January 2002, 2 February 2002; *International Herald Tribune,* 19 February 2002.

72. See, for instance, Chinara Jakypova and Vladimir Davlatov, "US Campaign Poses Threat to Central Asia," *IWPR's Reporting Central Asia* 103 (8 February 2002; www.iwpr.net).

73. See, for instance, *Economist,* 2 February 2002; Joshua Machleder, "Confusion and Cynicism Mark Uzbek Referendum," *Eurasia Insight,* 28 January 2002 (*www.eurasianet.org*).

74. Rashid, *Jihad,* 81–82.

75. RFE/RL *Central Asia Report* 1:13 (18 October 2001).

76. Jane's Sentinel: Tajikistan, 30 May 2002.

77. Jane's Sentinel: Russia, 30 May 2002; Jane's Sentinel: Tajikistan, 30 May 2002. The 201st Motor Rifle Division according to some currently has a strength of only 6,000 to 7,000 troops.

78. Lena Jonson, *The Tajik War: A Challenge to Russian Policy* (London: Royal Institute of International Affairs, 1998), 1; Anette Bohr, *Uzbekistan: Politics and Foreign Policy* (London: Royal Institute of International Affairs, 1998), 51–54.

79. International Crisis Group (ICG), *Tajikistan: An Uncertain Peace* (Osh/Brussels: International Crisis Group, Asia Report 30, 24 December 2001), 4–5.

80. Bakhrom Tursunov and Marina Pikulina, *Severe Lessons of Batken* (Sandhurst: Conflict Studies Research Centre, November 1999), Internet edition. See also Ahmed Rashid, "Namangani's Foray Causes Concern Among Central Asian Governments," *Eurasia Insight,* 5 February 2001 (*www.eurasianet.org*).

81. Anthony Davis, "Tensions in Central Asia," *Jane's Defence Weekly,* 1 September 1999, 20.

82. Tursunov and Pikulina, *Severe Lessons of Batken;* Jane's Sentinel: Kyrgyzstan, 31 October 2000. See also "Central Asia's Narcotics Industry."

83. Tursunov and Pikulina, *Severe Lessons of Batken;* Rashid, "Namangani's Foray."

84. Jonson, *Tajik War,* 9–12, 37–38; Herzig, *Iran and the Former Soviet South,* 31.

85. Tursunov and Pikulina, *Severe Lessons of Batken;* Rashid, "Namangani's Foray;" Alexander Kniazev, "Afghanistan: Religious Extremism and Terrorism, the Year 2000," *Central Asia and the Caucasus* 5, 2000, 82.

86. *Economist,* 29 September 2001. See also Cooley, *Unholy Wars,* 80, 95; Isby, *War in a Distant Country;* Reeve, *New Jackals,* 167–168; regarding the embassy, see ICG, *Tajikistan,* 24.

87. Viktor Korgun, "Afghanistan on the Threshold of Peace," *Central Asia and the Caucasus* 1 (13), 2002, 7–13, on 11. Korgun refers to *Izvestiya,* 18 September 2001.

88. See, for instance, Jakypova and Davlatov, "US Campaign."

89. Jane's Sentinel: Kyrgyzstan, 30 May 2002.

90. Rashid, *Jihad,* 234–235; Jane's Sentinel: Kyrgyzstan, 30 May 2002, 28 August 2001.

91. Jane's Sentinel: Kyrgyzstan, 30 May 2002; Tamara Makarenko, "Central Asia Commits to Military Reform," *Jane's Intelligence Review* 12:9 (September 2000), 29–32, on 31.

92. See, for instance, John Anderson, *Kyrgyzstan: Central Asia's Island of Democracy*

(Amsterdam: Harwood, 1999); International Crisis Group (ICG), *Kyrgyzstan at Ten: Trouble in the "Island of Democracy"* (Osh/Brussels: ICG Asia Report 22, 28 August 2001); International Crisis Group (ICG), *Kyrgyzstan's Political Crisis: An Exit Strategy* (Osh/Brussels: ICG Asia Report 37, 20 August 2002); Rashid, *Jihad,* 66–73.

93. See Rashid, *Jihad,* 71–73.

94. Chinara Jakypova, "Kyrgyzstan: US Bolsters Strategic Plans for Region," *IWPR's Reporting Central Asia* 98 (11 January 2002; www.iwpr.net); Asel Sagynbaeva, "Kyrgyzstan: Mixed Reactions to US Base," *IWPR's Reporting Central Asia* 100 (25 January 2002; www.iwpr.net).

95. Jane's Sentinel: China, 24 October 2001.

96. Ibid., 13 May 2002; 9 April 2002.

97. See, for instance, Burles, *Chinese Policy,* 5.

98. Ibid., 23, 39. See also Fredholm, "The Tatmadaw: Burma's Armed Forces and Prospects for the Future," *The Democracy Movement in Burma since 1962* (conference on 25–26 September 1999 organised by the Center for Pacific Asia Studies at Stockholm University).

99. Anthony Davis, "Xinjiang Learns to Live with Resurgent Islam," *Jane's Intelligence Review,* September 1996, 417–421.

100. Burles, *Chinese Policy,* 18.

101. See Gohari, *Taliban,* 139.

102. See Cooley, *Unholy Wars,* 65–79; Reeve, *New Jackals,* 167, 176, note 32.

103. Rashid, *Taliban,* 232.

104. *Washington Post,* 20 October 2001, referring to a conversation between two alleged Al-Qaida members secretly taped by Italian police. See also Bergen, *Holy War,* 122.

105. Jane's Sentinel: Russia, 30 May 2002.

106. Ibid. The strength in Tajikistan may currently be lower because the units have been reduced.

107. Melvin, *Uzbekistan,* 91, 102.

108. See, for instance, Melvin, *Uzbekistan,* 100. Alexander Solzhenitsyn argued in his *Rebuilding Russia* (London: Harvill, 1991) that Russia had to "shed the onerous burden of the Central Asian underbelly."

109. See Reuters, 15 November 2001 (on Pakistan); AP, 19 November 2001; *International Herald Tribune,* 19 February 2002 (on Uzbekistan); RIA Novosti, 11 December 2001; RFE/RL *Central Asia Report,* 7 March 2002 (on Kyrgyzstan); and RFE/RL *Newsline,* 10 January 2002 (U.S. restrictions on the transfer of military equipment to Tajikistan lifted).

110. *Economist,* 15 December 2001; Igor Torbakov, "Putin Faces Domestic Criticism over

Russia's Central Asia Policy," *Eurasia Insight*, 26 February 2002 (www.*eurasianet.org*).

111. See, for instance, Ahmed Rashid, "Hamid Karzai Moves from Lightweight to Heavyweight in Afghan Politics," *Eurasia Insight*, 10 December 2001 (www.*eurasianet.org*).

112. See *Economist*, 17 November 2001; *Guardian* (UK); Interfax, 15 November 2001.

113. See, for instance, Isby, *War in a Distant Country*.

114. Barry Turner, ed., *The Statesman's Yearbook: The Politics, Cultures and Economies of the World* (London: Macmillan, 2000).

115. Ibid.

116. Zbigniew Brzezinski, *The Grand Chessboard: American Primacy and Its Geostrategic Imperatives* (New York: BasicBooks, 1997), 148–150. See, however, Gregory Gleason, *The Central Asian States: Discovering Independence* (Boulder, Colo.: Westview Press, 1997), 155; Charles Fairbanks et al., *Strategic Assessment of Central Eurasia* (Washington, D.C.: Atlantic Council of the United States and the Central Asia-Caucasus Institute, 2001), 96–100. Compare also the early enthusiasm of Ariel Cohen, "U.S. Policy in the Caucasus and Central Asia: Building a New "Silk Road" to Economic Prosperity," *Heritage Foundation Backgrounder* 1132, 24 July 1997, with the more subdued Ariel Cohen, "U.S. Interests in Central Asia: Testimony before the Subcommittee on Asia and the Pacific/House International Relations Committee, 17 March 1999" (Washington, D.C.: United States House of Representatives, 1999), and Ariel Cohen, "U..S. Interests in Central Asia and the Caucasus: The Challenges Ahead," *Central Asia and the Caucasus* 2, 2000, 12–25. Cohen's frequently changing views on Central Asia often reflect and thereby serve as a reliable guide to the changing realities of current U.S. policy.

117. See, for instance, Jonson, *Russia and Central Asia*, 14–15.

118. Menashri, *Central Asia Meets the Middle East*, 9–10.

119. Rashid, *Taliban*, 176–177, 182.

120. Jakypova, "Kyrgyzstan."

121. See, for instance, Ralph A. Cossa, *The Major Powers in Northeast Asian Security* (Washington, D.C.: Institute for National Strategic Studies, National Defense University, McNair Paper 51, August 1996). Although the U.S. occupation force was withdrawn from Korea in 1949, a small group of military advisors remained in place, and in the following year U.S. forces returned on the side of the United Nations in the Korean War. Sohn Pow-key, Kim Chol-choon, and Hong Yi-sup, *The History of Korea* (Seoul: Korean National Commission for UNESCO, 1970), 332.

122. See, for instance, Rashid, *Taliban*, 160–182.

PART III
The War on Terror

CHAPTER 11

The Intelligence War against Usamah bin Ladin and Al-Qaida

The United States is the stupidest country in the world about Afghanistan.
—Abdul Haq, veteran Afghan mujahidin commander
(killed by the Taliban on 26 October 2001 as he
single-handedly tried to form a Pashtun anti-Taliban alliance)

A major problem for the United States is that its military and political intelligence far too often is not its own, but rather is derived from states that it regards as loyal allies. In some cases, the loyalty is mostly genuine, for instance in intelligence cooperation with Great Britain. In other cases, however, the supposedly loyal allies have their own agendas—which more often conflict with rather than support U.S. interests. Even if the quality of the delivered intelligence appears to be high, the underlying basis of the intelligence may well be biased—and thus unreliable. Nowhere is this more obvious than in the Middle East, where the U.S. intelligence agencies since 1984 seem to rely considerably on information and opinions provided by Israeli intelligence.[1] This is one reason the United States continues to treat Iran as a major evil rather than a geopolitical opportunity. But it remains hard to understand how any U.S. administration, even the most religiously minded, can seriously believe that the Israeli government and intelligence services provide unbiased intelligence and opinions about Israel's particular set of enemies.[2]

In Central and South Asia, the United States has until recently (and perhaps even now) relied chiefly on Pakistani intelligence. During the 1980s and 1990s, most of the intelligence from

Afghanistan—not to mention the opinions and subjective judgements on what was going on there—was derived almost exclusively from Pakistani sources.[3] Amazingly, U.S. intelligence never seemed to have realised that Pakistan was far more interested in furthering its own national interests than those of the United States. This, at least, is the obvious conclusion one can draw from the repeated U.S. attempts to kill or capture Usamah bin Ladin: plans formulated in Washington, D.C., or Langley, Virginia, and repeatedly compromised by Pakistani intelligence services.

Following the November 1995 terrorist attack on a joint Saudi and U.S. facility in Riyadh, the CIA's Counterterrorist Center formed a special Usamah bin Ladin task force in January 1996 (also based on evidence that suggested a connection with the 1993 World Trade Center bombing).[4] Several plans on how to get bin Ladin were put together, the first half-hearted attempt being made at the end of June 1997. Bin Ladin was known to have moved from the eastern Afghan province of Nangarhar to the southern city of Kandahar. A party of three U.S. diplomats and CIA officers stationed in New Delhi reportedly flew to Peshawar to make contact with representatives of several Afghan (probably exclusively Pashtun) tribes as well as the Taliban to spread the word that the United States would pay generously for information on bin Ladin's whereabouts or, preferably, his capture and delivery to U.S. representatives. For at least 10 days, the U.S. diplomats met with elder tribal warlords and a senior Taliban minister; in the end, however, they had to return to India without having achieved anything.[5]

The next attempt was made in mid-April 1998. Bill Richardson, the U.S. ambassador to the United Nations, travelled to Pakistan and then Afghanistan for talks with senior Taliban officials. He reportedly suggested that they hand over bin Ladin to the United States in exchange for international recognition. His attempt did not succeed. The word in the Afghan camps was that teams of U.S. special forces troops had arrived in Pakistan at the same time that Richardson was moving into the U.S. consulate in Peshawar in preparation for a cross-border raid (other versions of this story mentioned deployment of CIA or FBI special teams in not only

Pakistan but, even more unlikely, Tajikistan as well).[6] This rumour is unlikely to have been true because any attempted armed infiltration was by then regarded by the Clinton administration as too hazardous (the Pakistani ISI knew all about such risk aversion, as will be shown).[7] In addition, the Clinton administration probably reasoned that bin Ladin had not yet caused a sufficient number of American deaths to warrant the risk of the United States' suffering further casualties.

Following the August 1998 bombings of the U.S. embassies in Kenya and Tanzania, the United States made several additional, and no doubt more serious, attempts to get bin Ladin. President Clinton issued highly classified directives (i.e., a presidential finding to authorise covert action and three memorandums of notification that authorised the killing of Usamah bin Ladin and several of his lieutenants and the downing of any private aircraft in which he was flying) designed to give the CIA maximum leeway to operate against Al-Qaida. The directives, while technically adhering to the legal ban on the assassination of foreign leaders, did authorise the use of lethal force for self-defence or to prevent terrorist attacks against U.S. targets.[8] Perhaps due to their singular lack of success, no details on these covert operations were released to the public. Only in December 2001, after the fall of the Taliban government, did the CIA disclose that since the 1998 embassy bombings its directorate of operations had, upon orders from President Clinton, recruited, trained, paid, and equipped proxy forces in Pakistan, Uzbekistan, and among tribal militias in Afghanistan with the sole purpose of capturing or killing Usamah bin Ladin.[9]

President Clinton also ordered one overt attack on Usamah bin Ladin: the 20 August 1998 cruise missile attack on what proved to be largely empty Al-Qaida camps in Afghanistan.[10] The cruise missile attacks may have been secret to the American public, but they were clearly anticipated in Pakistan and Afghanistan. As early as two or three days before the missile strike, the ISI warned bin Ladin about the possibility of an attack but pointed out that there would be no commando raid because the United States regarded it as too risky.[11] ISI suspicions had probably been raised when the

U.S. State Department ordered hundreds of nonessential U.S. personnel and dependents out of Pakistan four days before the operation.[12] In less than two days, the ISI, in a highly professional intelligence operation, learned the reason for the State Department order and successfully transmitted a warning to bin Ladin. This, incidentally, also proves that ISI knew all about the Clinton administration's aversion to possible U.S. casualties.

The CIA was probably also involved in at least the last of what appears to have been the series of failed Saudi attempts to assassinate bin Ladin, although any U.S. engagement in assassination attempts at that time are unlikely to be acknowledged. On 19 March 1997, a bomb exploded inside a police station in Jalalabad, killing more than 50 people but not bin Ladin.[13] In November 1998, yet another attempt was made, and this time the CIA may have been involved. An assassin called Siddiq Ahmad was reportedly paid $267,000 to poison bin Ladin. The attempt was only partly successful: bin Ladin survived but, if the story is true, suffered acute kidney failure. The true facts of the incident remain unknown to outsiders, since the region by then abounded in rumours of conspiracies against bin Ladin. There are stories that tell of covert attempts by Arab and Afghan mercenaries to assassinate the infamous Saudi. If the rumours can be believed, which is doubtful, several of the putative assassins were caught and executed by the Taliban. A number of Westerners were also supposedly caught in Afghanistan, as they engaged in surveillance of bin Ladin on behalf of the CIA, but these stories are almost certainly untrue, even though Western intelligence activities aimed at bin Ladin did intensify.[14] Certainly none of the various U.S. plans to seize bin Ladin appears to have included the insertion of U.S. intelligence personnel into Afghanistan. Yet another Saudi attempt to murder bin Ladin may have taken place in the spring of 1999.[15] At least two separate assassination attempts were also reported in the summer of 2000.[16]

The operation that ostensibly showed the most promise, and probably the one in which the CIA put its chief trust, was the Pakistani option. In early 1999, Pakistani Prime Minister Nawaz Sharif established a small, secret commando team with orders to remain ready to cross into Afghanistan together with U.S. operatives to kill or capture Usamah bin Ladin. This was perhaps a genuine offer, but more likely, Nawaz Sharif was pressed by the United States into undertaking the operation and had no choice but to comply. In mid-1999, the CIA commenced a secret training program for approximately 60 commandos from the ISI to enter Afghanistan to liquidate or capture bin Ladin. The CIA supplied the team with all necessary equipment. In 1999, the CIA's Special Activities Division also dispatched a surveillance aircraft into Afghanistan's air space (without landing) to ascertain whether a desert airstrip, probably the one at Dolangi near Kandahar, was suitable for the extraction of bin Ladin, if he could be captured. These activities probably took place in August, since U.S. military aircraft then landed at a Pakistani base and cordoned it off against outsiders.[17] At the latest, by October 1999 (but probably much earlier), the team was deemed ready for initiating the operation. Unfortunately, the whereabouts of bin Ladin could never be determined, and following the 12 October 1999 military coup by General Musharraf, the commando team was disbanded. In any case, the operation would have had precious little chance of success even if launched. Although trained and equipped by the CIA, the commando team remained under the full control of the ISI—which at this time continued to support the Taliban and Al-Qaida and so was less than likely to be cooperative. It is hardly a coincidence that bin Ladin's location could never be verified.[18]

The CIA by then, or soon afterward, also turned to Uzbekistan, where the agency established links with Uzbek forces, which were hoped to eventually be able to kill or capture Usamah bin Ladin. The Uzbeks, as well, apparently accomplished nothing.[19] Although the identity of the Uzbeks involved in this effort was never made public, there is little doubt that they involved Uzbekistani intelligence, with which the CIA was cooperating at least as early as 2000, if not before (certainly in the months before the Clinton administration declared the IMU a terrorist group in September 2000; see Appendix 11).[20] The CIA was also, no doubt, in contact with forces loyal to the Afghan Uzbek warlord Abdul Rashid Dostum.[21]

In October 1999, the CIA—for the first time ever—arranged a meeting with Ahmad Shah Masud, the military leader of the Northern Alliance.[22] Nothing seems to have been achieved by this meeting, probably because of continued Pakistani hostility toward Masud and the Northern Alliance and the CIA's wish not to antagonise the Pakistanis. Indeed, one may speculate about whether the CIA did not in fact first attempt to forge an alliance with Abdul Rasul Sayyaf, who was the only ethnic Pashtun leader within the Northern Alliance and also had amicable relations with Saudi Arabia, which might have made him more palatable to the ISI. However, the details of the meetings remain classified.

It may have been to placate the Pakistanis that the CIA instead, in 2000, established links with a number of southern Pashtun tribal leaders.[23] Among these, the CIA recruited about 15 Afghans, several of whom belonged to the same, undisclosed clan.[24] This clan was willing, and claimed to be able, to kill Usamah bin Ladin. All evidence indicates that this was the Karzai clan, many members of which were by then living in the United States and for this reason were regarded as suitably loyal to the U.S. cause. Although it twice claimed to have attacked bin Ladin's forces, the Afghan group never inflicted any verifiable damage on Al-Qaida. It is not known if the clan members ever actually made the attempt. In light of the CIA's dismal record until then, it seems most likely that the agency merely paid those who claimed to be able to do something, presumably in the hope that at least one of these groups or individuals really had the requisite capability.[25]

More important, a number of intelligence-gathering operations took place in Afghanistan. Operatives (of unknown nationality, but apparently not Americans) of the Special Collection Service, a joint project of the CIA and the National Security Agency (NSA), entered Afghanistan and managed to place radio-monitoring equipment within range of what the CIA referred to as Al-Qaida's "tactical radios." In August and September 2000, an RQ-1 Predator, a propeller-driven, unmanned reconnaissance drone (launched from a base in Uzbekistan),[26] was on several occasions flown at medium altitude over Afghanistan. Once, the Predator's cameras filmed a "tall bearded man in flowing robes" accompanied by a security team, who some believed may have been Usamah bin Ladin. However, on a subsequent mission the drone crashed, and no further attempts were undertaken. The CIA also apparently had a contact in an informer from the Kandahar Taliban who from time to time sent in reports with hearsay information about bin Ladin and his whereabouts. These reports never arrived in time to mount a strike, even if they had been credible—which they apparently were not.[27]

None of these various operations, it should be pointed out, entailed the running of agents within the Al-Qaida network inside Afghanistan. And none could provide credible, up-to-date information on bin Ladin's whereabouts so that cruise missiles could be launched against him, which was the primary objective of the activity. The insertion of commandos, although never completely ruled out by President Clinton, continued to be seen as too risky.[28] Despite every effort, the CIA never appears to have succeeded in gathering substantial intelligence on Usamah bin Ladin and his organisation.[29]

The Planned Assassination of President Clinton

Usamah bin Ladin is the chief suspect in a plan to assassinate President Bill Clinton when he visited the Philippines on 12 November 1994. Apparently Ramzi Yousef was approached for the job, since he made several contingency plans for the attempt. Initially, Yousef considered firing a missile or placing explosives along the route of the president's motorcade. He may have considered whether a Stinger missile could be used, either against the president's airplane as it landed or in a ground attack on his motorcade. Another option he appears to have considered was the use of phosgene gas, which kills by paralysing the lungs of the victim, in a chemical warfare attack. However, after due consideration, Yousef realised that security around the president would be too tight and abandoned his plans.[30]

However, there was, perhaps, one major victory in the intelligence war. In mid-May 1997, a businessman named Sidi al-Madani al-Ghazi Mustafa al-Tayyib (also known variously as Sayyid Tayyib al-Madani, Abu Fadel, and Muhammad bin Moisalih) reportedly defected to Saudi intelligence and the CIA. Sidi Tayyib was either a helpful business acquaintance who just happened to be married to a relative of Usamah bin Ladin, or, as some claim, bin Ladin's chief financial aide. Much remains unclear to Western analysts about Tayyib's role. Some claim that Tayyib was a Saudi intelligence agent all along, others that he was arrested by the Saudi security forces and chose to talk to save himself. In any case, Tayyib proved a highly cooperative source of information, talking at length about bin Ladin's bank accounts and various business interests in Pakistan and Afghanistan. He also talked about the transfer of money to Islamic extremist groups in London, Brooklyn, Jersey City, and Detroit. He also named several of those involved in the money flow. The information, which contained some important facts (although much of it proved flawed and of dubious value), was handed over to the FBI and British intelligence. Some of the details of Al-Qaida's financial operations were reportedly of sufficient value to enable U.S. law enforcement agencies to identify and confiscate key Al-Qaida assets in various banks.[31] However, this claim begs further answers. According to the U.S. Treasury Department's report on terrorist assets for 2000, no assets had yet been firmly linked to Usamah bin Ladin, in the United States or elsewhere, and hence none were frozen.[32] Sources close to Al-Qaida assert that bin Ladin knew in advance that Tayyib was going to betray him and therefore had time to liquidate the exposed assets, although suffering losses while doing so.[33]

As for the NSA (responsible for U.S. signals intelligence), there is no evidence that this organisation was better prepared than the CIA for locating Usamah bin Ladin. Its capability to handle Afghanistan-related communications intercepts was "almost nonexistent": the NSA in September 2001 reportedly had no more than three, if even that many, linguists with the required language skills in Dari and Pashto.[34]

This suggests that the activities of bin Ladin and the other Arab Afghans remained little known among intelligence services for a long time, in the West as well as in Russia and the Middle East. For obvious reasons, the results of these services' interest in the Arab Afghan movement were not widely publicised before the fall of the Taliban, and often not even then. When George Tenet, head of the CIA, delivered his annual statement to the Senate Select Committee on Intelligence in February 2000, he could only claim that in 19 months (since July 1998), his agency (with its vast resources and the full backing of the U.S. government as well as working with foreign governments) had "helped to render more than two dozen terrorists to justice." Of these, "more than half" belonged to bin Ladin's organisation, and "in some cases" their apprehension had prevented planned attacks from occurring.[35] This probably referred to the seven bomb attacks that the CIA in February 1999 claimed to have prevented through the monitoring by satellite of bin Ladin's communications network.[36] These claims might be true, even though signals intelligence of this kind is not usually associated with the CIA but with the NSA. And one then wonders why the agency never managed to locate bin Ladin himself—if it really had that kind of insight into his communications procedures. To locate a person through communications intelligence is admittedly often more difficult than to listen in on his communications. But it can be done over a period of time, especially if the communications reveal clues on the location. It should be noted that the NSA in October 1999 admitted to a lamentable track record in locating bin Ladin.[37]

The NSA has also disclosed that it, with the help of its British partner, the Government Communications Headquarters, was able to listen in on bin Ladin's personal Inmarsat (International Maritime Satellite Organization) satellite telephone for about two years, from the time of his move to Afghanistan in 1996 until August 1998. However, bin Ladin apparently never discussed specific terrorist activities on the phone (its number was 00873-682-505-331, incidentally).[38] A French source listed another telephone number used by Usamah bin Ladin as 925-12 53 06, while Taliban leader Mullah Omar used 928-18 37 825.[39] Unfortunately for the eavesdroppers, the Afghanistan-based Islamic extremists realised in 1998 that foreign and local intelligence services were able to intercept and locate both satellite telephones and the various communications methods that use the Internet. As it became clear during the war with the Soviet forces that regular radio communications could be intercepted, the extremists appear to have switched to the use of couriers for more important messages.[40]

Considering the hundreds and hundreds of Islamic extremists who are arrested or killed in war zones every year, the CIA's claim of having participated in the arrest of about a dozen men (apparently throughout the world) can hardly be called a spectacular result. In February 2001, Tenet again gave the same audience his views, but then he was only able to say that the United States and its allies had "scored some important successes against terrorist groups and their plans," although he mentioned that he would elaborate during the closed session later.[41] The conclusion to be inferred from this is that no major intelligence service in the West or among its allies (including Russia, with its own extremist threat in northern Caucasus) had managed to penetrate more than isolated elements of the Arab Afghan movement—making it a true black hole in today's increasingly connected world. The full extent of the extremists' influence appeared to remain unknown, probably even to the movement's leaders and proponents.

The challenge posed by Islamic extremists to the intelligence services has been summarised, somewhat naively, by Oliver Revell, former associate deputy director of the FBI: "What makes these groups so troublesome is that they hide under a religion, do not have a traditional linear hierarchy, speak a foreign language, and generally go about as far as they can in pushing the limits of the law without our being able to track them when and if they go over the line."[42] To this litany of difficulties can be added the increased reliance on computer databases within the intelligence services. Many Muslims share the same names, and different agencies transcribe Arabic in different ways (Muhammad, Mohammed, or Muhammed? Usamah bin Ladin or Osama bin Laden?), often even within the same agency. These are two factors that do not facilitate the searching for particular extremists in the huge databases of collected intelligence.

It appears that among major intelligence services in the West or those of their allies, Russian intelligence may have been most successful in collecting substantial intelligence on Al-Qaida and its sponsors. Even so, the seven-page Russian intelligence summary presented to the UN Security Council on 9 March 2001 provided far less intelligence on bin Ladin and Al-Qaida than on the Taliban and their Pakistani sponsors. Although the report provided "extremely explicit intelligence" on 55 alleged Al-Qaida bases and offices in Afghanistan, its emphasis was on the 31 senior Pakistani officers who, the report claimed, at the time were actively involved with bin Ladin and the Taliban. Among these were eight ISI generals and various other military officers of senior rank based at Pakistan's embassy in Kabul, as well as others reportedly attached to military units or acting as advisers to the Taliban. The report also named six Pakistani officers who allegedly held senior positions within the Taliban military and security apparatus, including head of intelligence. The Russian report also gave 16 examples of regular units of the Pakistani armed forces that, it claimed, were based in Afghanistan (including parachute and commando units), and what was described as an airborne warning and control system reconnaissance aircraft—probably a reference to a more common reconnaissance aircraft—that operated out of Mazar-e-Sharif. The report also named the seven top Taliban officials, including the chief of the general staff, who controlled Afghanistan's narcotics production.[43] Far less was known about the inner workings of Al-Qaida.

When Usamah bin Ladin and his organisation rose to prominence in the early 1990s, the U.S. intelligence community was slow to recognise the new, emerging threat. For most of its agencies, in particular the CIA, interest in Afghanistan had waned with the fall of the Soviet Union. Sunni Islamic extremism was simply not taken seriously, as efforts along this line of inquiry were—upon guidance from Israel—aimed almost exclusively against Iran, the traditional bogeyman of the CIA and the various presidential administrations.

If American policy toward Afghanistan during the 1990s gives the impression of having been shortsighted, the CIA's reliance on the Pakistani ISI arguably was the main failure.[44] During the war against the Soviet Union, the CIA was content to act as a quartermaster to the Pakistani ISI, which handled the distribution of money and goods to its own favoured Afghan parties. Exactly who received the goods was beyond the CIA's control. Very few CIA officers were involved in the enterprise, and it appears that not one CIA officer even went into Afghanistan during this war (unlike, for instance, British and French intelligence, which sent several operatives into the country). In fact, the first CIA officer who had even a minimal command of any Afghan language did not arrive in Pakistan until 1987, when the war was almost over. No CIA officer ever visited Ahmad Shah Masud in Afghanistan during the war against the Soviet Union (although British and French intelligence personnel frequently did), and in fact did not do so until the already mentioned meeting in October 1999. After the Soviet withdrawal, the CIA appears to have lost the little interest it once had in Afghanistan.[45]

In all fairness, however, the agency probably found its resources barely sufficient to cover the disintegration of the Warsaw Pact and the Soviet Union, which no doubt—and justifiably—was regarded as more important to U.S. policy-makers. Still, the advantage of hindsight is not required to see that the agency, after arming and training a large force of fanatic Muslim holy warriors for a God-decreed crusade against those perceived as hostile to Islam, at least should have devoted minimal attention to what these men were doing with their new weapons and lethal training after the war ended. This clearly did not happen. According to a former CIA analyst, the one CIA case officer who repeatedly asked headquarters for permission to collect intelligence inside Afghanistan through the access offered by the Northern Alliance was always ordered not to. The reason was that the Pakistani ISI loathed Masud, and the CIA did not wish to offend the ISI, believing that the Pakistani agency was the United States' trusted friend. Other U.S. intelligence organs reacted similarily. One U.S. Defense

Intelligence Agency analyst, Julie Sirrs, was even fired in 1999 for meeting with Masud, even though she had previously received permission for the trip (though this dismissal may also have been due to interagency rivalry, that being the year in which the CIA also sent its first representative to Masud). When the August 1998 U.S. Embassy bombings in Tanzania and Kenya finally shook the CIA out of its complacency toward Afghanistan-based Sunni Islamic extremists, its officers for too long found themselves unable to develop useful networks against Al-Qaida. Only a handful of CIA officers had spent even a few days in Afghanistan, and the necessary experience was thus simply not available. Besides, the bias in favour of the ISI and against Masud remained. Apparently the Taliban, being primarily Pashtuns and thus—in the view of the Pakistanis and, accordingly, most U.S. Intelligence chiefs— favourably disposed toward the United States, would eventually calm down and hand over Usamah bin Ladin. As late as October 2000, the CIA reportedly had not sent a single operative to search for intelligence on Al-Qaida within Afghanistan,[46] although the agency, as already noted, had established contacts with various groups outside the country. As for the 10 months prior to the September 2001 attacks, there is no evidence to suggest that the CIA made any substantial effort to move into Afghanistan. With the exception of a few and not very reliable local sources (such as that informer within the Kandahar Taliban),[47] the agency appears to have had no presence in Afghanistan on the eve of the September 2001 attacks: it subsequently had to begin its war-related operation in Afghanistan from scratch.

One reason the CIA did not itself attempt any infiltration of Al-Qaida was no doubt an employment practice that emerged within the agency during the 1990s: the agency much preferred hiring young, inexperienced people than older, seasoned ones.[48] While inexperienced employees are more likely to obey their superiors without asking disturbing questions and to follow the dictates of current political correctness, they are seldom independent-minded and knowledgeable enough to resolve anything but routine tasks. This practice was exacerbated by internal squabbles that resulted in the resignation of several senior people within the directorate of operations. The employment policy thus gave rise to a culture in which "operations that include diarrhoea as a way of life don't happen," as one CIA officer put it.[49] Needless to say, a penetration of Al-Qaida would have been neither routine, politically correct, nor necessarily good for one's health.[50]

This culture of glorification in inexperience and bureaucracy did not dissappear overnight after 11 September 2001. As late as the end of October 2001, former national security adviser Robert C. McFarlane (by then acting as informal adviser to the late Abdul Haq, whose requests for weapons, a helicopter airlift, and a field radio he claimed the CIA had turned down) angrily pointed out that he had yet to meet any Dari speaker in the CIA, or indeed anyone who spoke any Afghan dialect or had real knowledge of Afghanistan.[51] McFarlane's allegations against the CIA were probably right on the mark; when Kabul fell to Dari-speaking Tajik troops of the Northern Alliance in November 2001, the CIA team on the spot had not yet hired any Dari interpreter. According to sources inside the CIA, the agency had only a single Afghan analyst when the war in Afghanistan began.[52]

Yet, despite the various internal problems and previous mistakes, the CIA did successfully rise to the challenge of a war in Afghanistan following the 11 September attacks. Already by 15 September, CIA Director George Tenet presented and received the president's approval for a covert plan to strike back against Al-Qaida. Outside of stepped-up intelligence cooperation with various other countries, the plan envisaged the insertion of half a dozen small CIA paramilitary teams into Afghanistan. These would eventually link up with U.S. Army Special Forces to aid the opposition in Afghanistan.[53]

Little time was wasted. Realising that the Northern Alliance, which kept a base in Tajikistan, formed the only independent gateway into Afghanistan free from ISI interference, CIA officials immediately attempted to establish an understanding with the government of Tajikistan. This had to have been a premature hope at such an early stage. It is unlikely that Taijikistan's Rahmonov government would have been able to immediately agree to such a request, depending on the good will of Moscow as it was. Even though Russian President Putin, as soon became evident, was ready to accept a U.S. presence in the region, few governments are eager to allow a foreign intelligence service to initiate a war from their territory.

However, the CIA had an unexpected ally in Tajikistan. It soon turned out that the Northern Alliance, which operated an embassy in Tajikistan's capital, was quite ready to form an alliance with the United States. Indeed, it appears that the first successful contacts with Tajikistan's government came about through the good offices of those Northern Alliance leaders who retained links with British intelligence (many of them were once trained by members of the British army's Special Air Service, SAS), as well as memories of U.S. support during the war against the Soviet Union.[54] With such assistance, as well as encouragement from Putin, the CIA by 23 September 2001 had acquired permission from Tajikistan to use the country as a base for the invasion of Afghanistan.[55] There were also reports, impossible to verify though not implausible, that Japan also applied pressure on Tajikistan to allow the Americans into the country. Considering that Japan is one of Tajikistan's main donors, the United States may well have requested Japanese support for its request.[56] On 24 September 2001, small groups of CIA paramilitary operatives began arriving in Dushanbe. So did, apparently, the first British SAS troops.[57]

The CIA paramilitary units, whose existence had not previously been disclosed, belonged to the CIA's Special Activities Division, which reports to the deputy director for operations, the clandestine arm of the CIA. Before 2000, the division was called the Military Support Program, which existed for decades but had atrophied after the Cold War. The paramilitary units consist of teams of about half a dozen men who do not wear military uniforms. The Special Activities Division is made up of about 150 men (fighters, pilots, and specialists), mostly military veterans. The division's inventory includes helicopters and aircraft as well as the Predator drones armed with Hellfire antitank missiles.[58] Dressed in civilian garb, the CIA teams almost certainly operated under the cover of journalist or, less likely at this particular time, aid worker. (Although this was an operationally sound tactic also used by the United States' Western allies during the Soviet Afghan war, it most likely endangered legitimate journalists attempting to cover the war within Afghanistan. No fewer than eight journalists were killed in the period from September to December 2001).[59]

On 26 or 27 September 2001 (almost certainly during the night),[60] the first CIA paramilitary unit entered Afghanistan, being the first U.S. force on the scene. Its mission (probably in conjunction with the British SAS) was to work with the Northern Alliance to pave the way for U.S. Special Forces expected to arrive later.[61] The Northern Alliance Liaison Team (NALT), as this unit became known, was eventually followed by five additional six-man teams: Alpha in the northwest, Bravo at Mazar-e-Sharif, Charlie in the west, and Echo and Foxtrot in the south.[62] Unconfirmed reports mentioned that SAS commandos were active near Kabul at around the same time (the end of September), so it is likely that they entered together with the U.S. teams.[63] The war on the ground had begun.

End Notes

1. For details on U.S.-Israeli defence and intelligence cooperation, see Lewis, "United States and Israel," 373–375.

2. Another dubious ally is of course Saudi Arabia, the country of origin of 15 of the 19 hijackers on 11 September 2001, which consistently has since refused to freeze assets belonging to Islamic extremist and terrorist organisations. Despite this, the Bush administration apparently continues to regard Saudi Arabia as a reliable ally. See, for instance, *Economist,* 3 November 2001. Saudi Arabia, however, is not a major source of intelligence because it has precious little intelligence-gathering capability of its own.

3. See, for instance, Rubin, *Fragmentation of Afghanistan,* 251–252; Bergen, *Holy War,* 73.

4. Reeve, *New Jackals,* 184–185; *Washington Post,* 3 October 2001.

5. Ibid., 193–194. Reeve, it should be noted, appears to have had access to information and sources within British intelligence. Although he occasionally refers to interviews with U.S. and British intelligence officials, he offers no source for several nuggets of information that could come only from intelligence reports (in some cases he has even copied peculiarities in the spelling of foreign names, forms that would not have been

used by most academics or journalists). In addition, the information has not, so far as I have been able to ascertain, previously been released to the public.

6. Bodansky, *Bin Laden,* 341.

7. Reeve, *New Jackals,* 195; Jacquard, *Osama Bin Laden,* 52.

8. *Washington Post,* 14 September 2001, 19 December 2001.

9. Ibid., 19 December 2001.

10. Some have suggested that the purpose of the attack was merely to frighten Usamah bin Ladin. This seems unlikely; bin Ladin was not a head of state like Muammar al-Qadhafi of Libya or Saddam Hussein of Iraq. Yet claims have been made that the U.S. intelligence agencies knew that bin Ladin was absent from the Zhawar Kili al-Badr camps at the time of the attack because of their monitoring of his radiotelephone traffic, and so it was a deliberate decision not to kill him and so make him a martyr. Cooley, *Unholy Wars,* 217. The truth, if any, in these claims has been impossible to verify.

11. Bodansky, *Bin Laden,* 287–288.

12. *Washington Post,* 3 October 2001. Nonessential personnel and dependents were apparently also evacuated from the embassies in Albania, Eritrea, Uganda, Egypt, Yemen, and Malaysia because U.S. officials feared further embassy bombings after the ones in Africa on 7 August 1998.

13. Alexander and Swetnam, *Usama bin Laden's al-Qaida,* 41.

14. Reeve, *New Jackals,* 204. Usamah bin Ladin's alleged kidney and liver disease was also the subject of speculation in the news media in March and April 2000. Alexander and Swetnam, *Usama bin Laden's al-Qaida,* 47.

15. Jacquard, *Osama Bin Laden,* 87.

16. Alexander and Swetnam, *Usama bin Laden's al-Qaida,* 48.

17. Tara Kartha, "Pakistan and the Taliban: Flux in an Old Relationship?" *Institute for Defence Studies and Analyses* 24:7 (New Delhi, October 2000). The news also appeared on Al-Jazeera, 10 August 1999.

18. *Washington Post,* 3 October 2001, 19 December 2001; *Time,* 6 May 2002.

19. Ibid., 19 December 2001.

20. Ibid., 31 January 2002.

21. The CIA has since claimed that it gave the Northern Alliance "very limited financial and technical covert support" at a cost of several million dollars a year over the "past four years" (that is, since 1998–1999), handled by the CIA's paramilitary teams. If this claim is true, which seems doubtful (the sum mentioned might possibly indicate the part of the CIA budget spent on its ongoing operation against Usamah bin Ladin in Afghanistan, not the funds actually being transferred to the Northern Alliance), the

support almost certainly went exclusively to Dostum, who after all was an important member of the Northern Alliance. *Washington Post,* 29 January 2002.

22. Reuel Marc Gerecht, "Counterterrorist Myth," 38–42.
23. *Washington Post,* 31 January 2002.
24. Ibid., 23 December 2001.
25. Ibid., 19 December 2001.
26. Ibid., 31 January 2002.
27. Ibid., 19 December 2001.
28. Ibid.
29. At least one CIA intelligence report on bin Ladin has since been made public. Dated by its contents to the period from late July to early November 1995, before the CIA's Counterterrorist Center in January 1996 formed a special Usamah bin Ladin unit (Reeve, *New Jackals,* 184–185; *Washington Post,* 3 October 2001), the report contains little but general news agency material. This suggests (but does not prove) that the various intelligence efforts up to then, at least, had been largely ineffectual. See the undated report "Usama bin Ladin: Islamic Extremist Financier" released through the National Security Archive (www.*gwu.edu/~nsarchiv/NSAEBB*).
30. Reeve, *New Jackals,* 76–77.
31. Bodansky, *Bin Laden,* 243; Reeve, *New Jackals,* 204–205.
32. Department of the Treasury, *2000 Annual Report to Congress on Assets in the United States Belonging to Terrorist Countries or International Terrorist Organizations* (Washington, D.C.: Office of Foreign Assets Control, Department of the Treasury, January 2001).
33. Interview with Dr. Saad al-Faqih and the anonymous document given to a PBS reporter, both displayed on the Web site, *http://pbs.org/frontline*
34. James Bamford, *Body of Secrets: Anatomy of the Ultra-Secret National Security Agency* (New York: Anchor Books, 2002), 648. See also James Bamford, "Too Much, Not Enough," *Washington Post,* 2 June 2002.
35. "The Worldwide Threat in 2000: Global Realities of Our National Security," Statement by Director of Central Intelligence George J. Tenet Before the Senate Select Committee on Intelligence, 2 February 2000 (*www.cia.gov*).
36. Rashid, *Taliban,* 137.
37. *Intelligence Newsletter* 372 (16 December 1999), 5.
38. *Komsomolskaya Pravda,* 13 March 2002, referring to the Indian newspaper *Statesman,* 12 March 2002; *Washington Post,* 2 June 2002.
39. Jacquard, *Osama Bin Laden,* 48, 260.

40. Jane's World Insurgency and Terrorism 13, 27 November 2001.

41. "The Worldwide Threat in 2001: National Security in a Changing World," Statement by Director of Central Intelligence George J. Tenet Before the Senate Select Committee on Intelligence, 7 February 2001 (*www.cia.gov*; www.usembassy.org.uk/terror128.html).

42. Reeve, *New Jackals,* 232.

43. *Jane's Intelligence Digest Special Report: Why Was Russia's Intelligence Coup on Al-Qaeda Ignored?* (*Jane's Intelligence Digest,* 12 October 2001).

44. In September 1989, the head of the CIA Afghan Task Force was dismissed due to charges in Congress of CIA incompetence and acquiescence in ISI politics by the organisation's complete reliance on its Pakistani counterpart. Rubin, *Fragmentation of Afghanistan,* 251–252.

45. Gerecht, "Counterterrorist Myth," 38–42. Gerecht, "Terrorists' Encyclopedia," 84–85. Although Gerecht appears to hold a grudge against the CIA, his is the only independent public account of the CIA interest, or lack thereof, in Afghanistan prior to the 11 September 2001 attacks. The generally favorable reports on CIA activities in Afghanistan, leaked by the agency to various newspapers after the fall of the Taliban government, only contradict Gerecht in self-congratulatory optimism, never in the details of CIA activities actually revealed. See, for instance, *Washington Post,* 19 December 2001; 31 January 2002.

46. Gerecht, "Terrorists' Encyclopedia," 84–85.

47. *Washington Post,* 19 December 2001.

48. See, for instance, *Economist,* 6 October 2001. The hiring policy was a prominent part of the CIA's Web site (*www.cia.org*).

49. Gerecht, "Counterterrorist Myth," 38–42.

50. For CIA overreliance on inexperienced desk officers without overseas experience, see, for instance, Robert Baer, *See No Evil: The True Story of a Ground Soldier in the CIA's War Against Terrorism* (New York: Random House International, 2002), although his conclusion about Iranian complicity in virtually all Islamic terrorism seems somewhat exaggerated. As for health problems, this writer can vouch for the likelihood of catching dysentery in Afghanistan.

51. *Newsweek,* 5 November 2001.

52. *Time,* 11 March 2002.

53. *Washington Post,* 31 January 2002.

54. *Economist,* 29 September 2001. See also, for instance, Cooley, *Unholy Wars,* 80, 95; Isby, *War in a Distant Country;* Reeve, *New Jackals,* 167–168; regarding the embassy, see ICG, *Tajikistan,* 24.

55. *Washington Post,* 24 September 2001.

56. Rashid, *Jihad,* 185.

57. RIA Novosti, 24 September 2001, referring to ABC News.

58. *Washington Post,* 18 November 2001.

59. For more information on the number of journalists killed, see *Washington Post,* 3 May 2002, referring to the annual report of Reporters Without Borders.

60. On 26 September according to *Newsweek,* 29 April 2002, but on 27 September according to *Washington Post,* 18 November 2001, 3 April 2002.

61. *Washington Post,* 18 November 2001.

62. *Newsweek,* 29 April 2002.

CHAPTER 12
The Military Campaign
in Afghanistan

When the military campaign began with the first air raids on Taliban and Al-Qaida targets in Afghanistan on 7 October 2001, the British SAS and U.S. CIA paramilitary forces had already been in the country since 27 September 2001. To move these light, mobile troops had been an exercise in diplomacy but was logistically simple; to bring the main force of U.S. and British military might to bear on Afghanistan demanded logistical work of a far higher magnitude. The latter effort, undertaken by thousands of staff planners, supply officers, junior officers, and noncommissioned officers, was not particularly glamorous but formed the real achievement of the Afghan war. In comparison, most combat operations in Afghanistan were undemanding.

While U.S. policy toward Afghanistan and Sunni Islamic extremism had remained inconsequential and frequently misguided for most of the 1990s, the United States immediately after the 11 September 2001 terrorist attacks showed that it could still act decisively, fully utilising all the various powers at its disposal. By early October, U.S. and coalition forces in the theatre had reached substantial numbers, although the bulk consisted of troops and vessels normally deployed there and already present at the time of the 11 September attacks. In fact, the U.S. Central Command, which was responsible for operations in the region, maintained a normal operating strength there that typically varied between 20,000 and 25,000 troops on any given day. The bulk of this force was at sea, but there were also substantial numbers in various bases throughout the area. It was also common for large U.S. forces to participate in war games in the vicinity. One such multinational exercise, Bright Star, was scheduled for October 2001 in Egypt, with a planned U.S. participation of 23,200 troops, including units of the 1st Marine Expeditionary Brigade and the 26th Marine Expeditionary Unit.[1] Partly for this reason, the United States had a larger than usual military presence in the neighbourhood. In addition, one carrier battle group was in the process of relieving another, which added further to the available military strength.

British troops in the region included 23,000 troops (8,500 naval personnel, 12,000 soldiers, and 2,500 Royal Air Force [RAF] personnel) and a Royal Navy task group of reportedly about three dozen warships based around Britain's largest aircraft carrier, HMS *Illustrious*, carrying a squadron of British Aerospace Sea Harrier FA Mk2 attack aircraft with vertical takeoff and landing capability. There was, too, the assault ship HMS *Fearless*, with Royal Marines and army commandos aboard, taking part in a preplanned exercise with Omani forces (Operation *Sarif Sareea* [Swift Sword] II).[2] Britain too had unusually large numbers of troops in the theatre; the troops conducting the exercise in Oman constituted the biggest British deployment of forces since the Gulf War.

Central Command was headed by Gen. Tommy R. Franks for about a year. General Franks came under criticism in the media for being a senior army officer reluctant to deal with the media. Some observers regarded him as plodding and unimaginative and, it was claimed, he displayed a singular lack of interest in intelligence and special operations, despite the emphasis that the war obviously would put on these.[3] General Franks may also have had a strained relationship with Secretary of Defense Donald H. Rumsfeld. On 7 December, Rumsfeld even made public the fact that he had overruled the general's first war plan for its being unimaginative.[4] Franks had, apparently, wanted to move large numbers of conventional forces into Afghanistan following the pattern of the Gulf War against Iraq, while Rumsfeld wished to emphasise special forces and unconventional warfare. In the end, the United States chose the special forces option. However, faced with the actual conduct of war in Afghanistan, General Franks seems to have displayed none of the negative tendencies he had been accused of. And he did lead the coalition that defeated the Taliban.

The U.S. forces usually stationed in the area, or brought there in the initial deployment (6,000 additional U.S. troops were soon moved into the region, including special forces),[5] can be divided into two groups: those at sea and those on bases in allied countries.

AMERICAN AND BRITISH FORCES AT SEA

The U.S. military might in the theatre primarily consisted of the forces at sea. By mid-September 2001, the manpower alone was about 20,000 navy personnel and 6,000 marines. These forces were distributed among aircraft carrier battle groups, which rotated through the theatre at regular intervals. Each battle group was centred on an aircraft carrier with about a dozen combat and support ships and an air wing of about 70 to 80 aircraft: the aircraft included up to 20 Grumman F-14 Tomcat strike fighters, 36 McDonnell Douglas F/A-18C/D Hornet multirole strike interdictors, 4 Grumman EA-6B Prowler electronic warfare aircraft, and 4 Grumman E-2C Hawkeye AWACS (airborne warning and control system) aircraft used for direction of air defence and strike operations. Furthermore, there were 6 Lockheed Martin S-3B Viking antisubmarine warfare aircraft also useful as refueling tankers, 2 Lockheed Martin ES-3A Shadow signals intelligence aircraft (primarily for electronic intelligence), as well as 4 Sikorsky SH-60F Seahawk helicopters typically used for antisubmarine warfare, and 2 Sikorsky HH-60H Seahawk helicopters used in a strike role and for special warfare support, as well as search-and-rescue operations.

Each carrier had about 5,000 to 6,000 crew members, as well as the crews of the accompanying ships of the battle group. In addition, a battle group was typically accompanied by an amphibious squadron with about 3,000 personnel, including a Marine Expeditionary Unit (MEU) of 2,200 troops, commanded by a colonel. Each MEU consisted of a reinforced ground battalion with 31 light armoured vehicles, a mortar unit, an antitank unit, 6 howitzers, and 4 M-1A1 tanks, as well as a support force with 63 Humvee light trucks, heavy trucks, forklifts, and 2 water purification plants. The MEU also had its own dedicated air support in the form of an aviation squadron with McDonnell Douglas AV-8B Harrier attack aircraft as well as both attack and transport helicopters: AH-1W Super Cobra attack helicopters, Vertol CH-46 Sea Knight helicopters, Sikorsky CH-53 Sea Stallion helicopters (used for assault, support, and transportation purposes; a Sea Stallion can carry 38 Marines), and Bell UH-1N Iroquois utility helicopters.[6]

Three carrier groups, based on the USS *Enterprise*, the USS *Carl Vinson*, and the USS *Theodore Roosevelt*, respectively, were already in or near the zone of deployment, while a fourth, based on the USS *Kitty Hawk*, was eventually dispatched from its base in Japan.

British Royal Navy vessels in the area included the aircraft carrier HMS *Illustrious* and a helicopter carrier, HMS *Ocean*. These vessels carried the 40 and 45 Commando of the Royal Marines, which both had participated in the Oman exercise, as well as most of the 60 British aircraft in the vicinity.[7] The British naval assets also included three nuclear attack submarines in the Gulf of Oman. Three Royal Navy nuclear-powered fleet submarines of the *Swiftsure* and *Trafalgar* classes were deployed for the start of operations in October: HMS *Superb,* HMS *Trafalgar,* and HMS *Triumph*, the latter two equipped with Tomahawk cruise missiles.[8]

U.S. MILITARY ASSETS PRESENT

The USS Enterprise Battle Group
(Carrier Air Wing Eight, CVW 8)

Location: On 11 September 2001 exiting the Arabian Sea and in the process of being relieved by the USS *Carl Vinson* Battle Group. Needless to say, the USS *Enterprise* Battle Group received orders to remain in the neighbourhood and did so, taking part in the air operations, until November 2001, when the group left the northern Arabian Sea and returned to port. Some units of the Amphibious Ready Group (ARG) already returned to port in mid-October, after having been replaced by the ARG with the USS *Carl Vinson* Battle Group, while others remained, ending up with the USS *Theodore Roosevelt* Battle Group.

Strike Aircraft: two Grumman F-14A Tomcat strike fighter and two McDonnell Doiuglas Hornet F/A-18C/D multirole strike interdictor squadrons, one Grumman EA6B Prowler squadron.

The USS *Enterprise* Battle Group

USS *Enterprise* (CVN 65)	Aircraft carrier	Enterprise class
USS *Philippine Sea* (CG 58)	Guided missile cruiser	Ticonderoga class
USS *McFaul* (DDG 74)	Guided missile destroyer	Arleigh Burke class
USS *Nicholson* (DD 982)	Destroyer	Spruance class
USNS *John Ericsson* (T-AO 194)	Oiler	Henry J Kaiser class
USS *Arctic* (AOE-8)	Fast combat support ship	Supply class
USS *Jacksonville* (SSN 699)	Attack submarine	Los Angeles class
USS *Providence* (SSN 719)	Attack submarine	Los Angeles class

The following returned to home ports before combat operations began:

USS *Gettysburg* (CG 64)	Guided missile cruiser	Ticonderoga class
USS *Stout* (DDG 55)	Guided missile destroyer	Arleigh Burke class
USS *Gonzales* (DDG 66)	Guided missile destroyer	Arleigh Burke class
USS *Thorn* (DD 988)	Destroyer	Spruance class
USS *Nicholas* (FFG 47)	Guided missile frigate	Oliver Hazard Perry class

Note: Ticonderoga-class cruisers, Arleigh Burke-class destroyers, Spruance-class destroyers, and Los Angeles-class submarines are cruise missile platforms; the vessels in the battle group as originally constituted had the capacity to launch roughly 500 conventional land-attack Tomahawk cruise missiles.

Attached to the USS *Enterprise* Battle Group was also an

ARG, consisting of three ships. All were in the Mediterranean on 10 September 2001. The U.S. Marine component of the group was the 24th MEU.

USS *Kearsarge* (LHD 3)	Amphibious assault ship	Wasp class
USS *Ponce* (LPD 15)	Amphibious transport dock	Austin class
USS *Tortuga* (LSD 46)	Amphibious cargo ship	Whidbey Island class

The USS Carl Vinson Battle Group
(Carrier Air Wing Eleven, CVW 11)

Location: The Persian Gulf, in the process of relieving the USS *Enterprise* Battle Group. The USS *Carl Vinson* Battle Group was itself relieved on 15 December 2001 by the USS *John C. Stennis* Battle Group.[9]

Strike Aircraft: one Grumman F-14D Tomcat strike fighter and three McDonnell Douglas F/A-18C/D Hornet multirole strike interdictor squadrons, one Grumman EA6B Prowler squadron.

The USS *Carl Vinson* Battle Group

USS *Carl Vinson* (CVN 70)	Aircraft carrier	Nimitz class
USS *Antietam* (CG 54)	Guided missile cruiser	Ticonderoga class
USS *Princeton* (CG 59)	Guided missile cruiser	Ticonderoga class
USS *John Paul Jones* (DDG 53)	Guided missile destroyer	Arleigh Burke class
USS *O'Kane* (DDG 77)	Guided missile destroyer	Arleigh Burke class
USS *O'Brien* (DD 975)	Destroyer	Spruance class
USS *Sacramento* (AOE 1)	Fast combat support ship	Sacramento class
USS *Niagara Falls* (T-AFS 3)	Combat stores ship	
USS *Olympia* (SSN 717)	Attack submarine	Los Angeles class
USS *Key West* (SSN 722)	Attack submarine	Los Angeles class

Some reports also mentioned the following as attached to the battle group:

USS *Ingraham* (FFG 61)	Guided missile frigate	Oliver Hazard Perry class

Note: The battle group also probably included an oiler.

Attached to the USS *Carl Vinson* Battle Group was an ARG, initially located in the Arabian Sea, consisting of three ships. The marine component of the group was the 15th Marine Expeditionary Unit, Special Operations Capable (MEUSOC), normally stationed at Camp Pendleton, California. The MEUSOC was commanded by Col. Thomas Waldhauser.[10]

Marine Air Wing: McDonnell Douglas AV-8B Harrier attack aircraft, Bell AH-1W Super Cobra attack helicopters, Vertol CH-46 Sea Knight helicopters, Sikorsky CH-53 Sea Stallion helicopters, and Bell UH-1N Iroquois utility helicopters.

USS *Peleliu* (LHA 5)	Amphibious assault ship	Tarawa class
USS *Dubuque* (LPD 8)	Amphibious transport dock	Austin class
USS *Comstock* (LSD 45)	Amphibious cargo ship	Whidbey Island class

The USS Theodore Roosevelt Battle Group
(Carrier Air Wing One, CVW 1)

Location: The USS *Theodore Roosevelt* Battle Group left Norfolk, Virginia, on 19 September for the Mediterranean Sea. The battle group transited the Suez Canal on 13 October 2001 and arrived in the Arabian Sea on 15 October. The USS *Theodore Roosevelt* was to be replaced by mid-January 2002 by the USS *John F. Kennedy* (CV 67). However, repairs to the latter delayed her deployment until 20 February 2002. She finally relieved the USS *Theodore Roosevelt* on 7 March.

Strike Aircraft: one Grumman F-14B Tomcat strike fighter and three McDonnell Douglas F/A-18C/D Hornet multirole strike interdictor squadrons, one Grumman EA6B Prowler squadron.

The USS *Theodore Roosevelt* Battle Group

USS *Theodore Roosevelt* (CVN 71)	Aircraft carrier	Nimitz class
USS *Leyte Gulf* (CG 55)	Guided missile cruiser	Ticonderoga class
USS *Vella Gulf* (CG 72)	Guided missile cruiser	Ticonderoga class
USS *Ramage* (DDG 61)	Guided missile destroyer	Arleigh Burke class
USS *Ross* (DDG 71)	Guided missile destroyer	Arleigh Burke class

USS *Peterson* (DD 969)	Destroyer	Spruance class
USS *Hayler* (DD 997)	Destroyer	Spruance class
USS *Elrod* (FFG 55)	Guided missile frigate	Oliver Hazard Perry class
USS *Carr* (FFG 52)	Guided missile frigate	Oliver Hazard Perry class
USS *Detroit* (AOE 4)	Fast combat support ship	Sacramento class
USS *Springfield* (SSN 761)	Attack submarine	Los Angeles class
USS *Hartford* (SSN 768)	Attack submarine	Los Angeles class

Note: According to some reports, perhaps three of the destroyers and one of the frigates followed later, joining the battle group en route.[11] The battle group also probably included an oiler and a combat support ship.

Attached to the USS *Theodore Roosevelt* Battle Group was an ARG consisting of three ships. The marine component of the group was the 26th Marine Expeditionary Unit, Special Operations Capable (MEUSOC), normally stationed at Camp Lejeune, North Carolina. The MEUSOC was commanded by Col. Andrew Frick.

USS *Bataan* (LHD-5)	Amphibious assault ship	Wasp class
USS *Shreveport* (LPD 12)	Amphibious transport dock	Austin class
USS *Whidbey Island* (LSD 41)	Amphibious cargo ship	Whidbey Island class

Marine Air Wing: McDonnell Douglas AV-8B Harrier attack aircraft, Bell AH-1W Super Cobra attack helicopters, Vertol CH-46 Sea Knight helicopters, Sikorsky CH-53 Sea Stallion helicopters, and Bell UH-1N Iroquois utility helicopters.

When the USS *Enterprise* Battle Group returned home, its ARG vessels stayed in place. For this reason, around 17 November 2001 an additional marine unit, at first deployed in the Mediterranean Sea, was joined to the *Theodore Roosevelt* Battle Group. This unit, apparently another 1,500 to 2,000 marines from the 26th MEU, had originally left their base on 20 September for Bright Star, a regularly scheduled mission in the Arabian Sea.[12] This was a 10-nation exercise in October 2001 that included a total of 70,000 troops, including the 1st Marine Expeditionary Brigade and the 26th MEU (marines from Camp Pendleton, Miramar Marine Corps Air Station and Twentynine Palms Marine Base, as well as 21,000 other U.S. troops). When the exercise was concluded by early November, it was reported that the units in Egypt would return home. However, the bulk of the marines, 2,200 troops, remained in Egypt for potential deployment under Operation Enduring Freedom.

This ARG consisted of three ships. The new marine component of the Group became the 26th MEUSOC, normally stationed at Camp Lejeune, North Carolina.

USS *Kearsarge* (LHD 3)	Amphibious assault ship	Wasp class
USS *Ponce* (LPD 15)	Amphibious transport dock	Austin class
USS *Carter Hall* (LSD 50)	Amphibious cargo ship	Harpers Ferry class

Marine Air Wing: McDonnell Douglas AV-8B Harrier attack aircraft, Bell AH-1W Super Cobra attack helicopters, Vertol CH-46 Sea Knight helicopters, Sikorsky CH-53 Sea Stallion helicopters, and Bell UH-1N Iroquois utility helicopters.

The USS Kitty Hawk Battle Group
(Carrier Air Wing Five, CVW 5)

Location: The battle group left its homeport of Yokosuka, Japan, bound for the Arabian Sea on 1 October. The USS *Kitty Hawk* eventually departed the northern Arabian Sea for its home port in Japan on 8 December 2001.

Strike Aircraft: Only a limited contingent (reportedly a total of eight Grumman F-14 Tomcat strike fighters and McDonnell Douglas F/A-18C/D Hornet multirole strike interdictors) of her normal complement of about 75 aircraft;[13] the navy wanted to leave sufficient deck space to carry special forces helicopters and other aircraft.[14]

Special Operations Aircraft: Flight deck cleared for various tactical aircraft and helicopters to support special forces operations, including a dozen special operations Sikorsky MH-60 Black Hawk Special Forces transport helicopters, a half-dozen Boeing MH-47

Chinook medium-lift transport helicopters, and several Sikorsky MH-53J Pave Low special forces transport helicopters. Reportedly more than 1,000 special forces personnel were based on the carrier, including the army's 160th Special Operations Aviation Regiment (Task Force Falcon), known as the "Night Stalkers," Navy SEALS, and air force special forces. The USS *Kitty Hawk* picked up the special forces helicopters and some of the personnel in Oman and then moved to the Arabian Sea off the coast of Pakistan, whence the helicopters flew to a base in Pakistan, where they were loaded with additional special forces troops flown in on Lockheed Martin C-130 transports.[15]

The USS *Kitty Hawk* Battle Group

USS *Kitty Hawk* (CV 63)	Aircraft carrier	Kitty Hawk class
USS *Vincennes* (CG 49)	Guided missile cruiser	Ticonderoga class
USS *Chancellorsville* (CG 62)	Guided missile cruiser	Ticonderoga class
USS *Curtis Wilbur* (DDG 54)	Guided missile destroyer	Arleigh Burke class
USS *Cushing* (DD 985)	Destroyer	Spruance class
USS *Gary* (FFG 51)	Guided missile frigate	Oliver Hazard Perry class
USNS *Rappahannock* (T-AO 204)	Oiler	Henry J Kaiser class
USS *Bremerton* (SSN 698)	Attack submarine	Los Angeles class

Note. Some reports indicate that an additional cruiser joined the battle group on the way from Japan:

USS *Cowpens* (CG 63)	Guided missile cruiser	Ticonderoga class

Attached to the battle group was an ARG, consisting of three vessels. The marine component was the 31st MEU. The ARG, which landed in East Timor on 30–31 October, did not take part in Afghan operations.

USS *Essex* (LHD 2)	Amphibious assault ship	Wasp class
USS *Juneau* (LPD 10)	Amphibious transport dock	Austin class

USS *Fort McHenry* (LSD 43)   Amphibious cargo ship   Whidbey Island class

BRITISH MILITARY ASSETS PRESENT

The HMS *Illustrious* Battle Group
HMS *Illustrious*   Aircraft carrier
HMS *Fearless*   Assault ship

The carrier was also supported by at least six other ships and two submarines. The HMS *Illustrious,* in addition to a complement of aircraft, carried the 40 Commando Royal Marines.

The HMS *Ocean* Battle Group
HMS *Ocean*   Helicopter carrier

The carrier was supported by at least seven other ships. The HMS *Ocean* also carried the 45 Commando Royal Marines.

U.S. AND BRITISH FORCES ON BASES WITHIN THE REGION

The United States also had a substantial military presence at bases within the theatre of war. Most of it belonged to the air force. Even before reinforcements were sent from home, about 175 operational aircraft were in place on bases in allied countries, together with many aircraft and much equipment in prepositioned storage.

Saudi Arabia
Personnel: About 4,800 air force, 650 army, 250 marines, and 20 navy. About 1,000 British troops[16] (including 280 RAF personnel).
Equipment: One Patriot surface-to-air missiles battery; McDonnell Douglas F-15 Eagle, Lockheed Martin F-16 Fighting Falcon, and Lockheed Martin F-117 Nighthawk fighters; Lockheed Martin C-130 Hercules transports; Lockheed Martin KC-130 tankers; Lockheed Martin U-

2 high-altitude reconnaissance aircraft; and Boeing E-3 Sentry AWACS surveillance aircraft based at Prince Sultan Air Base at Al-Kharj, roughly 50 miles (80 kilometres) southeast of Riyadh, with a new sophisticated Combined Air Operations Center (CAOC) opened in June 2001. About 200 U.S. aircraft stored at the Eskan Village Air Base. A British RAF squadron of six Panavia Tornado F Mk3 fighters.[17]

Kuwait

Personnel: About 4,800 to 5,100, mostly U.S. Army and Air Force personnel. The army has since 1992 rotated battalion-size units through the Camp Doha Army Base. About 430 British RAF personnel at Ali al-Salem Air Base.

Equipment: The U.S. Air Force has deployed aircraft with the mission of enforcing the no-flight zone over southern Iraq, based at Ahmed al-Jabar Air Base and Ali al-Salem Air Base. The RAF also deployed a few combat aircraft, usually eight Panavia Tornado GR Mk1 strike interdictors, at Ali al-Salem for the same purpose. Prepositioned reinforced brigade with two tank battalions, a mechanised infantry battalion, and an artillery battalion. Two Patriot air defence batteries.[18]

Bahrain

Personnel: About 1,000, including about 680 U.S. Navy personnel and 220 U.S. Marines. The U.S. Fifth Fleet is based in Manama. Central Command also maintains a forward headquarters in Bahrain.[19]

Equipment: The Fifth Fleet headquarters commands a force that in recent years has averaged 15 vessels, including an aircraft carrier. The U.S. Air Force periodically deploys fighter and support aircraft at Shaikh Isa Air Base, typically McDonnell Douglas F-15C Eagle or Lockheed Martin F-16C Fighting Falcon fighters as well as Boeing KC-135 Stratotanker refueling tankers.

Several warehouses of prepositioned equipment and supplies. In addition, there is a small RAF presence in Bahrain, usually centred on one or two BAC VC-10 tanker aircraft from 101 Squadron, RAF Brize Norton.[20]

United Arab Emirates

Personnel: About 400, mostly U.S. Air Force, at Al-Dhafra Air Base. Small U.S. Navy and Air Force facilities at Fujairah.
Equipment: U.S. Navy equipment prepositioned at Jebel Ali Naval Base.[21]

Oman

Personnel: About 630 U.S. Air Force and 60 Navy personnel.
Equipment: Prepositioned equipment at Thumrait Air Base, Masirah Air Base, and Seeb Air Base to supply a force of 25,000 troops. A U.S. signals intelligence interception facility on the island of Masirah.[22]

Qatar

Personnel: About 1,000, mostly U.S. Army personnel.
Equipment: Prepositioned equipment for one armoured brigade at the Al-Udeid Air Base.[23]

Turkey

Personnel: About 2,000, mostly U.S. Air Force personnel (Incirlik Air Base). Base for the patrols of the northern no-flight zone over Iraq.
Equipment: 40 McDonnell Douglas F-15 and Lockheed Martin F-16 Fighting Falcon fighter aircraft; Grumman EA-6B Prowler electronic warfare aircraft.

Diego Garcia Navy Support Facility
Personnel: About 600, mostly U.S. Navy personnel.
Equipment: Equipment for a U.S. Marine expeditionary brigade.

Deployment Orders

Among immediate deployments, nearly 50 U.S. combat aircraft were ordered to the British base on Diego Garcia, in the Indian Ocean.[24] This included an undisclosed number of Boeing B-52 bombers from the 5th Bomb Wing at Minot Air Force Base, North Dakota, and the 917th Reserve Wing at Barksdale Air Force Base, Louisiana (nine of them left Barksdale on 21 September); and B-1B bombers from the 28th Bomb Wing at Ellsworth Air Force Base, South Dakota, and the 34th Bomb Squadron at Mountain Home Air Force Base, Idaho. By the end of November, eight B-1B and ten B-52 bombers were deployed to Diego Garcia, together with Col. Edward Rice, previously commander of Ellsworth Air Force Base. From Diego Garcia, Colonel Rice commanded what became known as the 28th Air Expeditionary Wing, a unit consisting of B-1B bombers from Ellsworth and B-52 bombers from other bases.

In late September, Lt. Gen. Charles F. Wald, commander of air forces assigned to the Middle East and South West Asia, flew to Prince Sultan Air Base, Saudi Arabia. This base became the headquarters for air operations during the entire Afghan campaign. The Prince Sultan Air Base, also known as Al-Kharj, is very large and has extensive landing and aircraft storage facilities. It has often been compared to a large parking lot. (During the 1991 Gulf War, Al-Kharj—then little more than a runway and parking ramp—was often referred to as "Al's Garage.") The base has since been extensively developed—paradoxically by the Saudi Binladin Group[25]—and due to the threat of terrorism became the main American base in Saudi Arabia. In June 2001, a new CAOC was opened at Prince Sultan Air Base, being fully operational in mid-July. This has since served as the primary command and control, or C2, facility in the theatre. In October

2001, the Saudi government agreed that United States would be able to use the command center to coordinate air operations against targets in Afghanistan, although the Saudis did not want any combat mission to be launched from Saudi territory.[26] By then, almost the entire U.S. C-5 and C-17 transport fleet, a total of about 140 aircraft, was engaged in the relocation of troops and supplies to the region.

On 19 September 2001, U.S. Air Force aircraft began flying into the area, primarily bound for bases in Kuwait, Saudi Arabia, Oman, and the Diego Garcia Navy Support Facility in the Indian Ocean. The aircraft included F-15Es, intended for deployment to Uzbekistan. This never took place, however, and the F-15Es remained in Kuwait, where they operated out of Ali al-Salem Air Base. Other aircraft deployed to the zone of operations included F-16 fighters, B-1B long-range bombers, E-3 AWACS aircraft, KC-135s, and other support aircraft.[27] The number of aircraft deployed rose steadily, soon reaching roughly 150 aircraft in addition to those already in the neighbourhood, including reportedly some two dozen bombers and support aircraft. The total of U.S. aircraft in the theatre was brought up to more than 300. U.S. and British KC-10 Extender and Boeing KC-135 tankers, operating primarily from bases in Diego Garcia, Oman, Bahrain, and elsewhere in Southwest Asia, were on almost constant call in the air, being concentrated in several orbits over southwestern Pakistan. By early November, almost 500 aircraft were involved in the operation, including reconnaissance and other support aircraft from not only Britain but Australia, Canada, and France.

Within days of the 11 September 2001 terrorist attacks, Secretary of Defense Donald H. Rumsfeld signed deployment orders for a variety of units, including some that were already in the area of operations:

2d Bomb Wing, Barksdale Air Force Base, Louisiana
5th Bomb Wing, Minot Air Force Base, North Dakota
   (Boeing B-52)

28th Bomb Wing, Ellsworth Air Force Base, South
Dakota (B-1B)
509th Bomb Wing, Whiteman Air Force Base, Missouri (B-2)
917th Reserve Wing, Barksdale Air Force Base,
Louisiana (B-52)
34th Bomb Squadron, Mountain Home Air Force Base,
Idaho (B-1B)
22d Air Refueling Wing, McConnell Air Force Base,
Kansas
141st Air Refueling Wing, Fairchild Air Force Base,
Washington (KC-135E)
Air Refueling Wing from Beale Air Force Base,
California
1st Fighter Wing, Langley Air Force Base, Virginia (F-15)
20th Fighter Wing, Shaw Air Force Base, South Carolina
(F-16)
27th Fighter Wing, Cannon Air Force Base, New
Mexico (F-16)
388th Fighter Wing, Hill Air Force Base, Utah
355th Wing, Davis-Monthan Air Force Base, Arizona
(EC-130E Airborne Battlefield Command and
Control Center [ABCCC]; Fairchild OA-10
Thunderbolt II forward air controllers)
366th Wing, Mountain Home Air Force Base, Idaho
(McDonnell Douglas F-15 Eagle fighters from
Kadena Air Base, Okinawa)
552d Air Control Wing, Tinker Air Force Base,
Oklahoma (E-3 Sentry AWACS and KC-135)
9th Reconnaissance Wing, Beale Air Force Base,
California (U-2 high-altitude reconnaissance aircraft;
probably operating out of Al-Dhafra Air Base,
United Arab Emirates; included in a second deploy-
ment order)
55th Reconnaissance Wing, Offutt Air Force Base,

Nebraska (RC-135 Rivet Joint signals intelligence aircraft; included in a second deployment order)

193d Special Operations Wing, a unit of the Pennsylvania Air National (EC-130E Commando Solo II Airborne Psychological Warfare, essentially flying radio and television stations used for broadcasting messages to the enemy in psychological warfare operations)

USS *Enterprise* Carrier Battle Group, Norfolk Naval Base, Virginia

USS *Carl Vinson* Carrier Battle Group, Bremerton Naval Base, Washington

USS *Theodore Roosevelt* Carrier Battle Group, Norfolk Naval Base, Virginia

USS *Kitty Hawk* Carrier Battle Group, Yokosuka Naval Base, Japan

USS *Bataan* Amphibious Assault Group, Norfolk Naval Base, Virginia

USS *Kearsarge* Amphibious Assault Group, Norfolk Naval Base, Virginia

USS *Peleliu* Amphibious Assault Group, San Diego Naval Base, California

15th Marine Expeditionary Unit, Camp Pendleton, California

24th Marine Expeditionary Unit, Camp LeJeune, North Carolina

26th Marine Expeditionary Unit, Camp LeJeune, North Carolina

10th Mountain Division, Army, Fort Drum, New York

Units under the Army Special Operations Command: an undisclosed number of units belonging to Special Operations Command Central, including but not limited to the army's 5th Special Forces Group (Fort Campbell, Kentucky),[28] 75th Ranger Regiment (Fort Benning, Georgia), the 528th Special Operations

Support Battalion, and the 112th Special Operations
Signal Battalion.[29]

The 160th Special Operations Aviation Regiment
and the 101st Airborne Division (both based at Fort
Campbell, Kentucky; the 101st commanded by Maj.
Gen. Richard A. Cody) were notified to be prepared to
deploy overseas by 16 October 2001.[30] So were, almost
certainly, the other special units that would take part in
the Afghan war: Delta Force, Navy SEALs, 5th Special
Forces Group (army Green Berets, based at Fort
Campbell, Kentucky),[31] and 23d Special Tactics
Squadron (air force, based at Hurlburt Field in
Florida).[32] Later, the 82d Airborne Division (Fort Bragg,
North Carolina) was ordered to deploy as well.[33]

The 10th Special Forces Group, 3d Special Forces
Command, Special Operations Command Europe, based
at Stuttgart, Germany, did not take part in the Afghan
operations, but some of its units were sent to the
Caucasian republic of Georgia in a War on Terror-related
mission in February 2002.

Less conspicuous but of great importance to the campaign
was the RQ-1 Predator: a propeller-driven, unmanned reconnaissance drone armed with two Hellfire laser-guided missiles. In
Afghanistan, these were under the control of the CIA but actually
operated by the U.S. Air Force.[34] The Predator has an endurance
of 24 hours and a range of 500 miles, which enabled the craft to
reach Afghanistan from bases in Uzbekistan or Pakistan. The
Predator was reportedly able to produce still photographs and live
videos of activities on the ground from more than 10,000 feet up,
as well as strike targets with its Hellfire missiles. Although highly
useful in reconnaissance, as many as 20 Predators were lost in the
campaign. Another, larger unmanned surveillance drone, the RQ-
4A Global Hawk, was also used. Having a greater range, it was

operated by a joint air force and Northrop Grumman contractor crew from Al-Dhafra Air Base in the United Arab Emirates.[35]

Uzbekistan became the first country in the vicinity of Afghanistan where the United States acquired new basing rights. The first regular military deployment in Central Asia took place on 22 September 2001, when two C-130 transport aircraft with about 100 U.S. troops landed in Uzbekistan (at Tuzel, just outside Tashkent).[36] On 24 September, they were followed by at least two other C-130s with several hundred U.S. troops (referred to as army commandos).[37] Major deployments took place only in early October, before the air raids began. On the evening of 2 October, a reinforced battalion of light infantry (more than a thousand troops) from the 10th Mountain Division landed at the previously nonoperational Uzbekistani air base of Qarshi/Khanabad, 152 kilometres (94 miles) north of the Afghan border (in Qashqadaryo [Kashkadarya] region, not to be confused with the regular Uzbekistani air base Khanabad near Tashkent). This deployment was later denied[38] and said to have taken place only on 6 October 2001 after an official agreement had been negotiated between the two states.[39] The word in the U.S. Army was that the 10th Mountain Division had been selected because it had not had the opportunity to serve in Iraq during the Gulf War (this was likely a key reason for the unit's deployment; most of the units that eventually served in Afghanistan were among those not deployed at the time of the Gulf War). The army mission was to provide base security for the expected air force fighter deployment and combat search-and-rescue units. In addition, the unit would form a rapid reaction force ready to come to the aid of any U.S. Special Forces unit that found itself in trouble in Afghanistan. The initial deployment, which within a month was reinforced by another thousand troops from the 10th Mountain Division, lasted for six months, after which the 10th Mountain Division was expected to send another battalion as replacements (but this order was cancelled; other troops may have been sent instead).[40] Later the United States was also allowed the use of the airfield in Termiz, on the Afghan border.[41] The United States was, as noted, expected to base F-15s and F-16s in Uzbekistan,[42] but this never took place.

By early November, more than 50,000 U.S. servicemen were deployed throughout the area of operations: a vast area reaching from the shores of the Red Sea to the Indian Ocean and northward to Uzbekistan and Tajikistan. About half were aboard naval ships operating in the northern Arabian Sea. Approximately 3,000 U.S. troops were reportedly in Oman, including soldiers from the 3d Battalion, 75th Ranger Regiment. Another 1,500 to 2,000 Americans, including soldiers from the 10th Mountain Division and special operations forces, were, as noted, based at Qarshi/Khanabad air base in Uzbekistan. On 11 November, the Third Army, the ground component of Central Command, also moved its forward headquarters from Fort McPherson, Georgia, to Camp Doha, Kuwait. This headquarters (Coalition Forces Land Component Command) from early December on controlled ground operations in Afghanistan.[43]

Britain also made a substantial contribution to the early deployment of forces. Britain has the second largest air-to-air refuelling tanker force in the world after the United States. The RAF accordingly contributed a combat support force to the operation consisting of Lockheed Martin L-1011 Tristar K Mk1 and Tristar KC Mk1 dual-role refuelling and transport aircraft. These have refuelling systems compatible with U.S. Navy and Marine Corps aircraft. This tanker force offered support in particular to the U.S. carrier-borne air assets and was retained in theatre to support the continuing operations in the area.

Royal Air Force units taking part in the operation included the following:

10th Squadron, RAF Brize Norton, Oxfordshire (VC-10 tanker aircraft)
101st Squadron, RAF Brize Norton, Oxfordshire (VC-10 tanker aircraft)
216th Squadron, RAF Brize Norton, Oxfordshire (L-1011 Tristar K Mk1 and Tristar KC Mk1 dual-role refuelling and transport planes)

1312 Flight, Falkland Islands (VC-10 tanker aircraft)
8th Squadron, RAF Waddington, Lincolnshire (Boeing E-3D
Sentry AEW Mk1 surveillance and control aircraft (airborne
early warning radar platform))
23d Squadron, RAF Waddington, Lincolnshire (Boeing E-3D
Sentry AEW Mk1 surveillance and control aircraft [airborne
early warning radar platform])
51st Squadron, RAF Waddington, Lincolnshire (British Aerospace
Nimrod R Mk1 signals intelligence aircraft)
RAF Kinloss (home of three Nimrod squadrons, including the
120th and 206th; Nimrod MR Mk2 maritime reconnaissance
and antisubmarine warfare aircraft)
39th Squadron, RAF Marham, Norfolk (English Electric/BAC
Canberra PR Mk9 reconnaissance aircraft)
RAF Lyneham, Oxfordshire (primarily C-130 transport aircraft and,
apparently, some C-17 heavy airlifters)
RAF Brize Norton, Oxfordshire (primarily C-130s and, apparently,
some C-17s)

End Notes

1. When no other source is given, this section is based on United Kingdom Ministry of Defence (*www.mod.uk*); French Ministry of Defence (*www.defense.gouv.fr*); Center for Defense Information (summaries prepared by Rear Admiral (Ret.) Stephen H. Baker, U.S. Navy (www.*cdi.org*); and in particular the invaluable summaries provided by John Pike at his Web site, *www.globalsecurity.org* For the details on the U.S. and coalition order of battle, see the relevant issues of Jane's Sentinel; *New York Times,* 21 September 2001; *Economist,* 29 September 2001; and the U.S. Navy Web site (www.*chinfo.navy.mil*).

2. *New York Times,* 30 September 2001; *Economist,* 29 September 2001; *Washington Post,* 3 October 2001, 8 October 2001.

3. For background information on General Franks, see *Washington Post,* 9 November 2001.

4. *Washington Post,* 9 December 2001.

5. *New York Times,* 30 September 2001.

6. See also Jane's Information Group, *Jane's Fighting Ships 2002–2003.*

7. *Economist,* 26 January 2002.

8. *Washington Post*, 8 October 2001. All three submarines later returned to Britain, being replaced by other Royal Navy submarines in regular rotation.

9. The USS *John C. Stennis* (CVN 74) battle group, based in San Diego, included six warships: USS *Lake Champlain* (CG 57), the USS *Port Royal* (CG 73), the USS *Decatur* (DDG 73), USS *Elliot* (DD 967), the USS *Jarrett* (FFG 33), and the USS *Bridge* (AOE 10)), two attack submarines, the USS *Salt Lake City* (SSN-716) and the USS *Jefferson City* (SSN 759), and one supply vessel. En route, the battle group was joined by a Canadian frigate, the HMCS *Vancouver*. The USS *John C. Stennis* battle group left port on 12 November 2001, heading for the Indian Ocean by way of Hong Kong, which the battle group visited in the first week of December. The battle group arrived in the Arabian Sea on 15 December 2001, where it divided air operations with the USS *Theodore Roosevelt* into day and night shifts, respectively.

10. *Washington Post*, 2 November 2001, 3 November 2001.

11. See, for instance, *Washington Post*, 20 September 2001; *Washington Times*, 24–30 September 2001 (National Weekly Edition).

12. *Washington Post*, 20 September 2001, 9 November 2001.

13. Reportedly four F/A-18C/D multirole strike interdictor squadrons and one EA6B squadron with a full air wing aboard, but not on this mission.

14. *Washington Post*, 2 October 2001.

15. *Washington Times*, 1–7 October 2001 (National Weekly Edition); *Washington Post*, 9 October 2001, 24 December 2001.

16. *Economist*, 26 January 2002.

17. Jane's Sentinel: Saudi Arabia, 28 May 2002.

18. Ibid.: Kuwait, 29 April 2002.

19. Ibid.: Bahrain, 29 October 2001.

20. Ibid.

21. Ibid.: United Arab Emirates, 28 May 2002.

22. *Washington Times*, 8–14 October 2001 (National Weekly Edition); Jane's Sentinel: Oman, 28 May 2002; *Washington Post*, 5 October 2001.

23. Jane's Sentinel: Qatar, 28 May 2002.

24. *New York Times*, 30 September 2001.

25. Jacquard, *Osama Bin Laden*, 17.

26. Despite reassurances to the contrary, some key U.S. policy makers, after the 11 September 2001 attacks, were just as disillusioned by the reluctance of their Saudi ally to move against the extremists as they were with Pakistan. In the autumn, the United States accordingly began an extensive upgrading of the facilities at Al-Udeid Air Base

in Qatar, a huge airfield about 35 kilometres south of Doha, in order to establish an alternative command centre. By early 2002, the number of U.S. aircraft and personnel at the base had increased substantially. By mid-March, several thousand U.S. troops were stationed there in support of the Afghan war, staffing a large contingent of U.S. aircraft, including F-16 fighters, JSTARS reconnaissance aircraft, and KC-10, KC-130, and KC-135 tankers. By late March 2002, additional communications and control equipment was moved to Al-Udeid from Prince Sultan Air Base in Saudi Arabia, in a move intended to provide long-term operational flexibility in the region. Within a few days, the United States had set up a new alternative CAOC at Al-Udeid. By April 2002, around 2,000 U.S. troops were living in a large military tent city at the base. While Central Command denied that the new emphasis on Al-Udeid was a sign that the United States was leaving Prince Sultan Air Base in Saudi Arabia, the U.S. agreement with Qatar allows a wider range of military operations than is permitted by the agreement with Saudi Arabia. Qatar has, for instance, indicated that it would not place limits on rules of engagement.

27. *Washington Post,* 20 September 2001.
28. On 4 December 2001, three Green Berets from the 3d Battalion of this unit were killed and 16 wounded by friendly fire while guarding Hamid Karzai. *Washington Post,* 6 December 2001.
29. John Pike, *www.globalsecurity.org*
30. *Washington Post,* 9 October 2001.
31. On 1 April 2002, it was disclosed that most of the Army's 5th Special Forces Group by the end of March had returned to Fort Campbell, Kentucky, having turned over in-theatre duties to the 3d Special Forces Group, based at Fort Bragg, North Carolina, and geared toward action in Eastern Africa and the Middle East. *Washington Times,* 1–7 April 2002 (National Weekly Edition).
32. On 4 December 2001, four Air Force special operations controllers from this unit were wounded by friendly fire while on duty with Green Berets of the 3d Battalion, 5th Special Forces Group. *Washington Post,* 6 December 2001.
33. It was also initially speculated whether the 18th Airborne Corps (Fort Bragg) and the 3d Infantry Division (Fort Stewart, Georgia) would be deployed. *Washington Times,* 24–30 September 2001 (National Weekly Edition).
34. *Washington Post,* 18 October 2001.
35. Center for Defense Information (www.*cdi.org*); Jane's Sentinel: United Arab Emirates, 28 May 2002.
36. *Washington Post,* 23 September 2001, referring to Interfax and Agence France Presse.

37. RIA Novosti, 24 September 2001, referring to ABC News.

38. *Washington Post,* 4 October 2001.

39. Ibid., 6 October 2001.

40. Ibid., 3 October 2001.

41. Korgun, "Afghanistan on the Threshold of Peace," 11–12.

42. *Washington Post,* 6 October 2001.

43. Jane's Sentinel: Kuwait, 29 April 2002; Jane's Sentinel: Afghanistan, 31 May 2002.

CHAPTER 13

The Coalition Deploys

Great Britain was the first U.S. ally to send forces to the area of operations, but other allies soon followed. After Britain, the most important was arguably France, which at an early stage had also agreed to allow U.S. (and some coalition) forces operate out of its military base at Djibouti, a republic and port in the Horn of Africa, on the Gulf of Aden. France also offered the use of its naval forces in the Indian Ocean and by early October announced that French undercover intelligence agents were active in Afghanistan, working with the Northern Alliance. In addition, French special forces units were ready to join the war from the French base in Djibouti. A French refuelling ship and a missile cruiser were already patrolling with U.S. and British fleets off the coast of Oman.[1]

By early November 2001, France had assigned 2,000 military personnel to the operation in Afghanistan, divided among 1,200 navy troops, 200 air force personnel, 100 logistics personnel, and 500 military intelligence officers (although some of the latter operated out of France). Aircraft in the neighbourhood included Dassault Mirage IV-P reconnaissance aircraft and a Transall C-160G Gabriel signals intelligence aircraft. The Mirage IV-P operated out of Manas, Kyrgyzstan, from 23 October to 8 February 2002, being virtually the only nontransport or tanker aircraft that did so in this period.[2] France reportedly requested permission to base six Dassault Mirage 2000 multirole combat fighter aircraft/fighter-bombers, two Lockheed Martin C-130 Hercules tanker aircraft, and 200 technicians in Kyrgyzstan and Tajikistan. On 1 December, the French nuclear-powered aircraft carrier (the only carrier in the French navy), the recently modernised *Charles de Gaulle*, left Toulon for the northern Indian Ocean. After going through the Suez Canal on 11 December 2001, the French carrier battle group, designated CTF 473, was a substantial force with an air contingent of 16 Dassault Super Etendard reconnaissance and strike aircraft, two Dassault Rafale M multirole fighter-bombers, and two Grumman E-2C Hawkeye air surveillance aircraft. Along with the *Charles de Gaulle* (R 91), the carrier group included the antiaircraft frigate *Jean Bart* (D 615), the antisubmarine frigates *Jean de Vienne* (D 643) and *La Motte-Piquet* (D 645), the supply tanker *Meuse* (A 807), and the nuclear attack submarine *Rubis* (S 601).[3] With the American and British heavily involved in combat operations, the French force (as well as those of most other coalition members) undertook the less glamorous but equally important task of maritime patrolling, thus preventing Al-Qaida and Taliban members from moving large amounts of explosives or other weapons of terrorism overseas for retaliatory strikes. French forces also took part in combat operations, however. On 2 December, French units (apparently 200 men from the 21st Marine Infantry Regiment) were deployed to Mazar-e-Sharif airfield to provide security for the outer perimeter of the airfield.[4]

The military buildup continued throughout the autumn. On 8 October, the day after the air war began, NATO pledged five German-manned AWACS aircraft from Geilenkirchen Air Base, Germany, to the emerging coalition.[5] On 1 November, Turkey announced that it would send 90 special forces troops to help train Northern Alliance troops.[6]

On 7 November, Italy pledged 2,700 troops, including naval, air, and ground units. The forces included the aircraft carrier *Giuseppe Garibaldi* (C-551) with 8 McDonnell Douglas AV-8B Harrier attack aircraft and 4 GKN Westland Sea King transport/antisubmarine warfare helicopters, the 2 frigates *Zeffiro* (F-577) and *Aviere* (F-583), the supply ship *Etna* (A-5326), from 6 to 10 Panavia Tornado reconnaissance aircraft, a Boeing 707 refuelling plane, a C-130 Hercules transport plane, 4 Agusta A 129 Mangusta attack helicopters, and 1,400 ground troops to be employed primarily in escort and humanitarian missions, although the troops also included about 150 paratroopers.[7]

A Japanese contingent of three warships, the destroyers *Kurama* (DDH-144) and *Kirisame* (DD-104) as well as the supply ship *Hamana* (AOE-204), left Japan on 9 November in what was Japan's first military deployment since World War II in support of combat forces. Later in the month, the supply ship *Towada* (AOE-422), the minesweeper *Uraga* (MST-463), and the destroyer *Sawagiri* (DD-157) left Japan to join the other warships. As with most other allied forces, their main task was maritime patrol, operating out of Diego Garcia. At the end of March 2002, when the combat operations in Afghanistan were basically concluded, the Japanese contingent returned home.[8]

On 9 November, the Netherlands also pledged 1,200 troops to the coalition, as did the Czech Republic and New Zealand.[9]

As early as 8 October, Australia had committed 1,000 troops, including 150 elite commandos of the Special Air Service Regiment, as well as refuelling and surveillance aircraft.[10] By mid-November 2001, Australia had also committed a guided missile frigate (HMAS *Kanimbla*), 4 McDonnell Douglas AF-18A Hornet multirole strike interdictors, 2 Lockheed Martin P-3C Orion long-range maritime surveillance aircraft (more typically used in anti-submarine warfare operations), 2 Boeing 707 air refuelling aircraft, and 1,500 troops to the operation.[11]

On 27 November 2001, Germany commenced operations in support of the coalition: the first deployment of German troops outside Europe since World War II. The German contingent included three Transall C-160 transport aircraft, as well as up to 100 troops from the army's Special Operations Command (*Kommando Spezialkräfte,* KSK), and eventually some naval assets.[12]

Canada, having already deployed the frigate HMCS *Halifax* to the gulf, pledged 2,000 troops, including a commando unit (a component of the Canadian counterterrorism/special operations unit Joint Task Force 2), 6 warships (the *Halifax*, a destroyer, a supply ship, and Sea King helicopters were immediately directed to the Persian Gulf; another frigate, HMCS *Vancouver*, was deployed later, arriving to the theatre with the USS *John C. Stennis* Battle Group), and 6 aircraft (3 RCAF C-130s, an Airbus, and 2 CP-140 Aurora maritime patrol aircraft) to the coalition.[13] On 7 January 2002, Canada also announced the immediate deployment of 800 troops from the 3d Battalion, Princess Patricia's Canadian Light Infantry (3 PPCLI) Battle Group to Kandahar. By mid-February, these troops (2 rifle companies from 3 PPCLI, support elements, and a reconnaissance squadron from Lord Strathcona's Horse [Royal Canadians] equipped with Coyote light armoured reconnaissance vehicles) operated in conjunction with the U.S. troops.[14]

The coalition allies also provided additional special operations forces. By January 2002, special operations forces from not only Britain but also Australia, France, Denmark, Germany, and Turkey had deployed to Afghanistan, where they conducted operations in conjunction with the U.S. forces.[15]

By early March 2002, more than 17,000 military personnel from 17 coalition countries had been sent to the region, although only a few of these were actually involved in combat operations in Afghanistan. Most were, as noted, involved in maritime patrol. To cover the vast Indian Ocean between Pakistan and the shore of Africa, a fleet of about 100 ships (40 U.S. and 60 allied, including those from Australia, Bahrain, Britain, Canada, France, Germany, Italy, Japan, and the Netherlands) had been amassed. This was reputedly the largest international naval task force assembled since World War II.[16]

THE NEW BASES

The most important of the various traditional means of winning wars in Afghanistan was to bribe local leaders with cash

and weapons.[17] It was well known that the Taliban movement
frequently bought the loyalty of enemy commanders during its
offensives across Afghanistan—occasionally referred to as
checkbook campaigns.[18] The funding for this no doubt came
from abroad, probably Saudi Arabia and, especially after the
Saudis cut their support, private sources among Muslims.
Unfortunately for the Taliban, two could play this game, and
after 11 September, the United States was in an infinitely more
powerful position to buy any support it desired. This, as will be
shown, included several Pashtun warlords in Afghanistan and a
number of largely mercenary Pashtun military forces. The United
States was also in a position to provide support to the Northern
Alliance. But even more important in the long run, the United
States could acquire basing rights in the neighbouring countries
in exchange for financial aid, political and military support, and
in some cases probably outright bribes to individual political
leaders. By September, U.S. aid and other forms of economic
assistance had begun to flow into the region to procure the active
assistance from, as well as territory for military bases in,
Pakistan, Uzbekistan, Tajikistan, and Kyrgyzstan. From October
on, as the war eventually got under way on the ground in
Afghanistan, U.S. officers also seem to have handed out cash
payments in Afghanistan itself to persuade local leaders, often
Taliban, to switch allegiance to the coalition.[19]

On the international level, the United States did not need to
hand out all rewards by itself. It could, and did, pressure the
International Monetary Fund (IMF) and the World Bank to increase
financial help to those countries deemed worthy by the United
States. One likely candidate was Uzbekistan, despite its lack of
interest in economic reform. Much of the aid was bound to be
wasted on useless projects or disappear into the pockets of those in
power, but as a means of waging war, the payments did fulfill their
purpose. The United States, accordingly, was able to line up an
impressive coalition of neighbouring states that fully supported the
U.S.-led war in Afghanistan. Although the United States formally
cannot direct IMF policy (it has only 17 percent of the board's

votes), in actual practice, it is able to influence many other industrialised countries to vote along with it and has often done so.[20]

Most U.S. aid and support for obvious reasons went to the countries whose support was vital for the military campaign, but the United States did not forget more distant Muslim allies. Before the end of September, the United States passed a long-delayed free-trade agreement with Jordan and offered to expand Indonesia's special trade preferences.[21]

Pakistan

The first regional power that the United States needed to align (or perhaps more likely, rein in) with U.S. policy was Pakistan. Despite the United States' formerly relying on Pakistan (and still wishing to do so), the 11 September attacks made it clear to most U.S. policymakers that Pakistan was dangerously out of control.

On 13 September 2001, Secretary of State Colin Powell formulated seven demands to Pakistan. These were presented to the Pakistani leader, Pervez Musharraf, together with a warning that the demands were not negotiable and that he must accept all of the following seven demands:

- Stopping of Al-Qaida operatives at the Pakistani border, interception of arms shipments through Pakistan, and cessation of *all* logistical support for Usamah bin Ladin.
- Blanket overflight and landing rights.
- Access to Pakistan, naval bases, air bases, and borders.
- Immediate intelligence and immigration information.
- Condemnation of the 11 September attacks and curbing of all domestic expressions of support for terrorism against the United States, its friends, or its allies.
- Cut-off of all fuel shipments to the Taliban and halting of Pakistani volunteers going into Afghanistan to join the Taliban.
- Breaking-off of diplomatic relations with the Taliban government, cessation of support for the Taliban, and assistance to the United States as above to destroy Usamah bin Ladin and his Al-Qaida network should the evidence strongly implicate their

presence in Afghanistan *and* should Afghanistan and the
Taliban continue to harbour them.

Musharraf immediately replied that Pakistan would support the
United States and comply with all of the demands.[22]
On the following day, Musharraf called a meeting with all
senior military and intelligence officers to discuss the U.S.
demands. The ISI leaders expressed different opinons. For example, Javed Alam Khan, since March 2000 deputy director-general
of the ISI and regarded by some as the real power in the ISI,
reportedly advised Musharraf to break with the Taliban. However,
the director-general of the ISI, Lt. Gen. Mahmood Ahmad, probably argued against giving in to the U.S. demands and spoke out to
continue support to the Taliban—although this has been denied in
official statements. After the meeting, Ahmad went to Kandahar,
reportedly to discuss the possibility with the Taliban leadership of
handing over bin Ladin to the United States. Again, this is the
official version. It is more likely that he instead—and probably on
his own initiative—expressed his and Pakistan's support for the
Taliban in the struggle against the West. The latter seems far more
likely than the official version, since he brought with him 10
Pakistani clerics, who subsequently endorsed the Taliban decision
not to co-operate.[23]
On 7 October 2001, hours before the first air raids on
Afghanistan began, Musharraf, apparently fearful that the ISI was
plotting his assassination, removed from their posts Ahmad and
Taliban sympathisers in the army, including the deputy chief of
staff of the army, Lt. Gen. Muzzafar Usmani. Lt. Gen. Muhammad
Aziz Khan, a strong supporter of the Islamic extremist groups, was
promoted away from the key post of deputy chief of staff of the
army to the largely ceremonial position of chairman of the joint
chiefs of staff. Musharraf also appointed new commanders in the
strategically important Baluchistan and North-West Frontier
Province, both on the Afghan border.[24] On the following day,
Pakistani security forces detained three influential pro-Taliban
extremist leaders, Fazlur Rahman (released later that day), Sami ul-

Haq, and Azam Tariq.[25] Rahman and ul-Haq were the leaders of the recently established Council for the Defence of Afghanistan, a public charitable organisation in Pakistan that vowed to assist the Taliban against the United States, while Tariq was the head of the Pakistani extremist group *Sepah-e Sahaba Pakistan* (SSP, Army of the Companions of the Prophet of Pakistan).[26]

At around this time, the United States had already worked out a mutually favourable understanding with Pakistan (which soon came to include substantial aid payments to Pakistan as well as rescheduled or written-off debt, reduced tariff barriers, soft loans, and the removal of sanctions) in exchange for the deployment of U.S. troops in Pakistan.[27] Before the end of September 2001, the United States had lifted economic sanctions on Pakistan (and for geopolitical reasons, its rival India), as well as rescheduling $379 million of Pakistan's bilateral debt. It was expected that Pakistan would get further relief on its $37 billion in external debts.[28]

By the end of September 2001, the United States and Pakistan had discussed the possibility of U.S. use of five airfields in Pakistan: Bareder, Quetta, Dalbandin, Pasni, and Chitral.[29] The two sides eventually negotiated an agreement according to which U.S. troops could use commercial or second-rate military airports in the towns of Pasni, Panjgur, and Dalbandin (all in Baluchistan), as well as Jacobabad (in Sind, close to the Baluchistan border). By 11 October (when U.S. and Pakistani officials made public the fact that U.S. forces were using Pakistani airfields),[30] if not before, troops from the United States had been dispatched to these bases.[31] U.S. Marines were assigned for base security. This was a prudent move because some of the bases subsequently came under threat from local Islamic extremist groups (this threat seems to have made the U.S. forces on the smaller bases move at least once).[32]

According to the agreement with Pakistan, coalition forces could use the Pakistani bases for search and rescue missions, but not for direct attacks on the Taliban. In reality, the bases were chiefly used by special forces personnel. Chief among them was Jacobabad, also known as Pakistani Air Force Shahbaz, designated a Forward Operational Base, which would become fully operational in case of war, located about 300 miles north of Karachi and 300 miles southeast of Kandahar. Both Jacobabad and Pasni bases were sealed off, and a five-kilometre cordon was set up around the bases by Pakistani security forces. By mid-October 2001, seven U.S. C-130 Hercules cargo/troop transport aircraft were at the airbase at Jacobabad, together with some helicopters. About 250 U.S. Marines were stationed at Jacobabad, along with perhaps 200 special forces personnel. By the end of November, the marines were replaced by the first of several hundred troops from the U.S. army's 101st Airborne Division. The marines were first recalled to their ships in the Arabian Sea, then, as will be shown, redeployed to southern Afghanistan.

The arrival of U.S. troops in Jacobabad caused several violent protests by members of the Pakistani Islamic extremist mass movement *Jamaat-e Islami*, who threatened to storm the base. On 14 October, these protesters tried to march to the Jacobabad base and clashed with local police. One person was killed and 24 injured in the resulting fighting. However, by the end of October the protests had largely subsided. In early December, the United States requested and received Pakistani permission for a long-term presence at Jacobabad, as well as materials to reinforce, refurbish, and fully cordon off the base. The United States demanded a continued presence at the Pasni and Dalbandin airfields as well. A smaller airfield, Shamsi, was also in use after November (perhaps as a replacement for Panjgur?): it was believed to be employed by certain special operations units. However, in late December, when base improvement work had already begun, Pakistan notified the United States that the bases at Jacobabad and Pasni might be needed by the Pakistani Air Force due to the emerging conflict with India. The bases were therefore partly reclaimed by Pakistan, and by early January 2002, both Pakistani and U.S. forces were operating at the two airfields. The Americans retained exclusive use of the Dalbandin and Shamsi bases until at least late April and continued to launch operations from them.

By 11 January 2002, U.S. forces (special operations teams, marine combat search-and-rescue teams, support aircraft, and units of the 101st Airborne Division) used four bases in Pakistan: Pasni, Dalbandin, Shamsi, and Jacobabad. Dalbandin was used as a forward refuelling base for U.S. special forces helicopters flying into Afghanistan. The smaller Shamsi was believed to be used by only a few special operations units.[33]

Tajikistan and Kyrgyzstan

Although intelligence and special forces troops arrived early in Tajikistan, it took considerable time before any conventional U.S. or Western forces were based there. On 3 November, Tajikistan authorised U.S. military engineers to immediately begin assessing conditions at the Kulob, Qurghonteppa (Kurgan-Tyube), and Khojand air bases for possible use.[34] The United States finally appears to have negotiated a mutually profitable deal with President Rahmonov by the end of November. On 4 December 2001, he publicly announced Tajikistan's readiness to admit foreign access to its air bases.[35] The bases in question were probably three, including the one at Kulob already being used by the Northern Alliance (the other two bases were probably Qurghonteppa and either Dushanbe or Ayni).[36] Unlike the other states in the region, Tajikistan does not appear to have received any significant amounts of foreign aid or soft loans as a reward for the privilege of establishing bases on its territory. One might thus speculate about whether other types of payment were involved, directed to individual leaders such as President Rahmonov rather than state structures; yet, no evidence either way seems to be available.

Details of the coalition's presence in Tajikistan were regarded as sensitive and not widely publicised. By early December, a handful of Italian, U.S., and French air and ground crews were stationed in Tajikistan. Almost all were with airlift or tanker units, since the Tajikistani bases came to be almost exclusively used for supply purposes. Dushanbe airport seems to have been the one most often used. The French contingent was far larger than the others and at least somewhat later appears to have been stationed separately from the other Western units, probably in Ayni and Qurghonteppa. French Transall C-160G Gabriel signals intelligence aircraft were also sent to Tajikistan. Most Americans and Italians may have been at Kulob air base, although it appears that Qurghonteppa was also used.[37] Kulob air base was also used by Russian troops (who, among other duties, resupplied the Northern Alliance),[38] and there appears to have been some tensions between the U.S. and Russian units; the United States had demanded, but not received, exclusive access to the base.

Tajikistan was not the only choice for coalition air bases, nor was it the most attractive. In early November 2001, a coalition team including representatives from the United States, Britain, Turkey, Canada, and the Netherlands was inspecting air bases in Kyrgyzstan, Kazakhstan, and Azerbaijan as well to determine their suitability as future coalition bases. Uzbekistan had, as noted, already been surveyed. On 28 November, General Franks announced that attack aircraft from at least the United States and France would be sent to Central Asia in early December. These, it was believed at the time, would include F-15E fighter-bombers and A-10 ground attack aircraft (commonly referred to as Warthogs). The U.S. Air Force hoped to base them in Uzbekistan or Tajikistan, but in the end, none of these aircraft were deployed.

In December 2001, the United States concluded an agreement with Kyrgyzstan, receiving very favourable conditions for a military base at Manas International Airport, close to Kyrgyzstan's capital of Bishkek and about 1,500 kilometres or three hours by air from Kandahar. The agreement, as noted, allowed extensive use of the country's only international airport and a 37-acre military base and included the provision that U.S. military personnel were immune to prosecution by the Kyrgyzstani government, were free to enter and leave the country without hindrance, wear uniforms, and carry arms.[39] Plans were therefore made to base a squadron of 24 combat aircraft in Kyrgyzstan: 6 F-15E fighter-bombers originally intended for Uzbekistan or Tajikistan, 6 marine F/A-18C/D multirole strike interdictors, and 6 other jets (either the A-10s intended for Central Asia or F-16 fighters). At about the same time, France requested permission to base 6 Mirage 2000 multirole fighter-bombers, two C-130 tankers, and 200 technicians in Kyrgyzstan, a request granted in early January 2002.[40] In late December 2001, engineers arrived at Manas to prepare for the deployment; airlift and tanker aircraft began arriving in mid-January 2002. The base was expected to eventually have a staff of 3,000. The French troops were at first expected to stay until 2003, although they pulled out on 2 October 2002, when the main combat operations in Afghanistan were concluded. They were relieved by a European force of Norwegian, Danish, and Dutch air units.[41] The U.S. troops remained, no doubt because Manas was seen not only as an excellent key base in former Soviet Central Asia but also a means of encroaching on the Russian zone of influence.

From the outset, it was clear that the dispatch of combat aircraft to the Central Asian bases would be of use not so much in the Afghan operations as in future conflicts in the area. By mid-February 2002, it became known that the strike aircraft were not expected to arrive until March, along with five KC-135 tankers and four C-130 transports. By that time Manas was already serving as a refuelling hub for C-17 transports coming from Afghanistan. Eventually, the six French Mirage 2000D fighter-bombers arrived on 26–27 February 2002: their purpose was to fly fighter and reconnaissance missions in support of the operation in Afghanistan. The six U.S. Marine F/A-18C/D strike interdictors and their crews arrived only on 16 April 2002.[42] As for the A-10 Warthogs intended for Central Asia, they were instead sent to Jacobabad. The six F-16s and the six F-15E fighter-bombers (from the 48th Fighter Wing at Lakenheath, Britain) were only deployed later, apparently in May 2002, but by then the war was largely over.

End Notes

1. *Washington Post,* 9 October 2001; *Economist,* 13 October 2001.
2. John Pike (*www.globalsecurity.org*); French Ministry of Defence (*www.defense.gouv.fr*).
3. As of early March 2002, the composition of the carrier group CTF 473 had changed slightly. With the *Charles de Gaulle* (R 91) were the frigates *Jean Bart* (D 615), *De Grasse* (D 612), and *La Motte-Picquet* (D 645), the tanker *Somme* (A 831), and the nuclear attack submarine *Rubis* (S 601). The electronic surveillance vessel *Bougainville* (L 9077) was also in the region but operated independently.

THE COALITION DEPLOYS

4. John Pike; French Ministry of Defence.
5. *Washington Post,* 9 October 2001.
6. Ibid., 2 November 2001.
7. Reuters, 7 November 2001; *Washington Post,* 8 November 2001; John Pike.
8. John Pike.
9. *Washington Post,* 11 November 2001.
10. Ibid., October 2001.
11. John Pike; Center for Defense Information (*www.cdi.org*).
12. Ibid.
13. *Washington Post,* 9 October 2001.
14. Ibid., 19 April 2002; John Pike (*www.globalsecurity.org*).
15. Ibid.
16. Ibid.
17. Hiro, *Islamic Fundamentalism,* 263.
18. Davis, "How the Taliban Became a Military Force," Fundamentalism Reborn, 49–51; G.D. Bakshi, *Mono-Ethnic Solutions: The Taliban's Cheque Book Campaign, Autumn 1998.* Bakshi is an Indian army officer, and his work should be read in the context of Indian-Pakistani rivalry.
19. On the buying over of Taliban defectors, see *Economist,* 27 October 2001.
20. Ibid., 22 September 2001.
21. Ibid.
22. *Washington Post,* 29 January 2002.
23. Arif Azad, "Musharraf Feared Rebellion," *IWPR's Reporting Central Asia* 79 (30 October 2001; *www.iwpr.net*).
24. *Washington Post,* 8 October 2001; Arif Azad, "Musharraf Feared Rebellion," *IWPR's Reporting Central Asia,* 79. For a more unfavourable analysis of Musharraf's policy, see ICG, *Pakistan.*
25. RFE/RL, 9 October 2001.
26. Jane's World Insurgency and Terrorism 13, 28 November 2001.
27. *Washington Post,* 2 October 2001; BBC, 11 November 2001; Reuters, 15 November 2001; and for a useful summary, *Economist,* 9 March 2002.
28. *Economist,* 22 September 2001.
29. John Pike (*www.globalsecurity.org*). Pasni is also known as Basni. As a curiosity, the first World Trade Center bomber, Ramzi Yousef, appears to have been a resident of Pasni. Mylroie, *War Against America,* 75.
30. *Washington Post,* 11 October 2001.

31. See, for instance, VOA News, 11 October 2001; RIA Novosti, 19 October 2001, 22 October 2001.

32. See, for instance, RIA Novosti, 19 October 2001.

33. *Washington Post,* 11 January 2002.

34. Ibid., 4 November 2001.

35. RFE/RL, 5 December 2001.

36. ICG, *Tajikistan,* 25.

37. Interfax, 5 December 2001; Reuters, 13 December 2001.

38. See, for instance, Maley, *Fundamentalism Reborn?,* 115.

39. Jakypova, "Kyrgyzstan;" Sagynbaeva, "Kyrgyzstan."

40. RFE/RL, 13 February 2002.

41. Independent Bishkek TV (Kyrgyzstan), 21 January 2002; French Ministry of Defence.

42. Center for Defense Information; French Ministry of Defence By 26 April, about 2,000 troops were reportedly based at Manas, half of them U.S. forces, half allied forces from Australia, Denmark, France, the Netherlands, Norway, South Korea, and Spain. *Washington Post,* 27 April 2002.

CHAPTER 14
Operation Enduring Freedom

There never was any real chance that the Taliban would survive the combined onslaught of U.S., British, coalition, and Northern Alliance units. Neither the predominantly Pashtun Taliban movement, nor its ethnic foundation among the Pashtuns, formed a united force. A Taliban victory over the other ethnic groups, if it had occurred, would no doubt only have led to further fragmentation and a new civil war, this time among the Pashtuns who dominated the movement.[1] The reasons were several. First, while the Taliban regarded Mullah Omar as their supreme leader, many senior Taliban commanders enjoyed considerable autonomy. Second, the Pashtuns remained (and remain) fragmented into different ethnic subgroups. Third, Taliban troops were customarily kept in separate units based on territory, district, or tribe, and in the case of foreign volunteers, nationality, to minimise frictions.[2] This policy could easily have backfired and split the movement in any leadership crisis. Finally, the Taliban never succeeded, or indeed appeared to be much interested, in building any viable type of civil government that could accommodate the needs of the state when not at war.[3] Afghanistan was so devastated that even a complete Taliban victory was unlikely to give the Pashtuns unquestioned control over Afghanistan's entire territory. Vast areas of territory nominally controlled by the Taliban remained susceptible to troop movements and sudden strikes by opposition forces from bases either at the borders or in remote locations deep inside Afghanistan. Even though the Taliban government claimed control over most of Afghanistan's territory, this in many areas such as central Hazarajat amounted to little more than a small armed presence in the major towns.[4] (For a full chronology of the war, see Appendix 2.)

THE WAR IN THE AIR

Operation Enduring Freedom formally began on 7 October 2001, only 26 days after the 11 September attacks on the United States. The operation began with an impressively orchestrated air attack on Taliban positions in Afghanistan, controlled from the Combined Air Operations Center at Prince Sultan Air Base, Saudi Arabia. Most notable about the operation was that Afghanistan is a landlocked country far away from all U.S. and reliable allied military forces. The capital, Kabul, is about 600 miles from the nearest navigable shore. Even with forward deployment from aircraft carriers and bases in the region, distances to be flown are very long and need a carefully prepared refuelling operation. U.S. Navy jets operated from aircraft carriers in the Arabian Sea, roughly 500 miles from the area of operations in southern Afghanistan alone, and even longer from northern Afghanistan. U.S. Air Force bombers had to fly six-hour round-trip missions from Diego Garcia in the Indian Ocean, while fighter-bombers flew eight- to nine-hour missions from bases in the Persian Gulf.

On 7 October, the United States and Britain launched the first of many consecutive air raids on Kabul, Kandahar, Jalalabad, and Mazar-e-Sharif. The strikes included the use of 50 Tomahawk cruise missiles (launched from both a U.S. and a British submarine, the U.S. destroyers USS *John Paul Jones*, *McFaul*, *O'Brien*, and the cruiser USS *Philippine Sea*).[5] Fifteen land-based bombers also participated, including a pair of B-2 "stealth" bombers from the 509th Bomb Wing at Whiteman Air Force Base near Kansas City, Missouri, which were sent to hit any Taliban early-warning radar installations (a sensible move, though it is doubtful whether any operational ones existed). The others were B-52 and B-1B bombers from Diego Garcia, which flattened abandoned Taliban and Al-Qaida camps in eastern Afghanistan.[6] The B-2 missions were the most remarkable from a logistical point of view. Of the total number of 21 B-2 bombers of the 509th, only about 11 (reportedly 55 percent) were mission-capable on 7 October. These flew a total of six missions on the first three days of air raids. Each mission took 70 hours to reach Afghanistan, drop bombs, continue to the Diego Garcia support facility in the Indian Ocean to get a new crew, and return home.[7] During each mission, the bombers needed to refuel in the air several times.[8] Twenty-five carrier-based aircraft participated in the air raids as well. The first wave from the USS *Carl Vinson*, southeast of the Strait of Hormuz, included S-3B antisubmarine warfare aircraft equipped for air refuelling operations (from the Sea Control Squadron 29 Dragonfires), followed by several E-2C AWACS aircraft, four F-14 fighters and six F/A-18C/D multi-role strike interdictors, and several EA-6Bs to jam and attack any Taliban air defence radar systems. Another wave flew from the USS *Enterprise*. At the same time, two air force C-17 transports were poised to depart Ramstein Air Base to air-drop food containers over Afghanistan in an attempt to win over the population to the U.S. cause.[9]

On the following day, the air strikes were more limited, reportedly consisting of only 15 Tomahawk cruise missiles, 3 B-1B bombers from Diego Garcia, 2 B-2 bombers from Whiteman Air Force Base, and 10 carrier-based F-14s and F/A-18C/Ds. No British forces participated on this day, which instead saw the first of what would become a major psychological warfare operation. Lockheed Martin EC-130E Commando Solo II aircraft, operated from a base in Oman by the 193rd Special Operations Wing of the Pennsylvania Air National Guard, were dispatched to broadcast messages to Afghanistan to cease supporting the Taliban. Aircraft operated by the 4th Psychological Operations Group at Fort Bragg were preparing to drop propaganda leaflets. The Voice of America radio station expanded its broadcasts to the region as well. Because of local conditions in Afghanistan, the EC-130Es, though technically capable of television broadcasts, were primarily engaged in transmitting short-duration tactical military radio messages to warn ordinary Afghans to stay away from terrorist camps, roads, bridges, and the like. The aircraft were also used to broadcast more questionable propaganda, for instance, referring to the Taliban as "cowards that hide in shadows and strike at the weak," as well as accusing them of striking out "at expectant mothers, the elderly, and little children." Other propaganda efforts included dropping leaflets with similar content over Afghanistan, as well as Dari- and Pashto-language radio programs from what the Department of Defense referred to as "information radio" broadcasts from the U.S. Special Operations Command.[10]

Within a few days, the allies destroyed almost the entire Taliban air force. The air raids, however, at first studiously avoided assisting the Northern Alliance. Instead the U.S. aim was to appease Pakistan, induce divisions in the Taliban leadership (which did not succeed), and prepare for a future, Pashtun-dominated government in Kabul. The fact that the United States did not target front-line Taliban troops in order to favour what some hoped to be a Pashtun alternative to the Northern Alliance was eventually acknowledged on 31 October 2001.[11] The overly cautious strategy of the first month was also intended to encourage Pashtun defectors. But this strategy proved self-defeating: many in Afghanistan got the impression that the United States was not prepared to use its full strength and indeed might give up and pull out, as U.S. forces had done in Somalia after losing a few men in 1993. The southern strategy, as the Pashtun option became known, was an approach championed especially by the State Department and the CIA.[12]

Another feature of the war in the air was the reliance on precision-guided munitions. Unlike in earlier air campaigns, seemingly more than half (around 55 percent by 7 February 2002, or 10,000 out of 18,000 bombs, missiles, and other ordnance, according to General Franks) of the munitions used against the Taliban and Al-Qaida were precision guided. (In mid-January 2002, Vice Admiral John Nathman reportedly claimed that more than 90 percent of all bombs dropped were laser-, TV- or satellite-guided munitions; if so, this only applied to the navy.) Of the precision-guided munitions, about half were laser-guided bombs, and the other half consisted of GPS satellite-guided bombs. The greatest number of precision-guided munitions appears to have been used early in the campaign, probably at least in part because of supply problems. Yet, a major portion of the munitions was delivered by the 10 venerable B-52s and 8 B-1Bs of the 28th Air Expeditionary Wing operating out of Diego Garcia. By the end of November 2001, they had delivered no less than 72 percent of the total bombs dropped on Afghanistan. The 8 B-1Bs did 4 sorties per day, while 5 B-52s flew daily—on missions from 12 to 15 hours. The ground crews at Diego Garcia worked around the clock because mission planning mainly took place at night. Early targets included suspected early-warning radar stations, Taliban airfields and aircraft, and what was generally referred to as command and control facilities (although facilities as such hardly existed in Afghanistan). When, following a very cautious initial air campaign, the threat to the bombers was deemed to have been obliterated, Taliban and Al-Qaida ground units and infrastructure were targeted. As it became increasingly clear that few fixed targets existed in Afghanistan, war planners divided Afghanistan into engagement zones and assigned fighter-bombers to patrol them. Within the assigned geographic area, pilots were authorised to choose their own targets and fire at will.

The air war demanded refuelling on an unprecedented scale. In addition to the obvious refuelling positions on carriers and nearby bases (such as the Kuwait-based F-15Es, which managed to carry out strikes in Afghanistan with the aid of up to six refuellings),[13] a massive tanker operation also took place over the Black Sea to serve long-distance missions to the theatre. In the first month of air operations, no fewer than 211 U.S. Air Force planes flew over Ukraine, Bulgaria, and Romania: 78 C-17 transports, as well as 5 C-130 and 128 KC-135 tankers. Many of the latter were based at Burgas Air Base, Bulgaria, where about 200 U.S. servicemen were stationed, flying about six refuelling missions a day.

In comparison, the number of combat aircraft involved in the air war on Afghanistan was comparatively small: 40 on the first day, barely half that number on several subsequent days, then rising to around 100 on most days in subsequent weeks. While the U.S. forces certainly waged the war in a cautious, risk-averse way, logistics too probably dictated the number of sorties, as most were launched from aircraft carriers. In contrast, the U.S.-led air war on Serbia in 1999 involved 300 aircraft, later rising to 1,000, while as many as 2,500 were deployed in Operation Desert Storm in 1991.[14] Compared with Desert Storm, when about 3,000 sorties were flown per day, Operation Enduring Freedom saw only about 200. Actual combat missions were of course only a part of this total amount. Yet, according to General Franks, the number of targets hit each day was about the same, primarily due to more efficient weapon systems. In the roughly 6,500 strike missions flown from 7 October to 23 December 2001, when air operations decreased in number, carrier-based aircraft flew 4,900 of the 6,500 strike sorties, or about 75 percent of the total. However, the air force, flying 25 percent of the sorties, delivered more than 70 percent of the total munitions. This was obviously because of the B-1Bs and B-52s, which flew only 10 percent of the sorties but delivered 11,500 of the 17,500 total munitions expended during the period. In fact, the eight B-1Bs reportedly dropped more bombs on Afghanistan than any other aircraft.

Although much media attention was devoted to the U.S. basing rights in the countries around Afghanistan, no air force combat aircraft were actually stationed until well after the fall of the Taliban government. The bulk of tactical air strikes were launched from the USS *Carl Vinson* and *Theodore Roosevelt* in near 24-hour-a-day operations. Because the sorties were long, often demanding refuelling more than once, they took a heavy toll on both aircraft and crew members. General Franks realised that he needed a fourth carrier and thus had the USS *John C. Stennis* depart San Diego already on 12 November, well ahead of her scheduled January deployment.[15]

THE SPECIAL FORCES WAR

Most prominent in the Afghan war were the small teams of army Green Berets, who became the first regular U.S. troops to infiltrate Afghanistan. Their task was to advise and train local anti-Taliban forces. Divided into five commands of 1,200 soldiers each, the Green Berets operate in small teams that include specialists in reconnaissance, communications, demolition, unconventional warfare, and weapons. The 5th Special Forces Group, based at Fort Campbell, Kentucky, was known to have practised for operations in Central Asia. Some of the troops speak local languages and know the culture and political situation.[16] Special Forces from this group were, for instance, involved in the training of Kyrgyzstani special forces in early 2000, as well as Uzbekistani troops.[17] From July 2001, they also deployed to Kazakhstan to train troops there.[18]

Other special units that took part in operations in Afghanistan included the U.S. Army's Delta Force, a secretive unit of perhaps 360 (or possibly 800) men formed in the 1970s for counterterrorism operations. This unit has drawn on the experiences of special operations forces in Britain, France, Germany, and Israel. Delta Force was under the control of the Joint Special Operations Command, headquartered at Pope Air Force Base, which borders Fort Bragg, home to army Special Operations Command and the Delta Force. Also participating were the similarly trained Navy SEALs.[19] The SEALs, so named for being capable of operations at sea, in the air, and on land, are divided into 16-man groups, with larger teams often divided into cells (an evasion and recovery cell, a force protection cell, a reconnaissance cell, a sniper cell, and so on).

The U.S. Army Rangers, of which there is one active

regiment and three battalions, specialise in rapid
infantry assault, night fighting, and airfield seizure,
often in conjunction with—and as a diversion for—the
more exclusive Delta Force.

In special forces operations, air support was often
provided by the Army 160th Special Operations
Aviations Regiment, the "Night Stalkers."

The U.S. Air Force provided its special operations
units, specialising in the rescue and evacuation of
downed aircrews and the coordination of air strikes. Air
controllers from these units operated together with the
Green Berets and fulfilled an important role in
Afghanistan from the outset of the air war.

The most famous of the coalition special forces was
arguably the British Army's Special Air Service (SAS)
Regiment, a counterterrorism and counterinsurgency
unit. As noted, SAS teams had already penetrated
Afghanistan at the outset of the war, together with the
CIA paramilitary teams. In Afghanistan the SAS worked
closely with the Northern Alliance. Australia also provided its own SAS units.

On 15 October 2001, two U.S. Special Forces AC-130H
Spectre gunships entered the air war for the first time, flying in
from Oman in a raid on Kandahar. The slow-moving gunships, a
heavily armed version of the ubiquitous Hercules transport with a
150mm cannon based on an army howitzer, a Bofors 40mm gun,
and a 25mm, six-barrel Gatling gun, were able to engage Taliban
units at close range, and short of SAMs or plenty of antiaircraft
artillery, there was little the Taliban could do to harm them.[20] Soon
six AC-130Hs were flying missions from Oman. Eventually, however, the distance from Oman to Afghanistan was found to be too
great, so on 21 November the Pentagon requested and received permission from Uzbekistan to station three AC-130Hs there.[21]

U.S. Army Special Forces were also operating on the ground.

On 18 October it was disclosed that small groups of Special Forces had begun operations in southern Afghanistan. This statement almost certainly referred to the insertion into Afghanistan of 11 Green Berets from the 5th Special Forces Group's Operational Detachment-Alpha 574 (ODA-574), led by Capt. Jason Amerine. This appears to have been the first Special Forces team to be inserted into Afghanistan. Prior to the 11 September attacks, Amerine and his team had been in Kazakhstan, training that country's troops in small-unit tactics and counterterrorism. Amerine and his men joined Hamid Karzai in Afghanistan "in mid-October," with orders to assist in various ways and, perhaps most important, keep Karzai alive.[22]

Karzai was almost certainly the Bush administration's first choice as future leader of Afghanistan. He and his family had many ties to the United States. Two of his seven brothers owned restaurants in Boston, San Francisco, Baltimore, and Glenwood, Maryland. Another was a university professor on Long Island, New York, while an uncle, Shah Karzai, lived in Silver Springs.[23] Probably most important, however, is that he was a former consultant for the oil company Unocal. This company had, as noted, projected a trans-Afghan pipeline that, if built, would ensure substantial profits to the company itself, guarantee the United States a non-Arab source of gas and oil, and, of even greater value to the Bush administration, restrict Iran's influence in the region.[24] By 30 September 2001, if not before, the Karzai clan's friends and supporters in Washington had eagerly told journalists how enthusiastic Hamid Karzai, the Karzai clan, and its "several hundred thousand-strong Popalzai tribe—strategically located east and north of Kandahar, the Taliban's de facto capital"—were to cooperate in overthrowing the Taliban and getting Usamah bin Ladin.[25]

It soon became clear that the United States favoured Hamid Karzai financially and politically the expense of other Pashtun anti-Taliban leaders. On 26 October, Abdul Haq, a veteran Afghan mujahidin commander of far higher domestic renown, was captured by the Taliban while on a clandestine trip in the country to raise a Pashtun anti-Taliban force. Although he was in touch with the

Americans, he had received no Special Forces escort and the CIA belatedly sent a token force (an armed Predator drone) in a vain attempt to rescue him. Haq was executed by the Taliban.[26] A few days later, on the evening of 1 November, Hamid Karzai found himself in a similar situation while trying to raise tribal support inside Afghanistan. As he came under threat of Taliban forces, Captain Amerine immediately had U.S. aircraft sent to his aid.[27] Within one or two days, Taliban forces still got too close, and Karzai had to ask the U.S. forces to pick him up by helicopter and return him to Pakistan. He was taken out on 4 November yet continued to claim in interviews with the BBC and CNN that he remained in southern Afghanistan.[28]

Although Karzai lacked substantial personal support and essentially was a political tool, he did have some military uses. Through him, for instance, satellite telephones were distributed to several locals who were willing to act as spotters for air raids. Their work proved invaluable for the war effort because they could go where foreigners could not.[29] Yet, Karzai's lack of a serious fighting force eventually made the military commanders realise that stronger allies had to be found elsewhere.

While working with local allies was doubtless the most important of the various special forces missions, public opinion, if nothing else, demanded that they also show their raiding skills. On 19 October, U.S. Army Rangers and a Delta Force unit, reportedly more than 100 men altogether, mounted the first ground attacks in Afghanistan in two related raids (one by Rangers, a smaller one by Delta Force).[30] About 100 Rangers parachuted down near a small airfield in the vicinity of the southern city of Kandahar that had formerly been used by Gulf Arab hunting parties (almost certainly the Dolangi airstrip surveyed by a CIA aircraft in 1999) and secured the facility. They landed unopposed and shot some film for propaganda use (it was later shown on the main television networks). Fighting eventually broke out as Taliban troops belatedly arrived. Although they apparently inflicted some casualties, the Rangers soon withdrew—which of course was the plan from the outset. They were picked up by C-130s. The entire raid, it should be noted, was a diversion for the second raid in which a team of Delta Force commandos rode 160th Special Operations Aviation Regiment helicopters to a compound believed to have been occupied by Mullah Muhammad Omar. They landed, secured the compound (which was empty), reportedly gathered some documents, and left. One helicopter used in conjunction with the raid crashed in Pakistan, killing two men identified as Rangers.[31] The two raids, though successful, served little purpose and were never repeated. They did not kill or capture any Taliban leader, and it is unlikely that they brought back much intelligence. (The Taliban maintained few records and did not operate a conventional military bureaucracy, thus producing few if any documents that could be captured and used to provide useable intelligence. Mullah Omar was in fact known to write down his orders on any piece of scrap paper, and these were not filed for future reference.) The well-known investigative writer Seymour Hersh later claimed in the *New Yorker* that the raids were a failure. The claims were disputed by the Pentagon.[32]

On the same day, however, army Special Forces had a more enduring but less television-friendly success in northern Afghanistan. The 5th Special Forces Group's ODA-555, led by CWO Dave Diaz, went into Afghanistan in two MH-53J helicopters. ODA-555 consisted of 11 Green Berets and an air force combat controller from the 720th Special Tactics Group. (Diaz himself had some experience from Central Asia, having spent seven months on the Afghan-Pakistani border, though without entering Afghanistan, on a CIA-led mission training mujahidin in 1987.) ODA-555's orders were to identify targets for air attack. Once in Afghanistan, the detachment was met by and then worked with CIA paramilitary teams and the Northern Alliance forces under Muhammad Fahim Khan. The team remained in Afghanistan until 4 January 2002. For nearly a week, ODA-574 under Amerine and ODA-555 under Diaz were the only Special Forces teams in Afghanistan. In the second half of October, three more A-teams infiltrated the country: ODA-553 in Bamian Province, ODA-585 in the area around Kondoz, and ODA-595 in Dara-e-Suf (Uzbek warlord Abdul Rashid Dostum's headquarters in Samangan Province, where the Green Berets had to take up horseback riding). These were joined by others around 5–6 November. In total, eighteen A-teams, four company-level units, and three 15-man-strong battalion-level commands (altogether 316 men) entered Afghanistan. Almost every team included one or two CIA paramilitary operatives and an air force special operations combat controller. All teams reported to a Joint Special Operations Task Force at Khanabad Air Base in Qarshi, Uzbekistan, 100 miles north of the Afghan border. The Special Forces teams were monitored and controlled from the CAOC at Prince Sultan Air Base. The Special Forces were treated well by their Afghan hosts, who in most cases did not even allow the American troops to fight or take risks: like the Taliban they believed that any U.S. casualties would cause the teams to be withdrawn.[33] The first sustained ground combat operations in Afghanistan began to take place around 5 November, working with the Northern Alliance in the north and reportedly conducting night raids and ambushes in the south.[34]

The Special Forces team with Dostum was the first one to be disclosed to the news media, which shows the emphasis on the Uzbek front then displayed in the U.S. strategy. Dostum, being part of the Northern Alliance as well as enjoying the support of Uzbekistan, unlike Hamid Karzai, had a significant military force. ODA-595 apparently consisted of eight U.S. troopers and a foreign national and reportedly arrived in Dara-e-Suf after mid-October.[35] The team probably did not take part in operations until 25 October, however.[36]

By late October, several mutually antagonistic, predominantly Pashtun exile groups vied for the honor of leading the so-called Afghan peace process. Among the more important were the Rome group, the Cyprus group, and the Peshawar group. The Rome group was centred around ex-King Zahir Shah (resident in Rome) and backed by the United States. The Cyprus group consisted of those Afghans opposed to the monarchy. Its detractors (and therefore most Western media) claimed that the Cyprus group was backed by Iran. Iran certainly was opposed to monarchism, but this group was attached to some extent on the Islamist leader Gulbuddin Hekmatyar who subsequently was expelled from Iran for his Taliban sympathies—which indicates that the Iranian support may have been exaggerated.[37] The Cyprus group was led by Homayoun Jarir, son-in-law of Hekmatyar.[38] The Peshawar group was backed by Pakistan and headed by Pir Sayyid Ahmad Gailani at the subsequent Bonn conference. Gailani was at first seen by the West as a possible prime minister.[39] On the diplomatic scene, there was also a "working group" consisting of the United States, Italy, Iran, and Germany that met in Geneva. This unlikely partnership would eventually acquire lasting influence in the process through its capacity to organise the subsequent Bonn conference.[40]

Pakistani intelligence sources later claimed that the principal beneficiaries of U.S. funding were four Pashtuns: Hamid Karzai, Abdul Khaliq (a leader of the Noorzai tribe and the self-appointed representative of ex-King Zahir Shah in Quetta), former Gen. Abdul Rahim Wardak (Zahir Shah's military advisor in Pakistan, known to be friendly to the United States), and Gul Agha Shirzai (a mercenary warlord and former self-appointed governor of Kandahar). But by late October the military—though clearly not the State Department—had all but given up on Karzai's (and the others') ability to deliver a Pashtun victory. A more substantial Afghan force had to be found. To support Dostum was fine, but even he was only one leader in the Northern Alliance, which after all was the only serious anti-Taliban force in the country.

Having failed to find credible Pashtun opposition to the Taliban, General Franks met General Khan on 30 October in Dushanbe for secret talks on closer cooperation between U.S. and alliance forces.[41] U.S. distrust of the Northern Alliance remained, however, and Pakistan took the opportunity to spread some anti-Northern Alliance propaganda, swiftly (and falsely) claiming that Khan had been the KGB-trained head of the Soviet-supported Afghan communist intelligence service during the Soviet involvement in Afghanistan. (Actually he had been the intelligence chief of the Northern Alliance under Masud.) Apparently some American officials and many reporters believed the Pakistani claims because the false information was widely, though briefly, published. When asked on American television the following day whether the Northern Alliance could be trusted, General Franks replied, "Well, we're not sure."[42]

However, on 31 October the United States acknowledged that the policy against targeting front-line Taliban troops in order to favour what some had hoped to be a Pashtun alternative (in the words of the administration: "not to favor rebels of the Northern Alliance, who are rivals of other potential members of a post-Taliban government") to the Northern Alliance had finally been abandoned, and that air raids were currently directed against Taliban troops along the front line.[43] U.S. Secretary of Defense Donald Rumsfeld later explained that the first month of air strikes had made little apparent impact on the Taliban, since most strikes had been directed against such conventional targets as airfields and antiaircraft emplacements. Rumsfeld pointed out that the turning point came only when, upon his personal insistence, special operations target spotters in early November began to work with the Northern Alliance.[44]

Finally supported by coalition air power, the Northern Alliance quickly broke through the Taliban lines. On 13 November, units of the Alliance moved into Kabul.

THE WAR ON THE GROUND

For the coalition's conventional troops, the war on the ground was mostly over before they even entered Afghanistan. When the Northern Alliance took the capital on 13 November, most of northern Afghanistan had already fallen to the Northern Alliance. The last Taliban stronghold, Kandahar, surrendered on 7 December.

The importance of deploying conventional forces to Afghanistan should not be underestimated, however. There were still large Taliban forces in the country. In addition, nobody really knew at first whether the Taliban were defeated or had merely withdrawn into the country to wage guerrilla warfare. There were several precedents in Afghan history for abandoning Kabul to an enemy invader. When the British appeared before the walls of Kabul in early July 1839, they found that Afghan ruler Dost Muhammad had fled and surrendered the capital without a shot being fired.[45] In 1996, supreme northern commander Ahmad Shah Masud abandoned the capital to the invading Taliban without attempting its defence when he realised that the tactical situation was untenable.[46]

After the Northern Alliance's capture of Kabul, on 15 November Britain flew in a company-sized unit of Special Boat Service commandos in a C-130 to Bagram Air Base, located approximately 7 miles (11 kilometres) southeast of the city of Charikar and 27 miles (44 kilometres) north of Kabul. Since the British had no permission to land, the commandos and the Northern Alliance units that guarded Bagram came within an ace of opening fire on each other.[47] Negotiations between the respective political leaders were soon successfully concluded, however, and on the following day, the first British conventional troops (about 200 Royal Marines) arrived at Bagram to provide base security.[48]

The first deployment of U.S. conventional troops in Afghanistan took place around 19 November, when a platoon from the 10th Mountain Division commanded by Lt. Col. Paul LaCamera flew in to Bagram from Uzbekistan. Additional troops soon followed, and within days LaCamera commanded a company at Bagram of more than a hundred men.[49]

While these units were the first conventional forces to deploy to Afghanistan, the first major conventional fighting force to deploy to the country consisted of the U.S. Marines. On 25 November, the first several hundred of a force that soon grew into about 1,300 began to move into a bridgehead named Forward Operating Base Rhino (FOB Rhino) at the Dolangi airfield 55 miles (89 kilometres) southwest of Kandahar in southern Afghanistan, which earlier had seen Arab hunting parties, CIA reconnaissance operators, and the inconclusive Rangers' raid on 19 October.[50] The airstrip had earlier been captured by allied Afghan mercenary forces under the Pashtun warlord Gul Agha Shirzai. Exactly why the Americans favoured him for the venture remains unclear to most outside observers; not only did he have an unsavoury past, but he was also a traditional rival of the Karzai family. In addition, his military strength in the area was fundamentally mercenary rather than tribal, apparently made up mostly of men recruited from Pakistani refugee camps and among local bandits. Maybe the explanation is no more complicated than that he happened to be there at the right time—and was willing to make a deal.[51]

The marines were picked from the two MEUs in the area of operations: the 15th from Camp Pendleton, aboard the USS *Peleliu*, and the 26th from Camp Lejeune, aboard the USS *Bataan*. They were combined into a brigade under the command of Brig. Gen. James N. Mattis.[52] The marines were not alone at Base Rhino. In late November or early December, around 120 Australian Special Air Service commandos, with transportation in the form of Perentie long-range patrol vehicles, arrived as well to conduct raids against Taliban-held caves in the alongside the marines.[53] In addition, an undisclosed number of army special operations troops, SEALs, and U.S. Navy Seabee engineers and construction teams arrived at Rhino. By early December 2001, C-130 and C-17 transports maintained a nightly air bridge to Rhino, averaging at least 10 flights in and out every night.[54]

Subsequently, several thousand additional troops from the United States and coalition countries were deployed in Afghanistan, the latter chiefly but not exclusively British and French. Most operated out of Bagram Air Base near Kabul and Mazar-e-Sharif.[55]

The command structure also changed. The U.S. Third Army, the ground component of Central Command (CENTCOM), had moved its forward headquarters from Fort McPherson, Georgia, to Camp Doha, Kuwait, in November. From early December on, this headquarters, under Lt. Gen. Paul Mikolashek, commander of the Third Army and recently transferred to the new headquarters from Atlanta, directed ground operations in Afghanistan.[56] By early January 2002, the total number of U.S. ground forces deployed in Afghanistan had grown to nearly 4,000 troops.[57]

The Tora Bora Debacle

The ground operations so far had been successful, but problems developed in December 2001. After discovering substantial Taliban and Al-Qaida forces in late November hiding near a complex of fortified caves at Tora Bora ("Black Dust") and Milawa, south of Jalalabad in eastern Afghanistan, the coalition leaders decided to surround and destroy them. There was some hope that bin Ladin himself was in the area; it was known that he had earlier made his headquarters in one of the caves. Besides, radio intercepts seemed to indicate that he was there. On 3 December, several U.S. air raids began on the cave complexes, and on the following day Afghan warlord and mercenary troops moved into Tora Bora along with U.S. and British special forces. In hindsight, it was a mistake not to back up this force with large numbers of conventional coalition units. Despite a gruesome campaign in the snowbound mountain country, the available forces were unable to seal the nearby border with Pakistan. The United States had not yet pressured Pakistan into rendering decisive support, and the Afghan warlord and mercenary troops often seem to have had personal connections with the Taliban they were fighting—or were simply not sufficiently motivated to engage in the desperate fighting needed to root out the enemy forces in the Tora Bora area. In the end, hundreds of Taliban and Al-Qaida troops fled across the border, possibly also including several key leaders, and perhaps bin Ladin himself. Pakistan made no attempts to stop them.[58]

The possibility that bin Ladin had successfully fled into Pakistan was of course a major disappointment. Some analysts, with the benefit of hindsight, have since questioned whether the radio intercepts that seemed to demonstrate bin Ladin's presence in the Tora Bora and Milawa cave complex in late 2001 were not in fact faked.[59] After all, for security reasons, Usamah bin Ladin since 1998 appeared to rely far less on telecommunications than on couriers. However, at the time of this writing it is simply not known whether he was at Tora Bora or, if so, whether he successfully escaped.

The Coalition Bases at Kandahar, Bagram, and Khost

By the beginning of January 2002, the marines from the 15th and 26th MEUs had been redeployed from FOB Rhino to Kandahar Airport. The marines did not remain long at Kandahar, however, their landing party mission being to all effects accomplished. After 4 January, they gradually began to pull out, being replaced by a regiment of the 101st Airborne Division. The last hundred marines from the 26th MEU left Kandahar on 5 February. The new troops formed what would become known as Task Force Rakkasan. By early February, Task Force Rakkasan consisted of 3,600 troops, including more than 1,600 from the 2d Battalion, 3d Brigade, 101st Airborne Division, (another 700 troops of 1st Battalion, 3d Brigade, were then based in Pakistan), 800 troops from the 3d Battalion of the Princess Patricia's Canadian Light Infantry Battle Group, and 1,200 other U.S. and coalition troops.

Another task force was set up at Bagram Air Base. This had been an important Soviet air base and was now an important U.S. base. The detachment from the 10th Mountain Division had by mid-December increased to some 300, and by early January 2002 reached about 400. By late January, there were about 500 U.S. troops at Bagram, as Special Operations Command officers from CENTCOM in Florida and troops from the 82d Airborne Division from Fort Bragg arrived as well. By mid-March, U.S. troops had begun to renovate the facilities at Bagram. As many as 50 army helicopters, including CH-47 Chinooks, AH-64 Apaches, AH-1F Huey Cobra attack helicopters, and UH-60 Black Hawks were eventually based at Bagram. In addition, transports such as the C-17 used the base frequently.

In mid-January 2002, approximately 100 U.S. troops were also stationed at the Khost airfield, located 60 miles from Gardez in Paktia Province, eastern Afghanistan, and about 20 miles from the Pakistani border. By mid-February nearly 200 U.S. soldiers were stationed there. Their main task appeared to be the formation and training of a 400-strong allied Afghan force. However, Khost was in the Taliban heartland. On 20 March, the base at Khost was attacked by hostile forces in one of the few anti-coalition offensive operations during the war; however, the attack was repulsed. By late January 2002, the total number of U.S. troops in Afghanistan was reportedly more than 4,000, including conventional forces and engineers to repair and protect bases as well as interrogators and other intelligence personnel. By 9 February, there were around 3,000 U.S. troops in Kandahar, somewhat less than 1,000 in Bagram, and around 200 (from the 10th Mountain Division) at an airfield outside Mazar-e-Sharif, in addition to the contingent at Khost. By then, the U.S. presence in the region was substantial. There were more than 1,000 U.S. troops in Uzbekistan (in Khanabad) and 1,500 in Pakistan (in Shamsi, Dalbandin, Pasni, and Jacobabad). In Tajikistan, troops were stationed at bases in Khojand, Kulob, and Qurghonteppa.[60]

Operation Anaconda

U.S. conventional troops launched only one major ground offensive in the war. This was Operation Anaconda, commanded by army Maj. Gen. Franklin L. "Buster" Hagenbeck, and it commenced on 1 March 2002 against what was reported to be a concentration of several hundred Taliban and Al-Qaida troops south of Gardez in Paktia Province, in eastern Afghanistan. This time, it was argued, the debacle in Tora Bora would not be repeated. A sufficient number of conventional units would be used, so that the Afghan mercenary and warlords' troops would not be able to let the enemy withdraw unpunished. With Operation Anaconda, additional air power more suitable for the new type of operations became necessary. In early March 2002, the first air force A-10 Thunderbolt ground-support aircraft arrived from their base in Kuwait. Deployed to Jacobabad in Pakistan, they soon took part in operations.[61]

Operation Anaconda was essentially a large-scale offensive in the Mezzai Mountains around Gardez, especially the Shah-e-Kot Valley, by a task force consisting of 800 to 900 men from the 101st Airborne Division and 10th Mountain Division, as well as more than 100 Rangers, Special Forces, and Navy SEALs, working with about 200 coalition commandos from Australia, Canada, Denmark, France, Germany, and Norway.[62] The 160th Special Operations

Aviation Regiment took part as well. The operation was fundamentally a commando sweep: the ratio of commandos to conventional troops being unusually high, about 1:3, even though the army contingent from the 101st and 10th can hardly be called run-of-the-mill troops. In addition, the coalition units were supported by a force of from 1,000 to 1,500 Afghan mercenary troops, mostly under the warlord Bacha Khan Zadran, paid and armed by the United States. A considerable number of combat aircraft flew daily missions over the battlefield: 10 heavy long-range bombers, 30 to 40 fighters, 2 to 4 AC-130H gunships, 16 army AH-64 Apaches (subordinated the 101st Airborne Division), and 5 marine Bell AH-1W Super Cobras, formerly based on the USS *Bonhomme Richard*, in the northern Arabian Sea.[63] In support of the operation, a previously unacknowledged U.S. helicopter base at Pol-e-Kandahar, about 20 miles west of Kabul, was used as a base for the attack helicopters and as many as 15 Chinook transport helicopters. These flew sorties in support of the operations around Gardez and Shah-e-Kot, about 50 miles (80 kilometres) to the south.[64] More than half the fighters that supported the operation from the air were French: 16 Super Etendard reconnaissance and strike aircraft and 2 Rafale M multirole fighter-bombers from the aircraft carrier *Charles de Gaulle* in the Arabian Sea, as well as 6 Mirage 2000 multirole fighter-bombers, sent in late February to Kyrgyzstan.[65]

This was the first time that U.S. and coalition conventional forces were at the forefront of ground combat. Despite reassuring press releases and claims of victory, independent observers generally regarded the operation as inconclusive if not outright unsuccessful. Despite the considerable air support as well as reportedly heavy fighting on the ground (U.S. troops suffered at least eight dead and forty wounded during the first four days of the operation), it remains unclear to most exactly how successful the operation was. A number of enemy troops were killed, but many others appear to have escaped. In addition, the mercenary Afghan forces again did not fulfill expectations. After about a week of fighting, Northern Alliance commander Muhammad Fahim Khan had to send more than 1,000 regular Northern Alliance troops to reinforce the coalition forces in the operation. By then, any Taliban forces in the area had largely withdrawn, and fighting ebbed out around 13 March.[66] Operation Anaconda was declared over on 18 March.[67] As before, the fluid nature of the Afghan irregular troops had prevented any decisive battle. The Taliban and Al-Qaida fighters simply dispersed and withdrew, many of them into Pakistan, when the battle turned against them. After the operation, Maj. Gen. Hagenbeck indicated the need to engage in hot pursuit into Pakistan, but on 25 March he was overruled by Secretary of Defense Rumsfeld, who claimed that he was satisfied with Pakistani border security and that U.S. troops would not pursue the enemy across the border.[68] It was also probably in part an intelligence failure. It is unlikely that there ever were so many enemy troops in the area as the various intelligence sources claimed.

The End of Active Combat Operations

By April 2002, combat operations were to all effects concluded in Afghanistan. There was still plenty of activity, as U.S. and coalition forces in several heavily hyped operations continued to search for the reclusive enemy. Few enemy fighters were ever found, and most searches quickly turned into the mere confiscation of weapons from local villagers. Most search missions were conducted by commandos from the United States, Britain, Canada, Australia, New Zealand, Norway, Germany, and Denmark.[69]

It was also a time for troop rotation. On 23–24 March, the first group of the planned deployment of some 1,700 Royal Marines arrived at Bagram.[70] The remainder joined during the following two weeks. These were the ground forces of the HMS *Ocean* battle group. Early in 2002, the helicopter carrier HMS *Ocean* (which had been in the area of operations since the outset of the campaign) relieved the carrier HMS *Illustrious* and assault ship HMS *Fearless*, which had formed the core of the original task group. This also signified a rotation of the Royal Marines because the *Ocean* carried Royal Marines from 45 Commando, who took over the task of providing an in-theatre contingency reserve force from 40 Commando, on the HMS *Fearless*. The replacement force included elements from 45 Commando Royal Marines (about 650

men from Arbroath near Dundee, a subunit of the 3 Commando
Brigade, commanded by Brig. Roger Lane); 7 (Sphinx) Commando
Battery Royal Artillery (from Arbroath; armed with three 105mm
howitzers); 59 Independent Commando Squadron Royal Engineers
(from Chivenor near Barnstaple); a detachment from Commando
Logistics Regiment (from Chivenor; consisting of marine, navy,
and army personnel); and the Royal Air Force 27 Squadron
(Chinook helicopters from RAF Odiham). The British troops,
forming a task force under Brigadier Lane, were housed in a part
of Bagram that came to be called Camp Gibraltar.[71] By the end of
April, 4,000 coalition force members were based at Bagram,
including troops of the Australian SAS.[72]

Of the 12,000 coalition forces then in Afghanistan, perhaps
10,000 were Americans, including 3,000 paratroopers from the
101st Airborne Division. Two 10th Mountain Division battalions,
the 1st Battalion, 87th Infantry Regiment and 4th Battalion, 31st
Infantry Regiment, returned home in mid-April. As replacements,
additional troops from the 101st Airborne Division were sent
(although the recently arrived Royal Marines had assumed responsibility for Bagram).[73] The troop rotation caused some fluctuation
in strength, however, and within days, reportedly only 6,500 to
7,000 U.S. combat troops (of whom nearly half were from the
101st) were in Afghanistan.[74] By late May, 1,000 U.S. troops
remained on three military bases in Pakistan. At the same time,
7,200 U.S. troops were deployed in Afghanistan.[75] Pakistan was
estimated to have stationed about 6,000 troops along the Afghan
border, ostensibly involved in helping coalition forces hunt down
what remained of the Taliban and Al-Qaida there.[76]

It had, however, become clear that the United States would
probably maintain a lasting military presence in Afghanistan. On
30 April, it was announced that U.S. forces (150 men from the 92d
Engineering Battalion at Fort Stewart) were building a garrison for
2,500 soldiers at Bagram Air Base to last until December 2004.
According to independent reports, the buildings were designed to
last for five years, which may indicate a projected presence of U.S.
forces in Afghanistan until 2007.[77]

THE INFORMATION WAR:
UNITED STATES VERSUS AL-JAZEERA

From the point of view of the investigative reporter, the news coverage of the war in Afghanistan was largely a failure. Western news agencies in most cases found themselves unable to report from the front lines. The reasons were several, not least of which was the fact that the U.S. and British political and military leadership were strongly opposed to independent reporting. This was perhaps understandable; in most wars, after all, independent reporting can compromise security and reveal the deployment of one's forces, thus causing unnecessary loss of life. Besides, propaganda continues to play an important role in any serious war, in fact growing in importance because the mass media can make or break a president's future career, cause widespread resentment sufficiently strong to start—or end—most small wars, and, with global television, serve as the true moulder of public opinion. All wars include incidents of civilian casualties, by mistake or design, but modern public opinion being what it is, most war leaders prefer such reports to go unchallenged and thus easily forgotten. There was a real possibility that widespread reports of Afghan women and children dying in droves on prime television time would force the U.S. and British administrations, not to mention most of their allies, to back down without having secured a conclusive victory. Thus, from the outset both the Bush and Blair administrations expressed a wish that the U.S. and British media would maintain a certain level of self-censorship and not report any news that might be damaging to the conduct of the military or political part of the war. Ari Fleischer, the White House press spokesman and formerly Bush's campaign spokesman, warned U.S. reporters to "watch what they say." British Prime Minister Tony Blair, on his side, pointed out that there was still a propaganda war to be won, while the British Ministry of Defence initially asked war correspondents to clear their stories before publishing them.[78]

Another reason for the failure of most independent news agencies to report from the front lines was the unavoidable fact that,

Afghanistan being what it is, no Western reporters were stationed in the country from the outset. This was almost certainly not because of an unwillingness among journalists to cover the events, but rather the reluctance of news services—and their insurance companies—to face the risk of losing employees as war casualties. While equally understandable as the desire for self-censorship, this could only aggravate the impotence of Western media to report objectively what happened in Afghanistan.

What further politicised the media coverage of the war was that with the Western media unwilling or unable to enter Afghanistan, the only television network with a presence in Kabul was the Qatar-based Arabic-language news network Al-Jazeera. This network's Kabul correspondent, Tayseer Allouni, reported the bombing of Kabul and regularly uploaded television images via Al-Jazeera's 24-hour satellite link to the network's headquarters in Doha, Qatar. As other networks picked up the Al-Jazeera television broadcasts, they were shown throughout the world, becoming the major journalistic scoop of the war.[79] Allouni did a good job of reporting events as seen in Kabul. Many in the West indeed believed that he was too efficient. As his reporting seemed to challenge the official version of events, Al-Jazeera turned into a public relations problem for the Western anti-Taliban coalition, especially in the generally hostile Arab world.

But things soon got worse. Al-Jazeera came into possession of a videotape of Usamah bin Ladin, in which he expressed joy at what had happened and asserted that the West was involved in a war with Islam. This was bad enough, but then a second bin Ladin videotape arrived, with similar content. To suppress the broadcasting of the tape to a domestic American audience, Condoleezza Rice, national security adviser to President Bush, called the presidents of the big five American television news networks (CNN, NBC, ABC, CBS, and Fox News Channel), demanding that the broadcasting of messages from bin Ladin be stopped. The reason offered was that the tapes might contain coded messages to terrorists already in the United States, spurring them into action.[80] Although superficially plausible, this explanation does not hold water: Al-Qaida easily could transmit such messages, and in far greater detail, by other means, including telephone and e-mail. Any code that would not be detected in a videotape would be unlikely to be found in a telephone conversation, especially one conducted in a foreign language (though such one-way communication as a video is admittedly safer for the operative in hostile territory because he does not need to reveal that he takes part of the information). As noted, the linguistic capabilities of the U.S. intelligence and security organs were very limited.

The success of Al-Jazeera in covering the war from the Afghan side forced the Western networks to devote increasing efforts to broadcasting something that at least had the feel, if not quality, of genuine news from the front. This posed some difficulties. "It was all window-dressing," one BBC producer later admitted. In London, the BBC's news reporters learned from Al-Jazeera that Kabul was being bombed. They immediately called their journalists on the ground: three correspondents, including John Simpson, stationed with the Northern Alliance in northern Afghanistan. They, too, knew nothing of the attacks. However, being in Afghanistan, they could within minutes report the attacks by satellite uplink to the viewers in Britain and elsewhere. The impression was that the news came from the BBC team in Afghanistan, although the broadcast could just as well have been made by a junior reporter in a London studio.[81]

On 9 October, the United States seriously entered the field of information warfare against the Taliban and Al-Qaida. First, the State Department complained that the Al-Jazeera network had become a platform for Usamah bin Ladin. Al-Jazeera certainly had broadcast interviews with and video recordings from bin Ladin, but what especially irked the State Department was that the Qatari network—unlike its U.S. counterparts—refused to engage in self-censorship on behalf of the United States. On the same day, President Bush nominated counterterrorism chief Richard A. Clarke to the newly created position of special adviser for cyberspace security, a part of the newly created Office of Homeland Security.[82] Presumably as a result of this, in an act not widely publicised, the

United States also closed all American Internet servers for access to a large number of Web sites deemed controlled by Islamic extremists. Britain reacted in a similar way, at least with some sites.[83] This move, it was claimed, was warranted by the fear that Al-Qaida would send hidden instructions through these Web sites to its agents in the United States to initiate further terrorist attacks.[84] While the fear might have been real, the move also (presumably an additional boon) ensured that the public would not be able to learn the enemy point of view regarding the military operations. In this, the government was largely successful. Predictably, however, the move did not cut all access to the Web sites from the United States; it remained possible to reach many of them either through shadow sites or through servers in Asia and Europe.

The official as well as public American anger at the Al-Jazeera network grew increasingly strong. In mid-October, a New York journalist named Zev Chafets advocated a military attack on the Al-Jazeera station in Kabul.[85] On 13 November, hours before the first Northern Alliance units entered Kabul and when the Taliban had already withdrawn, a U.S. air raid on Kabul hit and severely damaged the Kabul offices of Al-Jazeera. It was never disclosed who had ordered the attack, and the explanation for this deliberate attack on a television network station was turned into a public relations fiasco when a U.S. spokesman claimed that "compelling" evidence indicated that the building was being used by Al-Qaida and that there was no intelligence that claimed otherwise.[86] Even worse, the air raid was not an isolated incident. On the following day, Al-Jazeera's Washington correspondent, Muhammad al-Alami, was detained in Waco, Texas. Local officials falsely alleged that the correspondent's company credit card was "linked to Afghanistan," implying that he was a terrorist suspect.[87]

The preeminence of Al-Jazeera was not for lack of trying by Western reporters: thousands of them flocked to the region to cover the war. For the Western journalist Afghanistan was—like any war zone—often a frustrating experience. Most reporters wishing to reach the front lines in Afghanistan entered through Tajikistan, where they could find representatives of the Northern Alliance. The Tajikistani capital Dushanbe enjoyed an unprecedented boom during the combat operations. Western journalists were everywhere, throwing dollars at ramshackle hotels (most stayed in the Tajikistan Hotel), eager taxi drivers, and anybody else who knew, or claimed to know, something of the conditions in Afghanistan.

To go there was easy, although the journalist needed to fulfill a few basic requirements. First, he needed serious amounts of dollars to pay for the privilege of wading through bureaucracy and to find knowledgeable sources who could tell him something of what was actually going on. To find any source was not a problem; scores of people would always crowd around the foreigner, trying to sell some information (usually of dubious authenticity). Second, he had to learn to disregard all Western standards of living and sanitation. Third, he would hand out about $250 for a ride in the escorted convoy of vehicles that left Dushanbe for the Afghan border every Tuesday and Saturday. At the border, numerous Afghan entrepreneurs would offer continued transport for another $200 to $300. The border guards would take another $10 to $20 to get around border-crossing formalities. Few Western journalists would travel further into the country than Khwaja Bahauddin, 35 kilometres (22 miles) from the border and the site of a Northern Alliance base. During the war, the town's normal population of about 10,000 inhabitants was augmented by the presence of some 2,000 journalists. There drivers and interpreters could be found who would take the journalist into what were claimed to be, and sometimes were, real battle zones. The price would be another $200 to $300 a day for a driver and an interpreter.[88]

End Notes

1. Rashid, *Taliban,* 104, 212–213

2. Jane's Sentinel: Afghanistan, 30 August 2000.

3. Rashid, *Taliban,* 213.

4. Jane's Sentinel: Afghanistan, 17 October 2000.

5. The British submarines HMS *Trafalgar* and HMS *Triumph* fired Tomahawks on the first night of operations on 7/8 October and 13 October, respectively. The other Tomahawks were fired by U.S. vessels. *Washington Post,* 8 October 2001.

6. Ibid., 8 October 2001.

7. *Washington Times*, 28 January–3 February 2002 (National Weekly Edition).
8. Ibid., 24–30 September 2001 (National Weekly Edition).
9. *Washington Post*, 8 October 2001.
10. Ibid., 9 October 2001; *Jane's Defence Weekly*, 24 October 2001.
11. Reported in an interview with Northern Alliance commanders in the *Washington Post*, 9 October 2001, as well as in several subsequent issues of the *Washington Post*. See also *Washington Post*, 23 October 2001, and in particular, 1 November 2001.
12. Ibid., 11 November 2001.
13. Jane's Sentinel: Kuwait, 29 April 2002.
14. *Economist*, 13 October 2001.
15. *Washington Times*, 12–18 November 2001 (National Weekly Edition), 3–9 December 2001; John Pike (*www.globalsecurity.org*).
16. It was originally speculated whether the 10th Special Forces Group, based at Fort Carson, Colorado, and in Germany, should be sent to Afghanistan as well, since this unit specialized in cold-weather missions. It was instead used in the War on Terror-related mission to the Caucasian republic of Georgia.
17. Rashid, *Jihad*, 170, 193.
18. Ibid., 235.
19. *Washington Times*, 26 November–2 December 2001 (National Weekly Edition).
20. *Washington Post*, 16 October 2001, 17 October 2001.
21. John Pike (*www.globalsecurity.org*).
22. *Washington Post*, 19 October 2001, 11 December 2001, 23 December 2001.
23. Ibid., 2 November, 2001, 6 December 2001, 31 January 2002.
24. Ron Callari, "Energy Interests, the U.S. Government, and the Post-Taliban Trans-Afghan Pipeline," *Central Asia—Caucasus Analyst Biweekly Briefing*, 22 May 2002 (*www.cacianalyst.org*).
25. See, for instance, Bergen, *Holy War*, 229, 281 note 21.
26. *Washington Post*, 27 October 2001.
27. Ibid., 3 November 2001.
28. Ibid., 7 November 2001.
29. Ibid., 13 January 2002.
30. The Rangers probably came from the 3d Battalion, 75th Ranger Regiment, reportedly deployed to Oman as of 8 November 2001. John Pike (*www.globalsecurity.org*).
31. *Washington Post*, 20 October 2001, 21 October 2001; *Washington Times*, 5–11 November 2001 (National Weekly Edition).
32. Seymour M. Hersh, "Escape and Evasion: What Happened When the Special Forces

Landed In Afghanistan?" *New Yorker,* 6 November 2001; *Washington Post,* 6 November 2001. For a rebuttal of Hersh, see *Washington Times,* 12–18 November 2001 (National Weekly Edition), which points out that there were only 21 AC-130H Spectre gunships in the entire U.S. Air Force inventory and that Delta Force operates in troops and squads, not companies—errors suggesting that the story was based on a rumour. Even so, it is hard to conclude that the raids were a military success, and little has been heard of them since.

33. *Washington Post,* 20 February 2002, 3 April 2002.
34. *Washington Times,* 26 November–2 December 2001 (National Weekly Edition).
35. *Washington Post,* 20 October 2001.
36. Ibid., 16 November 2001.
37. Ibid., 25 November 2001; Korgun, "Afghanistan on the Threshold of Peace," 7–13.
38. *Washington Post,* 4 November 2001.
39. Ibid., 25 November 2001; Korgun, "Afghanistan on the Threshold of Peace," 7–3.
40. Ibid., 1 November 2001.
41. Ibid.
42. *Washington Post,* 2 November 2001, which also reports the Pakistani claims without questioning or verifying them.
43. Ibid., 1 November 2001.
44. Rumsfeld made the remarks on 7 December. *Washington Post,* 9 December 2001.
45. Hopkirk, *Great Game,* 200.
46. Anthony Davis, "Anguish Continues in Afghanistan," *Jane's Intelligence Review* 7:12 (December 1996), 551.
47. See, for instance, *Washington Post,* 16 November 2001, 18 November 2001, and especially 22 November 2001; *Washington Times,* 23 January 2002.
48. *Washington Post,* 17 November 2001.
49. Ibid., 29 November 2001, 24 February 2002.
50. Ibid., 26 November 2001, 1 December 2001.
51. Ibid.
52. Ibid..
53. *Washington Post,* 2 December 2001, 5 December 2001; Jane's Sentinel: Afghanistan, 31 May 2002.
54. John Pike (*www.globalsecurity.org*).
55. See, for instance, Bidar, "US Set For Long Stay;" RIA Novosti, 2 December 2001; *Daily Yomiuri* (Japan), 11 December 2001; U.K. Ministry of Defence (*www.mod.uk*); French Ministry of Defence (*www.defense.gouv.fr*).

56. Jane's Sentinel: Kuwait, 29 April 2002.

57. John Pike (*www.globalsecurity.org*).

58. *Washington Post,* 28 November 2001, 5 December 2001, 6 December 2001, 13 December 2001, 14 December 2001, 17 December 2001, 18 December 2001, 10 February 2002; *USA Today,* 15 April 2002, 18 April 2002.

59. *Newsweek,* 13 May 2002.

60. *Washington Post,* 9 February 2002; Center for Defense Information (www.cdi.org).

61. John Pike (*www.globalsecurity.org*).

62. No British troops took part in Operation Anaconda. *USA Today,* 15 April 2002; *New York Times,* 28 May 2002.

63. *Washington Post,* 3 March 2002, 4 March 2002, and several later issues, especially 5 March 2002, 8 March 2002, 14 March 2002; see also *Economist,* 9 March 2002; *USA Today,* 2 May 2002; John Pike, *www.globalsecurity.org*). For a vivid account of the ambush in which several Americans lost their lives during this operation, see *Washington Post,* 24 May 2002, 25 March 2002. The marine contingent came from the 13th MEU from Camp Pendleton embarked on the three ships of the USS *Bonhomme Richard* ARG. They had left their home base on 1 December 2001 to relieve the 15th MEU.

64. *New York Times*, 7 March 2002.

65. *Washington Post,* 8 March 2002.

66. Ibid., 13 March 2002.

67. Center for Defense Information.

68. See, for instance, Center for Defense Information.

69. *USA Today,* 17 April 2002.

70. *Washington Post,* 25 March 2002.

71. *USA Today,* 15 April 2002, 17 April 2002.

72. Ibid., 30 April 2002.

73. Ibid., 15 April 2002.

74. Ibid., 11 April, 2002, 17 April 2002.

75. Ibid., 30 May 2002.

76. Associated Press, 1 June 2002.

77. *USA Today,* 30 April 2002.

78. *Observer* (London)/*Japan Times* (Tokyo), 27 October 2001.

79. See, for instance, Mohammed el-Nawawy and Adel Iskandar, *Al-Jazeera: How the Free Arab News Network Scooped the World and Changed the Middle East* (Cambridge, Mass.: Westview Press, 2002).

80. *Washington Post,* 11 October 2001, 16 October 2001. See also *Observer*

(London)/*Japan Times* (Tokyo), 27 October 2001; *Guardian*, 15 October.

81. *Observer* (London)/*Japan Times* (Tokyo), 27 October 2001.
82. *Washington Times*, 15–21 October 2001 (National Weekly Edition).
83. This was not widely reported, although details of the suppression were occasionally published. See, for instance, *Washington Post*, 11 October 2001.
84. Ibid., 11 October 2001, 16 October 2001. See also *Observer* (London)/*Japan Times* (Tokyo), 27 October 2001.
85. *New York Daily News*, 14 October 2001 (*www.nydailynews.com*).
86. *Washington Post*, 14 November 2001.
87. Ibid., 15 November 2001.
88. See, for instance, Avazbek Atakhanov, "Afghan Press Odyssey," *IWPR's Reporting Central Asia* 91 (7 December 2001; *www.iwpr.net*). Atakhanov is a local journalist who, unlike most of his Western colleagues, speaks a couple of the languages of Afghanistan.

CHAPTER 15

After the War: Implications for Afghanistan

He is as great an enemy as a cousin.

—Afghan proverb

As the Taliban government collapsed under the combined onslaught of the Northern Alliance, the United States, and the coalition, the victors installed a new interim government in Afghanistan. The United States and Pakistan pushed through the demand that a Pashtun had to head the new government. Eventually, Hamid Karzai was chosen, in a process not dissimilar to that when the Soviet Union in 1986 appointed Muhammad Najibullah, another ethnic Pashtun, president of Afghanistan, then in 1989 left him on his own as the Soviet troops moved out of the country. Najibullah had to seek shelter in a United Nations diplomatic compound in Kabul in 1992, where he remained until the Taliban dragged him out to be castrated and killed in 1996.[1] How long Hamid Karzai can survive the eventual pull-out of U.S. and other Western forces remains to be seen.

Despite rhetoric to the contrary, the Taliban forces were not annihilated by U.S. air attacks or by the advancing forces of the Northern Alliance. The Taliban had ample time to move out of the cities before the air raids began, and the Taliban leaders had pulled out of at least Kandahar and Jalalabad already by mid-September 2001.[2] Besides, the U.S. air campaign was initially designed neither to destroy the Taliban forces nor to dislodge them from their positions between the Northern Alliance and Kabul, but rather to intimidate them into surrender.[3] The United States wished to preserve an organised Pashtun military force as a counterweight to the Iranian- and Russian-supported Northern Alliance, as well as to prevent the latter from occupying Kabul. When the Northern Alliance did take Kabul on 13 November 2001, perhaps advised to do so by their Iranian or possibly Russian backers, this humiliated President Bush who had earlier promised Pakistani leader Musharraf that he would not permit it to happen.[4] While the Taliban certainly took some losses early on in the war, the Taliban collapse was rather the effect of the sudden switching of allegiance of most Taliban commanders and units from the Taliban government, first to various Pashtun local leaders, then to the interim government of Hamid Karzai. Due to support from the United States and Pakistan, Karzai was widely regarded as the guarantor for continued Pashtun dominance.

Although the exact number of former Taliban troops who currently support Karzai is unknown to outside observers and possibly even to Karzai, reports indicate that at a very minimum of several thousand are being recruited into the new Afghan army, where they are being armed with Russian weapons and uniforms provided by Turkey and the United States. In Kandahar alone, it is estimated that as many as 6,000 former Taliban will form part of the new army.[5] It seems reasonable to assume that most former Taliban soldiers, unless they find other employment opportunities, will eventually enlist. This is worrisome for two reasons. First, these men will not have transformed themselves overnight into a pro-Western and pro-democracy force for secular government. Second, it seems likely that rivalry, possibly of a violent kind, will continue to characterise the situation between the Pashtun and non-Pashtun components of the new army.

The Formation of the New Afghanistan National Army
There are plans to establish a 75,000-strong police force and an army of 80,000 to protect the central government against local warlords. This is easier said than

done. Potential recruits are certainly available, perhaps as many as 200,000. To form them into a unified force is another matter.[6]

Germany has undertaken to recruit and train an Afghan police force. In late August 2002, a force of about 900 recruits was expected to begin a three-year course in the newly restored police academy in Kabul.[7]

British instructors from ISAF trained the first battalion, 600 men, of the Afghan National Guard. They completed six weeks of basic training on 3 April 2002, in uniforms donated by Turkey. They were supposed to be used mainly to guard offices in the capital.[8]

The United States, meanwhile, began to build a new national army. More than 500 men were recruited to the 1st Battalion of the Afghanistan National Army (ANA). Following a 10-week training course that began in May 2002 and relied on instructors from the Army Special Forces (1st Battalion 3d Special Forces Group) under Lt. Col. Kevin McDonnell, their number had dropped to about 300 men, who graduated as the first battalion. The dropouts left for various reasons, not the least of which was the revelation that they would only be paid $30 a month, rising to $50 upon graduation. The Americans also trained Afghan instructors who will eventually assume responsibility for training the new army. French instructors on 8 June commenced training of the 2d Battalion of the Afghan army, which graduated on 14 August with a strength of 330 men.[9] Two border patrol battalions were also to be formed and trained, each 300-men strong.[10]

In May 2002, the Indian Ministry of Defence announced that India would train officers for the Afghan armed forces. In addition and perhaps more importantly, Indian technicians would service the Afghan Air Force's

surviving fleet of Mikoyan-Gurevich MiG-21 "Fishbed" interceptor/ground attack fighters.[11]
By mid-July 2002, the Afghan air force included nine MiG-21 fighters and two Czech Aero L-39C Albatros jet trainers (probably none of Taliban origin; more likely, they had earlier been saved and mothballed by the Northern Alliance in Tajikistan or Uzbekistan). The inventory also included eight Mi-8/17 transport helicopters earlier used by the Northern Alliance and five Mi-24 attack helicopters received from Russia in April 2002.[12]

Despite the efforts of the United States and Pakistan in installing and supporting Karzai's interim government, it is by no means certain that his leadership will ensure the survival of Afghanistan as a unified country. None of the tensions between the various ethnic groups of the country, exacerbated by more than two decades of civil war, has been satisfactorily resolved.[13] As noted, the Pashtuns are the largest ethnic group in Afghanistan (about 40 percent of the population), followed by Tajiks, Hazara, and Uzbeks (together roughly 50 percent).[14] However, since 60 percent of the country's agricultural resources and 80 percent of its industrial, mineral, and gas wealth are in the chiefly Uzbek and Tajik north, the Pashtuns wish to recover their leading position, while the non-Pashtuns try to keep their natural resources beyond Pashtun control.[15]

Some feel that Afghanistan's territorial integrity is inviolable, and that the Pashtuns should form the backbone of any future government as they mostly did in the past.[16] However, any policy to try to return Afghanistan to the situation in 1979 is bound to fail. Besides, a Pashtun-dominated Afghanistan would by no means ensure a period of peace in Afghanistan. The Pashtuns remain fragmented into different subgroups. Many senior Taliban commanders enjoyed considerable autonomy, and their predominantly Pashtun troops were kept in separate units based on region, district, or tribe to minimise friction.[17] As the Taliban government fell, most of its

Pashtun commanders and forces were not annihilated but merely switched allegiance. Besides, considering the common practice in Afghanistan—also taken advantage of by the Taliban in their heyday—of buying over enemies instead of fighting them,[18] it is likely that payments to local Taliban commanders played a substantial part in the transferring of their allegiance to Hamid Karzai.

The Bonn agreement included the eventual convening of a *Loya Jirga* (Grand Assembly). This is an institution developed in the 1920s in an attempt to reinvent Pashtun tribal tradition to legitimise state power. The Loya Jirga since then has been regarded as the highest representative body of the Afghan state, although its composition frequently changed in accord with current state interests. The purpose of this most recent Loya Jirga was to form a broadly based transitional government. This would then be followed by elections of some kind, the disarmament (if possible) of all groups, and the formation of a regular army.[19] A new government, though still headed by Hamid Karzai, was accordingly selected on 19 June 2002.[20] Unfortunately, current ethnic divisions and the history of mistrust limited the authority of the new government and rendered disarmament all but impossible except by force. The new government will additionally, no doubt, subject the formation of a regular army to those ethnic leaders who happen to gain control of its units. Minorities will want strong and credible guarantees before disarming and exposing themselves to a possibly vindictive Pashtun military. Such guarantees are unlikely to be forthcoming.

Instead, a viable case of autonomy within a federation or outright independence can be made for several ethnic and religious groups.[21] These include the northern Tajiks and Uzbeks, the Shia Heratis, as well as the Ismailis of the Wakhan Corridor, and probably the Shia Hazara. Most of these groups have a tradition of cooperation with their ethnic cousins on the other side of the border. Besides, their territories probably have the natural or economic resources to create statelets that in due time could choose to reunite, remain independent, or join their compatriots in the neighbouring countries.

The Ismailis, although a fairly small group, retain extensive contacts abroad due to their contacts with overseas Ismailis through their leader, the Agha Khan. Ismailism, although not as well known as other branches of Islam, emerged in the 8th century as a major Islamic movement, currently with over 20 million followers. These are scattered throughout the world, but major concentrations of Ismailis live in, among other countries, India, Pakistan, Afghanistan, Tajikistan, and Iran. They are headed by Aga Khan, who through the Aga Khan Foundation dispenses aid and support to projects designed to improve and assist economic development, health, and education in several third world countries, but in particular in East Africa and Central Asia where there are numerous Ismailis. In Afghanistan, there are two large Ismailitic communities. One is the Ismailis of Badakhshan (in Darwaz, Shugnan, Ishkashim, Wahan, and Munjan) headed by hereditary religious leaders known as *pirs* and *khalife* (pir deputies). They live close to their compatriots in Tajikistan's Gorno-Badakhshan Autonomous Region. The other is the Ismailitic Hazara community in Kabul and the district of Doshi, Baghlan Province, headed for the past two centuries by a hereditary pir, Sayyid Shah Naser Nadiri of the Kayani clan in Hazarajat. Some of their leaders have maintained close connections with the Uzbek warlord Dostum.[22]

There are also non-Ismailitic Hazara. They present a special though not unsolvable problem. Their territory, generally known as the Hazarajat, is often regarded to cover portions of the three central provinces of Bamian, Oruzgan, Ghowr, as well as parts of Herat, Farah, Kandahar, Ghazni, Parwan, Baghlan, Balkh, and Badghis. The Hazara-majority Sar-e-Pol Province was created in 1988 by the Afghan leader Muhammad Najibullah in the southern part of the Jowzjan Province. It became an economic and political base for the northern Hazara. The Hazara speak a Persian dialect known as Hazaragi.[23] If autonomy is granted to the other groups, the Hazara could probably achieve the same status, since they could then gain access to the present international border through the territories of other groups.

This leaves the Pashtuns, who straddle the border between Afghanistan and Pakistan. A Pashtun state could easily be set up in

southern Afghanistan, but this may leave Pakistan vulnerable to separatism among its own Pashtuns. Pakistan has long feared that the
Pashtuns in its North-West Frontier Province would unite with the
Afghan Pashtuns to declare an independent Pashtunistan. The threat
of Pashtun separatism would be exacerbated if major elements of
the defeated Taliban resumed their struggle in Pakistan. Pakistan can
accordingly be counted on to attempt to maintain a degree of influence in Afghanistan, by proxy if not direct involvement. (Another
Pakistani concern is the potential of Baluchi separatism: there are
Baluchis as well in both Afghanistan and Pakistan.)

Even as the Pashtuns perceive themselves as the rightful rulers
of Afghanistan and are unlikely to accept a ruler from one of the
other ethnic groups, they too suffer from fragmentation based on
their culture of tribalism and blood feuds. Some Pashtun clans and
tribes, especially in the border areas beyond the immediate control
of any central government, have a history of rowdy independence
and fairly egalitarian societies. Even so, there were influential
Pashtun leaders, usually from the powerful, entrenched Pashtun lineages that controlled the trade routes east and south of Kabul.[24]
While no government of Afghanistan could be formed without at
least some form of Pashtun participation, currently there do not
seem to be any Pashtun tribal leaders who (1) wield sufficient influence to be accepted by all Pashtun clans, and (2) remain untouched
by association with the Taliban or Islamic extremism. A few moderate Islamic parties that took part in the war against the Soviet Union
remain in Pakistan, but most of their leaders are getting on in years
and may have lost much of their influence in Afghanistan.[25]

The Northern Alliance has also seemingly played out its part in
the drama of Afghan politics. The alliance was primarily united by
its resistance to the Taliban, its mujahidin leaders being fragmented
according to personal, frequently ethnically based, power bases and
without sharing any common ideology. By September 2001, there
no longer appeared to be (if there ever was) any long-term strategy
or objectives beyond mere personal survival. The only—but perhaps decisive—point in favour of the Northern Alliance leaders is
that they long have received support from first the West, then

Russia, Iran, India, and several Central Asian states. This gives them some understanding of contemporary international politics and the outside world. Unfortunately, this aid—and its use to resist the Pashtuns—has widened the chasm between the ethnic groups. The older leaders of the Northern Alliance formed part of the Kabul government from 1992 to 1996, but their record was, to say the least, not inspiring. Several of them from time to time resorted to military action against each other in Kabul and elsewhere, and most have less than impeccable records.

Be that as it may, the United States will probably maintain a lasting military presence in Afghanistan. On 30 April 2002, it was announced that U.S. forces were building a garrison for 2,500 soldiers at Bagram Air Base. As noted, independent reports indicated that the buildings were designed to last for as long as five years, which may indicate a projected presence of U.S. forces in Afghanistan until 2007.[26]

It is clear, then, that some resolute decisions need to be taken regarding the policy of the West in Afghanistan. It seems as if the West is no closer to formulating an effective policy now than a century ago. In 1909, an anonymous analyst summarised the problems of dealing with Afghanistan in the following way:

> In short, to manage a country without occupying it is no less impossible than to steer a boat without taking a seat in it. The process of subordinating the Afghan tribes to effective control will probably go forward slowly and at intervals. It may be that when one part of the country is taken resolutely into hand, the rest will be overawed and quieted; but we doubt whether any other remedy can be found for the feuds and forays that from time immemorial have distracted this borderland, which has preserved the primitive conditions of life and habits that have long disappeared from the frontiers of all other civilised nations. Yet the objections to pushing forward our landmarks into these mountains are great and manifest, while the disadvantages of the present system are

equally patent. The attempt to protect our subjects by a line of outposts, to adopt the tactics of stationary defence, varied by occasional sallies forth from our cantonments to pursue assassins or to punish depredators by destroying houses and crops, is to assume a somewhat impotent and undignified attitude, hardly creditable in the case of a mighty empire worried by mere highland caterans. The [British] Indian Government, therefore, finds itself placed in a dilemma: to advance or to stand still is equally difficult; nor is any practicable issue out of this situation to be foreseen.[27]

The present concept of respect for territorial integrity regardless of the costs in dead and wounded is a fairly recent phenomenon. In 1880, as soon-to-be Afghan king Abdul Rahman crossed the Oxus into Afghanistan with a small force of supporters, the consensus in London and Calcutta was that Afghanistan should be broken up, thereby making it more difficult for the Russians or any other potential enemy to gain control of the country. A permanent occupation was expected to bring an enormous cost in lives and money.[28] As late as in 1951, a British diplomat suggested the partitioning of Afghanistan. Because British officials doubted the viability of Afghanistan as an independent country and suspected that the country eventually would fall into chaos and anarchy, they discussed the possibility of dividing a failed Afghanistan among the Soviet Union, Pakistan, and Iran along the line of the Hindu Kush mountain range.[29]

To resolve the Afghan conflict, the international community is faced with a stark choice. One must either accept the fact that Afghanistan is already—and under current conditions perhaps irreversibly—fragmented along ethnic lines and divide the failed country into independent or at least fully autonomous territories, or prepare for a long period of direct government by an outside administration, backed by foreign or UN forces. The alternative of installing an ostensibly broad-based government and pulling out all foreign forces will amount to mere abandonment of Afghanistan to further warfare. Unfortunately, breaking up the country may well cause further, though temporary, regional instability, as neighbouring countries will attempt to influence or even assume control of the territories inhabited by their ethnic cousins in Afghanistan. The rule by foreign troops, however, despite the facade of respect for Afghanistan's territorial integrity, will only postpone the conflict between different ethnic groups. Such a policy will alienate existing military and tribal leaders, who would regard the foreign forces as competitors instead of a guarantee for disarmament. This policy, or the abandonment of Afghanistan to renewed warlordism, will cause further resentment against the West and will no doubt encourage the very extremism and terrorism that the international community wishes to eradicate.

Any attempts at conflict resolution in Afghanistan must take this possible fragmentation into account. The Afghan civil war was to a large extent sustained by foreign aid agencies. The provision of humanitarian aid has weakened rather than strengthened the stability of the state by allowing warlords the means to prolong the war. Rather than arguing about who has the right to form a legitimate government of Afghanistan and, if an undemocratic regime assumes power, whether to impose sanctions or not, the West needs to realise that Afghanistan has failed as a state and there is currently very little point in pretending otherwise. This situation was not rectified by the mere fall from power of the Taliban or the installment by foreign powers of a more amenable government.

There is a further point to be kept in mind. Any return to the historic legacy of the Afghan state, as established by Amir Abdul Rahman Khan in the late 19th century, implies that existing local community structures, identities, and loyalties must be suppressed or (if possible) destroyed, if they are expected one day possibly to conflict with those of the state. In other words, what little civil society there is in Afghanistan has to be sacrificed to reinforce the power of the central government. If the state is to be based on the Pashtuns, this legacy is especially threatening to the non-Pashtun citizens of the state. Ironically, the government of Hamid Karzai is often perceived by the Pashtuns to be dominated by Tajiks—which in a new twist causes the Pashtuns to see this very legacy as a threat to themselves, even though they earlier profited from it. The historic legacy is also counterproductive because both old and recent history shows that it is not the state, invariably dependent on foreign donors as it was and is, that assured national independence, but the presence of well-armed local community structures that were willing to fight against foreign intrusions.

Disarming the local communities in favour of an autocratic central government dependent on foreign aid may well make the latter's life easier, but it will not guarantee long-term security in the provinces and it will not provide any guarantees in the face of lingering Islamic extremism or foreign threats.[30] This argument should of course not be taken to endorse the presence of lawless warlords, but it is a strong argument, seldom mentioned, in favour of local autonomy. At present several Western governments are in the process of creating, outfitting, and training an Afghan national army. This is all good and well, but it will take years, if not decades, before this rag-tag band will be able to assume responsibility for anything but paramilitary police actions. To successfully disarm the local communities will take far stronger security guarantees than this.

End Notes

1. Rashid, *Taliban,* 49–50.

2. *Afghanistan: OCHA Situation Report* 1 (18 September 2001; *www.reliefweb.int*).

3. See, for instance, *Economist,* 13 October 2001; 20 October 2001.

4. See *Economist,* 17 November 2001; *Guardian*; Interfax, 15 November 2001.

5. See, for instance, Tim Reid, "Mullah Omar's Troops Enlist in Afghan Army," *Times* (U.K.), 17 January 2002; *Time,* 10 December 2001.

6. *Economist,* 10 August 2002.

7. *Economist,* 10 August 2002.

8. *Washington Post,* 4 April 2002; *USA Today,* 11 April 2002.

9. Michael Drudge in an untitled article at *www.globalsecurity.org*, 21 July 2002; *Economist,* 10 August 2002; Jane's Sentinel: Afghanistan, 18 July 2002; French Ministry of Defence (*www.defense.gouv.fr*). The French instructors on 7 September

2002 began to train the 4th battalion of the ANA, then about 420 men.

10. Center for Defense Information (*www.cdi.org*).

11. Jane's Sentinel: Afghanistan, 18 July 2002.

12. Jane's Sentinel: Afghanistan, 18 July 2002.

13. See, for instance, Kenneth Weisbrode, "Afghanistan Interim Government 'Solution' Could Leave Regional Problems Intact," Eurasia Insight (*www.eurasianet.org*), 4 December 2001.

14. CIA, *The World Factbook 2001.*

15. Rubin, *Fragmentation of Afghanistan,* 237–238; Rashid, *Taliban,* 55.

16. There seems to be an implicit belief among many contemporary political leaders that the maintenance of the status quo equals peace, while its disturbance, even for good reasons, would be a move towards war. Unfortunately, it is debatable what exactly is the meaning of the term status quo when it comes to Afghanistan. The Latin *status quo* means "the state of things as they are," referring to the existing state of, for instance, a society's social system, state structure, or form of government. It has also often been used with regard to a state's geographical location and borders. The term might even refer to the existence or not of actual statehood. All these variables are debatable for a country such as Afghanistan, which for decades was torn apart by civil war. Clearly, the term status quo is meaningless with regard to Afghanistan. The variant *status quo ante* means the previous state of things, while *status quo ante bellum* means the state of things before the war. However, even the latter variant brings forth a host of problems. The state before which war? This is not easy to tell, and in any case it would be overly optimistic to attempt to turn the clock back a quarter of a century.

17. Jane's Sentinel: Afghanistan, 30 August 2000.

18. See, for instance, Anthony Davis, "Afghanistan's Taliban," *Jane's Intelligence Review* 7:7 (July 1995), 315–321; Maley, *Fundamentalism Reborn?,* 50–51.

19. See, for instance, *Economist,* 8 December 2001.

20. *IWPR'S Afghan Recovery Report* 15 (19 June 2002; *www.iwpr.net*).

21. The advantages for Afghanistan of a federal system have been argued elsewhere. See, for instance, Maley, *Fundamentalism Reborn?,* 195–197, with references.

22. Saidanwar Shokhumorov, "Ismailism: Traditions and the Present Day," *Central Asia and the Caucasus* 2 (2000): 130–138.

23. Mousavi, *Hazaras,* xiii; Rubin, *Fragmentation of Afghanistan,* 259.

24. For Pashtun tribalism in a historical context, see, for instance, Christine Noelle, *State and Tribe in Nineteenth-Century Afghanistan: The Reign of Amir Dost Muhammad Khan (1826–1863)* (Richmond, Surrey: Curzon Press, 1997), 125–158, 291–294.

25. While a member of the former royal family might conceivably form a token government that on the surface would reunite the country despite the decades of ethnic fragmentation, it is unlikely—though not impossible—for this to heal the rifts among the ethnic groups. What some claim speaks in favour of a royal participation in a future Afghan government is the reported feeling among certain Afghans that the time under royal rule was a golden age. However, most Afghans are young (more than 40 percent of the population is under the age of 15) and accordingly have no personal memories of the monarchy. Besides, ex-King Muhammad Zahir Shah was born in 1914, has not ruled since he was deposed in a coup in July 1973, and the Afghan administration under his rule was not noted for its efficiency.

26. *USA Today,* 30 April 2002.

27. "Frontiers Ancient and Modern," *Edinburgh Review* (1909): 219.

28. Hopkirk, *Great Game,* 396.

29. The relevant official files were only made public on 2 January 2002. See, for instance, *Japan Times,* 4 January 2002, based on Associated Press report.

30. M. Nazif Shahrani, "The Future of the State and the Structure of Community Governance in Afghanistan"; Maley, *Fundamentalism Reborn?,* 237–238.

CHAPTER 16
Can the War on Terror Be Won?

Islam is peace. Hence there can be no peace with the Jews until they are converted.

—From a communiqué of the Islamic Society (Morocco), signed by the movement's emir, Abu Abdullah al-Sharif

It is, of course, impossible ever to declare that a war on terror has been won: it would only take a single madman with a gun, some explosives, or a box-cutter to disprove the claim. The cynic would also point out that an ongoing war is convenient for the government—any government—to introduce all sorts of emergency regulations that are unacceptable in times of peace and to justify large expenditures on defence and the intelligence and security structures. It is thus unlikely that the Bush administration ever will declare a victory in the current war on terror, which seems destined to join the old wars on drugs and money laundering as a permanent fixture in national policy.

It might, however, be possible to win the war against Sunni Islamic extremism. In a way, Islamic extremism can be said to have been defeated in Afghanistan. Surely, many extremists remain in the country, but a return to Taliban rule seems increasingly unlikely—whether the future belongs to a democratic government or the traditional warlords. Unfortunately, Islamic extremism remains alive and well in other parts of the world. So do, perhaps, Usamah bin Ladin and his chief associates. Key supporters of Islamic extremism and terrorism also remain—fundamentally unaffected by the war—in Saudi Arabia and Pakistan (see Appendices 3 and 4).

Three conclusions can be drawn, none of which offers hope for an easy solution to the problem of Sunni Islamic terrorism. First, if the Saudi government were to renounce extremist views that are widespread among the Saudi elite as well as the general population, this could lead to the fall of the House of Saud. The ensuing turmoil might require Western military intervention. But if not, Saudi Arabia is likely to remain a source of funds as well as recruits for the jihad against the West.

Second, the Pakistani government remains vulnerable to Islamic extremism. Although Musharraf hitherto has been successful in containing his country's large numbers of extremists, these have not gone away and may even have been reinforced by Al-Qaida and Taliban survivors from Afghanistan. If Pakistan ever were to follow Afghanistan's descent into civil breakdown and extremism, whoever wins control over the country's nuclear weapons program will be of more than passing interest to the international community.

Third, the question of the fate of the Al-Qaida top leadership remains unresolved. At the time of this writing, very little is known about the current activities of bin Ladin. If he died while in hiding or simply disappeared, he would yet remain as a highly evocative front for the Arab Afghan movement. However, even were he to be killed or captured, this would not signify the end of the Arab Afghan movement. Usamah bin Ladin is a key player in the movement, but its various components always conducted many if not most operations without his involvement, leadership, or financing. Simply having him killed or punished for his role in terrorist activities will change nothing, aside from possibly providing a highly inspiring martyr for the extremists. To have bin Ladin punished for his role in terrorist activities makes legal and, according to most interpretations, moral sense, but his death or imprisonment will in no way solve the problem of the Arab Afghan movement and Sunni Islamic terrorism.

Terrorist supporters also remain among local Muslims in the United States and Europe. While the leading members of the Islamic extremist movement were educated elites, the chief recruitment base was, as noted, among young, unemployed men living in poverty or without clear prospects for the future. Not all of them live in third-world countries. There is also a "hip hop" generation of Islamic extremists: young men, often petty criminals and in the West frequently the sons of immigrants, who have no real Islamic background but want to imitate bin Ladin because he is seen as a rebel opposed to Western society. A typical representative of the new generation of Islamic extremists in the West is a fairly ordinary young man named Anwar Khan, who was born in Britain and grew up in Manchester. According to his own statement when he was captured by the Northern Alliance, he got into trouble with the police, so his parents sent him to relatives in Pakistan to "clean up his act." Instead, soon after arriving, he joined the extremist group Harakat ul-Ansar, which sent him to Afghanistan to fight in a Taliban unit.[1] Anwar Khan was fortunate; he was captured before the War on Terror got under way.

There are many young men like Anwar Khan. Britain, with a total population of nearly 60 million, is the home of some 2 million Muslims, the majority Pakistanis and Bangladeshis, but also including many recent immigrants from Afghanistan, Iraq, and Somalia. London's role as a centre for Islamic extremists has already been described. France, with a total population of around 60 million people, is the native land of at least 4.2 million Muslims, most of them North Africans or their offspring. Germany, with a total population of 82 million, is the fatherland of some 3.2 million Muslims, although some 2.5 million of these are Turks and long-time residents, more secular and less likely to get involved in Islamic extremist movements than most others.[2] Yet, there are groups affiliated with Al-Qaida in Germany, including one that was involved in the 11 September attacks, as well as various Palestinian and Algerian groups such as Hamas, FIS, and GIA. Spain, with a total population of 40 million, is the abode of around 500,000 Muslim legal residents and perhaps another 200,000 Muslim illegal residents, mostly from North Africa. Al-Qaida cells have been found there as well. Italy contains well-established groups of the FIS, GIA, Al-Qaida, and the Egyptian Islamic Society. There are proportionally large Muslim communities in most other Western countries, in particular the Netherlands and the Scandinavian countries. The Netherlands has a community of 400,000 Muslims, including numerous recent immigrants from North Africa and the former Yugoslavia. Denmark has a population of 80,000 Muslims: extremist groups based in Denmark include the Hizb ut-Tahrir and Islamic Society. In Sweden, there are cells belonging to a number of groups, including FIS, GIA, and the Tunisian En-Nahda. Belgium has a Muslim population of more than 300,000, including groups belonging to the Muslim Brotherhood, FIS, GIA, and En-Nahda. Besides, the Muslim population in all these countries is invariably young: in Britain, for instance, half of the Muslims are probably under 18.[3] Their youth and background in a not yet integrated immigrant community make them doubly vulnerable to Islamic extremism.

As for the 6-million-strong Muslim population in the United States, it differs considerably from the Muslim population of the Middle East. The largest contingent of U.S. Muslims is black, not Arab. Among the Arab-Americans, fully three-quarters are not Muslims at all but Christians.[4] Yet, in the United States, too, there are recent immigrants, whether of legal, refugee, or illegal status, of the type common in Europe (see Appendix 18). Even so, the FBI for years hesitated to investigate radical Islamic clerics, even in cases involving the advocacy of terrorism and the murder of their opponents. This situation did not immediately change after the 11 September 2001 terrorist attacks, as the Bush administration consistently attempted to play down the fact that many Muslims actually supported the terrorist attacks.[5] However, from late 2002 several FBI investigations were under way. On 20 February 2003, the FBI arrested Sami al-Arian, a Palestinian professor at the University of South Florida in Tampa, charged with the support of terrorism. He had been identified as a fundraiser for Islamic Jihad as early as 1994.[6]

Islamic extremists and the Western governments play by different rules; each can declare victory. The West destroyed the Taliban government, but the Islamic extremist might argue that the West could not destroy Islam. He might also see the war as a good thing, a catharsis that roused many Muslims who because of the Western aggression realised that they too had to take up the gun to defend the word of God. If so, continued safe havens in countries such as Saudi Arabia will enable the extremists to rebuild their shattered organisations.

It will not be sufficient for the West merely to create a system of deterrence based on military force. Deterrence depends on the existence of credible retaliatory capabilities (the ability to inflict unacceptable levels of damage). Deterrence works against opponents who are rational and make predictable relative-value judgements. It means nothing to opponents who seek negative values such as glorious martyrdom. Military deterrence also means little to those who have no values vulnerable to attack, or no values that are worthy of attack. Such men—or their spiritual descendants—are likely to attack again. The world is no more safe from Islamic terrorism than it was before 11 September 2001.

Airline Security and Terrorism

Because of the obvious risks of commercial airline travel, most security measures introduced after the 11 September 2001 attacks have involved raising airport security. Although these served to calm the fears of the public, most are of dubious value because they are almost wholly aimed at the passengers, not the airport or airline staff. While it is important to search for car bombs, it is, for instance, childish to order the National Guard to protect airport car parking lots as long as nobody is checking the contents of all large trunks and bags brought into the airport terminals but never checked in for a flight. Increased airport security can of course, if successfully implemented, prevent copycat terrorism and attempts by amateur supporters of the various terrorist groups. The security measures introduced are, however, unlikely to prevent serious terrorists from accomplishing their goals. Most successful airline hijackings against hard targets, that is, airports outside the United States (American airports were until recently regarded as easy to infiltrate—and they probably still are) were inside jobs. A typical example was the GIA hijacking of the Air France flight on 24 December 1994.[7] The terrorists acquired the uniforms, badges, and other paraphernalia of airport workers. They learned the security procedures from genuine airport employees. It is surprising, and somewhat falsely reassuring, that the men who executed the 11 September attacks in most ways acted as amateurs rather than professionals. However, the existence of such Arab Afghans as Ramzi Yousef shows that there are men in Al-Qaida who have the technical knowledge to carry out far more sophisticated attacks. Although security has been improved since 2001, much remains to be done.

USAMAH BIN LADIN AND WEAPONS OF MASS DESTRUCTION

There is no doubt that bin Ladin attempted to acquire weapons of mass destruction. "We don't consider it a crime if we tried to have nuclear, chemical, biological weapons," he once said. "Our holy land is occupied by Israeli and U.S. forces. We have the right to defend ourselves and to liberate our holy land." He added: "Acquiring weapons for the defence of Muslims is a religious duty. If I have indeed acquired these weapons, then I thank God for enabling me to do so. And if I seek to acquire these weapons, I am carrying out a duty. It would be a sin for Muslims not to try to possess the weapons that would prevent the infidels from inflicting harm on Muslims."[8]

As early as 1992 bin Ladin had tried to obtain components for nuclear weapons, including enriched uranium. An alleged Al-Qaida operative named Mahmoud Salim was arrested in September 1998 in Munich and was accused of involvement in this attempt as well as other terrorism-related crimes. Unfortunately, few details of this and other similar incidents have been released. For instance, small amounts of Russian weapons-grade uranium and plutonium that fell into the wrong hands have been confiscated on various occasions, but no such cases have been reported after 1995.[9]

By late 1993, Al-Qaida is believed to have hunted for a complete nuclear missile from the former Soviet Union, apparently through black-market contacts within Russian organised crime. When this search yielded nothing, bin Ladin instead appears to have instructed his followers to attempt the acquisition of highly enriched uranium and nuclear weapons components, spending large amounts in the process. According to some reports, the Al-Qaida operatives acquired, or were offered, low-grade reactor fuel unusable for a weapon—but which the sellers claimed to be enriched uranium. It appears that the Al-Qaida men frequently were conned out of their money by unscrupulous officials or criminal gangs offering anything from chemical waste to low-grade nuclear reactor fuel, impossible to use in the construction of a nuclear bomb. Another scheme involved the sale of "red mercury," radioactive waste supposedly used in the manufacture of nuclear weapons that never seem to have existed—but for which Al-Qaida operatives probably paid large amounts of cash. Although useless for weapons purposes, "red mercury" had by then acquired a mythical status among the agents of powers such as Iraq and others that attempted the manufacture of nuclear weapons.[10] There were also rumours that Al-Qaida commissioned some Chechens to obtain by theft or capture nuclear "suitcase bombs," small Russian nuclear devices that, although considerably larger and heavier than a suitcase, were still portable. Such weapons were developed during the Cold War for possible use by Soviet special forces or agents in the West.[11]

It would, of course, be conceivable for terrorists to build a radiological dispersal device commonly known as a "dirty bomb." This is a contraption that would scatter radioactive materials over a limited area by using conventional explosives. A dirty bomb is built by packing radioactive materials around conventional explosives. A terrorist could, for instance, use materials such as cesium 137 or cobalt

60. These materials are dangerous to handle and more radioactive than enriched uranium but are widely used for medical and industrial purposes. These and other suitable radioactive materials can be found in many laboratories, food irradiation plants, medical centres, and oil-drilling operations. The radioactive materials per se would be unlikely to cause immediate fatalities, although they would likely cause cancer in the long term. However, the area affected would need to be decontaminated, or demolished and abandoned, because radioactive materials can bind to concrete or asphalt. This might result in the total abandonment of a major city centre, with all that this would entail in financial and material losses.[12]

Although Al-Qaida probably acquired various radioactive substances that could conceivably be used in a dirty bomb, its operatives never appear to have acquired true nuclear weapons. Bin Ladin may eventually have realised that his agents had been had. Al-Qaida instead appears to have settled for chemical or biological weapons, since they were easier to manufacture.[13] This is at least in theory far easier. Al-Qaida members operating from Albania reportedly obtained anthrax and the lethal viral agent botulism from a laboratory in the Czech Republic for $7,500 a sample. Similar biological agents have no doubt been obtained elsewhere as well. The real problem for Al-Qaida, though, is to develop a system of delivering these weapons.[14] However, Al-Qaida has a history of reasonably successful experiments with chemical or biological weapons in at least the form of poison gas. The group has been linked to the production of the persistent nerve agent VX in Sudan and the biological agent ricin.[15] In a cache of 64 videotapes spanning more than a decade, several were found to be recordings of poison tests on animals.[16] The latest Al-Qaida laboratory for such experiments was reportedly established in Kurdistan, the part of northern Iraq beyond the control of Saddam Hussein's Baghdad regime and paradoxically under the protection of the West. It was apparently set up by Al-Qaida members from a local Islamic extremist group known as *Ansar al-Islam* (Helpers of Islam), which in December 2001 split from an earlier extremist group, *Jund al-Islam* (Soldiers of Islam), which itself had emerged only around

September 2001, when the loosely organised Islamic Movement of Kurdistan (IMK) broke up. Even the IMK was not expected to have had a strength of more than, 1,500 men, at most, and the successor groups are unlikely each to field more than a few hundred men, mostly Kurds. Yet, Jund al-Islam and Ansar al-Islam clearly subscribed to extremist beliefs, having declared a jihad against all secular and apostate forces, as well as Jews and Christians.[17]

There was also a disturbing—and potentially far more serious—link between Al-Qaida and the Pakistani nongovernmental organisation called *Ummah Tamir-e Nau* (Foundation for Reconstruction, UTN), which until the war also had offices in Taliban-controlled Kabul. The president of UTN, Bashiruddin Mahmood, one of Pakistan's leading nuclear scientists as well as a radical Muslim, was held in detention for some time in Pakistan due to his links with the Taliban. Although the UTN officially assisted the Taliban government with flour mills, school textbooks, and road repair, evidence left in the organisation's Kabul office when its personnel fled together with the Taliban seems to indicate that it was involved in various biological weapons projects, including the use of anthrax.[18] U.S. forces also discovered a half-finished laboratory near Kandahar, which they believe was ultimately intended to produce anthrax. No biological agents were found, however.[19] Unfortunately, the surviving evidence in either case seems insufficient to indicate whether this project predated the limited anthrax outbreaks in the United States, or perhaps more probably, was only initiated in imitation, inspired by the outbreaks.

Yet the threat from terrorism in the form of weapons of mass destruction is real. This includes chemical and biological, as well as nuclear, weapons. Lorries full of poisonous or radioactive materials (if obtainable) can be used as suicide bombs. Even simpler might be to fly an aircraft into repositories of such materials. To actually manufacture weapons of mass destruction is far from easy. Yet, organisations such as Al-Qaida seem to be able to attract sufficiently qualified technical personnel (e.g. Bashiruddin Mahmood), which means that this might yet happen.

An additional concern is that acts of terrorism could target nuclear power plants, in effect blowing them up—by conventional explosives, flying aircraft into the plant, or through inside sabotage—to release nuclear radiation in the vicinity. Depending on wind speed, direction, and the ambient temperature, such an attack might disrupt a large area, with tens of thousands of casualties.

However, a less known but almost greater danger is posed by chemical, petroleum, and hazardous-materials plants. Again the scale of disaster in case of a terrorist attack would depend on the above-named factors. Compared with nuclear power plants, however, which are comparatively few (the United States has 103 commercial nuclear power reactors) and often heavily guarded, chemical plants are far more numerous and usually without adequate protection. Being in most cases commercial entities, they have less incentive to spend large amounts on security aimed at protecting against an attack that might, after all, never come. There is no federal counterterrorism security standard for chemical plants or refineries. They are also often located in close proximity to major residential areas. Even worse, dangerous chemicals are often transported by rail or road without any form of protection whatsoever, leaving them vulnerable to attack as they are passing through major population centres. According to an analysis from the Environmental Protection Agency (EPA), at least 123 plants each keep sufficiently large amounts of toxic chemicals that, if released, could put more than 1 million people in danger. Locations include Los Angeles and Orange counties in California, New Jersey next to New York City, Philadelphia, and Detroit. Medium-sized and small plants are typically even less secure than the major plants. Of these, 709 plants store sufficient amounts to put at least 100,000 people at risk, and 3,015 plants are located in areas where they might endanger at least 10,000 people.[20]

Not all Al-Qaida members are poorly educated. In addition to university-educated Arabs from the Middle East or the West, technical knowledge for this kind of sophisticated operation may exist in Al-Qaida among two comparatively new groups: Pakistanis, disillusioned by the defeat of the Taliban, and Chechens, disillusioned by the West's acquiescence in the Russian reoccupation of Chechnya.

An Iraqi Connection?

Many investigators have searched for evidence of Iraqi involvement in the terrorist activities of the Arab Afghans. So far, after several years (since the first suggestions of Iraqi involvement in Islamic extremism and terrorism) and despite exhaustive investigations by a whole slew of U.S. intelligence and security agencies, no conclusive evidence has been released—or leaked—to the public. Considering that elements within the Bush administration have staked much political capital on the need for an attack against Iraq, it seems unlikely that any evidence, if found, would not eventually have been made public. The conclusion then appears inevitable: there is no Iraqi involvement in the Arab Afghan movement and Al-Qaida. The connection would indeed be remarkable, if it existed, considering the deep hatred of the Arab Afghans toward the kind of secular rule embodied by Saddam Hussein and Iraq's ruling party—and Saddam Hussein's deep distrust of Islamists. Yet, there are indications that suggest that although Iraqi leader Saddam Hussein should not be blamed for crimes he did not commit (after all, those that he did commit would be quite sufficient for almost any human rights or war crimes tribunal), the West needs to remain vigilant on the activities of some of his intelligence officers. Such men could, perhaps, establish working relationships with their counterparts in Al-Qaida.[21]

First, there are indications that Iraq may have been behind Ramzi Ahmed Yousef's bombing of the World Trade Center in 1993, even though Iraq does not appear to have been involved in any of his subsequent activities. The date of the bombing, 26 February, was the second anniversary of the liberation of Kuwait. Ramzi Yousef later told the investigating officers that the date of the attack was forced upon him, as he and his fellow terrorists could not afford to pay rent for the next month. Yet he could afford to escape New York on a first-class airline ticket, and the FBI discovered $2,615 in cash in the apartments of the conspirators. Furthermore, one of the conspirators, an Iraqi named Abdul Rahman Yasin, who when interviewed by the FBI pretended to cooperate and then fled to Iraq, has since lived openly in Baghdad, where he apparently works for the Iraqi government, despite the $5 million bounty offered for his head. Another conspirator, Muhammad Salameh, had an uncle living in Baghdad who was a former PLO terrorist leader and formerly received funds from the Iraqi government. In the six weeks before the attack, Salameh made 46 telephone calls to Baghdad, most of them to his uncle. Ramzi Yousef himself only arrived in the United States on 1 September 1992. It has been suggested that he may have been free-lancing as an Iraqi agent, or perhaps was working for the *Mujahidin-e Khalq* (The People's Mujahidin), an anti-Iranian terrorist group run from and supported by Iraq.[22] Reports from Iraqi defectors claim that foreign Arabs have been trained by Iraqi intelligence for terrorist attacks against U.S. targets.[23]

Second, Saddam Hussein's Iraq has a history of attempted attacks in revenge for the Gulf War. Most serious was probably the attempted assassination of former U.S. President George Bush during a visit to Kuwait between 14 and 16 April 1993 to celebrate the Gulf War victory. Kuwaiti police arrested 16 people connected with the attempt (which was exposed and thereby aborted), including 11 Iraqis, apparently led by a colonel in the Iraqi General Intelligence Directorate. Large amounts of explosives were also seized.[24]

Third, in light of the obsessive hostility against Iran

in some U.S. lobbying groups, it would not take a great leap of faith to come to the decision that a new and inexperienced presidential administration would jump to the conclusion that Iran must be responsible for any serious act of terrorism against the United States. A U.S. military action against Iran would suit nobody better than Saddam Hussein. There is some evidence that Iraq has made plans to falsely implicate Iran in acts of terrorism.[25]

Fourth, the availability of anthrax in Iraq has suggested to some that Iraq was behind the anthrax outbreaks in the United States. Although this was never proven and seems somewhat unlikely, the mere possibility of future anthrax attacks must be taken seriously.[26]

WAYS TO SUCCESSFULLY COMBAT ISLAMIC EXTREMISM AND TERRORISM

Such people must be shot in the head. If necessary, I will shoot them myself.
—Uzbekistani President Islam Karimov on 2 May 1998,
on how to deal with Islamic extremists and terrorists

Although the Arab Afghan movement and its associate organisations in Central Asia had the capacity, and will, to ignite armed conflicts and terrorism in most Central Asian states, and accordingly constituted the chief threat to security and stability in the region, they did not have any united foreign policy objectives except a will to fight fundamentally anybody who did not follow their own interpretation of what constitutes a good Muslim's life. They accordingly could not be neutralised by policy means such as international sanctions (imposed on Afghanistan's uncompromising Taliban regime but obviously without effect on the Taliban's policy decisions).[27] Their involvement in narcotics trafficking and subversion gave the impression that law enforcement means could be used against them. However, such means were attempted by Uzbekistan, Kyrgyzstan, and Tajikistan against the Islamic Movement of

Uzbekistan and Hizb ut-Tahrir with no apparent result except radicalising constitutional elements of the Islamic opposition and pushing them into the Arab Afghan movement.[28] Finally, military means have been used with varying degrees of success. Examples include the United States' 20 August 1998 cruise missile strikes aimed at Usamah bin Ladin, which achieved nothing,[29] Uzbekistan's somewhat more effective use of warlords to fight separatists abroad,[30] and of course the mostly successful Operation Enduring Freedom.

Although decisive military means clearly were the most immediately effective in fighting the Arab Afghans and far superior to sanctions and law enforcement means, to successfully undermine Islamic extremism and terrorism, one must be prepared also to deal with its fundamental, underlying factors.

To successfully strike against Islamic extremism and terrorism, the extremist movements must be attacked where they are most vulnerable: funding and recruitment. Most extremist groups of this kind appear to be funded partly by donations from like-minded religious groups in various countries and partly from involvement in narcotics trafficking. It will be necessary to reduce their disposable income. Without ready cash, they cannot purchase weapons, ammunition, and most importantly, maintain the networks of informers and accomplices needed to move men and goods across state borders. This is not only a question of confiscating monetary assets in foreign banks, which the United States and its allies have been doing since at least September 2001, if not before. An extremist movement is also required to spend very large amounts of cash to support its members and their dependants financially, as well as those locals who come to rely upon the extremist movement for handouts. This is, in fact, typically such a movement's major cause of expenditure. However, in Afghanistan's capital Kabul, the majority of the population has for years depended on the World Food Program (WFP) for food supplies, thus freeing any feuding warlords from the need or compulsion to actually deal with the deplorable supply situation.[31] No warlord or extremist leader can remain in power very long if he spends his funds on ammunition rather than food for his local supporters and dependents—unless an idealistic foreign aid agency steps in to help. In failed states such as Afghanistan, it will accordingly become necessary for Western aid agencies and nongovernmental organisations to terminate, or at least reformulate, their international aid programs, as the existence of such aid relieves the extremist leaders and warlords from the otherwise necessary obligation to feed the population under their control. Such a policy will appear highly impalatable to the international community but has nonetheless been considered due to the belated realisation that such is really the case.[32]

Second, any long-term solution to the threat of Islamic extremism must address the question on how to reduce the recruitment base of the extremists among young, unemployed men living in poverty and without prospects for the future. In countries such as Pakistan and Afghanistan, this base is found among poor, uneducated young men, often orphans, who have absolutely nothing to lose and view membership in a well-funded international, extremist Islamic organisation with pretensions of equality and brotherhood, as well as good political connections in certain Arab countries, as a viable career move far better than remaining in poverty at home. "These boys were a world apart from the Mujaheddin [mujahidin] whom I had got to know during the 1980s—men who could recount their tribal and clan lineages . . . and recounted legends and stories from Afghan history," wrote the well-known Pakistani journalist Ahmed Rashid about the Taliban. "These young warriors did not even know the history of their own country or the story of the jihad against the Soviets. . . . They admired war because it was the only occupation they could possibly adapt to. Their simple belief in a messianic, puritan Islam which had been drummed into them by simple village mullahs was the only prop they could hold on to and which gave their lives some meaning. . . . Moreover, they had willingly gathered under the all-male brotherhood that the Taliban leaders were set on creating, because they knew of nothing else. . . . The mullahs who had taught them stressed that women were a temptation, an unnecessary distraction from being of service to Allah."[33] A very similar recruitment base is, as noted, paradoxically to be found in the West and the more developed Muslim countries:

the "Hip Hop" generation of Islamic extremists consisting of young men, often petty criminals and in the West frequently the sons of immigrants who have no real Islamic or national background, did not fight against the Soviet troops in Afghanistan, but want to imitate Usamah bin Ladin and earn a modicum of respect by engaging in violence.[34]

To fully eradicate extremism, this recruitment base will have to be eliminated. This may well be an impossible task. Even if the international community agreed to eradicate poverty in the affected third world countries by flooding them with foreign aid, which is very unlikely, this would in the short term work directly against the need to force the extremist leaders to spend their funds on the improvement of social conditions rather than arms and ammunition. Nonetheless, if means can be found to provide locals with education that can be used to offer an alternative to fighting and dying for somebody else's cause, it may in the long run reduce the recruitment base for the extremist movements.

However, while such means may well work in Afghanistan and Pakistan, at least for now, the recruitment base in less tribal states, such as those of the former Soviet Central Asian republics and much of the Middle East, is typically found among young people who have achieved higher levels of learning—but see their expectations crushed soon after graduation because of very high levels of unemployment. Islamic extremism—as well as any other type of extremism—has been known to gain widespread support on university campuses.[35] This shows that any education provided also needs to give the recipient the opportunity to actually support, even enrich, himself to make extremism a less tempting career. A high rate of unemployment obviously works against this. An example is provided by Uzbekistan, which suffers from a stagnant economy despite a strong, universal education system. Of those Uzbekistani Islamic extremists who have been arrested and convicted for political reasons, more than 80 percent had secondary and vocational education, and the rest had higher education. Moreover, the highest number of arrests were made in regions with large and urban populations such as Tashkent, Andijon, Namangan, and Khorezm provinces—people who had seen their hopes go unfulfilled because of unemployment and economic stagnation.[36] A vast majority of the Islamic groups with extremist beliefs that were founded in Central Asia since the dissolution of the Soviet Union were founded in the urban centres of the densely populated Ferghana valley. Examples included the Islamic Movement of Uzbekistan and Hizb ut-Tahrir.[37]

Disaffected young people frequently turn to religion, whether it be Islam, Marxism, or militant vegetarianism. Islam promises paradise, in the form of a perfect Islamic society here and now or, this failing, in the after-life. The conclusion seems to be that to fully eradicate Islamic extremism, the state needs to eradicate unemployment, provide higher education for anybody who desires it, and create a vibrant, never-failing economy in which everybody can enjoy a life of fulfilment and enrich himself without the need to do any menial or hard work, in short, paradise on Earth. For this is what the extremists want—and are prepared to die for. Yet, not all young people are disaffected, and those who are frequently grow up to join the rat race of full-time work, the raising of a family, and the saving of money for a home. In the process, they tend to shed any extremist ("idealist") beliefs. A prerequisite is, of course, that there is a rat race to join.

Islamic extremism also had a disturbing tendency to turn up among, then hijack legitimate opposition or separatist movements among, Muslim populations. This included separatist movements in areas that happened to belong to an existing state, but where a majority had elected a representative government that subsequently declared independence. Kashmir was the first example of this type of development, but Palestine, the Philippines, Chechnya, and Chinese Xinjiang saw it happen as well. Similar developments took place in countries were opposition was suppressed, such as Uzbekistan. A case could also be made for including Algeria in this group (see Appendix 8).

A number of states share the will to eradicate Wahhabi Islamic extremism with and are useful allies to the West. Most, of course, have their own agendas, which typically include the crushing of domestic dissent and separatism. Russia and China (which coincidentally would love to crush separatist movements to some extent infiltrated by Islamic extremists in Chechnya and Xinjiang, respectively) are obvious allies of the West. However, Wahhabi Islam is also intrinsically hostile to Shia Islamic Iran. Now may be the optimal time for the United States to mend fences with Iran, realising that the two countries share a common enemy. Other less than democratic states also feel the need to eradicate Islamic extremism. Whether the West really should court oppressive dictatorships such as Uzbekistan and much of the Middle East is another matter. India and Israel are also eager to help the West, but they have their own agendas, which include the often brutal repression of Kashmiri and Palestinian separatists.

Despite everything, there is some hope for those fighting Islamic extremism. As a political movement, Islamic extremism is in almost global retreat (although many extremists seem unwilling to share this conclusion). Even in Algeria, where Islamic extremism caused a bloody civil war, it appears that the extremists are failing against the military government. Wahhabism gained a powerful position in Saudi Arabia, but the House of Saud has, so far, managed to keep the extremists in check at home if not abroad. Sunni Islamic extremists only managed to gain political power in three countries: Afghanistan, Sudan, and Yemen, all of which were afflicted by civil wars. In Afghanistan, the most intractable extremists have been driven out of government, while the military rulers of Sudan and Yemen have reasserted their power against the domestic extremist parties. The coalition victory over the Taliban shattered a number of widely believed Muslim myths. First, millions of devout Muslims did not rise against their corrupt governments and the West to defend Usamah bin Ladin. Second, the Taliban emirate was not the beginning of a global Islamic revival—and the sight on television screens of Afghan Muslims taking joy in the fall of the Taliban proved beyond doubt that the Taliban had been yet another in a long line of brutal oppressor regimes. Third, Afghanistan did not prove the graveyard for infidel invaders, as it often was claimed to be—and most coalition forces on the ground were Afghan Muslims, not Western infidels.

End Notes

1. See, for instance, Sirrs, "Taliban's International Ambitions," 65.

2. The 11 September 2001 attacks were at least in part planned in Germany. Christoph Bluth, "War against Terrorism: The Hamburg Connection," *Jane's Intelligence Review* 13:11 (November 2001), 15–17. For some additional details and much gossip see *Der Spiegel* magazine, and *Inside 9–11: What Really Happened* (New York: St. Martin's Press, 2002).

3. See, for instance, Jacquard, *Osama Bin Laden,* 113–117; *Economist,* 20 October 2001, 10 August 2002. See also Ed Blanche, "Europe Cracks Down on Algerian Islamists," *Jane's Pointer,* May 1998, 12; Ed Blanche, "Worldwide Arrests," *Jane's Intelligence Review* 13:8 (August 2001), 49–51.

4. *Economist,* 22 September 2001.

5. *Washington Post,* 29 October 2001.

6. *Guardian* (UK), 21 February 2003. For more information on Sami-al-Arian, see Emerson, *American Jihad,* 86, 109–25, 205–6, 214.

7. See Department of State, *Patterns of Global Terrorism 1994* (Washington, D.C.: Department of State, April 1995); *Seattle Times,* 23 June–7 July 2002 (*www.seattle-times.com*).

8. Reeve, *New Jackals,* 214, referring to *Newsweek,* 11 January 1999; *Time,* 11 January 1998. The interview took place on 23 December 1998. PBS (*www.pbs.org/frontline*).

9. Cooley, *Unholy Wars,* 218–219. However, the National Intelligence Council has claimed that several cases in which Russian radioactive materials were lost to theft or negligence probably have occured since, and that unreported cases of smuggling may have taken place. National Intelligence Council, *Annual Report to Congress on the Safety and Security of Russian Nuclear Facilities and Military Forces* (Washington, D.C.: National Intelligence Council, February 2002). See also Stefan Leader, "Osama bin Laden and the Terrorist Search for WMD," *Jane's Intelligence Review* 11:6 (June 1999), 34–37.

10. Leader, "Osama bin Laden and the Terrorist Search for WMD," 34–37; *Time,* 21 December 1998; Jacquard, *Osama Bin Laden,* 144.

11. Reeve, *New Jackals,* 214–216.

12. Leader, 34–37; *Washington Post,* 11 June 2002.

13. *Time,* 21 December 1998; Jacquard, *Osama Bin Laden,* 144.

14. Reeve, 216–218.

15. Alexander and Swetnam, *Usama bin Laden's al-Qaida,* 32.

16. Agence France Presse, 19 August 2002.

17. See, for instance, Associated Press, 20 August 2002; *Washington Times,* 22 August 2002; *International Herald Tribune,* 22 August 2002; *Guardian,* 23 August 2002; Jane's Sentinel: Iraq, 18 March 2002.

18. *Economist,* 24 November 2001.

19. Ibid., 30 March 2002.

20. *Washington Post,* 16 December 2001.

21. Reeve, 216–219, details some Western intelligence reports that claim contacts between Al-Qaida and Iraq. Jacquard, *Osama Bin Laden,* 111–113, perhaps referring to French intelligence sources, notes that Al-Qaida approached Iraq several times but was rebuffed in public—so that a clandestine operational connection could be established afterward. This may well be so. However, considering that it would be in the interest of some Western intelligence services to find a connection between bin Ladin and Saddam Hussein, these claims are impossible to verify independently.

22. Mylroie, *War Against America, passim,* in particular 253–234. The evidence is also summarised in Reeve, 40, 140, 246–247. Laurie Mylroie is the original and chief proponent of the theory of the Iraqi connection.

23. So did, for instance, a high-ranking defector from Iraq, a lieutenant general and former senior officer of the Iraqi General Intelligence Directorate (Dairat al-Mukhabarat al-Amah) in late 2001 claim that he had worked at a secret Iraqi government camp that trained Islamic terrorists since 1995. The general said that the men being trained in the camp, known as Salman Pak and located on the Tigris River, came from a number of countries, including Saudi Arabia, Yemen, Algeria, Morocco, and Egypt. He did not, however, claim that any were linked to Al-Qaida. RFE/RL *Crime, Corruption, and Terrorism Watch* 1:3 (16 November 2001).

24. Mylroie, 113–114, 195–196; Reeve, 247–248.

25. Mylroie,, 104, 281, note 20.

27. See, for instance, *Guardian,* 15 October 2001.

27. *Jane's Defence Weekly,* 30 August 2000, 8.

28. See, for instance, Melvin, *Uzbekistan,* 54–57; RFE/RL *Newsline,* 4 January 2001, 20 February 2001; Jane's Sentinel: Kyrgyzstan, 31 October 2000; Rashid, "Namangani's Foray."

29. Statement by the president, White House Office of the Press Secretary, 20 August 1998.

30. Fredholm, *Afghanistan and Central Asian Security.*

31. Jane's Sentinel: Afghanistan, 17 October 2000.

32. See, for instance, Peter Marsden, *The Taliban: War, Religion and the New Order in*

Afghanistan (London: Zed Books, 1998), 106–113. See also Edward N. Luttwak, "Give War a Chance," *Foreign Affairs,* July/August 1999, 36–44.

33. Rashid, *Taliban,* 32–33.
34. Rashid, "From Deobandism to Batken."
35. See, for instance, Hiro, *Islamic Fundamentalism*, 75–76.
36. International Crisis Group, *Central Asia: Islamist Mobilisation and Regional Security* (Osh/Brussels: International Crisis Group, Asia Report 14, 1 March 2001), 18.
37. Babadzhanov, "Fergana Valley," 112–123.

PART IV
Appendices

APPENDIX
Key Events of the Arab Afghan Movement and Al-Qaida

1992

- On 29 December 1992, bombs aimed at some hundred U.S. servicemen en route to Somalia in support of UN relief operations and billeted in Aden, Yemen, exploded outside the city's best hotels, the Mövenpick Aden Hotel and Golden Moor Hotel. The Americans had already departed, but a tourist and a hotel worker were killed. Almost simultaneously, a small group of men allegedly trained by Al-Qaida was caught at Aden airport preparing to launch rockets at U.S. military transport aircraft.[1]

1993

- On 5 January 1993, Mir Aimal Kansi, an Arab Afghan, gunned down six people, including five CIA employees, two of whom died, outside the main gate of CIA headquarters in Langley, Virginia.[2] (Mir Aimal Kansi was arrested in Pakistan in June 1997.)[3]
- On 26 February 1993, a bomb in a van exploded in the underground parking garage of the World Trade Center in New York. Six people were killed and 1,042 wounded in the first terrorist attack on the World Trade Center. The perpetrators, a group of Islamic extremists led by Ramzi Yousef, were later linked to Usamah bin Ladin.[4]

- In June 1993, bin Ladin was allegedly involved in an attempt to murder Crown Prince Abdullah of Jordan.[5]
- On 24 June 1993, the first of several Arabs were arrested for conspiring to bomb the United Nations Headquarters, the Lincoln and Holland Tunnels, the George Washington Bridge, and the Federal Building in New York. This plot, which was allegedly planned for 4 July but might never have been carried out, was essentially a FBI sting operation. Without the FBI mole who claimed bombing expertise, the conspiracy would probably never have taken place.[6]
- On 3–4 October 1993, two U.S. Black Hawk helicopters were shot down and 18 U.S. soldiers on a peacekeeping mission in Somalia were killed in battle. In addition, 76 U.S. soldiers were wounded. Fighters under bin Ladin, allegedly advised or led by Muhammad Atef, later claimed responsibility for the incident, although it is unclear to outsiders what role, if any, they actually played.[7]

1994
- In February or March 1994, Ramzi Yousef developed a (subsequently foiled) plan to bomb a number of U.S. and Israeli embassies in Asian capitals simultaneously.[8]
- On 20 June 1994, Ramzi Yousef was probably implicated in the bombing of the shrine of Reza, one of the holiest Shia sites, in Mashhad, Iran. At least 26 pilgrims died.[9]
- On 12 November 1994, Ramzi Yousef and, perhaps, the Abu Sayyaf group, both linked to Al-Qaida, plotted to assassinate U.S. President William Clinton while he visited Manila. Yousef aborted the plan because security was too tight.[10]
- On 11 December 1994, Ramzi Yousef exploded a bomb on a Philippine Airlines flight from Cebu to Tokyo, killing one and injuring several.[11]
- On 24 December 1994, four Algerian terrorists, members of the Phalange of the Signers in Blood, a subsidiary of the GIA, hijacked an Air France passenger airliner from Algiers. They demanded that

it be flown to Marseille, where it was to be refueled for a flight to Paris. The terrorists also demanded that the aircraft, an Airbus A300, be loaded with 27 tons of fuel, three times what was needed for the flight. French troops successfully stormed the airplane on the ground. It was subsequently determined that the terrorists had intended either to explode the aircraft over Paris or to crash it into the Eiffel Tower.[12]

1995

• In mid-January 1995, Ramzi Yousef and the Abu Sayyaf group, both linked to Al-Qaida, plotted to assassinate Pope John Paul II during a visit to Manila. The plot was exposed and abandoned.[13]

• In January 1995, a not yet fully developed plan to blow up as many as 11 passenger airliners in a single day, known as the Bojinka Plot and involving Ramzi Yousef, was accidentally exposed to the security forces and thus aborted. The plot was at the planning stage only. It is unlikely that all parts of the plot would ever have been attempted. The plot has since come to be regarded by Philippine investigators as the creation of Khalid Shaikh Muhammad, a Kuwaiti Al-Qaida member of Pakistani ancestry who since appears to have gone into hiding in Pakistan (and was recently captured there).[14]

• On 8 March 1995, two U.S. consular officials in Karachi were killed and a third wounded in an ambush of their embassy vehicle, perhaps in revenge for the arrest and extradition of Ramzi Yousef to the United States on 7 February 1995.[15]

• On 26 June 1995, a heavily armed team (probably belonging to the Islamic Society, which claimed responsibility) attempted to assassinate Egyptian President Hosni Mubarak in Addis Ababa by attacking his motorcade with heavy weapons. Usamah bin Ladin allegedly helped to fund the attempt.[16]

• On 13 November 1995, Saudi terrorists attacked Saudi Arabia's National Guard (known as such as in the West; actually the Royal Guard) Communications Centre, a joint Saudi and U.S. military facility in central Riyadh, with a car bomb. Two Indians and five U.S. military and civilian advisers for National Guard training were killed. Responsibility was claimed by a fictitious front organisation calling itself the Tigers of the Gulf, with follow-up communiqués by the Islamic Change Movement and a previously unheard of group calling itself the Militant Partisans of God Organisation. Four Saudi men were captured by the security forces and quickly beheaded before they could be interrogated by U.S. investigators. Three of the men were Arab Afghans, and the fourth had fought with Bosnian Muslim forces in the civil war in the former Yugoslavia; all expressed their admiration of and support for bin Ladin.[17]

1996
- On 25 June 1996, a bomb aboard a fuel truck exploded outside the Khobar Towers housing complex on the U.S. air base in Dhahran, Saudi Arabia. Nineteen U.S. servicemen were killed and 515 people were wounded, including 240 Americans. Al-Qaida is believed to have been involved in planning the attack, although bin Ladin (probably for tactical reasons) denied personal involvement. Saudi Arabia loudly blamed Iran or Iranian-backed domestic Shia Muslims, but then quietly arrested 600 Arab Afghans. The United States followed the Saudi lead: a federal grand jury in June 2001 claimed that Iran had "directed" the attack.[18]
- On 23 August 1996, bin Ladin issued his first fatwa, a declaration "to His Muslim Brothers in the Whole World and Especially in the Arabian Peninsula: Declaration of Jihad Against the Americans Occupying the Land of the Two Holy Mosques; Expel the Heretics from the Arabian Peninsula." This has since been regarded as bin Ladin's formal declaration of war against the United States.[19]

1997
- On 11–12 April 1997, another attempt to kill Pope John Paul II took place, when 23 antitank mines were placed under a bridge on the route the Pope was to travel to Sarajevo. Usamah bin Ladin was reputedly linked to the incident.[20]
- On 17 November 1997, Islamic extremists (probably an Islamic Society cell) massacred 58 foreign tourists (the majority Japanese,

Swiss, British, and Spanish) and about 10 Egyptians, and wounded another 26, in Luxor, Egypt.[21]

1998

- On 23 February 1998, Usamah bin Ladin's World Islamic Front for Jihad Against the Jews and Crusaders issued a fatwa demanding attacks on Americans.[22]

- On 7 August 1998, terrorist bombs destroyed the U.S. Embassies in Nairobi and Dar es Salaam, Tanzania, in two terrorist operations known respectively as Operation Holy Kaaba and Operation Al-Aqsa Mosque. In Nairobi, 291 people were killed, including 12 Americans, and more than 5,000 were wounded (including 6 Americans). In Dar-es-Salaam, 11 were killed and about 85 wounded (including 1 American). Al-Qaida was accused of planning and financing the attacks, as well as a similar attack, never carried out, on the U.S. Embassy in Kampala, Uganda (if true, this would have been Al-Qaida's Operation Nabavi Mosque, named after the remaining of Islam's three most holy sites).[23] As before, several unheard of front organisations, such as the Liberation Army of the Islamic Sanctuaries, claimed responsibility.[24] Plans were reportedly also made around this time to destroy the U.S. Embassies in Bangkok; Baku, Azerbaijan (by an Egyptian group); and Tirana, Albania (by members of the Egyptian Islamic Jihad, arrested in June 1998), but these were abandoned or exposed to the security forces and never carried out.[25] In retaliation, the United States on 20 August 1998 launched 80 Tomahawk cruise missiles from five U.S. warships in the Arabian Sea and two in the Red Sea in a secret attack code-named Operation Infinite Reach. Their targets were two: the Zhawar Kili terrorist training camps in Afghanistan, associated with Al-Qaida, and the Al-Shifa ("Healing") pharmaceutical plant in Khartoum, Sudan. However, bin Ladin had left the camp, almost certainly alerted by the ISI. As for the pharmaceutical plant, it probably had nothing to do with Al-Qaida.[26]

1999

- On 10 June 1999, bin Ladin again called for a holy war against the United States, in an interview with the Al-Jazeera satellite television network. This was the first interview with him to be broadcast in the Middle East and the Persian Gulf.[27]
- On 14 December 1999, Ahmed Ressam, an Algerian who had lived in Montreal for five years, was arrested in Port Angeles, Washington, when he tried to enter the United States from Canada. In his rental car, agents found 130 pounds (60 kilograms) of bomb-making chemicals and detonator components. Intelligence officials later concluded that he was part of what subsequently came to be known as the millennium plot. This was a plan to unleash at least three attacks during the millennium celebrations, one aimed at a U.S. Navy ship in Yemen, the second on tourist sites and the Radisson Hotel in Amman, Jordan (frequented by Israelis and American Christians who visit an area of the Jordan River associated with St. John the Baptist), and the third on unknown targets in the United States, perhaps Los Angeles International Airport. Ressam had in the previous year received training at an Al-Qaida camp.[28]
- There may also have been a plan to attack targets in Senegal as part of the millennium plot. On 22 January 2000, Mouhamedou Ould Slahi, a Mauritanian electrical engineer suspected of being a supporter of Usamah bin Ladin, was arrested, believed to have planned December 1999 bomb attacks there aimed at the millennium celebration. Mouhamedou Ould Slahi from the mid-1990s to September 1999 lived in Germany, after which he moved to Canada, from which he went to Senegal. Because of this as well as a connection with Ahmed Ressam, U.S. and Canadian officials had him arrested at Dakar Airport, Senegal, and extradited to Mauritania. The truth in the allegations, if any, has not been verified. (Mouhamedou Ould Slahi was after a month released for lack of evidence. Following the 11 September 2001 terrorist attacks, President George Bush telephoned the Mauritanian president, asking him to have Mouhamedou Ould Slahi rearrested. The Mauritanian government complied on 29 September 2001.)[29]

2000
- On 3 January 2000, would-be suicide bombers in Aden over-loaded a small boat with explosives and accidentally sank it. They thus lost their chance of attacking the USS *The Sullivans*, an Arleigh Burke-class destroyer, which was then visiting Aden.[30]
- On 12 October 2000, terrorists in a boat laden with explosives carried out a suicide bombing of the USS *Cole*, another Arleigh Burke-class destroyer, in the harbour of Aden. They killed 17 U.S. servicemen and wounded 39. Al-Qaida was accused of having planned the attack, which was executed by a group led by an Arab Afghan named Muhammad Omar al-Harazi (also known as Abdul Rahman al-Saafani), of Yemeni origin but born in Saudi Arabia.[31]

2001
- On 15 June 2001, two men, one of them a Sudanese named Abdul Rauf Hawas, were arrested by Indian police in Bihar, eastern India, with six kilograms of RDX, a high explosive, and some improvised explosive devices. The two were allegedly planning to blow up the visa section of the U.S. Embassy in the diplomatic neighbourhood of Chanakyapuri in the capital New Delhi. Al-Qaida was accused of planning the operation, which was reportedly led by Muhammad Omar al-Harazi, who was also behind the attack on the *Cole*.[32]
- In August 2001, Islamic extremists with connections to Al-Qaida planned a terrorist attack on the U.S. Embassy in Jakarta, or so it appeared based on evidence in the form of a map found by Indonesian police.[33]
- On 11 September 2001, three hijacked passenger airliners crashed into the World Trade Center in New York and the Pentagon in Washington. A fourth plane was also hijacked, probably destined for the White House in Washington, although it crashed in Pennsylvania. On 13 September, U.S. Secretary of State Colin L. Powell named Usamah bin Ladin the prime suspect.[34]
- By late November 2001, the Al-Qaida leadership still in Afghanistan was believed to have fled to a network of caves near Tora Bora in the White Mountains 35 miles (56 kilometres) south

of Jalalabad, together with between 1,000 and 2,000 Al-Qaida members and Taliban soldiers, according to some estimates. Leaving the Tora Bora in secret, the survivors moved into Pakistan and other neighbouring countries to continue the struggle there. Within a couple of months, the remaining members of two banned Pakistani extremist movements, Jaish-e Muhammad and Lashkar-e Tayyiba, joined with other extremists, probably including fugitive elements of Al-Qaida and possibly even the Taliban, in a new coalition of extremist organisations known as *Lashkar-e Umar* (Army of Caliph Umar). Although many extremists remained in Pakistan, some went to Saudi Arabia, and others went to Kashmir to continue the jihad.[35]

• On 22 December 2001, on an international flight from Paris to Miami, Richard Colvin Reid tried to blow up the passenger airliner in which he was flying with explosives hidden in his shoes.[36]

2002

• In late February 2002, Italian police arrested four Moroccans suspected of planning an attack with bombs or cyanide gas against the U.S. Embassy in Rome.[37]

• In early May 2002, an alleged Al-Qaida plot to launch suicide attacks on NATO ships in the Strait of Gibraltar was foiled in Morocco.[38]

• On 8 May 2002, a car bombing in Karachi killed 14 people, including 11 French workers. Suspicions fell on Al-Qaida.[39]

• On 10 June 2002, Attorney General John Ashcroft announced that he had broken up a terrorist plot to detonate a "dirty bomb" in the United States. American-born Jose Padilla, also known as Abdullah al-Muhajir, was named the chief suspect. He had been arrested in Pakistan, then released and returned to the United States, where he was re-arrested on 8 May upon arriving from Pakistan. The prosecution was unable to build a case against Padilla, so he was named an "enemy combatant" and turned over to the military to be locked up indefinitely until he admitted to something.[40]

- On 14 June 2002, a car bomb exploded outside the U.S. Consulate in Karachi. Twelve Pakistanis were killed. Although a spokesman for a previously unheard of group referring to himself as *tarjuman al-Qanoon* (spokesman for the Law) claimed responsibility, Lashkar-e Umar was believed to have been involved.[41]

- On 12 October 2002, a bomb at a discotheque on the crowded Kuta Beach on the Indonesian island of Bali killed more than 190 people, including many foreign (mostly Australian) tourists. Several intelligence and law enforcement agencies accused Al-Qaida of involvement.[42]

End Notes

1. Reeve, *New Jackals.* 182; Bergen, *Holy War,* 172.

2. Cooley, *Unholy Wars,* 220; Emerson, *American Jihad,* 29.

3. Reeve, *New Jackals.* 201; U.S. Department of State, Diplomatic Security Service (www.dssrewards.net).

4. Reeve, *New Jackals,* 6–22; Center for Defense Information, Washington, D.C. (www.cdi.org).

5. Reeve, *New Jackals,* 183.

6. See, for instance, Mylroie, *War Against America,* 4, 182–92; Emerson, *American Jihad,* 29.

7. Reeve, *New Jackals,* 182; Bergen, *Holy War,* 82–3.

8. Reeve, *New Jackals,* 63–5.

9. See, for instance, Reeve, *New Jackals,* 65–67.

10. Reeve, *New Jackals,* 76–7.

11. Reeve, *New Jackals,* 78–81.

12. See, for instance, *Patterns of Global Terrorism 1994*; Gunaratna, "Terror from the Sky," 7.

13. Reeve, *New Jackals,* 78, 86–9.

14. Reeve, *New Jackals,* 84–91; *Times of London,* 24 June 2002.

15. Reeve, *New Jackals,* 188; Mylroie, *War Against America,* 202, 295.

16. See, for instance, Alexander and Swetnam, *Usama bin Laden's al-Qaida,* 40; James Wyllie, "Egypt: Staying the Course?" *Jane's Intelligence Review* 7:11 (November 1995), 499–500.

17. Reeve, *New Jackals,* 183–4; Cooley, *Unholy Wars,* 220; Center for Defense Information, Washington, DC (www.cdi.org).

18. Reeve, *New Jackals,* 187; Bergen, *Holy War,* 87–8; Center for Defense Information,

Washington, DC (www.cdi.org); *Economist,* 22 September 2001; Bodansky, *Bin Laden,* 151.

19. See, for instance, http://pbs.org/frontline/.

20. See, for instance, Cable News Network (CNN), 12 April 1997; Catholic World News, 15 April 1997 (www.cwnews.com).

21. Cooley, *Unholy Wars,* 183–5; Gerges, "End of the Islamist Insurgency in Egypt?" 594.

22. See, for instance, Cooley, *Unholy Wars,* 224–5; Reeve, *New Jackals,* 270. For the full text of the fatwa, see Reeve, *New Jackals,* 268–70; FAS Intelligence Resource Program (www.fas.org).

23. Reeve, *New Jackals,* 198–201; Bergen, *Holy War,* 105–13; Center for Defense Information, Washington, DC (www.cdi.org).

24. See, for instance, Mirskiy, "Islamic Fundamentalism," 34.

25. Cooley, *Unholy Wars,* 7; *Time,* 21 December 1998.

26. Statement by the President, White House Office of the Press Secretary, 20 August 1998; Reeve, *New Jackals,* 1, 201–2; Bergen, *Holy War,* 118–26; Bodansky, *Bin Laden,* 285–90.

27. Reeve, *New Jackals,* 265.

28. Bergen, *Holy War,* 139–40, 185.

29. *Washington Post,* 1 October 2001.

30. Bergen, *Holy War,* 185.

31. *Jane's Defence Review,* 20 December 2000, 17; Bergen, *Holy War,* 184–7, 273 n.81.

32. Bergen, *Holy War,* 197; *Tribune* (Chandigarh, India), 17 June 2001.

33. *International Herald Tribune,* 14 January 2002.

34. *Washington Post,* 12 September 2001, 14 September 2001.

35. *Jane's Intelligence Digest,* 31 May 2002; Jane's Sentinel: Pakistan, 18 July 2002; Jane's World Insurgency and Terrorism 13, 27 November 2001.

36. *Washington Post,* 23 December 2001. For more details on Reid, see *Washington Post,* 31 March 2002.

37. Reuters, 25 February 2002.

38. *Washington Post,* 16 June 2002.

39. See, for instance, *Washington Post,* 9 May 2002, and especially 1 June 2002.

40. *Washington Post,* 11 June 2002; *Newsweek* (Asia edn), 19 August 2002.

41. *Washington Post,* 15 June 2002; Jane's Sentinel: Pakistan, 18 July 2002.

42. See, for instance, *Japan Times,* 14 October 2002; VOA, 14 October 2002.

APPENDIX

Chronology of the War on Terror

2

___

September 2001

9 September—Ahmad Shah Masud, the Afghan military leader regarded as the main threat to the Taliban movement, was assassinated in a suicide attack by two North Africans (Algerians or Moroccans). Posing as journalists, during an interview with him in Khwaja Bahauddin, they detonated a bomb hidden in a video camera.[1] Masud was succeeded by Muhammad Fahim Khan.[2]

11 September—Terrorists in a well-coordinated operation hijacked four recently departed passenger airliners (consequently loaded with full fuel tanks) and successfully crashed them into the World Trade Center in New York (two airliners, one aimed at each tower) and the Pentagon in Washington, D.C. (one airliner). The fourth, probably aimed at the White House, crashed in Pennsylvania as passengers attempted to regain control over it, having learned the fate of the other aircraft. More than 3,000 people were killed. The burning aircraft fuel generated such intense heat that steel girders supporting the World Trade Center buildings melted, causing the two towers to collapse.[3] Within hours, suspicions fell on Usamah bin Ladin, although at first he was only one of several suspects.[4] Within a day or two of the attacks, the United States began to prepare its response by intensifying the training schedule on its major air bases.[5] British security forces were reportedly put on alert as well. Political leaders throughout the world condemned the attacks, including President Muhammad Khatami of Iran (as did Iranian supreme leader Ayatollah Khamenei on 18 September in his first public statement on the attack). A notable exception was Iraqi state television, which hailed the attacks as the "operation of the century" and announced that the United States deserved it because of its "crimes against humanity" (Iraq blames the United States for prolonging UN sanctions imposed after Iraq's 1990 invasion of Kuwait and the 1991 Persian Gulf War).[6]

12 September—Elements within the Northern Alliance avenged the murder of Masud by launching missiles against Kabul, an act which numerous news networks mistook for a U.S. cruise missile attack.[7] In the United States, the aircraft carrier USS *John F. Kennedy*, based at Mayport, Florida, provided close air patrols over New York City, together with the USS *George Washington*, based at Norfolk, Virginia.[8]

13 September—The North Atlantic Treaty Organization (NATO) and Russia urged efforts to combat global terrorism.[9] An emergency meeting was held in Dushanbe, Tajikistan, among representatives from Russia, Iran, Tajikistan, India, Uzbekistan, and the Northern Alliance regarding the succession of the assassinated Ahmad Shah Masud and its likely impact on future developments in Afghanistan.[10] In the United States, Secretary of State Colin L. Powell named bin Ladin the chief suspect.[11] Powell also formulated seven demands to Pakistan, which would ensure full and complete Pakistani cooperation in the war against the Taliban. These were presented to Pakistani leader Pervez Musharraf together with the warning that the demands were not negotiable and that he must accept all seven. Musharraf immediately replied that Pakistan would comply.[12]

15 September—U.S. President George W. Bush declared the United States at war against terror.[13] CIA Director George J. Tenet presented, and received the president's approval for, a covert plan to strike against Al-Qaida, which included stepped-up intelligence cooperation with the services of various other countries but also the insertion of half a dozen small CIA paramilitary teams into Afghanistan, with orders eventually to link up with U.S. Army Special Forces to aid the opposition in Afghanistan.[14]

16 September—The first group of U.S. servicemen, reportedly 50 men and perhaps CIA paramilitary troops, were reported to have landed in Peshawar, Pakistan.[15] Little is known of this deployment, and it may, in fact, only have been a rumour. On the same day, the carrier USS *Carl Vinson* (having departed Bremerton on 23 July) arrived in the Persian Gulf, where she was supposed to relieve the USS *Enterprise* in the northern Arabian Sea. Because of the expected war, the *Enterprise* remained in the theatre.[16]

17 September—President Bush announced that bin Ladin was wanted "dead or alive."[17] The Taliban government banned and vowed to shoot down all foreign aircraft over its territory as soon as they were detected, including flights by international organisations such as the United Nations (the aircraft of which henceforth did not receive flight clearance). By then, the Taliban leaders had already left at least Kandahar and Jalalabad, anticipating air raids.[18]

18 September—Russian President Vladimir Putin told Tajikistan to allow the United States to use its airspace.[19] On 19 September, Gen. Anatoli Kvashnin, chief of the Russian General Staff, flew to Dushanbe, capital of Tajikistan.[20] On the following day, Vladimir Rushailo, head of the Russian Security Council, arrived there as well.[21] On 22 September, Kvashnin held a meeting with the Northern Alliance in Tajikistan.[22] On 25 September, the Russian minister of defence, Sergei Ivanov, announced that the United States could use an airport in Dushanbe.[23]

19 September—The United States began flying additional military aircraft into the Persian Gulf region for bases in Kuwait, Saudi Arabia, Oman, and the Diego Garcia Navy Support Facility in the Indian Ocean. Eventually, as many as roughly 150 additional aircraft were moved to the region.[24] The USS *Theodore Roosevelt* departed Norfolk for the Mediterranean and the Persian Gulf.[25]

21 September—The Bush administration promised that it would waive economic sanctions on Pakistan for its support.[26] Sanctions had first been imposed because of Pakistan's nuclear weapons tests in 1998; penalties were also imposed in 1999 because of Musharraf's military coup.[27]

22 September—The United Arab Emirates severed diplomatic relations with the Taliban government.[28] Two C-130 Hercules military transport aircraft with about 100 U.S. troops landed in Uzbekistan (Tuzel just outside Tashkent).[29] On 24 September, they were followed by at least two other C-130 transports with several hundred U.S. troops (referred to as army commandos).[30] Major deployments had to wait, however, taking place only on 2 October.[31]

23 September—Following President Putin's request to allow a U.S. military presence in Tajikistan and General Kvashnin's meeting with Northern Alliance leaders in Dushanbe, the United States and Tajikistan apparently reached an understanding on the matter.[32] President Bush signed an executive order, effective from 24 September, freezing the bank accounts and other assets (whenever known) of a large number of organisations believed linked, however tenuously, to Usamah bin Ladin. Among them were Al-Qaida, the Abu Sayyaf (Philippines), Islamic Jihad (Egypt), Harakat ul-Mujahidin (Pakistan and Kashmir), Islamic Movement of Uzbekistan, Asbat al-Ansar (Lebanon), GIA (Algeria), GSPC (Algeria), Islamic Fighting Group (Libya), Al-Itihaad al-Islamiyyah (Somalia), and Aden-Abyan Islamic Army (Yemen). Other governments soon followed the U.S. example.[33]

24 September—The first small groups of troops from the United States and NATO countries, CIA paramilitary troops, and probably British Special Air Service Regiment (SAS) commandos, arrived in Tajikistan.[34]

25 September—Saudi Arabia severed diplomatic relations with the

Taliban government. Defense Secretary Donald H. Rumsfeld renamed the military operation in the War on Terror, hitherto referred to as Operation Infinite Justice (following the pattern of the 1998 Operation Infinite Reach). This term was belatedly deemed insensitive and upsetting to Muslims, for only God is capable of infinite justice. The war henceforth became known as Operation Enduring Freedom.[35] In Britain, the British contribution to the military operation was named Operation Veritas.[36]

26/27 September—The first U.S. force entered Afghanistan: a CIA six-man paramilitary unit named the Northern Alliance Liaison Team (NALT). This unit was eventually followed by five additional six-man teams: Alpha in the northwest, Bravo at Mazar-e-Sharif, Charlie in the west, and Echo and Foxtrot in the south.[37] Unconfirmed reports mentioned that British SAS commandos were active near Kabul at around the same time (the end of September), so it is likely that they entered together with the U.S. teams.[38]

30 September—Mullah Abdul Salam Zaeef, Taliban ambassador to Pakistan, declared that the Taliban were hiding bin Ladin for his own safety.[39]

October 2001

1 October—The carrier USS *Kitty Hawk* departed Yokosuka, Japan, bound for the Arabian Sea.[40]

2 October—A reinforced battalion of light infantry from the U.S. Army's 10th Mountain Division landed at the previously non-operational Uzbekistani air base Qarshi/Khanabad.[41] Its mission was to provide base security for any U.S. Air Force units deployed there and manpower for combat search-and-rescue units.[42] Later the Americans were also allowed the use of the likewise unused airfield in Termiz, on the Afghan border.[43] The air force expected to base combat aircraft (F-15 and F-16 fighters) in Uzbekistan, but this deployment never took place. The base was, however, used by transports of various kinds.[44]

5 October—An editor at a Florida tabloid newspaper died of inhaled anthrax infection, being the first of five Americans, including two postal workers, who eventually died in the 18 confirmed cases of anthrax infection. The culprit or culprits remain unknown to law enforcement agencies. Henceforth, the anthrax scare came to dominate domestic U.S. news reporting.[45]

6 October—Uzbekistan gave official permission for the U.S. deployment (which had then already taken place) and the use of an Uzbekistani air base.[46] In return, the United States proposed to triple aid to Uzbekistan.[47] The Uzbekistani government has subsequently claimed that the agreement (which for undeclared reasons apparently was not signed until on 7 October, unclear where or by whom, and in any case remained secret except for the vague formula that the two countries had entered into "a qualitatively new relationship based on a long-term commitment to advance security and regional stability")[48] contained secret terms including a long-term U.S. commitment to Uzbekistan.[49] In Pakistan, Fazlur Rahman, a leader of the *Jamiat-e Ulama-ye Islami* (Society of Islamic Scholars, JUI) party, was detained for one day and then released.[50]

7 October—Musharraf, apparently fearful that the ISI was plotting his assassination, removed Lt. Gen. Mahmood Ahmad, the director general of the ISI, as well as Taliban sympathisers within the army.[51] By late September, the United States had already worked out a mutually favourable understanding with Pakistan. This soon came to include substantial aid payments to Pakistan as well as rescheduled or written-off debt, reduced tariff barriers, soft loans, and the removal of sanctions.)[52] These were offered in exchange for the deployment of U.S. troops in Pakistan, where second-rate military airports in the towns of Pasni, Panjgur, Dalbandin, and Jacobabad by 11 October, if not before, came to be used by U.S. troops.[53] The United States and Britain launched the first air raids on Kabul, Kandahar, Jalalabad, and Mazar-e-Sharif.[54]

8 October—Following violent protests against the United States, Pakistani security forces detained three influential pro-Taliban extremist leaders. Fazlur Rahman, a leader of the JUI, was detained for the second time since 6 October, when he was held for a day and released (he was again released later in the day). Sami ul-Haq, a leader of one of the other factions of the JUI, was placed under house arrest. Azam Tariq, head of the Sunni extremist group SSP, was also detained.[55] Fazlur Rahman and Sami ul-Haq were the leaders of the recently established Council for the Defence of Afghanistan, a public charitable organisation in Pakistan that vowed to assist the Taliban against the United States.[56] Meanwhile, NATO pledged five German-manned AWACS aircraft from Geilenkirchen Air Base, Germany. Canada pledged 2,000 troops, including a commando unit (a component of a unit called Joint Task Force 2), six warships, and six aircraft to the anti-Taliban coalition. France offered the use of French naval forces in the Indian Ocean and announced that French intelligence agents were working with the Northern Alliance. Australia committed 1,000 troops, including 150 elite commandos of its Special Air Service, as well as refuelling and surveillance aircraft.[57]

9 October—The U.S. military declared air supremacy over Afghanistan. The air raids continued.[58] In a separate development, the United States seriously entered the field of information warfare against the Taliban and Al-Qaida. First, the State Department complained that the Qatari Al-Jazeera satellite television network had become a platform for Usamah bin Ladin. While Al-Jazeera certainly had broadcast interviews and video recordings from bin Ladin, what especially irked the State Department was that the Qatari network—unlike its U.S. counterparts—refused to engage in self-censorship on behalf of the Americans. On the same day, President Bush nominated White House Counterterrorism Chief Richard A. Clarke to the newly created position of Special Adviser for Cyberspace Security, a part of the newly created Office of Homeland Security.[59] Presumably as a result of this, the United States also, in an act not widely publicised, closed all U.S. Internet servers to access to a large number of Web sites deemed controlled by Islamic extremists. Britain reacted in a similar way, at least with some sites.[60]

10 October—An Islamic nations' emergency meeting condemned the 11 September attacks but said that retaliation should not harm civilians (reports of which had already appeared). On the same day, the Shanghai Cooperation Organization (consisting of China, Russia, Kazakhstan, Kyrgyzstan, Tajikistan, and Uzbekistan) began a two-day emergency meeting in Kyrgyzstan's capital, Bishkek, to discuss the U.S.-led air strikes on Afghanistan.[61] Meanwhile, the *Kitty Hawk* arrived in the Arabian Sea, where the *Carl Vinson* was operating as well.[62] On 12 October, the *Kitty Hawk* reached the area of operations. Almost immediately, special forces troops and their equipment waiting in Oman were loaded onto the ship.[63]

11 October—U.S. and Pakistani officials made public the fact that U.S. forces were using Pakistani airfields.[64]

13 October—The USS *Theodore Roosevelt* Battle Group transited the Suez Canal.[65]

15 October—The USS *Theodore Roosevelt* Battle Group arrived in the Arabian Sea.[66] Two U.S. AC-130H Spectre gunships entered the air war for the first time (coming from Oman) in a raid on Kandahar.[67]

16 October—Pentagon officials acknowledged that the United States focused its support on the Mazar-e-Sharif front, but without mentioning it, the forces led by the Uzbek warlord Abdul Rashid Dostum.[68] Considering the Uzbekistani and to some extent Turkish support to Dostum, as well as the presence of U.S. ground forces in Uzbekistan, this was hardly surprising. The intention was also no doubt, at least to some extent, to open up a land route for bringing in supplies and troops.

17 October—Thirty-one U.S. Senate staff members tested positive for anthrax exposure. Much of the U.S. Capitol was closed until further notice.[69]

18 October—The United States disclosed that small groups of Special Forces troops had begun operations in southern Afghanistan. This statement almost certainly referred to the insertion into Afghanistan of 11 Green Berets from the army's 5th Special Forces Group's Operational Detachment-Alpha 574

(ODA-574), led by Capt. Jason Amerine. This appears to have been the first Special Forces team to be inserted into Afghanistan. Amerine and his men joined the Afghan-American leader Hamid Karzai in Afghanistan "in mid-October," with orders to assist in various ways and, perhaps most importantly, keep Karzai alive.[70] Hamid Karzai was almost certainly the Bush administration's first choice as future leader of Afghanistan.[71]

19 October—U.S. Army Rangers and other special forces troops belonging to Delta Force, reportedly more than 100 men, in two related raids (one by Rangers, a smaller one by Delta Force) mounted the first ground attacks in Afghanistan. One U.S. helicopter used in conjunction with the raid crashed in Pakistan, killing two men identified as Rangers.[72] The two raids, although successfully carried out, in themselves served little purpose and were never repeated. On the same day, however, the Special Forces had a more enduring but less television-friendly success in northern Afghanistan. The Army's 5th Special Forces Group's Operational Detachment-Alpha 555 (ODA-555), led by CWO Dave Diaz, infiltrated into Afghanistan with orders to identify targets for air attack. Landing in Afghanistan, they were met by and then worked with CIA paramilitary teams and the Northern Alliance forces under Muhammad Fahim Khan. In the second half of October, three more A-teams infiltrated the country: ODA-553 in Bamian Province, ODA-585 in the region around Kondoz, and ODA-595 in Dara-e-Suf (Dostum's headquarters, Samangan province, about 55 miles southeast of Mazar-e-Sharif). Around 5–6 November these were joined by others. In total, 18 A-teams, four company-level units, and three 15-men battalion-level commands (316 men altogether) entered Afghanistan.[73] The team with Dostum was the first one to be disclosed to the news media, which shows the emphasis on the Uzbek front displayed in the U.S. strategy.[74] The team was probably not taking part in operations until 25 October, however.[75] The first sustained ground combat operations in Afghanistan began to take place around 5 November: working with the Northern Alliance in the north and reportedly conducting night raids and ambushes in the south.[76]

25 October—Italian police disclosed that an Egyptian suspected terrorist, Rizik Amid Farid, had been caught in Italy a few days earlier locked inside a shipping container destined for Canada. The container had its own bed and rest room facilities, and among the man's possessions were a Canadian passport, airport maps, airport security passes, and other documentation, as well as two mobile telephones and a laptop computer.[77]

26 October—Abdul Haq, a veteran Afghan mujahidin commander attempting to raise a Pashtun anti-Taliban force, was captured and executed by the Taliban. Britain declared that its ground forces had joined the coalition.[78]

27 October—A paramilitary force belonging to the Pakistani organisation Tanzim-e Nifaz-e Shariat-e Muhammadi, reportedly comprising around 10,000 people, of which many were unarmed or only poorly armed, assembled at the village of Leghari, around 4 miles (7 kilometres) from the Afghan border, planning to enter Afghanistan to assist the Taliban.[79]

29 October—Some Russian news agencies reported that Russian special forces had been deployed to positions near Kabul.[80] If so—and the information, though not quite implausible, has been impossible to verify—no more was heard of them before the arrival of Russian transports on 26 November 2001.

30 October—Having failed to find a credible Pashtun opposition to the Taliban, army Gen. Tommy R. Franks, the U.S. commander in charge of operations in Afghanistan, met Gen. Muhammad Fahim Khan, commander of the Northern Alliance, in Dushanbe for secret talks on closer cooperation between U.S. and Alliance forces. On the following day, the United States acknowledged that the policy to not target front-line Taliban troops had been abandoned. This policy was supposed to have encouraged what some had hoped to be a Pashtun alternative to the Northern Alliance. Air raids were thus currently being directed against Taliban troops along the front line.[81] In a separate development, on 30 October, President Bush called President Heydar Aliev of Azerbaijan and President Robert Kocharian of Armenia to discuss settling the two countries' dispute over the territory of Nagorno-Karabakh, so that sanctions against Azerbaijan could be waived to permit immediate U.S. use of an air base there. The base was to be used for resupply operations or as a backup to bases in Uzbekistan and Pakistan. Both countries had previously offered assistance in the War on Terror.[82] However, no deal was ever concluded, nor did the base become available. In a separate development, a major blunder was announced: the air-dropped yellow food packages to Afghan civilians were inadvertently quite similar to unexploded yellow cluster bombs. This was thought to have led to casualties.[83] After some soul-searching, it was announced that henceforth, the colour of the food packages was to be blue—but first all of the already manufactured packages would be air-dropped.[84]

November 2001

1 November—Concerned that they were losing the war for international public opinion, the United States and Britain somewhat belatedly launched a public relations effort to, among other tasks, counter Taliban claims of massive civilian casualties.[85] The *Enterprise* departed the northern Arabian Sea (returning to Norfolk Naval Base on 10 November).[86] Turkey announced that it would send 90 special forces troops to help train the Northern Alliance.[87]

2 November—The Tabligh opened its annual convention at Raiwind, near Lahore, Pakistan. About a million Muslims gathered. The convention lasted until 4 November.[88]

3 November—Tajikistan authorised U.S. military engineers to immediately begin assessing conditions at the Kulob, Qurghonteppa (Kurgan-Tyube), and Khojand air bases for possible use by U.S. forces.[89]

4 November—Confronted by approaching Taliban forces, Hamid Karzai asked the Americans to pick him up by helicopter. He was extracted and returned to Pakistan. Karzai continued to claim in interviews with the BBC and CNN that he remained in southern Afghanistan.[90]

6 November—German Chancellor Gerhard Schroeder pledged up to 3,900 troops, including special forces, for the coalition.[91]

7 November—The United States began to take punitive action against not only terrorist groups but also organisations, corporations, and individuals suspected of links to Al-Qaida. In particular, the United States cracked down on the numerous companies that served immigrants from the Middle East and South Asia by wiring small amounts of cash to and from these regions in the time-honoured system known as *hawala*. These companies had hitherto been quite legal but were not licensed as banks and so did not keep full records on transactions. Not only could terrorists use their services, it was realised, but hawala could also be used to evade taxes. Among those whose assets were frozen was the hawala company Al-Barakaat.[92] In a separate development, Italy pledged 2,700 troops, including naval, air, and ground units. The forces included the aircraft carrier Giuseppe Garibaldi and two frigates, as well as ground troops and paratroopers.[93]

9 November—The Northern Alliance in the first significant gain of the campaign—no doubt assisted by the belated air support—reconquered the city of Mazar-e-Sharif, attacking from the south (probably under Dostum).[94] The Netherlands pledged 1,200 troops to the coalition. The Czech Republic and New Zealand also pledged troops. Japan dispatched naval forces.[95]

10 November—The Northern Alliance captured most of the northern province of Takhar and important towns throughout the north.[96] The Green Berets team ODA-555 for the first time called in air strikes to facilitate Muhammad Fahim Khan's march on Kabul, according to its leader Chief Warrant Officer Diaz, who claims to have been the one to encourage Fahim Khan to take Kabul (if so, probably in blissful unawareness that this was in conflict with the wishes of the Bush administration).[97]

11 November—U.S. air raids for the first time targeted Taliban forces opposing the western Northern Alliance commander, Ismail Khan.[98] The Northern Alliance reconquered Taloqan, capital of Takhar Province.[99] In a separate development, the U.S. Third Army, the ground component of Central Command, moved its forward headquarters from Fort McPherson, Georgia, to Camp Doha, Kuwait. This headquarters (Coalition Forces Land Component Command) after early December controlled coalition ground operations in Afghanistan.[100]

12 November—The Northern Alliance reconquered the city of Herat.[101] In a separate development, as Pakistani leader Musharraf returned home after a visit to the United States, U.S. intelligence said reports had reached it about a planned Pakistani military coup during Musharraf's absence. Other intelligence reports apparently claimed that a small number of Pakistani army personnel had defected to Afghanistan to fight with the Taliban.[102] Neither piece of information could be verified. The carrier USS *John C. Stennis* departed San Diego Naval Base, well ahead of her scheduled January deployment, since the carriers *Carl Vinson* and *Theodore Roosevelt*, launching the bulk of tactical strikes in near 24-hour-a-day operations, were in severe need of relief and reinforcement.[103]

13 November—Northern Alliance units advanced into Kabul, despite U.S. objections, after the Taliban had withdrawn. Hours before the Northern Alliance advance, a U.S. air raid on Kabul severely damaged the Kabul offices of Al-Jazeera. In what was soon described as a public relations fiasco, a U.S. spokesman falsely claimed that "compelling" evidence indicated that the building was being used by Al-Qaida and that there was no intelligence that claimed otherwise.[104]

14 November—Warlord politics reasserted itself in Pashtun-dominated eastern Afghanistan. Various hitherto exiled Pashtun warlords, having moved into Afghanistan, claimed to control the eastern Pashtun areas. Hamid Karzai professed to control Oruzgan Province (a claim he by 30 November had modified into the somewhat more truthful statement "almost all" of

Oruzgan Province[105]), while Muhammad Yunus Khalis claimed likewise in Jalalabad and the surrounding province of Nangarhar. Yunus Khalis, being 82 years old, was represented by his local commander Haji Abdul Qadir, the pre-Taliban governor of Nangarhar and a brother of the late Abdul Haq. However, Abdul Qadir was immediately challenged by Muhammad Zaman Ghun Shareef, the Pakistan-based head of an alliance known as the Eastern Shura, who had returned from exile in France after the 11 September terrorist attacks.[106] Abdul Qadir was also challenged by Hazrat Ali, an ethnic Pashai who was a Northern Alliance commander and led the 5,000-strong Nuristani militia. Eventually, the three contenders agreed to share power with Abdul Qadir as governor.[107] In a separate development, the U.S. Treasury Department claimed that funds with the value of more than $56 million linked to Al-Qaida and the Taliban had been frozen.[108] In another public-relations failure, an Al-Jazeera correspondent was detained at Waco, Texas, reportedly because officials alleged, falsely, that his company credit card was "linked to Afghanistan."[109]

15 November—Around 120 British troops (a company of Special Boat Service commandos) landed at Bagram Air Base in a C-130 Hercules. The British troops were at first stopped by Northern Alliance forces who held the air base and prevented them from bringing in more troops until negotiations between the political leaders were successfully concluded. Since the British had no permission to land, the two sides came within an ace of opening fire on each other.[110] French troops from the 21st Marine Infantry Regiment, meanwhile, planned to land at and take control of Mazar-e-Sharif airport on 18 November. This move was postponed until 2 December, probably because of the sticky reception at Bagram.[111]

16 November—The Muslim fast of Ramadan began. Additional British troops (about 200 Royal Marines) arrived at Bagram Air Base, where they remained to provide base security. The United States claimed that bin Ladin's top aide Muhammad Atef was killed in a U.S. air strike on Kabul (but his name remained on the "wanted" lists distributed by the FBI).[112] Several Taliban commanders and their troops, reportedly 600 men, crossed on foot from Tora Bora into Pakistan.[113]

18 November—Kabul Television was back on air after five years of Taliban suppression.[114] U.S. officials begin a public-relations campaign to publicise the successes of the CIA paramilitary units in Afghanistan and the insertion into the country of "some" of the "10 to 20" CIA case officers from the Near East Division "with Afghan experience, knowledge of the terrain and languages, and contacts with anti-Taliban groups and tribes."[115]

19 November—Around this time (described variously as "a few days before" 22 November and "more than a week" before 28 November), the first conventional U.S. ground forces entered Afghanistan. This was a platoon from the Tenth Mountain Division commanded by Lt. Col. Paul LaCamera, which flew from Uzbekistan to Bagram Air Base, secured a few days earlier by British troops. Additional troops were soon flown in, and within days, LaCamera commanded a company at Bagram of more than 100 men.[116]

20 November—Bush promised to help the Philippines in the war on the Abu Sayyaf group, somewhat rashly offering to send combat troops. The Philippines politely declined, noting that the Philippine constitution prohibits foreign troops from fighting on the nation's territory.[117]

21 November—The Taliban leadership claimed that it no longer had contact with Usamah bin Ladin.[118]

22 November—Pakistan ordered the Taliban government to close its Islamabad embassy.[119]

24 November—Most Taliban in Kondoz surrendered, after repeated air raids and sustained artillery barrages.[120] The remaining fought on until 26 November, when the Northern Alliance captured Kondoz, the last Taliban stronghold in the north.[121]

25 November—The first several hundred (of a force that would grow into about 1,200) U.S. Marines began to move into a bridgehead named Forward Operating Base (FOB) Rhino at the Dolangi airfield 55 miles southwest of Kandahar in southern

Afghanistan. The airfield had earlier been captured by allied Afghan mercenary forces under the Pashtun warlord Gul Agha Shirzai. The marines were picked from the two Marine Expeditionary Units (MEUs) in the region: the 15th from Camp Pendleton, California, aboard the USS *Peleliu*, and the 26th from Camp Lejeune, North Carolina, aboard the USS *Bataan*. They were combined into a brigade under the command of Brig. Gen. James N. Mattis.[122] The marines were not alone at FOB Rhino. In late November or early December, about 120 Australian SAS commandos arrived to conduct raids against Taliban-held caves in the area together with the marines.[123] In yet another development, about 500 mostly foreign prisoners linked to Al-Qaida revolted in a Mazar-e-Sharif prison (the fort Qala-e-Jhangi). Several hundred prisoners and guards died in the fighting, including one U.S. CIA officer. Nine U.S. Special Forces troops and six British SAS troops participated in the battle. The fighting grew serious, and air strikes were called in against the mutinying prisoners. On 26 November, five guards were killed by a 2,000-pound "smart bomb" supposed to strike the prison but mistakenly aimed at a Northern Alliance tank. On the same day, conventional troops from LaCamera's force at Bagram also arrived to help quell the prison revolt. The allies regained control of the fort only on 28 November.[124] In a possibly separate development, IMU commander Juma Namangani was on 25 November reported to have died "recently" in a Kabul hospital due to wounds suffered from air bombing when the Northern Alliance took Mazar-e-Sharif on 9 November.[125]

26 November—A Russian humanitarian centre belonging to the Ministry for Emergency Situations was established in Kabul, being flown into Bagram Air Base in the previous week by 12 Ilyushin Il-76 military transport aircraft.[126] Faced with a fait accompli, U.S. officials could only express their concern.[127]

27 November—A UN-sponsored meeting on a post-Taliban interim government opened in Bonn.[128] The United Nations ordered the assets of Taliban leaders to be frozen.[129]

28 November—Taliban leader Mullah Muhammad Omar ordered

his men not to surrender any territory.[130] U.S. officials voiced suspicions that bin Ladin and up to 2,000 of his men were hiding in a complex of fortified caves at Tora Bora, south of Jalalabad near the Pakistani border.[131] According to some analysts, bin Ladin had crossed to Pakistan on foot along with four supporters sometime between 28 and 30 November,[132] or in the first 10 days of December.[133] A Pashtun leader eventually claimed that he had crossed from Tora Bora into Pakistan on 9 December.[134]

29 November—The Northern Alliance agreed to an international peacekeeping force.[135]

30 November—U.S. air raids targeted Kandahar, especially Taliban positions at Kandahar airport. Pakistani intelligence sources said that the four principal beneficiaries of U.S. funding had been four Pashtuns: Hamid Karzai, Abdul Khaliq (a leader of the Noorzai tribe who was the self-appointed representative in Quetta of ex-King Zahir Shah), former general Abdul Rahim Wardak (Zahir Shah's military advisor in Pakistan, known to be friendly to the United States), and Gul Agha Shirzai (the former self-appointed governor of Kandahar). Karzai, who had received two U.S. military airdrops of weapons and materiel, claimed that he had assumed control of "almost all" of Oruzgan Province. Gul Agha Shirzai claimed, no doubt truthfully, to have been given automatic rifles and grenade launchers by "people working for the U.S. government" (likely the CIA) as well as desert camouflage uniforms, communications equipment, and daily food drops from the U.S. military.[136]

December 2001

1 December—The Russian Ministry of Emergency Situations opened a humanitarian field hospital in downtown Kabul.[137]

2 December—The first unit of 60 French troops out of about 250 were dispatched to Mazar-e-Sharif airport, flying in from Uzbekistan. They stayed there until 2 February 2002.[138]

3 December—U.S. air raids targeted Usamah bin Ladin's suspected headquarters, cave complexes in Milawa and Tora Bora south of Jalalabad.[139]

4 December—In Bonn, the Afghan parties initialled a deal for an interim government to be headed by Hamid Karzai. In Afghanistan, a U.S. B-52 mistakenly dropped a bomb on friendly troops, killing three U.S. Special Forces troops and six Afghans, as well as slightly wounding Karzai, whose forces were advancing south toward Kandahar. About 2,500 allied Afghans under Hazrat Ali (the Jalalabad warlord favoured by U.S. support and money) and Muhammad Zaman Ghun Shareef (reportedly assisted by British special forces) commenced the attack on the Tora Bora complex. Later another warlord, Zahir, the son of Abdul Qadir, also arrived with some men.[140]

6 December—In a deal negotiated by Hamid Karzai, the Taliban leadership offered to surrender Kandahar in exchange for guarantees for the safety of Mullah Muhammad Omar and other top leaders; however, the United States pressured Karzai not to offer any amnesty and the deal fell through. The State Department declared that it had put 39 groups, charity organisations, and companies on a "terrorist exclusion list" in order to deport or deny the issuance of visas to their members. In a separate development, Afghan leaders Ismail Khan and Pir Sayyid Ahmad Gailani, as well as several other leaders, criticised the Bonn agreement but said they would accept it. Dostum declared that he would boycott the interim government.[141]

7 December—Taliban forces surrendered the border town of Spin Boldak as well as the southwestern province of Helmand with the provincial capital, Lashkar Gah. The Taliban also surrendered their last stronghold in Kandahar but not Mullah Muhammad Omar, who had gone into hiding. Hamid Karzai put Naqibullah Akhund, a traditionalist mullah of the Alikozai tribe, in charge of Kandahar, but the mullah was immediately pushed out by Gul Agha Shirzai, who declared himself governor and installed himself in the governor's palace. Other local Pashtun leaders also assumed control of various places in the area.[142]

8 December—The USS *Kitty Hawk* departed the Arabian Sea. She returned to Yokosuka on 24 December.[143] UN peacekeeping experts arrived in Kabul to plan the deployment of a multinational force there. The UN World Food Program raised its food distribution in Kabul to unprecedented levels.[144]

9 December—A Northern Alliance helicopter crashed in unexplained circumstances at Farkhar, Takhar Province, killing 20 Afghans, including two anti-Taliban commanders.[145] The State Department reported that Dostum would cooperate with the interim government. Uzbekistan opened a border bridge for aid deliveries to Afghanistan.[146]

10 December—Britain agreed to lead an international peacekeeping force in Afghanistan for three months, with a possible extension of up to six months.[147] On 17 December, Britain formally accepted to assume command of an 18-nation peacekeeping force in Afghanistan (to be known as the International Security Assistance Force, ISAF), which was to be established by the UN Security Council on 20 December.[148]

13 December—In India, suicide bombers attacked the Indian parliament, resulting in the death of 14 people. The terrorists were linked (by India) to the Pakistani extremist groups Lashkar-e Tayyiba and Jaish-e Muhammad.[149] The terrorists may have wanted to discredit Musharraf so as to encourage an Indian military attack on Pakistan.[150] In the United States, President Bush, after about two weeks of deliberation, released a videotape in which Usamah bin Ladin seemingly implicated himself in the 11 September 2001 terrorist attacks.[151]

15 December—The marines began preparations to leave FOB Rhino and instead move into Kandahar airport. The *John C. Stennis* relieved the *Carl Vinson*, which returned to Bremerton on 23 January 2002. The *John C. Stennis* Battle Group, including the 13th MEU from Camp Pendleton, embarked on the three ships of the USS *Bonhomme Richard* Amphibious Ready Group. The 13th MEU eventually relieved the 15th MEU. The *John C. Stennis* stayed in the theatre until some point in April–May 2002, when she departed the northern Arabian Sea. She returned to San Diego on 28 May 2002.[152] In Azerbaijan's capital Baku, U.S. Defense Secretary Donald Rumsfeld told the presidents of Azerbaijan and Armenia that he expected the United States to lift sanctions against them in the following week, thus paving the way for a resumption of military ties with the United States.[153]

17 December—Anti-Taliban forces (by then only about 1,000 men, since many had returned home) finally captured what was believed to have been bin Ladin's base (not the Tora Bora cave complex but the nearby Milawa cave complex) in the mountains of eastern Afghanistan. Usamah bin Ladin was not found. Although only Afghans took part in the battle on the ground until 11 December, as many as 60 British SAS troops and 40 U.S. Special Forces troops reportedly took part in the final stages of the assault. Despite these efforts, hundreds of surviving Taliban and Al-Qaida troops escaped into Pakistan.[154]

19 December—According to an arrangement worked out between Britain and the United States, the U.S. Central Command (CENTCOM) would have formal authority over the international peacekeeping force, although the former would have day-to-day control over the peacekeeping mission in Kabul.[155]

20 December—The Security Council duly authorised the British-led ISAF for peacekeeping in Kabul. The force was to be under the command of the British Maj. Gen. Sir John McColl. An advance team of 50 Royal Marines landed at Bagram.[156]

22 December—Hamid Karzai's six-month interim government was inaugurated in Afghanistan. On an international flight from Paris to Miami, Richard Colvin Reid tried to blow up the passenger airliner in which he was flying with explosives hidden in his shoes.[157]

24 December—Dostum was appointed deputy defence minister in the interim government. Pakistan froze the bank accounts of Lashkar-e Tayyiba.[158] A "senior U.S. official" claimed that China had supplied SA-7 Grail manportable surface-to-air missiles and small-arms ammunition to Al-Qaida after the 11 September 2001 attacks.[159] This is unlikely, to say the least, although supplies to the Taliban (not Al-Qaida) in exchange for whatever China may have wanted might be plausible.

25 December—Maulana Masood Azhar, founder of Jaish-e Muhammad, was arrested in Pakistan.[160]

January 2002

4 January—The 15th MEU was pulling out of Kandahar, to be replaced by a regiment of the 101st Airborne Division.[161] The latter assumed control of the base on 19 January.[162]

9 January—Several former ministers of the Taliban government, including Mullah Haji Obaidullah Akhund, minister of defence, and Mullah Nuruddin Turabi, minister of justice, both of whom were wanted by the United States, surrendered in Kandahar but were allowed by Kandahar governor Gul Agha Shirzai to go free after swearing fealty to the interim government.[163]

11 January—Pakistan began to reclaim the U.S. bases in Pakistan, ostensibly because of the brewing conflict with India.[164]

12 January—Musharraf stated that Pakistan no longer would cultivate extremism; he unveiled plans and new regulations to eradicate terrorism and extremism from Pakistani society and conceded to most of the demands made by India after the 13 December attack on the Indian parliament. He also announced an immediate ban on the two groups (Lashkar-e Tayyiba and Jaish-e Muhammad) alleged by India to be responsible as well as two other extremist organisations (SPP and Tanzim-e Nifaz-e Shariat Muhammadi), and their leaders and hundreds of followers were detained. However, Musharraf did not agree to the extradition to India of Pakistani nationals wanted by India on charges of terrorism.[165] Eventually as many as 2,000 militants were arrested, of which about half remained in custody by late May 2002.[166]

16 January—President Bush for the first time extended the War on Terror to include a region outside Central Asia, as the United States sent the first of 650 soldiers, including 160 Special Forces troops, to the Philippines for a (eventually mostly postponed) military exercise. These troops were expected to begin working with Philippine troops on Basilan, where about 5,000 Philippine troops were hunting for about 80 Abu Sayyaf guerrillas (although most media, following the official lead, by then claimed that the Abu Sayyaf numbered 1,000 men, which was patently untrue).[167] Within about a month, President Bush also moved the War on Terror into the Caucasian republic of Georgia (see below, under 27 February).

18 January—The United States began what could only be called a propaganda war on Iran. The Bush administration's envoy to Afghanistan, the former Unocal consultant Zalmay Khalilzad,[168] accused Iran of supplying arms, money, and Iranian-trained Afghan soldiers to Ismail Khan, with the purpose of discouraging him from submitting to the interim government.[169] U.S. officials also claimed that Iran had sent 200 to 300 Afghan fighters from Iran to the area around Mazar-e-Sharif during the previous several weeks. These were alleged to be covert members of the Shia group *Sepah-e Muhammad* (Soldiers of Muhammad), reputed to have been trained in Lebanon by Hezbollah. The group was also reputedly known as the Afghan Hezbollah. The Bush administration also claimed that Iranian special forces troops, members of the Al-Qods division of the Revolutionary Guards Corps, were in Afghanistan working with the Shia group. Another claim was that this group worked independently of Iranian intelligence and military personnel in two other parts of Afghanistan as well: around Herat and near Bamian. Finally, U.S. officials alleged that Iran wished to gain control over the important Shia shrine in Mazar-e-Sharif.[170] Most of these claims cannot be verified, although it seems likely that Iranian intelligence was active in Afghanistan, which after all was an unstable neighbouring state.

27 January—Hamid Karzai arrived in Washington for a three-day visit to the United States.[171]

28 January—President Bush pledged that the United States would help establish and train a new Afghan army and police force.[172]

29 January—President Bush made the bold assumption that states that may attempt to develop chemical, biological, or nuclear weapons—and are not close allies of the United States—also must be in the process of sponsoring terrorism. In his first official State of the Union address, Bush accordingly declared that an "axis of evil" consisting of the three disparate countries of Iran, Iraq, and North Korea threatened world peace.[173]

30 January—Rival Pashtun warlords, including Bacha Khan Zadran, who was aligned with and named governor by Hamid Karzai, commenced hostilities over Gardez.[174]

31 January—In an advisory and training role, U.S. troops commenced operations against the Abu Sayyaf together with the Philippine army, in what was referred to as Joint Task Force 510. This was, as noted, the first War on Terror-related military operation outside Central Asia. U.S. troops were permitted to assist in an advisory role only and could not participate in combat, except in self-defence, because the Philippine constitution precluded it.[175] It was later disclosed that U.S. Navy and Air Force intelligence-gathering aircraft, based on Okinawa and elsewhere in Asia, had flown missions over the southern Philippines. The aircraft may have been navy P-3C Orion maritime patrol aircraft, which were also being flown from bases in Oman for surveillance purposes in Somalia.[176] In Afghanistan, P-3Cs were additionally used as a platform for special operations with the task of radioing enemy positions to troops on the ground, but this probably did not happen in the Philippines.[177]

February 2002

5 February—Defense Secretary Rumsfeld noted that the United States had spent $7 billion in the war's first four months and needed another $10 billion to pay for the first five months of war projected in 2003.[178] This amount did not include the political payments in aid and other benefits in exchange for base rights.

8 February—Afghan interim leader Hamid Karzai visited Pakistan, where he declared that the construction of a pipeline carrying natural gas from Turkmenistan across his country to Pakistan was "very essential." The pipeline was the project in which Karzai had been involved as a Unocal consultant and one he knew was dear to the Pakistani leaders.[179]

14 February—Karzai ceased his support of Bacha Khan Zadran in Gardez and in a compromise deal with local leaders appointed Taj Muhammad Wardak (an 80-year-old exile in California) new governor. At Kabul Airport, angry pilgrims waiting for a flight to Mecca attacked and beat to death the minister for civil aviation and tourism, Abdul Rahman, as he went to the airport for a flight to New Delhi.[180] On the following day, Hamid Karzai attempted to take advantage of the killing by announcing that the minister had in fact been assassinated in a plot by 20 members of the government, including five high-ranking officials from the defence, intelligence, and justice ministries. Of these, three were named: Gen. Abdullah Jan Tawhidi, a second-ranking official at the intelligence department; Qalander Beg, a senior defence official; and Sananwal Abdul Halim, a senior prosecutor in the Ministry of Justice. Karzai claimed that all three had fled to Saudi Arabia after the killing. However, all those named were ethnic Tajiks as well as members of the Northern Alliance and, therefore, political rivals of Karzai. It later became clear that they had gone to Saudi Arabia as part of the pilgrimage, not as fugitives.[181] On 24 April, an official investigation finally concluded that there had been no plot and that Minister Rahman had indeed been killed by the mob.[182] Hamid Karzai did not further comment on the incident.

16 February—An incident that probably was the first armed attack on the international peacekeeping force in Kabul took place, resulting in the death of one Afghan civilian.[183]

19 February—Iranian newspapers reportedly announced that the government had decided to expel the Afghan Islamist Gulbuddin Hekmatyar, due to his outspoken support for the Taliban.[184]

20 February—The carrier *John F. Kennedy* departed Mayport, bound for the Arabian Sea.[185]

24 February—Hamid Karzai visited Iran. Ayatollah Khamenei publicly endorsed the Afghan interim government.[186]

26 February—Iran, as expected, expelled Hekmatyar because of his outspoken support for the Taliban.[187]

27 February—It was disclosed that President Bush had extended the War on Terror to the Caucasus through a military assistance program to Georgia. The assistance program included two parts: military helicopters (which had already been arranged in October 2001, around the time when an assistance agreement was concluded between the two countries) and training for Georgian pilots and ground support personnel, as well as the creation and training of a Georgian rapid-deployment force specialising in antiterrorist operations. The latter was to include about 1,500 Georgian troops, who would participate in various U.S. training programs conducted by about 200 Special Forces military instructors and staged at different military bases throughout the country. The United States would also equip the units undergoing training. The transferred materiel included 10 UH-1H combat helicopters (similar to the AH-1 Huey Cobra of Vietnam fame—six for operations and four for spare parts), which had already been provided to Georgia. The aim was to fight Chechen separatists from Chechnya, a few of whom were believed to be linked to Al-Qaida. About 40 U.S. military personnel, including Special Forces troops (from 3d Special Forces Command, Special Operations Command Europe, based at Stuttgart, and probably the 10th Special Forces Group from Fort Carson, Colorado, which specialised in cold-weather missions), had already visited Georgia in February. [188]

28 February—General Franks described the ongoing operation in the Philippines as a model for future military and counterterrorism assistance to Yemen and other countries.[189]

March 2002

1 March—U.S. troops under army Maj. Gen. Franklin L. "Buster" Hagenbeck launched the only major ground offensive in the war, Operation Anaconda, against what was reported to be a concentration of several hundred Al-Qaida and Taliban troops south of Gardez in Paktia Province, eastern Afghanistan.

Despite reassuring press releases and claims of victory, independent observers generally regarded the operation as inconclusive, if not outright unsuccessful. Fighting in the area ebbed around 13 March. Operation Anaconda was declared over on 18 March.[190]

2 March—Following General Franks' remarks on 28 February, the Pentagon disclosed plans to bring the War on Terror to Yemen, as well. It had been decided to send several hundred U.S. Special Forces troops (from 5th Special Forces Group, Special Forces Command, CENTCOM) to assist the Yemeni government in the fight against Islamic extremists, in an operation modelled on the one in the Philippines.[191]

3 March—The carrier *John F. Kennedy* transited the Suez Canal on her way to relieve the *Theodore Roosevelt*, which on the same day departed the northern Arabian Sea (she returned to Norfolk on 27 March).[192]

7 March—The *John F. Kennedy* formally relieved the *Theodore Roosevelt*.[193] By 18 March, the *John F. Kennedy* was off the coast of Pakistan.[194]

20 March—U.S. forces released 12 men detained for two weeks at Kandahar; they at first were thought to be Iranian agents but later were found to be Afghans.[195]

23 March—The first group of the planned deployment of 1,700 Royal Marines, code-named Operation Jacana, arrived at Bagram.[196]

28 March—In an early-morning raid apparently based on FBI communications intercepts (reportedly telephone calls to Afghanistan and e-mail;[197] or less likely, a tracking device on a car followed by an ISI tip),[198] Abu Zubaydah (real name Zayn al-Abidin Muhammad Hussain, born to a Palestinian family in Riyadh), a high-ranking Al-Qaida and Islamic Jihad member believed to have been the organisation's chief of overseas operations, and some 50 other suspected Al-Qaida members (the majority Pakistanis) were captured at a safe house in Faisalabad, Pakistan.[199] Some claim that Abu Zubaydah was replaced within Al-Qaida by Saif al-Adil, a former Egyptian army officer wanted in connection with the 1998 embassy bombings.[200]

April 2002

1 April—It was disclosed that by the end of March that most of the Army's 5th Special Forces Group had returned to Fort Campbell, Kentucky, having turned over in-theatre duties to the 3d Special Forces Group, based at Fort Bragg, North Carolina, and geared toward action in East Africa and the Middle East.[201]

3 April—The 1st Battalion, 600 men, of the Afghan National Guard completed six weeks of basic training by British instructors from ISAF, in uniforms donated by Turkey.[202] At around this time, the United States began work to build a new national Afghan army. Between 500 and 600 men were recruited to the first battalion of the Afghanistan National Army (ANA). The new units would be the only military force directly under the control of the Karzai government (Hamid Karzai controlled no personal forces), and the Afghan National Guard was supposed to be used to guard offices in the capital.[203] However, by mid-May about 250 men (mainly Pashtuns) had dropped out of the 10-week-training program, and only about 300 men eventually graduated as the 1st Battalion.[204]

4 April—Afghan officials disclosed that about 300 political opponents of the interim government had recently been arrested in Kabul, the majority accused of being part of an attempted coup led by the Islamist leader Gulbuddin Hekmatyar. Among the suspects was Wahidullah Sabawoon, the Northern Alliance finance minister and formerly a close associate of Hekmatyar. He escaped capture.[205]

8 April—The Afghan Defense Minister Muhammad Fahim Khan, an ethnic Tajik, survived a bomb blast as he made his first official visit to Jalalabad, a city dominated by ethnic Pashtuns.[206] Coalition forces operating from a military base on Khost air field, where several dozen U.S. Special Forces troops were based, renewed the search for Al-Qaida forces around Gardez near the Pakistani border (in the same area where U.S. forces a month earlier had conducted Operation Anaconda).[207] U.S., British, and Australian special forces also began operations on the Pakistani side of the border.[208] This was only confirmed on 25 April, however, when U.S. military officials disclosed that U.S. special forces (apparently including Delta Force) "in recent weeks" had been conducting operations there, as well.[209] By then, this was hardly a secret; Pakistani Foreign Minister Abdul Sattar had already on 26 March stated that Pakistan was prepared to let U.S. troops cross the border in pursuit of Al-Qaida suspects. However, U.S. officials had repeatedly denied that there were any such plans; this was to spare the feelings of Pakistani leader Musharraf, who had been pressured by the United States into allowing U.S. personnel to engage in hot pursuit across the border, something he still vehemently opposed. On 29 April, Musharraf finally confirmed the presence of U.S. troops operating with Pakistani forces in the hunt for Al-Qaida members on the Pakistani side of the border.[210]

16 April—It was announced that several hundred British commandos had deployed to the border area near Pakistan to hunt remaining Taliban and Al-Qaida forces, in what became known as Operation Ptarmigan.[211] They did not find any, and U.S. officials as well as defence sources in London later characterised the deployment, which was concluded on 18 April, as little more than a training exercise.[212]

18 April—After several delays caused by security concerns in Afghanistan, ex-King Zahir Shah returned to Afghanistan under heavy guard. He arrived in one of a group of three identical Italian C-130 transports: two of the three aircraft served as decoys in case of missile attack.[213]

27 April—Factional fighting among rival Pashtun warlords again broke out at Gardez, Paktia Province, in eastern Afghanistan.[214] The main contenders were Bacha Khan Zadran, who in January had unsuccessfully claimed the governorship of Paktia Province by force; the elderly Taj Muhammad Wardak, who had been appointed governor by and received a provincial government from Hamid Karzai; Said Muhammad Isshaq, the

Gardez security chief; and Hakim Taniwal, a retired sociologist who had been living in Australia but now was appointed governor of Khost.[215]

29 April—Turkey officially agreed to assume command of the ISAF. The takeover eventually took place on 20 June. There were currently 270 Turkish troops in the peacekeeping force, which was chiefly responsible for patrolling Kabul. Turkey announced that it expected to enlarge the Turkish contingent to about 1,000 troops upon assuming command.[216] In a separate development, U.S. forces began to set up a training facility in the former, and heavily damaged, military academy at Kabul, with the declared goal of training 18,000 soldiers for the new ANA in the coming year and a half.[217] Formal training may have started as late as 14 May. In yet a separate development, 1,000 Royal Marines, backed by some Afghan troops and with U.S. air support, commenced Operation Snipe in the mountainous southeast of Afghanistan, near the Pakistani border. The operation lasted until 13 May.[218]

30 April—The coalition launched Operation Mountain Lion, a long-term operation (which also included Operation Snipe) in which elite British and Australian units, as well as parts of two battalions of the U.S. 101st Airborne Division, backed by AH-64 Apache helicopters, searched various suspected Al-Qaida hideouts in the Mezzai Mountains, probably in Pakistan as well as in Afghanistan.[219] However, participation by the 101st was later denied by military officials at Bagram.[220] In a separate development, it was announced that U.S. forces (150 men from the 92d Engineering Battalion at Fort Stewart, Georgia) were building a garrison for 2,500 soldiers at Bagram Air Base to last until December 2004. According to independent reports, the buildings were designed to last for five years, which may have indicated a projected presence of U.S. forces in Afghanistan until 2007.[221] Meanwhile, the first 20 of about 200 U.S. Special Forces instructors (from the army's 10th Special Forces Group, based at Fort Carson and in Germany, and specializing in cold-weather missions[222]) arrived in the Caucasian republic of

Georgia to train Georgian security forces in counterinsurgency operations, with the avowed purpose of hunting down Islamic extremists among guerrillas from neighbouring Chechnya. The United States also promised to provide small arms, ammunition, uniforms, communications equipment, medical supplies, fuel, and construction materials.[223]

May 2002

6 May—The CIA tried to assassinate Gulbuddin Hekmatyar with a Predator missile attack. He escaped, though several of his followers were reportedly killed.[224] In a separate development, it was reported that the British SAS was involved in raids on suspected safe houses for heroin processed in Afghanistan.[225] Meanwhile, it was announced that around 400 Canadian troops, around 90 men from the 101st Airborne, and some allied Afghans were engaged in a week-long search in Tora Bora, codenamed Operation Torri. Apparently, after the December offensive there, the 50 U.S. troops left in the area had not themselves searched what was left of the fortified caves, instead trusting to their Afghan mercenaries to do so. This omission was now rectified, although admittedly after a four-month delay. No enemy fighters were found.[226]

8 May—A car bombing in Karachi killed 14 people, including 11 French workers. Suspicion fell on Al-Qaida.[227]

16 May—It was announced that about 3,000 troops from the U.S. 82d Airborne Division would be sent to Afghanistan in June to replace units from the 101st Airborne Division and were likely to remain until the end of the year.[228] Within days, the first elements of the 101st began withdrawing.[229]

17 May—Following an engagement between an Australian SAS team and hostile forces of unknown allegiance north of Khost on the previous day, around 1,000 troops, mostly Royal Marines, launched a major sweep, code-named Operation Condor. The operation lasted around a week.[230]

21 May—Canada announced the return of 850 troops from the 3d Battalion, Princess Patricia's Canadian Light Infantry Battle

Group, in July or August, after completing a six-month tour of duty in Afghanistan. 1,300 Canadian troops would remain in Afghanistan.[231]

24 May—The Canadian frigate HMCS Toronto returned to St. John's, Newfoundland.[232]

29 May—About 300 Royal Marines commenced Operation Buzzard, an attempt of several weeks to patrol the plains south and east of Khost, near the Pakistani border. The operation's purpose was to cut Taliban and Al-Qaida forces communications routes and to prevent those who went into hiding in Pakistan from returning to Afghanistan. One of the targets was reportedly Gulbuddin Hekmatyar.[233]

31 May—Lt. Gen. Dan K. McNeill, commander of the U.S. Army's 18th Airborne Corps, assumed command of the new Combined Joint Task Force 180 (Afghanistan; CJTF-180 [AFG]), based at Bagram Air Base. The U.S. command structure also changed, so that McNeill from June on would report directly to General Franks, head of the U.S. CENTCOM at MacDill Air Force Base, Florida. This eliminated the Third Army forward headquarters (Coalition Forces Land Component Command) at Camp Doha, from the chain of command.[234]

June 2002

1 June—It became clear that much of the frozen money allegedly belonging to terrorist groups was gradually being released because the United States did not release evidence to justify the legal blocking of accounts.[235]

5 June—Omar al-Faruq, probably an Iraqi, was arrested in Indonesia and handed over the United States. After more than three months of interrogations, he reportedly confessed to being Al-Qaida's representative for Southeast Asia.[236]

10 June—U.S. officials announced that they had broken up a terrorist plot to detonate a "dirty bomb" in the United States. U.S.-born Jose Padilla, also known as Abdullah al-Muhajir, was named the chief suspect. He had been arrested in Pakistan, then released and returned to the United States; on 8

May, upon arriving from Pakistan, he was rearrested. The prosecution was unable to build a case against Padilla, so he was named an "enemy combatant" and turned over to the military to be locked up indefinitely until he admitted to something.[237] In Afghanistan, the Loya Jirga (Grand Assembly) was supposed to convene to choose a new Afghan government. Because of widespread confusion, the meeting could only open on 11 June.[238]

13 June—Hamid Karzai was elected transitional head of state for the following 18 months to two years.[239]

14 June—A car bomb exploded outside the U.S. consulate in Karachi. Twelve Pakistanis were killed. Although a spokesman for a previously unheard of group referring to himself as tarjuman al-Qanoon ("spokesman for the Law") claimed responsibility, the new extremist coalition known as Lashkar-e Umar was believed to have been involved. To have a fictional group assume responsibility was classical Al-Qaida tactics.[240]

19 June—Among other appointments, Hamid Karzai retained Muhammad Fahim Khan as minister of defence and Abdullah Abdullah as minister for foreign affairs. He replaced Yunus Qanooni, who previously had resigned as interior minister, with the 80-year-old Taj Muhammad Khan Wardak, and appointed Yunus Qanooni minister of education. Hamid Karzai appointed Muhammad Fahim Khan, Karim Khalili, and Haji Abdul Qadir vice presidents.[241]

20 June—Turkey formally assumed command of the ISAF. Gen. Hilmi Akin Zorlu took command in Kabul.[242] In a separate development, the carrier *George Washington* left Norfolk.[243]

22 June—The six-month mandate of the interim government expired.

July 2002

6 July—The Afghan vice president, former warlord Abdul Qadir, was assassinated. This further eroded the Pashtun faith in Karzai's government, which the Pashtuns argued contained too many Tajiks.[244]

13 July—The *George Washington* transited the Suez Canal.[245]

14 July—August Hanning, head of the German Federal Intelligence Service (*Bundesnachrichtendienst*), stated that bin Ladin was still alive was hiding in the Afghan-Pakistani border region.[246]

19 July—The *George Washington* relieved the *John F. Kennedy*, which went through the Suez Canal on 24 July, left the Mediterranean on 8 August, and returned to Mayport on 17 August.[247]

31 July—U.S. and Philippine troops formally concluded six months of joint exercises, and the U.S. Army Special Forces pulled out of the country.[248]

End Notes

1.   AP, 9 September 2001. See, for instance, Vladimir Davlatov, "Northern Alliance Face Uncertain Future," London: Institute for War and Peace Reporting, RCA 69, 14 September 2001 (www.iwpr.net); *Economist*, 15 September 2001.

2.   RFE/RL *Central Asia Report* 1: 9 (20 September 2001).

3.   See, for instance, *Economist*, 15 September 2001. For a final confirmation that the White House was the final target, see *Washington Post*, 23 May 2002.

4.   *Washington Post*, 12 September 2001.

5.   Personal observation, 12 September 2001.

6.   *New York Times*, 12 September 2001, 21 September 2001.

7.   *Washington Post*, 12 September 2001.

8.   John Pike, www.globalsecurity.org.

9.   Reuters, 13 September 2001.

10.   RFE/RL *Newsline*, 14 September 2001.

11.   *Washington Post*, 14 September 2001.

12.   *Washington Post*, 29 January 2002.

13.   *Washington Post*, 16 September 2001.

14.   *Washington Post*, 31 January 2002.

15.   NTV (Russia), 16 September 2001, referring to Pakistani sources.

16.   John Pike, www.globalsecurity.org.

17.   AFP, 17 September 2001.

18.   *Afghanistan: OCHA Situation Report* 1 (18 September 2001; www.reliefweb.int).

19.   Korgun, "Afghanistan on the Threshold of Peace," 11. Korgun refers to *Izvestiya*, 18 September 2001.

20.   *Kommersant* (Russia), 20 September 2001.

21. *Washington Post,* 20 September 2001.
22. *Washington Post,* 24 September 2001.
23. *On-Line Pravda,* 25 September 2001 (www.english.pravda.ru).
24. *Washington Post,* 20 September 2001.
25. John Pike, www.globalsecurity.org.
26. *New York Times,* 22 September 2001.
27. *Economist,* 22 September 2001.
28. *Economist,* 29 September 2001.
29. *Washington Post,* 23 September 2001, referring to Interfax and Agence France Presse.
30. RIA Novosti, 24 September 2001, referring to ABC News.
31. *Washington Post,* 4 October 2001.
32. *Washington Post,* 24 September 2001.
33. Presidential Executive Order 13224, 23 September 2001. See also, for instance, *New York Times,* 25 September 2001.
34. RIA Novosti, 24 September 2001, referring to ABC News.
35. *Washington Post,* 26 September 2001.
36. UK Ministry of Defence (www.mod.uk).
37. *Washington Post,* 18 November 2001; *Newsweek,* 29 April 2002.
38. *Economist,* 29 September 2001, 6 October 2001.
39. Reuters, 30 September 2001.
40. John Pike, www.globalsecurity.org.
41. *Washington Post,* 4 October 2001.
42. *Washington Post,* 3 October 2001.
43. Korgun, "Afghanistan on the Threshold of Peace," 11–12.
44. *Washington Post,* 6 October 2001; John Pike, www.globalsecurity.org.
45. Reuters, passim; Andy Oppenheimer, "All Quiet on the Anthrax Front?" *Jane's Chem-Bio Web,* 5 June 2002.
46. *Washington Post,* 6 October 2001.
47. See, for instance, *International Herald Tribune,* 19 February 2002.
48. RFE/RL, 12 October 2001; RFE/RL *Central Asia Report* 1:13 (18 October 2001).
49. Rashid, *Jihad,* 184.
50. RFE/RL, 9 October 2001.
51. *Washington Post,* 8 October 2001; Azad, "Musharraf Feared Rebellion." For a more unfavourable analysis of Musharraf's policy, see ICG, *Pakistan.*
52. *Washington Post,* 2 October 2001; BBC, 11 November 2001; Reuters, 15 November 2001; and for a useful summary, *Economist,* 9 March 2002.

53. See, for instance, *Washington Post,* 11 October 2001; VOA News, 11 October 2001; RIA Novosti, 19 October 2001, 22 October 2001.
54. *Washington Post,* 8 October 2001.
55. RFE/RL, 9 October 2001.
56. Jane's World Insurgency and Terrorism 13, 28 November 2001.
57. *Washington Post,* 9 October 2001.
58. *Washington Post,* 10 October 2001.
59. *Washington Times,* 15–21 October 2001 (National Weekly Edn).
60. This was not widely reported, although details of the suppression were occasionally published. See, for instance, *Washington Post,* 11 October 2001.
61. Sultan Jumagulov, "Uzbekistan 'Rebuffs' Shanghai Pact," *IWPR's Reporting Central Asia* (19 October 2001; www.iwpr.net).
62. John Pike, www.globalsecurity.org.
63. *Washington Post,* 24 December 2001.
64. *Washington Post,* 11 October 2001.
65. John Pike, www.globalsecurity.org.
66. John Pike, www.globalsecurity.org.
67. *Washington Post,* 16 October 2001, 17 October 2001.
68. *Washington Post,* 17 October 2001.
69. Reuters, 17 October 2001.
70. *Washington Post,* 19 October 2001, 11 December 2001, 23 December 2001.
71. Ron Callari, "Energy Interests, the U.S. Government, and the Post-Taliban Trans-Afghan Pipeline," *Central Asia – Caucasus Analyst Biweekly Briefing,* 22 May 2002 (www.cacianalyst.org).
72. *Washington Post,* 20 October 2001, 21 October 2001; *Washington Times,* 5–11 November 2001 (National Weekly Edn).
73. *Washington Post,* 20 February 2002, 3 April 2002.
74. *Washington Post,* 20 October 2001.
75. *Washington Post,* 16 November 2001.
76. *Washington Times,* 26 November – 2 December 2001 (National Weekly Edn).
77. *Times* (London), 25 October 2001.
78. *Washington Post,* 27 October 2001.
79. *Nation* (Pakistan, Lahore edn as available on Internet), 1 November 2001.
80. www.allnews.ru, 29 October 2001.
81. *Washington Post,* 1 November 2001.

82. *Washington Post,* 2 November 2001.
83. *Washington Post,* 30 October 2001.
84. *Washington Post,* 2 November 2001.
85. *Washington Post,* 1 November 2001.
86. *Washington Post,* 11 November 2001; John Pike, www.globalsecurity.org.
87. *Washington Post,* 2 November 2001.
88. *Economist,* 3 November 2001.
89. *Washington Post,* 4 November 2001.
90. *Washington Post,* 7 November 2001.
91. *Washington Post,* 7 November 2001.
92. *Washington Post,* 8 November 2001. The ever-growing list of blocked companies and individuals under Presidential Executive Order 13224, 23 September 2001, is available from the Office of Foreign Assets Control, U.S. Department of the Treasury. For further details on the *hawala* (also known as *hundi* and, in China, *fei qian*) system of money transfers, see, for instance, *Economist,* 24 November 2001.
93. Reuters, 7 November 2001; *Washington Post,* 8 November 2001.
94. *Washington Post,* 10 November 2001.
95. *Washington Post,* 11 November 2001.
96. *Washington Post,* 11 November 2001.
97. *Washington Post,* 3 April 2002.
98. *Washington Post,* 11 November 2001.
99. *Washington Post,* 12 November 2001.
100. Jane's Sentinel: Kuwait, 29 April 2002; Jane's Sentinel: Afghanistan, 31 May 2002.
101. *Washington Post,* 13 November 2001.
102. *Washington Times,* 19–25 November 2001 (National Weekly Edn).
103. *Washington Times,* 12–18 November 2001 (National Weekly Edn), 3–9 December 2001 (National Weekly Edn); John Pike, www.globalsecurity.org.
104. *Washington Post,* 14 November 2001.
105. *Washington Post,* 1 December 2001.
106. *Washington Post,* 15 November 2001, 16 November 2001, 10 February 2002.
107. *Washington Post,* 19 November 2001. On Hazrat Ali, see also *Washington Post,* 18 February 2002.
108. Reuters, 14 November 2001.
109. *Washington Post,* 15 November 2001.
110. *Washington Post,* 16 November 2001, 18 November 2001, 22 November 2001; *Times,* 23 January 2002.

111. *Washington Post,* 16 November 2001; French Ministry of Defence (www.defense.gouv.fr).

112. *Washington Post,* 17 November 2001.

113. *Newsweek* (Asia edn), 19 August 2002.

114. Reuters, 18 November 2001.

115. *Washington Post,* 18 November 2001.

116. *Washington Post,* 29 November 2001, 24 February 2002.

117. *Washington Post,* 21 November 2001; *Time,* 28 January 2002.

118. Reuters, 21 November 2001.

119. *Washington Post,* 23 November 2001.

120. *Washington Post,* 25 November 2001.

121. *Washington Post,* 27 November 2001.

122. *Washington Post,* 26 November 2001, 1 December 2001.

123. *Washington Post,* 2 December 2001, 5 December 2001; Jane's Sentinel: Afghanistan, 31 May 2002.

124. *Washington Post,* 26 November 2001, 2 February 2002; *Time,* 10 December 2001. Others estimated that as many as 40 Special Forces troops and 10 to 12 British commandos were in the area around the prison at the time. Center for Defense Information (www.cdi.org).

125. *Washington Post,* 26 November 2001.

126. *Washington Post,* 28 November 2001, 29 November 2001. For the initial announcement, see AVN, 23 November 2001. For the Ministry of Civil Defence, Emergency Situations, and the Elimination of the Consequences of Natural Disasters, as its full name goes, see the ministry's Web site, www.emercom.gov.ru.

127. *Washington Post,* 29 November 2001.

128. *Washington Post,* 27 November 2001.

129. Reuters, 27 November 2001.

130. Reuters, 28 November 2001.

131. *Washington Post,* 28 November 2001.

132. *Christian Science Monitor,* 4 March 2002.

133. *Washington Post,* 17 April 2002, citing U.S. intelligence officials.

134. Arnaud de Borchgrave in *Washington Times,* 29 April–5 May 2002 (National Weekly Edn).

135. Reuters, 29 November 2001.

136. *Washington Post,* 1 December 2001.

137. Reuters, 1 December 2001.

138. *Washington Post,* 30 November 2001; French Ministry of Defence (www.defense.gouv.fr).

139. *Washington Post,* 5 December 2001.

140. *Washington Post,* 6 December 2001. On the first two warlords, see *Washington Post,* 18 February 2002. On Zahir, see *Washington Post,* 10 February 2002.

141. *Washington Post,* 7 December 2001.

142. *Washington Post,* 8 December 2001.

143. John Pike, www.globalsecurity.org; *Washington Post,* 24 December 2001.

144. Reuters, 8 December 2001.

145. Reuters, 9 December 2001.

146. *Washington Post,* 11 December 2001, 12 December 2001.

147. *Washington Post,* 11 December 2001.

148. *Washington Post,* 21 December 2001.

149. See, for instance, *Economist,* 15 December; *Washington Post; International Herald Tribune; Wall Street Journal Europe,* 14 January 2002.

150. Ahmed, "Pakistan in Crisis."

151. *Washington Post,* 14 December 2001; Transcript and annotations of the video tape independently prepared by George Michael, translator, Diplomatic Language Services; and Dr. Kassem M. Wahba, Arabic language program coordinator, School of Advanced International Studies, Johns Hopkins University, 13 December 2001.

152. On 28 November 2001, the Navy announced that the 13th MEU would deploy on 1 December. John Pike, www.globalsecurity.org.

153. *Washington Post,* 16 December 2001.

154. *Washington Post,* 13 December 2001, 14 December 2001, 17 December 2001, 18 December 2001. See also *Washington Post,* 10 February 2002.

155. *Washington Post,* 20 December 2001.

156. *Washington Post,* 21 December 2001; Center for Defense Information (www.cdi.org).

157. *Washington Post,* 23 December 2001. For more details on Reid, see *Washington Post,* 31 March 2002.

158. *Washington Post,* 25 December 2001.

159. *Washington Times,* 24–30 November 2001 (National Weekly Edn).

160. *Washington Post,* 26 December 2001.

161. *Washington Post,* 4 January 2002.

162. *Washington Post,* 20 January 2002.

163. *Washington Post,* 10 January 2002.

164. *Washington Post,* 11 January 2002.

165. See, for instance, *Financial Times; International Herald Tribune; Wall Street Journal Europe,* 14 January 2002. Musharraf also banned a Shia party, unconnected with Sunni Islamic extremism.

166. *Economist,* 19 January 2002; Associated Press, 28 May 2002.

167. *Washington Post,* 16 January 2002.

168. Ron Callari, "Energy Interests, the U.S. Government, and the Post-Taliban Trans-Afghan Pipeline," *Central Asia–Caucasus Analyst Biweekly Briefing,* 22 May 2002 (www.cacianalyst.org). Khalilzad, an Afghan-American scholar with a deep interest in the Iranian Revolution and its effect on Afghanistan, in 2001 served as the Program Director for Strategy, Doctrine, and Force Structure at the RAND Corporation's Project Air Force. See for instance, Zalmay Khalilzad, "Iranian Policy Toward Afghanistan Since the Revolution," David Menashri (ed.), *The Iranian Revolution and the Muslim World* (Boulder, Colorado: Westview Press, 1990).

169. *Washington Post,* 19 January 2002.

170. *Washington Times,* 25 February – 3 March 2002 (National Weekly Edn).

171. *Washington Post,* 27 January 2002.

172. *Washington Post,* 29 January 2002.

173. *Washington Post,* 30 January 2002.

174. *Washington Post,* 31 January 2002, 1 February 2002.

175. *Washington Post,* 1 February 2002.

176. *Washington Post,* 21 February 2002.

177. *Washington Times,* 8–14 April 2002 (National Weekly Edn).

178. *Washington Times,* 11–17 February 2002 (National Weekly Edn).

179. RFE/RL *Central Asia Report* 2:6 (14 February 2002), Internet edn.

180. *Washington Post,* 15 February 2002.

181. *Washington Post,* 16 February 2002, 17 February 2002.

182. *Washington Post,* 25 April 2002.

183. *Washington Post,* 17 February 2002.

184. *Washington Times,* 25 February–3 March 2002 (National Weekly Edn).

185. John Pike, www.globalsecurity.org.

186. Entekhabi-Fard, "Afghan Leader's Visit to Iran."

187. Jane's Sentinel: Afghanistan, 17 October 2000; IRNA, 26 February 2002.

188. *Washington Post,* 27 February 2002, 2 March 2002; Jaba Devdariani, "U.S. and Georgian Officials Move to Next Phase of Military Deployment," *Eurasia Insight,* 16 March 2002 (www.eurasianet.org).

189. *Washington Post,* 28 February 2002.

190. *Washington Post,* 3 March 2002, 4 March 2002, and several later issues, especially 5 March 2002, 8 March 2002, 13 March 2002, 14 March 2002; Center for Defense Information (www.cdi.org).

191. *Washington Post,* 2 March 2002.

192. John Pike, www.globalsecurity.org.

193. John Pike, www.globalsecurity.org.

194. *Washington Times,* 18–24 March 2002 (National Weekly Edn).

195. Center for Defense Information (www.cdi.org).

196. *Washington Post,* 25 March 2002.

197. *Time,* 15 April 2002.

198. *Time,* 6 May 2002.

199. For details on the raid, see, for instance, *Washington Post,* 4 April 2002; *Newsweek,* 13 May 2002; *Time,* 15 April 2002.

200. *Time,* 3 June 2002.

201. *Washington Times,* 1–7 April 2002 (National Weekly Edn).

202. *Washington Post,* 4 April 2002.

203. *USA Today,* 11 April 2002.

204. Michael Drudge in an untitled article at www.globalsecurity.org, 21 July 2002; *Economist,* 10 August 2002; Jane's Sentinel: Afghanistan, 18 July 2002.

205. *Washington Post,* 5 April 2002.

206. *Washington Post,* 9 April 2002.

207. *Star Tribune,* 14 May 2002, based on Associated Press; *USA Today,* 25 April 2002.

208. Center for Defense Information (www.cdi.org).

209. *Washington Post,* 25 April 2002.

210. *Washington Times,* 1–7 April 2002 (National Weekly Edn); *USA Today,* 25 April 2002; *Post-Bulletin* (Minneapolis), 29 April 2002, based on Associated Press.

211. *Washington Post,* 17 April 2002; *USA Today,* 17 April 2002.

212. *Washington Post,* 3 May 2002; Center for Defense Information (www.cdi.org); Jane's Sentinel: Afghanistan, 31 May 2002.

213. *Washington Post,* 18 April 2002, 19 April 2002.

214. *Washington Post,* 28 April 2002.

215. *Washington Post,* 4 May 2002

216. *Post-Bulletin,* 29 April 2002, based on Associated Press; *Washington Post,* 30 April 2002.

217. *Post-Bulletin,* 29 April 2002, based on Associated Press.

218. Center for Defense Information (www.cdi.org); Jane's Sentinel: Afghanistan, 31 May 2002; Associated Press, 14 May 2002.
219. *Washington Post*, 1 May 2002; *Newsweek*, 13 May 2002.
220. *Washington Post*, 3 May 2002
221. *USA Today*, 30 April 2002.
222. *Washington Post*, 11 June 2002.
223. *Washington Post*, 1 May 2002; *USA Today*, 30 April 2002.
224. *Washington Post*, 10 May 2002; *Time*, 3 June 2002.
225. *Washington Times*, 6–12 May 2002 (National Weekly Edn).
226. Center for Defense Information (www.cdi.org).
227. See, for instance, *Washington Post*, 9 May 2002, and especially 1 June 2002.
228. *Washington Post*, 16 May 2002.
229. *Washington Times*, 27 May–2 June 2002 (National Weekly Edn).
230. See, for instance, Center for Defense Information (www.cdi.org).
231. *Washington Post*, 22 May 2002.
232. *Chronicle-Journal* (Thunder Bay, Ontario), 25 May 2002.
233. *Washington Post*, 30 May 2002; Center for Defense Information (www.cdi.org).
234. *Washington Post*, 22 May 2002; *USA Today*, 28 May 2002; *Washington Times*, 3–9 June 2002 (National Weekly Edn).
235. *Washington Post*, 1 June 2002.
236. *Far Eastern Economic Review*, 3 October 2002.
237. *Washington Post*, 11 June 2002; *Newsweek* (Asia edn), 19 August 2002.
238. See, for instance, *IWPR'S Afghan Recovery Report* 9 (11 June 2002; www.iwpr.net); *IWPR'S Afghan Recovery Report* 15 (19 June 2002).
239. *Washington Post*, 14 June 2002.
240. *Washington Post*, 15 June 2002; Jane's Sentinel: Pakistan, 18 July 2002.
241. *IWPR'S Afghan Recovery Report* 15 (19 June 2002; www.iwpr.net); *Washington Post*, 20 June 2002.
242. *Washington Post*, 21 June 2002.
243. John Pike, www.globalsecurity.org.
244. See, for instance, *International Herald Tribune*, 15 July 2002.
245. John Pike, www.globalsecurity.org.
246. *Welt am Sonntag*, 14 July 2002.
247. John Pike, www.globalsecurity.org.
248. *Economist*, 3 August 2002.

Islamic Extremism in Pakistan

Maududi

Islamic extremism in Pakistan can be said to have begun with the *Jamaat-e Islami* (Islamic Society), founded in 1941 by Sayyid Abul Ala al-Maududi (1903–1979) in what was then British India. When India was partitioned upon independence in August 1947, Maududi moved to Pakistan where he re-established the organisation.[1] Maududi argued that Islam was self-sufficient, separate from, and indeed opposed to Western capitalism as well as socialism. He regarded the West as morally decadent and corrupt. Since the West was opposed to Islam, he argued, it was permissible and even obligatory to struggle against Western influences, and by extension the West itself and any secular society. Yet Maududi did believe that there could be compromise between Islam and the non-Islamic world, which set him apart from more radical Muslim thinkers such as Sayyid Qutb.[2] In 1953, Maududi was sentenced to death for militant activities, though he was subsequently amnestied and died in exile in the United States in 1979.[3] The Jamaat-e Islami continued to grow. It is currently a political mass movement with millions of members, led by Qazi Hussain Ahmed (a Pashtun; in charge of the movement's Afghan affairs during the 1970s and appointed amir of the movement in the late 1980s)[4] and based in Lahore. Its aim is the full Islamisation of Pakistani society. The organisation began to receive official patronage after Gen. Muhammad Zia ul-Haq's military coup in 1977. Numerous high-ranking Pakistani military officers have since become linked with the movement. Although not itself directly engaged in terrorism and irregular warfare, it is clear that it advocates jihad to create an Islamic transnational state and has inspired and supported the more violent groups that emerged later.[5] It is widely believed that Saudi Arabia is the major financial backer of the organisation.[6]

The *Tanzim ul-Ikhwan* (Movement of the Brotherhood) was another Islamic mass movement, led by Maulana Akram Awan. It drew its main strength from the Punjab and also included many army officers.[7]

Extremism in Pakistan was boosted by the vast resources pumped into the country during the 1980s to fuel the Afghan groups fighting the Soviet Union.[8] Since 1988, however, when widespread insurgency broke out in Indian Kashmir,[9] most Pakistani extremist groups have turned to, or were indeed founded for, the struggle for a united Kashmir under Pakistani rule. It appears that the Kashmir issue soon became the prime cause, as well, for Pakistan's Afghanistan and, eventually, Taliban policy. Most Pakistani extremist groups had military training camps in Taliban-controlled parts of Afghanistan, even though their chief interest was in Kashmir and most of the groups maintained headquarters in Muzzafarabad, near the border between Azad ("Free") Kashmir and Indian Kashmir.[10] In the autumn of 1988, following an initiative from Hamid Gul, the ISI director-general of the time, all Pakistani diplomatic facilities abroad were instructed to issue special tourist visas to any Muslim expressing an interest in studying in a Pakistani madrasah and fighting in the Afghan or Kashmiri jihad. Airline tickets were often provided as well. A lack of proper travel documents, or indeed any travel documents at all if the recruit was wanted for terrorism and offered a false name, did not prevent the trip to Pakistan.[11]

Later Extremist Groups

The first Pakistani modern extremist group, the *Harakat ul-*

Ansar (Movement of Helpers, named after the first supporters of the Prophet Muhammad), was founded in 1980 to participate in the Afghan war as part of the U.S.-led effort to fight the Soviet Union. After a number of splits, the factions again merged in 1987 and, again, after new splits, in October 1993, when two factions of the group (*Harakat ul-Mujahidin,* or Movement of Mujahidin, and *Harakat ul-Jihad al-Islami,* or Movement of Islamic Jihad) began to operate as a military organisation with 450 to 500 members. Although based in Pakistan (Muzaffarabad and Rawalpindi) and Taliban-controlled eastern Afghanistan, the group operated in Kashmir. Designated a terrorist organisation by the United States in October 1997 due to the kidnapping and killing of five Western tourists in Kashmir in July 1995, the group resumed the name Harakat ul-Mujahidin in 1998. Responsibility for the kidnappings was claimed by a previously unheard of group known as *Al-Farhan* (The Delightful), which was believed to be a front for the Harakat ul-Ansar. As already noted, the use of fictitious front organisations is a classical Al-Qaida tactic.[12] The Harakat ul-Mujahidin was also associated with the 24 December 1999 hijacking of an Indian passenger airliner, which was flown to Kandahar. On 30 December 1999, India agreed to release Harakat ul-Mujahidin leader Maulana Masood Azhar and two followers in exchange for the surviving hostages.[13] The Harakat ul-Mujahidin was led by Fazlur Rehman Khalil, one of the Islamic extremist leaders who, on behalf of the Harakat ul-Ansar, and together with Usamah bin Ladin, set up the World Islamic Front for Jihad Against Jews and Crusaders in February 1998.[14] He stepped down in February 2000 in favour of his second-in-command, Faruq Kashmiri, probably in connection with the formation of yet another faction, the Jaish-e Muhammad (see below).[15] While Harakat ul-Mujahidin was mainly involved in Kashmir, it was also linked to various acts of terrorism in other Muslim countries throughout the world.[16] A splinter group was *Harakat ul-Mujahidin al-Alamiya* (Movement of Global Mujahidin), which fought in Afghanistan on the Taliban side.[17]

A number of Deobandi clerics, including Sami ul-Haq and Fazlur Rahman, set up a political party, *Jamiat-e Ulama-ye Islami,*

(Society of Islamic Scholars, JUI). The JUI currently consists of three main factions, led respectively by Fazlur Rahman, Ajmal Qadri, and Sami ul-Haq, the latter as the party's secretary general. The party remained politically isolated until Pakistan's 1993 elections, when it became part of Prime Minister Benazir Bhutto's ruling coalition. The JUI then established close links with the army, the ISI, and the Interior Ministry. Soon the JUI was closely involved in Afghanistan, in 1994 guiding and nurturing the emergence of the Taliban movement. In 1996, the Taliban handed over control of training camps to the JUI and several of its many breakaway factions, which became the chief recruiters of Pakistanis and others for the Taliban forces. It has been estimated that as many as 80,000 to 100,000 Pakistanis trained and fought in Taliban units in Afghanistan between 1994 and 1999 (independently of those regular Pakistani troops who also reportedly served with the Taliban). After returning home, these battle-hardened men were poised to take the war to their own country. By 1998, neo-Taliban groups had already become a major influence in the Pashtun-dominated Pakistani provinces of Baluchistan and the North-West Frontier Province, banning television, imposing punishments under *shariah*, and killing Shia Pakistanis. Their influence was also being spread to Punjab and Sind.[18]

Two extremist Punjabi splinter groups of the JUI were the *Sepah-e Sahaba Pakistan* (Army of the Companions of the Prophet of Pakistan—SSP) and the *Lashkar-e Jhangvi* (Army of Jhangvi). The SSP was founded in September 1984 (as the *Anjuman-e Sepah-e Sahaba Pakistan* (Society of the Army of the Companions of the Prophet of Pakistan) by Haq Nawaz Jhangvi, head of the Punjab branch of the JUI, with funding from Saudi Arabia and Iraq. The purpose was to combat the Shia minority in Pakistan, the presence of which Jhangvi and his associates detested. The SSP was subsequently led by Azam Tariq, with Abdul Khaliq Siddiqi as secretary general. The Lashkar-e Jhangvi was formed in 1994 as an armed faction of SSP and received its name in 1996 in honour of Jhangvi (who died in a revenge killing in 1990). Both maintained close ties with the Taliban, as well as with Usamah bin Ladin, and many of their followers joined the Taliban army. The leaders of the two groups, accused of the killings of many Pakistani Shias, eventually took refuge in Kabul. The leader of the Lashkar-e Jhangvi, Riaz Basra, was killed in May 2002.[19]

The *Jaish-e Muhammad* (Army of Muhammad) was founded in February–March 2000 as an offshoot of Harakat ul-Mujahidin by Maulana Masood Azhar, the Islamic cleric with close links with bin Ladin who was released from an Indian jail following the December 1999 hijack of an Indian passenger airliner. Many Harakat ul-Mujahidin fighters, reportedly three quarters, followed Masood Azhar into the new organisation. It had 300 to 400 members in Kashmir and was based at Peshawar and Muzaffarabad in Pakistan. The group also had close ties to the SSP. Masood Azhar has since been placed under house arrest.[20]

In addition to the Jaish-e Muhammad, the group that in recent years caused most headlines was the *Lashkar-e Tayyiba* (Army of the Pure), based in Mudrike, near Lahore. The headquarters, built with Saudi funding in the 1980s, covered a vast area and was sealed off and in effect outside Pakistani law. The Lashkar-e Tayyiba became the militant branch of the Pakistani Wahhabi organisation *Markaz al-Dawa wa'l-Ershad* (Center for Proselytising and Guidance, established in 1987), the most influential of the Wahhabi organisations in Pakistan. It is a loose group that also includes the *Jamiat-e Ahl-e Hadith* (Society of the People of the Prophetic Tradition) and *Jamiat-e Ulama-ye Ahl-e Hadith* (Society of the Islamic Scholars of the People of the Prophetic Tradition). The Lashkar-e Tayyiba had been formed as early as 1980 and took part in the Afghan war during the 1980s; after 1993 it began operations in Kashmir. It had between 300 and 400 members and was based in Pakistan, although it also enjoyed the use of Afghan training camps associated with bin Ladin. Operations were led by Zaik ul-Rehman Lakhvi, while the overall leader of the movement was Hafiz Muhammad Sayeed, a professor at Lahore's University of Engineering and Technology, who was founding member and amir of Markaz al-Dawawa'l-Ershad. Hafiz Sayeed has since been placed under house arrest.[21] Among the group's spokesmen were Abdullah Muntazir (at least in 1999) and the group's information secretary, Yahya Mujahid.[22]

On 13 December 2001, Islamic extremists attacked the Indian Parliament in New Delhi, and India accused Jaish-e Muhammad and Lashkar-e Tayyiba. On 30 December 2001, Pakistani police reported the arrest of Hafiz Sayeed and more than a dozen members of Lashkar-e Tayyiba and Jaish-e Mohammed.[23] But more was to follow. On 12 January 2002, Pakistani leader Musharraf, in a speech that some diplomats referred to as historic, stated that Pakistan no longer would cultivate extremism. Musharraf also unveiled plans and new regulations to eradicate terrorism and extremism from Pakistani society, acceded to most of the demands made by India since the attack on the Indian parliament, and announced an immediate ban on Lashkar-e Tayyiba and Jaish-e Muhammad. Four Jihadist organisations (i.e., Lashkar-e Tayyiba, Jaish-e Muhammad, SPP, and Tanzim-e Nifaz-e Shariat Muhammadi) were proscribed. The organizations' leaders were detained and the Indian Muslims (but not Pakistani citizens) reportedly extradited to India. More than 700 people were detained, including hundreds of Pakistan-based Kashmiri militants, many of them members of the two banned groups.[24] Eventually as many as 2,000 militants were arrested, of whom about half remained in custody by late May 2002.[25] Musharraf has since also banned the Lashkar-e Jhangvi and Harakat ul-Mujahidin.[26]

The remaining members of the banned Jaish-e Muhammad and Lashkar-e Tayyiba, and probably the other groups, appear to have since joined with other extremists (perhaps including fugitive elements of Al-Qaida and possibly even the Taliban) in a new coalition of extremist organisations known as *Lashkar-e Umar* (Army of Caliph Umar). The new grouping is believed to have been responsible for the bombing of the U.S. Consulate in Karachi on 14 June 2002, which killed 12 Pakistanis.[27]

The *Hizb ul-Mujahidin* (Mujahidin Party), founded in 1989 and led by Syed Salahuddin (real name Muhammad Yusuf Khan), was for most of the 1990s Kashmir's largest insurgent group, with 1,000 to 1,200 members, in Kashmir. It was established by the ISI and the Jamaat-e Islami as a pro-Pakistani movement to compete with the Jammu and Kashmir Liberation Front, a local insurgent group fighting for independence but currently dormant after declaring a cease-fire in 1994. The Hizb ul-Mujahidin, regarded as the militant wing of the Jamaat-e Islami, was based in Muzaffarabad, Rawalpindi, and Islamabad. The party was divided into a public *tanzimi* (political) wing and a clandestine *askari* (military) wing which was engaged in terrorism in Kashmir. The military wing was organised into army-like units; while engaged in operations, members increasingly dressed in military uniforms. Its commanders were designated by formal military ranks. Being the premier extremist party active in Kashmir, all foreign groups that operated there depended on the Hizb ul-Mujahidin for logistic support. Syed Salahuddin was also the leader of the United Jihad Council, a Pakistani charitable organisation set up in 1990 to support the jihad in Kashmir. The Hizb ul-Mujahidin was clearly a Wahhabi organisation, banning (and violently enforcing) a broad range of vices that included cinemas, cable television, beauty parlours for women, and the production and consumption of alcoholic drinks. The party also established its own news agency, Kashmir Press International, based in Rawalpindi, and acquired the support in the United States of Ghulam Nabi Fai's Kashmir American Council.[28]

Al-Badr Mujahidin was founded in 1998 in Peshawar as an offshoot of Hizb ul-Mujahidin. The group, first believed to have been led by Naseer Ahmed and Bhakat Aaman but currently led by Emir Bakht Zamin Khan, has grown from only 40 to 50 members while it coordinated its activities with the Lashkar-e Tayyiba to 250 to 300 men in Kashmir, where it has been engaged since 1999. About 70 members of Al-Badr Mujahidin were arrested in Musharraf's crackdown on Jaish-e Muhammad and Lashkar-e Tayyiba in January 2002[29]

Other Pakistani extremist groups active mostly in Kashmir—but also at home—included the nebulous All Parties Hurriyat Conference, founded in the early 1990s as a pro-Pakistan umbrella organisation for more than 20 Kashmiri groups and led by Abdul Ghanit Butt.[30] Yet other groups included offshoots or perhaps only individual members of extremist groups of Middle Eastern origin such as *Al-Jihad* (The Jihad), *Al-Umar Mujahidin* (Mujahidin of Caliph Umar, apparently led by Mushtak Ahmed Zargar), and *Ikhwan ul-Muslimin* (Muslim Brotherhood), and perhaps *Hizbullah* (Party of God).[31]

The *Tanzim-e Nifaz-e Shariat-e Muhammadi*, or TNSM (Movement for the Enforcement of the Law of Muhammad)[32] led by Sufi Muhammad was another Islamic extremist movement, clearly inspired by the Afghan Taliban. The movement, a tribally based Deobandi party active in the North-West Frontier Province that grew to prominence with an armed uprising north of Peshawar in 1994,[33] was until its proscription in January 2002 prominent in the Pashtun areas of Pakistan, especially Malakand. Unlike the other Pakistani extremist groups, this one was apparently not involved in Kashmir. Its members wore a uniform white *shalwar kameez* (long shirt and baggy trousers, the Pakistani national dress) with a black turban and carried black and white flags, as did the Afghan Taliban. One of its prominent leaders was Painda Khan.[34]

On 27 October 2001, the TNSM tribal army, reportedly of around 10,000 men mostly from Swat, Buner, Shanglapar, Dir, and Malakand Agency, assembled at the village of Leghari, a bit over four miles (seven kilometres) from the Afghan border. The TNSM leaders planned to enter Afghanistan to assist the Taliban in the ongoing war. However, many of the tribal army's members were armed poorly or not at all. As a consequence, the local price of used Kalashnikovs rose from PR6,000–7,000 to PR10,000–11,000 (Pakistani Rupees)—that is, from just above $100 to more than $180 at the then exchange rate. The price of new Kalashnikov rifles rose from PR11,000 to PR17,000–18,000—from $180 to more than $300. The price of a packet of 10 bullets rose from PR50 to PR70 (from about $.85 to $1.20). Likewise, local supplies of black and white cloth soon ran out, as the militants procured black or white turbans, the typical attire of Taliban soldiers.[35] Those who eventually crossed into Afghanistan mainly died or disappeared. A TNSM spokesman later admitted that around 3,000 fighters had gone missing. Survivors claimed that more than 5,000 had died, while thou-

sands remained in Afghan prisons or were being held for ransom in Afghanistan. Sufi Muhammad apparently gave himself up for arrest in Pakistan to avoid being killed in revenge by his own tribesmen.[36]
The exact number of militants belonging to the multitude of Pakistani extremist groups is unknown to Western observers, although the Indian government estimates that 3,000–4,000 fighters are active in Kashmir at any given time. Much larger numbers remain in Pakistan, which boasts an estimated 40,000–50,000 madrasahs (religious boarding schools), of which an estimated 10 to 15 percent (about 5,000 to 6,000) espouse extremist beliefs and continually teach and inspire the spiritual obligation to engage in jihad against the enemies of Islam.[37] The madrasah that created the Taliban, Jaamiah Dar ul-Ulum Haqqaniyah, located in Akora Khattak, outside Peshawar, and headed by Sami ul-Haq, in 2000 expanded its capacity to house 500 foreign students, from Afghanistan (nearly half of the student body), Uzbekistan, Tajikistan, Russia, and Turkey. The Haqqaniyah has traditional ties with the University of Medina in Saudi Arabia.[38] The madrasahs and extremist movements are funded from private sources, often of the same type (or precisely the same) that funds the Arab Afghan movement. The families of killed extremist fighters often receive financial assistance either from the militant groups or something like the *Shuhda-e Islam* (Martyrs of Islam) Foundation, founded in 1995 by Jamaat-e Islami for this purpose. Other Islamic charities as well are suspected of giving financial assistance to militants, among them the *Ummah Tamir-e Nau*. Many extremists fight for one or two seasons and then return home, but without severing their links with the extremist movement. After liberating Kashmir, they will wish to rebuild Pakistan as a proper Islamic state. It is also common for the extremists to hire criminals to carry out acts of violence. The groups also sometimes turn to petty or organised crime themselves. As in the Arab Afghan movement, the various extremist movements share madrasahs, training camps, and members.[39]

Extremism and Pakistani Military Strategy
The activities of Pakistani extremists in Kashmir have tied

down significant large Indian military forces and resources there, which indeed appears to be one of the chief reasons why Pakistan does not seem willing to suppress the extremist movements. However, by facilitating the activities of militants in Kashmir and Afghanistan, Pakistan inadvertently promotes internal sectarianism on its own territory, as well as damaging its international standing—both threatening the cohesion of Pakistani society and statehood.[40] The extremist groups, if not deployed in Kashmir or Afghanistan, are likely to turn inward, which will increase violence and turmoil inside Pakistan and undermine internal order. Signs inside Pakistan indicate growing sectarian tension and unrest, alongside the steady Islamisation of society.[41]

The Islamisation of Pakistan has also turned the country into a safe haven for foreign Islamic extremists, who did not hesitate to bring their own struggles into Pakistan. On 19 November 1995, the Egyptian embassy in Islamabad was almost destroyed in a suicide truck-bomb attack by Islamic Jihad, under the leadership of Ayman al-Zawahiri. Fifteen people died, and more than 60 were injured.[42]

Pakistan's leader, Gen. Pervez Musharraf, seems to have been involved in the training of Arab Afghans during the Afghan war as well as the infiltration of guerrillas into Indian Kashmir. He is also reputed to have had ties to bin Ladin, criminal syndicates involved in narcotics trafficking in the North-West Frontier Province, and a number of military officers who have close links with the Harakat ul-Mujahidin.[43] Whether this makes Musharraf a closet extremist or a man uniquely qualified to deal with the problem is anybody's guess.

As a child, Musharraf lived for seven years in Turkey. He speaks Turkish, admires the founder of secular Turkey, Mustafa Kemal Atatürk (1881–1938), and drinks alcohol.[44] However, Musharraf has yet to take decisive action against the extremists. While he handled the anti-American demonstrations with a minimal loss of life and sacked a number of high-ranking military officers regarded as too close to the militants, he seems more uncertain on how to deal with the various extremist organisations. A few militant groups have been banned, but others have suffered no government interference. Certain extremist leaders have been detained, but by no means all, or even the majority. Musharraf's hesitation was clearly shown when in early October 2001 he first had the influential extremist leader Fazlur Rahman detained, then had him released, but had him held again after a few days.[45] In spring 2002, when Pakistan made an attempt, obviously without putting too much effort into it, to freeze the accounts of several banned extremist organisations, the government effort secured the equivalent of less than $100.[46]

Some 20 percent of the Pakistani army is made up of ethnic Pashtuns, of whom many would be reluctant to confront their cousins in Afghanistan or elsewhere.[47] Many are high-ranking officers such as former army chief Gen. Abdul Waheed and the head of military intelligence, Lt. Gen. Ali Kuli Khan, who both were involved in the Taliban movement. Besides, most operational ISI field officers involved with the Taliban were Pashtuns.[48] Furthermore, it is estimated that approximately 30 to 35 percent of the military officers in Pakistan have sympathies with the jihadi movement.[49]

The extremists' ambition to achieve full control over the government of Pakistan has probably more to do with domestic reasons than any serious plan to gain an international role. However, Pakistan's frequent references to its "Islamic bomb" no doubt have inspired the extremists in terms of what can be achieved against neighbouring, and perhaps more distant, states regarded as enemies of Pakistan and Islam. Until the 11 September 2001 terrorist attacks, Pakistan tolerated and even encouraged Islamic extremist groups such as the Afghan Taliban, but Islamic extremism poses a severe threat to Pakistan as well. Facing a tough ultimatum from President Bush, Musharraf declared Pakistan's support for the United States against Usamah bin Ladin and Afghanistan-based Islamic terrorism. Musharraf knew, however, that were the Pakistani government to rally decisively behind the United States in an extended military campaign, it might fall victim to the very Islamic extremism that it had nurtured elsewhere. This might lead to violent popular unrest, civil breakdown, and the eventual destruction of the state. Even though the West persuaded the Pakistani government to turn against its former disciples, this may result in a very severe cost to the latter. The internal cohesion of Pakistan remains at stake, and the decision has already cost lives lost in violent street demonstrations. The 5,000 to 6,000 religious seminaries that espouse extremist beliefs and continually teach and inspire the spiritual obligation to engage in jihad against the enemies of Islam are not likely to meekly abide any government reaction against them. The inherent conflict between secular rulers and Wahhabi Islam, no longer possible for the Pakistani government to sidestep, has not been resolved.

End Notes

1. Hiro, *Islamic Fundamentalism*, 242, 246–8. For further information on Pakistan, see also Christophe Jaffrelot (ed.), *Pakistan: Nationalism without a Nation?* (London: Zed Books, 2002).

2. Hiro, *Islamic Fundamentalism*, 66–7, 141, 247. Maududi's writings include hundreds of works, among others, Sayyid Abul Ala Maududi, *Towards Understanding Islam* (Lahore: Islamic Publications, 1960); Sayyid Abul Ala Maududi, *A Short History of the Revivalist Movements in Islam* (Lahore: Islamic Publications, 1963); Sayyid Abul Ala Maududi, *Purdah and the Status of Woman in Islam* (Lahore: Islamic Publications, 1972, 1979); Sayyid Abul Ala Maududi, *The Prophet of Islam* (Karachi: Islamic Research Academy, 1970). While influential, Maududi is not universally popular among Muslims and indeed despised by many of them.

3. Cooley, *Unholy Wars*, 43.

4. Olivier Roy, "Has Islamism a Future in Afghanistan?" Maley, *Fundamentalism Reborn?* 199–211, on 201.

5. See, for instance, Jamaat-e Islami web page, www.jamaat.org; Anthony Davis, "Musharraf's Dilemma," *Jane's Intelligence Review* 13:3 (March 2001), 38–41, on 39; Rahul Bedi, "Kashmir Peace Talks Collapse," *Jane's Intelligence Review* 12:10 (October 2000), 34–7, on 36.

6. Hiro, *Islamic Fundamentalism*, 141.

7. Davis, "Musharraf's Dilemma," 39–40.

8. Cooley, *Unholy Wars*.

9. Ishtiaq Ahmed, *State, Nation and Ethnicity in Contemporary South Asia* (London:

Pinter, 1998), 154–155.

10. Rashid, *Taliban*, 186–187; Bergen, *Holy War*, 212.

11. Bodansky, *Bin Laden*, 24–25.

12. Davis, "Musharraf's Dilemma," 40; Bedi, "Kashmir Peace Talks," 36; Rahul Bedi, "Clashes in Kashmir Stretch Indian CI Ops," *Jane's Intelligence Review* 11:8 (August 1999), 30–33, on 32; Viacheslav Belokrenitskiy, "Islamic Radicalism in Pakistan: Evolution and Regional Role," *Central Asia and the Caucasus* 6, 2000, 104–116; *Intelligence Newsletter* 261 (30 March 1995), 7; Ahmed Rashid, "Taliban Aided Terrorism and Regional Instability," Central Asia-Caucasus Institute, 19 January 2000 (Internet publication); Department of State Web site, www.state.gov.

13. Bergen, *Holy War*, 208–12; *Patterns of Global Terrorism 1994*.

14. For the full text of the fatwa, see Reeve, *New Jackals*, 268–70; FAS Intelligence Resource Program (www.fas.org).

15. Katzman, *Terrorism*, 15.

16. Rashid, "Heart of Darkness," 8–12; Rashid, "Taliban: Exporting Extremism," 22–35; Jessica Stern, "Pakistan's Jihad Culture," *Foreign Affairs* 79:6 (2000), 115–126.

17. Jane's Sentinel: Pakistan, 18 July 2002.

18. Rashid, "Taliban: Exporting Extremism," 22–35; Rashid, *Taliban*, 187, 194–5; Davis, "Musharraf's Dilemma," 39; ICG, *Pakistan: Madrasas*, 6.

19. Stern, "Pakistan's Jihad Culture," 115–126, in particular 124; Belokrenitskiy, "Islamic Radicalism," 104–116; Rashid, "Heart of Darkness," 8–12; Rashid, "Taliban: Exporting Extremism," 22–35; Rashid, *Taliban*, 92; Davis, "Foreign Fighters," 14–17; Davis, "Musharraf's Dilemma," 39; Roger Howard, "Probing the Tiesthat Bind Militant Islam," *Jane's Intelligence Review* 12:2 (February 2000), 36–9, on 38; Anthony Davis, "Pakistan: State of Unrest," *Jane's Intelligence Review* 11:1 (January 1999), 33–8, on 35. Current SSP leadership: Jane's Sentinel: Pakistan, 18 July 2002; Richard Behar, "Kidnapped Nation," *Fortune* 145: 9 (29 April 2002), 84–92, on 85. Riaz Basra: ICG, *Pakistan: Madrasas*, 18 n.102, 33.

20. Davis, "Musharraf's Dilemma," 40; Bedi, "Kashmir Peace Talks," 36; Rashid, "Taliban Aided Terrorism;" Bergen, *Holy War*, 217; ICG, *Pakistan: Madrasas*, 22. The Jaish-e Muhammad maintained a Web site, www.jaish-e-muhammad.org.

21. Stern, "Pakistan's Jihad Culture," 115–126; Belokrenitskiy, "Islamic Radicalism," 104–116; Davis, "Musharraf's Dilemma," 40; Bedi, "Kashmir Peace Talks," 34, 36; Howard, "Probing the Ties," 38–9; Bedi, "Clashes in Kashmir," 32; ICG, *Pakistan: Madrasas*, 22. The Lashkar-e Tayyiba maintained a Web site, www.markazdawa.org.

22. Bergen, *Holy War,* 39; *International Herald Tribune* (Tokyo), 1 January 2002.

23. *International Herald Tribune* (Tokyo), 1 January 2002.

24. See, for instance, *Washington Post; Financial Times; International Herald Tribune; Wall Street Journal Europe,* 14 January 2002. Musharraf also banned a Shia party, unconnected with Sunni Islamic extremism. This was the *Tehrik-e Jafaria Pakistan* ("Movement for the Shia of Pakistan"), since 1988 the name of the originally *Tehrik-e Nefaz-e Fiqh-e Jafaria* ("Movement for the Defence of Jafari [Shia] Law"), formed in 1979 inspired by the Iranian Islamic Revolution. See, for instance, Davis, "Pakistan," 34. The party has since been renamed *Millat-e Jafaria Pakistan* ("Shia Nation of Pakistan"). ICG, *Pakistan: Madrasas,* 34.

25. *Economist,* 19 January 2002; Associated Press, 28 May 2002.

26. Musharraf also banned a smaller group, *Sepah-e Muhammad* ("Army of Muhammad"). ICG, *Pakistan: Madrasas,* 21, 22.

27. Jane's Sentinel: Pakistan, 18 July 2002.

28. Bedi, "Kashmir Peace Talks," 34, 36; Bedi, "Clashes in Kashmir," 32–3; Belokrenitskiy, "Islamic Radicalism," 104–116; Bergen, *Holy War,* 215–16.

29. See, for instance, *Washington Post; International Herald Tribune; Wall Street Journal Europe,* 14 January 2002; Davis, "Musharraf's Dilemma," 40; Bedi, "Kashmir Peace Talks," 36; Bedi, "Clashes in Kashmir," 32; Jacquard, *Osama Bin Laden,* 124.

30. Bedi, "Kashmir Peace Talks," 36.

31. Jane's Sentinel: Pakistan, 14 November 2000, 18 July 2002, 31 July 2002.

32. Also sometimes referred to as Tehrik-e Nifaz-e Shariat Muhammadi, with fundamentally the same meaning.

33. Davis, "Musharraf's Dilemma," 39–40; Davis, "Pakistan," 36.

34. "In the Shadow of the Taliban," *The Economist,* September 2001.

35. *Nation* (Pakistan; Lahore edn as available on Internet), 1 November 2001.

36. ICG, *Pakistan: Madrasas,* 21–2.

37. Stern, "Pakistan's Jihad Culture," 115–126.

38. Stern, "Pakistan's Jihad Culture," 123; ICG, *Pakistan: Madrasas,* 11. For more information on Haqqaniyah, see, for instance, Jeffrey Goldberg, "The Making of a Terrorist," *New York Times Magazine,* 25 June 2000.

39. Stern, "Pakistan's Jihad Culture," 115–126.

40. Stern, "Pakistan's Jihad Culture," 115–126.

41. Rashid, *Taliban,* 186–7, 194–5.

42. Reeve, *New Jackals,* 166–67, 236; Bergen, *Holy War,* 200–201.

43. Jane's Sentinel: Pakistan, 14 November 2000.

44. Ahmed, "Pakistan in Crisis."
45. RFE/RL, 9 October 2001.
46. ICG, *Pakistan: Madrasas*, 21, 22.
47. Rashid, *Taliban*, 26.
48. Ahmed Rashid, "Pakistan and the Taliban," Maley, *Fundamentalism Reborn?* 72–89, on 86; Rashid, *Taliban*, 262 n.7.
49. Ahmed, "Pakistan in Crisis."

Islamic Extremism in Kashmir

4

The Pakistani-Indian Rivalry

When India and Pakistan were formally created out of British India in 1947, the technically independent principality of Jammu and Kashmir, predominantly Muslim but with a reigning Hindu maharaja, had the option of choosing either new nation for its allegiance. However, the internal situation of the still independent state soon grew messy.

First a tribal revolt broke out among pro-Pakistani Muslim separatists from certain Muslim-majority areas, primarily Poonch. The separatists in September 1947 invited large numbers of tribesmen from the North-West Frontier Province of Pakistan to invade Jammu and Kashmir. By 20 October 1947, more than 1,000 primarily Pashtun tribesmen (Mahsuds, Mohmands, Wazirs, Daurs, Bhittanis, Khattaks, Turis, and some Afridis from Tirah, as well as men from the former princely states of Swat and Dir) were moving into Kashmir. On 23 October 1947, they captured Domel. They continued along the Jhelum River road, the traditional route used by invading Afghan armies, toward Baramula, the entry point into the Vale of Kashmir, whence the road led directly to the Kashmiri capital of Srinagar. As a result, in a series of events murky to this day, the maharaja fled the country in a panic after signing over his

state to India, and Indian troops went into Kashmir. The first two
Indian military units arrived there on 27 October 1947, the same
day the Pashtun tribesmen reached Baramula. Soon the Indian air
force began air raids against the tribesmen, destroying men, vehicles, and ammunition supplies.[1]

The Kashmir dispute had by then, in the words of a diplomat,
"assumed a strong Islamic aspect," and allegations that Pakistani
officers and soldiers, conveniently on leave from the army, were
fighting alongside the tribesmen and insurgents circulated widely.
Pakistani arms, ammunition, and supplies were also made available
to the tribesmen. Considering the state of the newly created
Pakistani army at the time, the real importance of the Pakistani
support was less in numbers and more in terms of experience.
Certainly some retired officers of the old Indian National Army,
Muslims and hence pledging their allegiance to Pakistan, were
available to assist the insurgents.[2] In other words, a pattern was
established that was to characterise Pakistani policy toward first
Kashmir, then also Afghanistan.

Pakistan responded to the maharaja's submission to India by
sending its own troops into Kashmir, but to assist the Muslim
forces. This resulted in a war that ended with a cease-fire imposed
by the United Nations in January 1949 and the separation of the
two forces along a line of control which since then divides the formerly independent princely state into Azad (Free) Kashmir, ruled
by Pakistan, and Jammu and Kashmir, ruled by India. Roughly
two-thirds of the state are held by India, one-third by Pakistan.[3]
Kashmir turned into an important issue in international politics,
being a prime cause behind the three wars (in 1947, 1965, and
1971) fought by India and Pakistan since independence. Like similar indigenous, fundamentally secular insurgent movements in
Muslim regions elsewhere, the insurgency was in the years following the anti-Soviet Afghan jihad hijacked by Arab Afghans.
Kashmir is the single most important reason relations remain very
poor between Pakistan and India.[4]

Some Kashmiri groups advocate outright independence, often
pointing to the state's former independence and the irregular cir-

cumstances in which India took control of Kashmir. While independence may well be the only way to create peace in Kashmir, the third option, an independent Kashmir consisting of both Pakistani and Indian Kashmir, was forgotten in the 1949 UN resolution.[5] Such a solution may today be acceptable to Pakistan, but probably not to India. Yet, Indian Kashmir remains mostly Sunni Islamic. Indian Jammu has a population consisting of approximately 35 percent Sunni Muslims, the rest being Hindus. India also controls the comparatively small Ladakh, which has a population (small in actual numbers) of which more than half are Buddhists and 46 percent are Shia Muslims. The question of the future status of Kashmir will thus be difficult to resolve, even if India would ever allow the oft-demanded plebiscite. A further complication is that Kashmir (the portion currently held by India) is important for its water resources, being the source of all important rivers in the region.[6]

For Pakistan, Kashmir is an emotional issue. The demand for a separate homeland for the Muslims of British India was first proposed by Chaudhuri Rahmat Ali in 1933. He envisaged a "PAKstan" for the Muslims, taking its name from the initial letters in the three main provinces of Punjab, Afghan Province (better known as the North-West Frontier Province), and Kashmir. The initial letters of the provinces of Sind and Baluchistan were not used.[7] Pakistan can also be translated from Urdu as "Land of the Pure."[8]

Pakistan and India fought their second war over Kashmir in August–September 1965. The Pakistani leadership had devised a plan in which Maj. Gen. Akhtar Hussain Malik would command task forces to enter Kashmir secretly in early August and gain the support of the discontented population that would declare for Pakistan. The plan failed in various ways, notably the fact that the Pakistani forces had not bothered to make advance contact with the Muslim political leaders in Kashmir, who were not at all inclined to side with Pakistan. Then the Pakistani government replaced General Malik in the middle of the operation, causing further confusion. In retaliation, on 6 September, Indian army columns moved toward Lahore, where, incredibly, the local Pakistani troops had not been alerted that India might invade. A third column crossed into

West Punjab towards Sialkot, and the Indian air force bombed
Pakistani air bases. A Pakistani counteroffensive failed, losing nearly 100 tanks. China secretly offered Pakistan unconditional support,
on the understanding that Pakistan would be prepared to fight an
extended war. However, Pakistan was already beaten, and a UN-
imposed cease-fire came into force on 22 September 1965.[9]

The third war between India and Pakistan was fought in 1971,
resulting in the break-up of Pakistan, which until then also had
encompassed the territory of Bengali East Pakistan (present
Bangladesh). On 16 December 1971, the Pakistani armed forces
there surrendered at Dhaka, and Bangladesh eventually was made
an independent country.[10]

In 1999, Pakistani and Indian soldiers fought each other in a
fourth bitter conflict between the two countries. Hostilities were
initiated by a major Pakistani intrusion, planned and led by the current Pakistani president, Pervez Musharraf, into the remote Kargil
region of Kashmir. Nearly 1,200 combatants died before the fighting ended.[11]

Kashmiri Separatism
After the 1947 war, little happened in Kashmir for two
decades. Although the leading Kashmiri activists, Muhammad
Saraf, Sardar Qayum Khan, and Ghulam Abbas, had already
formed the Kashmir Liberation Movement in 1958 with the intent
of crossing into Indian Kashmir, the Pakistani government, not
wishing to provoke India, reacted by detaining hundreds of
activists, including Ghulam Abbas.[12] However, in 1965, at the time
of the second war between India and Pakistan, some Kashmiri
nationalists, including Amanullah Khan and Maqbool Butt (who
had first come to Pakistan in 1958) formed a new party in Azad
Kashmir known as the Plebiscite Front. Inspired by the Algerian
struggle for independence, the party established an armed wing
called the Jammu and Kashmir National Liberation Front. In June
1966, Butt returned to the Kashmir valley, where he spent four
months organising secret cells and training locals in sabotage, until
he was arrested by Indian security forces in September 1966. He

was sentenced to death in September 1968 but escaped and fled to Azad Kashmir in January 1969.[13]

The tactics used have remained unchanged since then. Kashmiri militants have attacked Indian political, military, and administrative targets in ambushes and hit-and-run raids, typically at night. Most of their targets have been in Indian Kashmir. They have attempted to disrupt Indian rule through bombings, attacks on military patrols and police, and the cutting of communications.[14]

From 1970 on, protests, demonstrations, and systematic violence became increasingly common in the Vale of Kashmir. India blamed a shadowy group known as *Al-Fatah* (The Conquest), which supposedly was working for Pakistan. In January 1971, an Indian passenger airliner was hijacked by two Kashmiris and diverted to Lahore (Maqbool Butt, almost certainly falsely, claimed responsibility for the hijacking). In 1976, Butt returned to Kashmir and was again captured and imprisoned. This time he could not escape. Amanullah Khan, on the other hand, soon afterwards moved to Britain. Because Britain had proscribed organisations that advocated armed struggle, Amanullah Khan renamed his organisation the Jammu and Kashmir Liberation Front (JKLF). For 10 years the renamed organisation operated out of Birmingham, Amanullah Khan's place of residence.[15]

By 1984, the Kashmir Liberation Army, believed to be associated with the JKLF, was active in Kashmir, with the objective, among others, of getting Butt released in exchange for the victim of a desperate last-minute kidnapping. This attempt failed, however, and Butt was executed on 11 February 1984.[16]

Although the situation in the Vale of Kashmir was volatile and resistance to the Indian presence was common, the situation had not yet developed into widespread armed hostilities. However, all this changed with the elections of 23 March 1987, widely claimed to have been rigged by India, which led to renewed armed insurgency, especially after 1988. By then, Amanullah Khan had returned to Pakistan. (In 1985 he had been arrested in Britain and charged with the possession of illegal chemicals that the prosecution alleged could be turned into explosives but that Amanullah claimed were to be used as insecticides. Although acquitted in September 1986, he was deported three months later, possibly due to pressure from India. If so, the Indians had made a strategic error. In Pakistan, Amanullah Khan linked up with four young Kashmiris belonging to the Srinagar-based Islamic Students League to form the new generation of Kashmiri military leaders: Ashfaq Majid Wani, Sheikh Abdul Hamid, Javed Ahmad Mir, and Muhammad Yasin Malik, known collectively as the Haji group. This effectively merged Amanullah Khan's Pakistan-based organisation and supply of arms and training with an organised network among Kashmir's disaffected urban youth.

From May 1987 on, Amanullah Khan began to direct military operations with these men in Indian Kashmir: sniper attacks, bombings, and sabotage became increasingly common. By 1988, a number of resistance factions had emerged in Kashmir, with their members usually referred to as "militants." The JKLF was believed to still be the main group. Political protests became increasingly common, too, showing that the militants had considerable popular support. A general strike took place on 27 October 1988, the anniversary of India's airlift of troops into Srinagar in 1947. A strike was also called for India's Republic Day on 26 January 1989. Many other strikes followed as well. The year 1988 is accordingly regarded as the real beginning of the Kashmir insurgency.[17]

Militant groups were especially active in the towns of Srinagar, Anantnag, Baramula, and Sopore. Most prominent was the JKLF, led locally by the Haji group. However, several local Kashmiri political parties also formed militant wings. Abdul Ghani Lone's People's Conference had links with *Al-Barq* (The Glimmer [of hope]). One faction of Shabir Shah's People's League relied on *Al-Fatah* (led by Zain ul-Abdeen, a contender in the 1987 elections) as its armed wing; the group was different from the Al-Fatah allegedly in operation during the 1970s. Another faction of the People's League formed the armed group *Al-Jihad*. Azam Inquilabi, general secretary of the *Mahaz-e Azadi* (Independence Front), attempted to create a united front for Kashmir's right to self-determination.[18]

Islamic Extremists Hijack the Separatist Movement

Kashmir began to receive its share of the "blowback" from the anti-Soviet jihad in Afghanistan. Some individuals and groups in Kashmir started to advocate an Islamic, as distinct from national, state. New groups also appeared, more Islamic and more militant than those that then formed part of what can be called the mainstream of Kashmiri militancy. Such groups were generally formed in Pakistan, often with Pakistani veterans of the Afghan jihad as key leaders. The Allah Tigers attacked video shops and beauty salons for being un-Islamic. Most important became the *Hizb ul-Mujahidin* (Mujahidin Party), founded in 1989 in Sopore by Ahsan Dar (eventually arrested in India) but currently led by Syed Salahuddin (real name Muhammad Yusuf Khan). It was for most of the 1990s Kashmir's largest insurgent group with from 1,000 to 1,200 members in Kashmir, led by the group's military leader Abdul Majid Dar. The Hizb ul-Mujahidin was established by the ISI and the mass movement *Jamaat-e Islami* as a pro-Pakistani movement to compete with the JKLF. The Hizb ul-Mujahidin, doubtless a Wahhabi organisation, was in Kashmir regarded as the militant wing of the Pakistani Jamaat-e Islami. Pakistan also became the home of the United Jihad Council, a charitable organisation set up in 1990 to support the jihad in Kashmir.[19]

Another Pakistani Wahhabi organisation, which after 1993 became increasingly active in Kashmir, was *Lashkar-e Tayyiba* (Army of the Pure). The early 1990s, in fact, saw numerous new small groups, all believed to favour unification with Pakistan. Among them were groups with names that suggested links with the Middle East such as *Hizbullah* (Party of God), *Ikhwan ul-Muslimin* (Muslim Brotherhood), *Al-Umar Mujahidin* (Mujahidin of Caliph Umar, still active in early 2001), *Hizb ul-Muminin* (Party of Believers), and *Tehrik ul-Mujahidin* (Movement of Mujahidin).[20] Other groups established at this time were *Al-Hadith* (The Prophetic Tradition), established in 1994; *Karwan-e Khalid* (Caravan of Mercy); *Hezb-e Islami* (Party of Islam); and *Mujahidin-e Jammu wa Kashmir* (Mujahidin of Jammu and Kashmir).[21] By 1990, India claimed to have identified more than

46 camps throughout Azad Kashmir, and the existence of the camps was not disputed by Kashmiri militants.[22]

Within a few years, differences arose between the secular nationalist movements and the Islamic extremist groups, such as the Hizb ul-Mujahidin. Murders of separatist leaders who supported the JKLF took place, and the Islamic extremist groups were the chief suspects. Among the murdered was Mirwaiz Maulvi Farooq, an important pro-Pakistani Kashmiri traditional political leader and the chief preacher at the Jamah Masjid in Srinagar, who was assassinated on 21 May 1990.[23] The JKLF leaders soon found that the Hizb ul-Mujahidin was receiving increased support in Pakistan at their expense. Amanullah Khan complained that his recruits were being diverted, indeed coerced, into joining the Hizb ul-Mujahidin and similar groups. In December 1991, he claimed that the Hizb ul-Mujahidin was killing JKLF members and revealing their hideouts to the Indian security forces. He also began to voice claims for Kashmiri independence outside Pakistan, an activity that made Pakistan briefly detain him along with 300 of his supporters. Nonetheless, for a while these activities increased the popular Kashmiri support for his movement.[24]

In February 1993, more than 30 political parties formed the umbrella organisation known as the All Parties Hurriyat (Freedom) Conference (APHC). A chairman was chosen—by then primarily as a figurehead—Muhammad Umar Farooq, the teenage son of Mirwaiz Maulvi Farooq. More important APHC leaders at this time were Syed Ali Shah Gilani of the Jamaat-e Islami, Abdul Ghani Lone (killed in 2002) of the People's Conference, Maulvi Abbas Ansari of the Liberation Council, and Professor Abdul Ghani of the Muslim Conference, though all of them were under arrest for most of this period. Umar Farooq also assumed his father's position as *mirwaiz* (chief preacher) of the Jamah Masjid. The unifying factor behind the APHC was the demand for Kashmiri self-determination and a plebiscite: some APHC leaders wanted independence, while others wanted unification with Pakistan.[25]

The APHC, however, soon developed increasingly Islamic extremist views, with matters simply decided by whether they were

ISLAMIC EXTREMISM IN KASHMIR

un-Islamic and therefore forbidden. At the same time, the original Kashmiri militants grew increasingly weary of the struggle. The Indian Kashmiri government in 1994 released almost 300 political detainees, including such leaders as Shabir Shah, who had been in prison intermittently for nearly 20 years; Syed Ali Shah Gilani; Abdul Ghani Lone; and Yasin Malik (of the JKLF Haji group). The latter, upon his release in May 1994, renounced armed struggle, offered a unilateral cease-fire, and suggested political negotiations. In 1995, Azam Inquilabi of Operation Balakote left Azad Kashmir, returned to Srinagar, and declared in favour for a political rather than a military solution. In June 1994, the JKLF admitted part of the guilt for the many atrocities committed in the struggle. Some conciliation then appeared to be possible.

The JKLF has since remained dormant, no longer taking part in the conflict. However, by 1993 the JKLF was no longer the main militant movement, its place having been taken by the extremist Hizb ul-Mujahidin. Besides, the JKLF had for all intents and purposes divided into two factions: while Yasin Malik reaffirmed the secular nature of the JKLF, Amanullah Khan continued to operate from Rawalpindi and Muzaffarabad as JKLF chairman *in absentia*. At the end of 1995, Amanullah Khan unilaterally removed Yasin Malik as president of the JKLF. Yasin Malik, equally petulant, retaliated by expelling Amanullah Khan as chairman, and Shabir Ahmed Siddiqi temporarily took over leadership of Amanullah's faction. The Pakistani government, possibly in response to the confused situation, continued to recognise Yasin Malik as the leader of the JKLF.[26]

When the JKLF ceased active involvement in the conflict, there was no longer any question that the Islamic extremist organisations had hijacked the Kashmir insurgency. Due to support from the Pakistani mass organisation Jamaat-e Islami, the Hizb ul-Mujahidin came to dominate the smaller pro-Pakistani groups in the mid-1990s. The Hizb ul-Mujahidin by then had an active strength of 1,000 to 1,200 members inside Kashmir (closer to 2,500 by Indian estimates). Through the Jamaat-e Islami, the Hizb ul-Mujahidin also dominated the APHC. By 1993, the *Harakat ul-Ansar*

(Movement of Helpers) operated alongside the Hizb ul-Mujahidin. Most Arab Afghans fighting in Kashmir by then belonged to the Harakat ul-Ansar. Most were, of course, not Arabs at all but men from Pakistan or Azad Kashmir, and a substantial group also came from Afghanistan. Smaller numbers came from Sudan, Egypt, Lebanon, and probably other Muslim countries.[27] Two other groups, Al-Barq and Al-Jihad, which both remained active in the Doda, Poonch, and Rajauri regions, also operated alongside the Hizb ul-Mujahidin.[28] So did yet another newly formed group: *Tehrik-e Jihad* (Jihad Movement), founded in 1997 and led by Salim Wani, originally a member of the United Jihad Council. The new group, an amalgam of several smaller organisations, was head-quartered in Islamabad and Muzaffarabad.[29]

The APHC remained of little consequence. Its leadership split between two broad factions. Yasin Malik, Abdul Ghani Lone, and Syed Ali Shah Gilani formed one faction; Umar Farooq, Abdul Ghani, Maulvi Abbas Ansari, and Shabir Shah (at least tacitly) the other. In 1996, the Indian government had attempted to form an alternative to the APHC by opening a dialogue with four former militants, including two from the Hizb ul-Mujahidin, as well as Baba Badr, a former chief of the group Muslim *Janbaz*, and Bilal Lodhi, former leader of Al-Barq.[30] Yet, the APHC remains a legal political organisation. In November 1995, it even established an office in New Delhi.[31]

Violence has since continued in Kashmir. On 1 October 2001, terrorists set off a car bomb outside Srinagar State Assembly, then opened fire within the building, killing 38 and wounding about 75.[32] On 21 May 2002, Abdul Ghani Lone, the senior leader of the APHC, was shot dead in Srinagar.[33]

End Notes

1.   Schofield, *Kashmir in the Crossfire*, 141–64.
2.   Schofield, *Kashmir in the Crossfire*, 157, quoting a Commonwealth Relations Office note from 1 December 1947.
3.   Schofield, *Kashmir in the Crossfire*, 3.
4.   Schofield, *Kashmir in the Crossfire*, xii–xiii, 289. For further information, see also

Jaffrelot, *Pakistan;* Sumit Ganguly, *Conflict Unending: India-Pakistan Tensions since 1947* (New York: Columbia University Press, 2001); Edward W. Desmond, "The Insurgency in Kashmir (1989–91)," *Contemporary South Asia* 4:1 (March 1995); Anthony Davis, "The Conflict in Kashmir," *Jane's Intelligence Review* 7:1 (January 1995), 40–46; International Crisis Group (ICG), *Kashmir: Confrontation and Miscalculation* (Islamabad/Brussels, ICG Asia Report 35, 11 July 2002).

5. Schofield, *Kashmir in the Crossfire*, 286.

6. Ahmed, "Pakistan in Crisis."

7. Schofield, *Kashmir in the Crossfire*, 109.

8. Cooley, *Unholy Wars,* 49.

9. Schofield, *Kashmir in the Crossfire*, 201–5.

10. Schofield, *Kashmir in the Crossfire*, 211.

11. Rahul Bedi, "Paying to Keep the High Ground," *Jane's Intelligence Review* 11:10 (October 1999), 27–31.

12. Schofield, *Kashmir in the Crossfire*, 187.

13. Schofield, *Kashmir in the Crossfire*, 208–9.

14. Schofield, *Kashmir in the Crossfire*, 270.

15. Schofield, *Kashmir in the Crossfire*, 210.

16. Schofield, *Kashmir in the Crossfire*, 226.

17. Schofield, *Kashmir in the Crossfire*, 230–4, 237–41; Davis, "Conflict in Kashmir," 44. Ashfaq Majid Wani was killed in March 1990, while Abdul Hamid Wani was killed on 17 April 1998.

18. Schofield, *Kashmir in the Crossfire*, 230–4, 237–41.

19. Belokrenitskiy, "Islamic Radicalism," 104–116; Bergen, *Holy War,* 215–16; Rahul Bedi, "Kashmir's Future," *Jane's Intelligence Review* 7:7 (July 1995), 6–9; Roger Howard, "Evolving Rather Than Receding, the Killing in Kashmir Continues," *Jane's Intelligence Review* 11:1 (January 1999), 39–42; Bedi, "Clashes in Kashmir," 30–33; Anthony Davis, "Decision-Time for Pakistan as Kashmir Conflict Threatens," *Jane's Intelligence Review* 12:5 (May 2000), 30–32; Bedi, "Kashmir Peace Talks," 34–7. For the various border disputes, see Rahul Bedi, "India's Borders Prove Hard to Pin Down," *Jane's Intelligence Review* 13:10 (October 2001), 28–31.

20. Schofield, *Kashmir in the Crossfire*, 230–4, 237–41.

21. The last three, and Hizb ul-Muminin, were apparently banned in Pakistan in early 2001. Jane's World Insurgency and Terrorism 13, 28 November 2001.

22. Schofield, *Kashmir in the Crossfire*, 249.

23. Schofield, *Kashmir in the Crossfire*, 247.

24. Schofield, *Kashmir in the Crossfire*, 249–54.
25. Schofield, *Kashmir in the Crossfire*, 249–54.
26. Schofield, *Kashmir in the Crossfire*, 259–62, 267–9.
27. Schofield, *Kashmir in the Crossfire*, 272.
28. Jane's Sentinel: Pakistan, 31 July 2001; Belokrenitskiy, "Islamic Radicalism," 104–116; Schofield, *Kashmir in the Crossfire*, 269.
29. Bergen, *Holy War*, 215–16; Howard, "Evolving Rather Than Receding," 41.
30. Schofield, *Kashmir in the Crossfire*, 269.
31. Ibid., 293.
32. *Washington Post,* 2 October 2001, referring to Associated Press, 1 October 2001.
33. PPA, 21 May 2002 (www.MiddleEastWire.com); *Washington Post,* 22 May 2002.

APPENDIX
Islamic Extremism in Yemen

5

Northern Yemen became independent of the Ottoman Empire in November 1918. It was ruled by a mostly hereditary line of *imams*, religious leaders. Its relations with neighbouring states were mostly hostile. Border disputes soon led to a conflict with Britain, which as early as 1839 had set up a protectorate around the strategically important port of Aden. In 1933–1934, Yemen also fought and lost a war with Saudi Arabia, ceding the provinces of Najran, Asir, and Jizan.

Yemen's tribal structure could not keep up with the times. Internal unrest grew, culminating in a coup in the capital San'a on 26 September 1962 by young military officers with a revolutionary leftist orientation, who proclaimed a people's republic. This resulted in a period of civil war and tribal rebellions; after 1962 the leftists received the support of what grew to be a 70,000-strong Egyptian expeditionary military force, while the followers of the traditional line of imams received support from Saudi Arabia. For all purposes, it was a proxy war fought between Egypt and Saudi Arabia. However, the Egyptians pulled out following their defeat in the Six-Day War against Israel in June 1967, and a new regime assumed power in Yemen, this time based on the military power of the tribes. Further fighting followed, however, as members of the royal family (who wanted to revive the hereditary imam-dominated structure) continued to receive support in the form of materiel and gold from Saudi Arabia. Both republicans and royalists depended on the constantly shifting allegiances of the tribes. The war only ended when the imam and the princes, finally out-maneouvred by their opponents, went into exile in 1970.[1]

In 1978, Lt. Col. Ali Abdullah Salih (born 1942), the chief of staff, assumed power in Yemen. President Salih, of the powerful Hashid tribe, survived a number of assassination attempts and eventually succeeded in establishing a stable government.

The British protectorate in south Yemen developed in a similarly tortuous way. When Britain pulled out of south Arabia in November 1967 after years of Marxist-inspired insurgency, North Yemen (known as the Yemen Arab Republic) suddenly found itself the neighbour of newly independent South Yemen. The latter's leaders, after developing close relations with the Soviet Union and China, turned South Yemen into a virulently revolutionary, Marxist-Maoist nation, which soon became known as the People's Republic of South Yemen. Aden became the main Soviet naval base in the Middle East, and the country was renamed the People's Democratic Republic of Yemen in November 1970, in effect claiming to represent northern Yemen as well.

South Yemen had poor relations with most of its neighbours. Saudi Arabia, already involved in northern Yemen, early on claimed the Hadhramaut region of southeastern Yemen and at first refused to recognise South Yemen. By 1965, leftist guerrillas of what was to grow into the Popular Front for the Liberation of the Occupied Arab Gulf rebelled in the neighbouring principality of Oman. Within a few years, it became clear that they were operating out of South Yemen and receiving substantial South Yemeni support. Their ultimate goal may have been to overthrow not only the government of Oman but most of the Persian Gulf principalities. The revolt simmered on, while Oman received military support from Britain, the United States, Iran, and Jordan. In 1975, South Yemen was forced to cease its support to the rebels, who then soon faded from the scene.[2]

Clashes between the two Yemens, both of which claimed the other's territory, soon escalated. The conflict was further aggravated by tribal and border disputes, as well as what appears to have been a massive exodus of hundreds of thousands of Yemenis from the south to the north. In September 1972, the continuing rivalry led to a short war. In February 1979, another short war (known as the Ten-Day War) broke out. Yet, despite the many grievances and occasional military clashes, eventually the two closely related countries in theory agreed to merge. They were formally unified as the Republic of Yemen on 22 May 1990.[3]

However, the unification took place in an atmosphere of increased violence and numerous killings.[4] While the south, and in particular the port of Aden, to some extent still remained secular, the north was a hotbed of Islamic extremism. In fact, during the Afghan war against the Soviet Union, Yemen was one of the primary sources of Arab Afghan volunteers. After unification, the northern elite had assumed all positions of power, much to the chagrin of the southerners. Among the considerably more secular southerners, feelings of being discriminated against, as well as traditional tribal rivalries, led to the establishment of a southern secessionist movement in April 1994. The northern and southern armies had not yet been amalgamated, and serious fighting involving air and tank units broke out. The southerners, under Gen. Ibrahim al-Bidh in Aden, declared a new Democratic Republic of Yemen in May 1994, but received only limited foreign support, primarily from Saudi Arabia. In the north, the situation was different. Perhaps as many as 2,000 battle-hardened Arab Afghans had returned to northern Yemen, and some had brought comrades from other Muslim countries as well.[5] Upon their return, President Salih recruited them and like-minded fighters from throughout the Arab world to fight a jihad against the ungodly south.[6] In addition, Usamah bin Ladin and Al-Qaida, which maintained a camp in Mudiyah, Abyan Province,[7] began to move weapons and money into the country.[8] The importance of the Al-Qaida support, if any, is hard to gauge. An estimated third of bin Ladin's recruits at this time were believed to be Yemenis. In Yemen, there were also many refugees, including some 80,000 Somalis and 38,000 Arabs from Palestine, Sudan, and Iraq who formed a pool of ready recruits for Al-Qaida.[9] The northern military already had significantly more manpower than its southern rival but the southern forces benefitted from high morale and a more efficient air force and navy.[10] But the war was largely fought on the ground. By July 1994, the northern army had defeated its southern rival and successfully bombarded and invaded the city of Aden. (The Arab Afghans promptly burned down the country's only brewery.)[11]

Having won the war, President Salih introduced legal reforms, strongly influenced by Islamic law (which was regarded as "the source" of the new legislation). He appointed Sheikh Abdul Majid al-Zindani, the founder of the Muslim Brotherhood in Yemen and an Arab Afghan, as presidential counsellor. He carefully moulded the tribal areas of Yemen into strongholds of Islamic extremism through the political vehicle of the extremists, the *Islah* (Reform) Party, established in 1990.[12]

Smaller extremist groups, too, found a haven in Yemen. For instance, around 1993 bin Ladin assisted Tariq al-Fadhli, the son of the deposed sultan of Abyan, in founding the Yemeni Islamic Jihad movement. There was nothing clandestine about the establishment of this movement; it was part of the Yemeni government's integration of Arab Afghans into the armed forces.[13] Fadhli himself was an Arab Afghan who had spent about two years fighting the Soviets.[14] However, he had also organised the bombings of Aden's best hotels, the Mövenpick Aden and Golden Moor, on 29 December 1992, killing a tourist and a hotel worker. The bombs were in fact aimed at U.S. servicemen in Aden, Yemen, who had been billeted in the hotels to support UN relief operations in Somalia and had already departed. Almost simultaneously, a small group of men allegedly trained by Al-Qaida was caught at Aden airport carrying RPG-7 rocket launchers and preparing to fire rockets at U.S. military transport aircraft parked nearby. Usamah bin Ladin was linked to the attacks.[15] The Yemeni government responded by sending an armored brigade against Fadhli's hereditary mountain fortress. He surrendered on 8 January 1993. Another

Arab Afghan, Fadhli's deputy Jamal al-Nahdi, was also allegedly involved in the attacks. However, with the foundation of Yemeni Islamic Jihad, all was forgiven. President Salih soon appointed Fadhli a member of his personally selected consultative council, and Fadhli's sister married into President Salih's family (she married Gen. Ali Muhsin al-Ahmer, more of whom below). Nahdi is currently a respected businessman in San'a and a member of the permanent committee of Yemen's ruling party.[16]

The most active Islamic extremist group in Yemen has since been the *Jaish Aden Abin al-Islami* (Aden-Abyan Islamic Army, AAIA), founded sometime in 1997 as an offshoot of the Yemeni Islamic Jihad. Apparently disillusioned with the legitimate political process, the AAIA aims to establish an Islamic state in Yemen. The AAIA was founded by an Arab Afghan and probable Al-Qaida trainee, Zain al-Abdin Abu Bakar al-Mihdar, but better known as Abu Hassan. The Yemeni government, however, has accused Sheikh Abu Hamza al-Masri, based in London, of being the AAIA's spiritual and organisational leader. He certainly was the group's spiritual leader, and he may well have played some part in the formation and operations of Abu Hassan's group. Abu Hamza (real name Mustafa Kamal) was born in Egypt in 1958. He graduated in civil engineering from Brighton University in 1986 but then became a cleric based in the Finsbury Park Mosque in northern London, where he in 1993 set up an organisation known as *Ansar al-Shariah* (Supporters of Sharia, or sometimes Partisans of Sharia). The AAIA was hardly noticed until 1998, when the group threatened to attack U.S. interests in Yemen in retaliation for the U.S. cruise missile attacks against suspected Al-Qaida targets, yet it was probably active during most of the 1990s. The group, which contained a few Arab Afghans and several less motivated local men, has since committed a number of kidnappings, several of which resulted in the death of the victims, and a number of bombings in Yemen. The group has probably maintained contacts with other Yemeni extremist groups, including "Muhammad's Army" and the "Islamic Deterrence Force," as well as Al-Qaida. Yemen also claims that Abu Hamza's Supporters of Sharia is behind the AAIA. In

December 1998, the Yemeni government charged five British Muslims with entering the country to carry out acts of terrorism and claimed that Abu Hamza had sent the men to join the AAIA. In 1999, Yemeni security forces arrested and quickly executed the entire known AAIA leadership. This, incidentally but perhaps not coincidentally, removed any chance of determining the veracity of an offered testimony that Gen. Ali Muhsin al-Ahmer, a relative of President Salih who reportedly met bin Ladin in Afghanistan at some point during the 1980s, also was involved in the group. The AAIA survived, however, and in October 2000, the group claimed involvement in the bombing of the USS *Cole*.[17] Assets of the AAIA in the United States have since been frozen.[18]

From 1994 to 1997, President Salih's General People's Congress (GPC) governed in coalition with Sheikh Abdullah bin Hussain al-Ahmar's Islah. However, President Salih, not himself an Islamic extremist, successfully pushed through a law that allowed women to vote in parliamentary elections. Perhaps in part because of this reform, the GPC in the April 1997 legislative election won a landslide victory, allowing Salih to end the coalition with Islah. However, Islah under Sheikh Abdul Majid al-Zindani remains Yemen's largest opposition party and controls 64 out of 301 seats in parliament, retains a military wing, and has members in the Political Security Office (the intelligence service) and the army.[19]

The GPC victory was probably fortunate for Yemen. It enabled Salih to begin military cooperation with the United States as early as autumn 1998, when U.S. special forces began to train the Yemeni army.[20] U.S. military advisers were brought in to train the Yemeni coastguard and security forces. The FBI also maintains a presence in Yemen.[21] At the outbreak of the U.S. War on Terror, Salih pledged to help the United States to suppress Al-Qaida, and Yemeni special forces rounded up dozens of suspected foreign Islamic extremists. These were deported to such countries as Egypt, Saudi Arabia, Sudan, and Algeria.[22] Some observers believe that President Salih cooperates with the United States merely as a way to enhance his power and turn Yemen into a one-party state.[23] On 18 December 2001, Yemeni armed forces, includ-

ing helicopters and tanks, attacked tribal forces in the central
Marib and Shabwah regions after local leaders of the Jalal tribe
had refused to hand over five suspected Al-Qaida members, some
of whom were suspected of having taken part in the attack on the
Cole. The battles resulted in the death of at least a dozen people.[24]

By late March 2002, U.S. and British troops began three
months of military exercises with Yemeni forces in the remote
Hadhramaut region, near areas where Al-Qaida fighters and other
Islamic extremists were expected to enjoy considerable support. In
preparation of this deployment, in mid-March a U.S. 20-member
special forces team arrived in Yemen to coordinate U.S. military
assistance and training. Another 30 U.S. military instructors were
due to arrive at the end of March 2002.[25]

Meanwhile, Yemen's relations with Saudi Arabia have at times
remained tense. There is some evidence that Saudi Arabia encouraged insurgents in South Yemen in the early 1980s.[26] During the
1990 Persian Gulf crisis, recently unified Yemen took what the
international community regarded as a tacit stand for Iraq rather
than Saudi Arabia, although Yemen refrained from actively assisting Iraq. Saudi Arabia retaliated by expelling about 800,000
Yemeni workers and introduced economic sanctions. At other
times, such as 1995, clashes along the frontier have taken place. In
June 2000, Saudi Arabia and Yemen agreed to a delimitation of
their common border, though final demarcation required adjust-
ments based on tribal considerations. And Yemen could conceivably
challenge Saudi Arabia, politically and militarily, for hegemony in
the Arabian Peninsula. Besides, Yemen contains a sizeable Shia
minority—which in Saudi eyes brings the horror of a southern
neighbour at some point siding with Iran in the rivalry for the
hearts and minds of Islam.[27]

End Notes

1.   When no other source is given, this section is based on Sela, *Political Encyclopedia,*
     652–3, 682–6, 800–808; Cooley, *Unholy Wars,* 117, 122–4. See also *Intelligence
     Newsletter* 309 (17 April 1997), 6–7.

2.   Cooley, *Unholy Wars,* 95; Sela, *Political Encyclopedia,* 577, 618.

3. See also James Wyllie, "Saudi Arabia's Other Front," *Jane's Intelligence Review* 4:6 (June 1992), 265–8.

4. Joseph Kostiner, *Yemen: The Tortuous Quest for Unity, 1990–94* (London: Royal Institute of International Affairs), 1996.

5. Sue Lackey, "Yemen: Unlikely Key to Western Security," *Jane's Intelligence Review* 11:7 (July 1999), 24–9, on 26.

6. *Economist,* 16 February 2002.

7. Lackey, "Yemen," 26.

8. Cooley, *Unholy Wars,* 122. See also *Intelligence Newsletter* 366 (23 September 1999), 7.

9. Lackey, "Yemen," 27.

10. For a comparison and evaluation of the two military forces, see Kostiner, *Yemen,* 79–85.

11. Cooley, *Unholy Wars,* 124; Bergen, *Holy War,* 174.

12. *Economist,* 16 February 2002.

13. Bodansky, *Bin Laden,* 374.

14. Cooley, *Unholy Wars,* 123–4; Bergen, *Holy War,* 173.

15. Reeve, *New Jackals.* 182; Bergen, *Holy War,* 172.

16. Bergen, *Holy War,* 173.

17. Lackey, "Yemen;" Reeve, *New Jackals,* 211–12; Bergen, *Holy Wars,* 176–83 (General Ahmer's alleged involvement: 183).

18. *New York Times,* 25 September 2001.

19. *Economist,* 16 February 2002.

20. Lackey, "Yemen."

21. *Economist,* 16 February 2002.

22. *Washington Post,* 19 December 2001, 2 January 2002.

23. *Economist,* 16 February 2002.

24. *Washington Post,* 19 December 2001, 2 January 2002.

25. *Washington Post,* 2 March 2002; John Pike, www.globalsecurity.org.

26. See, for instance, Bodansky, *Bin Laden,* 13. Bodansky's assertion of Usamah bin Ladin's participation seems less well founded.

27. See, for instance, James Wyllie, "Perpetual Tensions: Saudi Arabia and Yemen," *Jane's Intelligence Review* 7:3 (March 1995), 118–19.

Islamic Extremism in Sudan

6

The Muslim Brotherhood had already established a substantial presence in Sudan by the late 1940s, before the country acquired independence in 1956. The organisation became a leading force in Sudanese politics during the 1970s and formed part of the government in 1977. The Muslim Brotherhood acquired loyal supporters and key positions throughout Sudanese society, including the military. In 1983, Islamic law was introduced in Sudan, including the non-Muslim south (although this decision was subsequently suspended). This provoked further enmity from the south, where an already ongoing civil war had re-erupted shortly before the hotly disputed legal reform.[1] Sudan has for decades been in a state of civil war between the Islamic northern government, supported by the Muslim Arab population, and the predominantly black, Christian and animist south, which continues to resist the imposition of an Islamic state. It is estimated that the war and its associated famines have resulted in at least 1.5 million deaths, as well as millions of refugees.[2]

Since 1964, the Muslim Brotherhood in Sudan had been headed by Sheikh Hassan Abdullah al-Turabi, who was born in February 1932 in Kassala, a city on the border between Sudan and Eritrea. (One of his ancestors had proclaimed himself *mahdi*, or

spiritual guide, in the 17th century.) After studies in the Sudanese
capital of Khartoum and in London, Turabi graduated from the
Sorbonne in 1964. Back in Sudan, he was jailed in 1969 but was
released after seven years and appointed attorney general by the
same president who had imprisoned him. In the early 1980s, Turabi
married the sister of Sadiq al-Mahdi, who conveniently seized
power in April 1985.[3] In the same year, Turabi and the most powerful elements of the Muslim Brotherhood formed a new political
wing of the brotherhood called the National Islamic Front (NIF),
which eventually grew into the largest political party in Sudan.[4]
However, Turabi entertained higher ambitions. On 30 June 1989, a
military junta with an Islamic orientation led by Lt. Gen. Omar
Hassan Ahmad al-Bashir seized power from Sadiq al-Mahdi in a
military coup widely believed to have been engineered by Turabi,
who henceforth became the main supporter of the new regime.
Turabi made sure that the government was dominated by members
of the NIF.[5] The Bashir government, no doubt with the active help
of Turabi, activated the Popular Defense Forces (PDF), tribal militias of young Muslim fanatics as well as semi-autonomous units of
mujahidin, to assist the army against the non-Muslim, black southern insurgents.[6] Bashir assumed the post of president on 16
October 1993, retained power through several transitional governments, and was even elected president in March 1996.[7]

In April 1991, Turabi, along with some 50 other Islamic movements in Africa and Asia, established a new pan-Islamic body
named the Popular Arabic Islamic Conference.[8] He aimed to build
an alternative to the worldwide Muslim Brotherhood, which to his
regret remained dominated by Egyptian leaders. In 1992, Usamah
bin Ladin and many Arab Afghans loyal to him moved to
Khartoum, where he already had several business interests. They
were all welcomed by Turabi.[9] Many Egyptian Arab Afgans ended
up in Sudan, where Turabi, with bin Ladin's logistical support, was
conducting a violent jihad against the southern part of the country.
The Egyptians also found Sudan useful as a base for their own
activities back home.[10] And many Arab Afghans ended up in the
camps of the PDF.[11]

With Turabi as the power behind the military regime, Sudanese intelligence organs developed intimate ties with Al-Qaida. On at least one occasion, there was a planned but never executed second New York bombing for 1993 for which Sheikh Omar Abdul Rahman was indicted, and Sudanese diplomats (Siraj Yousef and a certain Muhammad) were directly involved in further acts of terrorism. For instance, they conspired to assassinate Egyptian President Hosni Mubarak at the time of his visit to New York in 1993, and a Sudanese intelligence officer in 1997 was working out of the Washington offices of the America Muslim Council, a large American Muslim organisation.[12]

The relations between Sudanese President Bashir and the Islamic extremists, though mutually profitable, gradually deteriorated. In May 1996, the UN Security Council imposed sanctions on Sudan, including a travel ban, to force Bashir to extradite three Egyptian extremists suspected of complicity in the attempted assassination of Hosni Mubarak in Ethiopia in June of the previous year. (the United Nations also suspected official Sudanese involvement in the attempt).[13] In early March 1996, Bashir was willing to comply, and to turn over Usamah bin Ladin as well, to the United States or Saudi Arabia. However, neither was willing to take him.[14] Usamah bin Ladin instead left Sudan for Afghanistan in 1996, and the United States imposed its own sanctions in November 1997.[15] Sudan has since cooperated with U.S. intelligence covertly, although little was made public until late September 2001, and the Sudanese government still seems to be reluctant to admit any cooperation to its domestic audience.[16]

In March of 1996, Turabi had become speaker of the National Assembly. This took place against the background of rumours of growing disagreements between Bashir and Turabi. In 1999, Sudan began exporting oil.[17] With the resultant new revenues, President Bashir no doubt felt less dependent on the Islamic extremists. On 12 December 1999, Bashir decisively moved against Turabi by dismissing the entire National Assembly.[18] The following year, he also manoeuvred Turabi out of government (on 27 June 2000, Turabi attempted to hold on to power by founding a new party, but this availed him little). On 23 February 2001, Bashir had Turabi put under house arrest.[19]

Sudan may still sponsor and train Islamic extremists for the PDF, but in far smaller numbers than when Usamah bin Ladin had stayed in Khartoum. The United States has no embassy in Sudan, which is one of the countries on the State Department's list of states that sponsor terrorism.[20]

The government of Sudan, however, has continued to cooperate with the United States in the War on Terror. In September 2001, Sudan reportedly arrested about 30 suspected associates of bin Ladin. As a reward, the UN travel ban was lifted on 28 September 2001. Sudan still aims to take control of the non-Muslim south, and it may eventually succeed because the oil revenues can be used to re-equip the Sudanese army. However, the Islamisation of the army, seen through by Turabi before he was ousted, has overburdened it with officers who may be pure in faith but remain poorly trained. As for the conscripts, they seem to find increasingly less interest in the jihad against the infidel south. Peace is unlikely to come soon.[21]

End Notes

1. Where no other source is given, this section is based on Sela, *Political Encyclopedia,* 374, 544, 692–5, 745–7.
2. Paul Harris, "Cycle of Conflict Continues in Sudan," *Jane's Intelligence Review* 10:10 (October 1998), 42–6, which also describes the civil war and the south in additional detail.
3. Bodansky, *Bin Laden,* 32–3; Jacquard, *Osama Bin Laden,* 30.
4. Sela, *Political Encyclopedia,* 374, 544, 692–5, 745–7; Bodansky, *Bin Laden,* 32–3; Jacquard, *Osama Bin Laden,* 30.
5. See, for instance, *Washington Post,* 10 December 2001; Cooley, *Unholy Wars,* 120; CIA, *World Factbook 2001;* Sela, *Political Encyclopedia,* 165–6, 746.
6. Sela, *Political Encyclopedia,* 693.
7. CIA, *World Factbook 2001.*
8. Jacquard, *Osama Bin Laden,* 31.
9. Sela, *Political Encyclopedia,* 746; Cooley, *Unholy Wars,* 120; Frank Smyth, "Culture Clash: Bin Laden, Khartoum and the War against the West," *Jane's Intelligence Review* 10:10 (October 1998), 22–5.

10. Cooley, *Unholy Wars,* 183–4.
11. Cooley, *Unholy Wars,* 211.
12. Mylroie, *War Against America,* 191–2; Emerson, *American Jihad,* 142–4.
13. Sela, *Political Encyclopedia,* 696–7; *Economist,* 6 October 2001.
14. *Washington Post,* 3 October 2001.
15. *Economist,* 22 September 2001; Harris, "Cycle of Conflict," 46.
16. See, for instance, *Economist,* 6 October 2001.
17. CIA, *World Factbook 2001.*
18. CIA, *World Factbook 2001;* Sela, *Political Encyclopedia,* 166.
19. See, for instance, Jacquard, *Osama Bin Laden,* 33; *Economist,* 6 October 2001.
20. Reeve, *New Jackals,* 230; *Economist,* 22 September 2001. See also Harris, "Cycle of Conflict."
21. *Washington Post,* 29 September 2001; *Economist,* 6 October 2001.

APPENDIX

Islamic Extremism in Somalia

7

Although Al-Qaida has a base of supporters in Somalia, the major Somali contribution to the Islamic extremist movement was the de facto victory over the United States and the United Nations in 1993 by an Islamic warlord, Muhammad Farah Hassan Aidid. In addition, many of the combat techniques that were developed in the Somali clan wars from 1994 on also became characteristic of the Taliban in Afghanistan. This was most clearly shown in the tactical use of four-wheel-drive pickup trucks mounted with antiaircraft guns and other automatic support weapons, a military innovation pioneered in Somalia. Arab Afghans therefore appear to have formed a significant, if not necessarily very large, component of the fighting force in Somalia.[1]

The developments in Somalia in many ways mirrored those of Afghanistan. An often nomadic and fundamentally clan-based society, Somalia had little in the ways of national ethnic identity and was formed from the merging of British and Italian Somaliland into an independent Somali Republic on 1 July 1960. From late 1969 until early 1991, Somalia was ruled as a one-party state by the powerful Gen. Muhammad Siad Barre. Somalia remained severely underdeveloped, but Barre managed to take advantage of Somalia's strategic importance in the Cold War. He received huge amounts of aid and military supplies first from the Soviet Union, then—after the Soviets in 1977 switched support to rivalling Ethiopia—the United States. As in Afghanistan, the government relied on the arms supplies and the manipulation of clan rivalry to keep the country calm. As in Afghanistan, the government kept the clans quiet by distributing weapons and other perquisites to those affiliated with the clan of Siad Barre.

Unfortunately for Barre, the end of the Cold War also signified the end of the generous arms and aid handouts. Civil war erupted in the 1980s and grew increasingly problematic. In 1989, Barre was challenged by a group called the United Somali Congress, led by the warlord Aidid and recipient of military aid from Libya. On 26 January 1991, Barre was forced out of the capital, Mogadishu. What little remained of national government and state institutions fell apart within months. The clan rivalry prompted violent struggles between clans, factions, and sub-clans throughout the country. Two Hawiye clan warlords, Ali Mahdi Muhammad and General Aidid, fought each other for control of Mogadishu, with neither being able to push out the other. In May 1991, northern Somalia (the administrative regions of Awdal, Woqooyi Galbeed, Togdheer, Sanaag, and Sool) declared independence as the Republic of Somaliland, which in a few years managed to form a comparatively stable government. Eventually, two neighbouring regions (Bari and Nugaal) did likewise as the self-declared Republic of Puntland. Neither was recognised by foreign governments. Internationally recognised southern Somalia, meanwhile, reverted to what can only be described as constant tribal war. Hundreds of thousands of Somalis fled to refugee camps in Kenya and Ethiopia or crossed the sea to Yemen. Those with substantial wealth flew to Western Europe, the United States, and Canada to claim refugee status.

By April 1992, the international community decided to attempt to rebuild a national government in Somalia, prompted by widespread starvation caused by war and drought, a major refugee problem, and the consistent lack of national Somalian authority. By then, southern Somalia had lost all traces of the formal local, regional, or national government and the various southern clans and subclans showed no interest in any superior government. The armed forces in the country included nine major ethnic-based factions, many of which included substantial numbers of former Somali Army soldiers, and numerous smaller armed gangs aligned with the factions or operating on their own. The largest Somali force, and also the one that controlled most territory among the numerous factions, was the loosely organised alliance under Aidid. The large number of mutually hostile factions, combined with the general lack of infrastructure, doomed the international intervention from the outset. The fundamental problem, the fact that there was no national leadership but merely a number of divided clans that constantly battled each other, remained unsolved. The international intervention, known as UNOSOM (United Nations Operation in Somalia), never succeeded in pacifying the country, and the relief work brought its own series of miscalculations. A major mistake was that aid workers early on hired armed Somalis (referred to as "technical assistance" or "technicals") for protection of foreign personnel as well as relief convoys and supplies. Since these men invariably came from the armed contingents of local warlords and gang leaders and owed their allegiance to them rather than the aid workers, the protection operation was in all but name a protection racket. It soon became impossible for the aid agencies to get rid of these gangsters, whose looting, stealing, and extortion of relief supplies in exchange for the use of vehicles and armed guards simply increased.

Although regular military support weapons in the form of tanks and artillery remained in common use, the most innovative weapon—and the one that formed the backbone of most Somali forces—was what soon became known as the "technical" (named after the armed Somalis hired by aid workers). This was a four-wheel-drive pickup truck mounted with antiaircraft guns or other automatic weapons.

Due to the already severe situation in conjunction with the poorly executed relief effort, between 300,000 and 500,000 Somalis died by December 1992 and some 1.5 million were refugees within or outside the country, out of an estimated prewar population of 7.5 million. The resulting media outcry resulted in a new, reorganised, and much increased (although strictly time-limited) UN intervention in Somalia, the Unified Task Force (UNITAF). In December 1992, more than 38,000 troops from more than 20 countries, including 28,000 U.S. troops, were sent to Somalia under the command of U.S. Army Lt. Gen. Robert Johnston. The force was authorised to secure the airfield, seaport, and capital city of Mogadishu, a certain number of towns identified as relief centers (Baidoa, Belet Weyne, Gialassi, and Oddur), and areas in the south that included Bardera, the route from Baidoa to Bardera, the port cities of Kismayo and Merca, and Baledogle, which had one of the largest aircraft runways in Africa. The UN force was also supposed to provide for the transfer of responsibility to a subsequent, presumably smaller UN peacekeeping force. The strong military force was largely successful in pacifying its areas of operations. By January 1993, when a UN conference was held during which some southern Somali leaders agreed to a nationwide cease-fire and general disarmament, there were reported to be almost no weapons visible on the streets of Mogadishu.

The mighty UNITAF left in April 1993, leaving authority to a smaller and militarily much less impressive UN force, UNOSOM II. The southern Somali warlords, who had largely kept quiet during the powerful UNITAF intervention, did not hesitate to reopen hostilities. The UNOSOM II command somewhat naively assumed that because the Somalis had not attacked the powerful UNITAF, they would also respect the weaker UNOSOM II. This was a severe miscalculation. On 5 June 1993, Aidid responded to a UN attempt to seize his radio station and a weapons depot by attacking a peacekeeping force, killing 24 Pakistani UN soldiers. Because of this incident, UNOSOM II increasingly focused on the arrest and detention of Aidid, rather than the safekeeping of what remained of the cease-fire and distribution of humanitarian aid. This caused further confusion. The U.S. components of UNOSOM II saw the capture of Aidid and his lieutenants as their main objective, while other key participants, such as France, Italy, Zimbabwe, and Botswana ordered their forces not to participate but to concentrate on the original objectives of the peacekeeping operation. As a consequence, UNO-

SOM II largely failed. Throughout the summer of 1993, Somali militias continued to fight each other, especially in Mogadishu and the Kismayo area, while a virtual state of war erupted between Aidid and the United Nations. This culminated in the 3 October 1993 clash between Aidid's forces and U.S. units in which 18 U.S. soldiers were killed, 78 wounded, and one taken hostage (over a thousand Somalis were also killed or wounded). Two UH-60 Black Hawk helicopters were shot down, and a third one crashed at the Mogadishu airport. This incident, extensively covered by the media and eventually becoming the inspiration for the movie *Black Hawk Down*, marked the end of the U.S. intervention in Somalia. President Clinton announced that the U.S. forces would leave Somalia by March 1994, and the United States ceased support to the UN operation and began to pull out its forces—as did the other participating member states.

In a 12 November 1993 report by the UN secretary general, it was admitted that the entire peacekeeping operation had largely been a failure and actually had provoked many Somali factions to prepare for a future of renewed fighting. To the surprise of the world, and the glee of Islamic extremists everywhere, the United States—and the United Nations—seemed to have been defeated by a single Muslim Somali warlord. It was also noted that the operation had been largely led by the media. Extensive news coverage of starving Somali children in the fall of 1992 had brought in the powerful UNITAF, while coverage of dead U.S. soldiers being dragged through the streets in the aftermath of the 3 October 1993 clash was the direct cause of the UN withdrawal.

Despite the failure of the UN operation, the international community continued in its attempts to create a government in southern Somalia. In October 2000, at a meeting in Arta, Djibouti, several southern Somali factions eventually managed to create a Transitional National Government (TNG) under President Abdikassim Salad Hassan, with a three-year mandate to create a permanent national Somali government and form a national army out of the many existing militias. The southern TNG also claims the territory of northern Somaliland and Puntland. These, however, remain outside the control of the TNG, which wishes to include the comparatively orderly northern territories in its own unstable southern territory. Yet, despite the several attempts at peacemaking, numerous clan and political conflicts continue in the country, and warlords and factions go on fighting for control of Mogadishu and the other southern regions.[2] Moreover, Islamic influences, some of the extremist variety, are growing increasingly common, partly because of influence from foreign Islamic charities.[3]

General Aidid died in 1996. He was succeeded by his son Hussein Muhammad Aidid, a former U.S. Marine reservist who currently lives in the United States.[4]

British intelligence has since claimed that Usamah bin Ladin (then in Sudan) dispatched Muhammad Atef to Somalia to organise the resistance to the UN forces. In 1992 and 1993, he is supposed to have travelled to Somalia on several occasions. In the spring of 1993, Atef, another senior Al-Qaida member named Saif al-Adil (a former Egyptian army officer), and several others reportedly began to provide military training to Somalis who opposed the UN presence. Some of them may have participated in the clash with U.S. forces on 3 and 4 October 1993, although this is by no means certain.[5]

The most likely Somali link to Al-Qaida was a radical Somali group, *Al-Itihaad al-Islamiyyah* (Islamic Alliance, AIAI). This group, which emerged in 1991 as an armed movement among followers of the Muslim Brotherhood, ran several towns in the Gedo region of Somalia until 1997. The group is suspected by some of attempting to assume control of the self-proclaimed Republic of Puntland and has also been accused of terrorist bombings and assassination attempts in neighbouring Ethiopia, the rulers of which are Orthodox Christians. The attacks aimed to destabilise Ethiopia's central government and support a rebellion among ethnic Somali Muslims in Ethiopia's Ogaden region. However, Ethiopia sent troops into Somalia in 1996 and 1997 and destroyed the AIAI military strongholds. Survivors retreated to camps on the Kenyan border, where they appear to have melted into the local population. The movement has survived but at present is apparently more involved in running Islamic schools, courts, and clinics.[6] The AIAI was among the organizations and individuals whose assets were frozen by President Bush on 24 September 2001. Subsequently, a number of Somali individuals, as well as Al-Barakaat Group of Companies Somalia, Ltd., were added to the list.[7] On 31 October 2001, TNG President Hassan denied any links between his administration and the AIAI. Although his Transitional National Government did not control the whole country (in fact only about half of the capital Mogadishu[8]), President Hassan claimed it had a good information network to keep abreast of developments. Eventually, the TNG also established an anti-terrorism task force. As for the charges against Al-Barakaat Group, President Hassan expressed surprise and set up a commission to look into its records.[9] However, several opposition groups have alleged that the leadership of the Transitional National Government remains in favour of the AIAI and indeed itself was linked to Al-Qaida.[10]

By early November 2001 if not before, U.S. intelligence reports indicated that Al-Qaida was building a new base for its activities, with arms and equipment, in Somalia.[11] The truth, if any, in these allegations has not been possible to confirm.

End Notes

1. Where no other source is given, this section is based on Lynn Thomas and Steve Spataro, "Peacekeeping and Policing in Somalia," Robert B. Oakley, Michael J. Dziedzic, and Eliot M. Goldberg (eds.), *Policing the New World Disorder: Peace Operations and Public Security* (Institute for National Strategic Studies (INSS), at the Web site www.ndu.edu). Lieutenant Colonel Steve Spataro served as Provost Marshal during the main United Nations operation (UNITAF) in Somalia.

2. See, for instance, United Nations Security Council, *Report of the Secretary-General on the Situation in Somalia* (United Nations Security Council S/2002/189, 21 February 2002). See also CIA, *World Factbook 2001*.

3. *Economist,* 22 September 2001.

4. *Washington Times,* 4–10 February 2002 (National Weekly Edn).

5. Bergen, *Holy War,* 82; *Washington Times,* 22–28 October 2001 (National Weekly Edn).

6. *Washington Post,* 4 November 2001 (referring to a recent paper by Ken Menkhaus), 24 February 2002; *Economist,* 22 December 2001.

7. See, for instance, United Nations Security Council, *Report of the Secretary-General on the Situation in Somalia* (United Nations Security Council S/2002/189, 21 February 2002).

8. *Economist,* 22 December 2001.

9. See, for instance, United Nations Security Council, *Report of the Secretary-General on the Situation in Somalia* (United Nations Security Council S/2002/189, 21 February 2002).

10. See, for instance, United Nations Security Council, *Report of the Secretary-General on the Situation in Somalia* (United Nations Security Council S/2002/189, 21 February 2002).

11. *Washington Times,* 26 November–2 December 2001 (National Weekly Edn).

Islamic Extremism in Algeria

8

When the Muslim Brotherhood was first banned in Egypt in 1948, and again after its attempted assassination of Nasser in 1954, hundreds of members moved abroad, establishing overt or covert branches throughout the Middle East and North Africa. In Algeria, the brotherhood became known as the *Ahl al-Dawa* (People of the Call).[1] Even though Algeria was then involved in a bloody campaign for independence from France, the seeds sown by the brotherhood remained viable. Three decades later the implanting has resulted in yet more violence, this time with the purpose of transforming Muslim Algeria into a Salafi Islamic emirate.[2]

During the 1970s, Algeria was politically stable under the ruling party that had led the country to independence, the *Front de Libération Nationale* (National Liberation Front, FLN). Algeria enjoyed a comparatively high standard of living because its petroleum-based economy, one of the most centrally planned in the Arab world, included a generous welfare sector. The export of oil produced 95 percent of the country's income. The decline in oil prices after 1982, and in particular in 1986, shattered the Algerian economy and caused large-scale unemployment (by the late 1980s, about 70 percent of the male population age 17 to 23 was out of work). As the government slashed its welfare spending, the standards of living fell as well. Economic mismanagement and widespread corruption exacerbated the economic decline. Popular resentment grew, increasingly in the form of Islamic militancy. From 1984 to 1987, the veteran FLN fighter Mustapha Bouyali led an armed insurgency to establish an Islamic state. The revolt ended when he was killed in an ambush and his group was crushed by government forces. To save credibility as well as to attract desperately needed foreign investment, the government headed by President Chadli Ben Jedid introduced various economic reforms, including severe cuts in public welfare. In 1988, for the first time, the ruling FLN went so far as to allow a democratic opposition. However, the reforms backfired because they encouraged Islamic extremists. With the help of substantial funds from unknown sources, almost certainly in Saudi Arabia, these Islamists built new mosques and schools, and through Islamic charities administered from the mosques created substantial welfare programs for the urban poor.

In October 1988, social unrest escalated into violent urban mass riots, as Islamic preachers, inspired by the legacy as well as current activities of the Muslim Brotherhood throughout the Arab world, advocated a *jihad* against not only the Algerian government but those of the other North African states.

On 18 February 1989, 28 leading clerics gathered in the Bab al-Oued mosque in Algiers to establish the *Front Islamique du Salut* (Islamic Salvation Front, or FIS) in a merger of four smaller Islamic groups, one of which was the local branch of the international Muslim organisation, Tabligh. The new organisation was based on the rapidly growing network of mosques and Islamic charities throughout the country. The Bab al-Oued mosque's imam, Sheikh Abbasi Madani (born 1931), who earlier had spent a year in prison for declaring the ruling party "anti-Islamic," became the leader of the new organisation, while Ali Belhadj (born 1956), who lacked formal education but was known for his fiery, populist preaching, was appointed Madani's deputy. Both soon acquired a reputation for strong Salafi/Wahhabi beliefs. Funding came from Saudi Arabia, initially from the Saudi government but at some point after August 1990, when Madani visited Saddam Hussein in Baghdad to express his support for the Iraqi leader, from private financiers as well, believed by some to include bin Ladin. The generous funding brought results. In the Algerian municipal and local elections of 1990 and the parliamentary election of 26 December 1991, no other party had a local organisation that could rival that of the FIS, based as it was on a network of 8,000 mosques and Islamic charities. The FIS, which was particularly strong in the northern cities, saw spectacular gains in the first round of the parliamentary election, winning 180 out of 231 seats.

However, the FIS victory, as well as vociferous FIS support of Iraq at the time of the Persian Gulf War, caused the army to intervene in January 1992 (forcing President Ben Jedid to dissolve the National Assembly and resign on 11 January 1992) and postpone the decisive second round of the election. In February 1992, the army declared martial law and launched a massive offensive on the FIS, which was banned in April the same year. The FIS responded by launching its own attacks on the government.

The FIS had a strong ally in the returning Arab Afghans, at first led by Mansouri Meliani (arrested in July 1992 and executed the following year). These provided a major source of eager and experienced manpower for the FIS leaders.[3] However, the most militant extremists refused to accept the FIS insistence on elections and preferred to fight for a Salafi emirate. In particular the Arab Afghans were soon out of control.

In fact, the Arab Afghans had begun hostilities even before the army cancelled the election. On 29 November 1991, for example, a returning Arab Afghan who also was a FIS member had led a group of militants in a surprise raid on a border guard post in Guemmar. Killing the soldiers in their sleep, the attackers seized their weapons and escaped into the desert. Although the militants were subsequently tracked down, tried, and executed, the raid inspired many Islamic extremists and, in late 1992, gave rise to numerous armed extremist groups. Unlike the FIS, these groups rejected the political process and regarded Salafi Islam as the only solution to the country's problems. On 13 May 1994, many of these organisations (together with several militant FIS leaders, but not the mainstream FIS) merged as the *Groupe Islamique Armé* (Armed Islamic Group, in Arabic *Jamaat al-Islamiyyah al-Musallahah*), or GIA, the most brutal of the many Algerian Islamic extremist groups. The GIA, whose first leader is generally thought to have been an Arab Afghan named Abdelhaq Layada (although he was arrested in Morocco in July 1993), in retrospect claimed that the Guemmar raid marked the birth of the organisation as well as the beginning of its armed insurgency.

GIA members and followers adopted Afghan dress and manners, and the Belcourt area of Algiers, where many GIA cells were based, soon came to be called "Kabul." Not only Algerian Arab Afghans came here from Afghanistan; such other Islamic extremists as Pakistanis and Sudanese turned up. Many had also fought in Bosnia and Kashmir.[4] Despite its many followers, though, the GIA never developed into more than a network of separate groups loosely unified by common objectives. The groups varied in size from 20 or fewer to as many as 300 members. Most fighters were recruited among impoverished urban youths. As early as 1993, the GIA expanded its list of targets to include not only military and government officials but foreigners, intellectuals, and journalists as well. After 1994, the GIA also began to kill leaders of rival extremist groups, including the FIS.

The FIS responded to this rival by forming its own armed wing. An earlier *Mouvement Islamique Armé* (Armed Islamic Movement, MIA) appears to have been formed as early as in 1990, then again in 1993. In July 1994, the FIS merged the MIA with several other, smaller Islamic groups to form the *Armée Islamique du Salut* (Islamic Salvation Army, AIS). In March 1995, the FIS appointed an Arab Afghan named Madani Mezraq national amir of the AIS.

By then, the country was in a state of virtual civil war. Although the Algerian crisis was caused by domestic factors and not directly by the return of the Arab Afghans, Algeria was probably the country hardest hit by the return of the veterans. At least 2,000 to 3,000 Algerians had gone to fight in Afghanistan, many being deserters from the army. So when they returned home, they were already fugitives from justice.[5] From 1992 to 1994, somewhere between 600 and 1,000[6] Afghan veterans returned to Algeria in three waves. Forming the core of Algeria's Islamic fighters (though the majority seem to have joined the GIA), the FIS too had its share of Arab Afghans), they initiated a series of massacres that escalated, provoking government troops into the use of the same methods, until certainly more than 65,000 people, perhaps as many as 100,000, were killed during the 1990s. Militant Islamic extremists and government forces that included the *Sécurité Militaire,* which responded in kind, waged a savage campaign of terror aimed as much, if not more, at the civilian population as each other. Extremists and government forces in effect competed in killing and terrorising the population in a vicious war.[7]

Although the root causes of the Algerian civil turmoil included the inept economic policies of what was regarded as a corrupt government as well as the inspiring example of the Muslim Brotherhood, it is highly unlikely that the disturbances would have turned into a virtual civil war without the participation of Islamic extremists funded from abroad and the returning Arab Afghans. After 1992, many Algerian extremists, especially those of the GIA, enforced policies identical to those of other Sunni extremist movements. Musical entertainment was proscribed, several leading Algerian pop stars were assassinated, and vineyards, wine presses, and distribution facilities, despite being a major source of export income, were attacked. Other targets included unveiled women, teachers, journalists, and writers. Some 600 schools and several universities were burned down.[8]

Another reason for the continued warfare was the invariable tendency among Algerian Islamic groups to divide into factions and, eventually, into splinter groups. Since each new division was autonomously led, it soon split, as well, into yet a smaller formation. Not only did these breakups cause considerable confusion and difficulties in coordinating military operations and political demands, they also gave rise to violent infighting within the Islamic movement. The absence of an acknowledged leadership made negotiations with the government impossible, which also served to prolong the war. The continuous civil war between the FIS and the secular state apparatus, which nonetheless allowed elections involving pro-government and moderate religious parties (though a party law banning political parties based on religion was enacted in March 1997), did not subside until 21 September 1997. Then the armed wing of the FIS, the AIS, and a smaller group which had split from the GIA in November 1995, the *Ligue Islamique de la Daawa et du Djihad* (Islamic League for Call and Jihad), or LIDD, announced a truce to start in October 1997. Yet another group, the *Front Islamique du Djihad Armé* (Islamic Front for Armed Jihad), or FIDA, joined the LIDD. Algerian President Abdelaziz Bouteflika, elected in April 1997, responded by extending amnesty to many extremists.

In January 2000, the AIS under Sheikh Madani Mezraq disbanded itself and many of its members surrendered under an amnesty program designed to promote national reconciliation. The Islamic extremist movement split into two broad factions: French-speaking, technocratic, and political Djazarists and the Arabic-speaking, revolutionary Salafists. The Djazairists (from *jazaira,* "Algerianist," a title used since the early 1980s for those who wished to adapt Islamist ideas to an Algerian context) emphasised the national aspect of the struggle, while the Salafists (*salafiyyah*) saw the struggle as an international Salafi jihad. The two factions soon were at each other's throats.[9]

Fighting with government forces continued, as well, since many extremists, in particular the GIA and its leader Antar Zouabri, refused to surrender. The FIS was still banned. Among its main leaders, two (Ali Belhadj and Dr. Abassi Madani) remained in prison, and two (Rabeh Kebir, the FIS representative abroad, and Kamreddine Kherbane, a member of the *Instance Exécutive du Front Islamique du Salut à l'Étranger* (the foreign executive organisation of the FIS), or IEFE, are in voluntary exile abroad.[10]

There have been many connections between Algerian extrem-

ists and Al-Qaida, and they continue. GIA leader Bounoua
Boudjemaa (also known as Abu Anes or Abdullah Anas) married
a daughter of Abdullah Azzam. After the murder of Azzam on 24
November 1989, Boudjemaa grew increasingly close to Usamah
bin Ladin, who is said subsequently to have relied mostly on
Algerians as personal bodyguards—which is why he provided
substantial support to the Algerian extremists.[11] Al-Qaida is
reported to have contributed funds to the GIA until bin Ladin,
who was horrified by the group's attacks on civilian Muslims,
switched his support to a GIA commander named Hassan Hattab.
Bin ladin encouraged the latter in 1996 to form his own group,
Jamaat al-Salafiya li'l-Dawa wa'l-Qital (*Le Groupe Salafiste
pour la Prédication et le Combat;* Salafi Group for Call and
Combat), or GSPC.[12]

Antar Zouabri was killed in February 2002.[13] Yet, despite the
amnesty and national reconciliation program, many extremist
groups continue to engage in violence. (One such group, the
GSPC, was among the Al-Qaida-related terrorist groups whose
assets the United States ordered frozen on 24 September 2001.)[14]
The GSPC seems to have gained popular support in Algeria, eclips-
ing the GIA and indeed co-opting the GIA's networks abroad since
about 1998. The group's current strength is unknown to Western
observers but is estimated at several hundred to several thousand in
Algeria alone, in addition to supporters abroad, particularly in
Western Europe.[15] Another such group is *Al–Baqun ala al–Ahd*
(*Mouvement des Fidèles au Serment;* Those Who Keep Their
Oath), or MFS.

However, Algeria's key problem remains. The country has the
fifth largest reserves of natural gas in the world and is the second
largest international gas exporter. It ranks fourteenth in oil
reserves. These constitute the the key sector of the economy, with
petroleum and natural gas accounting for roughly 60 percent of
budget revenues, 30 percent of gross domestic product, and more
than 95 percent of export earnings. The economy, therefore,
remains vulnerable and is badly in need of diversification.[16]

End Notes

1. Hiro, *Islamic Fundamentalism*, 86–7.

2. When no other source is given, this section is based on Mohammed M. Hafez, "Armed Islamist Movements and Political Violence in Algeria," *Middle East Journal* 54:4 (Autumn 2000), 572–91; Luis Martinez, *La Guerre Civile en Algérie, 1990–1998* (Paris: Karthala, 1998; published in English in 2000 by Columbia University Press, New York, as *The Algerian Civil War 1990–1998*); Michael Willis, *The Islamist Challenge in Algeria: A Political History* (Reading: Ithaca Press, 1996; republished in 1999 by New York: New York University Press); Séverine Labat, *Les Islamistes Algériens, entre les Urnes et le Maquis* (Paris: Seuil, 1995); Cooley, *Unholy Wars,* 192–3, 200–201; Sela, *Political Encyclopedia,* 28–33, 379; CIA, *World Factbook 2001.*

3. See, for instance, Cooley, *Unholy Wars,* 6, 192–3. The movement maintained a Web site, www.fisalgeria.org.

4. Cooley, *Unholy Wars,* 201–7, 212; Maley, *Fundamentalism Reborn?* 203.

5. Cooley, *Unholy Wars,* 85, 201.

6. Cooley, *Unholy Wars,* 201.

7. See, for instance, Reeve, *New Jackals,* 3–4; *Patterns of Global Terrorism 1999.*

8. Cooley, *Unholy Wars,* 199–200, 207.

9. The two broad factions, or rather points of view, had existed for years. Two Djazarist FIS leaders, Muhammad Said and Abdelrazak Rejjam, were executed by the GIA already on 2 November 1995.

10. CIA, *The World Factbook 2001;* Cooley, *Unholy Wars,* 203, 208. Yet another FIS leader, Abdelkader Benouis, who soon moved to Saudi Arabia for fund-raising, probably with Al-Qaida, was in May 1993 sentenced to death *in absentia* in Algeria, together with the two sons of Sheikh Abbasi Madani, Usamah and Iqbal, and Rabeh Kebir. Usamah Madani was later jailed in Germany. Benouis had left Algeria already in 1992 and, after looking for refuge in several countries, ended up in Britain. In 1998, the Algerian government demanded his extradition. Rabeh Kebir remains in Germany, where he was once jailed. Cooley, *Unholy Wars,* 203. Kamreddine Kherbane, a former air force officer who left the Algerian armed forces and went to Peshawar in 1983 to organise Arab Afghans, in 1991 sought asylum in Britain and acquired British citizenship. Moroccan news agency MAP Web site, 21 September 2001. See also Jacquard, *Osama Bin Laden,* 59.

11. Cooley, *Unholy Wars,* 202, 223; Reeve, *New Jackals,* 169. Boudjemaa went on to edit the GIA's *Jihad News* from Poland.

12. Reeve, *New Jackals,* 209.

ISLAMIC EXTREMISM IN ALGERIA

13. BBC *News,* 9 February 2002.
14. *New York Times,* 25 September 2001.
15. FAS Intelligence Resource Program (www.fas.org).
16. CIA, *The World Factbook 2001.*

.

Islamic Extremism in Tunisia

9

In Tunisia, a former French colony, the Muslim Brotherhood became known as the *Hizb al-Islami* (Islamic Party). This organization was subsequently banned, as were all other opposition parties.[1] Led by President Habib Bourguiba after independence (ruled 1957–1987), Tunisia until the late 1960s was regarded as a fundamentally secular state, indeed being among the most Westernised of the Arab countries. However, urban Islamic movements began to emerge in the 1970s, and they soon became radical. Most important was *Mouvement de la Tendance Islamique* (Islamic Tendency Movement), or MTI, founded in 1981.[2] After a number of bombings of government buildings, the Tunisian government in 1986 ruthlessly suppressed the extremist movement.[3]

Islamic militancy did not disappear, however. During the 1980s, the international Muslim organisation Tabligh recruited at least 160 Tunisians, mainly from the universities, for religious training in Pakistan. Roughly half also received military training, and a handful fought in Afghanistan together with several hundred other Tunisians who had joined the Afghan jihad through other means. Some eventually returned home, where they organised around the remnants of the MTI, in early 1989 renamed *Parti de la Renaissance* (*Hizb al-Nahda,* better known as En-Nahda, or

Renaissance Party, led by Rashid al-Ghanoushi. The government actively suppressed the extremist groups, however, and in 1989 Ghanoushi went into voluntary exile in London (for a while, he enjoyed the use of a Sudanese diplomatic passport).[4] The Tunisian government, from 1987 on headed by President Ben-Ali Zein Al-Abidin, jailed several other leaders, imposed life sentences *in absentia* on Ghanoushi and the exiled leaders in 1992, and refused to legalise any radical Islamic group. The government suppression was largely successful. With the exception of a number of attacks in the late 1980s, primarily on foreign tourists, and an incident in the summer of 1992 in which members of the international Islamic extremist movement Hizb ut-Tahrir, which had apparently gained a role in En-Nahda, were accused of plotting a coup d'etat, Tunisia has remained stable. The explanation is no doubt found in the fact that Tunisia has been the most successful of the North African countries economically. By the late 1990s, national security forces had largely contained the remaining extremists.[5]

End Notes

1.   Hiro, *Islamic Fundamentalism*, 86–7.

2.   Cooley, *Unholy Wars,* 82–5; Jacquard, *Osama Bin Laden,* 61.

3.   Cooley, *Unholy Wars,* 82–5; Jacquard, *Osama Bin Laden,* 61. For further information on Tunisia, see, for instance, Sela, *Political Encyclopedia,* 734–45; CIA, *World Factbook 2001.*

4.   Pipes, "Islamic Movements in Northern Africa."

5.   Cooley, *Unholy Wars,* 6, 85, 210–11. The Hizb ut-Tahrir involvement is poorly documented and possibly only an allegation.

Hizb ut-Tahrir

The *Hizb ut-Tahrir al-Islami* (Islamic Liberation Party) was founded in 1953 in Jordan, allegedly but improbably in (the Muslim) East Jerusalem, by Sheikh Taqiuddin al-Nabhani (1909–1979), a Palestinian graduate of Al-Azhar and former member of the Muslim Brotherhood.[1] Working as a teacher and local Islamic judge, Nabhani had settled in Jordan after being forced to leave Palestine. Nabhani's dream was to create an Islamic caliphate and rid the Islamic world of all Western influences. The organisation was outlawed in Jordan in 1969. In the 1970s, the Hizb ut-Tahrir spread to Egypt (where it was also known as *Shabab Muhammad,* or Youth of Muhammad) and North Africa, especially Tunisia (where it achieved considerable influence in the 1980s). Some elitist cells within the party eventually appear to have penetrated the ruling circles in the Arab states, endeavouring but invariably failing to initiate a forceful change to Islam through military coups. In June 1974, Hizb ut-Tahrir members attempted an armed attack on the military academy in Cairo to capture weapons with which to overthrow the government. They killed 30 soldiers but failed to achieve their objective. In the summer of 1992, other members, under the name of *Hizb al-Nahda* (also known as *Parti de la Renaissance*) were accused of plotting a coup d'etat in

Tunisia. In 1993, members of the group were accused of planning a coup against King Hussein of Jordan.[2] As the organisation was banned in most parts of the Middle East, its leaders established the organisation in Europe, in particular Germany, Denmark, and Britain, where London is believed to be a major centre. The first Hizb ut-Tahrir branch in Britain was founded in 1986 by Omar Bakri Muhammad. Muslim students in British universities currently form an important segment of the organisation's membership.

The Hizb ut-Tahrir is also popular in Turkey and is establishing a presence in Pakistan.[3] The modern Hizb ut-Tahrir is an international movement, active in various parts of the Islamic world and based on Wahhabi thought. It works for the reestablishment of the caliphate (*khilafah*). The movement engages in various campaign activities even though it tries to operate in strict secrecy.[4] The successor of Nabhani and current leader of the Hizb ut-Tahrir is Sheikh Abdul Qadeem Zaloom, another Palestinian and former Al-Azhar professor whose location is kept a well-guarded secret. He is probably based in Europe.[5]

The members of the Hizb ut-Tahrir are organised in small cells (Arabic *daira*, Uzbek *halqa*, Tajik *ziyofat*, English "circle") of five to seven people, headed by a *mushrif*. The regular members only know the other members of the circle, since the *mushrif* is the only one who maintains contact with the next higher stage of the organisation. The top leader in a country is the *mutamad*. Directly below him are regional or city leaders (*masul*, "responsible, in charge"), each with his own group of district leaders, or *musond*. New member are expected to take an oath on the Koran, vowing never to betray the interests of Islam, never to reveal information about the Hizb ut-Tahrir to the public, and to fight for the establishment of a caliphate until the very end. After new members have completed about two months of training, they are expected to form a new cell (women's and men's cells are kept separate for religious reasons; women's cells are regarded as less political and militant than those of the men). Each aspirant must first be carefully investigated, including his place of work and home address, so as to avoid government infiltrators.[6] The organisation follows the Marxist practice of establishing clandestine organisations based on secret cells, which is not surprising considering the time and place of the movement's original establishment. The Hizb ut-Tahrir maintains a Web site with information in Arabic, Turkish, Russian, English, German, Danish, French, Urdu, and Malay.

The organisation's centre in Central Asia is Uzbekistan, where it claims 80,000 members.[7] Unlike the Islamic Movement of Uzbekistan, which primarily recruited in rural areas, the Hizb ut-Tahrir appears to draw its supporters primarily from the educated urban elite as well as college students, educated but unemployed youth, and skilled factory workers. Most of the arrested Hizb ut-Tahrir members are educated urban men in their 20s. They are not necessarily deprived or living in poverty. Quite a few, perhaps most, appear to have been introduced to Islam for the first time through the Hizb ut-Tahrir. The Hizb ut-Tahrir, known in Central Asia as *Hezb-e Tahriri Islomiya*, has become the most popular underground movement in Uzbekistan, Kyrgyzstan, and Tajikistan.[8]

According to Uzbekistani officials, the Hizb ut-Tahrir was established in Uzbekistan only as late as 1995, the first cell being set up in Tashkent by a Jordanian named Salahuddin with the help of two Uzbeks. The first Hizb ut-Tahrir pamphlets in Uzbekistan, then written in Arabic, apparently appeared in 1995–1996. Cells were then established elsewhere in Tashkent as well as in the Ferghana Valley, whence the movement spread throughout the country and to Kyrgyzstan and Tajikistan.[9] In Kyrgyzstan, the Hizb ut-Tahrir is reputed to be very active in the Osh and Jalalabad regions, where local Uzbeks have distributed leaflets calling for the overthrow of existing governments in Central Asia and the establishment of a pan-Islamic state. The first secret cells in these regions appeared in 1997–1998, and since 1999, the activists there have worked openly. Almost 300 such activists were arrested in southern Kyrgyzstan in 2000 for distributing religious literature. Kyrgyzstani security forces believe that 90 percent of the members are ethnic Uzbeks, the rest ethnic Kyrgyz, and some claim that there are more than 60,000 Hizb ut-Tahrir supporters (not necessarily members) only in Osh. In Tajikistan, more than 150 Hizb ut-

Tahrir activists were arrested in 2000. The Hizb ut-Tahrir seems to be especially strong in the northern part of the country (the movement claims 20,000 members in Sughd Province, formerly Leninabad),[10] probably because most Uzbeks live there.[11] The movement has been banned in all three countries.[12] The Hizb ut-Tahrir is also gaining popularity in Kazakhstan, at least in the south and in Almaty, Kazakhstan's largest city.[13] The movement even appears to have spread into China. In June 2001, two Hizb-ut Tahrir cells were reportedly found by Chinese security forces: one in Urumqi and one in Khotan.[14]

At present, the Hizb ut-Tahrir makes full use of videos, computer CDs, and e-mail to publish its beliefs. Another favourite form of propaganda is the *shabnama* (Persian "night letter"), printed at night and pushed under people's doors. Posters are also produced and displayed on walls at night.[15] Originally, all publications were in Arabic, but this has changed, and in Central Asia, most of the literature is currently in Uzbek, with some in Tajik and a bit in Kyrgyz.[16] The contents and the high quality of printing evidenced by its leaflets and other literature indicate that much of it comes from abroad, some apparently from Libya. The movement also seems to receive funding from abroad: at least the rank-and-file members of the organisation, mainly young men 17 to 25 years of age, from time to time reportedly receive rewards of $50 to $100.[17] Members with regular jobs are instead expected to contribute from 5 to 20 percent of their income to the party every month. The movement also runs small businesses to get additional funds.[18]

The IMU is believed to have sought a rapprochement with Hizb ut-Tahrir, but the latter appears to have rejected the proposal. The two movements are, however, reputed to share the same values and opinions (i.e., that Uzbekistani President Karimov is a Jew, an infidel, an enemy of Islam, and a servant of the West).[19] Propaganda against Israel and the "worldwide Zionist conspiracy" is another popular topic, as is the demand that all Shia Muslims be expelled from Central Asia (and presumably the world).[20] In addition, several hundred Hizb ut-Tahrir members reportedly fled to Afghanistan, where they subsequently joined the IMU. Hizb ut-

Tahrir literature was reportedly found on several killed IMU fighters. There is little doubt that the two organisations maintained close contacts, at least on the individual level.[21]

The views of the Hizb ut-Tahrir are simplistic and single-minded as in all other Wahhabi groups; the imposition of Islamic law is in itself believed to resolve all ethnic, social, and economic problems and create a perfect, frankly utopian society without further ado. When a European non-governmental organisation attempted to fight AIDS by propagating the use of condoms among local women, the Hizb ut-Tahrir characteristically protested by claiming that the NGO was encouraging prostitution.[22]

Uzbekistan began to move against the Hizb ut-Tahrir in May 1998, after the Law on Freedom of Conscience and Religious Organisations had been passed. Despite its name, this law severely restricted religious worship, banning the use of unregistered mosques and requiring that all Muslim preachers be registered.[23]

Although the Hizb ut-Tahrir remains suppressed, its very aura of resistance appears to encourage new converts to the movement. This, together with the possibility that some of them will adopt violent methods to bring an Islamic state into being, means that the Hizb ut-Tahrir remains a strong threat to secular rule in Uzbekistan. It should be noted that the Hizb ut-Tahrir sees its mission as consisting of three phases: inviting people to Islam, establishing an Islamic state, and finally, the expansion of the Islamic state through jihad. In the Islamic state, military conscription and training in preparation for jihad would be mandatory for all Muslim men over 15.[24] This shows that even though it currently advocates nonviolent methods, the Hizb ut-Tahrir does not rule out the use of force. As noted, the organisation has already attempted violent actions elsewhere. In 1988, at least, it also published literature advocating the hijacking of aircraft of countries considered to be opposed to Islam. Chief among such countries is the United States, but other states with "imperialistic motives" such as Britain and Russia remain "potential" enemies, while Israel is regarded an "actual" enemy.[25] In addition, many individual members of the Hizb ut-Tahrir have expressed sympathy with the armed struggle of the IMU and say that they are willing, in some cases apparently eager, to fight. The Hizb ut-Tahrir finds many new recruits in prisons.[26] If these are already hardened militants or even criminals, they will provide an increased propensity for violence. The clandestine nature of the Hizb ut-Tahrir also means that the organisation is prone to factionalism. At least two cases are known in which significant Hizb ut-Tahrir subgroups established separate political movements independent of the Hizb ut-Tahrir leadership. In early 1997, a group in the Ferghana region of Uzbekistan led by a certain Yu. Akramov left the Hizb ut-Tahrir after a dispute with local leaders. In 1999, another split took place in Uzbekistan's capital Tashkent, where a significant group of Hizb ut-Tahrir members reportedly set up its own party, called *Hizb an-Nusra* (Assistance Party), possibly because they were dissatisfied with only nonviolent means of political struggle. Factional splits have also been reported in Kyrgyzstan.[27]

In light of the U.S. military presence in Uzbekistan, it should be noted that from 1992 to 1999 the Hizb ut-Tahrir had a branch in California, known as the Islamic Cultural Workshop, which appears to have ceased activities.[28] The Hizb ut-Tahrir has announced that it supports actions against the "infidel powers" (the United States and Britain) engaged in military operations in Afghanistan.[29]

End Notes

1. Rashid, *Jihad,* 116. See also Muminov, "Traditional and Modern Religious-Theological Schools," 101–111; Babadzhanov, "Fergana Valley," 112–123; the movement's Web site, www.hizb-ut-tahrir.org. In Britain as well as Pakistan (where the movement is banned), the movement maintained a Web site under the name *Khilafah* (www.khilafah.com; www.khilafah.com.pk). As the Hizb ut-Tahrir was banned in most British universities, the movement also operated under the name Islamic Heritage Society. On the Internet, the Hizb ut-Tahrir was also active under the name Muslim Student's Website or Muslim Student Home Page (www.acgnet.co.uk/islam.htm). Michael Whine, "Islamist Oganizations on the Internet," *Terrorism and Political Violence* 11:1 (spring 1999), 123–32, on 129. Some independent observers, not necessarily well-informed, suggest that the party was founded in 1952.

2. Hiro, *Islamic Fundamentalism,* 3, 70–1; Sela, *Political Encyclopedia,* 234, 374, 545,

HIZB UT-TAHRIR

742; Emerson, *American Jihad,* 195–6. See also Erkin Kurmanov, "Hizb ut-Tahrir in Kyrgyzstan," *Central Asia and the Caucasus* 3 (15), 2002, 119–26. The Hizb ut-Tahrir involvement in the 1974 coup attempt is well documented, the Tunisian connection less so.

3. Rashid, *Jihad,* 118–19; interview with Omar Bakri Muhammad on Danish television, 2002. Hizb ut-Tahrir's spokesman in Copenhagen is Fadi Abdullatif.

4. Muminov, "Traditional and Modern Religious-Theological Schools," 101–111; Babadzhanov, "Fergana Valley," 112–123; the movement's Web site, www.hizb-ut-tahrir.org.

5. Rashid, *Jihad,* 116, 119. Books by the founder and the present leader of the Hizb ut-Tahrir include Taqiuddin an-Nabhani, *The Islamic State* (Lahore: Hizb ut-Tahrir, 1998; first published in 1962); Taqiuddin an-Nabhani, *Islamic Concepts* (np, UK: Al Khilafah, nd); Abdul Qadeem Zaloom, *How the Khilafah Was Destroyed* (Lahore: Hizb ut-Tahrir, 1998). Another book by one or both of these two authors include *The Economic System in Islam.* The Hizb ut-Tahrir also publishes a magazine, *Al-W'ai* ("Consciousness").

6 . Alima Bissenova, "Is Hizb-ut-Tahrir Going Public in Its Struggle?" Central Asia-Caucasus Analyst, 18 July 2001; Rashid, *Jihad,* 119; International Crisis Group (ICG), *The IMU and the Hizb-ut-Tahrir: Implications of the Afghanistan Campaign* (Osh/Brussels: International Crisis Group, Central Asia Briefing, 30 January 2002), 7; Kurmanov, "Hizb ut-Tahrir in Kyrgyzstan," 120.

7. Bissenova, "Is Hizb-ut-Tahrir Going Public;" Rashid, *Jihad,* 119, 120; ICG, *IMU and the Hizb-ut-Tahrir,* 7.

8. Rashid, *Jihad,* 111, 115–36.

9. Rashid, *Jihad,* 120–21, 130–31.

10. Rashid, *Jihad,* 131.

11. Kurmanov, "Hizb ut-Tahrir in Kyrgyzstan." For more details on the regional membership of the Hizb ut-Tahrir, see ICG, *IMU and the Hizb-ut-Tahrir.*

12. RFE/RL *Newsline,* 4 January 2001, 20 February 2001; Jane's Sentinel: Kyrgyzstan, 31 October 2000; Rashid, "Namangani's Foray."

13. Rashid, *Jihad,* 130–31.

14. *Economist,* 29 September 2001, 30 March 2002.

15. Rashid, *Jihad,* 120–21, 130–31.

16. Kurmanov, "Hizb ut-Tahrir in Kyrgyzstan."

17. Babadzhanov, "Fergana Valley," 112–123.

18. Kurmanov, "Hizb ut-Tahrir in Kyrgyzstan," 121.

19. ICG, *Central Asia: Islamist Mobilisation*, 6–7.
20. Rashid, *Jihad*, 123.
21. Rashid, *Jihad*, 133.
22. Rashid, *Jihad*, 121, 129.
23. Rashid, *Jihad*, 125, 146.
24. Rashid, *Jihad*, 117–18.
25. Emerson, *American Jihad*, 196–7.
26. ICG, *IMU and the Hizb-ut-Tahrir*, 8–11.
27. ICG, *IMU and the Hizb-ut-Tahrir*, 9; Kurmanov, "Hizb ut-Tahrir in Kyrgyzstan," 123.
28. Emerson, *American Jihad*, 193–7.
29. Kurmanov, "Hizb ut-Tahrir in Kyrgyzstan," 122.

APPENDIX

The Islamic Movement of Uzbekistan

11

Origins of the Movement

The Islamic Movement of Uzbekistan (IMU), or *O'zbekiston Islom Harakati* as it is known locally (*Harakat ul-Islamiyyah* in Arabic),[1] can be said to have formed part of the Arab Afghan network and shared a recruiting base (primarily unemployed young men) as well as attitudes to Wahhabism with the Taliban and the Arab Afghans. The movement relied on bases in Afghanistan (Mazar-e-Sharif, Kondoz, and Taloqan) and Tajikistan (Hoit in the Karategin Valley and Sangvor in the Tavildara Valley).[2]

The groups that constituted the IMU had their origin in the public manifestation of the Islamic movement *Adolat* (Justice). Adolat arose in the city of Namangan in the Uzbek part of the Ferghana Valley in 1990 as a response to perceived widespread corruption and social injustice exposed by the liberal perestroika era. As well, it was part of the resurgence in Islamic activities no longer prohibited by the Soviet government. The movement, funded by sources in Saudi Arabia and therefore inspired by Wahhabism, was led by two young men: the passionate college drop-out and local mullah Tohir Yuldosh and the former conscript soldier Jumaboy Khojiev (later known as Juma Namangani). In 1990, the movement built the first of several mosques and madrasahs. From November

1991 to the spring of 1992, the movement, which consisted of as many as 5,000 mostly unemployed young men, went on to organise protest meetings and occupy government buildings. The movement formed its own vigilante religious police force that administered summary justice in the streets. In April 1991, Uzbekistan's President Karimov, having come to talk to the militants, was shouted down. In December 1991, the militants occupied the Communist Party of Uzbekistan headquarters. In no time, branches of Adolat rose across the Ferghana valley, in Andijon, Margilan, Kuva, Farghona, and Osh (in Kyrgyzstan).[3]

Tohir (or Tohirjon) Abduhalilovich Yuldosh (in Russian, Tahir Yuldashev; in Arabic Tahir Farooq [Farukh in Russian]) was born in 1968.[4] His father died when he was five, and he was brought up by his mother, Karomat Asqarova.[5] An early member of the Uzbekistani branch of the All-Union Islamic Renaissance Party (IRP), founded in Astrakhan in June 1990, he had grown disillusioned with the party's refusal to demand an Islamic state. Together with other like-minded young Uzbeks, Yuldosh formed Adolat as a platform for his demand for an Islamic revolution.[6]

Jumaboy Ahmadjonovich Khojiev, an ethnic Uzbek born in 1968 in Namangan, graduated from agricultural vocational school before he was drafted into the Soviet army in 1987. He reportedly served as an airborne soldier in Afghanistan during the last phase of the Soviet war there, eventually being promoted to sergeant, unless the elite airborne episode too is part of the myth that soon grew up around his person. He is said to have become interested in Islam during his term in Afghanistan.[7]

Although Wahhabism was unknown among most government leaders at this early stage, it was clear to them that Adolat was becoming out of control. Adolat was banned in March 1992; the Uzbekistani government restored order and dissolved the movement. Several Adolat leaders, including Yuldosh and Khojiev, who now took the name Juma Namangani after his hometown, fled to Tajikistan in 1992, where they joined the Tajikistani branch of the IRP, which was by then preparing to launch a civil war there.[8] There the two young men embarked upon very different careers, though they continued to aim for the same broad goals.

Yuldosh began what can only be called a political career. When the civil war went against the IRP, he joined the other key IRP leaders in exile in Afghanistan. He also travelled to Pakistan and Saudi Arabia, and later to Iran, the United Arab Emirates, Turkey, and perhaps the Caucasus as well, to make contacts with other radical groups and to request funding from the intelligence services in these countries. Pakistan's ISI offered continuous funding and a base in Peshawar, the centre of the Arab Afghans. Yuldosh kept Peshawar as his base from 1995 to 1998, as well as getting funding from various Islamic charities and, according to Russian and Uzbekistani officials, the intelligence services of Saudi Arabia, Iran, and Turkey. (In Saudi Arabia were many descendents of members of the Uzbek diaspora produced by the 1918–1928 Basmachi revolts against the Soviets. Now this generation encompassed many committed Wahhabis who eagerly offered support to Yuldosh.)[9]

When Namangani arrived in Qurghonteppa (Kurgan-Tyube), Tajikistan, in 1992, he brought with him some 30 Uzbeks and several Arabs, who had served as emissaries to Adolat from Saudi Islamic charities. These men formed the core of Namangani's force, which within months attracted additional recruits from Uzbekistan, soon totalling some 200, as well as additional Arabs from Afghanistan. Namangani then volunteered the services of his men and himself, as a subordinate commander, to the IRP-supported United Tajik Opposition (UTO) during Tajikistan's civil war. The IRP, in turn, attached several Tajiks to Namangani's group and moved the volunteers to a camp in the village of Sangvor in the Tavildara valley, which became Namangani's base after 1993. Namangani, a charismatic leader and tough disciplinarian, though erratic, temperamental, and authoritarian, was a useful field commander for the UTO. He also made several valuable friends in the Tajik IRP: Hakim Kalindarov, who led the Tavildara groups together with Namangani, and, most important, Mirzo Zioev, the IRP's army chief of staff from 1996 and thereby Namangani's direct superior. Zioev was the nephew of Said Abdullo Nuri, head of the IRP, and after the civil war became minister of emergency situations in the new coalition government. Further, Namangani learned some Tajik and married an Uzbek woman, with whom he had a daughter. (In early 2001, he also married a Tajik widow with two sons whose husband, an IRP member, had been killed in Tajikistan's civil war and thus was regarded as a martyr; Namangani's Uzbek wife and daughter were then in Afghanistan.[10] He also occasionally travelled to Afghanistan to meet the IRP political leadership.[11]

After Tajikistan's civil war ended in 1997, Namangani at first refused to accept the end of the jihad against the government. Zioev finally persuaded him to cease fighting, and Namangani settled his men into his camp in the Tavildara valley. As for himself, he acquired a residence in Hoit, a small village north of Garm in the Karategin valley. It appears that he soon became heavily involved in transporting heroin from Afghanistan to Tajikistan and on to Russia and Europe, at times travelling to Afghanistan himself. Namangani also formed a substantial personal military force of mostly Uzbeks but also Arabs, Tajiks, and Chechens. Many of his men were accompanied by their families.[12]

Yuldosh and Namangani Establish the IMU

In 1997, Yuldosh travelled to Hoit to meet with his old associate Namangani. Neither was pleased with the end of the jihad, and so they agreed to form a new group to continue the jihad against their native country and other states in Central Asia. Some claim that Usamah bin Ladin was the one who urged them to create the group. Be that as it may, it seems clear that Al-Qaida contributed funds to the new movement. Both Yuldosh and Namangani certainly favoured Wahhabi Islam and agreed with bin Ladin's anti-Western rhetoric. In 1998, Yuldosh settled in Afghanistan, in a building offered by the Taliban in Wazir Akbar Khan, the diplomatic quarter of Kabul. He also received a residence in Kandahar. It was in the summer of 1998 that Yuldosh and Namangani met in Kabul to formally establish the IMU. From among the Wahhabis of Uzbek descent from the Arabian Peninsula, they (though most probably Yuldosh) picked Zubayr ibn Abdul Raheem, reputedly a descendant of the Mangit family that had ruled Bukhara, as head of the religious leadership of the IMU. On 25 August 1999, Raheem declared a jihad against the government of Uzbekistan, in which he also proclaimed that foreign tourists coming to Uzbekistan would be attacked.[13] Yuldosh also pledged to set up an Islamic state, while Namangani returned to Taijikistan.

On 16 February 1999, in what possibly was an attempt on the life of President Karimov, there were six car-bomb attacks in Uzbekistan's capital, Tashkent, which in any case killed 16 and injured more than 130 people.[14] Uzbekistani intelligence accused Yuldosh of having organised the attacks from the United Arab Emirates, and Uzbekistan subsequently applied pressure on Tajikistan to expel Namangani and his men. Namangani, however, had left Hoit in early summer of 1999 and moved to his camp in Sangvor in the Tavildara valley to prepare for war. In August 1999 (a date no doubt coordinated with the declaration of jihad the same month), he left his Sangvor camp and moved into Kyrgyzstan. Meanwhile, Yuldosh dispatched supplies and new recruits provided by the Taliban, Al-Qaida, Pakistan, and various groups in the Arabian Peninsula, including members of the Uzbek diaspora there. Additional funds came from profits in the heroin trade.[15]

In August 1999, Namangani dispatched several small IMU guerrilla groups into Kyrgyzstan toward Uzbekistan's Sukh and Tajikistan's Vorukh enclaves, two regions inside Kyrgyzstan that, while physically separated from Uzbekistan and Tajikistan, remained part of their territory. On 9 August, a 21-man group kidnapped the mayor and three officials of a small village west of Osh. The group demanded $1 million in ransom, supplies, and a helicopter to fly to Afghanistan. On 13 August, the Kyrgyzstani government gave in, granting the guerrillas safe passage back to Tajikistan—and probably a ransom of $50,000—in exchange for the hostages. This enraged President Karimov, who retaliated by ordering air raids on the towns of Tavildara and Garm in Tajikistan, where the IMU enjoyed considerable support—an attack vigorously protested against by the Tajikistani government. Other IMU guerrilla groups, comprising approximately 50 to 150 fighters, then moved into the area around Batken in Kyrgyzstan. They briefly occupied three villages and in an amazing coup also kidnapped a major general of the Kyrgyzstani Interior Ministry—the commander of the Interior Forces, no less.

On 23 August 1999, the IMU achieved international fame when one of its groups seized seven additional hostages, including four Japanese geologists. In addition, the IMU was recruiting more men among the local Kyrgyz. The confusion was now considerable because most observers by then had no idea who the IMU fighters really were, not to mention what they wanted or where they were going. In addition, Japanese agents and negotiators descended on Kyrgyzstan, a major recipient of Japanese aid, demanding the immediate release of the four geologists. By 4 September, negotiations were somehow opened, apparently through a Pakistani who was a member of the extremist organisation Sipah-e Sahaba (several Pakistanis from the two extremist groups Sipah-e Sahaba and Lashkar-e Jhangvi had by then joined Namangani), although at first without results. The Uzbekistani air force again went into action, this time launching attacks on the IMU-held villages around Batken and Osh in Kyrgyzstan. The Kyrgyzstani army launched its own offensive against the guerrillas as well. This situation continued until 25 October 1999, when the hostages were released, probably in exchange for a ransom of $2 million to $6 million (different sources suggest different amounts, probably because some money disappeared on the way to the IMU), paid by Japan to Kyrgyzstani officials, who then handed it (or at least parts of it) over to the IMU. As winter approached, threatening to close the mountain passes through snowfall, the IMU guerrillas prepared to return to Tajikistan.[16]

Under intense pressure from Uzbekistan, senior representatives of the Tajikistani government including Mirzo Zioev were dispatched to persuade Namangani to leave for Afghanistan. Arriving even before the IMU guerrillas returned, they persuaded Namangani to accept a Tajikistani government rescue and transportation operation. In the first week of November 1999, some 600 IMU guerrillas (one-third from Hoit, the rest from

Sangvor), together with their families, were flown in Zioev's
Ministry of Emergency Situations helicopters (at least wounded
IMU fighters were almost certainly rescued by Zioev)[17] to the
Afghanistan border, where they were received by Yuldosh and
his Taliban protectors.

The IMU guerrillas settled in Mazar-e-Sharif, and their dependents were given quarters in an abandoned UN refugee camp at
Kamsachi (originally set up to house Tajik refugees from
Tajikistan), about 15 miles from Mazar-e-Sharif. In addition to
Mazar-e-Sharif, the IMU opened offices in the residences in Kabul
and Kandahar provided by the Taliban to Yuldosh.[18] However, having quite independently formed the military wing of the IMU,
Namangani became the movement's main military leader, and thus
the most influential one.

In July 2000, Namangani returned to the Tavildara valley along
with several hundred IMU guerrillas. Then, in August, several IMU
guerrilla groups, each probably of no greater strength than at most
100 men (and probably no more than 50), set out in what looked
like a skillfully coordinated diversionary offensive in several direc-
tions at once. By thus dividing the poorly coordinated enemy
forces, Namangani managed to provide security for other IMU
groups that probably were smuggling narcotics and weapons into
enemy territory. The main fighting group again moved towards
Batken, Sukh, and Vorukh in Kyrgyzstan. Another group appears to
have remained in Tajikistan, moving through the Zeravshan Valley
toward Penjikent, where it turned south into the poorly defended
Surkhondaryo (Surkhandarya) Province of Uzbekistan. There a
base was established with some 170 IMU guerrillas, most probably
from already established sleeper cells or recent recruits from the
local population. Yet another group appears to have gone to
Khojand in northern Tajikistan and somehow crossed into
Uzbekistan, ultimately taking up positions in the mountains north
of Tashkent. Fighting, and considerable confusion among civilians
and government forces, broke out on all three fronts. Namangani
proved himself a master guerrilla leader, able to cause significant
mayhem with only a handful of men.[19]

On 12 August 2000, the Batken guerrillas kidnapped first 12 mountaineers of various nationalities, and then an additional four—specifically Americans. The IMU guerrillas held onto the American mountaineers but either abandoned or lost track of the others. The Americans were rescued within days. However, upon their return to the United States, they in a lucrative deal sold their account of their heroic struggle against and escape from the extremists to Random House and the movie rights to the tale to Universal Studios. The Clinton administration responded to the media attention (and as noted, to the burgeoning Uzbekistani cooperation with the CIA) on 25 September 2000 by declaring the IMU, which it had barely noticed, a terrorist organisation. When the IMU withdrew the surviving guerrillas in late October, and Namangani himself apparently went to Afghanistan, the United States was already flying in military supplies and counterinsurgency equipment to Uzbekistan and Kyrgyzstan. And so were Russia, China, Turkey, France, and Israel.[20]

In late November 2000, Namangani left Afghanistan and returned to Tajikistan with a force of some 300 guerrillas. Zioev was again dispatched to Tavildara to negotiate Namangani's return to Afghanistan. In January 2001, Namangani and most of his men (a small garrison was left in the Sangvor camp) were again airlifted by Zioev's government transport helicopters to the Afghan border.[21]

IMU Strategy
Why had the IMU, which wished to overthrow the government of Uzbekistan, instead invaded Kyrgyzstan for two years in a row? Two explanations are possible. The first may be found in the geography and social situation of the region. The population of Kyrgyzstan includes large numbers of ethnic Uzbeks, and the country is located between the areas held by extremists in Tajikistan (the Garm, Jirgatal, and Tavildara districts) and the populous Ferghana Valley, shared by Tajikistan, Uzbekistan, and Kyrgyzstan and one of the suspected targets of the IMU intrusions.[22] Due to the valley's large population and its conservative Islamic attitudes, it may be the only area in Uzbekistan where Islamic extremists are likely to gain a

wide following—and from which they may be able to create an uprising sufficiently strong enough to have any impact on Uzbekistan's government. The Ferghana Valley, which saw considerable resistance to Russian forces before their conquest and occupation of the valley in 1876, has a history of violent uprisings. In 1898, peasant unrest in Andijon was used by local religious and secular groups to challenge local administrators as much as Russian control. A new uprising, again partly of a religious character, took place in 1916 in response to the mobilisation decree calling for Central Asian men to be drafted for the Russian effort. This was followed by the 1918–1928 Basmachi movement (branded as bandits by Soviet propaganda), a response to the brutal Soviet suppression of local autonomy. Violence again erupted in June 1989 when bloody riots took place in the valley in a conflict between ethnic Uzbeks and Meskhetian Turks, which was fundamentally engendered by economic decline. Later, in June 1990, ethnic violence occurred between ethnic Uzbeks and Kyrgyz in the Osh district of Kyrgyzstan's part of the valley.[23]

In Kyrgyzstan, there are, as noted, two Uzbekistani enclaves that are geographically separated from Uzbekistan: Sukh and Shah-e Mardon. The Sukh enclave, with a predominantly Tajik population of some 43,000 people, was favourably disposed toward the IRP during Tajikistan's civil war. Later many of these Tajiks transferred their loyalty to the IMU. The fact that there is no land route between the enclave and Uzbekistan's main territory created conditions favourable for the IMU's de facto occupation of a piece of Uzbekistani territory. This was a territory in which they could expect to win popular support, and the Uzbekistani army could not defeat or even react to this except by a risky airlift operation. The other enclave inside Kyrgyzstan, Vorukh, is the home to a predominantly Tajik population of some 25,000 people. It, too, is a hotbed of Islamic extremism and support for the IMU.[24]

Another explanation for the IMU raids is equally possible. The raids were perhaps less connected with the Islamic revolution than with attempts to maintain transportation routes for narcotics traf-

ficking. There is a growing flow of narcotics from and through
Kyrgyzstan (drugs from Afghanistan but also locally produced opi-
ates and marijuana from the Ferghana valley), and Osh has become
a particularly important way station.[25] Since the raids certainly had
geographical objectives in the vicinity of known smuggling routes,
this explanation cannot be ruled out. When small groups of raiders
engaged the security forces in certain districts, the latter—too thin-
ly stretched to keep complete control over the border—certainly
left a number of routes unguarded, thus allowing the extremists the
opportunity to move large amounts of narcotics through the
region.[26] So it also became possible to move weapons, ammunition,
and military supplies to the IMU sleeper cells in Uzbekistan.[27]

Whether such movements actually took place seems to be
known only to the IMU leadership. However, fuel and ammunition,
not to mention wages to fighters, cost large amounts of cash, especially if the extremists recruit criminals and former soldiers, which
appears to be the case, as well as inexperienced and uneducated
volunteers.[28] The extremists need money and cannot rely only on
sympathisers abroad. To distinguish between political and criminal
activities and objectives when discussing the extremist movement
may be impossible and indeed regarded as irrelevant by the movement's leaders themselves as long as both activities are directed
against infidels.

IMU in the War on Terror

By early 2001, the IMU had bases in Afghanistan as well as
Tajikistan. There also seem to have been substantial numbers of
IMU sleeper cells in Uzbekistan. Yuldosh had reportedly formed
IMU cells in the Ferghana Valley and in Surkhondaryo, in southeastern Uzbekistan on the border with Tajikistan.[29] It seems more
likely, however, that the latter were formed by Namangani during
his stay in the area.

In Afghanistan, the base at Kamsachi was commanded by Tal
Udeshev, who escaped from Uzbekistan immediately after the
Tashkent bombings of February 1999 and, after a brief stay in
Peshawar, moved to Kamsachi with the blessings of the Taliban.

His group consisted of 300 to 400 people, including as many as 50 Uighurs from China.[30] It has been suggested that the Taliban sent diplomatically embarrassing recruits such as Uighurs and Chechens to the IMU when they or their sponsor Pakistan were under pressure from either China and Russia to cease their support to such groups. Pakistani extremists wanted by the Pakistani security forces were also quietly dispatched to the IMU.[31] There were bases in Kondoz, and since the autumn of 2000 a large IMU contingent (estimated at 800) had formed part of the Taliban garrison in Taloqan.[32]

However, the main military leader of the IMU, and thereby the movement's most influential leader, was clearly Namangani. (He was reputed to not get along very well with Udeshev.)[33] The total strength of the movement is not known. It has been estimated that the majority of the Arab Afghans in Central Asia were (at the very most, 2,000 in Afghanistan and another 2,000 in Tajikistan, but probably far less on both accounts because these figures probably included dependents. Most likely the bulk of these forces in fact consisted of IMU members, except perhaps 500 to 1,000 Arabs who served directly under Usamah bin Ladin.[34] In the spring of 2001, an eyewitness reported some 400 men in Namangani's base at Sangvor. The membership of the IMU was predominantly Uzbeks and Tajiks from Uzbekistan and Tajikistan. All the same, it was believed that many Kyrgyz, ethnic Uzbeks and Tajiks from Afghanistan, some Arabs, Pakistanis, Uighurs, and Chechens, and even Slavs were part of the camp's forces.[35] Some reports indicate that the IMU used Russian as a common language.[36] Morale was high, and like Al-Qaida's Arabs, few IMU guerrillas ever surrendered, even when cornered by government troops.[37]

Despite this, the IMU can be differentiated from the Arab Afghans because the movement had principally fought the neighbouring governments of Uzbekistan and Kyrgyzstan. Thus the IMU formed a native fighting force rather than being part of the global movement espoused by bin Ladin. It should, however, be noted that many members of the IMU appeared to come from Afghanistan and even the Arabian Peninsula.

The IMU also had a greater propensity for terrorist activities in the region than the members of bin Ladin's network. The IMU was, as noted, accused of perpetrating the car-bomb attacks in Tashkent on 16 February 1999.[38] For this reason alone, the IMU could be regarded as the key terrorist threat in Central Asia.

In contrast to the often eloquently argued global aspirations of the Arab Afghans, presented on the Internet and in various publications, only limited amounts of information specifically from the IMU ever reached the West. Nonetheless, the motivation, means, and background of the IMU so far appear to be essentially identical to those of the Arab Afghans. Another similarity with the Arab Afghans is that the IMU forged intimate links with the Taliban. Namangani, in return for the patronage of Al-Qaida and the Taliban, not only allowed his forces to protect narcotics smuggled from Afghanistan into Central Asia but also partly merged his units with the Taliban in the war against the Northern Alliance. Because of intimate ties with Al-Qaida and the Taliban, the IMU reportedly established contacts with most or all Islamic extremist groups with a presence in Afghanistan. These included the Algerian *Groupe Islamique Armé* (GIA) and *Groupe Salafiste pour la Prédication et le Combat* (GSPC); the Libyan Islamic Fighting Group (IFG); the Pakistani and Kashmiri group *Harakat ul-Mujahidin*, the Yemeni *Jaish Aden Abin al-Islami* (AAIA); the Somalian *Al-Itihaad al-Islamiyyah* (AIAI); and various radical Palestinian, Chechen, and Uighur groups.[39]

It is unlikely that the IMU received much funding from supporters in Uzbekistan. While Islamic charities often collect funds for extremist groups, such collection would be difficult to organise in Uzbekistan due to the strict controls the state has imposed on mosques and religious institutions. There is, however, reason to believe that Islamic charities elsewhere, particularly in Pakistan, supplied the IMU, since they also supplied the Taliban and Al-Qaida. For instance, the Al-Rashid Trust, run by Mullah Khail al-Rashid, was accused of smuggling weapons and supplies disguised as humanitarian aid to the Taliban and IMU.[40]

Due to its close association with the Taliban, the IMU was

known to be armed the same as any other Taliban unit. In addition, the IMU was reportedly armed with Russian sniper rifles, night-vision equipment, grenade launchers, pistols, and silencers, some of which were acquired from military units in Central Asia.[41] Although it seems beyond doubt that the Pakistani ISI supported the IMU, some senior ISI officers reportedly believed that the IMU instead was under the control of the Russian intelligence or security services. This probably erroneous belief was based on the apparent ease with which the IMU crossed Central Asian borders.[42]

The political structure of the IMU remains unknown to outside observers to this day and to some extent probably reflected the divisions within the organisation. Yuldosh was chief political leader. Zubayr ibn Abdur Raheem was head of the religious leadership and also appeared to be the chairman of the organization's supreme council. However, IMU military commander Namangani, who was known in Afghanistan as Juma Hakim[43] and also was one of the Taliban de facto defence ministers until his death in November 2001,[44] remained the most influential leader of the organisation. The structure of the group at the military level was also largely unknown to outside observers. While the IMU boasted brigades formed according to ethnic backgrounds, and did carry out joint operations with Al-Qaida and Taliban forces, most of the activities outside Afghanistan consisted of guerrilla raids and drug running by small units, typically of around 15 men, under what appear to have been local commanders.[45]

In mid-2000, a new group allied to the IMU was said to have been formed, the Islamic Movement of Tajikistan (IMT). There were also rumours about an Islamic Movement of Kyrgyzstan (IMK). So far, little is known about these groups, if they ever existed.[46] On 20 May 2001, however, it was reported that Namangani had launched a political party under the name of *Hezb-e Islami Turkestan* (Islamic Party of Turkestan), or IPT, as an umbrella organisation of the IMU with the avowed intention to include not only Uzbekistan but also Tajikistan, Kyrgyzstan, Kazakhstan, and Chinese Xinjiang in his movement's area of operations. Namangani appointed himself leader of the party, with Yuldosh as his deputy.

The IPT was reportedly formed in the Taliban-held town of Deh-e Dadi, south of Mazar-e-Sharif, that served as Namangani's headquarters among the IMU training camps along the Amu Darya River.[47] Some claimed that not all IMU leaders agreed with the change. These various structural changes may have indicated factional splits within the organisation.[48]

However, the existence of any such splits may now never become known. By late July 2001, IMU guerrillas were again attacking government forces on the Tajikistan-Kyrgyzstan border in the Batken region. Yuldosh, who assumed responsibility for the attacks in the name of the IMU, announced that what the Uzbekistani army had claimed to be military exercises earlier in the summer in Surkhondaryo (Surkhandarya) Province had actually been clashes with IMU guerrillas. Whether the guerrillas had passed through Tajikistan or been recruited from the sleeper cells already in place remained unclear to outsiders, although many observers believe the latter most likely.[49] Little else was heard of these skirmishes, before the 11 September 2001 terrorist attacks on the United States brought further attention to the region. For the governments of Uzbekistan and Kyrgyzstan, and to some extent Tajikistan, the 11 September attacks were a godsend. By offering intelligence and other cooperation, as well as the use of bases and air space, they quickly became the beneficiaries of American military aid.[50] When the Northern Alliance swept through Taliban-controlled Afghanistan, the IMU appears to have been swept aside with its Taliban sponsors.

Yet, it can be expected that the IMU to some extent survived the 2001 War on Terror in Afghanistan. The organisation has probably regrouped in Tajikistan, where it may easily go into hiding while reforming after the losses suffered during the war. Some survivors may also have escaped into Pakistan together with Al-Qaida. The defeat of the IMU and the death of Namangani in Afghanistan in late 2001 may signify the end of the movement. At the very least, its strength and power have been severely reduced. Nevertheless, the IMU remains popular among large segments of the religiously inclined part of the Uzbekistani population. The IMU may well rise again, either under surviving leaders from one of the factions of the original group or as a completely new group, which would simply assume the name of its renowned predecessor. The myth of the IMU remains alive and well, and it has merged with the already existing myths of anti-Russian resistance in Central Asia and the Caucasus. One example will suffice: the word has spread in the villages and army garrisons of Central Asia that the advance guard of IMU guerrilla groups consists of beautiful female snipers armed with sophisticated guns and night-vision goggles, equally prominent in seducing as killing enemy soldiers.[51] This myth probably derived from Chechnya, where many Russian soldiers swore that they were confronted by a legendary unit of Latvian (or Estonian, or both) women snipers known as the "White Tights"—a unit that has allegedly turned up in every post-Soviet war against Russia and its allies.[52]

The connection between the IMU and the well-funded international Wahhabi Islamic movement has also enhanced the group's popularity. In Uzbekistan, where any form of Islamic opposition is routinely labeled Wahhabism, this very persecution has given the Wahhabis a popular mystique that in fact encourages local Muslims to regard them as the only remaining true Muslims.[53]

Uzbekistan's demographic development suggests that Islamic extremism will continue to gain converts. Poverty is rising, and unemployment in the Ferghana Valley is reportedly as high as 80 percent. Each year, an additional 400,000 young people look for employment, often without finding any. Sixty percent of the population is under 25 years old, and this number is increasing.[54] This all makes for a fertile recruiting ground for extremist movements.

Other Uzbekistani Militant Islamic Groups

By 1999, there were also reported to be about 10 other, smaller militant Islamic groups active in the Ferghana Valley, with names such as *Tabligh* (Revelation), *Uzun soqol* (Long Beard), *Adolat uyushmasi* (Justice Union), *Islom lashkarlari* (Warriors of Islam), *Tavba* (Repentance), and *Nur* or *Nurchilar* (Ray of Light).[55] The number and names of these groups may well reflect old information, no longer reliable, or pure misunderstandings. Some groups of these names, such as the *Islom lashkarlari* of which Adolat was a faction, as well as their successor *Tavba* (also known as *Hizbullah*, or Party of God), were in fact groups crushed by the security forces in 1992 or 1995.[56] Others, such as *Uzun Soqol* (The Bearded Ones), are merely the popular nicknames of Islamic extremists.[57] Still others, including Tabligh, are Islamic missionary movements based in India and Pakistan. Even so, the Tabligh is known to have administered the recruitment of Islamic volunteers to the jihad in Afghanistan and the movement has been accused of subversive activities in Central Asia.[58] *Nurchilar*, finally, is a Sufi movement.[59] It probably has little to do with the other groups.

End Notes

1. ICG, *Central Asia: Islamist Mobilisation*, 4; Rashid, *Jihad*, 247.

2. See, for instance, Moldaliev, "An Incongruous War," 11–20; Rashid, *Jihad*, 137–86.

3. ICG, *Central Asia: Islamist Mobilisation*, 4; Rashid, *Jihad*, 137–40. See also Karen Dawisha and Bruce Parrott (eds.), *Conflict, Cleavage, and Change in Central Asia and the Caucasus* (Cambridge: Cambridge University Press, 1997), 382; Haghayeghi, *Islam and Politics*, 93–4.

4. Moldaliev, "An Incongruous War," 11–20; Rashid, *Jihad*, 247.

5. Rashid, *Jihad*, 146. She publicly disowned her son in 1999.

6. Rashid, *Jihad*, 138–9; Rashid, "Heart of Darkness," 8–12; Rashid, "Taliban: Exporting Extremism," 22–35; Rashid, "From Deobandism to Batken."

7. Moldaliev, "An Incongruous War," 11–20; Rashid, "From Deobandism to Batken;" *Washington Post*, 10 November 2001; Rashid, *Jihad*, 137–8. Khojiev was later publicly disowned by his sister Makhbuba Ahmedov and his brother Nasyr Khojiev (both arrested in 2000). Soon after, so did his mother. Rashid, *Jihad*, 147.

8. Rashid, *Jihad*, 140.

9. Rashid, *Jihad*, 138–41, 148.

10. Rashid, *Jihad*, 158.

11. Moldaliev, "An Incongruous War," 11–20; Rashid, "From Deobandism to Batken;" *Washington Post*, 10 November 2001; Rashid, *Jihad*, 137–8, 141–3.

12. Rashid, *Jihad*, 144, 145, 148.

13. Rashid, *Jihad*, 145–8. The declaration of jihad is reprinted in Rashid, *Jihad*, 247–9.

14. Melvin, *Uzbekistan*, 39, 57.

15. Rashid, *Jihad*, 151–5, 159.

16. Rashid, *Jihad*, 161–4, 175; Tursunov and Pikulina, *Severe Lessons of Batken.* See also ICG, *Central Asia: Islamist Mobilisation*, 7–9; and (although plagued by several errors) International Crisis Group (ICG), *Recent Violence in Central Asia: Causes and Consequences* (Central Asia/Brussels: International Crisis Group, Central Asia Briefing, 18 October 2000).

17. Tursunov and Pikulina, *Severe Lessons of Batken.*

18. Rashid, *Jihad*, 145, 164–7; Rashid, "Heart of Darkness;" Rashid, "Taliban: Exporting Extremism;" Rashid, "From Deobandism to Batken."

19. Rashid, *Jihad*, 167–70. See also ICG, *Central Asia: Islamist Mobilisation*, 7–9; and (although plagued by several errors) ICG, *Recent Violence.* For the narcotics situation, see ICG, *Central Asia: Drugs and Conflict* (Osh/Brussels: International Crisis Group, Asia Report 25, 26 November 2001).

20. Rashid, *Jihad*, 170–73, 258 n.13. For the media attention given to the American hostages, see, for instance, Michael Vig, "The Great Escape: Utah Climber Recalls Six Frightful Days in Kyrgyzstan," *Salt Lake Tribune*, 26 August 2000.

21. Rashid, *Jihad*, 176, 178.

22. Tursunov and Pikulina, *Severe Lessons of Batken;* Jane's Sentinel: Kyrgyzstan, 31 October 2000. See also "The Fergana Valley: A Magnet for Conflict in Central Asia," *IISS Strategic Comments* 6: 6 (July 2000).

23. Background: Melvin, *Uzbekistan*, 12–16. 1989 riots: Melvin, *Uzbekistan*, 25, 48; Lubin and Rubin, *Calming the Ferghana Valley*, 56. See also Shakhobitdin Ziiamov, "On the 1989 Ethnic Conflict in Uzbekistan," *Central Asia and the Caucasus*, 6, 2000, 134–8. 1990 riots: Melvin, *Uzbekistan*, 26.

24. Rashid, *Jihad*, 159–160; ICG, *Central Asia: Fault Lines*, 13.

25. Jane's Sentinel: Kyrgyzstan, 31 October 2000.

26. Tursunov and Pikulina, *Severe Lessons of Batken;* Jane's Sentinel: Kyrgyzstan, 31 October 2000. See also "Central Asia's Narcotics Industry."

27. Rashid, *Jihad*, 167.

28. Stern, "Pakistan's Jihad Culture," 122–3.

29. Rashid, *Jihad*, 141.

30. Rashid, "Heart of Darkness;" Rashid, "Taliban: Exporting Extremism;" Rashid, "From Deobandism to Batken."

31. Rashid, *Jihad*, 175–6.

32. Rashid, "Namangani's Foray."

33. Moldaliev, "An Incongruous War," 11–20; Rashid, "From Deobandism to Batken."

34. Fredholm, *Afghanistan and Central Asian Security.*

35. Rashid, *Jihad,* 158; Jane's World Insurgency and Terrorism 13, 27 November 2001.

36. Rashid, *Jihad,* 174.

37. Rashid, *Jihad,* 168, 171.

38. Melvin, *Uzbekistan,* 39, 57. See also the Department of State Web site, www.usembassy.org.uk/terror121.html; Michael Fredholm, "The Prospects for Genocide in Chechnya and Extremist Retaliation against the West," *Central Asian Survey* 19:3/4 (September–December 2000), 315–27.

39. Jane's World Insurgency and Terrorism 13, 27 November 2001.

40. *New York Times,* 25 September 2001.

41. Jane's World Insurgency and Terrorism 13, 27 November 2001.

42. Rashid, *Jihad,* 216.

43. *Dawn* (Pakistan), 21 May 2001.

44. *Washington Post,* 26 November 2001.

45. Jane's World Insurgency and Terrorism 13, 27 November 2001.

46. IMT: Jane's Sentinel: Tajikistan, 31 October 2000; IMK: Kiemiddin Sattori, "Tajik Press About the Youth and Islam," *Central Asia and the Caucasus* 3 (15), 2002, 126–34, on 131.

47. *Dawn* (Pakistan), 21 May 2001; Rashid, *Jihad,* 180–1.

48. Jane's World Insurgency and Terrorism 13, 27 November 2001.

49. Rashid, *Jihad,* 181–2; Interfax, 11 June 2001.

50. Fredholm, *Afghanistan and Central Asian Security.*

51. Rashid, *Jihad,* 10.

52. Anatol Lieven, *Chechnya: Tombstone of Russian Power* (New Haven: Yale University Press, 1998), 50.

53. Rashid, *Jihad,* 46.

54. Rashid, *Jihad,* 82.

55. ICG, *Central Asia: Islamist Mobilisation,* 18.

56. Muminov, "Traditional and Modern Religious-Theological Schools," 101–111.

57. Moldaliev, "An Incongruous War," 11–20.

58. Belokrenitskiy, "Islamic Radicalism," 104–116. For Jamaat-e Tablighi, see Cooley, *Unholy Wars,* 82–5.

59. Muminov, "Traditional and Modern Religious-Theological Schools," 101–111.

Islamic Extremism in Chechnya and the Caucasus

With the decline and fall of Soviet power, some northern Caucasian republics, most of them nominally Muslim and all part of the Russian Federation, declared sovereignty. Chechnya's first president, Jokhar Dudaev, went further and in 1991 declared independence. The Russian leaders could accept the break-up of the Soviet Union, but not the Russian Federation. The opposing Chechen and Russian policies ultimately led to the first Chechen war, which lasted from 1994 to 1996. Although unrecognized by the international community, Chechnya successfully defended its independence.[1] However, the economic carnage caused by the war caused the new Chechen president, Aslan Maskhadov, to lose control over parts of Chechnya that subsequently fell under the sway of militant Islamic extremists: Wahhabis supported by the Arab Afghan movement. Some of the Wahhabis in August 1999 assumed control over and spearheaded an uprising in neighbouring Dagestan, another Russian northern Caucasian republic with a Muslim population. The resulting fighting ultimately provoked a Russian invasion of Chechnya and the present war.[2]

Although Russian forces since have occupied most of Chechnya, the conflict between Chechnya and the Russian Federation shows few signs of being resolved soon. Nor is it likely to. Russia has again

embarked on war as the means to subdue the region, despite the fact
that the Chechens regularly have risen against their Russian rulers
since the region was first fully conquered by the tsarist armies in the
bloody wars of the 19th century.

Although Russia made the first moves toward the Caucasus in
1556, early attempts to conquer the region were unsuccessful and
Russia only seriously involved itself in the Caucasus from 1783 on.
In time, Russia conquered parts of Dagestan as well as territories
inhabited by Chechens and Ingush. Even though several northern
Caucasian groups united for the first time, from 1785 to 1791—
under Sheikh Mansur, a Chechen—to resist Russia, the tsarist
troops proved victorious. The Russian cause seemed less certain,
however, during the *ghazawat* (holy war) of 1830–1859, in which
the Dagestani religious leaders Ghazi Muhammad and Shamil united the mountain tribes of the eastern parts of the northern
Caucasus (a territory centered on Dagestan with some Chechen and
Ingush groups) into a religious state, an imamate. Shamil successfully resisted the Russian troops for three decades. Meanwhile, the
Cherkess (Circassians) in the western parts of the northern
Caucasus fought Russia in their own war. Divided by Christian
Ossetia and with little in common, the two northern Caucasian
resistance fronts never managed to cooperate efficiently against the
Russians. Shamil surrendered in 1859, and resistance by the
Cherkess, who never had a unified state, ended in 1864.

Russian occupation and the policy to settle large numbers of
ethnic Russians in the conquered territories led to a large exodus
of Cherkess, Chechens, Ingush, and Dagestanis to the Ottoman
Empire, where their descendants remain today in scattered communities. Unrest continued among those who stayed on, however,
and a major uprising took place in 1877–1878, in conjunction with
the Russian-Turkish War. In the Russian Civil War following the
1917 revolution, many northern Caucasians sided with the
Bolsheviks in an attempt to regain independence. A northern
Caucasian republic (the Mountain Republic) declared independence on 11 May 1918, but was crushed within a year by Gen.
Anton Denikin of the Russian White forces. More uprisings fol-

lowed and a second *ghazawat* broke out in 1920, again with most of the action in Dagestan. In 1921, an Autonomous Soviet Mountain Republic was formed. However, the Russian Soviets initiated a campaign against Islam, and the Mountain Republic lasted only until 1924. Further uprisings followed as regularly as the seasons changed (typically each spring) and were especially violent in 1924, 1926, 1928, 1929–1930, 1936, and 1941–1943. In earlier times the majority of the fighters had been Dagestanis, but after 1926 the Ingush and to some extent the Chechens became prominent. The vigorous Soviet campaigns to destroy Islam as a religious faith from 1924 had little effect.

In 1944, Soviet leader Joseph Stalin accused a number of northern Caucasian peoples, notably the Chechens and Ingush, of collaboration with the German invaders and deported them to Central Asia and Siberia. At the time, Stalin had made territorial demands on Turkey, a strategy that could have led to war, so he no doubt wished to remove potential Turkish allies from the Caucasus. And the uprising of 1941 probably influenced his final decision. Other mountain groups were forcibly resettled in the lowlands, and yet more ethnic Russians were settled in the urban areas of the region. However, Stalin's policy was reversed after his death, and from 1956 on the deported peoples began to return, causing frequent and occasionally violent disputes between the returnees and those who had been settled where the returnees used to live. Chechen and Ingush protests, for instance, took place in 1973.[3]

Stalin's policies, however, had served to break up the Chechen tribal structure: the Chechens of today are no longer tribesmen, and the majority—after more than 70 years of Soviet rule—are not militant Muslims. Most Chechens are urbanised, and the Chechen republic was fully industrialised in Soviet times. According to Soviet figures from 1989, Chechnya had a rural population of 63 percent, but this figure did not take into account the large numbers of Chechens who lived in cities outside Chechnya (nor for that matter that half the population of the capital Grozny at this time was made up of Russians).[4] Grozny was in Soviet times a major centre for research and the production of equipment for the petroleum industry. The city itself possessed major oil and gas refineries and even served as the main Soviet producer of aviation petrol. Although the early Dagestani, Chechen, and Ingush leaders had been imams, mullahs and sheikhs, that is, religious leaders, after 1940—when Chechen writer Hassan Israilov became the leading insurgent—the new generation was Soviet-educated and leadership was provided by the modern Chechen intelligentsia. This pattern has remained until the present. The Chechens of today have more in common with their Russian opponents than with the international Islamic extremists who nonetheless support Chechnya's struggle, often in ways directly opposed to the policies of Chechen president Maskhadov. Chechens have traditionally followed Sufi Islam, whereas the foreign Islamic extremists are Wahhabis, and are frequently accompanied by Wahhabi missionaries from the Middle East.[5]

What has confused the issue is that the most influential foreign Islamic extremists in Chechnya belong to the Chechen diaspora in the Middle East. They could thereby claim Chechen ethnicity, even though many of them speak only Arabic and virtually all are devoted Wahhabis who loathe traditional Caucasian Sufi Islam. Most notable among the Middle Eastern Chechens was the commander Habib Abdul Rahman Khattab. Reportedly born in Jordan (or perhaps Saudi Arabia; he may have held dual Jordanian-Saudi citizenship) in 1970, Khattab arrived in Chechnya with a small group of foreign volunteers in the spring of 1995, soon after the outbreak of the first of the two wars with Russia in the 1990s. Members of the Khattab group had already fought in places as diverse as Afghanistan, Tajikistan, and Bosnia as well as Abkhazia, Nagorno-Karabakh, and Ingushetia in the Caucasus. Khattab himself claimed to have fought in Afghanistan, Nagorno-Karabakh, and Tajikistan for eight years.[6] In Chechnya, he became the main commander of foreign Islamic extremists and remained so until his death in early 2002.[7]

Most Wahhabi missionaries concentrated their early activities not on Chechnya but neighbouring Dagestan.[8] The largest concentration of Wahhabis on the territory of Dagestan was situated in the

Buynaksk, Kazbek, Khasavyurt and Botlikh regions. They were led by well-funded missionaries from the Middle East who openly called themselves Wahhabis. The missionaries typically began by setting up mosques and Islamic boarding schools, often for orphans. Next the Wahhabis began to send young people abroad to study, with groups of between 15 to 30 young men going to Turkey, the United Arab Emirates, or Jordan. Upon their return, the students would drive from one village to another to propagate the faith among other young people. They distributed the appropriate literature and called upon Muslims to fight for the purification of Islam and evict the unbelievers from the villages. The Wahhabis then set up local communities that banned music as well as traditional celebrations, weddings, and funeral practices. They began to enforce Wahhabi dress, described earlier.

The Wahhabis often used material incentives to gain additional followers. Any preacher who agreed to propagate Wahhabism would receive a one-time payment of $1,000–$1,500, followed by an additional $100 to $150 every month, substantial sums in the Caucasus. Furthermore, he would receive another $50–$100 for each new recruit brought in.[9]

In August 1998, the Dagestani Wahhabis declared their villages independent from the secular authorities.[10] They had by then been involved in several armed clashes with local villagers and police in the period 1996–1997. The violence culminated in a battle with Dagestani police on 23 May 1998 that turned into a siege of several days of a Wahhabi village.[11] The Dagestani Wahhabis were apparently mostly killed or dispersed in the aftermath of the August 1999 uprising and during the second Chechen war.[12]

The Chechen Wahhabis, led by Khattab until his death, have been decimated by the current war but continue to launch operations against the Russian forces in Chechnya in conjunction with the Chechens under President Maskhadov, who seem to have no intention of giving up the struggle for independence. The Chechen Wahhabis can be said to form part of the Arab Afghan network and share a recruiting base (unemployed young men) as well as attitudes toward Islam with other Arab Afghans. Except for the

Caucasus, the Chechen and Dagestani Wahhabi movement also maintained a small presence in Central Asia. There the Wahhabi groups relied on bases in Afghanistan and, perhaps, those provided by the IMU in Tajikistan.[13] Despite this, the Chechen Wahhabis can be distinguished from the Arab Afghans because they, at least so far, principally fought a neighbouring government (Russia) and formed a native fighting force rather than joining the global movement promoted by Usamah bin Ladin.

In contrast to the often eloquently argued global aspirations of the Arab Afghans, presented on the Internet and in various publications, only limited amounts of information specifically from the Chechen Wahhabis have ever reached the West. The Chechens run a number of Web sites, but these have, so far, been concerned mostly with the war in Chechnya and do not fully reflect the Wahhabi position of the small minority of Islamic extremists.[14]

The Russian war in Chechnya has not eradicated Islamic extremism: the extremists were always a small minority in comparison with the secular or only moderately Muslim Chechen fighters who continue to oppose the Russian military presence. Although the extremists have attempted to hijack the Chechen nationalist-separatist movement,[15] they have not yet succeeded. However, Russian military operations in the northern Caucasus have always tended to cause the radicalization of Islam in the region. Today the same pattern is discernible, and extremist Islamic leaders with ties to groups in Saudi Arabia, Yemen, Afghanistan, and other centers of radicalism remain active in the Chechen war. Not only have leaders such as Khattab attracted militants from other volatile areas into Chechnya (many of whom have been apprehended in Georgia), such men as the Chechen politician Zelimkhan Yandarbiev, who travelled extensively in the Middle East and eventually visited the Taliban-sponsoring Pakistan, further strengthened the ties between Chechen radicals and other Islamic extremists. (In January 2000, the Taliban government of Afghanistan recognised the separatist government in Chechnya.)[16]

That Islamic extremism is gaining converts in Chechnya and the rest of the Caucasus is due neither to religion or nationalism but to demography. During the decade of *de facto* Chechen independence, a new generation of Chechens reached the age when they could bear arms. Of course, exact figures for the annual population growth are unknown, but comparable ones can be found in neighbouring Dagestan (e.g., 21 births per 1,000 in 1989) and Ingushetia (e.g., 13.4 per 1,000 in 1997).[17] In the 1970s and 1980s, the Chechen rate of annual population growth was as high as 31 to 40 per 1,000.[18] The young men and women of the new generation were never part of Russia and have no loyalties to Russia. Moreover, due to the economic devastation of Chechnya, which continues unabated, their chances of finding employment and a regular, peaceful life in Chechnya are nil and, due to prevalent suspicions of criminality and terrorism associated with Chechens in the Russian Federation, are not much better elsewhere. Their choice is between unemployment at home, work for criminal gangs in Russia, or enlistment in a religious brotherhood with international connections, monetary resources, and outspoken egalitarianism. That such a movement is regarded as extremist will hardly be a serious concern for the new generation of young Chechens, who have grown up in an environment of seemingly unending war.

The radicalisation of the Chechen youth may yet become a grave problem for the West as well. If the West allows Russia to gradually subdue Chechnya, the most radical Chechens are bound to turn up in the extremist Islamic circles that currently see the West as much as Moscow as their enemy. Wahhabism may yet win the day, although it is far too early to equate Chechen separatism with Islamic extremism and terrorism, as Russia commonly does.

Early in the conflict, many Chechen refugees and some Chechen insurgents fled to the Pankisi Gorge in neighbouring Georgia. The Pankisi Gorge already contained a large indigenous population of ethnic Chechens who had only limited contact with the rest of Georgia. The Georgian government, which has remained in turmoil since independence was granted in 1991, had neither the resources nor the inclination to deal with the problem—which in any case only affected Chechnya, not Georgia. Meanwhile, Russia threatened to send troops into the gorge to eradicate the Chechen fighters there.

The United States no doubt saw this as an opportunity to not only expand relations with Georgia but also to acquire a presence in the Caucasus. On 27 February 2002, it was disclosed that President Bush had extended the War on Terror also to this region through a military assistance program to Georgia. Among other undertakings, the United States promised to create and train a Georgian rapid-deployment force of about 1,500 troops.[19] On 30 April, the first 20 of about 200 instructors (from the U.S. Army's 10th Special Forces Group arrived to train Georgian security forces in counterinsurgency operations. The avowed purpose of such operations is eventually to hunt down Islamic extremists among the guerrillas from neighbouring Chechnya.[20]

End Notes

1. See, for instance, Carlotta Gall and Thomas de Waal, *Chechnya: A Small Victorious War* (London: Pan, 1997); Lieven, *Chechnya;* Stasys Knezys and Romanas Sedlickas, *The War in Chechnya* (College Station: Texas A & M University Press, 1999).

2. See, for instance, Lena Jonson and Murad Esenov (eds.), *Chechnya: The International Community and Strategies for Peace and Stability* (Stockholm: Swedish Institute of International Affairs, 2000); Fredholm, "Prospects for Genocide in Chechnya."

3. For further details on the historical background, see John F. Baddeley, *The Russian Conquest of the Caucasus* (London: Longman, 1908); Moshe Gammer, *Muslim Resistance to the Tsar: Shamil and the Conquest of Chechnia and Daghestan* (Frank Cass, 1994); Marie Bennigsen Broxup (ed.), *The North Caucasus Barrier: The Russian Advance towards the Muslim World* (London: Hurst & Company, 1992); John B. Dunlop, *Russia Confronts Chechnya: Roots of a Separatist Conflict* (Cambridge: Cambridge University Press, 1998); Ben Fowkes (ed.), *Russia and Chechnia: The Permanent Crisis-Essays on Russo-Chechen Relations* (London: Macmillan, 1998).

4. Anna Matveeva, *The North Caucasus: Russia's Fragile Borderland* (London: Royal Institute of International Affairs, 1999), 93.

5. See, for instance, Vakhit Akaev, "Religious-Political Conflict in the Chechen Republic of Ichkeria," Lena Jonson and Murad Esenov (eds.), *Political Islam and Conflicts in Russia and Central Asia* (Stockholm: Swedish Institute of International Affairs, 1999); Sanobar Shermatova, *The Role of Radical Islamic Groups in the North Caucasian Events,* unpublished paper.

6. Igor Dobaev, "Islamic Radicalism in the Northern Caucasus," *Central Asia and the*

Caucasus 6, 2000, 76–86, on 79. Dobaev refers to newspaper articles including one by Umar ben Ismail, amir of the Wahhabi *Jamaat* of the Chechen town of Urus-Martan. On Khattab, see also *Intelligence Newsletter* 364 (26 August 1999), 8.

7. See, for instance, *Guardian* (UK), 26 April 2002; Thomas de Waal, "Death of a Warlord," *IWPR's Caucasus Reporting Service* 127 (2 May 2002; www.iwpr.net).

8. See, for instance, Amri Shikhsaidov, "Islam in Dagestan," Jonson and Esenov, *Political Islam and Conflicts;* Enver Kisriev, "Dagestan: Factors of Conflict and Stability," Jonson and Esenov, *Chechnya;* Shermatova, *Role of Radical Islamic Groups.*

9. Charles W. Blandy, *Dagestan: The Gathering Storm* (Sandhurst: Conflict Studies Research Centre, nd (probably 1997); Shermatova, *Role of Radical Islamic Groups.*

10. RFE/RL *Newsline,* 18 August 1998.

11. RIA-Novosti, 24 May 1998, 25 May 1998; RFE/RL *Newsline,* 25 May 1998. See also Shikhsaidov, "Islam in Dagestan."

12. ITAR-TASS, 13 September 1999.

13. See, for instance, Moldaliev, "An Incongruous War," 11–20.

14. Web sites, www.kavkaz.org; www.qoqaz.net, connected to www.azzam.com.

15. See, for instance, *Intelligence Newsletter* 364 (26 August 1999), 1; *Intelligence Newsletter* 374 (20 January 2000), 6–7; the interview with Maskhadov on Deutsche Welle, 10 April 2000. See also Lackey, "Yemen," 24–29; *Intelligence Newsletter* 366 (23 September 1999), 7; Cooley, *Unholy Wars,* 175, 179–80.

16. RFE/RL *Newsline,* 17 January 2000.

17. Matveeva, *North Caucasus,* 91, 95.

18. Lieven, *Chechnya,* 323.

19. *Washington Post,* 27 February 2002, 2 March 2002; Devdariani, "U.S. and Georgian Officials."

20. *Washington Post,* 1 May 2002; *USA Today,* 30 April 2002.

APPENDIX 13

China and the
Uighur East Turkestan Movement

The membership of the East Turkestan movement is primarily made up of ethnic Uighurs and others of Turkic origin from China's westernmost province, Xinjiang, designated the Xinjiang Uighur Autonomous Region since 1955. The name of the movement as well as its aspirations derive from East Turkestan, earlier the common name for the region and from 1944 to 1950 the name of an independent, Uighur-led secular republic in the northern section of present Xinjiang (Ili, Tacheng, and Altay regions) that enjoyed support from the Soviet Union.[1] The founders of the movement were all leaders from this republic who had been forced into exile. There also was a brief state formation called the Turkish Islamic Republic of East Turkestan from 1933 to 1934—an unusually bloody and violent period even in this region's history—which the movement claims was the first republic of this name.[2] The ethnic Uighurs within the movement often refer to any future independent state as Uighurstan rather than East Turkestan.[3] The strength of the movement, or rather its two main components (secular and clerical) is unknown to Western observers.

About 60 percent of Xinjiang's approximately 16.9 million inhabitants belong to minorities. The region's largest ethnic group numbers 7.9 million. Most other minorities are also of Turkic origin, including a population of perhaps 1.3 million Kazaks, 165,000 Kyrgyz, and 13,000 Uzbeks. There are also 33,000 Persian-speaking Tajiks, as well as a significant population of Mongols. Han Chinese so far form only the second largest ethnic group, with a population of approximately 6 million (according to not necessarily reliable official statistics, since China for political reasons may wish to play down the Han Chinese presence in the region).[4]

There is also an Uighur exile community in Istanbul. This was dominated by Isa Yusuf Alptekin, commonly known as Isa Beg, former general secretary of the republic, until his death in 1995 (or perhaps 1993). Among the groups in Turkey championing Uighur independence were the East Turkestan National Salvation Committee, the East Turkestan National Revolutionary Front, and the East Turkestan Charity Fund.[5] Istanbul is also the headquarters of the Eastern Turkestan Refugees Association (*Dogu Türkistan Gocmenler Dernegi*), established in 1960 and first headed by Isa Beg, then Arslan Alptekin, although the latter, who was Isa Beg's son, was then only one of the group's several leaders. This organisation's emblem and flag (white star and crescent on blue) is the same as that of the failed Turkish Islamic Republic of East Turkestan. Also in Istanbul is the East Turkestan Foundation, headed by Mehmet Riza Bekin.[6] Some groups maintain a presence further afield, such as in Germany, where the first Uighur or East Turkestan National Congress assembled in October 1999. Germany is also the home of Erkin Alptekin, eldest son of Isa Beg.[7] There is an East Turkestan Information Center in Sweden, apparently headed by one Dilxat Raxit.[8]

Kazakstan has a substantial Uighur minority of around 200,000.[9] The largest of several Uighur political groups in the country are the Revolutionary Front of East Turkestan and the Uighurstan Liberation Organisation. The Revolutionary Front of East Turkestan (also known as the United Revolutionary Group for Eastern Turkestan or United National Revolutionary Front, unless either is yet another group, there being many Uighur factions), led by Modan Muglisi, advocates armed struggle against China. It claims to have nearly 30 armed units operating in

Xinjiang. The Uighurstan Liberation Organization, based in Kazakhstan's former capital of Almaty and headed by Hashir Vahidi, former commander of the republic's military forces, has renounced violent means. Almaty is also the base of the Committee for Eastern Turkestan, formed in 1992 and headed by Yusupbeg Muglisi. Yet another group advocating armed struggle is the Organization for East Turkestan Freedom. Several separatist parties were banned as early as 1996.[10]

There are also several Uighur groups in Kyrgyzstan that advocate an independent state in Xinjiang. Although some Uighurs in Kyrgyzstan are in favour of uniting with the Uighurs in Xinjiang, the mountainous nature of the Kyrgyz-Chinese border and the comparative lack of transportation infrastructure make this possibility far less acute than similar sentiments in Kazakhstan, where certain groups have demanded territory from both Kazakhstan and China for an independent Uighur state.[11] Nonetheless, it appears that Kyrgyzstan has faced Chinese pressure to deal with its separatist Uighurs: in May 2000 five Uighur separatists were ordered deported to China. Perhaps in retaliation, a leading Chinese businessman was kidnapped in the Kyrgyzstani city of Osh by what may have been Uighur separatists, demanding a ransom for his release. On 10 July 2000, the Kyrgyz government responded by arresting 10 members of the Uighur Liberation Front, among whom were reportedly Uzbeks, Uighurs, Turks, Kyrgyz, and Chinese (citizens of Uighur origin?) who allegedly had fought in Chechnya and trained in Pakistan and Afghanistan.[12]

There is a modest Uighur population in Uzbekistan.[13] However, due to the authoritarian government there, it is unlikely that these Uighurs could mobilise inside the country, even if they wanted to.

Some Uighur separatists built bases in Afghanistan, under Taliban protection. One such base at Kamsachi near Mazar-e-Sharif was shared with the Udeshev group of the IMU.[14] Some 200 to 300 Uighurs are believed to have received military training in Taliban camps.[15]

No Uighur movement appears to have maintained any presence in Xinjiang until the early 1990s; earlier ethnic violence directed against Han Chinese seemed spontaneous and of local origin. There are a few reasons for this. First, the fragmentation of the Soviet Union gave greater freedom in the new Central Asian republics, which allowed an increased level of Uighur political mobilisation, as well as making Uighurs in Xinjiang realise that the same could happen in China, too. Second, the Han Chinese immigration into Xinjiang, sponsored by the Chinese government, continually increased the non-Uighur population in Xinjiang from below 5 percent of the total population in 1950 to somewhere over 40 percent today, which has caused the Uighurs to feel swamped. Third, the spread of radical Islam inspired the Muslim population of Xinjiang to reassert itself, especially as Chinese policies on religion and minorities in the early 1980s grew increasingly liberal (cultural and religious reforms in 1978, followed by the opening of Xinjiang to foreign trade and tourism in 1985.)[16] Funding for new mosques and the opening of Islamic seminaries increasingly arrived from Saudi Arabia and the Persian Gulf states. Finally, the opening of the region to cross-border trade and economic growth has brought outside ideas, as well as funds, and at the same time caused further resentment as local Uighurs saw Chinese interests take in most of the new money.[17]

Since 1989, violent anti-Chinese riots have taken place in Xinjiang's capital Urumqi as well as in and around such major cities as Kashgar and Yining.[18] Beginning in early April 1990, violence began to spread over wide areas indicating a possible pattern of coordination, or at least a network of militant separatists. The Chinese government blamed a new, previously unheard of local Islamic group known as the Islamic Party (or Islamic Movement) of East Turkestan. Further unrest and bombings followed, and in 1993, the government blamed another group, the Islamic Reformists Party. The names of the groups indicate that both were clerical, not secular. The extremist groups were also reputed to be forging links with Uighur organised crime networks in Beijing, Guangzhou, and other major cities.[19] A series of terrorist activities connected with the movement followed, including a campaign of sporadic violence against ethnic Chinese in Xinjiang, the planting of bombs and attacks on police and military personnel, as well as bank robberies to finance the movement. The extremist movement also claimed responsibility for a bombing in Beijing in 1997 that caused approximately 30 casualties.[20] Eventually, on 21 January 2002, China's State Council released a report that named Hasan Mahsum, the leader of the East Turkestan Islamic Movement, as a beneficiary of Usamah bin Ladin's Al-Qaida network.[21] In anticipation of Chinese President Jiang Zemin's scheduled visit to the United States in October 2002 and as a reward for China's public announcement of its regulations for the export of missile technology, the United States in late August 2002 designated the East Turkestan Islamic Movement a terrorist group.[22] There were other local groups in Xinjiang, however. These apparently include (or included) bands known variously as the Wolves of Lop Nor, the Gulja (Yining) Liberation Movement, and the *Shaniyaz*.[23]

The East Turkestan movement may be the only truly native separatist organisation in northern Central Asia, having emerged from its own base rather than any Wahhabi-inspired international Islamic networks. However, there appear to be two, very different, strands in the movement's background. The exile groups in Istanbul and Germany still seem to be secular and nationalist, while the younger generation of the movement, and certainly the groups based in Central Asia, are clearly in sympathy and maintain links with the Wahhabi movement. While the older East Turkestan groups were nationalist and secular, the younger groups found Islam their unifying factor and drew inspiration from the Afghan war.[24] The Pakistani organisation Tabligh is believed to have sent supplies to Xinjiang and has provided religious instruction.[25] So has the Hizb ut-Tahrir. In June 2001, two Hizb-ut Tahrir cells were reportedly found by Chinese security forces: one in Urumqi and one in Khotan.[26]

The Islamic approach to insurgency in Xinjiang is probably more fruitful than the older, fundamentally intellectual nationalist ideology. Uighur intellectuals frequently describe themselves as Turkic and Uighurs, but the majority of the population appear to see themselves as Muslims first and Uighurs second. Besides, the

majority of Uighur intellectuals live in Urumqi, where they are isolated from and out of touch with the peasantry.[27]

To maintain stability in Xinjiang and to fight separatism, China
has emphasised the need for the economic development of
Xinjiang. One way to achieve this is through increased trade with
the Central Asian republics. However, this policy is a double-edged
sword: it also brings the risk of increased religious activity from
Islamic groups in those countries. Cross-border trade may also be
used by extremist groups to transmit financial or material aid to
their supporters in China. If separatist activity in Xinjiang or political instability in Central Asia were to increase, the Chinese leaders
may decide to restrict activity along the border, regardless of the
consequences for economic development.[28] The 1990s have already
seen sweeping purges of unauthorised Islamic clerics and mosques,
together with severe restrictions on Islamic activity in Xinjiang.[29]

So far, the Uighurs appear to be satisfied with fighting China.
Even though there is a considerable Uighur population in the former Soviet Central Asian republics, the movement's leaders appear
to regard these states as bases rather than targets for separatist
activities. This would indicate that there is little chance of the
movement instigating terrorism outside China's borders. On the
other hand, some Uighur separatists had built bases in Afghanistan,
and under Taliban protection established contacts with Islamic
extremists from the Arab Afghan movement (who in turn may have
got involved in Xinjiang).[30] This indicates that the Islamic wing of
the East Turkestan movement has the potential to turn into a more
general security threat to the region. Not even China's protégé
Pakistan has been successful in preventing its own Islamic extremists, such as the Jamaat-e Islami movement, from assisting separatists in Xinjiang.[31] Besides, strikes against Chinese interests in
such important cities as Hong Kong and Shanghai, and further
abroad, cannot be ruled out. These attacks might affect foreign,
including Western, interests.

Another problem for China is that the influx of Han Chinese
into Xinjiang appears to have come to an end. Recent years have
even seen a net outflow of Han Chinese because of the lifting of

residency controls and the establishment of a reasonably free labour market. Those Han Chinese who are able to migrate are increasingly attracted to the vibrant economies of the coastal, eastern regions of China, where many of them still have relatives.[32] For the Chinese leaders, who have noted the flight of ethnic Russians from the former Soviet Central Asian republics, this is a worrisome prospect.

End Notes

1. Justin Jon Rudelson, *Oasis Identities: Uyghur Nationalism along China's Silk Road* (New York: Columbia University Press, 1997), 29, 57, 159; Burles, *Chinese Policy*, 9. See also Linda Benson, *The Ili Rebellion: The Moslem Challenge to Chinese Authority in Xinjiang 1944–1949* (New York: M. E. Sharpe, 1990).

2. Rudelson, *Oasis Identities*, 6, 28; Roostam Sadri, "The Islamic Republic of Eastern Turkestan: A Comparative Review," *Journal of the Institute of Muslim Minority Affairs* 5:2 (1984), 294–319; Lars Erik Nyman, "Turkish Influence on the Islamic Republic of Eastern Turkestan (TIRET)," *Materiala Turcica* 2 (1976), 12–24; Erling Hoh, "Hear Our Prayer," *Far Eastern Economic Review*, 13 April 2000, 24–5.

3. Hoh, "Hear Our Prayer," 24–5.

4. Burles, *Chinese Policy*, 9; Davis, "Xinjiang," 417–21; Xu Tao, "Extremist Threat in Northwestern China," *Central Asia and the Caucasus* 5, 2000, 83–4; Rudelson, *Oasis Identities*, 21–3; Dodge Billingsley, "China Frets over Xinjiang Separatists," *Jane's Intelligence Review* 13:11 (November 2001), 36.

5. Davis, "Xinjiang," 417–21.

6. Hoh, "Hear Our Prayer," 24–5; Rudelson, *Oasis Identities*, 33.

7. *Intelligence Digest*, 5 December 1997; *The Economist*, 12 February 2000; Hoh, "Hear Our Prayer," 24–5. See also, for instance, Erkin Alptekin, "Eastern Turkistan After 32 Years of Exile," *Central Asian Survey* 1:4, 149–53.

8. *Washington Post*, 27 August 2002.

9. Davis, "Xinjiang," 417–21; Curtis, Glenn E. (ed.).Kazakhstan, *Kyrgyzstan, Tajikistan, Turkmenistan, and Uzbekistan: Country Studies* (Washington, D.C.: Library of Congress, 1997), 27.

10. Davis, "Xinjiang," 417–21; Jane's World Insurgency and Terrorism 10, 19 October 2000.

11. Jane's Sentinel: Kyrgyzstan, 31 October 2000; Jane's Sentinel: Kazakhstan, 2 January 2001; Davis, "Xinjiang," 417–21. See also Burles, *Chinese Policy*, 9–10, as well as 56–7.

12. Ahmed Rashid, "Central Asia Summary: Recent Developments in Kazakhstan, Kyrgyzstan and Turkmenistan," *Eurasia Insight* (eurasianet.org), 18 January 2001.

13. Burles, *Chinese Policy,* 8.
14. Rashid, "From Deobandism to Batken;" Rashid, "Heart of Darkness," 8–12; Joakim Enwall, "Towards a Sociolinguistic History of Sinkiang," Juntunen and Schlyter, *Return to the Silk Routes,* 129.
15. *Economist,* 29 September 2001.
16. Rudelson, *Oasis Identities,* 123.
17. Davis, "Xinjiang," 417–21.
18. Burles, *Chinese Policy,* 9–10.
19. Davis, "Xinjiang," 417–21.
20. Burles, *Chinese Policy,* 9–10; Rudelson, *Oasis Identities,* 170–171.
21. Mark Berniker, "China's Uighur Policy Draws Critics in Kazakhstan," *Eurasianet,* 29 January 2002 (www.eurasianet.org).
22. *Washington Post,* 27 August 2002.
23. Jane's World Insurgency and Terrorism 10, 19 October 2000; Jane's World Insurgency and Terrorism 11, 31 January 2001.
24. Davis, "Xinjiang," 417–21.
25. Jane's World Insurgency and Terrorism 10, 19 October 2000.
26. *Economist,* 29 September 2001, 30 March 2002.
27. Rudelson, *Oasis Identities,* 117–20, 133.
28. Burles, *Chinese Policy ,* 14, 57.
29. Davis, "Xinjiang," 417–21.
30. Zanini, "Middle Eastern Terrorism," 250. See also Burles, *Chinese Policy,* 18.
31. See, for instance, Burles, *Chinese Policy,* 18, based on "Unwelcome Traffic," *Far Eastern Economic Review,* 7 December 1995, 40.
32. *Central Asia: Islamist Mobilisation and Regional Security,* 25.

APPENDIX

Islamic Extremism in Palestine

14

This appendix will not deal with the key question of relations between Palestinians and the state of Israel but only with the active participation of Palestinian groups in the international Sunni Islamic extremist networks. Although both Jewish and Palestinian organisations in Palestine frequently have relied on terrorism as their chief weapon, they typically remained secular and nationalist rather than religious in outlook and, in the case of the Muslim groups, did not see Sunni Islamic extremism as their goal. Examples include Jewish terrorist bands, especially those active before the British left Palestine on 14 May 1948, such as *Irgun Zvai Leumi* (National Military Organisation), the *Haganah,* and Unit 101, from whence Israeli leaders such as the Menachem Begin emerged, as well as the Palestinian *Al-Fatah* (Conquest, the Palestinian National Liberation Movement) and Palestine Liberation Organization (PLO), founded in 1957 and May 1964, respectively, with the aim of destroying Israel. Contemporary Jewish terrorist groups such as *Kach* and *Kahane Chai* (Kahane Lives) are clerical in outlook but, of course, have nothing to do with Islamic extremism. All these groups remain beyond the scope of this book.[1]

The first Islamic extremist group in Palestine was the Muslim

Brotherhood. Hassan al-Banna had set up branches in many towns of Palestine already between 1942 and 1945. When the organisation was first banned in Egypt in 1948, and again after the attempted assassination of Nasser in 1954, thousands of brotherhood members moved abroad, many ending up in Palestine or among Palestinian refugees in Jordan. Although the Muslim Brotherhood in Palestine itself eventually collapsed, its numerous offshoots in time acquired major roles among the Palestinians in the Gaza Strip. Radicalism was further encouraged by the Israeli occupation of the Gaza Strip and the West Bank, as well as other territories, after the Six-Day War of 5 June 1967. (UN Resolution 242 still calls for Israeli withdrawal from the occupied territories). The many offshoots of the brotherhood among the Palestinians included the *Al-Majd* (intelligence) and *Al-Mujahidun* (commando) paramilitary organisation formed in 1983.[2]

Another, currently far more important offshoot of the brotherhood was Hamas (as well as an abbreviation of *Harakat al-Muqawama al-Islamiyyah,* or Islamic Resistance Movement, it means enthusiasm or zeal). Hamas emerged in the Gaza Strip in late 1987 under Sheikh Ahmad Yassin (who was paralyzed from illness and detained from May 1989 to October 1997) and was officially established in August 1988. The movement originated in the Palestinian uprising (intifada) against Israeli occupation, a period of violent protests that first erupted on 9 December 1987 in the Gaza Strip and soon expanded to the West Bank. Like other Palestinian organisations, Hamas advocates the destruction of Israel. At first a branch of the Muslim Brotherhood in the Gaza Strip and the West Bank, Hamas quickly developed into a serious rival to the established PLO. The fundamental difference between the two organisations was that the PLO embodied a national, secular view of a future Palestine, while Hamas offered to introduce an Islamic state based on Islamic law. Compared with PLO leaders, who were generally regarded as corrupt and compromising, the Hamas leadership appeared to be pure and dedicated to Islam. As in other Muslim countries with internal problems, this produced an immediate response among the Palestinian youth, especially those born as refugees and with little hope for the future. Hamas quickly found numerous recruits among the dissatisfied youths of the Palestinian slums and lower class neighbourhoods, especially since it promoted a strong social agenda, in addition to nationalism. Hamas set up a number of social functions to take care of health care, education, and grassroots political representation, gaining tens of thousands of supporters in the process.[3] Hamas soon established a military wing, the Qassam Brigades (named after Izz al-Din al-Qassam, a Syrian sheikh who had led an uprising in the early 1930s and was martyred on 19 November 1935 in Yabrod, Palestine, and continues to serve as a symbol for Palestinian resistance).[4] Among Palestinians, Hamas is currently the most important Wahhabi organisation.[5]

Qassam was also the main source of inspiration for yet another Palestinian Islamic extremist organisation, the Islamic Jihad movement formed in the 1980s by Fathi al-Shiqaqi (assassinated in October 1995, allegedly by Israeli agents) and inspired at least in part by the Iranian Islamic revolution of 1979. Islamic Jihad is currently led by Ramadan Abdullah Shallah, who used to be an adjunct professor at the University of South Florida.[6] Islamic Jihad was another offshoot of the Muslim Brotherhood, though apparently out of the brotherhood organisation in Egypt rather than Palestine.[7] Palestinian Islamic Jihad maintained a political wing centred around the Al-Qassam Mosque in the Gaza Strip.[8]

Hamas and Palestinian Islamic Jihad are vehemently opposed to Israel and carried out some 30 suicide bombings in Israel between October 1994 and 2001, with as many as 16 attacks in 2001 alone, all after the 28 September 2000 start of the second intifada.[9] Neither movement, however, was at first devoted to the Islamic extremist ideals. Neither has directly targeted the United States or Americans. The Palestinian Islamic Jihad in particular long appeared to be far less Wahhabi than other extremist groups, no doubt because it is politically closer to Iran than is Hamas.[10] However, not long before his death in 1995, Fathi al-Shiqaqi declared his intention to fight not only Israel but anybody opposed to Islam in Europe and Algeria.[11]

This is significant, because Islamic Jihad and Hamas together are believed to control the leading Muslim organisations and most of the mosques in Western Europe and North America.[12] Usamah bin Ladin has maintained occasional contacts with Hamas at least since 1994, when he offered some financial assistance. His funding of Hamas grew substantially in August 1997, after the United States had frozen the assets of Hamas wherever it could. Some Hamas members subsequently went for training in the Al-Qaida camps in Afghanistan. Hamas reportedly received emissaries from bin Ladin as late as September 2000 and January 2001.[13]

Still, it is too early to place with any surety Hamas and Islamic Jihad in the Al-Qaida camp. It is quite clear that both employ terrorism as a political weapon and ideologically follow Wahhabism, but there is in fact no real evidence to connect the two Palestinian groups with Al-Qaida on an organisational, rather than personal, level. The organisations, though sharing certain beliefs as well as an emphasis on terrorism and possibly even some members, seem to remain separate entities. While Al-Qaida strives for an international jihad, Hamas and Islamic Jihad, despite some Wahhabi tendencies, so far appear content in fighting for a national cause.

End Notes

1. When no other source is given, this section is based on the useful summary Katzman, *Terrorism*.

2. Hiro, *Islamic Fundamentalism*, 86–7.

3. Shaul Mishal and Avraham Sela, *The Palestinian Hamas: Vision, Violence, and Coexistence* (New York: Columbia University Press, 2000); Sela, *Political Encyclopedia*, 276–80. Hamas formed on 14 December 1987.

4. Emerson, *American Jihad*, 110.

5. See, for instance, Palazzi, "Islamists Have It Wrong," 3–11.

6. Emerson, *American Jihad*, 110.

7. Emerson, *American Jihad*, 118.

8. Emerson, *American Jihad*, 110.

9. Further information is available from the Terrorism Research Center (www.terrorism.com) and in particular, if read with care, International Policy Institute

for Counter-Terrorism (Israel; www.ict.org.il). Hamas maintained a Web site, www.palestine-info.net. Communiqués from Hamas have been presented on Assabeel Online, www.assabeel.com, and when of a military nature, www.demon.co.uk/alquds/more.htm. The *Palestine Times* Web site, www.ptimes.com, also promoted Hamas, as did The Liberty for the Muslim World, a London-based group, www.lmw.org. Other sites that seem to have connections with Hamas have been http://members.wbs.net/homepages/p/a/l/palestine2000.html and www.mynet.net/~msanews/Launchpad/hamas.html.

10. For more information on the Islamic Jihad, see, for instance, Sela, *Political Encyclopedia,* 377–8. The movement maintained a Web site, www.qudsway.com.

11. Jacquard, *Osama Bin Laden,* 63.

12. See, for instance, Palazzi, "Islamists Have It Wrong," 3–11.

13. Jacquard, *Osama Bin Laden,* 64, 282 n.8.

Islamic Extremism in the Balkans: Bosnia, Albania, Kosovo, and Macedonia

In the former Yugoslavia, the ethnic conflicts and the Muslim uprisings in Bosnia, Kosovo, and Macedonia attracted generous support from Saudi Arabia and the other Persian Gulf states. The formation of an Islamic support system in the Balkans was greatly facilitated by the Western media's generating public and government support for the Muslims, who were generally depicted as innocent victims forced to fight for their very lives against murderous Slav aggressors. Whether this one-sided media view was exaggerated or not is beside the point and beyond the scope of this book; however, the media greatly facilitated the work of the many Islamic extremists who hurried to the assistance of the Yugoslavian Muslims. Some were Shia and sponsored by Iran.; most, however, appear to have been Sunni. And some were Arab Afghans.

While U.S. policy towards Afghanistan in the 1990s was often was often ill-considered, Western policy toward the former Yugoslavia in the same period can only be described as hopelessly tied up with domestic Western concerns. Ultimately, its good sense is questionable and its intent, beyond making Western policymakers feel good, remains incomprehensible. There were undeniably real humanitarian concerns that prompted the Western support to the several Muslim uprisings in former Yugoslavia. Yet, it remains baffling that the West—which at first did little to ameliorate a real humanitarian disaster in Bosnia—in the end used the full military might of NATO to carve out an independent Muslim pseudo-state, Kosovo, only to hand it over to what until then was described as a band of terrorists and a supporting cast of Wahhabi missionaries. The latter promptly arrived to build mosques, teach Islamic law, and encourage anti-Western sentiments.

No present government in the Balkans can be said to form part of the Al-Qaida network, but there is considerable evidence that former Bosnian and Albanian governments, not to mention the ethnic Albanians in Kosovo and Macedonia, have benefitted from, and on occasion protected, members of the Arab Afghan movement. A further cause for worry is that thousands of Bosnians and Kosovo Albanians have been accepted throughout Europe and the United States as refugees. Among this large migrant population, there are likely to be quite a few Islamic extremists who can be counted on to share the ideals of Al-Qaida.

Bosnia

The vicious conflict in Bosnia, the causes of which are too complex to go into here, served all the needs of the Islamic extremist who was weary of fighting the same old war in Afghanistan. For some extremists, Bosnia was indeed a turning-point of the same magnitude that an older generation of holy warriors had experienced during the anti-Soviet jihad in Afghanistan (and as a subsequent generation did with the Taliban in the late 1990s). As elsewhere, the vast majority of Islamic extremists arrived under the cover of humanitarian organisations or Islamic charities. These included the Saudi High Commission for Relief (SHC) which according to some reports functioned as a logistical base and front for Al-Qaida activities in Bosnia. For instance, weapons were concealed in shipments of food and medicine into Bosnia. Other Islamic charities suspected of being used as cover for jihad activities were the Sudan-based Third World Relief Agency (TWRA), linked to Sheikh Omar Abdul Rahman and Usamah bin Ladin, and the Islamic Relief Agency.[1] Support networks grew up with connections in London, Turin and Milan, Istanbul, and Bursa, as well as in Macedonia.[2]

Since 1992, possibly as many as 4,000 Islamic extremists from North Africa, Lebanon, Turkey, Iran, and other places are believed to have fought in the wars of former Yugoslavia. Many were Muslims from Europe, some only recently converted. Some 3,000 international Islamic volunteers were admitted into the Bosnian armed forces during the 1992–1995 war. An independent mujahidin battalion of Islamic extremists, usually several-hundred strong, was formed and trained in camps near Zenica. This battalion, known as *El Mudahid* (Al-Mujahid) was under the honorary command of Bosnian President Alija Izetbegovic. Even though it may never have played a particularly important role on the battlefield, it was fully incorporated into the chain of command and formed part of the 7th Muslim Brigade (commanded by Abdelkader Mokhtari in Zenica) in the III Corps of the Army of Bosnia and Herzegovina. In 1993, the Bosnian presidency ordered that all volunteers were entitled to citizenship. Some reports (probably numerically exaggerated but not necessarily implausible) indicate that the Bosnian government quickly extended citizenship to as many as some 12,000 foreigners.[3]

According to other, less credible reports, the Bosnian government also gave the Islamic extremist groups that provided the manpower blank Bosnian passports to dispose of as they pleased.[4] Somewhat unconvincingly (considering the high value of even forged identity documents among extremists and terrorists), the Bosnian government has since claimed that no more than 70 foreign Islamic fighters took up the offer of citizenship. The present Bosnian government, attempting to play down the number of naturalised Muslim citizens, insists that only some 420 persons of North African and Middle Eastern origin were naturalised—and that all but 70 of these were settled, prewar residents of Bosnia. Be that as it may, the Muslim volunteer camps were closed following the Dayton Accords of 21 November 1995, and the El Mudahid battalion was disbanded in 1996.[5] The remaining volunteers isolated themselves in certain villages, such as Bocinja Donja near Zenica.[6]

Although few details are known about the identity of the
Muslim volunteers in Bosnia, most of the Algerian participants
belonged to the Abdullah Anas group, which was financed by
sources under Al-Qaida control. Abdullah Anas was a GIA leader
whose real name was Bounoua Boudjemaa, and who was known to
have married a daughter of the well-known Abdullah Azzam. One
of his commanders was Abu Abdul Aziz, known as Barbarossa
because of his henna-dyed beard and notoriety for displaying the
severed heads of Serbs.[7] Barbarossa seems to have been arrested in
Saudi Arabia in early 1996, where he operated under the name
Mahmud Abdul Aziz.[8] However, all Islamic extremist volunteers
did not leave the Balkans after the war. One of their key commanders, Muhammad al-Zawahiri, brother of Al-Qaida leader Ayman
al-Zawahiri and known as the "engineer," simply moved his headquarters to a suburb of the Bulgarian capital Sofia. He also began
using the name Muhammad Hassan Ali (and he was arrested on 7
April 2000 at Dubai Airport).[9]

By the mid-1990s, the Bosnian jihad had already ensured the
formation of a new generation of experienced Islamic jihad veterans, which was almost as important to the movement as the original
generation of Afghan veterans. In addition, numerous Islamic
extremists had been able to acquire Bosnian citizenship through
marriage or other means.[10] This then enabled some of them to
immigrate to Western countries under the cover of being Bosnian
refugees. Usamah bin Ladin himself was in 1993 reportedly offered
citizenship and a passport (with serial number 0801888 and valid
until 14 September 2003) by the Bosnian Embassy in Vienna.[11]
This embassy was the chief deal-making spot for all involved in the
smuggling of arms and funds into Bosnia from chiefly Saudi
Arabia, Iran, and Libya. This activity, though in defiance of the UN
arms embargo, was well known; however, the Clinton administration and the West quietly ignored the trade for geopolitical reasons
and concern about the news media.[12]

After the war, Wahhabi missionaries entered in the wake of the
fighters. The SHC, again with contributions from Al-Qaida, initiated a program to ensure that a new generation of Islamic extremists

would grow up in Bosnia. Since April 1996 the SHC has spent considerable efforts and resources to inculcate war orphans with the tenets of Wahhabi Islam. The emphasis is on creating a new, less secular, and Islamicised rather than Westernised generation to ensure that Bosnia is firmly bound to the Islamic world. Wahhabism is especially taught by the organisation known as Active Islamic Youth (AIO), which is particularly active in the Zenica and Bugojno areas.[13]

Islamic extremists have retained a presence in Bosnia. On 17 October 2001, the United States and Britain closed their embassies in the Bosnian capital of Sarajevo for three days in response to a terrorist alert. The following week, NATO officials claimed to have prevented an attack on an U.S. peacekeeping base in northeastern Bosnia. On 25 October, it was reported that at least one of the dozen terrorist suspects detained earlier in the month, an Algerian named Bensajeh Belkacem who had been arrested in Zenica on 8 October, had direct links to Al-Qaida. Five additional suspected terrorists were reportedly being hunted in the mountains of central Bosnia. Between 11 September and 30 October 2001, a total of 19 suspected terrorists were arrested in Bosnia and another 17 were closely monitored by the police.[14] On 20 March 2002, the U.S. Embassy in Sarajevo was again closed to the public following an intelligence report that Al-Qaida had planned attacks against the American and perhaps other European embassies. In addition, the eight Bosnian offices of Chicago-based Muslim charity Benevolence International Foundation (BIF, also referred to as the Benevolentia International Foundation, and occasionally even Bosnian Ideal Future) was raided by the police on 19 March 2002. It was revealed that the director of the Bosnian branch of BIF since mid-2000 was none other than Munib Zahiragic, the head of the Bosnian Muslim intelligence service, the Agency for Research and Documentation (AID), between 1996 and 2000. He was arrested on 22 March 2002 and charged with espionage. Evidence found at the BIF offices indicated the charity's involvement with Al-Qaida, and in late April 2002, the BIF headquarters in Chicago, headed by Enaam Arnaout, a Syrian-born U.S. citizen who was known to be bin Ladin's close friend since at least 1989, was formally accused of aiding Al-Qaida.[15]

Albania

When the officially atheist, communist state of Albania—a country where roughly 65 percent of the population were nominal Muslims—collapsed in 1991, religious delegations quickly rushed there from all over the Islamic world. Mosques were built or restored, and Islamic schools were set up to teach children Arabic and propagate the virtues of Islamic law. The fact that most Albanians were secular, with 25 percent nominally Orthodox and 10 percent nominally Catholic, was quietly forgotten.[16] As noted earlier, in April 1994 even Usamah bin Ladin visited Albania. He negotiated an agreement with Bashkim Gazidede, an Islamic intellectual who then was the head of the Albanian intelligence service, the *Sherbimet E Integruara Komunitare* (National Information Office). Probably in exchange for payments, Gazidede arranged entry into Albania for several Islamic extremists, including four men believed to be responsible for the 1993 assassination of Rifat el-Mahgoub, the speaker of the Egyptian Parliament.[17] Gazidede also likely arranged for Islamic extremists to acquire Albanian citizenship. Then, during a 1997 uprising, 100,000 blank Albanian passports disappeared without a trace. Some may well have ended up with Al-Qaida. Gazidede fled Albania after the uprising and is currently believed to have received sanctuary in Libya. The Albanian citizenship laws were tightened only following U.S. pressure after the 1998 embassy bombings in Africa. In 1998 and 1999, a number of Muslim terrorists were arrested and deported for plotting to attack the U.S. Embassy in the capital, Tirana.[18]

Al-Qaida reportedly set up a system of extremist camps and support facilities in Albania in early 1997, at least in part as a replacement for opportunities no longer available in Bosnia. As usual, a large number of Islamic charities and religious organisations were used as fronts for what appear to have been the introduction of more than a hundred Arab extremists into the country.[19] In 1998, a French citizen of probable Arab origin named Claude

Kader was arrested for murdering his interpreter in a row in a Tirana apartment. He confessed to being a follower of Usamah bin Ladin. He also admitted that he had been sent, with four others, to deliver weapons to the ethnic Albanian separatists in southern Serbia who had formed the Kosovo Liberation Army to start an armed uprising against the Serbs. Problems had ensued, however, and the deal had gone sour.[20]

Such problems were soon sorted out. Logistical support, including arms deliveries from Albania to ethnic Albanian guerrillas in not only southern Serbia (Kosovo) but also western Macedonia, soon took place. There is no suggestion that the Albanian government was involved; the borders were so poorly monitored that any competent smuggler could cross them.[21]

Kosovo

When a band of militant Muslim Albanians calling itself the *Ushtria Clirimtare E Kosoves* (Kosovo Liberation Army, UCK) rose against the Serbs in southern Serbia in 1998, the Western media quickly created widespread public and government support for the group in the same way that they had driven the war in Bosnia. In the excitement, everybody forgot that the UCK was the same band that the State Department only months before had classified as a terrorist organisation. Furthermore, it was also a group known to be financed by the international heroin trade (through its close links with Albanian organised crime) and through payments from Islamic countries and individuals, among them allegedly Usamah bin Ladin.

In 1999 the West set out to assist the UCK and the Kosovo Albanians to break free from Serbia and prepare for independence. Following a massive campaign of NATO air attacks on Serbian targets, involving no fewer than 1,000 aircraft,[22] Serbia was forced to concede defeat and the West propelled the UCK into power. Kosovo has since been a virtually independent state. The UCK has been renamed the *Trupat E Mbrojtjes se Kosoves* (Kosovo Protection Corps) and currently serves as the UN-sponsored police force in Kosovo. Although the West provided most of the muscle to build Kosovo's independence, Al-Qaida did its share—though far more subtly. Al-Qaida provided financial support, and some UCK officers received training in Al-Qaida camps in Afghanistan. Volunteers were also sent to assist the UCK. In late November 1998, a few dozen Arab combat veterans from the war in Bosnia joined the Kosovo Albanians. In addition, documents found on the corpse of a UCK soldier reportedly indicated that some fighters in his group were Islamic extremists of Saudi origin, all of whom carried Albanian passports.[23] There is no doubt that a number of Islamic extremists fought with the ethnic Albanian forces in Kosovo.[24] Interpol officials have stated that bin Ladin even supplied a top military commander for an elite UCK unit.[25]

After the fighters came the preachers. More than 30 Islamic charities are currently present in Kosovo, building mosques, distributing aid, and teaching Arabic and Islamic law. Several are believed to be linked with Islamic terrorist groups, and a number employ individuals suspected of having criminal records that include acts of terrorism. In addition, charities such as the Saudi Joint Relief Committee for Kosovo, for reasons of Wahhabi religious purity, engage in the destruction of local traditional Islamic architectural features seemed un-Islamic by the Wahhabis.[26] Whether the Wahhabis will succeed in establishing a lasting legacy remains to be seen. The West has indeed done its utmost to create a new Wahhabi state in the middle of the Balkans.

Macedonia
In Macedonia, amazingly, history is apparently repeating itself a third time. After the Kosovo Albanians had a state of their own handed to them on a platter, the ethnic Albanians in Macedonia saw the chance to acquire the same status. Rising against the majority Macedonian population, the ethnic Albanian *Armia Kombetare Shqipetare*, AKSh (better known as the National Liberation Army, or NLA), a UCK offshoot led by Ali Ahmeti, predictably received similarly favourable attention in the West as its predecessors in Bosnia and Kosovo. Although referred to as terrorists as late as in the first half of 2001 for atrocities against the Slavic Macedonian

population (which, unlike the Serbs, had not committed similar violence against ethnic Albanians), the West has since pressured the majority Macedonian government into rewarding the NLA with significant concessions. Yet, the NLA included international Islamic extremists,[27] and some believe that bin Ladin was the biggest financial supporter of the NLA.[28] The organization has since been officially disbanded.[29]

End Notes

1. Jacquard, *Osama Bin Laden,* 68, 70. See also, for instance, International Crisis Group (ICG), *Bin Laden and the Balkans: The Politics of Anti-Terrorism* (Brussels: ICG Balkans Report 119, 9 November 2001), 15, which although somewhat apologetic for the Islamic cause is a useful summary.

2. *Intelligence Newsletter* 347 (26 November 1998), 6–7.

3. See, for instance, ICG, *Bin Laden and the Balkans,* 10–11; Jacquard, *Osama Bin Laden,* 68, 70.

4. *Los Angeles Times,* 7 October 2001 (www.latimes.com).

5. See, for instance, ICG, *Bin Laden and the Balkans,* 10–12; Jacquard, *Osama Bin Laden,* 68, 70.

6. *Rzecspospolita* (Warsaw), 16 December 1997.

7. Cooley, *Unholy Wars,* 202, 223; Reeve, *New Jackals,* 169; Jacquard, *Osama Bin Laden,* 68, 70.

8. Bodansky, *Bin Laden,* 170.

9. Bodansky, *Bin Laden,* 155–6, 298; Jacquard, *Osama Bin Laden,* 108.

10. Jacquard, *Osama Bin Laden,* 69.

11. Jacquard, *Osama Bin Laden,* 71; Agence France Presse (AFP), 24 September 1999.

12. ICG, *Bin Laden and the Balkans,* 10–11.

13. Jacquard, *Osama Bin Laden,* 70–71. The AIO maintained a Web site, www.aiobih.org.

14. ICG, *Bin Laden and the Balkans,* 9, 14.

15. AP, 22 March 2002; *Washington Post,* 1 May 2002; *USA Today,* 1 May 2002.

16. ICG, *Bin Laden and the Balkans,* 3, 4.

17. Reeve, *New Jackals,* 180–81. See also *Intelligence Newsletter* 347 (26 November 1998), 6–7.

18. ICG, *Bin Laden and the Balkans,* 5, 8.

19. Bodansky, *Bin Laden,* 200.

20. *Scotsman* (UK), 21 September 2001.

21. ICG, *Bin Laden and the Balkans,* 8.

22. *Economist,* 13 October 2001.

23. Jacquard, *Osama Bin Laden,* 71–2; Bodansky, *Bin Laden,* 298–9. On the Albanian drug trade, see also *Economist,* 20 October 2001.

24. ICG, *Bin Laden and the Balkans,* 2.

25. *Independent* (UK), 21 October 2001.

26. ICG, *Bin Laden and the Balkans,* 20.

27. ICG, *Bin Laden and the Balkans,* 2, 22. The existence of the NLA was initially doubted by Western observers, as it was first reported by the Serbian state security service, *Resor Drzavne Bezhednost.* Zoran Kusovac, "AKSh: Macedonia's Unlikely Albanian Army," *Jane's Intelligence Review* 13:2 (February 2001), 3.

28. *Washington Times,* 22 July 2001.

29. ICG, *Bin Laden and the Balkans,* 22.

Islamic Extremism in the Philippines

The Moros

In 1988, Usamah bin Ladin sent his brother-in-law Muhammad Jamal Khalifa (also known as Muhammad Abdul Rahman Khalifa) to the Philippines to recruit men for the war against the Soviet Union. Khalifa, a Jordanian, by then headed the Jordanian branch of the Muslim Brotherhood. He had previously worked in Peshawar as local head of the Saudi-funded charity the Muslim World League. He had handled both jobs so well that he subsequently married one of bin Ladin's two full sisters. In the Philippines, Khalifa established a rattan-furniture business, as well as a series of Islamic organisations and charities, including the Daw'l Imam Al-Shafee Center (also known as the Imam Shafie Institute) in Patikul, a small village in the southern Sulu Archipelago. He married a Filipina there and recruited dozens of Muslims from the island province of Basilan in the southern Philippines, an island reachable by a 90-minute ferry crossing from Zamboanga on Mindanao.[1] In the early 1990s he also became the head of the Manila offices of various Islamic charities, including the International Islamic Relief Organization (IIRO) and Muslim World League, both of which received their main source of funding from the House of Saud. Both have from time to time been suspected of aiding Islamic extremist groups.[2]

By then, there were already two strong and very active indigenous Muslim insurgent movements in the southern Philippines, where relations between Filipino Muslims and Catholics had a long and complex history. In fact, the Mindanao civil war—Muslim separatists fighting the Philippine armed forces—has since its latest outbreak in 1969 produced the loss of at least 120,000 lives and caused more than half a million refugees.[3] The Mindanao Muslims, the Moros, were historically an autonomous and distinct people. They were also to some extent oppressed by corrupt local officials, typically Catholic Filipinos. Thus the civil war was caused more by a desire for independence than for an Islamic state.

The roots of the conflict, however, belong to the distant past. The Spanish, who first settled in the Philippines in 1565, had since 1578 fought continuously and usually victoriously against the Moro sultanates on Mindanao and in the Sulu Archipelago. When all Philippine islands, including the Moro lands in the south, were acquired by the United States following the 1898 Spanish-American War, the Moros disputed this. They resisted the Americans but were defeated in a brutal campaign of pacification. By the 1960s, the Moros had become a minority in many parts of their traditional lands due to a massive influx of Catholic Filipino settlers from the north. (This process has continued; the Moros currently form a majority in only 5 out of the 23 provinces of Mindanao and the Sulu islands.) The nation-building efforts of the dominant Filipino Catholics, heavily influenced by Spanish and American culture, required subordination of minorities, but the Moros were too many and culturally too different to comply. Violent confrontations took place almost as soon as the United States in 1946 ended its occupation of the Philippines in 1946.[4] Christian vigilante bands, often backed by the local police and military, frequently attacked Moros, and in 1969, the Mindanao Independence Movement (MIM) was established to fight for an independent Moro state on Mindanao, in the Sulu Archipelago, and on Palawan and adjacent islands.

The Moros were in contact with the Middle East, Indonesia, and Malaysia. This resulted in the construction of new mosques and (probably) the infusion of funds from abroad, but it also led to the formation of several other, more radical Muslim organisations. These included the Union of Islamic Forces and Organisations (UIFO) and the *Ansar al-Islam* (Helpers of Islam). In 1969, the first members of MIM and UIFO began military training in camps in Sabah, a Malaysian state on the island of Borneo. Another group apparently trained in a camp in peninsular Malaysia, close to the Thai border. Again the Malaysian support was considerable, the Moros receiving the support and tacit agreement to their presence by the Malaysian government. This was most likely a tit-for-tat decision in retaliation for the Philippines' territorial claim to Sabah and encouragement of a separatist rebellion there. In other words, the two countries encouraged each other's separatists.

Upon their return home, the Moros who had received training in Malaysia became crucial for the further development of the independence movement. One of them, Nur Misuari, a former political science lecturer at the University of the Philippines, and of humble Sulu islander origins, persuaded the MIM in 1972 to dissolve itself and founded the Moro National Liberation Front (MNLF) and the movement's military wing, the Bangsa Moro Army. Large-scale fighting soon broke out. The Moros also received additional support from abroad, particularly from Libya, which also provided military training to some Moro fighters. In December 1976, the Philippine government had to accept a negotiated settlement with Libya as mediator, the Tripoli Agreement. Misuari agreed to autonomy for 13 of Mindanao's 21 provinces and shelved the claims to independence. Unfortunately, the agreement soon fell through, and fighting recommenced.

The MNLF also split, as more radical factions broke off to form new groups. In 1982, the first dissenting MNLF leader quit to form the MNLF Reformist Group (MNLF-RG), based in Malaysia, and finally of little consequence. More important, the MNLF leadership was regarded as leftist, which did not suit those Moro leaders of a more Islamic bent. One of them, a cleric named Salamat Hashim, eventually saw no other recourse than to create a completely new Moro movement.

Hashim had first studied in Saudi Arabia, then in 1959 he won a scholarship to Al-Azhar University in Cairo. Strongly influenced by the writings of Sayyid Qutb and Maududi like so many other young Al-Azhar students, in 1962 he founded an association of Moro students in the Middle East. When Hashim returned to the Philippines in 1970, he did not like what he saw in the leftist MNLF leadership, which he broke away from in December 1977. In 1978, he instead established a "New MNLF" central committee, which become the core of his new movement. Most of his leaders were madrasah-trained clerics. In 1984, Hashim re-formed his group into the Moro Islamic Liberation Front (MILF) with himself as chairman. This was at first an exile organisation. Hashim based his group in Pakistan and soon embarked upon a training and fighting program in Afghanistan under the auspices of the *Ittehad-e Islami Bara-ye Azadi-ye Afghanistan* (Islamic Alliance for the Freedom of Afghanistan) of Abdul Rasul Sayyaf, a fellow Al-Azhar cleric, and *Hezb-e Islami-ye Afghanistan* (Islamic Party of Afghanistan) of Gulbuddin Hekmatyar. At least some 500 to 600 Moro fighters participated in the Afghan jihad against the Soviet Union. Hashim only returned to the Philippines in 1997. As the MILF resumed the demand for an independent state, reiterating the old claim that the Moro Muslims needed a separate state, it won over many MNLF members.

By the early 1990s, the MILF had indeed emerged as the main Moro insurgent movement. It had formed its own armed wing, the Bangsa-Moro Islamic Armed Forces. With officers trained in Sabah in the 1960s and many rank-and-file members with combat experience from Afghanistan in the 1980s, the movement was well established on Mindanao, where it enjoyed the support of 1.6 million Magindanaos, as well as the largest Muslim ethnic group, the 1.9 million Maranaos. (Hashim and his followers were mostly Magindanao or Maranao-speakers from the south-central provinces of mainland Mindanao.) The movement was well armed. By the mid-1990s, the MILF claimed a total armed strength of 120,000 men (unlikely but not quite implausible) in six separate divisions. While this number may have represented the total manpower available to the movement, independent observers estimated its standing force at 15,000 (most likely) to 35,000—in itself an impressive force. The movement, which by then controlled important parts of at least seven provinces in Mindanao where it acted as de facto government and cooperated with local officials, was well funded by Islamic organisations abroad, particularly in Malaysia, Pakistan, and the Middle East (reportedly also by associates of bin Ladin).[5] There were occasional clashes with government forces, but all in all this was a low-key conflict not eagerly pursued by either party. The two sides had simply fought each other to a standstill. In contrast, the MNLF was confined to the Sulu Sea islands, and because its leader, Misuari, was an ethnic Samal, it drew its support from others of the same ethnic background: the Tausug-speaking population on the island of Jolo.

Nevertheless, the Philippine government continued to concentrate on negotiations with the weaker, older, more secular, and internationally amenable MNLF under Misuari. Until 1987, it seemed that the Tripoli Agreement might eventually be implemented, after all. However, as it became increasingly clear that the Philippine government of Corazon Aquino remained unwilling to honour the agreement, negotiations were broken off. In 1990, Aquino established the Autonomous Region for Muslim Mindanao, but this encompassed only four provinces and was not accepted by the insurgents. But after 1993 negotiations resumed. The MNLF, suffering defections to the MILF and surrenders to the government's reconciliation programs, was weakened further. Further, several of its commanders refused to accept the cease-fire agreement and broke away from Misuari.

This was the background when Khalifa stepped in around 1991 to fund Muslim groups with bin Ladin's money, and the most hardened veterans from the war in Afghanistan returned to the Philippines.

Abu Sayyaf

The fresh infusion of cash and men caused a renewed, indeed increased, wave of Muslim extremism. Among the Afghan veterans was Abdurajak Abubakar Janjalani, an Islamic extremist born in 1963 in Isabela on the island of Basilan, apparently in a mixed

Christian-Muslim family. He had studied Islamic law in Saudi Arabia during the early 1980s, after which he became one of the Moro fighters in the Afghan jihad. He also appears to have studied in Libya. Soon after his return from Afghanistan in 1991, Janjalani (together with his companions Amilhussin Jumaani and Wahab Akbar) became the founder and leader of a group apparently named Harakat al-Islamiyyah (Islamic Movement) but soon better known as the Abu Sayyaf (Father of the Sword). This was the nom de guerre used by Janjalani (Kumander Abu Sayyaf) in the Afghan jihad. As deputy, he chose one Edwin Angeles, who later defected. Either directly or indirectly, bin Ladin offered him initial financial support. Ramzi Yousef turned up in the Philippines in 1991, too, introducing himself as an emissary from bin Ladin. All evidence indicates that Abu Sayyaf was bin Ladin's direct contribution to the Philippine jihad.

Although Abu Sayyaf was probably projected to become a more radical rival and the eventual successor to the two main Moro movements, this never happened, and Al-Qaida in 1995 lost control of the Philippine group. Abu Sayyaf remained a purely local group, concentrating its activities in the island province of Basilan and the nearby areas of Cotabato, Magindanao, Souo, and Tawitawi (an island near Sabah, Borneo). The group was primarily engaged in bomb attacks of local Christians and undertaking for-profit kidnappings, the main source of income. Despite its small size and limited influence, Abu Sayyaf soon achieved international notoriety—and equal fame among international Islamic extremists—due to its many brutal killings of civilians. However, Janjalani was killed in a police operation on Basilan on 18 December 1998. The group split into two factions, one of about 80 men based in Basilan, headed by his younger brother Khaddafy (or Gaddafi) Janjalani and Isnilon Hapilon (who, some claim, was the real leader); the other of more than 100 men based on Jolo and headed by Ghalib Andang, better known as "Commander Robot." Yet another commander was Mujib Susukan. The Commander Robot band made headlines in April 2000 by raiding a Malaysian diving resort, kidnapping 21 people including 19 foreign tourists. The hostages were eventually released after a payment of $25 million in a deal brokered by Libya. In 2001, the Janjalani faction in a similar way raided a Philippine beach hotel, kidnapping 20 people including three Americans, one of whom was subsequently beheaded and another who was killed in a gunfight with Philippine troops. The surviving hostages were by then held by a yet smaller faction, a mere handful of men led by Abu Sabaya, which had fled Basilan in April 2002 and moved to Mindanao.[11]

Although Abu Sayyaf once held the allegiance of perhaps 2,000 Muslims, 200 to 500 of whom were fighters, frequent clashes with the Philippine army shrank the group's number of active fighters to about 80.[12] By early 2002, the group certainly was a menace to society but had long since lost any pretensions to accomplishing an Islamic revolution.

The MNLF leader Nur Misuari signed a peace agreement with the government in September 1996, which incidentally also ensured that Misuari was elected governor of the Autonomous Region of Muslim Mindanao. The MILF denounced the agreement, formally assumed leadership of the Moro struggle for self-rule, and fought on. But the MILF in January 1997 also agreed to begin formal peace talks. However, in the same year fighting again intensified. By January 1999, Philippine President Joseph Estrada all but declared war against the Moros, and fighting escalated further. Formal peace negotiations recommenced only in October 1999. Clashes continued at least until April 2001, when the MILF finally agreed to a cease-fire. Yet peace remained beyond reach. On 19 November 2001, Nur Misuari—who had been ousted as MNLF leader in 2001 and to his further dismay seemed likely to lose his position as governor—and some 200 followers launched a surprise attack on army positions on Jolo. Although this probably had more than do with secular politics than Islamic extremism, some observers believed that at least some of his followers were allying themselves with Abu Sayyaf.[13] The attack failed, and Nur Misuari was arrested in Malaysia a few days later.[14]

On 20 November 2001, following Misuari's abortive attack and perhaps unable to distinguish between the two Muslim groups, President Bush immediately promised to help the Philippines in the war on the Abu Sayyaf group, which held a higher international profile because it still held American hostages. He also rashly offered to send combat troops. The Philippine government politely declined, noting that the Philippine constitution prohibits foreign troops from fighting on the nation's territory.[15] The Philippines had, after all, kicked the United States out of its two military bases in the country in 1991. There was nothing, however, in the Philippine constitution that prevented the United States from sending military units for joint military exercises. On 16 January 2002, the United States sent the first of 650 soldiers, including 160 Special Forces troops, for what was officially described as an exercise (though this was eventually postponed after the troops had arrived in the country). The U.S. contingent consisted mostly of conventional units sent for exercises to legitimate the military presence (though to boost morale, it was announced that at least some of them were expected to assist in the counter-insurgency effort as support and technical personnel). The key U.S. contribution, however, was the Special Forces contingent, which came from the Special Operations Command Pacific: troops from the 1st Special Forces Group; crew and MH-47 Chinook medium-lift transport helicopters from the 160th Special Operations Aviation Regiment (this contingent from a base in Taegu, South Korea); air force personnel of the 353d Special Operations Group (from Kadena Air Base, Okinawa); and Naval Special Warfare Group One.[16] Upon arriving in the country, they were expected to begin working with Philippine troops on Basilan, where about 5,000 of them were already hunting for about 80 Abu Sayyaf guerrillas.[17]

On 31 January 2002, U.S. troops commenced operations against the Abu Sayyaf together with units of the Philippines army in what was known as Joint Task Force 510. This was the first War on Terror-related military operation outside Central Asia.[18] U.S. Navy and Air Force reconnaissance and surveillance aircraft, based in Okinawa and elsewhere in Asia, flew missions over the southern Philippines. The aircraft may have been navy P-3C Orion maritime patrol aircraft, a type also being flown from bases in Oman for surveillance in Somalia.[19] In Afghanistan, such aircraft were also used as platforms for special operations to radio enemy positions to troops on the ground, and this may have been the intention in the Philippines as well.[20] In the end, however, the joint operation accomplished little. After six months, the U.S. and Philippine forces formally concluded the joint exercises on 31 July 2002, and the U.S. formations pulled out of the country.[21]

The situation in the Philippines shows several similarities with other areas where Islamic extremists and Arab Afghans had become active. As had happened in Kashmir and Chechnya, a secular native separatist movement seemingly ready to make peace had been displaced by a more violent and uncompromising Islamic extremist group based on veterans from the Afghan war. In addition, the first returnees from Afghanistan (Salamat Hashim and his MILF veterans), while Islamists, were considerably more moderate than the later group (Janjalani and the Abu Sayyaf) who received the support of bin Ladin and the uncompromising jihadists. As elsewhere, the complex background and local situation precluded easy solutions to resolve the conflict.

When U.S. troops arrived in the Philippines, bin Ladin's brother-in-law Khalifa had long since left. He has since had a checkered career. In April 1994, a Jordanian court issued a warrant for his arrest for the bombing of a theatre on the outskirts of Amman, an act which Khalifa allegedly financed. Khalifa fled to the United States. By the end of the year, however, U.S. officials had Khalifa arrested and extradited to Jordan, where he was made to stand trial. But he was acquitted and returned to Saudi Arabia, where he lived in Jeddah.[22] Khalifa was reportedly arrested in Saudi Arabia after the 11 September 2001 attacks.[23]

As for the U.S. involvement in the southern Philippines, it seems increasingly clear that it had little impact on the local situation. The training and re-equipping of the Philippine army may well eventually help it to deal with the lesser bands of bandits such as Abu Sayyaf. Yet, it remains uncertain whether U.S. aid really can assist in solving the intricate problem of relations between the

Catholic Filipinos and the Muslim Moros. By early 2003, it was decided that American troops again would take part in operations against the Abu Sayyaf in the Philippines. This time the emphasis was to be on combat operations.[24]

End Notes

1. Reeve, *New Jackals,* 136, 157–8; Bergen, *Holy War,* 54, 218.
2. *Washington Post,* 29 September 2001.
3. International Institute for Strategic Studies, "Separatist Rebellion in the Southern Philippines: A Simmering Crisis," *IISS Strategic Comments* 6:4 (May 2000); Andrew Tan, "Armed Muslim Separatist Rebellion in Southeast Asia: Persistence, Prospects, and Implications," *Studies in Conflict & Terrorism* 23:4 (October–December 2000), 267–88, on 268; Anthony Davis, "Islamic Guerrillas Threaten the Fragile Peace on Mindanao," *Jane's Intelligence Review* 10:5 (May 1998), 30–35.
4. *Time,* 28 January 2002; Tan, "Armed Muslim Separatist Rebellion," 267–88.
5. Jacquard, *Osama Bin Laden,* 122.
6. *Time,* 28 January 2002.
7. Reeve, *New Jackals,* 136, 157–8; Jacquard, *Osama Bin Laden,* 282 n.10; Peter Chalk, "Bin Laden's Asian Network," *Jane's Pointer,* December 1998, 6.
8. Interview with the chief of the National Intelligence Coordinating Agency (NICA) in *Manila Times,* 20 September 2001 (www.manilatimes.net).
9. Reeve, *New Jackals,* 136, 157–8.
10. See, for instance, Anthony Davis, "Arroyo Takes Hard Line on Abu Sayyaf," *Jane's Intelligence Review* 13: 5 (May 2001), 7.
11. *Time,* 28 January 2002; *Washington Post,* 7 February 2002, 11 June 2002.
12. *Time,* 28 January 2002.
13. *Economist,* 24 November 2001.
14. *Economist,* 1 December 2001.
15. *Washington Post,* 21 November 2001; *Time,* 28 January 2002.
16. *Washington Post,* 16 January 2002, 22 February 2002, 23 February 2002.
17. *Washington Post,* 16 January 2002.
18. *Washington Post,* 1 February 2002.
19. *Washington Post,* 21 February 2002.
20. *Washington Times,* 8–14 April 2002 (National Weekly Edn).
21. *Economist,* 3 August 2002.

22. Emerson, *American Jihad,* 156–7; *Washington Post,* 29 September 2001; Bergen, *Holy War,* 218.

23. Blanche, "Egyptians around Bin Laden," 21.

24. See, for instance, Washington Post, 21 February 2003.

Islamic Extremism in Indonesia, Malaysia, and Singapore

Indonesia

In Indonesia, the world's most populous Muslim country, a proportionally small but numerically large Muslim population has come to follow such extremist leaders as Usamah bin Ladin. (After the 1999 elections, nearly 35 percent of the seats in the parliament are held by Islamic parties.) This adherence to extremism was clearly visible in the aftermath of the 11 September 2001 terrorist attacks on the United States. For example, on 25 September Indonesia's highest Islamic authority, the Council of Ulama, called for a jihad against the United States if it retaliated against Afghanistan. In the days before this ruling, groups of Islamic extremists belonging to the Front Pembela Islam (Islamic Defenders Front), or FPI, headed by Habib Muhammad Rizieq bin Hussein Syihab, had already searched several hotels on the large island of Java in a hunt for Americans to kill, following a demand from the FPI leader that all U.S. and British citizens leave Indonesia. Although they did not find any, the violent search was a serious escalation from the movement's earlier, better-known exploits: raids on bars involved in prostitution and gambling dens.[1]

The FPI was not the only Islamic extremist group on Java. The island was home to a whole host of similar groups, most of which were involved in sectarian fighting with Christians and others. Among the groups was the self-styled Taliban Brigade, led by Muhammad Zainal Mutaqqien.[2] Perhaps most violent, however, was the *Laskar Jihad* (Jihad Army), founded in 2000 and led by a veteran from the Afghan jihad named Jafar Umar Thalib (arrested on 4 May 2002[3]). The Laskar Jihad is chiefly known for having sent thousands of fighters to the Moluccas and central Sulawesi to fight against the Christians there. The group was also believed to include several hundred foreign extremists. Its parent body, the *Ahl al-Sunnah W'al Jamaah* (People of the Beaten Path and Society) Communications Forum, was a Wahhabi organisation headquartered in a small village just north of Yogyakarta.[4]

The most nebulous, but also perhaps most influential, group was less an organised movement than a loose network. Named after the religious boarding school in which the network had its origin, Pondok Ngruki near Solo, in central Java, it is perhaps best known as the Ngruki network. The Pondok Ngruki was founded in 1971 and moved to its current home in 1973.

The network first began to coalesce in the late 1970s around the two founders of the school, Abdullah Sungkar (1937–1999) and Abu Bakar Ba'asyir (born in 1938). Interestingly, both were of Yemeni descent (like Usamah bin Ladin, who hails from Hadhramaut) though born in Java. Both fled to Malaysia in 1985 to avoid arrest at home, though subsequently returned, and their network retains a powerful presence in both countries. Founding its teachings on the writings of Hassan al-Banna, the Egyptian founder of the Muslim Brotherhood, the members of the network were united by the desire to create an Islamic state. The way to do this, they argued (in a process similar to ideas current in Egypt in the 1970s), was first to create an Islamic society (Malay, *jemaah islamiyah*; Arabic, *jamaah al-Islamiyyah*). (Most observers of the network mistook this for the name of an organisation, but an organisation as such does not yet exist.) Many members of the network are, however, on the executive committee of a group formed during a congress of Indonesian extremists in Yogyakarta on 5–7 August 2000 called the *Majelis Mujahidin Indonesia* (Indonesian

Mujahidin Council). The congress appointed Abu Bakar Ba'asyir head of the organisation, with the title of *amir ul-mujahidin* (commander of mujahidin).[5]

The background of the Ngruki network was to be found originally in several Muslim uprisings in Indonesia of the late 1940s and the 1950s. However, after the two founders' escape to Malaysia the network became increasingly international, and Malaysia became its new international centre. Furthermore, by 1987, at least six Ngruki followers had gone to Pakistan and Afghanistan. In the following year, their leader, Andi Muhammad Taqwa, moved to Sweden, where he was granted political asylum, which enabled him to continue his jihad activities from a safe base. Others likewise went to Germany and then the Netherlands. In Europe, the Ngruki extremists also renewed their contacts with Middle Eastern extremist groups with which they had come into contact during the Afghan jihad.

Inevitably, there were rumours that Ngruki extremists were in touch with Al-Qaida. They also talked about going to support the jihad in the Philippines and Thailand. The movement also attracted criminal elements, who committed robbery and murder to further the Islamic cause (which, incidentally, is allowed by the Koran as long as the crimes are directed at infidels). Other violent activities included armed clashes with the military and a series of bombings in Indonesia's capital Jakarta and other locations in 1984 and 1985. At least one of these was aimed at the Buddhist Borobodur temple, loathed by Islamic extremists as a symbol of everything that was un-Islamic.[6]

Abu Bakar Ba'asyir was arrested following the terrorist bombing of a discotheque on the crowded Kuta Beach on the Indonesian island of Bali on 12 October 2002, which killed more than 190 people, including many foreign tourists. Most Indonesians, however, refused to believe that Muslims were responsible for the attack: even educated Indonesians claimed that the CIA was behind the bombing in a conspiracy to frame Muslims everywhere.[7]

Yet another extremist group, although smaller, was *Laskar Jundullah* (Army of the Soldiers of God), one of whose leaders was Agus Dwikarna, who was arrested in Manila on charges of terrorism in March 2002. This was the militant wing of a Makassar-based organisation created in May 2000 called the *Komite Pengerak Syariat Islam* (Committee for Upholding Islamic Law). Dwikarna, who once before had been arrested (for attacking a karaoke bar in Makassar), also served as secretary of the Indonesian Mujahidin Council.[8]

Many of the Indonesian extremist parties and militias support bin Ladin, and according to Indonesian law enforcement and intelligence agencies, at least two major militia leaders were offered financial backing by Al-Qaida. In August 2001, Islamic extremists planned a terrorist attack on the U.S. Embassy in Jakarta, or so it appeared from evidence in the form of a map that was found by Indonesian police. Besides, in 2001 it had become increasingly clear that Islamic extremists of the Laskar Jundullah with connections to Usamah bin Ladin and Al-Qaida operated a jungle training camp near the port city of Poso on the island of Sulawesi. Several hundred Muslims, many from Europe, Pakistan, and the Middle East, had entered Indonesia over the year in the guise of aid workers with the purpose of rebuilding mosques. They carried letters of recommendation from an Islamic charity, the Crisis Prevention Committee (also known as the Committee to Overcome Crisis), known to have connections to Usamah bin Ladin and Al-Qaida. However, shortly after 11 September they went into hiding, either in or outside Indonesia.[9] At least two dozen people reportedly arrived there from the Philippines-based Moro Islamic Liberation Front.[10] And it looked as though a local extremist leader, Parlindungan Siregar, had gone into hiding.[11]

International Islamic extremists have made Indonesia their home as well: for instance, the international Islamic organisation Hizb ut-Tahrir established a budding presence in Indonesia, and the Hizb ut-Tahrir was among those represented in the Indonesian Mujahidin Council under Abu Bakar Ba'asyir.[12]

Malaysia

Islamic extremism is doing well in Malaysia. The religious

mass movement Al-Arqam, formed in 1967 by Ashaari Muhammad who in 1994 claimed 100,000 members, was known to have had relations with the Egyptian Muslim Brotherhood. Members of the movement also talked about overthrowing the secular state. Although banned in Malaysia in 1994 due to its increasingly irregular practices, its many supporters remain in Malaysia and elsewhere. (Ashaari Muhammad, for instance, claimed to have discussions with the Prophet Muhammad; he is since 1994 under house arrest.) Many members are believed to have established links with other militant Muslims on Sumatra, notably in Aceh.[13]

In September 1998, a similar Islamic movement was formed: *Al-Maunah* (Brotherhood of Inner Power), led by Sheikh Ikhwan Muhammad Amin Razali. The group, which had members in Singapore, Brunei, Egypt, and Saudi Arabia as well as in Malaysia, in July 2000 raided two Malaysian army bases to obtain weapons for the jihad. Some 50 of the movement's estimated 1,000 followers were subsequently arrested. Several turned out to be former servicemen.[14]

As noted, the Ngruki network also maintains a substantial presence in Malaysia. Its chief organiser in Malaysia was an Indonesian named Riduan Isamuddin, better known as Nurjaman or Hambali. Born in Cianjur, in western Java, Hambali is believed to be a key Al-Qaida operative in Southeast Asia. He is believed to have fought in Afghanistan during the late 1980s. At the time of this writing he remains at large, although he is suspected of being back in Indonesia. Hambali has been linked to several bombings in December 2000 in Indonesia as well as in Manila. Hambali was also linked to a plot to commit acts of terrorism in Singapore in late 2001 (see below). Hambali and his associates apparently wanted to overthrow all secular governments in the region and create an Islamic state consisting of the present territories of Malaysia, Indonesia, Singapore, Brunei, and the southern Philippines. As the suspected Al-Qaida point man in Southeast Asia, Hambali appears to have worked in the past with Ramzi Yousef and the latter's associate Wali Khan Amin Shah.[15] The Ngruki network in Malaysia has also been accused of being the "second wing" of the *Kumpulan Mujahidin Malaysia* (Malaysian Mujahidin Movement), which

Malaysian officials describe as a clandestine group working to over-throw the secular government and that reportedly has maintained contacts with Al-Qaida.[16]

Singapore

In the small island-state of Singapore, where Muslims (usually of Malay, but sometimes of Indian origin) constitute about 15 per-cent of the 4 million people, extremist groups with links to Usamah bin Ladin made several attempts in the late 1990s to recruit local Muslims for attacks primarily against U.S. interests. Singapore has strong military and economic ties with the United States and is the home of a U.S. Navy logistics unit. Singapore has one of only two piers in Southeast Asia where U.S. aircraft carriers are able to dock. In addition, from 2001 on Singapore has staunchly supported the U.S.-led War on Terror.[17]

Despite a strict and extensive law enforcement and domestic security apparatus, the Internal Security Department, the Singaporean security forces at first failed to understand the extent to which the state's Muslim population was ready to ally itself with Islamic extremist groups. However, among the many documents found in Afghanistan by U.S. forces were a few that documented Al-Qaida contacts with a Singaporean Islamic extremist group. The group was generally identified as the Jemaah Islamiyah (no doubt a misunderstanding on the part of the authorities; the use of this term for the group, which may never have had a proper name, in any case suggests that it was a part of the Ngruki network). The group was apparently led by one Ibrahim Maiden. In December 2001, 13 suspected terrorists of the group were arrested while allegedly planning to bomb Western embassies and businesses. (They were going to use trucks loaded with bombs made of ammonium nitrate fertilizer.) Among the group's possible targets were the U.S., British, Israeli, and Australian embassies. The group also had a list of more than 200 U.S. companies in Singapore, which may also have been potential targets. In addition, the group appears to have planned to blow up a shuttle bus that carried U.S. personnel to a naval dock on the northern coast of Singapore and to attack U.S.

ships using the harbour facilities. The suspects included 12 Singaporeans and one Malaysian, all of ethnic Malay or Indian descent. A worrisome factor was that several of those arrested were low-ranking former soldiers who were still in the reserves. At least eight had also received training in Al-Qaida camps in Afghanistan. The group reported to Hambali, the Indonesian Al-Qaida leader based in Malaysia.[18] Singapore in May 2002 identified Abu Bakar Ba'asyir as the overall leader of the terrorist cell, no doubt a correct conclusion if the cell was part of the Ngruki network.[19]

End Notes

1. *Washington Post,* 9 October 2001; *Economist,* 29 September 2001, 20 October 2001.
2. See, for instance, *Washington Post,* 4 May 2002
3. *Washington Post,* 5 May 2002
4. *Washington Post,* 9 October 2001; *Economist,* 20 October 2001.
5. The first, and at the time of writing only, serious description of the network is International Crisis Group (ICG), *Al-Qaeda in Southeast Asia: The Case of the "Ngruki Network" in Indonesia* (Jakarta/Brussels: ICG Indonesia Briefing, 8 August 2002), a report written by Sidney Jones.
6. ICG, *Al-Qaeda in Southeast Asia, passim.*
7. See, for instance, *Japan Times,* 14 October 2002; VOA, 14 October 2002; *Far Eastern Economic Review,* 31 October 2002.
8. *Observer* (London), 17 March 2002; *Washington Post,* 9 May 2002; ICG, *Al-Qaeda in Southeast Asia,* 17, 20.
9. *International Herald Tribune,* 14 January 2002.
10. *Washington Post,* 9 May 2002
11. *Newsweek,* 18 February 2002.
12. ICG, *Al-Qaeda in Southeast Asia,* 18.
13. Cheu Hock-Tong, "Islamic Cult Banned in Malaysia," *RMA Newsletter* (Tokyo: Kokugakuin University, 1999); Jacquard, *Osama Bin Laden,* 120.
14. Jestyn Cooper, "Rebel Group Threatens Malaysian Security," *Jane's Intelligence Review* 12:9 (September 2000), 2.
15. *Washington Post,* 3 February 2002, 7 February 2002, 9 February 2002; ICG, *Al-Qaeda in Southeast Asia,* 2. Two other key leaders of the group were reportedly the two brothers Faiz bin Abu Bakar Bafana and Fathi bin Abu Bakar Bafana, as well as Fikiruddin Muqti (also known as Muhammad Iqbal bin Abdul Rahman and Abu Jibril), who was

arrested in Malaysia in 2002. *Times of London,* 3 March 2002.

16. *Washington Post,* 9 May 2002; *Far Eastern Economic Review,* 26 September 2002. Malaysia was also reportedly the home of a branch of the *Al-Itihaad al-Islamiyyah* ("Islamic Alliance," AIAI), active in Somalia. *New York Times,* 25 September 2001.

17. *Japan Times,* 5 January 2002.

18. *Washington Post,* 12 January 2002, 3 February 2002; *Financial Times,* 14 January 2002.

19. ICG, *Al-Qaeda in Southeast Asia,* 2.

APPENDIX 18
Sunni Islamic Extremism in the Americas

The United States is by no means exempt from an Islamic extremist presence. The Muslim Brotherhood has established branches throughout the Middle East, and indeed claims branches in more than 70 countries, including the United States. Wahhabism has spread throughout the brotherhood's branches as well as the organisations under their control or influence, such as the Palestinian Hamas. These organisations are believed to control the leading Muslim organisations and most of the mosques in Western Europe and North America.[1] There are more than 1,200, and perhaps as many as 3,000 mosques in the United States. The number of Muslims in America is variously estimated to be between (probably) 3 million and perhaps as many as 8 million. Local imams are typically appointed by whoever funds the mosque. Since most mosques are funded with Saudi money, most imams are Wahhabis.[2] Sheikh Muhammad Hisham Kabbani, the head of the Islamic Supreme Council of America, on 7 January 1999 testified to the State Department that 80 percent of all mosques and Muslim charitable organisations in the United States had been taken over by extremists, in particular Wahhabis. Nine Muslim organisations subsequently jointly condemned Kabbani's testimony, accusing him of slandering all Muslims.[3]

The extremist control of the American Islamic organisations has not prevented them from being accepted as legitimate religious groups and rightful representatives of the Muslim American community despite their extremist ideology and ties with violent organisations such as Hamas. Steven Emerson, an American investigative journalist, has spent several years monitoring the large Islamic organisation in the United States. He has shown that several of them are broadly sympathetic to Islamic extremism of the Wahhabi variety and convincingly argued that many also support Islamic terrorist groups, including Al-Qaida. Although not directly engaged in actual terrorism, they raise funds that are used to "support an entire spectrum of services and activities that support the agenda of radical Islamic ideology." This includes the financial support of the dependents of so-called martyrs (such as suicide bombers) who have died during acts of terrorism. Emerson has shown that funds also get diverted to support jihad activities directly, for instance so that the extremist fighter "is equipped and given whatever he needs to fight for the cause of Allah. . . ." Among the several large and well-funded Islamic groups, Emerson cites nine:

- Council of American-Islamic Relations (CAIR), which, despite taking out full-page advertisements condemning the 11 September 2001 terrorist attacks, often "served as an ideological support group for militants
- American Muslim Council (AMC)
- Muslim Arab Youth Association
- Islamic Circle of North America
- Muslim Public Affairs Council
- American Muslim Alliance
- Islamic Society of North America
- Islamic Cultural Workshop (ICW), an American branch of Hizb ut-Tahrir (Islamic Liberation Party) which apparently has been inactive since 1999
- American Islamic Group, now defunct, which particularly endorsed the Committee for the Defense of Legitimate Rights, a militant Saudi opposition group that aimed to

overthrow the Saudi government and exterminate all Jews in Palestine[4]

The AMC even obtained the monopoly on the training of Muslim chaplains for the U.S. army.[5] Several Muslim organisations in the United States have been accused of actively championing Islamic extremist movements and associated terrorist groups. Those accused include the AMC, accused of being an umbrella group of the Muslim Brotherhood, and CAIR, accused of defending and rationalising the actions of extremist groups and leaders such as the convicted Sheikh Omar Abdel Rahman.[6]

The situation is similar in Canada. The Canadian branch of the Council for American-Islamic Relations, CAIR Canada, like the other American organisations, has been accused of receiving indirect support from extremists.[7] The situation may well be similar in South America.[8]

Islamic extremist groups known to have established themselves in the United States include the Muslim Brotherhood, Hizb ut-Tahrir, En-Nahda of Tunisia, the Algerian FIS (Islamic Salvation Front) and GIA (Armed Islamic Group), Egyptian Islamic Society, Hamas (operating largely, but not exclusively, under the names of the Islamic Association for Palestine and the Holy Land Foundation for Relief and Development), and Palestinian Islamic Jihad. Even such groups as Abu Sayyaf of the Philippines, the Taliban, and a possible Egyptian spin-off apparently named *Jamaat Muslimin* (Society of Muslims) from Pakistan and Bangladesh appear to have formed followings in the United States.[9] Wail Jalaidan, one of the founders of Al-Qaida and regarded as the logistics chief of the organisation, before his admission to Al-Qaida lived and worked at the Islamic Center of Tucson, Arizona.[10]

The large Islamic groups thrive because they have succeeded in establishing and maintaining a legal existence in North America. However, there is also a clandestine Islamic presence in the United States. The Al-Qaida network in the United States at first included groups in Tucson, Arizona; Brooklyn, New York; Orlando, Florida; Dallas, Texas; Santa Clara, California; Columbia, Missouri; and

Herndon, Virginia. The United States was also, until recently, an excellent place for extremist Web sites. Until 5 September 2001, when FBI agents raided the place, most of them used the Internet service provider InfoCom Corporation in Richardson, Texas. Among the more than 500 companies and nonprofit groups whose Web sites were hosted by InfoCom were many with Islamic extremist associations, including the Holy Land Foundation.[11]

According to data gathered by Emerson, by early 2002 current Islamic extremist groups (legal as well as banned) in the United States existed or had recently existed in the following locations (Emerson includes Hamas and Palestinian Islamic Jihad, although there is, as noted, little evidence to connect these essentially religious-nationalist organisations with the international Al-Qaida):[12]

Massachusetts

Boston — Al-Qaida
National Islamic Front (Sudan)

New York

New York (metro) — Al-Qaida
Islamic Society (Egypt)
Hamas (Palestine)
Harakat al-Muhajiroun (Britain)
Jamaat-e Islami (Pakistan)

Pennsylvania

Philadelphia — Islamic Society (Egypt)
Hamas (Palestine)
Harakat al-Muhajiroun (Britain)

Maryland

Laurel — Al-Qaida

District of Columbia

Hamas (Palestine)

Virginia

Herndon	Al-Qaida
	Islamic Jihad (Palestine)
Springfield	Hamas (Palestine)

North Carolina

Raleigh	Islamic Jihad (Palestine)

Florida

Orlando	Al-Qaida
Fort Lauderdale	Al-Qaida
Boca Raton	Al-Qaida
Tampa	Islamic Jihad (Palestine)

Ohio

Cleveland	Muslim Brotherhood
	Islamic Jihad (Palestine)

Indiana

Plainfield	Muslim Brotherhood
	Islamic Society of North America

Illinois

Chicago	Hamas (Palestine)
	Islamic Jihad (Palestine)

Michigan

Detroit	Muslim Brotherhood
	Islamic Society (Egypt)
	Hamas (Palestine)

Missouri

Columbia	Al-Qaida
	FIS (Algeria)
	Hamas (Palestine)

Kansas City	Hamas (Palestine)
	Advice and Reformation
	Committee (ARC), an apparently
	independent political branch of
	Usamah bin Ladin's organisation
	(since closed down)

Oklahoma

| Oklahoma City | Hamas (Palestine) |

Texas

Houston	Al-Qaida
	Muslim Brotherhood
	Hamas (Palestine)
Arlington	Al-Qaida
Dallas	Al-Qaida
	Hamas (Palestine)

Colorado

| Denver | Al-Qaida |

Arizona

| Tucson | Al-Qaida |
| | Hamas (Palestine) |

Washington

| Seattle | GIA (Algeria) |

California

San Francisco	Abu Sayyaf (Philippines)
Santa Clara	Al-Qaida
	Hamas (Palestine)
Los Angeles	Hamas (Palestine)
	Islamic Society (Egypt)
	GIA (Algeria)
San Diego	GIA (Algeria)

End Notes

1. See, for instance, Palazzi, "Islamists Have It Wrong," 3–11. The California branch of the Muslim Brotherhood maintains a Web site at www.ummah.net/Ikhwan.

2. Emerson, *American Jihad*, 40–41.

3. Muhammad Hisham Kabbani, "Islamic Extremism: A Viable Threat to U.S. National Security," An Open Forum at the US Department of State, 7 January 1999 (www.islamicsupremecouncil.org/radicalmovements/islamic_extremism.htm); Emerson, *American Jihad*, 159–60.

4. Emerson, *American Jihad, passim,* in particular 38, 183–220. Emerson appears mainly interested in the Palestinian groups, not all of which have been convincingly associated with Wahhabism or Al-Qaida.

5. See, for instance, Palazzi, "Islamists Have It Wrong," 10, where Palazzi also gives further references regarding the nature of CAIR and AMC. See also Emerson, *American Jihad*, 38.

6. Emerson, *American Jihad*, 167.

7. Emerson, *American Jihad*, 166.

8. Al-Qaida cells have been reported in Uruguay and Ecuador. Katzman, *Terrorism*, 13. In addition, Hamas is known to be established in Venezuela and Brazil, in the latter country also through the Holy Land Foundation for Relief and Development.

9. Reeve, *New Jackals*, 232 with 234 n.32. Reeve refers to Steven Emerson, prepared statement delivered before the Senate Judiciary Subcommittee on Terrorism, Technology and Government Information, 24 February 1998.

10. Emerson, *American Jihad*, 77.

11. Emerson, *American Jihad*, 104, 152.

12. Emerson, *American Jihad*, 178–80, and (on Hamas in the United States) 181.